Malawi,
Mozambique & Zambia

David Else

Malawi, Mozambique & Zambia

1st edition

Published by
Lonely Planet Publications
Head Office: PO Box 617, Hawthorn, Vic 3122, Australia
Branches: 155 Filbert St, Suite 251, Oakland, CA 94607, USA
10 Barley Mow Passage, Chiswick, London W4 4PH, UK
71 bis rue du Cardinal Lemoine, 75005 Paris, France

Printed by
Colorcraft Ltd, Hong Kong

Photographs by
Robert Drummond, David Else, Bruno Français, Doug Laing, Peter Robinson, David Wall

Front cover: Storks at sunset, Mozambique (Pete Turner, The Image Bank)

First Published
August 1997

National Library of Australia Cataloguing in Publication Data

Else, David
Malawi, Mozambique & Zambia

Includes index.
ISBN 0 86442 462 0.

1. Malawi – Guidebooks. 2. Mozambique – Guidebooks.
3. Zambia – Guidebooks. I. Title. (Series : Lonely Planet travel survival kit).

916.04329

text & maps © Lonely Planet 1997
photos © photographers as indicated 1997

David Else

After hitchhiking through Europe for a couple of years, David Else kept heading south and first reached Africa in 1983. Since then, he has travelled all over the continent, from Cairo to Cape Town, and from Sudan to Senegal, via most of the bits in between. He has written several guidebooks for independent travellers including Lonely Planet's *Trekking in East Africa*. He has also co-authored and contributed to several other Lonely Planet guides including *West Africa* and *East Africa*, plus *Africa – the South* and *Africa on a shoestring*. As part of the research for this book, David travelled through Malawi, Zambia, Mozambique and six other countries of Southern Africa.

When not in Africa, David lives in the north of England, where he's permanently chained to a word processor, and travel means driving to London and back.

From the Author

Firstly – a big thank you to my wife Corinne. Although my name goes down as author of this book, the seven-month research trip was very much a joint project. Corinne also wrote several of the historical, political and background items.

Many thanks also to the Higgs and Taylor families (and associates) of Dargle Dale, KwaZulu/Natal. They provided friendship, hospitality, a fax line, a magical device for saving camp fuel and (most appreciated) a base to come back to at the end of our trip.

In the UK, Roger Gook and Janet McDougal of Footloose Adventure Travel provided international flight and tour information. We'd also like to thank the friendly and helpful staff of Gulf Air in Durban, who swiftly arranged our emergency flights home at short notice.

Thanks also to: Mike Deady, a Kiwi traveller who suddenly found himself roped into Lonely Planet research duties when I was laid up with malaria in Beira; Geoff Perrott of Cape Town, for good company and various tips; Mike Slater of Johannesburg for information on Mozambique; Jane Jackson of Makuzi Beach, Malawi, who provided sound advice and Fansidar when it was Corinne's turn for malaria; Tim Truluck of Lusaka, Zambia, for a comprehensive lowdown on the city; Pam and Chris Badger for a base in Lilongwe; Carl Bruessow of the Wildlife Society of Malawi, for advice and information; and Ian Colclough, who joined us in northern Mozambique, masquerading as a linguist, mechanic and experienced traveller. He was a pretty good cook though, and we couldn't have done that bit of the trip without him.

In Malawi, Mozambique and Zambia, several local guides showed us the way, provided information, and shared their knowledge: Malcolm and Everlasting of Central Africa Wilderness Safaris in Lilongwe; Lovemore Ngoma of Kasungu National Park; Rabbie of Aqua Africa in Nkhata Bay; Austin Pindan, Raphael Maglas, Thomas Walusa, Daveson Goodwell and Oscar Kachina of Mulanje; Chá Omar of Nampula; and talkative Michael Virgilio of Beira.

Thanks to Deanna Swaney, author of several Lonely Planet guides including *Zimbabwe, Botswana & Namibia*, *Mauritius, Réunion & Seychelles* and

Madagascar & Comoros. Her input on Lusaka, the Zambezi and various other snippets from around the region were invaluable.

Thanks also to reader Hugh Dowling, of Rotherham, UK, who provided good hiking information about Malawi; to Robert Brierley of Switzerland for information on Zambia; and to Andrew Chilton of Portland, Oregon, who wrote a marvellously detailed and organised letter about his travels in the region.

From the Publisher

This first edition of *Malawi, Mozambique & Zambia* was edited in LP's Melbourne office by Richard Plunkett and Rachel Scully, with assistance from David Andrew, Katrina Browning, Justin Flynn, Carolyn Papworth and Jane Rawson. Mapping was co-ordinated by Sally Jacka, with assistance from Sandra Smythe, Geoff Stringer and Indra Kilfoyle. Sally was also responsible for the book design and layout. Thanks to David Andrew for the bird illustrations and to Indra Kilfoyle and Margie Jung for other illustrations. David Kemp designed the cover, and Adam McCrow was responsible for the back-cover cartography.

Warning & Request

Things change – prices go up, schedules change, good places go bad and bad places go bankrupt – nothing stays the same. So, if you find things better or worse, recently opened or long since closed, please tell us and help make the next edition even more accurate and useful.

We value all of the feedback we receive from travellers. Julie Young coordinates a small team who read and acknowledge every letter, postcard and email, and ensure that every morsel of information finds its way to the appropriate authors, editors and publishers.

Everyone who writes to us will find their name in the next edition of the appropriate guide and will also receive a free subscription to our quarterly newsletter, *Planet Talk*. The very best contributions will be rewarded with a free Lonely Planet guide.

Excerpts from your correspondence may appear in updates (which we add to the end pages of reprints); new editions of this guide; in our newsletter, *Planet Talk*; or in the Postcards section of our Web site – so please let us know if you don't want your letter published or your name acknowledged.

Contents

INTRODUCTION 9

FACTS ABOUT MALAWI 11

History 13	**Birds of Malawi 36**	Arts 42
Geography 26	Government & Politics 39	Society & Conduct 45
Climate 27	Economy 39	Religion 47
Ecology & Environment 27	Population & People 41	Languages 48
Flora & Fauna........................... 31	Education 41	

FACTS FOR THE VISITOR 50

Planning....................... 50	Radio & TV 67	Dangers & Annoyances 82
Suggested Itineraries 52	Photography & Video 68	Legal Matters 82
Highlights 53	Time....................................... 68	Business Hours 83
Tourist Offices 54	Electricity................................... 69	Public Holidays........................ 83
Visas & Documents 55	Weights & Measures................. 69	Activities.................................. 83
Embassies 56	Health.. 69	Accommodation........................ 85
Customs 57	Toilets.. 80	Food 87
Money....................................... 57	Women Travellers..................... 80	Drinks....................................... 87
Post & Communications 61	Gay & Lesbian Travellers......... 81	Entertainment........................... 88
Books.. 61	Disabled Travellers 81	Things to Buy........................... 88
Online Services.......................... 66	Senior Travellers...................... 81	
Newspapers & Magazines........ 67	Travel with Children................. 82	

GETTING THERE & AWAY 89

Air.............................. 89	USA & Canada 93	Organised Tours 99
UK & Ireland............................. 91	Land 95	

GETTING AROUND.. 103

Air.............................. 103	Car & Motorcycle................... 104	Boat... 106
Bus.. 103	Bicycle 105	Local Transport....................... 108
Train... 104	Hitching 106	Organised Tours 108

LILONGWE 109

History 109	Places to Stay..........................114	Getting Around 118
Orientation............................... 109	Places to Eat............................116	Around Lilongwe.................... 119
Information............................... 109	Entertainment...........................117	
Things to See & Do 113	Getting There & Away.............118	

CENTRAL MALAWI 121

Dedza....................................... 121	Ntchisi Forest Reserve............ 122	Kasungu National Park........... 123
Mchinji 122	Kasungu 123	Viphya Plateau 125

BLANTYRE & LIMBE.. 127

Orientation............................... 128	Places to Eat 133	Getting Around 135
Information............................... 128	Entertainment........................... 134	Around Blantyre 135
Places to Stay.......................... 131	Getting There & Away............. 134	

SOUTHERN MALAWI 138

Balaka 138
Liwonde 138
Liwonde National Park 138
Zomba 141
Zomba Plateau 142
Mulanje 147

Mt Mulanje **147**
Information 149
Places to Stay 150
Getting There & Away 151
Hiking & Trekking Routes 151
The Lower Shire **155**

Majete Game Reserve 155
Lengwe National Park 157
Bangula 158
Mwabvi Game Reserve 158
Elephant Marsh 158
Chiromo 159

NORTHERN MALAWI 161

Mzuzu 161
Rumphi 164
Vwaza Marsh Game Reserve 164
Livingstonia 166

Chitipa 169
Nyika National Park **169**
Flora & Fauna 171
Information 171

Things to See & Do 172
Places to Stay 174
Getting There & Away 174
Hiking & Trekking Routes 175

THE LAKE SHORE 178

The Northern Lake Shore 178
Karonga 178
Chilumba 179
Chitimba 179
The Central Lake Shore 180
Nkhata Bay 180
The Chintheche Strip 182
Dwangwa 184

Nkhotakota 184
Salima 186
Senga Bay 186
Chipoka 188
Mua 188
Monkey Bay & Cape
Maclear **188**
Monkey Bay 188

Cape Maclear 189
The Southern Lake Shore 194
The Monkey Bay-Mangochi
Road 194
Mangochi 195
Likoma & Chizumulu Islands 196

MOZAMBIQUE 201

Facts about the Country 203
Facts for the Visitor **212**
Getting There & Away **217**
Getting Around **219**
Maputo **220**
Around Maputo 226
Southern Mozambique ... **227**
Bilene 227
Praia de Závora 228
Maxixe & Inhambane 228
Tofu & Barra Beaches 228

Vilankulo 229
Bazaruto Archipelago 230
Inhassoro 231
Central Mozambique **231**
Beira 231
Chimoio 235
Tete 235
Northern Mozambique **237**
Quelimane 237
Mocuba 237
Milange 238

Molocuè 239
Nampula 239
Angoche 240
Cuamba 240
Lichinga 241
Mozambique Island 241
Chocas 243
Nacala 243
Pemba 244
Moçimboa da Praia 245
Palma 245

ZAMBIA 247

Facts about the Country 249
Facts for the Visitor **254**
Getting There & Away **258**
Getting Around **261**
Lusaka **262**
Eastern Zambia **269**
Chipata 269
South Luangwa National Park 269
Chirundu 271
Lower Zambezi National Park 272
Southern Zambia **274**
Victoria Falls 274
Livingstone 275

The Zambezi Riverfront 278
Choma 279
Lake Kariba 279
Siavonga 280
Lochinvar National Park 281
Western Zambia **281**
Sesheke 282
The Ngonye Falls 282
Senanga 283
Mongu 283
Kafue National Park 285
Northern Zambia **286**
Kapiri Mposhi 286

Ndola 286
Kitwe 287
Kasanka National Park 287
Lake Bangweulu 287
North Luangwa National Park 287
Shiwa Ngandu 287
Kasama 287
Mbala 287
Mpulungu 288
Sumbu National Park 288
Nakonde 288

GLOSSARY 289

INDEX 292

Maps 292

Boxed Text 292

Text 293

Map Legend

BOUNDARIES

.... International Boundary
.... Regional Boundary

ROUTES

.... Freeway
.... Highway
.... Major Road
.... Unsealed Road or Track
.... City Road
.... City Street
.... Railway
.... Underground Railway
.... Tram
.... Walking Track
.... Walking Tour
.... Ferry Route
.... Cable Car or Chairlift

AREA FEATURES

.... Parks
.... Built-Up Area
.... Market
.... Building
.... Cemetery
.... Reef
.... Beach or Desert
.... Rocks

HYDROGRAPHIC FEATURES

.... Coastline
.... River, Creek
.... Intermittent River or Creek
.... Rapids, Waterfalls
.... Lake, Intermittent Lake
.... Canal
.... Swamp

SYMBOLS

✪ CAPITAL		National Capital
◉ Capital		Regional Capital
🌐 CITY		Major City
● City		City
● Town		Town
● Village		Village
■	▼	Place to Stay, Place to Eat
⚓	▌	Cafe, Pub or Bar
✉	☎	Post Office, Telephone
❶	❸	Tourist Information, Bank
☻	☻	Transport Stations, Transport Stops
🏛	⛪	Museum, Youth Hostel
⌗	Å	Caravan Park, Camping Ground
✝	✚	Church, Cathedral
☪	✡	Mosque, Synagogue
♦♦	🅿	Border Crossing, Parking
✛	★	Hospital, Police Station
☻	☻	Embassy, Petrol Station
✈	✚	Airport, Airstrip
☰	✿	Swimming Pool, Gardens
❖	🐾	Shopping Centre, Zoo
⚑	⋔	Golf Course, Picnic Site
←	A25	One Way Street, Route Number
🏛	⚐	Stately Home, Monument
⚑	◪	Castle, Tomb
⌂	⌂	Shelter, Hut or Chalet
▲	☀	Mountain or Hill, Lookout
🌋	≚	Lighthouse, Shipwreck
)(	◉	Pass, Spring
⚐	⌒	Beach, Cave
∴		Archaeological Site or Ruins
		Ancient or City Wall
		Cliff or Escarpment, Tunnel
		Railway Station

Note: not all symbols displayed above appear in this book

Introduction

The tourist brochures bill Malawi as 'the warm heart of Africa' and, for once, the hype is true; Malawi's scenery is stunning and wonderfully varied, and (although we hate to generalise) Malawians really do seem to be among the friendliest people you could meet anywhere.

For most visitors, the country's main attraction is Lake Malawi, one of the Great Rift Valley lakes, stretching some 500 km down the eastern border. Two of the country's high-profile wildlife parks, Liwonde and Lake Malawi, are on or near the lake, and there's an ever-increasing number of hotels, lodges and campgrounds being built along the southern and western shores. The diving and snorkelling here are very highly rated.

Away from the lake are several more national parks and reserves, including

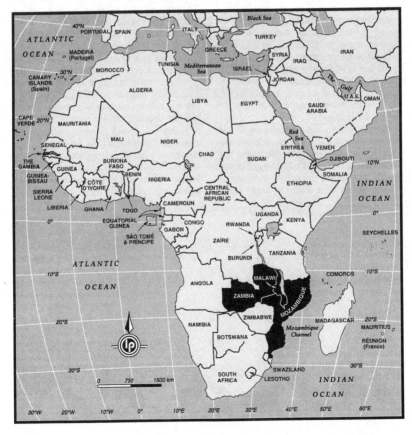

9

Kasungu, Lengwe, Vwaza Marsh and the Nyika Plateau – all different and with something special to offer. As well as mammals and fish, the birds of Malawi are a major attraction – very few countries have such a range of species in such a relatively small area.

Beyond the national parks, Malawi has forest reserves, isolated hills and the fantastic highland wilderness area of Mt Mulanje, where you find deep valleys, sheer escarpments and dramatic peaks, and some of the most enjoyable hiking routes in the whole of Africa.

Malawi's compact size is another advantage – the distances between places to see and visit are never too long. Add to this a system of roads which, although by no means perfect, is better than that of many other countries in the region, as well as an efficient public transport service, and a trip of any sort in Malawi becomes a real joy. The general lack of hassle so often associated with travel in the developing world has given the country another appropriate subtitle: 'Africa for beginners'.

Another welcoming aspect for visitors are the recent political changes. Malawi was once infamous for its leader, the nonagenarian President-for-Life Dr Hastings Kamuzu Banda, and for his restrictive dress code – women had to wear a skirt and men had to have short hair. These whimsical dictates were symptomatic of a much deeper malaise: Banda's iron grip on a terrorised population. But elections in 1994 ushered in a multiparty system and a level of freedom (albeit not without significant problems) never before enjoyed in the country.

Major changes have also occurred in Zambia and Mozambique, the two countries bordering Malawi to the west, east and south, which have long been off most travellers' routes. Civil war on one side and political chaos on the other meant Malawi was something of a peaceful retreat in a notoriously turbulent part of the world. But now both Zambia and Mozambique are welcoming tourists once again, and Malawi makes an obvious bridge or stepping stone for wider travels through the region.

Zambia has several world-class game parks, which outshine Malawi's in sheer size if not in accessibility, while Mozambique has a legendary tropical coastline and a colonial cultural heritage quite unlike its neighbours. Neither country can be called 'Africa for beginners' – travel is unpredictable and tourist facilities extremely limited, but the raw edge makes an intriguing contrast to Malawi's more approachable charms. A journey taking in all three countries would be like none other in Africa.

Map Index

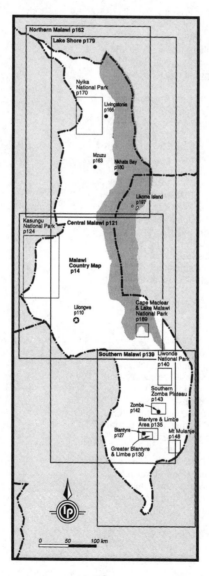

Northern Malawi p162

Lake Shore p179

Nyika National Park p170

Livingstonia p166

Mzuzu p163

Nkhata Bay p180

Likoma Island p197

Kasungu National Park p124

Central Malawi p121

Malawi Country Map p14

Lilongwe p110

Cape Maclear & Lake Malawi National Park p189

Southern Malawi p139

Liwonde National Park p140

Southern Zomba Plateau p143

Zomba p142

Blantyre & Limbe Area p135

Blantyre p127

Mt Mulanje p148

Greater Blantyre & Limbe p130

0   50   100 km

Facts about Malawi

HISTORY
Prehistory

Hominid species are known to have inhabited the area now called Malawi, along with many other parts of East and Southern Africa, between three and two million years ago. The oldest hominid ('human-like') remnant found in Malawi is a single jawbone of the species *Homo rudolfensis*, which palaeontologists calculate to be 2.5 million years old.

Most scientists agree that by about two million years ago, changing climatic and environmental conditions had resulted in the evolution of several hominid species, including *Homo habilis* and *Homo erectus*. By about 1.5 to one million years ago, the latter seems to have become dominant and developed basic tool-making skills, evolving into *Homo sapiens* (essentially the same as modern humans). This species led a nomadic existence, eventually spreading outwards from Africa to inhabit all parts of the world as it then was, slowly evolving further into various races, according to local environment and other factors.

The Stone Ages

Over the next million years it seems that *Homo sapiens* slowly improved the use of stone tools. At first these were large and clumsy, but by about 150,000 years ago people were using lighter stone points, spear heads, knives, saws and other finer tools useful for various hunting and gathering activities. Archaeologists classify this period of tool making as the Stone Age, divided into Early, Middle and Late stages. (The term applies to an individual group's level of technological development, rather than to a specific period of time within the whole of Africa or the world.)

Archaeological evidence suggests that Early Stone Age settlements existed along the lake shore in parts of central and northern Malawi around 100,000 years ago, while

Malawi
Area: 118,484 sq km (land area 94,080 sq km)
Population: 10 million
Population Growth: 3.5%
Capital: Lilongwe
Head of State: President Bakili Muluzi
Official Languages: English, Chichewa
Currency: Malawian kwacha
Exchange Rate: MK 15.2 = US$1
Per Capita GNP: US$180 (Purchasing power parity: US$750)
Literacy: 50%
Infant Mortality: around 20%

Middle Stone Age sites dating from 10,000 years ago have also been discovered in this area. The evidence further suggests that the early inhabitants of this area were the same Boskopoid people who inhabited much of this part of Africa: these were the ancestors of the pygmies in Central Africa and the San ('Bushmen') of Southern Africa who now survive only in isolated pockets.

The Iron Ages

About 2000 years ago, these 'Stone Age Malawians' came under pressure from another race of people, the Bantu, who were gradually migrating into the area. This movement was part of what has become known as the 'great migrations' – an important feature of East and Southern Africa's history. In the last 3000 years, waves of peoples have crossed and recrossed the region, some groups searching for new territory as their populations grew, others forced to move by climatic change. The movements inevitably had a knock-on effect too, as groups being invaded from one side expanded in the other direction. Most migrations took place over hundreds of years, and were made up of many short moves (from valley to valley, or from one cultivation area to the next), with dominant peoples slowly absorbing and assimilating other groups in the process.

MALAWI

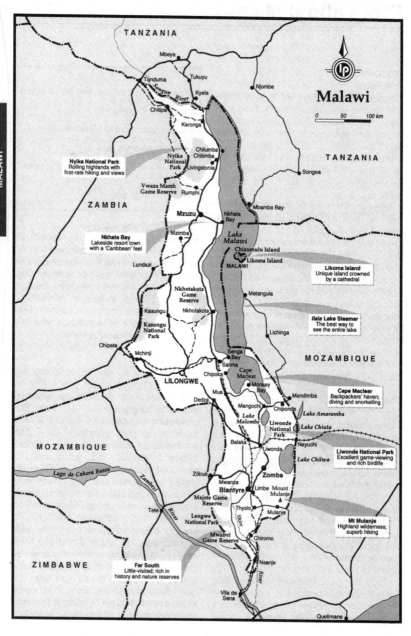

The Bantu migration was most significant because this group had knowledge of iron working. Armed with iron tools to clear forest and cultivate more effectively, the Bantu migrated from the area that is now Cameroun, through the Zaïre basin and onto the East and Southern African plateaux,

arriving in the region around 100 BC. Over the next 1000 years they spread across present-day Uganda, Kenya and Tanzania, and southward into Malawi, Zambia, Mozambique and several other areas.

It seems that in Malawi, as in other areas, the Stone Age and Bantu inhabitants co-existed for a long period (stories of 'little red men' still surviving in remote areas remain part of Bantu tradition) although the powerful newcomers eventually became completely dominant. In Malawi, rock and cave paintings remain as permanent reminders of the Stone Age people at a number of sites, including Dedza, Fingira Cave on the Nyika Plateau, and on Hora Mountain near Mzimba. Their designs tended to be shapes and patterns rather than figures, although some of these paintings are believed to be the work of the early Bantu inhabitants.

In Malawi, several Iron Age sites have been discovered, particularly around the south-western shores of Lake Malawi. The Bantu also had the technology to work clay, and remains from the places they inhabited consist principally of a number of distinctive types of pottery or 'ware'. The styles vary according to geographical area and age. For example, 'Nkope ware', the earliest style of Iron Age pottery, was found in the area around Mangochi, and can be broadly dated to between the 3rd and 10th centuries AD. The latest style – 'Mwudzu ware' – dates from as recently as the late 1550s.

Recent Migrations

Between the 14th and 16th centuries AD, waves of Bantu people called Tumbuka and Phoka migrated into the north of Malawi, probably from the Congo region, via Tanzania, although their traditions do not agree on this. By the 17th century they had settled around the highlands of Nyika and Viphya. Meanwhile, in the south, the Maravi/Chewa/Nyanja (see the boxed text on The Naming of Malawi) came in from present-day Zaïre and established a large and powerful kingdom that spread all over southern Malawi and parts of present-day Mozambique and Zambia.

The Naming of Malawi

During colonial times the country we now call Malawi was known as Nyasaland, but the derivation of both the old and new names are not entirely clear and the subject of some dispute.

When explorer David Livingstone first reached Lake Malawi he called it Lake Nyassa. Most authorities agree that 'Nyassa' is derived from the word *nyanja*, which means 'lake' in the language of the indigenous Chewa people. There is also a Nyanja people, but in Malawi this seems to be another name for the Chewa, although other authorities refer to the Chewa and the Nyanja as separate peoples. In colonial times and the early years of independence the language of the Chewa was called Chi-Nyanja (or Chinyanja) but was renamed Chichewa in 1968 when it became the national language.

Early Portuguese explorers who reached the area in the 16th century recorded a powerful kingdom called Maravi, which seems to have covered much of southern Malawi, as well as parts of Mozambique and Zambia. They also referred to the lake and the local people as Maravi, but it is not clear if the name of the people was derived from the lake, or vice versa. It seems the Chewa/Nyanja are descended from the Maravi. In his journals, Livingstone also mentioned people called Maravi inhabiting the area, although this may have been based on the Portuguese reports.

At independence a commission was established to find a new name for the new country. 'Malaŵi' was chosen officially inspired by the word *malavi*, which means reflected light, haze, flames or rays in Chichewa. (The word is also spelt *maravi* – 'l' and 'r' seem interchangeable in Chichewa.) This new name was seen as a reference to the sun rising over the lake, bringing a fresh light to the country. It may also be connected to the Maravi people, although no people of this name inhabit Malawi today.

The ŵ in Malaŵi is a 'soft v', and English speakers should pronounce a sound somewhere between 'w', 'v' and 'f'. Correctly, the ŵ should be used, but these days the name of the country is generally pronounced with the w (as in 'wee'), and the circumflex is often dropped. ∎

MALAWI

Smaller groups to migrate into Malawi during the 18th century included the Lambya, who moved from southern Tanzania, and the Ngonde people who came from the Congo/Zaïre region, to settle in the north of Malawi.

The early 19th century brought two more significant migrations. The Yao, from western Mozambique, invaded the highlands of southern Malawi, killing the more peaceful local inhabitants as they went, or capturing them for sale into slavery. An important factor in their successful conquest of this area was that they were armed with firearms supplied by Arab traders from the east coast of Africa (see The Rise of Slavery, following).

At about the same time, groups of Zulus were migrating northward as part of a great movement of peoples called the Difaqane (which translates 'the scattering of tribes'; the Zulu word for it, Mfecane, means 'the crushing'), initiated around 1820 by a powerful Zulu king called Shaka in present-day South Africa. A large number settled in Zimbabwe to become the Matabele. Others continued north, some as far as Tanzania. Around 1840, several groups settled in central and northern Malawi and became known as the Angoni or Ngoni. In their conquest of the local tribes, particularly the Chewa, the tendency of the Ngoni was to integrate captives into their own community, rather than selling them into slavery, as was the habit of the Yao.

The Rise of Slavery

Meanwhile, as the Bantu had been spreading across the interior of Africa, people from Arabia were slowly moving from the Gulf, trading goods down the east coast of Africa. By 700 AD the Arabs had founded several coastal trading settlements, the most notable being Kilwa in Tanzania. Trade flourished, and intermarriage with the local Bantu eventually gave rise to the Swahili people. Several powerful independent city-states were established on the coast, each ruled by a sultan. These city-states included Mombasa and Zanzibar, which eventually

---

The Horrors of Slavery

At the height of slaving in the mid-19th century, the Swahili-Arabs together with dominant tribes are reckoned to have either killed or sold into slavery 80,000 to 100,000 Africans per year. Those taken from the areas now called Malawi and Zambia would be brought to one of the Arab trading centres, such as Nkhotakota, Karonga or Salima, where they would be sold to 'wholesalers'. They were then crammed into dhows and taken across Lake Malawi. On the other side they were marched across Mozambique to the east coast, usually chained or tied to poles of wood to prevent escape. Many also carried elephant tusks, as ivory was another major commodity. Any slaves too ill to make the journey were simply abandoned, and died of dehydration or were killed by wild animals.

At the coast, the slaves were once more loaded back into dhows for the hazardous journey north to Zanzibar. They would be packed tightly lying down in several layers in the hold of the boat, jammed in place by the deck holding the layer above. For the duration of the voyage they would have no food or water, and would lie in their own excrement. Those who died – and there were many, particularly if journeys took longer than anticipated because of poor winds – could not be removed until the journey ended.

Those who managed to survive all this were sold once more in the large slave market in Zanzibar and then shipped to places such as Arabia or India. ∎

---

became major import and export centres for the transport of goods between the interior of Africa and various points around the Indian Ocean. Further south, the Swahili-Arabs established smaller ports and trading centres on the coast of present-day Mozambique, as far south as Sofala, south of modern-day Beira. (In fact, Mozambique is believed to be derived from the name of a local sultan called Mussa Mbiki – although there are many variations on the spelling.)

Slavery, and a trade in slaves, had existed in Africa for many centuries, but in the early 19th century demand from outside Africa increased considerably and the Swahili-Arabs began to push into the interior, in an attempt to increase the supply. They often used the services of powerful local tribes such as the Yao to raid and capture their unfortunate neighbours, and established

DAVID ELSE

ROBERT DRUMMOND

ROBERT DRUMMOND

ROBERT DRUMMOND

ROBERT DRUMMOND

DAVID WALL

DAVID ELSE

BRUNO FRANÇAIS

A	B	C
D		E
F	G	H

A: Elephants
B: Jackal
C: Kudu
D: Leopard

E: Zebras
F: Fish
G: Hippos
H: Cichlid fish

ROBERT DRUMMOND

ROBERT DRUMMOND

DOUG LAING

ROBERT DRUMMOND

ROBERT DRUMMOND

PETER ROBINSON

ROBERT DRUMMOND

ROBERT DRUMMOND

ROBERT DRUMMOND

A	B	C
D	E	F
G	H	I

A: Red bishop
B: Paradise flycatcher
C: Malachite sunbird

D: Pied kingfisher
E: Lilac-breasted roller
F: African fish eagle

G: Masked weaver
H: Red-collared widow
I: Giant kingfisher

ROBERT DRUMMOND

ROBERT DRUMMOND

ROBERT DRUMMOND

DOUG LAING

ROBERT DRUMMOND

DOUG LAING

A	B
C	D
E	F

A: Collared palm thrush
B: Hoopoe
C: Yellow-billed hornbill

D: Yellow-billed storks
E: Crowned crane
F: Carmine bee-eaters

ALL PHOTOGRAPHS BY PETER ROBINSON

A	B	C
D	E	
F	G	

A: Herschelia baurii
B: Sausage tree fruit
C: Kigelia africana (sausage tree)

D: Hibiscus rhodanthus
E: Adenium multiflorum (impala lily)
F & G: Helichrysum

several trading centres in Malawi, including Karonga and Nkhotakota – towns which still bear a strong Swahili-Arab influence today. (For example, large sailing boats on the lake are still built in the Arab dhow design, and many of the people in the northern lake shore regions are Muslim.)

The First Europeans

The first Europeans to arrive in Malawi were Portuguese explorers who reached the African interior from the east coast – present-day Mozambique – where trading stations had originally been established by Swahili-Arabs at places such as Quelimane and Ilha de Moçambique. The Portuguese also established trading posts in the Zambezi Valley, most notably at Vila de Sena and Tete. By 1540 both were sizeable settlements.

Although the Portuguese did establish trade links with the tribes in this area, only a few ventured inland or beyond the lower Zambezi Valley. One of these was Gaspar Bocarro; in 1616, he journeyed from Tete through the valley of the Shire River (then spelt Shiray, and still pronounced 'Shir-ee' today) to Lake Chilwa, through the south of what is now Tanzania and back into Mozambique.

The most famous explorer to reach this area was David Livingstone, a Scottish missionary, even though his claim to be the first European to see Lake Malawi is refuted by the records of another Portuguese explorer, Candido da Costa Cardoso, who sighted the lake in his travels during 1846. However, Livingstone's exploration heralded the arrival of Europeans in a way which was to change the nature of the region forever.

Livingstone & The First Missionaries

Between 1842 and 1856, Livingstone had been busy further south exploring the Kalahari Desert and the upper reaches of the Zambezi River, and also crossing the continent from the east to the west coast. On his return to Britain, he spoke at several public meetings about the 'undiscovered' interior of Africa, and the horrors of the slave trade. A speech at Cambridge University in 1857 led to the founding of the Universities Mission in Central Africa (UMCA), whose aim was to combat the slave trade by encouraging alternative commerce, and to establish missions for promoting the spread of Christianity.

Livingstone returned to Africa in 1858 to explore the Zambezi region in more detail. (This was his second major expedition, which was to last until 1864.) From Britain, he reached the area via the British Cape Colony (to eventually become South Africa) and the Portuguese port of Quelimane. Livingstone and his party travelled several hundred km up the Zambezi River on a small steamboat called the *Ma-Robert*, but their route was blocked by the vast gorge and rapids now called Cahora Bassa. Interpreting the obstacle as a sign from God, Livingstone changed plans and, with a few team-members, followed the Shire River (a major tributary of the Zambezi) upstream into the area now known as southern Malawi.

The river was navigable at first, but after about 300 km the explorers reached another series of rapids which blocked their way. Livingstone named these the Murchison Cataracts (after a notable geographer of the day,

Dr David Livingstone was a passionate opponent of Africa's slave traders.

MALAWI

MALAWI

who also has a large waterfall in Uganda named after him); today these are known as the Kapichira Rapids. The small party established a base camp here, while Livingstone and his companion John Kirk explored further north, reaching Lake Chilwa. The local people told them of an even larger lake to the north, so Livingstone returned to the Zambezi for more staff and supplies, then once again travelled north, through the Liwonde area and past Lake Malombe. In September 1859 they finally reached Lake Malawi, which Livingstone named Lake Nyassa, and explored much of its western shore.

Throughout this journey, Livingstone learnt from local people that the Swahili-Arab slavers and other powerful African tribes regularly raided the area. He even met a slaving party, complete with captives, and realised that a major slave route between the interior and the sea passed the narrow gap of land between lakes Malawi and Malombe (where today's town of Mangochi now stands).

Livingstone returned to the Shire River in 1861 accompanied by seven UMCA missionaries, including Charles Frederick Mackenzie and six priests, and a team of porters from Sesheke, a town on the Zambezi River in present-day Zambia. Retracing the earlier route, Livingstone and a few members of the party reached Lake Malawi and spent two months exploring the western shore of the lake. In his journals Livingstone noted and named several places including Cape Maclear (after an astronomer in the then Cape Colony) and 'Maclear Harbour' – the site of today's Cape Maclear village.

Meanwhile, Charles Mackenzie (who in Cape Town had been consecrated as the Missionary Bishop of Central Africa) attempted to establish the initial UMCA mission at a place called Magomero in the area of high ground to the north and east of the Shire River – called the Shire Highlands. Although the first mission was built, less than a year after taking up his post Mackenzie died from fever while travelling on the Lower Shire (the part of the river below the Kapichira

Rapids) and was buried near the village of Chiromo. His remains were later moved to Blantyre, after some international boundary alterations meant the site of his original grave was in Portuguese territory.

Through the rest of the early 1860s, more missionaries came to Malawi, undeterred, and built a new mission on the Lower Shire. However, they suffered terribly from malaria and other illnesses, and were in conflict with the local people. In 1864, the surviving missionaries withdrew to Zanzibar (the region's main trading centre) off the east coast of Africa.

Livingstone's Last Journey

Despite the problems encountered by the missionaries he'd inspired, Livingstone returned to the region around Lake Malawi once again in 1866, on his third major expedition in Africa, the main object of which was to find the source of the Nile River. He then travelled north to reach the southern end of Lake Tanganyika. During this time he was abandoned by several African followers he had recruited in Zanzibar. They made their way back to Zanzibar and reported that Livingstone had been killed by slave traders.

This story was not fully believed, so in 1867 the Livingstone Search Expedition, led by one Lieutenant Young (who had been with Livingstone on the Shire in 1862), was sent to find the missing explorer. (This later became known as the First Livingstone Search Expedition.) Young and his party retraced the now established route by boat up the Zambezi and Lower Shire to the Murchison Cataracts, then overland to the Upper Shire, and then by boat again onto Lake Malawi. From local chiefs on the west side of the lake, they discovered that Livingstone had continued north in safety, and the story was a fabrication. On their return voyage down the lake, they also anchored at Cape Maclear to shelter from a violent storm. Young noted that it made an excellent harbour and an ideal place for a settlement.

Meanwhile, Livingstone was in the area now called northern Zambia. In July 1869 he pushed even further north, intending to be gone for a few months (a short jaunt by his standards) but he was not seen or heard of for over two years. Livingstone was found by Henry Stanley (a Welsh-American journalist) on the banks of Lake Tanganyika in late 1871, when Stanley uttered the immortal words: 'Dr Livingstone, I presume'. Stanley was unable to persuade Livingstone to go with him, so returned to the coast alone. Livingstone doggedly continued on his quest for the source of the Nile, finally dying at the village of Chitambo, in the territory of the Ilala people, south-east of Lake Bangweulu in Zambia in 1873.

Two of his faithful followers called Juma and Suze (also spelt Chuma and Guze) buried his heart under a tree here, then embalmed the rest of his body and carried it over 1000 km eastward across present-day Zambia, Malawi and Tanzania to Zanzibar. From here it was shipped back to England, to be buried in Westminster Abbey in April 1874.

The Livingstonia Missionaries

If Livingstone's exploration heralded the arrival of the Europeans in Malawi, it was his death which confirmed their presence by rekindling missionary zeal in Britain and support for missions in this part of Africa. A leading figure in this new campaign was James Stewart, who had been with Livingstone on the Shire expeditions of the early 1860s.

On the basis of his earlier experience, Lieutenant Young was asked to lead the missionaries' return to Central Africa. In 1875, he returned to Lake Malawi with a group of missionaries from the Free Church of Scotland and built a new mission at Cape Maclear, which was named Livingstonia, after the great man himself. Second-in-command of this pioneering party was Dr Robert Laws. There were six other Europeans and four freed slaves who were recruited in Cape Town. They also had a new steam-powered boat, called the *Ilala*, specially designed to be taken apart and reassembled to allow easy transfer through the Murchison Cataracts.

The Free Church mission was reinforced by new arrivals in 1876, which included James Stewart. His arrival allowed Young to return to England. In the same party was William Black. They were accompanied by a group of missionaries from the Established Church of Scotland, who also wanted to found a mission in Central Africa. There was considerable co-operation between the two church groups. Using the skills of an experienced pioneer called Henry Henderson, who had helped Young and his party at Cape Maclear, the Established Church missionaries built a mission in the Shire Highlands which they called Blantyre, after Livingstone's birthplace. By 1891, Blantyre was a thriving community and the Church of St Michael and All Angels was completed. This important historical landmark can still be seen today – for more details see the Blantyre & Limbe chapter.

Meanwhile, back at Cape Maclear, the Free Church mission on the lake shore proved to be malarial. William Black died of fever in 1877, and in the following few years three other missionaries and a local follower also died. The five were buried in a small cemetery at the foot of the hills, which is still visible today (see Cape Maclear in the Lake Shore chapter). Despite the setbacks, a high point of the mission's history was the baptism of Albert Namalambe, the first African convert, in March 1881.

Later in 1881, the mission was abandoned

Hard Work
The first missionaries suffered horribly at their early sites along Lake Malawi but, inspired by their faith, they continued trying to convert the local African people to Christianity, which was met with a certain degree of understandable apathy and resistance. When they realised the second site at Bandawe was unsuccessful, the missionaries' leaders in Edinburgh tabulated the progress so far in laconic and typically Scottish terms:

- Liabilities: five European graves, five years expenditure (£20,000), five years hardship and toil.

- Assets: one convert, one abandoned mission. ∎

MALAWI

in favour of another site, further north along the lake shore at a place called Bandawe. This also proved unsuitable, so in 1894 the Livingstonia Mission was moved to an area of high ground in between the eastern escarpment of the Nyika Plateau and Lake Malawi. This site was successful; the mission flourished and is still there today (see Livingstonia in the Northern Malawi chapter).

The Colonial Period

The early missionaries blazed the way for various adventurers and pioneer traders, who saw Central Africa as a land of almost endless opportunity. Still following Livingstone's footsteps, these early arrivals usually disembarked from ocean-going ships at the Portuguese port of Quelimane from where they made their way by a small river and a section of overland travel to the Zambezi River. It was not possible to go directly to the Zambezi at that time as the mouth of the river was a vast delta of channels, swamps and sandbanks some 100 km wide. Once on the Zambezi it was possible to travel by boat upstream and into the Shire River. The furthest point which could be reached was once again the Murchison Cataracts (now called Kapichira Rapids), where a small staging post was established on the site of Livingstone's original camp. From here early travellers would continue overland to Blantyre, or to a place called Matope, above the rapids from where the Upper Shire could be followed to Lake Malawi.

In 1878 the Livingstonia Central African Mission Company was formed by private enterprise in Scotland. Its object was to develop the river route into Central Africa, and introduce trade to the area, working alongside the Livingstonia missionaries (see the boxed text on Mandala & the Africa Lakes Corporation in the Blantyre & Limbe chapter). Blantyre became the company base and trading centre, and by 1883 it had its own bank. On the Lower Shire, the company operated small steamboats up and down the river, with heroic Scottish names like *Bruce*

and *Scott*, ferrying goods and passengers between the interior and the coast.

In 1890 a navigable channel through the Zambezi Delta was discovered and the Livingstonia Central African Mission Company established a base here, called Chinde, which was recognised as a British Concession by the Portuguese who controlled the surrounding territory. By 1893, the company was renamed the African Lakes Company (later Corporation). Trade between the coast and the new territory continued to grow, and larger Mississippi-style paddle steamers, with names like *Cobra, Scorpion* and *Mosquito* were launched. Chiromo (then spelt Tshiromo) developed as an inland port; it was the highest point on the river that the larger boats could reliably reach (although even then in the dry season they often grounded) and it was also the first point which was entirely inside British territory.

The African Lakes Corporation went on to establish a successful commercial network along the upper and lower sections of the Shire River and the shores of Lake Nyasa (Lake Malawi). As intended, this had a serious effect on the Arab-controlled slave trade in the area, and after several clashes (the most notable being at Karonga – see that section in the Lake Shore chapter) many slave traders were forced to leave the area.

The Protectorate

By the 1880s the competition among the European powers in the area (known as the 'Scramble for Africa') was fierce. Britain was the dominant power in the Lake Malawi area, but Germany and Portugal both had claims. There had also been an increase in the slave trade again following the withdrawal of British naval ships from patrol on the East African coast. These factors together convinced the British Foreign Office that there was a need for greater protection of British interests in Malawi. They were therefore happy to accept the offer made by Cecil Rhodes in 1889, on behalf of his British South Africa Company (BSAC), to invest in and administer the Shire Highlands area. Thus, in 1889 the Shire district was proclaimed a British protectorate. In 1891 the British Central Africa Protectorate (BSAP), administered by Rhodes' BSAC, was extended to include much of the land along the west side of the lake. Sir Harry Johnston, formerly British Consul in Mozambique, was appointed first commissioner.

The colonial authorities made several attempts to stop the slave trade, but powerful local chiefs (mostly Yao and Ngoni) continued to prey on less-warlike tribes, capture slaves and send them to the east coast of Africa for shipment elsewhere. Forts were built to house garrisons of British and Indian soldiers to control the trade. These included Fort Anderson (which became Mulanje town), Fort Lister (near Phalombe, on the north side of Mt Mulanje) and Fort Johnston, which became Mangochi.

In 1907 the BCAP became the colony of Nyasaland, with all responsibility transferred to the British Colonial Office. These moves led to an increase in the number of settlers from Europe. The route they used was still the same as Livingstone's almost 50 years earlier: the early travellers would go from Quelimane or Chinde to Chiromo or Kapichira Falls by boat, from where they would continue by land, onto the higher ground or to Lake Malawi. The coastal territory was now formally Portuguese East Africa (later to be named Mozambique), but at the village of Chiromo these travellers entered the territory of the new British colony. Nyasaland's first post office was built at Chiromo and became a vital link in the communications network that developed across the region (for more details see the boxed text on Mail Runners in the Southern Malawi chapter).

Meanwhile, Chinde also grew in importance. In 1896 there were 20 permanent British residents (early records don't say how many locals), and by the first decade of the 20th century more than 20 ships a year were unloading here; almost 4000 passengers annually passed through Chinde on their way to the interior.

As the 20th century gathered pace, communications were improved by the construction of a railway between Beira, a Portuguese port south of Quelimane, and Port Herald (now called Nsanje) on the Shire River about 50 km downstream from Chiromo. Blantyre became an important staging post on the route between the Zambezi and Lake Malawi, and grew in importance as Chinde declined and (due to the effects of river erosion and a severe storm in 1922) slid literally into the sea. In 1923 the British Concession of Chinde was officially abandoned.

MALAWI

The Effects of Colonialism

Initially, colonial rule brought some positive effects to the Africans in the region. For a start, it brought an end to the slave trade. The inter-tribal conflicts which had plagued the area for so long also ceased, and other spin-offs included improvements in health care. However, as more European settlers arrived the demand for land grew, and vast areas were bought from local chiefs. The hapless local farmers found themselves labelled 'squatters' or tenants of a new landlord. A 'hut tax' was introduced and traditional methods of agriculture were discouraged. As a result, increasing numbers of Africans were forced to seek work on the white-settler plantations or become migrant workers in Northern and Southern Rhodesia (later Zambia and Zimbabwe) and South Africa. By the turn of the century some 6000 Africans were leaving the country every year. The trend continued through the colonial period. By the 1950s this number had grown to 150,000 a year. ∎

Early Protest

The first serious effort to oppose the colonial government in Nyasaland occurred in the early 20th century. This was led by the Reverend John Chilembwe, a Malawian who was educated first by a radical English missionary and later at a Baptist school in the USA, where he had become involved in a movement supporting black issues.

He returned to Nyasaland in 1900 as a priest. Encouraged by his experiences abroad and unhappy about the effects of colonialism, he started to protest in his preachings about white domination of the region. His outrage was further inflamed by the forced conscription of African men into the British colonial army at the outbreak of WWI in 1914, but his verbal and written protests were largely ignored.

Finally, in January 1915, he and his followers attacked the manager of a large estate neighbouring his mission near Magomero in the Shire Highlands. The manager, William Livingstone, was brutally decapitated, although his family was spared. Chilembwe followed up the attack by holding his usual Sunday service with Livingstone's head on the mission altar.

His plan had been to trigger a mass of uprisings, but they either failed or didn't materialise, and his rebellion was short-lived and swiftly crushed by the colonial authorities. His church was destroyed, many supporters were imprisoned or executed, and Chilembwe himself was shot in Mulanje.

Transition & Independence

After WWI, the British began to introduce ways for the African population to become involved in the administration of the country. Things happened slowly, however, and it wasn't until the 1950s that Africans were actually allowed to enter the government. On the economic front, events also moved slowly. Nyasaland proved to be a relatively unproductive colony with no mineral wealth and only limited plantations. Human labour proved to be a major export (see the boxed text on the Effects of Colonialism above).

In 1953, in an attempt to boost economic development in the region, Nyasaland was joined to the Federation of Northern and Southern Rhodesia (today's Zambia and Zimbabwe). At the same time there was a growing disenchantment with colonial rule among the African population, and the Federation was opposed by the recently formed pro-independence Nyasaland African Congress (NAC). The leading figure of this movement was Dr Hastings Banda.

Details about Banda's early life are confused. It is likely that he was born in about 1898. Few believe that it was as late as 1906 – his official birth date. He was brought up in Kasungu and initially trained as a teacher

at the Livingstonia Mission. It is unclear why he left there in 1915, but his travels then took him to Johannesburg (legend has it he walked all the way). While working as an interpreter for Chewa men in the South African mines, he came into contact with a group of American missionaries who arranged and paid for his training as a doctor in the USA. Following qualification in Ohio he moved to Britain, setting up practice in Liverpool and later in London. He also became an elder of the Church of Scotland. In the 1950s, as the rise of African nationalism grew, he became one of a group of prominent African nationalists based in London. His friends at the time included Jomo Kenyatta and Kwame Nkrumah. By the end of the 1950s he had moved to Ghana, and it was from here, after 40 years abroad, that he was to be invited home to lead the independence movement in Nyasaland. It was felt that he would give the movement a respectable front.

The NAC had been formed in 1944 and became the principal voice of opposition to colonial rule. Its strength and influence, however, remained limited until Banda took over leadership. He was so successful in gaining support that just one year after he took over, the colonial authorities declared a state of emergency. Banda and other leaders were thrown into jail and the authorities went on a rampage of suppression in which 52 Africans were killed.

Nevertheless opposition continued, and in April 1960 Banda was released. He stepped back into his position as head of the NAC, now renamed as the Malawian Congress Party. In 1961 the colonial authorities invited him to a constitutional conference in London. In the elections which followed, Banda's Malawi Congress Party (MCP) swept to victory. Shortly afterwards the Federation of Rhodesia and Nyasaland was dissolved and Malawi became independent in July 1964. Banda became prime minister and head of government while the former governor, Sir Glyn Jones, remained head of state for a transitional period. In July 1966, Malawi became a republic and Banda was made president.

Early Independence

Within weeks of taking power, Banda was consolidating his position. When major political differences began to surface between him and his ministers, Banda demanded they declare their allegiance to him. Rather than do this, many ministers resigned and took to opposition. Drawing his support from the peasant majority, Banda was quickly able to defeat this move by driving the opposition leaders into hiding or exile.

With the opposition muzzled, Banda continued to strengthen his dictatorial powers by having himself declared 'President for Life' in 1971, banning the foreign press whenever it suited him and waging pogroms against any group he regarded as a threat. His power was further increased by the establishment of two companies. Press Holdings was his personal company, part of which was the countrywide chain of PTC supermarkets. Admarc was the parastatal Agricultural Development and Marketing Corporation, to which all agricultural produce was sold at fixed rates. These two organisations between them controlled the country's economy – through them Banda gained total economic control.

Malawi's diplomatic ties with South Africa were established soon after Banda came to power. Unlike the leaders of the other front-line states, Banda was very conservative and shied away from the new socialist powers around him. He tended to encourage whites to remain in managerial positions, maintaining that they were better qualified for such roles. South Africa, concerned about the rise in socialism within the region and needing to defend its apartheid system, was delighted to have a relatively sympathetic neighbour, and initially rewarded Malawi with aid and trade. South Africans were established in top positions in some of Malawi's most important companies. South Africa, Israel and Taiwan were all involved in training the Malawi security forces. Money was also forthcoming. In particular, South Africa provided the initial loan financing the building of Lilongwe, declared Malawi's new capital in 1975. They also financed a new rail link from Malawi to Nacala in Mozambique (until then, Malawi's only rail link with the sea was the line to Beira, originally built in 1908).

There was a cooling of relations between South Africa and Malawi in the mid-1970s (Lilongwe was actually completed with funds from other donor countries), but by the mid-1980s things picked up and there was an increase in trade between the two countries again, principally of imports into Malawi rather than exports to South Africa. Malawi also became a base for South African backed Renamo units making incursions into northern Mozambique.

The Organization of African Unity (OAU) was furious at Banda's refusal to ostracise the South African regime. It could be argued, however, that at least his approach was honest and avoided charges of hypocrisy. This was unlike several other African countries who had outwardly condemned South Africa while secretly maintaining trade links.

At home, Banda's increasingly repressive regime resulted in innumerable political prisoners and little observation of basic human

The autocratic Dr Hastings Kamuzu Banda ruled Malawi from 1964 to 1994, eventually controlling the economy as well as the government.

MALAWI

rights. In a slight liberalisation in 1977 some 2000 detainees were released, but thousands more remained in jail.

In 1978, in the first general election to be held since independence, Banda personally vetted everyone who intended to stand as a candidate, demanded that each pass an English examination (thereby precluding 90% of the population). Even with these advantages, one Banda supporter lost his seat. He was simply reinstated.

Banda retained his grip on the country through the 1980s. The distinctions between the president, the party, the country, the government and Press Holdings became increasingly blurred. Quite simply, Banda *was* Malawi. Prominent figures were expected to give total support to 'His Excellency'. If this support was not forthcoming, they were relieved of their posts, or worse. The secretary general of the MCP (who was also the managing director of Press Holdings), and two cabinet ministers were fired for 'disciplinary offences', after they questioned presidential directives. In 1983 three other ministers died in a mysterious car crash. There was a small exiled opposition movement, the Socialist League of Malawi, but this lost momentum when their leader was murdered in Zimbabwe. It wasn't only high-profile people who suffered; one newspaper reported the disappearance and murder of more than 250,000 people during the 30 years of Banda's rule.

The 1990s brought increasing opposition to Banda's totalitarian one-party rule. The situation was also affected by the end of the Cold War era. As the strength and influence of the Soviet bloc withered, Europe, the USA and other western powers had no further interest in supporting 'friendly' countries such as Malawi (termed as such despite their distinctly unfriendly human rights records), and effectively propping up their leaders. Aid and preferential trade deals were still up for grabs, but now there were conditions, namely 'good governance', that is the principles of free-market economics and democracy (in that order of importance, according to some cynics).

But there were changes inside the country too, and it was the Catholic bishops of Malawi who finally triggered Banda's downfall. In 1992 they issued a pastoral letter which was read in every Catholic church. The letter condemned the regime and called for change. This was a brave action, for even bishops in Malawi could not be guaranteed immunity from Banda's iron grip of control. Demonstrations throughout the country, both peaceful and violent, added their weight to the bishops' move. As a final blow, donor countries cut off all non-humanitarian aid until Banda agreed to relinquish total control.

On 14 June 1993 a referendum was held in which the people of Malawi were asked to choose between a multiparty political system and Banda's autocratic rule. Over 80% of eligible voters took part. There was still a good deal of respect for the nonagenarian Dr Banda, but the desire for change was greater: the vote for a new system more than doubled the vote for the status quo. It was reported that some Malawians thought they were voting for an organisation *called* Multi Party. This was understandable, as voting was a new thing in Malawi, and an organisation with a similar name had recently come to power in neighbouring Zambia.

Banda accepted the vote, and constitutional changes were introduced to establish multiparty democracy in Malawi. The main political parties to emerge were the United Democratic Front (UDF), led by businessman Bakili Muluzi, and the Alliance for Democracy (AFORD), led by trade-unionist Chakufwa Chihana. Banda's MCP also remained prominent. A general election was called for the following year.

The End of the Young Pioneers

Through the 1980s and early 1990s the MCP youth organisation, the Young Pioneers, had been Banda's most ardent supporters – often with an enthusiasm bordering on the fanatical. Their activities ranged from organising spies and political informers to checking if market traders carried MCP party cards. They had become increasingly powerful and militarised and many were illegally armed, which caused considerable disquiet among senior figures in the army.

Prior to the general election, the Young Pioneers embarked on a programme of intimidation against voters in an attempt to maintain the MCP's dominant position. In late 1993, tension between the Young Pioneers and the army peaked after an attack on some soldiers by a group of Young Pioneers in Mzuzu. The army retaliated by attacking Young Pioneers offices in the north of the country, followed by helicopter attacks on their headquarters in Lilongwe. Some Young Pioneers took refuge in the MCP headquarters, but this was attacked as well. The Young Pioneers leaders were forced to flee the country and the organisation dissolved.

The country was ripe for an army take-over, but the generals ordered the troops back to barracks, and lent their support to the new democratic order.

Multiparty Democracy

Malawi's first full multiparty election was held on 17 May 1994. Essentially, it was a three-horse race between the MCP, the UDF and AFORD. All the parties' election promises were equally optimistic, so it was not surprising that voting was largely along ethnic and regional grounds: the MCP held in the centre of the country, and AFORD dominated the north, but support in the more heavily populated south of the country gave the UDF victory, although not an overall majority.

Once again, Banda accepted the result. Bakili Muluzi thus became Malawi's second president. He is a Muslim from Machinga in the south and was educated in England and Denmark. Although he rose through the MCP to become secretary-general in the early 1980s, he resigned from politics in 1982 to pursue business interests. It was not until the sanctioning of multiparty democracy that he re-entered the political scene.

Muluzi's first moves included the freeing of political prisoners, and offering ministerial posts to AFORD politicians in an attempt to form a coalition. This was rejected by

AFORD leader Chihana, who later also questioned Muluzi's constitutional right to free prisoners without consultation with parliament or the judiciary. (At the time nobody had questioned the move – everyone was so used to the president acting alone.) AFORD and the MCP went on to form a combined opposition alliance.

Despite these misgivings, the new president went on to introduce several more changes: the political prisons were closed, freedom of speech and a free press were permitted, and free primary school education was to be provided for all Malawian children. The unofficial night curfew which had existed during Banda's time was lifted. For tourists, the most tangible change was the repeal of Banda's notorious dress code which forbade women to wear trousers and men to have long hair.

The Muluzi government also made several economic reforms with the help of the World Bank and the International Monetary Fund, who had initiated a Structural Adjustment Programme (SAP) in 1993 – the last days of the Banda era. The kwacha (Malawi's unit of currency) had already been floated in February 1994, after many years of being artificially pegged high against foreign currencies. Effects of the SAP included the withdrawal of state subsidies and the liberalisation of foreign exchange laws. Further measures led to the closure of many private and state-owned businesses and a consequent rise in unemployment. A rationalisation of the civil service was also planned, which added to the job losses.

In September 1994, AFORD leader Chihana was made second vice-president and along with several other AFORD figures, took seats in Malawi's cabinet. The UDF described the move as a formation of a coalition government. AFORD and MCP maintained that their opposition coalition also remained intact. Observers also pointed out that this situation was made all the more unclear because there was no provision in the country's constitution for a second vice-president anyway. The obstacle was cleared with a bit of hasty rewriting.

In April 1995, Banda was brought to trial (with five others, including his former second-in-command John Tembo), accused of ordering the murder of three government ministers who died in a mysterious car accident in 1983. Banda's lawyers maintained he was too old and too ill to appear, but the trial went ahead in June. In December 1995 the trial ended in his complete acquittal and the result was greeted with general approval, especially when Banda went on to apologise publicly for any suffering he might have 'unknowingly caused'.

By 1996 the UDF's honeymoon period was well and truly over. Running the country was proving a tough job. Civil servants had gone on strike in mid-1995, following pay and job cuts. A scandal involving ministerial funds surfaced briefly, but was weathered. In April 1996, Chihana was sacked as second vice-president, and a month later pulled his AFORD party out of the coalition.

Outside the political arena, the effects of the post-election economic reforms, now optimistically named the Poverty Alleviation Programme, were hitting the average Malawian citizen very hard. Food prices soared as subsidies were reduced or withdrawn. For example, the price of bread doubled, and the price of maize flour (the country's staple) rose eight-fold between mid-1994 and mid-1996. Unemployment was now officially recorded at 50%, but may have been higher. There were reports of increased malnutrition, especially among the young. Crime, particularly robbery, often at night, increased in urban areas. Matters were made worse by the sluggish pace of the resumption of international aid, after it had been frozen in the final years of Banda's rule.

Modern Times

Although many of the problems Malawi now faces were inherited by the Muluzi government from Banda's time, there is growing dissatisfaction around the country. After 30 years to totalitarianism, the country is now in a state of bewilderment. Many Malawian people we spoke to during our research for this book ruefully admitted that the new

freedom of speech is marvellous, but then politely pointed out that they now have no money and no food. When well-fed politicians are frequently seen in large cars and helicopters, or reported to be voting themselves increased salaries and allowances, this does little to alleviate the resentment.

It hasn't escaped the attention of the newspapers that many of today's leading government figures are ex-MCP politicians. Charges of corruption and mismanagement of funds are frequently reported. The general feeling seems to be that little has changed since the old days. If anything, for the average Malawian, things are worse. This comes at a time when the economy is under strain from weak commodity prices (see Economy later in this chapter) and poor rural people (that is, the vast majority of Malawi's population) feel the pinch even more.

As so often happens in Africa (and elsewhere), the improvements promised by new politicians have simply not materialised. In Malawi, many people are already starting to hanker after the old days, and say they'd be happy if the MCP took control again. Thirty years of enforced allegiance to Banda is taking time to wear off, and there's still considerable respect for the 'old statesman'.

On the economic front there are some improvements after what's been seen as a slow period. International aid is also flowing back into the country once again. The challenge now for President Muluzi's government is to satisfy the heightened expectations of the Malawian people. The next presidential and parliamentary elections are due in 1999.

GEOGRAPHY

Malawi is a small country by the standards of the region, wedged between Zambia, Tanzania and Mozambique, with no direct access to the sea. The country is roughly 900 km long and between 80 km and 150 km wide, with an area of about 120,000 sq km.

The Great Rift Valley passes through Malawi, and the country's most obvious geographical feature – Lake Malawi – lies in a trough formed by the valley. This is the third largest lake in Africa, covering almost a fifth of Malawi's total area. A strip of low ground runs along the western lake shore, sometimes 10 or more km in width, sometimes so narrow there's only room for a precipitous footpath between the lake and the steep wall of the valley.

The lake shore is sandy in many places, with natural beaches, particularly in the south, where hotels and resorts have been built. Beyond the beaches and low plains, the Rift Valley wall rises steeply in a series of escarpments to high rolling plateaux that cover much of the country.

Malawi's main highland areas are the Nyika and Viphya plateaux in the north, and Mt Mulanje (also called the Mulanje Massif) in the south. Malawi's highest point is the summit of Sapitwa (3001m) at the centre of Mt Mulanje. There are also several isolated hills and smaller mountains dotting the country. The largest is the Zomba Plateau, near the town of the same name.

Malawi has three other lakes. The largest of these is Lake Chilwa, south-east of Lake Malawi. North of here is the remote Lake Chiuta, which spreads across the border into Mozambique. Less than 10 km south of Lake Malawi is Lake Malombe. Malawi's main river is the Shire; it flows out of the southern end of Lake Malawi, into and out of Lake Malombe and then southward as the plateau gives way to low ground, to flow into the Zambezi River in Mozambique. In this area, the lowest point is a mere 37m above sea level.

CLIMATE

Malawi has a single wet season, which runs from mid-October or early November to mid or late April, and a dry season from May to October/November. During the wet season daytime temperatures are warm and conditions humid in low areas, although much less rain falls along the shores of Lake Malawi than in the highlands. The dry season is cool from May to August, with July being the coolest month. At the end of the dry season, during September and October until the rains start, it can become hot and humid at midday, especially in low areas.

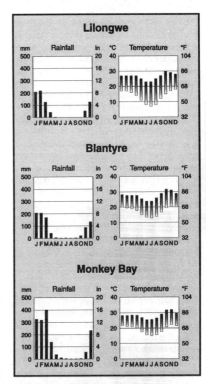

Daily temperatures in the lower areas do not fluctuate much, with average daytime maximums around 21°C in July and 26°C in January, although dry season highs of 38°C have been recorded in the Shire Valley. On the highland areas, average daytime temperatures in July are usually between 10°C and 15°C, while in September they get up to 20°C and above. Night-time temperatures on the highlands are low, sometimes dropping below freezing on clear nights in July.

ECOLOGY & ENVIRONMENT

The terms 'ecology' and 'environment' are bandied around a lot these days, and used in such a variety of contexts that actual meanings often become vague. Generally speaking, however, the factors relevant to

MALAWI

Malawi and other countries in East and Southern Africa are similar to those faced by the rest of the world. Environmental issues such as air and water degradation, industrial pollution, deforestation, soil erosion, urban encroachment, habitat and wildlife destruction, and the conservation of resources are becoming increasingly pertinent.

When discussing environmental matters there is often a danger of over-simplification. It is easy to regard the issues in isolation, when in fact they are all closely interrelated and linked to wider situations – economic, social and political – on a national, regional, and even global scale. Environmental and conservation issues are never straightforward. Experts often disagree on methods, solutions, and even on definitions.

For example, in Malawi, an ever-increasing human population puts great demands on the land and other natural resources. It is generally agreed that these resources need to be conserved, and one of the ways of doing this is to lower the rate of population growth. To suggest that the solution simply involves contraception, sterilisation or a change in cultural attitudes is a narrow view. Conservationists who prefer a broad perspective point out that the rapid population growth is closely linked to the problem of poverty, which in turn is linked to social issues such as lack of education and poor health. They argue that it is not reasonable to expect people with no money or little food to worry about conservation in its widest sense; the root of the problem – poverty – needs to be approached.

Poverty & Resources

One argument for the alleviation of poverty encourages poor (or 'Third World') countries to increase large-scale economic development, to provide income for their citizens which in turn will lead to a better standard of living and thus an interest in conservation. Against this, it could be argued that economic development can cause its own environmental damage: heavy industry leads to air and water pollution, and inevitably requires the use of natural resources,

while large-scale farming can also cause pollution and soil erosion.

When African environmental issues are being discussed, there is often a tendency to emphasise 'indigenous' situations. For example, in Malawi, the following problems are frequently cited: wood-burning stoves create deforestation, over-grazing by goats causes soil erosion, over-fishing in the lake reduces fish stocks, but it is important to recognise that on a global scale the countries of the 'First World' use a far greater proportion of the earth's resources than those in the 'Third World'. An urban citizen of Britain, Australia or the USA might consume over 50 times more natural resources than a poor rural inhabitant of Malawi, Zambia or Mozambique.

Thus, even with population growth stabilised, if everybody had the high standards (that is, high consumption) of the industrialised 'First World' countries, our planet's finite resources simply would not be able to support all the world's people. The 'broad' conservationists hold that this global imbalance in the use of resources is a major environmental factor which must be addressed.

Ivory, Elephants & Conservation

The debate about the conservation of elephants and the sale of ivory is particularly relevant in Africa, and provides another example of the complexity of environmental issues.

In the 1970s, various factors led to a massive increase in elephant poaching. At the end of the 1980s the price of one kg of ivory (US$300) was three times the *annual* income of more than two-thirds of Africa's population. Naturally the temptation to poach was great, although the real money was made not by poachers – often desperately poor villagers – but by the dealers who frequently acted with the full knowledge (and help) of senior government figures. In Malawi, Zambia, Mozambique and the countries of East Africa, elephant populations were reduced by up to 90% in about 15 years. In some other countries (notably Zimbabwe, South Africa and Botswana), where protected areas such as national parks were relatively well-managed, the elephant populations were not threatened by poachers to anything like the same degree.

In 1990, following a massive worldwide campaign from various conservation organisations, a world body called the Convention on International Trade in Endangered Species (CITES) banned the trade in ivory, and the global demand collapsed. At the same time there was an increase in funds for the protection of elephants. The improved law enforcement and closure of the trade were both seen as important steps in elephant protection.

But the issue does not stop there. In the countries which protected their herds successfully, there are increasingly strong arguments for the trade to be legalised again, and strictly controlled, so that funds raised from sales of ivory (including tusks of culled animals) could go to conservation projects that would benefit both animals and people. In this way the elephants would become a resource with a tangible value, giving governments and local people an incentive to ensure their survival.

The same 'pay to stay' arguments are now frequently applied to wildlife and protected wildlife areas throughout Africa. It is now recognised that protected areas such as national parks are unlikely to succeed in the long-term unless governments *and* local people can obtain real benefits from their presence. The argument goes like this: if the local people protect the animals, foreigners pay money to come and see them, and some of the money goes back to the local people. If there is no benefit, there is no incentive to conserve.

All over the region, there are increased moves to involve local people in wildlife conservation schemes. Examples include the WURCS (Wildlife Utilisation Raises Community Standards) schemes in Malawi, where assistance is given to locally-based initiatives to encourage the sustainable harvesting of natural resources, such as plant nurseries, forestry projects and the husbandry of 'wild' animals such as duiker and guineafowl. Another is the pioneering CAMPFIRE (Communal Areas Management Programme for Indigenous Resources) project in Zimbabwe, where local villagers 'own' the elephant and other animals which inhabit their traditional lands, and can generate funds from controlled hunting or photographic safaris which take place there. Income is also generated by the jobs that wildlife-tourism creates, such as game rangers, tour guides and various posts in the hotels, lodges and camps. Further spin-offs include the sale of crafts and curios – another way for local people to earn money direct from the tourists.

But even when such schemes are established, the issues still remain complicated. Despite success in elephant protection, the policy of establishing properly protected areas has created its own problems. Elephants eat huge quantities of foliage each day, and a large herd remaining within an unnaturally small area (even though it may be hundreds of square kilometres) will quickly destroy its surroundings. As the herd grows, the food supply for elephants and for other species dwindles.

In the past, the herd would have moved to another area, allowing time for vegetation regrowth, but with the increase in human population and the threat from poachers, this option is increasingly closed off. So, by successfully protecting a species, the authorities in various parks are now facing the problem of overpopulation by that species. A balance between the land and the animals must be maintained – but how? Solutions include relocation (where animals are taken to other areas) and a pioneering elephant contraception project (where breeding cows are injected with a 'pill' equivalent – so no jokes about condoms please). The most common alternative is to cull elephants, sometimes in large numbers. Killing elephants to conserve them seems a bizarre paradox, but at present the other options remain experimental and limited in their effect.

MALAWI

Tourism & the Environment

Although tourism can generate money, employment, and the incentive to conserve, it can also have very negative effects. Either way, tourism itself is a major environmental issue (it is one of the largest global industries), and is impossible to ignore. A problem arises when a destination cannot cope with the number of tourists attracted to it, which causes great damage to the natural and social environments. A classic example of this in Africa is Victoria Falls, shared by Zimbabwe and Zambia. In 1986 less than 80,000 visitors came to 'The Falls'; by 1996 it was almost 300,000. In another 10 years the figure could be 1.5 million. New hotels and lodges are being built or redeveloped on both sides of the falls, and upstream along the banks of the Zambezi. The population of Chinotimba township (on the edge of Victoria Falls town in Zimbabwe, but rarely seen by visitors) has also increased massively as local people are attracted by work opportunities. The town's water and sewage utilities reportedly can't cope with the numbers, so pollution ends up in the river. More visible are the vast amounts of plastic and metal rubbish that the burgeoning population generates. Local environmental campaigners say that the increase in river activities disturbs wildlife and damages the natural vegetation along the banks. Others point out that the woodcarvings for sale on every street corner mean that trees are being destroyed in a large area around the town.

Another issue, particularly relevant for visitors to Africa, is the growth of so-called eco-tourism. This is one of the most overused and meaningless terms around. Don't be fooled by travel companies blithely claiming to be 'eco-friendly' just because they do things outdoors. Activities such as camping, white-water rafting or game viewing (by car, foot or balloon), or sightseeing trips to remote or fragile areas *can be* more environmentally or culturally harmful than a conventional hotel holiday in a specifically developed resort.

Environmentalists point out that tourism relies on natural resources, such as healthy wildlife populations, clean rivers and rich cultural traditions, but quite often does little to maintain, sustain or restore them. A leading British environmentalist, perhaps surprisingly for those who like 'authentic adventure', reckons that Sun City in South Africa is one of the best examples of eco-tourism in the world: 'a purpose-built resort complex, creating 4500 local jobs, and putting wildlife back onto a degraded piece of useless veldt'.

If you want to support tour companies with a good environmental record, you have to look beyond the glossy brochures and vague 'eco-friendly' claims and ask what they are really doing to protect or support the environment (and remember that includes local people, as well as animals and plants).

When it comes to meaningless platitudes on tourism and the environment, governments are worse than the tour companies. A report in a 1995 issue of the Zimbabwe-based *Travellers Times* reported that South Africa, Zimbabwe, Namibia, Zambia, Swaziland and Malawi issued a joint declaration that they would implement environmentally friendly tourism policies. Observers say they look forward to a corresponding increase in action.

Visitors to Africa (or to any other part of the world) should consider the amount of money they pay during their holiday, and ensure that as much as possible stays within the 'host' country to the benefit of local people. With this in mind, opponents of the 'high-cost low-density' tourism policies adopted by countries such as Botswana and Zambia, point out that overland truck passengers, independent backpackers and other low-budget travellers on a long trip contribute just as much to local economies as high-rolling tourists who come to a country on a short all-inclusive trip paid for overseas.

The effect that tourists have on the environment is not just financial. It is important for visitors to behave in a manner which limits their impact on the natural environment and the local inhabitants – animal and human. Some ideas are listed below. To be a responsible tourist you have to question some of your own actions and those of tour companies providing the services and facilities you use. You also have to look pretty closely at the actions of governments, both local and around the world. Being a responsible tourist doesn't mean you have to get depressed and spoil your holiday. In fact, by asking a few questions and getting a deeper insight, it can make your trip even more rewarding.

Guidelines for Responsible Tourism

A British organisation called Tourism Concern has come up with several guidelines for travellers who wish to minimise negative impacts on the countries they visit. These include:

Save precious natural resources. Try not to waste water. Switch off lights and air-conditioning when you go out. Avoid establishments which clearly consume limited resources such as water and electricity at the expense of local residents.

Support local enterprise. Use locally-owned hotels and restaurants and support trade and craft workers by buying locally made souvenirs. But do help safeguard the environment by avoiding souvenirs made from local wildlife – ivory, fur, skins, etc – particularly endangered species.

Recognise land rights. Indigenous people's ownership of land they use and occupy is recognised by international law. This should be acknowledged irrespective of whether the national government applies the law or not. (Governments are among the principle violators of tribal rights.) When in tribal lands tourists should behave as they would on private lands at home.

Ask before taking close-up photographs of people. Don't worry if you don't speak the language. A smile and gesture will be appreciated.

Don't give money, sweets, pens, etc, to children. It encourages begging and demeans the child. A donation to a recognised project – a health centre or school – is a more constructive and meaningful way to help.

Show respect for local etiquette. Politeness is a virtue in most parts of the world, but remember that different people have different ideas about what's polite. In many places, tight fitting wear, revealing shorts or skimpy tops are insensitive to local feelings. Loose lightweight clothing is preferable. Similarly, public displays of affection are often culturally inappropriate.

Learn something about the history and current affairs of the country. This helps you understand the idiosyncrasies of its people, and helps prevent misunderstandings and frustrations.

Be patient, friendly and sensitive. Remember that you are a guest.

Tourism Concern (☎ 0171 753 3330; fax 0171 753 3331, Stapleton House, 277-281 Holloway Rd, London N7 8HN) is a membership organisation. If you want to support their work, it costs UK£18 per year to join. In the USA, the Centre for Responsible Tourism (☎ 415 258 6594; fax 415 454 2493, Box 827 San Anselmo CA 94979) is similar.

FLORA & FAUNA

Malawi's wide range of vegetation and animal habitats in a relatively small area make the country ideal for those with any interest in natural history. Many visitors come to Malawi specifically to observe or search for the country's animal and plant species. Malawi also stands at a 'biological crossroads' between Southern, Central and East Africa, with species occurring from all these regions. Various field guides are listed in the Books section of the Facts for the Visitor chapter.

Vegetation

Malawi's vegetation can be divided into several broad types or 'zones', each with characteristic plants (from tiny flowers to giant trees), as well as associated birds and animals. These zones are complex, and firm division lines are impossible to draw. There are considerable overlaps, pockets of one zone within another, and varying definitions among biologists. The following list of major zones is not exhaustive and, by necessity, is greatly simplified; but it will provide a useful overview.

Mopane This vegetation type occurs in hot lowland areas, including the middle Shire Valley and the plains along the southern shores of Lake Malawi and some of the smaller lakes. More than half of Liwonde National Park is covered by mopane woodland. It derives its name from the mopane tree, a tall multistemmed tree which characteristically grows well on soils with a high clay content. It has adapted well to the lack of rainfall and the heat in these areas; this is achieved through its shallow root system, which maximises water uptake, and through closing its distinctive butterfly shaped leaves together during the middle of the day, reducing water evaporation. When conditions are favourable these trees can reach up to 25m in height, although on poor soils they tend to grow as small shrubs. Other species in this zone include the broad-leafed shepherds tree, and the small and large sour plum tree. Most easily recognised is the baobab, which favours the same dry conditions, and frequently occurs in mopane woodland areas. (For more details on the baobab tree, see the boxed text in the Lake Shore chapter.)

Miombo Miombo woodland is the dominant vegetation type in Malawi, originally covering 70% of the land, although much of it has now been cleared for farming or plantations. It occurs up to an altitude of about 1500m in areas where the rainfall is higher and more reliable than in the mopane regions. The relatively poor soil that covers much of Malawi encourages the growth of small to medium height, well-spaced trees, producing an open canopy woodland. Enough sunlight penetrates through this to the ground to allow the growth of grasses and shrubs. Good examples of this can be seen on the slopes of Nyika Plateau and in Kasungu National Park. Apart from the diverse wildlife that miombo woodland supports, two of the most important functions of the woodland are maintaining water catchment areas and preventing soil erosion. Hence the reason that several areas of this type of woodland are now protected. The dominant trees of the open-canopy miombo are *Julbernadia globiflora* and several types of *Brachystegia*. Brachystegia is so dominant that miombo woodland is often called brachystegia woodland.

In areas of high rainfall, such as west of Nkhata Bay, and south of Mt Mulanje the trees tend to grow taller and closer together,

producing a closed canopy. The tall *Brachystegia spiciformis* is often the dominant species of this type of miombo woodland.

Evergreen Forest There isn't much indigenous forest left in Malawi as most has been cleared, but areas do exist which are thought to be remnants of the extensive evergreen forests that once grew all over Malawi, as well as southern Tanzania, northern Zambia, and Mozambique. Pockets of montane forest occur in the highland areas of Malawi, such as on Mt Mulanje and the Zomba, Nyika and Viphya plateaux. The variety of trees found in montane forest is enormous and the range of birds, animals and insects that they support is correspondingly great. Two notable, though uncommon, trees to be found in this type of forest are the Nyika juniper and the Mulanje cedar, both endemic to Malawi.

More extensive than the montane forest is the semi-evergreen forest, to be found in the Nkhata Bay area and on the slopes of the Zomba Plateau and Mt Mulanje. It is also found along river courses. This type of forest overlaps closely with the closed-canopy miombo woodland mentioned previously.

Montane Grassland This type of vegetation occurs generally above 1800m to 2000m, and predominantly occurs on the Nyika Plateau in northern Malawi, where the rolling hills are covered in grass. These grasslands are maintained by the annual fires, both natural and intentional, which sweep through, discouraging the growth of shrubs and trees. In the Nyika Plateau, the land below this altitude, in valleys and on the escarpment edges, is covered in light open miombo woodland, and in between the two vegetation zones you can often see areas of large protea bushes.

Riverine & Wetlands Along the shores of the lakes and the banks of the rivers that flow into them, the natural vegetation consists of dense riverine woodland or long reeds and grasses. In various parts of Malawi wide, marshy river courses, where reeds and grasses grow, are called *dambos*.

Plantation & Farmland Although this is not a natural vegetation, some naturalists refer to this as a separate zone or type because it covers most parts of Malawi. The vast majority of people are subsistence or small scale farmers (see Economy below). Plantation areas include the tea and fruit estates on the Thyolo Highlands between Limbe and Mulanje; rubber in the northern region; pine on the Viphya and Nyika plateaux; and sugar near Dwangwa, on the central lake shore.

Flowers

Malawi has a great diversity of indigenous wild flowers. This is due to the wide range of habitats, from high mountains and plateaux to tropical forest and low-altitude woodlands. There are numerous varieties of proteas, aloes, gladioli and helichrysums (also known as 'everlastings'). Malawi is particularly famous for its orchids: more than 280 terrestrial species and 120 epiphytic species have been recorded. (See the boxed text on the Orchids of Malawi.)

Good spots for flower enthusiasts include Nyika National Park, where montane grassland areas support many terrestrial orchid species and the patches of evergreen forest support epiphytics. Proteas and aloes are found on the lower slopes. Other highland areas include the Zomba Plateau and Mt Mulanje, where terrestrial and epiphyte orchids occur, plus proteas, aloes, stag's horn lily and various tree ferns. Kasungu National Park is also a good area; the miombo woodland is rich in tree species and the grassy dambos support orchids, gladioli, lilies and everlastings. Other forest areas supporting orchids include Dzalanyama, Dedza and Viphya. In miombo woodland areas, such as Liwonde and Majete, aloes also occur, plus the Sabi star (also called Impala Lily). The lagoons in Liwonde are also noted for their waterlilies and reedbeds.

For keen botanists, several local field-guides are available. Some are mentioned in the Books section of the Facts for the Visitor chapter. Others can be found at the Wildlife Society of Malawi bookshop in Limbe.

Mammals

Malawi lacks vast herds of popular easy-to-recognise animals, such as rhino and lion, so it is not considered a major game viewing country. However, for those less concerned with simply ticking off 'the big five', Malawi has plenty to offer. Most large mammals are found within the country's national parks and game reserves, although there are a few

Orchids of Malawi

Malawi is a relatively small country by regional standards but contains one of the largest number of orchid species of any African country. The current figure is over 400; this includes over 280 terrestrial species, divided into about 30 genera, and over 120 epiphytic species, with about the same number of genera. Botanists believe that several more hidden 'specials' wait to be catalogued. The reasons for this great number include a great diversity of habitat, including high montane grassland, various types of evergreen forest and lower altitude miombo woodland. Malawi also stands at a 'biological crossroads' with species common to the Central, Southern and East African regions.

The majority of terrestrial orchids flower in the rainy season, from November to early April, with a few species (mostly *Eulophia*) starting at the end of the dry season around October. The peak viewing time is January and February – the best place to see them is the Nyika Plateau and other high areas in the north such as the Viphya Plateau. Access to Nyika used to be a problem in the rainy season, but improvements are planned (see Nyika National Park in the Northern Malawi chapter for details) so keen botanists should be able to enjoy the flowers without too much difficulty. ∎

Eulophia speciosa stands up to 90 cm tall and is found throughout Malawi.

non-protected areas where certain species also occur.

The country's main national park is Liwonde, noted for its herds of elephant and antelope (including impala, bushbuck and kudu), and hippopotamus in the Shire River. Elephant also occur in Kasungu National Park, as do buffalo, zebra, hippopotamus and several antelope species.

In the north is Nyika National Park, renowned for roan antelope and the smaller reedbuck, as well as zebra, warthog, eland, klipspringer, jackal, duiker and hartebeest. There's also a chance of seeing hyena and leopard. Nearby Vwaza Marsh Game Reserve is renowned for its hippo, plus elephant, buffalo, waterbuck, eland, roan, sable, hartebeest, zebra, impala and puku. In southern Malawi, Lengwe National Park supports a population of nyala – at the northern limit of its distribution in Africa. The park also contains bushbuck, impala, duiker and kudu.

Fish

Lake Malawi has more fish species than any other inland body of water in the world, with a total of more than 500 of which over 350 are endemic, and new species are continually being discovered. The fish of Lake Malawi are netted by local people for food, fished for sport by anglers, goggled at by snorkellers, or simply left alone by everyone.

The largest family of fish in the lake is the *Cichlidae* (cichlids), which includes the small, brilliantly coloured and remarkably varied *mbuna* species, which are trapped and exported to aquariums all over the world. (For more details see the boxed text in the Lake Shore chapter.) They are easy to spot around rocky shores, and are the main reason snorkelling is so popular in Lake Malawi. In some areas, like Cape Maclear, the fish are so accustomed to being fed that they flock towards any swimmer, and nibble anything that moves – including your toes. In other areas they are still a bit timid, or simply ignore passing humans.

Other fish families in the lake include the *usipa* (also called lake whitebait), a small fish which collects in large schools, and is netted by local people from dug-out canoes. Anglers go for *mpasa* (also called lake salmon), *ncheni* (lake tiger), *sungwa* (a type of perch), *kampango* or *vundu* (both catfish).

As well as the lake, Malawi has many rivers, streams, smaller lakes and dams, which are also habitats to a wide variety of fish. For example, rainbow trout can be fished for on the Zomba Plateau and Mt Mulanje, and tigerfish can be hooked in the Lower Shire River. As most people come to catch these type of fish, rather than to simply look at them, more details have been included under Fishing in the Activities section of the Facts for the Visitor chapter.

National Parks & Game Reserves

Malawi has five national parks. These are (from north to south): Nyika; Kasungu; Lake Malawi Marine National Park (around Cape Maclear); Liwonde; and Lengwe. There are also four game reserves: Vwaza Marsh, Nkhotakota; Mwabvi; and Majete. Generally speaking, these are less developed than the national parks, with fewer accommodation options and a more limited network of roads and tracks (if any at all). Full details on the facilities of each park and reserve are given in the appropriate sections.

All national parks and game reserves have accommodation; this ranges from simple camp sites and rustic resthouses to self-catering chalets and comfortable (even luxurious) lodges. Until recently, the lodges and camps in Malawi's national parks and reserves were not of a good quality, mainly because they were run by the Department of National Parks and Wildlife, and any money they did make simply disappeared into central government coffers (along with about 90% of the revenue raised from national park entrance fees). There was very little reinvestment, and the poorly paid game-scouts and other staff had little incentive to improve standards or quality of service.

Despite lip service paid to wildlife conservation and management by the former government, poaching was rife through the 1980s and early 1990s, and game stocks in many parks and reserves were severely depleted. The new government promised to combat the poaching but a lack of resources and commitment meant little changed.

However, since the mid-1990s several parks and reserves have received development funds from international donor countries or organisations. For example the German government is assisting with development at Nyika National Park; the European Union is assisting at Kasungu National Park; Italian aid is received at Lake Malawi; South African aid is received at Liwonde; and aid from Japan is invested in Nkhotakota Game Reserve. This injection of foreign aid should result in improved access roads, management, anti-poaching and staff morale. Part of the deal in most cases is that accommodation should be leased out to private companies instead of being run by the Department of National Parks and Wildlife. One of the first places to change was Mvuu Lodge & Camp at Liwonde National Park, where the old park accommodation has been completely revamped and a new luxury lodge built, now run by Central African Wilderness Safaris. Wherever such schemes have been introduced, accommodation and general park standards have improved, although prices have also risen.

Accommodation Reservations for government-run accommodation in the parks and reserves should be made through the Department of National Parks & Wildlife in Lilongwe (see the Lilongwe chapter for details). Reservations for privately-run lodges and camps should be made direct or through an agent. It is not usually necessary to reserve camp sites, assuming you have your own tent. Details of accommodation options in each park and reserve are given in the relevant sections. However, as explained above, the situation is in a state of flux, so be prepared for some changes by the time you arrive.

Reservations for accommodation are recommended. However, if you prefer not to stick to a rigid itinerary, you can try your luck and turn up at parks and reserves without a

booking. In the popular parks this isn't recommended at weekends and during holiday times.

Costs All national parks and game reserves in Malawi have an entry fee of US$15 per person per day, plus US$15 per day per car (US$30 for larger vehicles). Other costs are optional: for example, the hire of a game scout for guiding in your vehicle is US$2. In parks where walking is permitted a game scout guide costs US$10 per day. A porter is US$15 per day. (These fees are paid to the park, so it is usual to tip the scouts extra for their services.) All these fees are payable in kwacha.

Forest Reserves

Malawi also has almost 70 forest reserves across the country, some of the largest and most famous for tourists being Mt Mulanje and the Zomba Plateau. Some forest reserves also have accommodation. These are usually log-cabin resthouses, simple and rustic (verging on the tumbledown), but often quiet and cheap, with a pleasant atmosphere. Forest resthouses include those at Dzalanyama and Dedza, near Lilongwe, Kasito and Luwawa on the Viphya Plateau, Chintheche on the northern lake shore, and on the Zomba Plateau. The Department of Forestry also has a series of huts on Mt Mulanje for hikers and trekkers (for more details see Mt Mulanje in the Southern Malawi chapter). There is usually no fee to enter a forest reserve.

Wildlife Society of Malawi

The Wildlife Society of Malawi (WSM) is an active conservation organisation, formerly called the National Fauna Preservation Society. It publishes several field guides to different parts of Malawi, and has close links with the Department of National Parks and Wildlife. You can contact the society directly (☎ 643428, PO Box 1429, Blantyre). For more information and a list of publications, or visit the WSM shop in Limbe (see the Blantyre & Limbe chapter for details).

MALAWI

Scimitarbills are agile climbers and often hang upside down to probe crevices for insects. Their black plumage has a purple sheen.

Birds of Malawi

Malawi is a popular destination for bird-watchers. For its size, Malawi contains more bird species than most African countries, reflecting its variety of natural habitats, ranging from mountain plateaux to lake shore. Some 645 species have been recorded in Malawi, and about 530 species probably breed here. Those that don't breed here are mainly long-distance migrants from Europe or Asia (mostly present in Malawi during the rains from about September to April).

Some of Malawi's breeding birds leave the region during the dry season, so probably the most productive time of year for bird-watching is November and December, but any time is likely to be very rewarding. There are many good places for bird-watching, some of the best being the national parks of Liwonde, Kasungu, Lengwe and the Nyika Plateau, and Dzalanyama Forest Reserve and Lilongwe Nature Sanctuary.

Some indication of the bird-watching opportunities in Malawi can be gleaned from the number and beauty of birds that you may well see in the gardens of the towns and cities. The lilac-breasted roller, little bee-eater, green loerie, a number of sunbirds, the paradise flycatcher and the African hoopoe are just a few of the parade of birds that you may see in the gardens of the Lilongwe Capital Hotel, for instance.

As with anywhere, the species of birds you are likely to see will depend on the surrounding habitat. Main vegetation zones are listed above. Below are some more details on the major habitats of Malawi, with a brief overview of the great variety of birds to be found within each. For more details, a good field guide is recommended. (See the Books section in the Facts for the Visitor chapter for suggestions.)

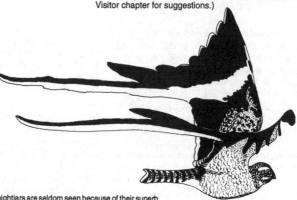

Although not uncommon, nightjars are seldom seen because of their superb camouflage and nocturnal habits. The pennant-winged nightjar is the most spectacular species. Only the male sports these eccentric plumes.

Mountains

The high open grasslands of the Nyika Plateau are home to wattled crane, Denham's bustard and red-winged francolin. Flowering plants in the grasslands may attract sunbirds such as the greater double-collared sunbird and the red-tufted malachite sunbird. Mountain cisticola and churring cisticola can be found in the bracken belts around the areas of forest. Nyika's patches of evergreen forest can be rewarding for birdwatchers, with beautiful species such as the bar-tailed trogon, starred robin and the cinnamon dove often seen.

Other mountain areas include Thyolo Mountain, to the east of Blantyre, which is home to several rare and threatened species such as the green-headed oriole, bronze-naped thrush and the Natal thrush. The forest on Zomba Plateau is also a good spot; species found here include the Thyolo alethe and the black-headed apalis. Ntchisi Mountain, north-east of Lilongwe, is topped with evergreen forest, which is a breeding site for birds such as the narina trogon.

Also known as the Stanley bustard, Denham's bustard is a large bird of the grasslands.

The white 'windows' in the wings of the black eagle are distinctive as it soars above the plains.

Rocky Hills

Rocky hills are scattered throughout Malawi, particularly in the area around Cape Maclear and near Dedza. They provide good vantage points from which to watch birds of prey such as lanner and peregrine falcons and black eagles. Other birds that may be seen in this type of habitat include the mocking chat, rock cisticola, large striped pipit and black stork. On rocky hills in the south of the country, you may see cape bunting.

Lake Shore Forest

The Kalwe Forest near Nkhata Bay closely resembles the coastal evergreen forests of East Africa. Bird-watching here is excellent – you may see birds such as the green coucal, red-capped robin, blue-mantled crested flycatcher and the local speciality, Cunning's akalat.

The blue-mantled crested flycatcher, like all fly-catchers, energetically pursues its insect prey.

Miombo Woodland

Miombo or brachystegia woodland occurs in several parts of Malawi, including on the lower slopes of the Nyika Plateau and Ntchisi Mountain, but probably the best examples are at Dzalanyama Forest Reserve and Kasungu National Park. Nearly every miombo bird species can be found in Dzalanyama, including such rarities as olive-headed weaver and Stierling's wood-pecker. Other more common species that are frequently seen include wood hoopoes and helmet shrikes.

Mopane Woodland

The best example of mopane woodland is found in Liwonde National Park. Birds typical of this habitat include the red-billed and crowned hornbill, long-tailed starling and white-browed sparrow-weaver. In Liwonde

Flocks of the gregarious white helmet shrike are commonly seen foraging in woodlands.

The comical-looking crested guineafowl roams the grassland in flocks.

The strange little hamerkop is related to herons and feeds on small aquatic animals.

you will also find Malawi's only population of Lilian's lovebird, and get your best chance to see Pel's fishing owl. There is also a good chance of seeing nightjars here, for example the fiery-necked nightjar and Mozambique nightjar.

Thicket
Dense deciduous thickets, most notably in Lengwe National Park, are yet another haven for ornithologists. Here you may find crested guineafowl, barred long-tailed cuckoo, black-and-white flycatcher and gorgeous bush-shrike, birds unlikely to be seen elsewhere in Malawi. You may also see African broadbill and the beautiful Boehm's bee-eater.

Mixed & Acacia Woodland
Two of the best areas for bird-watching in this type of habitat are Lengwe National Park and Lilongwe Nature Sanctuary. The yellow-billed hornbill is confined to this habitat, and other birds that may be seen include the red-winged warbler and the spectacular giant eagle owl.

Lake Malawi
The southern end of Lake Malawi is home to enormous numbers of the African fish eagle. The sound of its plaintive call and the sight of one of these magnificent birds perched in a tree overlooking the lake is for many one of the most enduring impressions of Malawi. The lake is also home to several large breeding colonies of white-breasted cormorant which nest offshore. Reedbeds along the shore support colonies of golden and brown-throated weavers. Other birds that are often seen include the palm swift and the collared palm thrush.

Rivers & Wetlands
There are several rivers in Malawi which are excellent for bird-watching. The Upper Shire River in Liwonde National Park is home to an enormous variety of birds, including several species of kingfisher, such as the pied, malachite and giant kingfisher, and a number of herons, including the white-backed night heron, and egrets and ducks. Further south, on the Lower Shire, near Chikwawa, are several large colonies of the beautiful carmine bee-eater which nests in the sandcliffs during the dry season. Mpatamanga Gorge and Kapichira Falls can also be rewarding; birds often seen include the rock pratincole and Livingstone's flycatcher. The Bua River in the Nkhotakota Game Reserve is another good spot.

Wetland areas support a great variety of waterfowl, and during the months of August to November they are often visited by a number of migrating Eurasian shore birds. Some of the best wetland areas in Malawi include Lake Kazuni in Vwaza Marsh Game Reserve and Lake Chilwa, near Zomba. In the far south of Malawi, the little-visited Elephant Marsh is an excellent bird-watching area; African skimmer and pygmy goose can be seen here, plus herons, storks and kingfishers. ■

The African skimmer feeds by trailing its lower mandible just below the water's surface.

GOVERNMENT & POLITICS

Until the elections of 1994, although a parliament existed, Malawi was effectively a dictatorship ruled by the President for Life, Dr Hastings Kamuzu Banda. There were elections for members of parliament, based on the British system, but all candidates came from the Malawi Congress Party – the only legal party in the country.

Following the move to multiparty politics, the parliamentary system of government is still the same. The big difference is that the people of Malawi now get representatives from different parties to choose from.

Elections are held every five years. Voters in each political constituency elect a representative to be their member of parliament. Separate presidential elections are held at the same time. There are between eight and 15 parties at any given time. The main parties are the Malawi Congress Party (MCP), Banda's old party, traditionally strong in the centre of the country; the Alliance for Democracy (AFORD) traditionally strong in the north; and the United Democratic Front (UDF) drawing most of its support in the more heavily populated south of the country.

There are no major ideological differences between the various parties, except that the MCP is considered more 'traditional' or 'conservative' (mainly because it's been around since independence, while the other parties are new on the scene). Party support is based largely on regional or ethnic allegiances, and although various matters are hotly debated in parliament, they often subside into personal accusations, with little genuine discussion on issues or policies.

Malawi's current head of state is President Bakili Muluzi, the leader of the UDF. He holds this position for a five year term, until the next elections, due in 1999.

ECONOMY

Malawi's economy is dominated by agriculture. Around 85% of the people are rural inhabitants; either subsistence farmers or workers on commercial farms and plantations. The main exports are tobacco, sugar and tea. Tobacco alone accounts for more than 60% of Malawi's export earnings (for more details see the boxed text in the Lilongwe chapter). Tea and sugar make up another 20%. The main cash crops are usually grown on large plantations, but tobacco is also grown on smaller farms cultivated by a single family.

Most rural people cultivate their own plot of land to provide food for their needs. Any surplus is sold in markets or to the government-run agricultural co-operatives. Maize, millet and rice are staple food crops. Until the 1970s Malawi was self-sufficient in food crops, and the economy was buoyant.

Through the 1980s the economy of Malawi suffered as a result of several factors. These included the general worldwide slump in trade following oil-price increases. There was also a fall in demand for tobacco and sugar, and an increase in international debt-servicing costs. Closer to home, the war in neighbouring Mozambique blocked land-locked Malawi's main access route to the sea (the railway line to the port of Nacala) so that imports and exports had to go by much longer and more expensive routes via Zimbabwe to South Africa, or through Tanzania. In the early 1990s there were also several years of bad drought; this hit agricultural output and also affected the rest of the manufacturing sector, which is largely agriculture-based. In early 1994, the flotation of the Malawi currency, the kwacha, caused it to plummet in value against international currencies, and inflation soared.

Since mid-1994 there have been a few bright spots. There was an increase in investor confidence when the rule of President Banda ended and a multiparty free-market economic system was introduced. At around the same time the war in Mozambique ended, which once again gave Malawi access to Nacala (although it took another couple of years for the railway to be fully repaired). A resumption of foreign aid, after it was frozen by many donors at the end of the Banda era, also helped boost the economy slightly. In 1996 favourable weather conditions meant a bumper tobacco crop was forecast. On the manufacturing front, several international companies promised to increase investment. Inflation has steadied, but was still running at around 20% at the time of research.

The new government has introduced various other economic changes including a liberalisation of foreign exchange laws, an easing of border tariffs, and a drive to encourage the diversification of cash crops. An ambitious and far-reaching privatisation programme is also in full operation, with more than 100 former state-owned businesses up for sale, including Air Malawi, the National Bank, plus various parts of Press Holdings, which was once more than 99% owned by former president Banda. Investment in mining and manufacturing is officially being encouraged, although critics say that in reality there is still too much government red tape and interference. Others point out that there is actually very little to mine.

Tourism is also seen as a great potential foreign currency generator. Although various international companies are poised to build new hotels and lodges on Lake Malawi and in national parks around the country, once again commentators report that there seems to be a lack of genuine will on the part of the government and its international advisors to positively encourage investment. An overnight 10% tax hike on hotels and restaurants in 1995 did little to alter this impression. These problems are not immediately apparent to visitors, but international observers in the tourism and aid industries have said it will have detrimental effects on the country as a whole unless government attitudes alter.

For the average Malawian, however, these economic changes and wranglings are irrelevant, as conditions for most people are extremely hard. By any yardstick, Malawi remains a poor country – one of the world's 10 poorest – with a per capita annual income of less than US$200. By the purchasing power parity method of assessing income (which works out how far the Malawian kwacha goes by comparing prices on basic consumer items) Malawians earn around US$750 per year (this is compared to an average of around US$20,000 in most industrialised western countries). Other socio-economic indicators paint a grim picture too: literacy rates

Economic Swings & Roundabouts

Former President Banda was undoubtedly a tyrant, but one of his policies which benefited Malawi and Malawians to a certain extent was the determination to keep the economy agriculturally based. He encouraged most of the population to remain in villages as subsistence farmers, and deliberately avoided promoting industrial development (although Malawi had little in the way of raw materials for industrialisation anyway).

'Cities breed poverty' he said, and compared to many other African countries the numbers of urban dwellers, and most particularly of the urban poor, was a small fraction of the population. Malawi also did not fall into the trap that caught other African countries: concentrating on industry and neglecting agriculture, only to spend export earnings on imported food. Malawi was self-sufficient in agricultural produce and staple foods were subsidised.

In recent times, following the political changes since 1994, what was a gradual drift from rural areas to urban areas has increased markedly: the 'informal settlements' or low-cost housing zones (townships) around Malawi's main cities have grown, and there has been an increase in crime. Some people, not only those with possessions to lose, bemoan the changes and wish the 'old man' would return, along with the status quo he enforced for 30 years.

Others point out that Banda's policy of keeping most of the population in scattered rural settlements meant that political opposition was harder to organise. They also recall that Admarc, the government's agricultural purchasing 'department', bought goods from farmers at fixed (usually low) prices. These goods were then sold (also cheaply) to private companies within the Press Holdings group, an organisation almost wholly owned by Banda. Now, they say, with the introduction of a free market economy, at least the farmers can get a fair price for the produce. The farmers agree, but go on to point out that now some of the locally produced food (such as maize flour) which was sold in PTC stores (part of Press Holdings) is more expensive, precisely because subsidies have been lifted. ∎

stand at about 50% and population growth at more than 3% a year. Infant mortality is around 20%, and Malawi has the second highest disparity between rich and poor in the world. Unemployment is over 50%.

There's still hell of a long way to go.

POPULATION & PEOPLE

Malawi's population in 1991 was estimated at around nine million, including almost half a million refugees from Mozambique. The population is growing by around 3.5% a year. Estimates in 1996 put the total at around 10 million, although most Mozambican refugees have now returned home.

Around 15% of the population inhabit towns and cities – the vast majority live in rural areas, in scattered villages and individual homesteads. Malawi's main urban centres are: Lilongwe, the administrative capital, in the centre of the country; Blantyre, the commercial capital (with its sister city, Limbe) in the south; Zomba, the political capital, between Lilongwe and Blantyre; and Mzuzu, the main town in the north. There are a few other small towns, mainly along the lake shore. In northern Malawi, where there's more high ground, the population is light and scattered. In the south and centre of the country the land is lower, densely populated and more intensively cultivated.

All the African people are of Bantu origin: the main ethnic groups ('tribes') are: the Chewa, dominant in the central and southern parts of the country; the Yao, also found in the south; and the Tumbuka in the north. Other groups include the Angoni (also spelt Ngoni) who inhabit parts of the central and northern provinces, and Chipoka (or Phoka) in the central area, the Lambya, the Ngonde (also called the Nyakyusa) in the northern region, and the Tonga mostly along the lake shore.

There are small populations of Asian and European people living mainly in the cities, and involved in commerce, plantations, aid and development, or the diplomatic service.

EDUCATION

Primary education in Malawi consists of eight years in school for pupils aged seven to 14. Officially, primary education is free of charge, but children must still provide books and materials, or be required to wear a uniform. The grades or classes are known as 'standards'. Thus a seven year old child starts school in standard one and goes on to finish in standard eight. There's an exam at the end of every year, and children who fail don't move up to the next standard. It is also common for children to take a year or longer out of schooling if they are needed at home or in the fields, or if the family simply cannot afford the necessary books and uniforms. Thus it is not uncommon to find 15 year olds still in standard five. Some standard eight pupils are almost 20.

During the days of President Banda

Malawians in South Africa

Historically, because there has been no industry in Malawi and insufficient employment to cater for the population, vast numbers of young men have gone to find work in South Africa, mainly in mining or related businesses. This process started at the end of the last century, when Nyasaland was administered by the British South Africa Company (BSAC), and local men were encouraged to work in the mines of Rhodesia and South Africa, also owned by the BSAC. The former president Banda was one of many who went to South Africa around 1915 (popular mythology had it he walked all the way), where he found work as a teacher and translator.

As you travel around Malawi you'll undoubtedly meet men who have spent time in South Africa, earning enough money to buy a farm or get married, sometimes returning several times to maintain their income. Despite the social disruption caused by absent fathers and husbands in Malawi, the source of revenue is greatly needed.

However, as the South African mining industry is itself in a state of flux requiring thousands of people to be laid off or 'retrenched', it's likely that workers from other countries, including Malawi, will be the first to go. ∎

primary education was not compulsory, and the whole education system was neglected (some observers say this was a deliberate policy to ensure the population remained docile). Even if every child had wanted to go, there were nowhere near enough schools – especially in rural areas. The result of this was the lowest literacy rate in Africa after Mozambique. After the multiparty elections of 1994, the new UDF government announced plans to provide genuinely free and universal primary education. Around 20,000 extra teachers were employed (some with just a few months training) and one million kwacha (then about US$70,000) was allocated for books and materials. Primary school enrolment in 1996 was reported up from under two million to over three million. Half of the standard one pupils were girls.

This was a great shock to the system, with up to 120 children in one classroom reported in many areas, but the move was generally seen as positive by most Malawians. Cynics noted that providing free education was actually quite easy, and not very expensive compared to other plans proposed by the new government. Others pointed out that the fact it was so cheap and easy means it should have been done years ago. Both sides agreed however that providing secondary schools or work for the school-leavers would be a much tougher battle.

Children who reach standard eight take a Primary School Leaving Certificate. If they pass they can officially go on to secondary education. However, even after passing the exam, this move up is not guaranteed as there are simply not enough secondary schools in the country. Generally, this means only those with the highest marks are selected. For those who are selected, secondary education usually means travel away from home, as each school serves a vast area. Children must board at the school, or find accommodation with relatives who live nearer. Once again, money is a major factor: school fees in a state-run secondary school are about US$10 per term (this includes boarding), but even this is too much for some families, so even children who pass the exam may miss out on secondary education for financial reasons. In reality less than 15% of Malawi's school-age population complete secondary education.

Secondary education lasts for four years: the grades are known as 'forms'. After two years pupils take their junior school certificate; if they pass, this takes them into form three and form four. At the end of form four, pupils take their final exam: the Malawi Secondary Certificate of Education. Ideally they are around 18 years old, but because of the 'years out' described above, many are in their early to mid-20s.

Pupils unable to get into state-run secondary schools can go to a private school. There are several in Malawi, but fees here are around US$170 per year (in a country where average annual income for many people is less then US$100), so only the relatively better-off families can send their children here.

This sector of Malawi's education system is also being tackled by the UDF government. Almost 250 new secondary schools have been promised, to absorb the increased numbers currently coming through primary level. They are all planned to be 'day-schools' so children can stay at home and walk each day to and from lessons. This plan is laudable, but even if it is fulfilled the new schools will still only cater for an extra 30% of secondary school-age children.

Tertiary education in Malawi consists of various colleges which make up the University of Malawi: Chancellor College, the School of Medicine, the Agricultural College and the Polytechnic. There are also three technical colleges – one in each province. University students are officially selected according to their secondary school performance, but once again fees are a considerable barrier for many. As part of the plans to expand tertiary education the government has announced plans to build a new 'university of the north' in Mzuzu.

ARTS
Visual Arts
The distinction between art and craft is often hard to determine, and this is the case in Malawi as elsewhere. All over the country,

visitors will see hand-produced items for sale in curio shops, markets and road-side stalls. If you're looking for cheap souvenirs, there's plenty to choose from: animals carved from wood or soapstone, clay figures, mats and baskets, model cars and bicycles made from raffia or wire, and Malawi's famous chief's chairs (for more details see Things to Buy in the Facts for the Visitor chapter). But in among the stuff that's hammered out in a hurry, you will also find works in wood and stone (and occasionally paintings) that have been created by artists of better-than-average talent. Salesmen often seem to make no distinction between work of good or mediocre quality, so it's always worth spending time to search the better pieces out.

Among places in Malawi where you can see artists in action, and buy their work, is Mua Mission (in Central Malawi, on the road between Salima and Balaka). A missionary named Father Boucher has established a school and studio here, providing the space and encouragement for local artists to explore and develop their own distinctive styles. Most of the artists work in wood, and while some of the work is strongly influenced by western Christianity, other pieces are of traditional African design. Other pieces are impossible to classify in this simplistic way, and are the result of the artist's personal inspiration.

Malawian artists who have achieved recognition for their work inside the country and abroad include Kay Chirombo, Willie Nampeya, Cuthy Mede, Charley Bakari and Louis Dimpwa. Between them they represent various media, producing carvings in stone and wood, batiks, and paintings, and many have exhibited outside Malawi. Some critics and commentators have discussed the evolution of a distinct Malawian style or 'school', but others point out that influences from Europe or other parts of Africa have precluded this.

Several of the artists mentioned above also teach at the University of Malawi, where the department of Fine and Performing Arts at Chancellor College (Zomba) trains students to degree standard, under the guidance of Professor Berling Kaunda, an internationally recognised artist in his own right.

Of the painters and sculptors inside Malawi, Cuthy Mede is possibly the best known, especially since he gave up his lecturing job to open Galerie Africaine in Lilongwe – the first high-profile art gallery in the country. Many of the works on display and for sale are his own, but some are by other local artists. He is also actively involved in the development and promotion of Malawian art within the country and around the world.

Other places to see locally produced art include the exhibitions which are regularly held at the National Museum in Blantyre, and at the French Cultural Centre.

Music & Dance

Traditional music and dance in Malawi, as elsewhere, are closely linked and often form an important social function, rather than being simply 'mere' entertainment. There are few country-wide traditions: the various tribes and areas have their own tunes and dances. Musical instruments are similar to those found in other parts of East and Southern Africa, with local names of special features. These include various drums, from the small hand-held *ulimba*, made from a gourd, to ceremonial giants carved from tree-trunks, and the *mambilira* similar to the western xylophone, with wooden keys, and sometimes played over hollow gourds to produce a more resonant sound. A single-string violin-type instrument called *zeze* is sometimes played, and various rattles and shakers called *maseche* are tied to dancers' legs and arms.

The most notable traditional dance in Malawi is the *Gule Wamkulu*, indigenous to the Chewa people (the largest and most dominant group in the country). The dance reflects traditional religious beliefs in spirits and is connected to the activities of secret societies. Leading dancers are dressed in ragged costumes of cloth and animal skins, usually wearing a mask, and occasionally on stilts.

Other groups have their own music and

dance traditions. For example, among the Tumbuka, in northern Malawi, the *vimbuza* is a curative dance performed by traditional healers ('witchdoctors') to rid patients of sickness. Local anthropologists report that the demand for vimbuza dancers has increased significantly in recent years, and healers from other northern tribes, such as the Ngoni, have adapted the dance into their own curative ceremonies.

More secular in origin are the *beni* dances of the Yao people in southern Malawi. During colonial times many men from the traditionally war-like Yao served as *askaris* (from the Swahili word for guard) in a regiment called the King's African Rifles (KAR). *Beni* is believed to be a corruption of 'band', and the dance originally satirised what the African soldiers saw as the European military obsession with marching and parades, before developing into a more specific form of its own. Other tribes served in the KAR, as soldiers or porters, and similar dances are performed in other parts of Malawi. For example in the north, the style is called *mapilenga*. Today, dancers still wear a costume inspired by the colonial military uniform (which originated in India), which includes white tunics and red caps – often made from local materials such as sardine tins.

For visitors to Malawi, it is often difficult to witness genuine traditional music and dance. By their very nature, such dances are not advertised for public participation, and usually take place in rural areas. Displays are often performed in large hotels, or at cultural centres in Lilongwe and Blantyre, but these may often be simplified and shortened to suit western tastes.

Modern home-grown contemporary music is not a major force in Malawi as it is in, say, Zimbabwe or South Africa. However, there are a few significant local musicians; you can find their work on cassettes sold at road-side stalls and markets. Most influential and popular is Allan Namoko, who successfully combines traditional and modern themes. He sometimes plays with the Chimvu River Jazz Band, and their albums

include *Ana Usiidwa* (The Orphans). Other names to look out for include Ethro Kamendo, one of Malawi's leading female singers, Lucius Banda, and the Sapitwa Band.

Literature

Like most other countries in Africa, Malawi has a rich oral tradition. Collections of traditional stories which have been transcribed into print include *Land of Fire – Oral Literature from Malawi* by Scoffeleers and Roscoe.

Since independence, a new breed of Malawian writers has emerged. In the early years several confident poets and novelists wrote with an enthusiasm not permitted or encouraged under colonial rule. However, as the country's despotic president, Dr Hastings Banda, became increasingly sensitive to criticism (real or imaginary) many writers found themselves under threat of imprisonment. Some simply abandoned their work, others continued in secret, while others were forced to leave the country. Until the mid-1990s, for their own safety, many of Malawi's leading literary figures continued to live abroad. Not surprisingly, common themes for many writers are oppression, corruption, deceit and the abuse of power.

Poetry is the most popular literary form, although the names of very few poets are known outside literary circles in Malawi and abroad. Most work is written in English, and nearly everything is published in English. Some anthologies which include Malawian writers are listed in the Books section of the Facts for the Visitor chapter.

Leading poets include Frank Chipasula, whose collections include *O Earth Wait for Me*, *Nightwatcher*, *Nightsong* and *Whispers in the Wings*. Another is Steve Chimombo, whose collections include *Napolo Poems*. His most highly acclaimed work is *The Rainmaker*, a complex poetic drama. But to many Malawians Chimombo is better known for his popular short stories that appear in newspapers and magazines – a strange but vivid combination of traditional themes and harsh urban settings. He is also a lecturer, critic and commentator on the wider arts scene.

Another leading figure is Jack Mapanje, who studied in Britain before becoming a lecturer and Head of the Department of English at the University of Malawi. His first poetry collection *Of Chameleons and Gods* was published in 1981, but much of the symbolism (chameleons play an important role in traditional Malawian beliefs) is obscure for outsiders. Not too obscure for President Banda though – in 1987 Mapanje was arrested and imprisoned without charge. He was released in 1991, and two years later published his second book *The Chattering Wagtails of Mikuyu Prison*. The title refers to Malawi's notoriously harsh maximum security jail, where Mapanje was imprisoned.

David Rubadi, another literary figure, has studied and taught in Kenya, Uganda and Britain. He has compiled an anthology called *Poetry from East Africa*, which includes a section on Malawi, and also writes poetry himself. His novels include *No Bride Price*, which discusses the familiar themes of corruption and oppression.

Most critics agree that Malawi's leading novelists include Legson Kayira, whose semi-autobiographical works *I Will Try* and *The Looming Shadow*, based on his journey from Malawi through Africa and eventually to the USA, earned him critical acclaim in the 1970s. A later work *The Detainee* on the surface describes how one man is influenced and controlled by the state, but the title also refers to the country as a whole, oppressed and imprisoned by a ruthless dictator. Also receiving high acclaim is James Ng'ombe, whose novel *Sugarcane with Salt* (1989) explores aspects of a changing African society.

Another more recently published writer is Sam Mpasu; his novel *Nobody's Friend* was ostensibly about a murder in a newly independent African country, but also a comment on the secrecy of Malawian politics. This criticism did not go unchecked and Mpasu was imprisoned for 2½ years. After his release he wrote *Prisoner 3/75*, about his imprisonment, and later became Minister for Education in the new UDF government. His comments on the time of Banda's rule sum up the situation for all writers, and the people of Malawi too: 'We had peace, but it was the peace of a cemetery. Our lips were sealed by fear.'

Banning the Press

It's worth noting that it wasn't only works of literature which incurred the wrath of former president Banda. Several books on contemporary history were also banned, including, perhaps not surprisingly, *The Theory and Practice of African Politics* and *Malawi – the Politics of Despair*. Newspapers from other countries and from within Malawi were also frequently barred from circulation, especially if they were seen to be critical, but sometimes even if they weren't. Any form of pornography was also prohibited, but this included several medical textbooks, on the ground that the diagrams were indecent. Even guidebooks didn't escape; an early Lonely Planet book called *Africa on the cheap* (forerunner of *Africa on a shoestring*) was critical of the regime in the Malawi chapter, and was promptly banned as well. In the early 1980s, travellers with a low-budget look about them often had bags specifically searched for the offending volume. ■

SOCIETY & CONDUCT

During your trip to Malawi, although you will meet citizens and expatriates of European and Asian origin, the society and culture is predominantly African, and most of the advice here assumes you're in an African situation.

As in any part of the world, the best way to learn about a society's conduct is to watch or listen to the locals. The first thing to remember is not to worry: Africans are generally very easy-going towards foreigners, and any social errors that you might make are unlikely to cause offence (although they may cause confusion or merriment). Having said that, there are a few things that are frowned upon wherever you go. These include: public nudity, open displays of anger, open displays of affection (between people of same or opposite sex), and vocal criticism of the government or country.

On top of these basics, a few straightforward courtesies may greatly improve your

MALAWI

chances of acceptance by the local community, especially in rural areas. Pleasantries are taken quite seriously, and it's essential to greet someone entering or leaving a room. Learn the local words for 'hello' and 'goodbye' and use them unsparingly. For those out of earshot, it is customary to offer a smile and a pleasant wave, even if you're just passing in a vehicle.

Great emphasis is also placed on handshakes. There are various local variations, involving linked thumbs or fingers, or the left hand touching the right elbow, which you'll pick up by observation, but these are reserved for informal occasions (not greeting officials). A 'normal' western handshake will do fine in most situations. Sometimes, people who know each other continue to hold hands right through their conversation, or at least for a few minutes.

As in most traditional societies, older people are treated with deference. Teachers, doctors, and other professionals (usually men) often receive similar treatment. Likewise, people holding positions of authority – immigration officers, government officials, police, village chiefs, and so on (also usually men) – should be dealt with pragmatically. In most of the countries in this book officials are normally courteous and fairly efficient, sometimes even friendly. On your side, manners, patience and co-operation will get you through most situations. Even if you meet somebody awkward or unpleasant, the same rules apply. It is one thing to stand up for your rights but undermining an official's authority or insulting an ego may only serve to waste time, tie you up in red tape and inspire closer scrutiny of future travellers.

At the other end of the spectrum, children rate very low on the social scale. They are expected to do as they're told without complaint and defer to adults in all situations. Unfortunately for half the region's population, the status of women is only slightly higher than for children. For example an African man on a bus might give his seat to an older man, but not normally to a woman, never mind that she is carrying a baby and luggage and minding two toddlers. In traditional rural areas, women are expected to dress and behave modestly, especially in the presence of chiefs or other esteemed persons. Visitors should act in the same way.

When visiting rural settlements, especially when away from areas normally reached by tourists, it is a good idea to request to see the chief to announce your presence and request permission before setting up camp or wandering through a village. You will rarely be refused permission. Visitors should also ask permission before drawing water from a community well. Avoid letting water spill on the ground, especially in dry areas. If you want to wash your body or your clothing, fill a container with water and carry it elsewhere, and try to minimise the water you use.

Most travellers will have the opportunity to share an African meal sometime during their stay and will normally be given royal treatment and a seat of honour. Although concessions are sometimes made for foreigners, table manners are probably different from what you're accustomed to. Before eating, a member of the family may pass around a bowl of water, or jug and bowl, for washing hands. If it comes to you first as honoured guest and you're not sure of the routine, indicate that the bowl should be taken to the head of the family, then do what they do when it comes to you. The African staple, maize or sorghum meal, is the centre of nearly every meal. It is normally taken with the right hand from a communal pot, rolled into balls, dipped in some sort of sauce – meat gravy or vegetables – and eaten. As in most societies, it is considered impolite to scoff food; if you do, your hosts may feel that they haven't provided enough. In fact, for the same reason, it may be polite *not* to be the one who takes the last handful from the communal bowl. If your food is served on separate plates, and you can't finish your food, don't worry; again this shows your hosts that you have been satisfied. Often containers of water or home-brew beer may be passed around from person to person. However, it is not customary to share coffee, tea or bottled soft drinks.

Dress Codes

None of the countries covered in this book have any specific regulations regarding clothing or behaviour. Malawi used to be a celebrated exception, because women visitors were required by law to wear skirts that covered the knees, while men were required to have short hair and tidy beards. The reason for this was partly because many women travellers used to tour Malawi wearing shorts, which offended the locals (men and women), particularly in the mainly Muslim north, but also in the centre and south where most people are pretty conservative.

The law was dropped in 1994, and although you are now *allowed* to wear what you like, it's still pretty insensitive to wander around with most of your legs showing (although this is no problem on the lake beaches, for hiking or for sports).

For women, the same applies in most other countries in the region: apart from the disrespect you are showing to local sensibilities, you also make things harder for yourself – don't be surprised if kids laugh, adults (men and women) treat you disdainfully, and some young guns see you as easy prey. From a practical point of view, keeping reasonably covered with loose-fitting clothes also helps prevent sunstroke.

What you wear is also important for men too. Look around you: the only people wearing shorts or tatty clothes are kids, labourers or the poor. Then ask yourself why some officials and other locals treat some bare-legged travellers with contempt. ■

MALAWI

If you do visit a remote community, please tread lightly and leave as little lasting evidence of your visit as possible. In some African societies it isn't considered impolite for people to ask others for items they may desire; but likewise it isn't rude to refuse. So if a local asks for your watch or camera, say 'no' politely, explaining it's the only one you've got, and all will be fine. If you start feeling guilty about your relative wealth and hand out all your belongings, you may be regarded as strange. Reciprocation of kindness is OK but indiscriminate distribution of gifts from outside, however well intentioned, tends to create a taste for items not locally available, erodes well-established values, robs people of their pride and in extreme cases, creates villages of dependent beggars.

On the other hand, when you're offered a gift, don't feel guilty about accepting it; to refuse it would bring shame on the giver. To politely receive a gift, local people may accept it with both hands and perhaps bow slightly, or they may receive it with the right hand while touching the left hand to your right elbow; this is the equivalent of saying 'thanks'. You can try this if you think it's appropriate. Spoken thanks aren't common and local people tend to think westerners say 'thank you' too often and too casually, so don't be upset if you aren't verbally thanked for a gift.

RELIGION

Most people in Malawi are Christian, usually members of one of the Protestant churches originally founded by the missionaries who came to Malawi in the late 19th century. There are Muslims in the north, particularly along the lake – a legacy of the Swahili-Arab slave-traders who operated in this area.

Alongside the established religions many Malawians also hold traditional beliefs, such as the intercedence of ancestors. There is also a belief in spells and magic (usually called witchcraft) which is a complex subject, hard for westerners to appreciate or understand. In brief simplistic terms it goes like this: physical or mental illnesses are often ascribed to a spell or curse having been put on the sufferer. A jealous relative or villager is usually suspected as being the 'witch' who placed the curse, and a traditional doctor, also called a diviner or witchdoctor, is then required to hunt out the witch and cure the victim. This is done in different ways in various parts of the country, and may involve the use of herbs, divining implements, prayers, chanting or dance. Services do not come free of charge, and many witchdoctors demand high payments – up to US$20, in a country where an average month's earnings is US$20 or less.

A witchcraft 'epidemic' was reported in Malawi in the mid-1990s. As the population increased, the standard of service in hospitals and clinics declined, and AIDS and other related illnesses took their toll.

Several medical relief organisations have described the use of and belief in witchcraft as a major impediment to their attempts to alter social behaviour, particularly in regard to the fight against AIDS, and even as a major hurdle in the development of the nation as a whole.

Islam in Malawi

In 1994 Bakili Muluzi, the leader of the UDF, became Malawi's second president. Although originating from the south of Malawi, he is a Muslim. Since the election several Islamic organisations have been invited to Malawi, and Islam is enjoying a revival. New schools, mosques and clinics have been opening in several towns and rural areas, supported by donations from various other Islamic countries in the world.

The new president differs sharply from his predecessor; Dr Banda was an elder of the Church of Scotland. Although the 'old man' had many faults, and maintained an oppressive regime, he did allow a certain degree of religious freedom and non-Christians were not actively persecuted. All signs indicate that this tradition of tolerance will be continued. ■

LANGUAGE

All the different ethnic groups in Malawi (see Population & People, earlier) have their own language or dialect. The Chewa are the dominant group and their language, called Chewa or Chichewa, is the national language and widely used throughout the country as a common tongue. (Chichewa is sometimes written ChiChewa – the 'Chi' prefix simply signifies 'language of').

English is the official language and is very widely spoken, particularly in the main towns. Even in remote rural areas, it's usually possible to find people who speak English, but a few words of Chichewa will always be useful, and certainly raise interest, particularly in rural areas.

Other groups also have their own languages. Of these, Tumbuka, spoken by about 500,000 people, is dominant in the north, and Yao, spoken by about 600,000 people is dominant in the south.

Some Basic Chichewa

Chichewa is a complex language: word prefixes and suffixes change according to context, so one single word cannot always be given for its English equivalent. The most common form is given here, but do remember that by using these words and phrases you may not be speaking 'proper' Chichewa. You will be understood though, as most Malawian people are accommodating and will be pleased to hear even a few words spoken by a foreigner.

Greetings & Civilities

Mazungu means 'white person', but is not derogatory. *Bambo* literally means 'father' but is a polite way to address any Malawian man. The female equivalent is *Amai* or *Mai*.

Hello.	*Moni.*
Thank you/Excuse me.	*Zikomo.*
Thank you very much.	*Zikomo kwambile/*
	Zikomo kwambiri.
Please.	*Chonde.*
Good/Fine/OK.	*Chabwino.*
Good night.	*Gonani bwino.*
Hello, anybody in?	*Odi.*
Come in/Welcome.	*Lowani.*
How are you?	*Muli bwanji?*
I'm fine.	*Ndili bwino.*

And you?
  Kaya-iwe? (to one person)
  Kaya inu? (to several people)
Goodbye. (to person staying; 'stay well')
  Tsala bwino.
Goodbye. (to person leaving; 'go well')
  Pitani bwino.
What is your name?
  Dzina lako ndani?
Where are you going?
  Ukupita kuti?
I'm going to Blantyre.
  Ndikupita ku Blantyre.

Useful Phrases

Yes.	*Inde.*
No.	*Iyayi.*
How much?	*Ntengo bwanji?*
	Ndalama zingati?
many	*zambile*
enough/finish	*bas*
Why?	*Chifukwa?*
I don't understand.	*Sindikunva.*
What's this?	*Ndi chiani?*
What's that (far away)?	*Icho ndi chiani?*
Where?	*Kuti?*
Here.	*Pano.*
Over there.	*Uko.*

I want ...	*Ndifuna ...*
I don't want ...	*Sindifuna ...*
to eat	*kudya*
to sleep	*kugona*
to buy	*kugula*
I am tired.	*Ndatopa.*

today	*lero*
tomorrow (early)	*m'mara*
tomorrow	*mara*
yesterday	*dzulo*

Women	*Akazi*
Men	*Akuma*

Food

Bring me ...	*Mundi passe ...*
bread	*buledi*
chicken	*nkhuku*
coffee	*khofi*
eggs	*mazira*
fish	*somba*
fruit (one)	*chipasso*
fruits (many)	*zipasso*
lake perch	*chambo*
meat	*nyama*
milk	*mkaka*
potatoes	*batata*
tea	*ti*
vegetables	*mquani*
water	*mazi*

In restaurants *nsima* is stiff maize porridge served with a sauce of meat, beans or vegetables.

Numbers

Chichewa speakers talking together will normally use English for numbers and prices. Similarly, time is nearly always expressed in English.

1	*chimonzi*
2	*ziwili*
3	*zitatu*
4	*zinayi*
5	*zitsano*

MALAWI

A Few Words of Tumbuka & Yao

Tumbuka is widely spoken in the north, and Yao is widely spoken in the south. But nearly all Tumbuka and Yao people speak Chichewa, and many also speak English, and they may use these as common languages.

English	Tumbuka	Yao
Hello.	*Yewo.*	*Quamboni.*
How are you?	*Muliwuli?*	*Iliwuli?*
Fine.	*Nilimakola.*	*Ndiri chenene.*
And you?	*Manyi imwa?*	*Qualinim we?*
What is your name?	*Zinolinu ndimwenjani?*	*Mwe linachi?*
Where do you live?	*Mmukukhalankhu?*	*Ncutama qua?*
My name is John.	*Zinalane ndine John.*	*Une linaliangu John.*
I live in England.	*Nkhula ku England.*	*Gutama ku England.*
Thank you (very much).	*Yewo (chomene).*	*Asante (sana).*
Goodbye.	*Pawemi.*	*Siagara gani ngwaula.*

Facts for the Visitor

PLANNING
When to Go

Malawi's wet season runs from October/November to late April, and its dry season is from April/May to October/ November (see Climate in the Facts about Malawi chapter). The best time to visit Malawi is during the dry season. It's cooler in the first months (July is the coolest time), increasingly warmer towards September, and positively hot in early October before the rains break.

When you go to Malawi will also be determined by your reason for coming. Late in the dry season is the best time for game viewing, as the vegetation is not so dense and animals converge at reliable water holes, but the heat can be unpleasant – especially in the lowland areas. May to July is not so good for seeing game, but the landscape itself is much more attractive and conditions less oppressive. August is a busy period, mainly because the weather is good, and also because it is school holiday time. During the rainy season, game viewing is usually not good, and it's also worth noting that in the rainy season or just afterwards, access roads in the parks (and other minor roads around the country) are often impassable, unless you've got a rugged 4WD vehicle.

If you come to Malawi specifically for the birdlife, October/November is the best time, as European migrants are also present. However, at this time, conditions are exceedingly hot or exceedingly wet (or both), so you have to be dedicated. The rest of the year is fine for most amateurs. If you've come for the angling, see Fishing in the Activities section later in this chapter.

If you come only to take landscape photographs, the later months of the dry season may not be the best time as the views, especially from the highland areas (such as Livingstonia and the Nyika Plateau), can sometimes be obscured by haze and smoke from grass burning on the lower plains. Views are at their sharpest during the wet season (when it isn't actually raining) or in the first few months of the dry season.

Although the views might be good, it's best not to consider hiking or trekking in the highlands during the wet season – stream crossings (particularly on Mt Mulanje) can be treacherous. Another factor to consider if you plan to visit southern Malawi, again especially Mt Mulanje, is a mist called *chiperone* (pronounced 'chiperoni') which occurs during the early months of the dry season, sometimes lasting up to five days at a time.

If you are planning to visit Mozambique or Zambia from Malawi, an idea of seasons here will also be useful. They are similar to Malawi's, although Mozambique's dry season runs from April to September, and weather conditions on the coast are also influenced by the ocean. This is the best time to visit Mozambique. Zambia has three seasons. May to August is dry and cool, and the landscape green and lush. By August vegetation becomes brown and more sparse, and is better for game viewing. September to October temperatures are uncomfortably hot, although game viewing is good. November to April is the rainy season: many rural roads are impassable and most national parks are closed. The best time for bird-watching is November to December, but conditions are good throughout the rest of the year.

It's worth noting that the weather patterns all over Southern Africa have become less predictable in the last decade or so. The rainy seasons have been arriving later, or finishing earlier (or sometimes later), and in Malawi the chiperones seem to be occurring less frequently.

Also worth considering when you travel in this region are the South African school holidays. In Malawi some lake shore resorts get busier, while the southern beaches of Mozambique and popular parks or tourist sights in Zambia can be crowded. The holiday periods are different in the various

South African provinces but occur roughly in the third week of March to mid-April; at the end of June to the third week of July; one week at the end of September; and early December to mid-January.

Maps

Maps of Malawi, suitable for general travelling, are not widely available outside the country. The choice seems limited to those produced by ITM Publishing: *Malawi Travel Reference Map* at a scale of 1:900,000, and a similar *Zambia Travel Reference Map* at 1:1,500,000. You should be able to locate these in good specialist shops (some are listed below).

The Michelin map *Africa Central & South* (Sheet 955) shows Malawi, and is good enough for general planning, especially if you're considering a visit to neighbouring countries too. The detail is good, given the limitations of scale (1:4,000,000), and the map is regularly updated. It's the kind of map that lingers in bookshops for ages though, so check you buy a recent version. (The date is on the cover, or in the bottom right-hand corner of the map.) Even so, you should expect a few discrepancies between the map and reality, particularly with regard to roads, as old tracks get upgraded and once-smooth highways become potholed disasters. In South Africa, Struik publishes *Central & Southern Africa*, which covers a similar area.

For more information, a specialist map supplier may be able to help. In the USA, a good source is Maplink (☎ (805) 965 4402), 25 E Mason St, Santa Barbara, CA 93101. In the UK, Stanfords (☎ (0171) 836 1321), 12-14 Long Acre, London WC2E has a similarly extensive collection, or use Latitude Map Mail Order (☎ (01707) 663090; fax 663029). In Australia, contact Map Land (formerly Bowyangs) (☎ (03) 9670 4383), 372 Little Bourke Street, Melbourne, Victoria 3000, or the Travel Bookshop (☎ (02) 9241 3554), 20 Bridge Street, Sydney, NSW 2000.

Once in Malawi, you can easily buy maps of the country in local bookshops (see the Lilongwe and Blantyre chapters for details). These include *Malawi* (1:1,000,000) which shows shaded relief features and most roads, including minor tracks, although light red lines on a brown background makes map reading tricky. The *Malawi Road & Tourist Map* (at the same scale) has one side showing all main roads and some minor roads, and national parks (but no relief details) plus street maps of the main towns and a very nice welcoming message from the Ministry of Information and Tourism. The other side contains some general information and another map of the country showing various features of interest to tourists. On both maps detail is not especially good, and the quality of roads is out of date, so you're probably better off using them together or using one of them alongside the Michelin 955.

For more detail, government survey maps (the most useful at scales of 1:50,000 and 1:250,000) are available from the Department of Surveys Public Map Sales Offices in Blantyre and Lilongwe (see Map Offices under Information in those chapters for details). In both places the staff are helpful, there are no formalities, and most maps cost about US$2. Maps of popular areas, such as Mt Mulanje, occasionally go out of stock.

Specific maps and guidebooks on individual national parks and hiking/trekking areas are covered in the relevant sections.

What to Bring

Clothes With such a variety of things to do in Malawi, it's hard to generalise about what to bring. You shouldn't carry too much, particularly clothes: anything you find yourself without can easily be bought along the way. In the cities and large towns, new clothes are comparably priced or cheaper than those in Europe, and in many markets you can find decent second-hand clothes (many originating from European charity stores – see the boxed text on Second-Hand Clothes). Note that in most places, especially in cities, local people dress smartly if they can afford to, so wearing some decent clothes will mean you get taken more seriously in 'official' situations. Generally, khaki or military-style clothing or baggage is not recommended, especially if you're also visiting Mozambique, as you may be mistaken for a soldier or a spy.

Second-Hand Clothes
In the last few years, all over Southern Africa, there has been a large increase in shops and market stalls selling second-hand clothes, mostly collected by charities and charity shops in Europe. You can also find factory overruns and items off-loaded by stores because they're out of fashion in western countries. The clothes are good quality, and a fraction of what they'd cost new, which means local people can avoid having to fork out hard-earned money for fancy gear. But there's a downside: the second-hand imports have wiped out any chance of the poorer countries of Southern Africa (especially Zambia, Malawi and Mozambique) having their own clothing industry. All over the region, market and street tailors, who used to run up shirts and trousers from local material, are going out of business. ■

Equipment To save money, or just to keep out of towns and cities, a tent and set of camping gear will be useful, and essential if you plan to do any hiking. Malawi has some marvellous places for camping. Even if you're not a camping fan, a sleeping bag and sheet liner will be useful in cheap hotels and cabins (and on overnight trains) where bedding might not be provided.

Absolute essentials include: basic medical kit, mosquito net, water bottle, purifying solution and water filter (all covered in detail under Health, later in this chapter); torch and spare good-quality batteries; several passport-sized photos (two or three for each visa application). Optional items include: camera and film (for more details see Photography & Video, later in this chapter); binoculars (for game and bird-watching); universal drain plug; small padlock to secure the contents of your pack from opportunistic riflers; travel alarm; Swiss Army-style knife; a clothes-drying line; a sewing kit.

Don't forget boring things such as a wash kit and towel (although some travellers class this as optional too).

Hiking Extras If you plan to visit the highland areas (such as Nyika or Mulanje), remember they get cold at night even in warm months, so a light jacket, a pullover or good sweatshirt, a hat, a pair of gloves and some warm socks would be worth taking. A thermal vest (T-shirt style), which has a good warmth-retaining capacity for its size and weight, is also a handy item.

A camping stove is essential, as fires are not allowed in many areas. One that runs on petrol will be the least hassle (don't rely on finding refined 'white gas' such as Shellite or Colemanfuel), but methylated spirits for Trangia-type stoves can usually be found in supermarkets, hardware shops or chemists.

Backpack To carry all your gear a backpack (rucksack) is most practical. Carry the sturdiest and best-made pack you can afford, paying special attention to the strength of zips and straps. Internal-frame packs are easier to handle, but some hikers prefer external-framed packs; they're cooler in hot conditions. Many travellers favour the type of travel-backpack that neatly turns into a normal-looking holdall. This is handy if you don't want to look like a backpacker, and particularly useful for keeping straps out of the way when your bag is loaded onto planes or bus roof racks. It's also wise to use plastic bags to protect the contents from moisture and dust.

SUGGESTED ITINERARIES

For a trip through Malawi, although the country is relatively compact, where you go and what you do depends on available time and money. Generally, it seems that (apart from the occasional footloose millionaire) the people with more time have less money, while those with healthy wallets can only ever take a few weeks off work.

The main factor affecting the number of places you can reach will be your form of transport. Many visitors use buses and trains for their entire trip, and can get to most places this way at a fairly low cost, albeit sometimes quite slowly. A hired car cuts these delays, and is also near essential

MALAWI

Highlights
The following list of highlights is naturally pretty subjective. It includes all our favourites, plus those from other travellers and from readers' letters.

Malawi
- Liwonde National Park – spotting elephant from a boat on the Shire River.
- Hiking on Mt Mulanje.
- The wildflowers and scenery of Nyika National Park, and the walk down to Livingstonia.
- Lake Malawi – budget travellers' good-times at Cape Maclear, smarter hotels for the more discerning at Nkopola and Club Makokola.
- The 'Caribbean' ambience of beautiful Nkhata Bay.
- Fascinating Likoma Island and it's incongruous cathedral.
- A ride on the lake steamer *Ilala*.
- The little-visited 'Far South' region.

Mozambique
- World Heritage-listed Mozambique Island.
- Pristine tropical reefs and beaches of the Bazaruto Archipelago.
- Legendary beaches of Tofu and Barra near Inhambane.
- Maputo's nightlife.
- The spectacular coastline around Pemba and Wimbi Beach in northern Mozambique.

Zambia
- Walking and night drives at South Luangwa National Park.
- A visit to the culturally intact and fascinating area of Barotseland.
- Canoe safaris on the Zambezi River.

---

for getting into some national parks, but is more pricey. Some travellers combine public transport with a few days or weeks in a hire car, sometimes teaming up with others to split costs.

Whatever your transport, if you've got plenty of time, then naturally you can see a lot. If time is limited, then it would be far better to concentrate on visiting just one or two places rather than rushing around to fit everything in, and only skimming the surface.

Where you go will also depend on your own interests. If you've come mainly to see wildlife, then a visit to Liwonde National Park is highly recommended. You might also want to visit Nyika, Lengwe and Kasungu national parks, plus Vwaza Marsh Game Reserve. If you simply enjoy wilderness, then any of the above parks can provide the required atmosphere. You could also visit the game reserves of Majete, Mwabvi and Nkhotakota. If you're a keen bird-watcher, then any of the above places will keep you

busy for days, plus of course the lake shore, and more obscure places like the Elephant Marsh or Dzalanyama Forest (for more details see Flora & Fauna in the Facts about Malawi chapter). If you're into water sports, particularly diving or snorkelling, then Lake Malawi will feature largely in your plans (for more details see Activities, later in this chapter). For hiking and trekking, the main highland areas are Mt Mulanje and the Nyika and Zomba plateaux. Nyika is also particularly well-known for its wild flowers.

Two Weeks
It's unlikely that visitors from Europe or further afield will come to Malawi just for a week, but for 10 days or two weeks a tour might go as follows: fly into Lilongwe, head for the lake shore (any or all of Senga Bay, Cape Maclear, Nkopola, Makokola), continue to the pleasant town of Mangochi, then visit Liwonde National Park and the Upper Shire area. From Liwonde go to Zomba, famous for its huge market and the nearby

Zomba Plateau, with good hiking, excellent views and several good places to stay. Continue to Blantyre, from where you can head east through the tea plantations to Mt Mulanje (then go walking for a day or trekking for a week according to your inclination), or south, down the escarpment to the Lower Shire area, taking in Lengwe, Majete and possibly Chiromo and the Elephant Marsh (if you're particularly keen on colonial history or birds). From there return to Blantyre and back to Lilongwe via Dedza.

Three Weeks

With three weeks available you could do the trip outlined above, then include a loop through northern Malawi too. (If you only had two weeks you could still visit the north by cutting down on some of the places you go in the south – missing out the Lower Shire area or Mt Mulanje, for example.) From Lilongwe, take the main road north, and visit Kasungu National Park, or stop over in a resthouse on the Viphya Plateau. Then go on to Mzuzu, from where you can reach Vwaza Marsh, the Nyika Plateau and the historical sites of Livingstonia, plus the beaches and quiet villages of the northern lake shore. Return to Mzuzu and then go back to the lake at the pleasant town of Nkhata Bay, before following the lake shore road south as fast or as slow as you want (there are plenty of places to stay along the way) to reach Nkhotakota or Salima, from where you can reach Lilongwe to finish.

Another loop from Lilongwe which is becoming increasingly popular is a visit to South Luangwa National Park in neighbouring Zambia, where you will see large-scale wilderness and sheer quantities of game that Malawi simply does not have. You can join an organised tour in Lilongwe, or go independently (the park caters for all budgets).

One Month

With more time at your disposal you might combine your trip in Malawi as outlined above with a tour of Zambia, by continuing west from South Luangwa National Park to Lusaka (which, to be brutal, has

little to make you stay long), and then going east to Lake Kariba, south to the scenic wonders of Victoria Falls or west into the culturally fascinating region of Barotseland.

Your other option could be to combine a trip in Malawi with some time in Mozambique. You can travel by train or road from various points in southern Malawi to reach the coastal town of Quelimane, or go east to Nampula, from where you can reach the fascinating Mozambique Island (Ilha de Moçambique). Alternatively, you could go south to the lively city of Beira; if time is limited, you can easily fly here from Malawi. South of Beira are the well-known beaches of the Vilankulo and Inhambane area, and of course the lively capital of Maputo itself, although to combine a visit here with some time in the north would take at least a month, possibly more.

Three Months

If you've got three months, then a journey through Malawi, Mozambique and Zambia would be a fascinating and rewarding trip, although in Malawi's neighbouring countries, distances are long and public transport not so well developed. However, these three countries between them offer a broad and contrasting (and very 'authentic') perspective on this region of Africa. If you've got your own vehicle, or take some regional flights (or simply leave out a few of the places mentioned here), you could still see something of all three countries in two months.

TOURIST OFFICES
Local Tourist Offices

Malawi has tourist offices in Blantyre and Lilongwe. Information is usually limited to glossy brochures produced for Malawi by a PR firm (featuring beautiful models and optimistic text), and leaflets on car hire and tour companies. However, the staff try to be helpful and can often assist with general inquiries on hotels, public transport, shops, hospitals and so on, if you explain exactly what you want to do, and how much money you want to spend. Making inquiries over the phone is hard.

In Lilongwe and Blantyre, the National Parks & Wildlife Offices have information on parks, reserves and other wildlife areas. You can also make bookings here for national park accommodation. For more details see the Information section in the Lilongwe and Blantyre chapters.

Tourist Offices Abroad

Malawi embassies and high commissions around the world (listed later in this chapter) each have a Tourism Department, which can help with inquiries and send out leaflets.

VISAS & DOCUMENTS
Passport

Your most important document is your passport. Some officials don't like passports near their expiry date, so it's better to have one which expires at least a few months after your trip ends.

Visas

A visa is a stamp in your passport, giving you permission to enter a country for a specific length of time – usually a month, but sometimes up to three. They are available from embassies of the country you wish to enter, and usually a fee is payable. For nearly every visa application you need two or three passport photos.

Not everyone needs a visa to enter every country – the rules change according to your nationality. For Malawi, visas are NOT required by citizens of Commonwealth countries, Luxembourg, Belgium, Denmark, Finland, Germany, Iceland, the Netherlands, Norway, Portugal, Ireland, South Africa, Sweden and the USA. Commonwealth citizens of Asian origin sometimes need visas that are not required by their black or white compatriots.

If you don't need a visa, when you enter the country at an airport or border you'll automatically be given a 30 day tourist pass, unless you can prove you need longer (for example, an air ticket showing a return date),

in which case getting up to two or three months is usually no problem.

If you do need a tourist visa for Malawi, they cost around US$25, or the equivalent in local currency. You also need two or three photos. It's usually issued in three days.

It is important to note that regulations are always liable to change, so it's best to check at your nearest Malawi embassy or high commission in your own country before you leave (or in a neighbouring country as you're travelling). Otherwise you may arrive at the airport or border without a visa only to find that the rules have changed.

Visa Extensions If your plans alter and you want to stay longer once you're inside the country you can get extensions at the immigration offices in Blantyre or Lilongwe, or at regional police stations. Wherever you go, the process is straightforward and free.

Photocopies

Photocopies of all your important documents (plus airline tickets and credit cards) will help speed up replacement if they are lost or stolen. Keep these (and a list of travellers' cheque numbers) separate from other valuables, or leave copies with someone at home so they can be faxed to you in an emergency.

Travel Insurance

A travel insurance policy to cover medical expenses is highly recommended (for more details see the Health section). If the policy also covers theft and loss, sometimes for an extra charge, that's a definite bonus. It's well worth shopping around: policies designed for short package tours in Europe are not going to suit a few months of backpacking in Africa. The international travel policies handled by STA Travel and other youth and student travel organisations are usually good value, and not always restricted to the young or studious. In the UK, a company called Worldwide Travel Insurance Services (☎ (01732) 773366; fax (01732) 368366) offers a long-term policy that can be extended while you're travelling – ideal if you fall in love with (or in) Malawi and want to stay longer. In other countries similar specialist policies may take some searching out.

Other Documents

Other documents you may need include: a vaccination certificate to show you've been jabbed for yellow fever, and possibly some other diseases (see Health, later in this chapter); a membership card for a youth hostel association which gets you cheap accommodation in affiliated hostels; your driving licence and an International Driving Permit (IDP); a student or young persons identity card (occasionally good for various discounts); your travel insurance policy.

EMBASSIES
Malawi Embassies Abroad

Countries with a Malawi embassy or high commission include Canada, France, the UK and the USA. Citizens of other countries should check in the phone directory of their own capital city. Malawi also has high commissions in Kenya, Mozambique, South Africa, Tanzania, Zambia and Zimbabwe. Generally speaking visa sections are open for applications in the morning only.

Canada
    Malawi High Commission, 7 Clemow Ave, Ottawa, Ontario K1F 2A9 (☎ (613) 236 8932)
France
    Malawi Embassy, 20 Rue Euler, Paris 75008 (☎ (01) 40 70 18 46)
Kenya
    Malawi High Commission, Waiyaki Way, Westlands, PO Box 30453, Nairobi (☎ 440569; fax 440568)
Mozambique
    Malawi High Commission, 75 Avenida Kenneth Kaunda, Maputo (☎ 491468)
South Africa
    Malawi High Commission, Sable House, 41 De Korte St, Braamfontein, Johannesburg (☎ (011) 339 1569)
Tanzania
    Malawi High Commission, 6th Floor, NIC Building, Samora Ave, Dar es Salaam (☎ 46673)
UK
    Malawi High Commission, 33 Grosvenor St, London (☎ (0171) 491 4172)

USA
    Malawi Embassy, 2408 Massachusetts Ave, Washington DC 20008 (☎ (202) 797 1007)
Zambia
    Malawi High Commission, Woodgate House, Cairo Rd, Lusaka (☎ 228296)
Zimbabwe
    Malawi High Commission, 42/44 Harare St, PO Box 321, Harare (☎ 705611)

Foreign Embassies in Malawi

These neighbouring nations have embassies, consulates or high commissions in Malawi:

Mozambique
    Commercial Bank Building, African Unity Ave, Capital City, Lilongwe (☎ 784100)
    Kamuzu Highway, Limbe (☎ 643189)
    Mozambique visas are available in both Lilongwe (quick and quiet) and Limbe (busy). Both offices are open Monday to Friday from 8 am to noon. Transit visas cost US$5 (or US$10 for double transit), require one photo and are issued within 24 hours. One month single-entry tourist visas cost US$9, require two photos and take one week to issue, although there is also a four day express service which costs US$15. A three month (minimum) multiple entry visa is US$30. All fees are payable in Malawi kwacha.
South Africa
    Impco Building (in Capital City Shopping Centre), Capital City, Lilongwe (☎ 783722)
    South African visas are free and take two days to issue. The embassy is open Monday to Friday from 8 am to noon.
Zambia
    Convention Drive, Capital City, Lilongwe (☎ 782100/635)
    Visas for Zambia cost US$20 and take two days to issue. The visa section is open Monday to Friday from 9 am to noon.
Zimbabwe
    Near Development House, off Independence Drive, Capital City, Lilongwe (☎ 784988)
    A visa for Zimbabwe, valid up to six months, costs US$8 (payable in Malawi kwacha) and takes a week to issue. The office is open from 8 am to 12.30 pm.

Other embassies in Malawi include:

Germany
    Convention Drive, Capital City, Lilongwe (☎ 782555)
UK
    Kenyatta Rd, Capital City, Lilongwe (☎ 782400)
USA
    Kenyatta Rd, Capital City, Lilongwe (☎ 783166)

Tanzania Be warned that there is no Tanzanian high commission in Malawi, so if you need a visa it must be obtained elsewhere. Lusaka and Harare are the closest places. (If you do need a visa and you're flying into Tanzania, you can get it at your airport of arrival.)

CUSTOMS

There are no customs restrictions on the amount of foreign ('hard') currency you can bring in or out of the country, but you are not allowed to import or export more than 200 kwacha (about US$14 at the time of going to print) of Malawian currency. Currency declaration forms are no longer used. All entry regulations are liable to change, so contact your nearest Malawi embassy, high commission or tourist office for up-to-date information.

Malawi immigration and customs officials are always polite and friendly, but they play strictly by the rules. If everything is in order you'll have no problems.

MONEY
Costs

Very generally speaking, costs of consumer items in Malawi are around 50% to 75% of what they are in Europe, Australasia or North America. Obviously there are exceptions: locally produced goods (including food and beer) may be much cheaper, while imported things may be twice what they cost in western countries.

Accommodation costs in Malawi range from less than US$1 per night for basic local resthouses, through US$3 to US$10 for camping, US$5 for hostel dorms, US$25 to US$50 for mid-range hotels, and up to US$100 or US$200 for top-end establishments. Couples can save on accommodation costs, as double rooms are cheaper than two singles. Often couples can share a single.

Transport options are equally varied: you can hitchhike for free or go by chartered plane at something like US$10 per minute. Most people, however, go by bus or train and these are comparatively cheap compared to western prices. (For more details see the Getting Around chapter.)

When working out your own costs, you should also take into account extra items such as visa fees (if you're travelling on to Mozambique or other countries in the region), national park entrance charges, plus of course the cost of any tours or activities (such as a wildlife safari or sailing trip).

Taking all of this into account, shoestring travellers could scrape by on US$5 per day, although most will have a good time on US$10. For a bit more comfort, US$20 to US$25 per day is a reasonable budget for living expenses, plus whatever optional extras you decide to do. For luxury travel, including car hire, top-end lodges, good food and wine, you could easily spend US$200 per day.

Carrying Money

To keep your money and other valuables (such as passport and air ticket) safe from pickpockets, the best place is out of sight under a shirt or skirt, or inside your trousers. You can make or buy a pouch that goes round your neck or waist. Some travellers go for 'invisible pockets', money belts and other imaginative devices.

Cash & Travellers' Cheques

Most travellers bring money in a mix of cash or travellers' cheques. Cash is quicker to deal with and gets better rates, but cannot be replaced if lost or stolen. If you lose your travellers' cheques you get a refund. When you buy your travellers' cheques make sure you know what to do if the worst happens – most companies give you a 24 hour international phone number to contact.

It's worth carrying a mixture of high and low denomination notes/bills and cheques. Thus, if you're about to leave a country, you can change for just a few days without having loads of spare cash to get rid of. Note also that, due to counterfeiting, old US$100 notes are not accepted at places which don't have a light machine for checking watermarks.

The most readily recognised international

currency in Malawi (and all over Southern and East Africa) is the US dollar (US$). Other currencies that are easily accepted include UK pounds and German marks. South African rand are also quick and easy to deal with all over the region, but unless you're from South Africa it's not worth changing your own currency into rand to then change again into kwacha and meticais (the currency of Mozambique).

Credit, Debit & Charge Cards

You can pay for expensive items such as flight tickets, car hire and top-end hotels with a credit, debit or charge card, but outside capital cities and other major centres, plastic is pretty near useless.

Officially, you can use a credit, debit or charge card to draw cash from banks in Malawi. Contact your own card company to see which banks in Malawi will accept your card.

You'll also need to ask your bank or card company about the charges, and arrange a way to pay off your credit and charge card bills if you're travelling for more than a month or so. The advantage of debit cards is there's no bill to pay off (if you have the money in your account of course), so they are more suited for longer travels.

However, in reality, when travelling in Malawi, Mozambique and Zambia it's normally not wise to rely totally on plastic for cash, as computer breakdowns can leave you stranded. Even if the system is up and running, it can still take more than a day to draw cash on a card.

International Transfers

If you think your finances may need topping up while you're travelling, ask your bank about international bank-to-bank transfers. This is usually a complicated, time-consuming and expensive business, especially when you get outside the major capitals, but if you're travelling for a long time it can save the worry (and sheer bulk) of carrying large wads of notes and cheques around.

Currency

Malawi's unit of currency is the kwacha (abbreviated to K, Kw, or MK), divided into 100 *tambala* (t). The largest bank note is MK 200. Others are MK 100, MK 50, MK 20, MK 10, MK 5. Coins include MK 1, 50t, 20t (called a 'florin'), 10t ('shilling'), 5t and 1t.

Currency Exchange

Inflation is high in Malawi, so quoting costs of transport, hotels and so on in Malawi kwacha is not always helpful, as prices will have undoubtedly changed by the time you arrive. Therefore we have used US dollars (US$) in this book.

Although the actual exchange rate will have changed by the time you reach Malawi, the cost of things in US dollars (or any other hard currency) will not have altered much. You can pay for most things in Malawi in hard currency or kwacha. As a guide, the exchange rates at the time of going to print were as follows (Australian, New Zealand and Canadian dollars are generally not accepted):

US$1	=	MK 15.2
UK£1	=	MK 25.1
SA R1	=	MK 3.5
DM1	=	MK 9.2
A$1	=	MK 12
NZ$1	=	MK 10.6
Can$1	=	MK 11

Changing Money

You can change hard currency (such as UK pounds and US dollars) into Malawi kwacha at branches of the National Bank of Malawi and the Commercial Bank of Malawi, which both have branches in cities and most towns all over the country. They will change cash and travellers' cheques although rates and charges vary, so it's worth going to branches of both banks if you can (in many towns they seem to be next to each other) to see which offers the best deal.

Banks in small towns may open only two or three mornings per week. You can still change money in smaller towns and rural areas, although usually no more than US$100 or US$200. The service here may be slow, but there's often less of a queue than in the city banks, so it works out about the same. If you arrive or leave by air at Lilongwe, the bank in the airport usually opens to coincide with international flights, but not always. See Business Hours later in this chapter for bank opening hours.

In rural areas, there's a system of 'roving' banks (basically an armoured van), which operate for about an hour on one or two days of the week only – and sometimes travellers' cheques are not accepted, so it's best not to rely on these.

You can also get cash advances with a Visa card at branches of the Commercial Bank of Malawi in Blantyre and Lilongwe. This is payable in kwacha, which you can then reconvert to US dollars or any other hard currency if required. The process takes a long time (sometimes more than a day), as the bank is not directly connected to Visa International and relies on confirmation faxes or telexes to/from your bank before giving you the cash, but you do get a better rate than for travellers' cheques (what your own card company charges though may cancel out this saving). However, with a Eurocheque card you can cash personal cheques at the National Bank of Malawi in Lilongwe, Blantyre, Mangochi and Mzuzu. The bank tellers are familiar with this process and you get a better rate than for travellers' cheques.

Recent currency deregulation has allowed private foreign exchange (forex) bureaux to open in the cities and large towns. These usually offer a slightly better rate than the banks, and have lower charges (or none at all), so are worth checking out. If you've got time, shop around the banks and bureaux, as rates and commissions can vary.

Currency deregulation also means you can change excess kwacha back into hard currency when you leave Malawi. Another aspect of currency deregulation is the absence of a real black market. You might get one or two kwacha more for your dollar on the street, but the chances of robberies or con men (there are many fake US$100 and US$50 bills in circulation) make this not worth the risk. Alternatively, shops which sell imported items sometimes need dollars and buy at rates around 5% to 10% more than banks or bureaux.

If you get stuck when banks and bureaux are closed, you can usually change money at a large hotel, although the rates are often poor so only change enough to get you by.

Black Market

In various parts of the world, artificial exchange rates mean you can get more local currency for your US dollars by changing outside the bank, on the so-called black market. This is illegal, morally questionable and sometimes dangerous. However, in Malawi (and Mozambique and Zambia) it's hardly an issue: due to currency deregulation all over the region, exchange rates are 'free'. Thus, banks (and the privately-owned 'forex' bureaux which have sprung up all over the region) can offer current market rates and the black market has virtually disappeared. You may be offered 5% or 10% more than bank or bureau rates by shady-looking characters on the street but it's very likely to be a set-up. If they offer more than 10% you *know* it's a set-up.

Tipping

In local, low-budget bars and restaurants, tipping is not expected (although always appreciated) by staff. In mid-range and top-end places tipping is usually expected – bar, restaurant and hotel bills have a 10% service charge added. However, only 4% of your total payment goes to the staff (the rest goes in taxes), so if you normally work on the 10% rule of thumb, then a tip of 5% or 6% is appropriate here. This is assuming the service has been good of course – you should never tip if the service has been less than satisfactory.

Resthouses in forest reserves and mountain huts are run by government departments and staffed by caretakers who are officially civil servants, but who get a very low wage.

MALAWI

Although the price you pay to spend the night technically covers their services, in most cases it's reasonable to tip an extra small amount (the equivalent of US$1 is fine). Again this assumes the service has been good, though.

At 'self-catering' camps and lodges the kitchen is often staffed by cooks and helpers. You can make your own food, but it's usual to give your stuff to the cook to prepare to your instructions. Even if you cook the food yourself, the kitchen hands usually wash up your pots and pans. Once again, the fee you pay to stay in the lodge or camp covers their services, but once again a small tip (US$1 to US$3) is appreciated, and usually appropriate (most of them are pretty good cooks!).

Bargaining

Visitors from western countries sometimes have difficulty with the concept of bargaining, especially when it comes to buying crafts and curios from road-side stalls. Westerners are used to things having a fixed value, whereas in Africa, commodities are considered worth whatever their seller can get for them. It really is no different to the concept of an auction and should be treated as one more aspect of travel in the region.

In markets which are frequented by foreigners, sellers will invariably put their asking price high. If you pay this – whether out of ignorance or guilt about how much you have compared to locals – you may be considered foolish, and you'll be doing fellow travellers a disservice by creating the impression that all foreigners are willing to pay any price named! You may also harm the local economy: by paying high prices you put some items out of reach of locals who generally have less disposable cash. And who can blame the sellers – why sell something to a local when foreigners will pay twice as much?

At craft and curio stalls, where items are designed to be sold to tourists, bargaining is very much expected, and should always be conducted in a friendly and spirited manner. The vendor's aim is to identify the highest price you're willing to pay. Your aim is to find the price below which the vendor will not sell. People have all sorts of formulae for working out what this should be, but there are no hard and fast rules. Some vendors may initially ask a price four (or more) times higher than what they're prepared to accept, although it's usually lower than this. Decide what you want to pay or what others have told you *they've* paid; your first offer should be about half this. At this stage, the vendor may laugh or feign outrage, but the price will quickly drop from the original quote to a more realistic level. When it does, begin making better offers until you arrive at a mutually agreeable price.

And that's the crux – *mutually agreeable*. You hear travellers all the time moaning about how they got 'overcharged' by souvenir sellers. When things have no fixed price, nobody really gets overcharged. If you don't like the price, it's simple – don't buy it.

There's no reason to lose your temper when bargaining. If you become fed up with intransigence or the effort seems a waste of time, politely take your leave. Sometimes sellers will call you back if they think their stubbornness may be losing a sale. Very few will pass up the chance of making a sale, however thin the profit.

If sellers won't come down to a price you feel is fair (or you simply can't afford), it probably means that many high-rolling foreigners have passed through and if you don't pay their prices, somebody else will. Remember the sellers are under no more obligation to sell to you, than you are to buy from them. You can go elsewhere, or (if you really want the item) accept the price. This is the raw edge of capitalism!

Taxes

In mid-range and top-end restaurants and hotels, your bill for food and accommodation attracts an extra 30% in taxes. Yes – 30%! And 26% of the total amount goes to the government. This is not always clear on menus and tariffs, so if in doubt, ask if the price includes tax or not, as it does make quite a difference. Wherever possible in this book we have shown prices inclusive of these taxes. For more information see the boxed text on taxes after the accommodation section of this chapter.

POST & COMMUNICATIONS
Postal Rates
Post around Malawi, and in and out of Malawi, is a bit of a lottery. Some letters have been known to get from Lilongwe to London in three days, while others take three weeks. Mail from Cape Town to Lilongwe or Blantyre can often take a month. Once letters have to get beyond the capital cities the service is even more uncertain; it can be quick or slow – you just never know.

Letters (less then 10 grams) inside Malawi cost 40 tambala (about three US cents). To other African destinations a letter costs US$0.10. To Europe, the Americas or Australasia it is US$0.20. Parcel rates used to be famously cheap in Malawi, allowing you to send home large wooden carvings at a very low price. However, it now costs about US$8 plus US$3 per kg to send stuff outside Africa.

Sending Mail
All towns (and many villages) have post offices, where you can simply and easily buy stamps. In the larger towns, post offices often have long queues, so a useful tip is to buy your stamps at a quiet rural office, but post your letters in Blantyre or Lilongwe to give them more of a chance of getting home. Note that if you're posting a parcel, the maximum weight allowed is 10 kg. Most chief's chairs (the favourite souvenir) are around 15 kg, but fortunately they come in two sections, so you just send two parcels. However, there is a one metre maximum length restriction, so keep your purchase relatively small if you want to post it home!

Receiving Mail
The post offices in Blantyre and Lilongwe have poste restante services. See the Post & Communications sections in those chapters for more details.

Telephone & Fax
International calls (to destinations outside Africa) from public Telcomms phone offices in main towns and cities (see relevant sections for details) cost around US$10 for a three minute minimum. Fax rates from these bureaux are the same. At hotels the service for phone calls and faxes may be quicker, but charges are often around US$10 for calls within Africa, and between US$20 and US$25 for three minutes anywhere outside Africa.

The international country code for Malawi, if you're phoning from abroad, is + 265 (that is, 00 265 from UK, 09 265 from SA etc).

Telephone calls within Malawi are inexpensive, and the network between main cities is reliable, although the lines to outlying areas are often not working. There are no area codes in Malawi, so wherever you dial within the country is just six digits. Numbers beginning with 7 are on the Lilongwe exchange; those starting with 6 are in Blantyre.

Telegrams
Telegrams can be sent from any post office, although those sent from Blantyre and Lilongwe will be faster. The cost for a telegram to Europe is US$1 per four words.

E-mail
Malawi's Internet service providers include Epsilon & Omega in ADL House, City Centre, Lilongwe (☎ 784444; fax 781231; e-mail: E&O@eo.wn.apc.org). If you need access to a terminal to send or receive e-mail, they can provide one for an hourly charge.

BOOKS
The following books cover all aspects of Malawi. Some will give you a general sense of the country and are good to read before you go or while you are travelling. Others are more detailed guidebooks and manuals which cater for travellers looking for deeper coverage on specific matters such as history or wildlife. Some larger books are too big to carry while travelling but make excellent trip souvenirs.

Most of the books listed here are available

outside Malawi (most notably in Britain, USA and South Africa). Inside Malawi there are good bookshops in the main centres, especially in Blantyre and Lilongwe, which are well stocked with imported and locally produced books (see Bookshops in these chapters for details). Malawi has a thriving home-based publishing industry, regularly turning out books on indigenous wildlife, local places to visit, and so on.

Note that most books may be published by different publishers in different countries – a hardcover rarity in one country may be a readily available paperback in another – so we have not included publishers in this list (unless particularly relevant). Fortunately, bookshops and libraries search by title or author, so your local bookshop or library is best placed to advise you on the availability of the following recommendations.

Good bookshops will stock most of the general titles listed below, especially those under Literature and Politics & Contemporary History. For more specialised titles you might have to hunt around. In the UK, a good mail order service for wildlife titles is Subbuteo Natural History Books (☎ (01352) 756551; fax 756004; e-mail sales@sub-books.demon.co.uk), Pistyll Farm, Nercwys, Mold CH7 4EW. In Australia, contact Andrew Isles (☎ (03) 510 5750), 115 Greville Street, Prahran, Victoria, 3181.

Lonely Planet

Lonely Planet's *Trekking in East Africa* has a good section on hikes and long-distance walks in Malawi, and also covers a wide range of routes in Kenya, Tanzania and Uganda. If you're travelling beyond the countries covered by this book, Lonely Planet has specific guidebooks on *Africa – the South*; *East Africa*; *South Africa, Lesotho & Swaziland*; *Zimbabwe, Botswana & Namibia*; and *Kenya*. If you're heading even further afield *Africa on a shoestring* will guide you across the continent.

Road Atlases

If you're coming to Malawi overland in your own vehicle the classic manual is the *Sahara*

Handbook, by Simon Glen. Although the routes it describes were closed to traffic at the time of research, much of the general information is relevant. Once beyond the Sahara, try *Africa Overland* by David Brydon.

If you're driving all the way across the continent, shipping a vehicle into South Africa, or including Malawi in wider travels around the region, *Africa by Road* by Bob Swain & Paula Snyder is recommended. The authors have done some solid ground work. Half the book is no-nonsense advice on everything from paperwork and supplies to driving techniques, while the other half is a complete country-by-country rundown.

Motorcyclists should get hold of *Desert Biking* by Chris Scott (published by The Travellers' Press). Although about regions in and around the Sahara, much of the general practical information applies anywhere.

Local Guides

Locally produced guidebooks include *Blantyre & the Southern Region of Malawi*, published by Central Africana – a general visitors' guide to the towns, parks, hotels and places of interest. Companion volumes are *Lilongwe & the Central Region* and *Mzuzu & the North*, but all three were written before the political changes of 1994.

Two highly recommended local books if you're loitering in the main centres for more than a few days are *Day Outings from Lilongwe* and *Day Outings from Blantyre*, both published by the Wildlife Society of Malawi, with suggestions on places to visit, things to see, local walks and so on, with an emphasis on wildlife. Well-written and researched, they cover a surprisingly wide area and are a good value investment. The only problem is they're aimed mostly at people with cars – thereby precluding many visitors and about 99% of Malawi's population. Another recommended read is *Guide to Mulanje Massif* by Frank Eastwood.

Lake Malawi's Resorts is a locally produced book by Ted Sneed covering every place to stay (more than 70) on the lake shore. It took so long to research that by the time Ted got to the south end, some new places had opened in the north!

History

Academic histories include *The Early History of Malawi* and *Malawi – the History of a Nation* by B Pachai, which cover the country from the Iron Age to colonial times, although both books were published in the 1970s and may be hard to find. More accessible might be *A Short History of Malawi* by BR Rafael, published in 1983. A classic volume is *Livingstone's Lake* by Oliver Ransford, but this was published in the 1960s and is hard to find these days.

European involvement with the area started with the arrival of Portuguese explorers. They were active in the region east of Lake Malawi from the 17th to 19th centuries, but this period is only sketchily covered by most histories. In contrast, many books have been written about the Scottish explorer David Livingstone, who travelled along the Shire River and into the area, now Malawi, in the late 19th century. Often reckoned to be the best of these books is *Livingstone* by Tim Jeal; this well-researched biography certainly avoids the adulatory nature of several others on Livingstone, presenting a complete picture of the great man, describing his obsessions, jealousies and weaknesses as well as his achievements.

Other local history books include:

Nyasa – A Journal of Adventures by ED Young. Written in the 1870s, reprinted in 1984; a missionary's account of his journey to help establish the original Livingstonia mission at Cape Maclear.

From Nyassa to Tanganyika by James Stewart (edited by J Thompson). Written as a journal between 1876 and 1879, reprinted 1989, describing the author's journey in the lands that were later to become Malawi and Tanzania. (This was the cousin of another James Stewart who inspired and helped to found the Livingstonia missions – see History in the Facts about Malawi chapter.)

A Lady's Letters from Central Africa by Jane Moir. Written in the 1890s by 'the first woman traveller in Central Africa', who came to Blantyre and the Shire Highlands as the wife of Frederick Moir, co-founder of the African Lakes Corporation. Reprinted 1991.

The Nyika Experience edited by F Dorwood, the chief ranger of Nyika National Park in colonial times. A collection of reminiscences from Dorwood and six other people who were involved with establishing and running the Nyika Plateau – Malawi's first national park.

Literature

To place Malawi in a wider context, you may like to try a regional anthology. These include *The Penguin Book of Southern African Stories*, edited by Stephen Gray, which collates stories from Malawi, Botswana, South Africa, and several other countries in the region; some are thousands of years old, and deliberately not classified by original language to show the similarities and common threads which exist in the various literary traditions.

General poetry anthologies include *The Heinemann Book of African Poetry in English*, edited by A Maja-Pearce, and *The Penguin Book of Modern African Poetry* edited by Moore & Beier.

The most useful book to get hold of is the *Traveller's Literary Companion – Africa*, edited by Oona Strathern, which contains over 250 prose and poetry extracts from all over Africa, including good sections on Malawi and Mozambique, plus a list of 'literary landmarks' – real features which appear in novels written about these countries.

Literature by local Malawian writers is covered in the Arts section of the Facts about Malawi chapter. Novels based in Malawi by non-Malawian writers include *Venture to the Interior* by the South African-born Laurens van der Post (who went on to write many more books about Southern Africa, most notably about the Kalahari). This early work based in Malawi describes the author's 'exploration' of Mt Mulanje and the Nyika Plateau in the 1940s, although in reality this was hardly trail-blazing stuff. Descriptions of the landscape are poetic, but this book is most interesting for its description of the quaint workings of the British colonial administration.

A more recent novel is *Jungle Lovers* by Paul Theroux, a light humorous work, which neatly captures several aspects of life in Malawi for locals and foreigners, and also pokes fun at a head of state which was remarkably similar to President Banda. Theroux was a Peace Corps Volunteer in Malawi in the 1960s. The book and the Peace Corps were later banned in Malawi by Banda.

Good for reading on long bus rides is *Elephant Song* by Wilbur Smith, a ripping yarn based partly in Malawi, covering conservation and the ivory trade, with Europeans and Africans united against corrupt regimes. It follows a familiar formula with perfect heroes, evil villains and a bit of sex and violence thrown in for good measure.

Politics & Contemporary History

For a wider perspective, several books mention Malawi and neighbouring countries in their coverage of the region, or the whole continent. These include *Fantastic Invasion – Dispatches from Africa* by Patrick Marnham, which was written soon after many African states achieved independence, and reveals the shambles created when western-style politics, boundaries, values and conservation efforts were imposed upon established African cultures. *Southern Africa Stands Up*, by Wilfred Burchett, was written at the end of the 1970s, covering the post-colonial revolutions in Mozambique, Namibia, Rhodesia (now Zimbabwe) and South Africa. *Beggar Your Neighbours*, by Joseph Hanlon, written in the mid-1980s, is informative and accessible, discussing South Africa's policies towards other states in the region, which normally boiled down to encouraging economic dependence or promoting destabilisation. *Fishing in Africa*, by Andrew Buckoke, is a depressing exposé of chaos, corruption and violence across the continent, enlightened only by moments when the author seeks out secret fishing holes – and real people – off the beaten track. *Blood on the Tracks*, by Miles Bredin, chronicles an essentially hopeless journey from Angola to Mozambique – a tale of war, bureaucracy, corruption and inefficiency neatly outlining the problems faced by modern Africa.

General

Zambezi – Journey of a River, by Michael Main, is a marvellous and immensely readable combination of history, geography, geology, anthropology, careful observation, humour, rumour and myth, following the great river from its source through Zambia, Angola, Zimbabwe and Mozambique, with side-tracks into Malawi.

Large Format Books

Two splendid coffee-table books are *Malawi – Lake of Stars*, a collection of fine photographs by Malawi-based photographer Frank Johnston, with text by local author Vera Garland, and *Between the Cape and Cairo*, a collection of sketches and paintings from all parts of Malawi by South African artist Tony Grogan. (Coincidentally, an early European explorer called Ewart Grogan, a forebear of the artist, passed through then-Nyasaland in 1899, whilst becoming the first man to walk from the Cape of Good Hope to Cairo, taking time out to shoot wildlife on the way. He wrote a book about it called *From the Cape to Cairo* and in it said 'Nyasaland is an exceptionally beautiful country, awaiting only a good artist to capture its true magnificence.' His descendant seems to have answered the call.) Another picture book to look out for is *Malawi* by Wils Nilwik.

If you are travelling in Zambia and Mozambique, as well as Malawi, you'll find the Zambezi River a major inspiration when it comes to coffee-table books. These include the interesting and attractive *Zambezi – River of the Gods*, by Jan & Fiona Teede, combining text, drawings and photographs, and *Zambezi – River of Africa*, by Mike Coppinger & Jumbo Williams, with skilful photography and intelligent text. More unusual is *Spirit of the Zambezi*, by Jeff & Veronica Sutchbury, which is a very personalised account of the Sutchbury's life on the Zambezi, and their pioneering work in tourism and wildlife conservation. Jeff died before the book was completed, but his stunning photos are a fitting memorial.

Conservation Issues

At the Hand of Man by Raymond Bonner is a study of the destruction of African wildlife, holding that conservation will only work if African people realise benefits, and that measures involving laws, force, threats and lack of consideration for local cultures and traditions only create animosity and suspicion. *Kakuli* by Norman Carr covers the same points, which the author (a leading figure in wildlife conservation in Zambia and the whole Southern African region) first raised more than thirty years ago. Carr was simply ahead of his time, and he still has points to contribute to the on-going 'people and conservation' debates. But this book is not a dry treatise; around the wider issues is a very readable personal account of life in the bush, working with animals, local people and tourists.

The conservation of elephants has come to symbolise wider issues, and there are many books which concentrate on this. *The Last Elephant*, by Jeremy Gavron, covers elephant poaching and culling, and the debates between advocates and opponents of a legal ivory trade. *To Save an Elephant*, by Allan Thornton & Dave Currey, is a gripping tale of undercover work for the Environmental Investigation Agency.

Regional Field Guides

Regional field guides to Southern Africa usually cover areas south of the Kunene, Okavango and Zambezi rivers, and thus not Malawi, Zambia or northern Mozambique. However, many species found south of these rivers also occur to the north, so a Southern African guide is often useful for Malawi, Zambia and Mozambique. Additionally, Malawi, Zambia and Mozambique also have species more common to Central or East Africa, which are covered in guides to those regions. Books which cover a larger area (ie the whole continent) tend to be less detailed, although this is not a problem for most 'amateurs'.

Mammals The *Field Guide to Mammals of Africa* by Haltenorth & Diller has been around for many years, and is very popular. Better, however, is the comprehensive and up-to-date *Field Guide to African Mammals* by Jonathan Kingdon with crisp design and accessible information, illustrated with colour maps and drawings. *Land Mammals of Southern Africa* by R Smithers is a rundown of 200 common species in the region. *Field Guide to the Mammals of Southern Africa* by Chris and Tilde Stuart is highly rated and well illustrated. The same authors also have *Southern, Central and East African Mammals* – a handy pocket guide, and *Tracks & Signs of Southern and East African Wildlife* – good for recognising animals by what they leave behind. Also good for a deeper insight is *The Safari Companion* or *The Behaviour Guide to African Mammals* by Richard Estes; a marvellous book for understanding animals' courtship rituals, territorial displays and so on.

Birds *Robert's Birds of Southern Africa* by Gordon Lindsay is *the* classic volume, but it's not a featherweight. *Sinclair's Birds of Southern Africa* by Ian Sinclair is another comprehensive tome. More portable, and ideal for most people, is *Newman's Birds of Southern Africa* by Kenneth Newman. The similarly sized *Field Guide to the Birds of East Africa* by J Williams & N Arlott may also be useful if you're in the northern part of the Southern Africa region (Malawi, Mozambique and Zambia). Even more portable is the slim *Birds of Southern Africa – a photographic guide* by Ian Sinclair (and the similar *Birds of Central Africa*); these pocket-sized volumes include only the most commonly observed species, and it can be frustrating when whatever you spot in the field never seems to be in the book.

Fish, Reptiles & Insects To learn more about the region's less fashionable wildlife, try the *Complete Guide to Freshwater Fishes of Southern Africa* by Paul Skelton, *Snakes and Other Reptiles of Southern Africa* by Bill Branch, and the *Butterflies of Southern Africa* by Ivor Migdoll.

Flora Highly recommended is *Flowers of Southern Africa* by Auriol Batten – a large-format book, more celebration than field guide, illustrated with superb and colourful paintings. *Trees of Southern Africa* by Keith Coates Palgrave is a classic volume, providing the most thorough coverage of the sub-continent's arboreal richness, illustrated with colour photos and paintings. *Southern African Trees – a photographic guide* by Piet van Wyk is a more portable work perfectly adequate for amateurs.

Malawi Field Guides

Malawi Wildlife, Parks and Reserves by Judy Carter (published by the Central Bookshop in Blantyre) is a beautiful book (although quite dated now), with concise and useful information, and good coverage of all Malawi's protected areas, although its large size makes it difficult to carry around. More portable, up-to-date and easier to find, is *Malawi's National Parks & Game Reserves* by John Hough (published by the Wildlife Society of Malawi) covering all parks and reserves in the country, with full details of flora and fauna occurring in each.

For bird-watching, one of the regional field guides listed above will cover most species. If you're keen, *Bridging the Bird Gap* by N Johnston-Stewart & J Heigham is a large-format booklet covering the 64 species found in Malawi that don't get coverage in *Robert's* and some of the other regional Southern Africa field guides. *Newman's Malawi Supplement* is similar, to be used with the main Newman's guide mentioned above.

Online Services
If you have access to the Internet, you can get hold of all sorts of information about Malawi and other parts of Africa. Places to start include:

Lonely Planet
www.lonelyplanet.com
The Lonely Planet website contains information on Africa as well as up-to-date travellers' tips on Malawi, Mozambique and Zambia (and the rest of the world).

WorldNet Africa
africa.cis.co.za:81/tourism/tourism.html
This is an extensive site with information on attractions and activities in Southern Africa (mostly Botswana, Namibia, South Africa, Zambia and Zimbabwe). As well as a wealth of country-specific information, the site has places to stay, national parks in the region and a travel booking service.

WildNet Africa
africa.cis.co.za:80/
A companion site to WorldNet Africa, this is a wildlife site, offering links to the national parks and game reserves of Southern Africa. Again, extremely informative and comprehensive.

Travelinfo Southern Africa
rapidttp.com/travel
This site wastes no time with graphics and is very ordinary looking, but full of good information on where to stay and what to do, getting around, health and safety, covering Botswana, Lesotho, Madagascar, Malawi, Mozambique, Namibia, Swaziland, South Africa, Zambia and Zimbabwe.

South Africa's Electronic Mail & Guardian
www.mg.co.za/mg
As well as daily news from one of South Africa's leading newspapers, this site contains an interesting and entertaining off-the-beaten-track guide to holidays in Southern Africa.

Africanet
www.africanet.com
Although still under development, Africanet looks to be a fairly impressive and comprehensive site. There's country specific information such as visa requirements and getting around, and the site has special interest information including beach resorts, photography in Africa, special events and exchange rates.

Trees of Malawi by JS Pullinger & AM Kitchen is a large format book with detailed colour illustrations.

Cichlids and all the other Fishes of Lake Malawi, by A Koning, is encyclopaedic (in size and coverage). *Guide to the Fishes of Lake Malawi* by L Digby (WWF, 1986) is more portable.

There are also several smaller books and leaflets devoted to subjects such as the fish of Malawi, the orchids, snakes, trees and so on, and to individual national parks (these are mentioned in the national park sections).

NEWSPAPERS & MAGAZINES
Foreign Press

For news on Malawi outside the country, you're best option is one of the magazines which cover Africa. These include *Africa Now, Africa Today, Business Africa* and the BBC's *Focus on Africa*.

You might be interested in a magazine called *Getaway,* published in South Africa (☎ (021) 531 0404; fax 531 7303, PO Box 596, Howard Place 7450, Cape Town), subtitled 'Holidays, adventure travel and ecotourism in Southern Africa'. Articles range from epic 4WD trips in Namibia or Zambia, through to active and not-so-active package tours of Zimbabwe or Malawi, to reviews of hotels and timeshare developments in South Africa. Most photos are excellent, the articles are informative (if not especially entertaining), and the advertisement section is a very useful source of ideas for places to go and things to do. Foreign subscriptions cost the equivalent of R100 (around US$28) for 12 issues.

Africa Environment & Wildlife (☎ (021) 686 9001; fax 686 4500, PO Box 44223, Claremont 7735, Cape Town) is published six times a year and covers a wide range of environmental and conservation issues, mostly on Southern Africa, with quality and even-handedness, plus excellent photography. Foreign subscriptions cost R105, US$32 or UK£21.

The two magazines mentioned above are available in bookshops in Malawi (Blantyre and Lilongwe). Many other foreign papers and magazines are available, including international titles like *Time* and *Newsweek,* various South African publications, and overseas editions of British and American papers like the *International Express* and the *International Herald Tribune.*

Malawian Press

For newspapers inside Malawi, there's a wide choice. During Banda's time, there were just two papers – both staunchly pro-government. Officially there was no censorship, but the slightest hint of non-support for the government or any of its ministries or parastatal bodies (which by extension meant a criticism of Banda) – usually landed editors and journalists in jail. Journalists who may have followed the line in print still risked detention if they discussed 'anti-government' matters in private conversation.

When Banda fell from power, the number of newspapers blossomed as enthusiastic writers and editors with access to paper and a printing press took advantage of the new-found freedom. In 1995 there were sometimes up to 20 different newspapers – most with only four or six pages, and mostly full of gossip or other rubbish – available on the streets of Blantyre and Lilongwe. Most disappeared as quickly as they'd arrived, leaving about eight papers which have managed to survive. These include *The Malawi Times* and *The Daily News,* survivors from the old days, and still MCP supporters. Newcomers include *The Chronicle, The Enquirer* and *The Nation,* all mostly pro-UDF, and *The Independent, The Democrat* and *Newsday* – not tied to any party.

RADIO & TV

Malawi's national radio station, produced by the Malawi Broadcasting Corporation, combines music news and chat shows in English, Chichewa and some other local languages. International news is brief but wide ranging. Until recently, Malawi was the only country in Southern Africa not to have a national TV station. In one of his wiser moves, Banda

MALAWI

MALAWI

decreed it was not necessary. The only TV available was picked up by people who could afford the necessary three metre satellite dishes, and had the time or inclination to channel-surf the globe. But with Banda gone, Malawi is set to join the rest of Southern Africa and national TV is on its way.

PHOTOGRAPHY & VIDEO

In Malawi, film, tapes and camera spares are generally only available in Blantyre and Lilongwe, although you may find some items in other large towns. Some sample film costs in the capitals are Fuji or Konika 200 ASA 36 exposure print film, US$7; 100 ASA 36 exposures, US$4; developing and printing: US$6 for 12, US$12 to US$15 for 36; US$7 for passport photos. Blank video tapes for VCRs cost about US$8. Tapes for video cameras are not available. For other photographic items your choice is often limited, so it's best to carry all you need with you. Places where you can buy stuff are listed in the Blantyre and Lilongwe sections.

As well as your camera, useful photographic accessories might include a small flash, a cable release, filters and a cleaning kit. Also, remember to take spare batteries. If you're using a video camera, you can recharge batteries in hotels as you go along, or in the cigarette-lighter socket of a bus or taxi (if you have a 12 volt adapter, and if the ride's a long one).

Most people find 100 ASA perfectly adequate for most situations, and possibly 400 ASA for long-lens wildlife shots. If you think you might need something slower or faster, for more specialist situations, then you don't need any more advice here. Consult a photographic manual.

TIME

Malawi's time is GMT/UTC + 2. The country does not have daylight saving. When

---

Photography Hints

Timing The best times to take photographs on sunny days are the first two hours after sunrise and the last two before sunset. This takes advantage of the colour-enhancing rays cast by a sun sitting low on the horizon.

Animals If you want to score some excellent wildlife shots, a good lightweight 35 mm SLR automatic camera with a lens between 210 mm and 300 mm should do the trick. Filters (for example, ultraviolet, polarising or 'skylight') can help; ask for advice in a good camera shop. If your subject is nothing but a speck in the distance, try to resist wasting film but keep the camera ready for the right moment (and subject) to arrive.

People Like people everywhere some Africans may enjoy being photographed, others do not. They may be superstitious about your camera, suspicious of your motives, or simply interested in whatever economic advantage they can gain from your desire to photograph them. If you can't get a candid shot, ask permission; don't just snap away.

People may agree to be photographed if you give them a picture for themselves. If you don't carry a Polaroid camera, take down their address and make it clear that you will send a copy of the photograph by post. Never say you'll send a photo, and then don't. Alternatively, you could just be honest and say that so many people ask you for photos that it makes it impossible to send copies to everyone.

Exposure When photographing animals or people, take light readings on the subject and not the brilliant African background or your shots will turn out underexposed.

Camera Care Factors that can spoil your camera or film include heat, humidity, very fine sand, saltwater and sunlight. Take appropriate precautions.

Restrictions You should definitely avoid taking photographs of bridges, dams, airports, military equipment, government buildings and *anything* that could be considered of strategic importance, particularly in Zambia and Mozambique. You may be put under arrest or have your film and camera confiscated. ∎

it's noon in Malawi, the time in the following cities is:

Los Angeles	2 am
New York	5 am
London	10 am
Sydney	8 pm
Auckland	10 pm

ELECTRICITY
Electricity in Malawi is 220V to 240V. Plugs are British-style three square pins. In Zambia they're the same, and Mozambique seems to use any plugs it can get its hands on: mostly British or South African (three round pins).

WEIGHTS & MEASURES
The metric system is widely used throughout Malawi, especially in supermarkets, shops and petrol stations. If you're used to pounds and gallons, refer to the conversion chart at the back of this book. In markets, items like firewood, fruit and vegetables may be sold by the bundle or pile. You can always see exactly what you're getting.

HEALTH
The most important specific aspect for this country is the presence of bilharzia in Lake Malawi (see boxed text – The Great Bilharzia Con). Most large towns have a hospital and pharmacy (part of the MPL chain) which are reasonably well stocked, although this can vary. The main centres (Mzuzu, Zomba, Lilongwe, Blantyre and Limbe) also have private clinics and hospitals. Malawi's main

---

The Great Bilharzia Con
Bilharzia (or schistosomiasis) is a disease transmitted by minute worms which are carried by infected humans and a certain species of water snail. Both 'hosts' need to be present for the worms to exist and transmit the disease. All over Africa bilharzia can be contracted if you swim or paddle in lakes, ponds, drainage ditches or any patch of standing water, where the worms already exist. (They do not occur in fast-flowing water or the sea.)

For many years the Malawi government's health and tourism departments stated that Lake Malawi was bilharzia-free. Only recently has evidence come to the public's attention that this claim was simply untrue. At one time the incidence may have been low, or restricted to more heavily populated areas less frequented by tourists, but bilharzia is definitely present. Its existence was denied probably because widespread knowledge of this disease would damage the country's vital tourism industry which depends heavily on its lake and water sports as an attraction.

A lot of people fell for it, including, it has to be said, Lonely Planet. Early editions of our *Africa on a shoestring* duly reported that Lake Malawi was free of bilharzia. Local tour companies and hotels were either hoodwinked also, or went along with the story. A British newspaper reported that a certain hotel on the shore of Lake Malawi sent its staff out early every morning to clear surrounding reeds of snails, without warning guests that the minute worms themselves might still be present.

But, although Lake Malawi definitely contains bilharzia, there's no need for visitors to panic. A report issued in late 1996 by the University of Malawi's Department of Community Health stated that 'there are areas, some of them very attractive to visitors, where the chances of catching the disease are negligible to the point of nonexistence. This is for a combination of reasons – topographical, ecological and environmental, as well as the result of continuing efforts to keep these areas free of the possibility of transmission'.

The report decries 'Don't go to Malawi' advice given to would-be visitors because of bilharzia dangers, and goes on to say that 'warnings against travel to Egypt (because of bilharzia in the Nile), to Tanzania (because of chloroquine-resistant malaria) or to Mozambique (because of sleeping sickness) are not thought necessary since 'precautions' can be taken. So they can in Malawi'.

Some of the up-market hotels along the lake shore have been involved in schemes to eradicate bilharzia in nearby areas, to the benefit of guests and local Malawians. These efforts should be applauded. There are community-based schemes in other areas too, however in many parts of the lake bilharzia undoubtedly remains.

The moral of the tale is this: enjoy your holiday, but if you decide to go swimming in Lake Malawi (or any other lake in Africa), recognise that you run the risk of acquiring the disease. If you have think you have been exposed to bilharzia (you may be particularly itchy after swimming), rubbing yourself down with alcohol is said to help. Have a check-up for the disease when you get home or reach a place with good medical services, but be aware that the disease may have a long incubation period and it can take weeks or even months before it shows up in blood tests. ■

hospitals are at Blantyre and Lilongwe: details are given in those chapters.

Travel health depends on your predeparture preparations, your daily health care while travelling and how you handle any medical problem that does develop. While the potential dangers can seem quite frightening, in reality few travellers experience anything more than upset stomachs.

Predeparture Planning

Immunisations Plan ahead for getting your vaccinations: some of them require more than one injection, while some vaccinations should not be given together. It is recommended you seek medical advice at least six weeks before travel. Be aware that there is often a greater risk of disease with children and in pregnancy.

Record all vaccinations on an International Health Certificate, available from your doctor or government health department.

Discuss your requirements with your doctor, but vaccinations you should consider for this trip include:

- **Hepatitis A** The most common travel-acquired illness after diarrhoea which can put you out of action for weeks. Havrix 1440 is a vaccination which provides long term immunity (possibly more than 10 years) after an initial injection and a booster at six to 12 months.
  Gamma globulin is not a vaccination but is ready-made antibody collected from blood donations. It should be given close to departure because, depending on the dose, it only protects for two to six months.
- **Typhoid** This is an important vaccination to have where hygiene is a problem. Available either as an injection or oral capsules.
- **Diphtheria & Tetanus** Diphtheria can be a fatal throat infection and tetanus can be a fatal wound infection. Everyone should have these vaccinations. After an initial course of three injections, boosters are necessary every 10 years.
- **Hepatitis B** This disease is spread by blood or by sexual activity. Travellers who should consider a hepatitis B vaccination include those visiting countries where there are known to be many carriers, where blood transfusions may not be adequately screened or where sexual contact is a possibility. It involves three injections, the quick-

est course being over three weeks with a booster at 12 months.
- **Polio** Polio is a serious, easily transmitted disease, still prevalent in many developing countries. Everyone should keep up to date with this vaccination. A booster every 10 years maintains immunity.
- **Meninogococcal Meningitis** Healthy people carry this disease; it is transmitted like a cold and you can die from it within a few hours. There are many carriers and vaccination is recommended for travellers to Mozambique. Travellers to Malawi and Zambia could consider this vaccination, but the risk of contracting it is low. A single injection will give good protection for three years. The vaccine is not recommended for children under two years because they do not develop satisfactory immunity from it.
- **Yellow Fever** You will need a yellow fever vaccination for Zambia. You usually have to go to a special yellow fever vaccination centre. Vaccination poses some risk during pregnancy but if you must travel to a high-risk area it is advisable; also people allergic to eggs may not be able to have this vaccine. Discuss with your doctor.
- **Rabies** Vaccination should be considered by those who will spend a month or longer in a country where rabies is common, especially if they are cycling, handling animals, caving, travelling to remote areas, or for children (who may not report a bite). Pretravel rabies vaccination involves having three injections over 21 to 28 days. If someone who has been vaccinated is bitten or scratched by an animal they will require two booster injections of vaccine, those not vaccinated require more.
- **Cholera** Despite its poor protection, in some situations it may be wise to have the cholera vaccine eg for the trans-Africa traveller. Very occasionally travellers are asked by immigration officials to present a certificate, even though all countries and the WHO have dropped a cholera immunisation as a health requirement. You might be able to get a certificate without having the injection from a doctor or health centre sympathetic to the vagaries of travel in Africa.
- **Malaria** Antimalarial drugs do not prevent you from being infected but kill the malaria parasites during a stage in their development and significantly reduce the risk of becoming very ill or dying.
  Expert advice on medication should be sought, as there are many factors to consider including the area to be visited, the risk of exposure to malaria-carrying mosquitoes, the side effects of medication, your medical history and whether you are a child or adult or pregnant. Travellers to isolated area in high risk countries may like to carry a treatment dose of medication for use if symptoms occur. See the Malaria section later under Insect-Borne Diseases for details.

Medical Kit Check List

Consider taking with you a basic medical kit including:

- ☐ **Aspirin** or paracetamol (acetaminophen in the US) – for pain or fever.
- ☐ **Antihistamine** (such as Benadryl) – useful as a decongestant for colds and allergies, to ease the itch from insect bites or stings, and to help prevent motion sickness. Antihistamines may cause sedation and interact with alcohol so care should be taken when using them; take one you know and have used before, if possible.
- ☐ **Antibiotics** – useful if you're travelling well off the beaten track, but they must be prescribed; carry the prescription with you.
- ☐ **Loperamide** (eg Imodium) or Lomotil for diarrhoea; prochlorperazine (eg Stemetil) or metaclopramide (eg Maxalon) for nausea and vomiting.
- ☐ **Rehydration** mixture – for treatment of severe diarrhoea; particularly important for travelling with children.
- ☐ **Antiseptic** such as povidone-iodine (eg Betadine) – for cuts and grazes.
- ☐ **Multivitamins** – especially for long trips when dietary vitamin intake may be inadequate.
- ☐ **Calamine lotion** or **aluminium sulphate spray** (eg Stingose) – to ease irritation from bites or stings.
- ☐ **Bandages** and **Band-aids**.
- ☐ **Scissors, tweezers** and a **thermometer** (note that mercury thermometers are prohibited by airlines).
- ☐ **Cold and flu tablets** and throat lozenges. Pseudoephedrine hydrochloride (Sudafed) may be useful if flying with a cold to avoid ear damage.
- ☐ **Insect repellent, sunscreen, chap stick** and **water purification tablets**.
- ☐ **A couple of syringes**, in case you need to have injections in a country with has medical hygiene problems. Ask your doctor for a note to explain the reasons why they have been prescribed.

Health Insurance Make sure that you have adequate health insurance. (See Travel Insurance under the Visas & Documents section of this chapter).

Travel Health Guides If you are planning to be away or travelling in remote areas for a long period of time, you may like to consider taking a more detailed health guide.

Staying Healthy in Asia, Africa & Latin America, Dirk Schroeder, Moon Publications, 1994. Probably the best all-round guide to carry; it's compact, detailed and well organised.

Travellers' Health, Dr Richard Dawood, Oxford University Press, 1995. Comprehensive, easy to read, authoritative and highly recommended, although it's rather large to lug around.

Where There is No Doctor, David Werner, Macmillan, 1994. A very detailed guide intended for someone, such as a Peace Corps worker, going to work in an underdeveloped country.

Travel with Children, Maureen Wheeler, Lonely Planet Publications, 1995. Includes advice on travel health for younger children.

There are also a number of excellent travel health sites on the Internet. From the Lonely Planet home page there are links at www.lonelyplanet.com/health/h-links.htm to the World Health Organisation, the US Centers for Disease Control & Prevention and Stanford University Travel Medicine Service.

Other Preparations Make sure you're healthy before you start travelling. If you are going on a long trip make sure your teeth are OK. If you wear glasses take a spare pair and your prescription.

If you require a particular medication take an adequate supply, as it may not be available locally. Take part of the packaging showing the generic name, rather than the brand, which will make getting replacements easier. It's a good idea to have a legible prescription or letter from your doctor to show that you legally use the medication to avoid any problems.

Basic Rules

Food There is an old colonial adage which says: 'If you can cook it, boil it or peel it you can eat it...otherwise forget it'. Vegetables and fruit should be washed with purified water or peeled where possible. Beware of ice cream which is sold in the street or anywhere it might have been melted and refrozen. Ice cream can be suspect in these countries, outside of reputable restaurants, and is best avoided unless you're sure. Shellfish such as mussels, oysters and clams should

MALAWI

MALAWI

be avoided as well as undercooked meat, particularly in the form of mince meat. Steaming does not make shellfish safe for consumption.

If a place looks clean and well run and the vendor also looks clean and healthy, then the food is probably safe. In general, places that are packed with travellers or locals will be fine, while empty restaurants are questionable. The food in busy restaurants is cooked, srved and eaten quite quickly with little standing around and is probably not reheated.

Water The number-one rule is *be careful of the water* and especially ice. In Malawi, Mozambique and Zambia it's best to assume the water is not safe. Reputable brands of bottled water or soft drinks are generally fine, although in some places bottles may be refilled with tap water. Only use water from containers with a serrated seal – not tops or corks. Take care with fruit juice, particularly if water may have been added. Milk should be treated with suspicion as it is often unpasteurised, though boiled milk is fine if it is kept hygienically. Tea or coffee should also be OK, since the water should have been boiled.

Water Purification The simplest way of purifying water is to boil it thoroughly. Vigorously boiling should be satisfactory; however, at high altitude water boils at a lower temperature, so germs are less likely to be killed. Boil it for longer in these environments.

A water filter is highly recommended. There are two main sorts. Total filters are high-tech gadgets which take out all the parasites, bacteria and viruses, and make your water safe to drink; these are very effective but can be expensive (although when compared to the price of bottled water bought over a long trip, their cost compares well). Simple filters (sometimes no more than an inexpensive nylon mesh bag) take out dirt and larger foreign bodies from the water, so that chemical solutions work much more effectively. In fact if water is dirty, chemical solutions may not work at all. It's very important when buying a filter to read the specifications, so that you know exactly what it removes from the water and what it doesn't.

Simple filtering will not remove all harmful organisms, so if you cannot boil water it should be treated chemically. Chlorine tablets (Puritabs, Steritabs or other brand names) will kill many pathogens, but not some parasites like giardia and amoebic cysts. Iodine is more effective in purifying water and is available in tablet form (such as Potable Aqua). Follow the directions carefully and remember that too much iodine can be harmful.

Nutrition

If your food is poor or limited in availability, if you're travelling hard and fast and therefore missing meals, or if you simply lose your appetite, you can soon start to lose weight and place your health at risk.

Make sure your diet is well balanced. Cooked eggs, tofu, beans, lentils and nuts are all safe ways to get protein. Fruit you can peel (bananas, oranges or mandarins for example) is usually safe (melons can harbour bacteria in their flesh and are best avoided) and a good source of vitamins. Try to eat plenty of grains (including rice) and bread.

Remember that although food is generally safer if it is cooked well, overcooked food loses much of its nutritional value. If your diet isn't well balanced or if your food intake is insufficient, it's a good idea to take vitamin and iron pills.

In hot climates make sure you drink enough – don't rely on feeling thirsty to indicate when you should drink. Not needing to urinate or small amounts of very dark yellow urine is a danger sign. Always carry a water bottle with you on long trips. Excessive sweating can lead to loss of salt and therefore muscle cramping. Salt tablets are not a good idea as a preventative, but in places where salt is not used much, adding salt to food can help. ■

Medical Problems & Treatment
Self-diagnosis and treatment can be risky, so you should always seek medical help. Although we do give drug dosages in this section, they are for emergency use only. Correct diagnosis is vital.

An embassy, consulate or five-star hotel can usually recommend a good place to go for advice. In some places standards of medical attention are so low that for some ailments the best advice is to get on a plane and go somewhere else. Antibiotics should ideally be administered only under medical supervision. Take only the recommended dose at the prescribed intervals and use the whole course, even if the illness seems to be cured earlier. Stop immediately if there are any serious reactions and don't use the antibiotic at all if you are unsure that you have the correct one. Some people are allergic to commonly prescribed antibiotics such as penicillin or sulpha drugs; carry this information when travelling eg on a bracelet.

Everyday Health
Normal body temperature is up to 37°C or 98.6°F; more than 2°C (4°F) higher indicates a high fever. The normal adult pulse rate is 60 to 100 per minute (children 80 to 100, babies 100 to 140). As a general rule the pulse increases about 20 beats per minute for each °C (2°F) rise in fever.

Respiration (breathing) rate is also an indicator of illness. Count the number of breaths per minute: between 12 and 20 is normal for adults and older children (up to 30 for younger children, 40 for babies). People with a high fever or serious respiratory illness breathe more quickly than normal. More than 40 shallow breaths a minute may be an indication of pneumonia. ∎

Environmental Hazards
Fungal Infections Fungal infections occur more commonly in hot weather and are usually found on the scalp, between the toes or fingers, in the groin and on the body (ringworm). You get ringworm (which is a fungal infection, not a worm) from infected animals or other people. Moisture encourages these infections.

To prevent fungal infections wear loose, comfortable clothes, avoid artificial fibres, wash frequently and dry carefully. If you do get an infection, wash the infected area at least daily with a disinfectant or medicated soap and water, and rinse and dry well. Apply an antifungal cream or powder like tolnifate (Tinaderm). Try to expose the infected area to air or sunlight as much as possible and wash all towels and underwear in hot water, change them often and let them dry in the sun.

Heat Exhaustion Dehydration and salt deficiency can cause heat exhaustion. Take time to acclimatise to high temperatures, drink sufficient liquids and do not do anything too physically demanding.

Salt deficiency is characterised by fatigue, lethargy, headaches, giddiness and muscle cramps; salt tablets may help, but adding extra salt ot your food is better.

Anhydrotic heat exhaustion, caused by an inability to sweat, is quite rare. It is likely to strike people who have been in a hot climate for some time, rather than newcomers.

Heat Stroke This serious, occasionally fatal, condition can occur if the body's heat-regulating mechanism breaks down and the body temperature rises to dangerous levels. Long, continuous periods of exposure to high temperatures and insufficient fluids can leave you vulnerable to heat stroke.

The symptoms are feeling unwell, not sweating very much (or at all) and a high body temperature (39°C to 41°C or 102°F to 106°F). Where sweating has ceased the skin becomes flushed and red. Severe, throbbing headaches and lack of coordination will also occur, and the sufferer may be confused or aggressive. Eventually the victim will become delirious or convulse. Hospitalisation is essential, but in the interim get victims out of the sun, remove their clothing, cover them with a wet sheet or towel and then fan continually. Give fluids if they are conscious.

Hypothermia Too much cold can be just as dangerous as too much heat. If you are hiking in mountain areas such as Mulanje you should be prepared.

Hypothermia occurs when the body loses heat faster than it can produce it and the core temperature of the body falls. It is surprisingly easy to progress from very cold to dangerously cold due to a combination of wind, wet clothing, fatigue and hunger, even if the air temperature is above freezing. It is best to dress in layers; silk, wool and some of the new artificial fibres are all good insulating materials. A hat is important, as a lot of heat is lost through the head. A strong, waterproof outer layer (and a 'space' blanket for emergencies) are essential. Carry basic supplies, including food containing simple sugars to generate heat quickly and fluid to drink.

Symptoms of hypothermia are exhaustion, numb skin (particularly toes and fingers), shivering, slurred speech, irrational or violent behaviour, lethargy, stumbling, dizzy spells, muscle cramps and violent bursts of energy. Irrationality may take the form of sufferers claiming they are warm and trying to take off their clothes.

To treat mild hypothermia, first get the person out of the wind and/or rain, remove their clothing if it's wet and replace it with dry, warm clothing. Give them hot liquids – not alcohol – and some high-kilojoule, easily digestible food. Do not rub victims, instead allow them to slowly warm themselves. This should be enough to treat the early stages of hypothermia. The early recognition and treatment of mild hypothermia is the only way to prevent severe hypothermia, which is a critical condition.

Jet Lag Jet lag is experienced when a person travels by air across more than three time zones (each time zone usually represents a one-hour time difference). It occurs because many of the functions of the human body (such as temperature, pulse rate and emptying of the bladder and bowels) are regulated by internal 24-hour cycles.

When we travel long distances rapidly, our bodies take time to adjust to the 'new time' of our destination, and we may experience fatigue, disorientation, insomnia, anxiety, impaired concentration and loss of appetite. These effects will usually be gone within

three days of arrival, but to minimise the impact of jet lag:

- Rest for a couple of days prior to departure.
- Try to select flight schedules that minimise sleep deprivation; arriving late in the day means you can go to sleep soon after you arrive. For very long flights, try to organise a stopover.
- Avoid excessive eating (which bloats the stomach) and alcohol (which causes dehydration) during the flight. Instead, drink plenty of non-carbonated, non-alcoholic drinks such as fruit juice or water.
- Avoid smoking.
- Make yourself comfortable by wearing loose-fitting clothes and perhaps bringing an eye mask and ear plugs to help you sleep.
- Try to sleep at the appropriate time for the time zone you are travelling to.

Motion Sickness Eating lightly before and during a trip will reduce the chances of motion sickness. If you are prone to motion sickness try to find a place that minimises movement – near the wing on aircraft, close to midships on boats, near the centre on buses. Fresh air usually helps; reading and cigarette smoke don't. Commercial motion-sickness preparations, which can cause drowsiness, have to be taken before the trip commences. Ginger (available in capsule form) and peppermint (including mint-flavoured sweets) are natural preventatives.

Prickly Heat Prickly heat is an itchy rash caused by excessive perspiration trapped under the skin. It usually strikes people who have just arrived in a hot climate. Keeping cool, bathing often, drying the skin and using a mild talcum or prickly heat powder or resorting to air-conditioning may help.

Sunburn In the tropics, the desert or at high altitude you can get sunburnt surprisingly quickly, even through cloud. Use a sunscreen, hat, and barrier cream for your nose and lips. Calamine lotion or stingose are good for mild sunburn. Protect your eyes with good quality sunglasses, particularly if you will be near water, sand or snow.

Infectious Diseases
Diarrhoea Simple things like a change of

water, food or climate can all cause a mild bout of diarrhoea, but a few rushed toilet trips with no other symptoms is not indicative of a major problem.

Dehydration is the main danger with any diarrhoea, particularly in children or the elderly as dehydration can occur quite quickly. Under all circumstances *fluid replacement* (at least equal to the volume being lost) is the most important thing to remember. Weak black tea with a little sugar, soda water, or soft drinks allowed to go flat and diluted 50% with clean water are all good. With severe diarrhoea a rehydrating solution is preferable to replace minerals and salts lost. Commercially available oral rehydration salts (ORS) are very useful; add them to boiled or bottled water. In an emergency you can make up a solution of six teaspoons of sugar and a half teaspoon of salt to a litre of boiled or bottled water. You need to drink at least the same volume of fluid that you are losing in bowel movements and vomiting. Urine is the best guide to the adequacy of replacement – if you have small amounts of concentrated urine, you need to drink more. Keep drinking small amounts often. Stick to a bland diet as you recover.

Lomotil or Imodium can be used to bring relief from the symptoms, although they do not actually cure the problem. Only use these drugs if you do not have access to toilets eg if you *must* travel. For children under 12 years of age Lomotil and Imodium are not recommended. Do not use these drugs if the person has a high fever or is severely dehydrated.

In certain situations antibiotics may be required: diarrhoea with blood or mucous (dysentery), any fever, watery diarrhoea with fever and lethargy, persistent diarrhoea not improving after 48 hours and severe diarrhoea. In these situations gut-paralysing drugs like Imodium or Lomotil should be avoided.

A stool test is necessary to diagnose which kind of dysentery you have, so you should seek medical help urgently. Where this is not possible the recommended drugs for dysentery are norfloxacin 400 mg twice daily for three days or ciprofloxacin 500 mg twice daily for five days. These are not recommended for children or pregnant women. The drug of choice for children would be co-trimoxazole (Bactrim, Septrin, Resprim) with dosage dependent on weight. A five-day course is given. Ampicillin or amoxycillin may be given in pregnancy, but medical care is necessary.

Amoebic dysentery is more gradual in the onset of symptoms, with cramping abdominal pain and vomiting less likely; fever may not be present. It will persist until treated and can recur and cause other health problems.

Another type of diarrhoea is **giardiasis**. The parasite causing this intestinal disorder is present in contaminated water. The symptoms are stomach cramps, nausea, a bloated stomach, watery, foul-smelling diarrhoea and frequent gas. Giardiasis can appear several weeks after you have been exposed to the parasite. The symptoms may disappear for a few days and then return; this can go on for several weeks. Tinidazole, known as Fasigyn, or metronidazole (Flagyl) are the recommended drugs. Treatment is a 2 gm single dose of Fasigyn or 250 mg of Flagyl three times daily for five to 10 days.

Hepatitis Hepatitis is a general term for inflammation of the liver. It is a common disease worldwide. The symptoms are fever, chills, headache, fatigue, feelings of weakness and aches and pains, followed by loss of appetite, nausea, vomiting, abdominal pain, dark urine, light-coloured faeces, jaundiced (yellow) skin and the whites of the eyes may turn yellow. **Hepatitis A** is transmitted by contaminated food and drinking water. It poses a real threat to western travellers. You should seek medical advice, but there is not much you can do apart from resting, drinking lots of fluids, eating lightly and avoiding fatty foods. People who have had hepatitis should avoid alcohol for some time after the illness, as the liver needs time to recover.

Hepatitis E is transmitted in the same way, and it can be very serious in pregnant women.

There are almost 300 million chronic carriers of **Hepatitis B** in the world. It is spread through contact with infected blood, blood products or body fluids, for example through sexual contact, unsterilised needles and blood transfusions, or contact with blood via small breaks in the skin. Other risk situations include having a shave, tattoo, or having your body pierced with contaminated equipment. The symptoms of type B may be more severe and may lead to long term problems.

Hepatitis D is spread the same way, but the risk mainly comes from sharing needles.

Hepatitis C can lead to chronic liver disease. The virus is spread by contact with blood - usually via contaminated transfusions or shared needles. Avoiding these is the only means of prevention.

HIV & AIDS HIV, the Human Immunodeficiency Virus, develops into AIDS, Acquired Immune Deficiency Syndrome, which is a fatal disease. HIV is a major problem in many countries. Any exposure to blood, blood products or body fluids may put the individual at risk. The disease is often transmitted through sexual contact or dirty needles – vaccinations, acupuncture, tattooing and body piercing can be potentially as dangerous as intravenous drug use. HIV/AIDS can also be spread through infected blood transfusions; some developing countries cannot afford to screen blood used for transfusions.

If you do need an injection, ask to see the syringe unwrapped in front of you, or take a needle and syringe pack with you.

Fear of HIV infection should never preclude treatment for serious medical conditions.

Intestinal Worms These parasites are most common in rural, tropical areas. The different worms have different ways of infecting people. Some may be ingested on food including undercooked meat and some enter through your skin. Infestations may not show up for some time, and although they are generally not serious, if left untreated some can cause severe health problems later.

Considering having a stool test when you return home to check for these and determine the appropriate treatment.

Meningococcal Meningitis This very serious disease attacks the brain and can be fatal. It is a problem in Mozambique, and it also occurs in Zambia and Malawi, but the risk to travellers is low. The disease is spread by close contact with people who carry it in their throats and noses, spread it though coughs and sneezes and may not be aware they are carriers.

A fever, severe headache, sensitivity to light and neck stiffness which prevents forward bending of the head are the first symptoms. There may also be purple patches on the skin. Death can occur within a few hours, so urgent medical treatment is required.

Treatment is large doses of penicillin given intravenously, or chloramphenicol injections.

Sexually Transmitted Diseases Gonorrhoea, herpes and syphilis are among these diseases; sores, blisters or rashes around the genitals, discharges or pain when urinating are common symptoms. In some STDs, such as wart virus or chlamydia, symptoms may be less marked or not observed at all especially in women. Syphilis symptoms eventually disappear completely but the disease continues and can cause severe problems in later years. While abstinence from sexual contact is the only 100% effective prevention, using condoms is also effective. The treatment of gonorrhoea and syphilis is with antibiotics. The different sexually transmitted diseases each require specific antibiotics. There is no cure for herpes or AIDS.

Typhoid Typhoid fever is a dangerous gut infection caused by contaminated water and food. Medical help must be sought.

In its early stages sufferers may feel they have a bad cold or flu on the way, as early symptoms are a headache, body aches and a fever which rises a little each day until it is around 40°C (104°F) or more. The victim's pulse is often slow relative to the degree of fever present – unlike a normal fever where the pulse increases. There may also be vomiting, abdominal pain, diarrhoea or constipation.

In the second week the high fever and slow pulse continue and a few pink spots may appear on the body; trembling, delirium, weakness, weight loss and dehydration may occur. Complications such as pneumonia, perforated bowel or meningitis may occur.

The fever should be treated by keeping the victim cool and giving them fluids as dehydration should also be watched for. Ciprofloxacin 750 mg twice a day for 10 days is good for adults.

Chloramphenicol is recommended in many countries. The adult dosage is two 250-mg capsules, four times a day. Children aged between eight and 12 years should have half the adult dose; and younger children one-third the adult dose.

Insect-Borne Diseases

Filariasis, leishmaniasis, sleeping sickness and typhus are all insect-borne diseases which occur in this region, but they do not pose a great risk to travellers. For more information on them see Less Common Diseases at the end of this Health section.

Malaria This serious and potentially fatal disease is spread by mosquito bites. In this region it is extremely important to avoid mosquito bites and to take tablets to prevent this disease. Symptoms range from fever, chills and sweating, headache, diarrhoea and abdominal pains to a vague feeling of ill-health. Seek medical help immediately if malaria is suspected. Without treatment malaria can rapidly become more serious and can be fatal.

If medical care is not available, malaria tablets can be used for treatment. You need to use a malaria tablet which is different to the one you were taking when you contracted malaria. The treatment dosages are mefloquine (two 250mg tablets and a further two six hours later), fansidar (single dose of three tablets). If you were previously taking mefloquine then other alternatives are halofantrine (three doses of two 250mg

tablets every six hours) or quinine sulphate (600mg every six hours). There is a greater risk of side effects with these dosages than in normal use.

Travellers are advised to prevent mosquito bites at all times. The main messages are:

- Wear light coloured clothing.
- Wear long pants and long sleeved shirts.
- Use mosquito repellents containing the compound DEET on exposed areas (prolonged overuse of DEET may be harmful, especially to children, but its use is considered preferable to being bitten by disease-transmitting mosquitoes).
- Avoid highly scented perfumes or aftershave.
- Use a mosquito net impregnated with mosquito repellent (permethrin) – it may be worth taking your own.
- Impregnating clothes with permethrin effectively deters mosquitoes and other insects.

Yellow Fever This viral disease, endemic in Zambia, is transmitted by mosquitoes. It is not a major risk to travellers if you are vaccinated against it. The initial symptoms are fever, headache, abdominal pain and vomiting. Seek medical care urgently and drink lots of fluids.

Cuts, Bites & Stings

Bedbugs & Lice Bedbugs live in various places, but particularly in dirty mattresses and bedding, evidenced by spots of blood on bedclothes or on the wall. Bedbugs leave itchy bites in neat rows. Calamine lotion or Stingose spray may help.

All lice cause itching and discomfort. They make themselves at home in your hair (head lice), your clothing (body lice) or in your pubic hair (crabs). You catch lice through direct contact with infected people or by sharing combs, clothing and the like. Powder or shampoo treatment will kill the lice and infected clothing should then be washed in very hot, soapy water and left in the sun to dry.

Insect Bites & Stings Bee and wasp stings are usually painful rather than dangerous. However in people who are allergic to them severe breathing difficulties may occur and

MALAWI

MALAWI

require urgent medical care. Calamine lotion or Stingose spray will give relief and ice packs will reduce the pain and swelling. There are various fish and other sea creatures which can sting or bite dangerously or which are dangerous to eat. Again, local advice is the best suggestion.

Cuts & Scratches Wash well and treat any cut with an antiseptic such as povidone-iodine. Where possible avoid bandages and Band-aids, which can keep wounds wet. Coral cuts are notoriously slow to heal and if they are not adequately cleaned small pieces of coral can become embedded in the wound. Avoid coral cuts by wearing shoes when walking on reefs, and clean any cut thoroughly with an antiseptic. Severe pain, throbbing, redness, fever or generally feeling unwell suggest infection and the need for antibiotics promptly as coral cuts may result in serious infections.

Jellyfish Local advice is the best way of avoiding contact with these sea creatures which have stinging tentacles. Dousing in vinegar will de-activate any stingers which have not 'fired'. Calamine lotion, antihistamines and analgesics may reduce the reaction and relieve the pain.

Leeches & Ticks Leeches may be present in damp rainforest conditions; they attach themselves to your skin to suck your blood. Trekkers often get them on their legs or in their boots. Salt or a lighted cigarette end will make them fall off. Do not pull them off, as the bite is then more likely to become infected. Clean and apply pressure if the point of attachment is bleeding. An insect repellent may keep them away.

You should always check all over your body if you have been walking through a potentially tick-infested area as ticks can cause skin infections and other more serious diseases. If a tick is found attached, press down around the tick's head with tweezers, grab the head and gently pull upwards. Avoid pulling the rear of the body as this may squeeze the tick's gut contents through the

attached mouth parts into the skin, increasing the risk of infection and disease. Smearing chemicals on the tick will not make it let go and is not recommended.

Snakes To minimise your chances of being bitten always wear boots, socks and long trousers when walking through undergrowth where snakes may be present. Don't put your hands into holes and crevices, and be careful when collecting firewood.

Snake bites do not cause instantaneous death and antivenenes are usually available. Immediately wrap the bitten limb tightly, as you would for a sprained ankle, and then attach a splint to immobilise it. Keep the victim still and seek medical help, if possible with the dead snake for identification. Don't attempt to catch the snake if there is a possibility of being bitten again. Tourniquets and sucking out the poison are now comprehensively discredited.

Women's Health
Gynaecological Problems Sexually transmitted diseases are a major cause of vaginal problems. Symptoms include a smelly discharge, painful intercourse and sometimes a burning sensation when urinating. Male sexual partners must also be treated. Medical attention should be sought and remember in addition to these diseases HIV or hepatitis B may also be acquired during exposure. Besides abstinence, the best thing is to practise safe sex using condoms.

Antibiotic use, synthetic underwear, sweating and contraceptive pills can lead to fungal vaginal infections when travelling in hot climates. Maintaining good personal hygiene, and loose-fitting clothes and cotton underwear will help to prevent these infections.

Fungal infections, characterised by a rash, itch and discharge, can be treated with a vinegar or lemon-juice douche, or with yoghurt. Nystatin, miconazole or clotrimazole pessaries or vaginal cream are the usual treatment.

Pregnancy It is not advisable to travel to some places while pregnant as some vaccinations normally used to prevent serious diseases are not advisable in pregnancy eg yellow fever. In addition, some diseases are much more serious for the mother (and may increase the risk of a stillborn child) in pregnancy eg malaria.

Most miscarriages occur during the first three months of pregnancy. Miscarriage is not uncommon, and can occasionally lead to severe bleeding. The last three months should also be spent within reasonable distance of good medical care. A baby born as early as 24 weeks stands a chance of survival, but only in a good modern hospital. Pregnant women should avoid all unnecessary medication, vaccinations and malarial prophylactics should still be taken where needed. Additional care should be taken to prevent illness and particular attention should be paid to diet and nutrition. Alcohol and nicotine, for example, should be avoided.

Less Common Diseases

The following diseases pose a small risk to travellers, and so are only mentioned in passing. Seek medical advice if you think you may have any of these diseases.

Cholera This is the worst of the watery diarrhoeas and medical help should be sought. Outbreaks of cholera are generally widely reported, so you can avoid such problem areas. *Fluid replacement is the most vital treatment* – the risk of dehydration is severe as you may lose up to 20 litres a day. If there is a delay in getting to hospital then begin taking tetracycline. The adult dose is 250 mg four times daily. It is not recommended for children under nine years nor for pregnant women. Tetracycline may help shorten the illness, but adequate fluids are required to save lives.

Filariasis This is a mosquito-transmitted parasitic infection found in this region. Possible symptoms include fever, pain and swelling of the lymph glands; inflammation of lymph drainage areas; swelling of a limb or the scrotum; skin rashes and blindness.

Treatment is available to eliminate the parasites from the body, but some of the damage already caused may not be reversible. Medical advice should be obtained promptly if the infection is suspected.

Leishmaniasis A group of parasitic diseases transmitted by sandfly bites, found in this region. Cutaneous leishmaniasis affects the skin tissue causing ulceration and disfigurement and visceral leishmaniasis affects the internal organs. Seek medical advice as laboratory testing is required for diagnosis and correct treatment. Avoiding sandfly bites is the best precaution. Bites are usually painless, itchy and are yet another reason to cover up and apply repellent.

Rabies Rabies is a fatal viral infection found in this region. Many animals can be infected (such as dogs, cats, bats and monkeys) and it is their saliva which is infectious. Any bite, scratch or even lick from a warm-blooded, furry animal should be cleaned immediately and thoroughly. Scrub with soap and running water, and then apply alcohol or iodine solution. Medical help should be sought promptly to receive a course of injections to prevent the onset of symptoms and death.

Sleeping Sickness In this region tsetse flies can carry trypanosomiasis or sleeping sickness. The tsetse fly is about twice the size of a housefly and recognisable by the scissor-like way it folds its wings when at rest. Only a small proportion of tsetse flies carry the disease but it is a serious disease which can be fatal without treatment. No protection is available except avoiding the tsetse fly bites. The flies are attracted to large moving objects such as safari buses, to perfume and aftershave, and to colours like dark blue. Swelling at the site of the bite, five or more days later, is the first sign of infection; this is followed within two to three weeks by fever.

Tetanus Tetanus occurs when a wound becomes infected by a germ which lives in soil and in the faeces of horses and other animals. It enters the body via breaks in the

MALAWI

skin. All wounds should be cleaned promptly and adequately and an antiseptic cream or solution applied. Use antibiotics if the wound becomes hot, throbs or pus is seen. The first symptom may be discomfort in swallowing, or stiffening of the jaw and neck; this is followed by painful convulsions of the jaw and whole body. The disease can be fatal.

Tuberculosis (TB) TB is a bacterial infection usually transmitted from person to person by coughing but may be transmitted through consumption of unpasteurised milk. Milk that has been boiled is safe to drink, and the souring of milk to make yoghurt or cheese also kills the bacilli. Travellers are usually not at great risk as close household contact with the infected person is usually required before the disease is passed on.

Typhus Typhus is spread by ticks, mites or lice. It begins with fever, chills, headache and muscle pains followed a few days later by a body rash. There is often a large painful sore at the site of the bite and nearby lymph nodes are swollen and painful. Typhus can be treated under medical supervision. Seek local advice on areas where ticks pose a danger and always check your skin (including hair) carefully for ticks after walking in a danger area such as a tropical forest. A strong insect repellent can help, and serious walkers in tick areas should consider having their boots and trousers impregnated with benzyl benzoate and dibutylphthalate.

TOILETS
In case this is the sort of thing you worry about, there are two main types of toilet in Malawi (and most other parts of Africa): the 'western' style, with a toilet bowl and seat; and the 'eastern' or African style, which is a hole in the floor, over which you squat. As with anywhere else, the standard of toilets can vary tremendously, from pristine to unusable. Some travellers complain that African loos are difficult to use, or that you have to remove half your clothing to use them. This is not so, and it only takes a small

degree of practice to master a comfortable squatting technique.

In some places (particularly rural areas, or in national parks) the squat toilets are built over a deep hole in the ground. These are called 'long-drops', and the stuff in the hole just fades away naturally over time, as long as too much other rubbish (such as paper or synthetic materials, including tampons) doesn't go down the hole as well. Therefore always use a bin if one is provided.

Other squat loos may be plumbed in and flush just like a 'western' loo. Conversely, some western loos are not plumbed in, but just balanced over a long-drop, and sometimes boxes or seats of one sort or another are constructed, supposedly to assist the people who can't have a crap unless they're sitting on something. The lack of running water usually makes such cross-cultural toilets a disaster. I'd rather have a non-contact squat loo than a filthy dirty 'western' one to hover over.

WOMEN TRAVELLERS
Generally speaking, women travellers in Malawi, whether travelling alone or in numbers, will not encounter specifically female problems (such as harassment from men) on a day-to-day basis any more than they might in other parts of the world. In fact, many women travellers report that, compared to North Africa (including Morocco and Egypt), South America, and numerous western countries, the whole Southern African region is relatively safe and unthreatening, and that friendliness and generosity are met far more often than hostility.

Southern Africa is one of few places in the developing world where it is possible for women travellers to meet and communicate with local men – of any race – without their behaviour automatically being misconstrued. That's not to say the 'loose foreigner' stigma that prevails in so many countries hasn't arrived to some degree but local white women (mostly South Africans, Namibians and Zimbabweans) have done a lot to refute the image that women of European descent are willing to hop into bed with the first taker.

Of course, there are places where mugging is a possibility and, as in any place worldwide, women (particularly lone women) are generally seen as easy targets, so it pays to keep away from these areas, especially at night. Such danger zones are listed in the individual country chapters under Dangers & Annoyances.

When it comes to evening entertainment, Southern Africa is very much a conservative, traditional, male-dominated society (among all races) and women travellers may come up against a few glass walls and ceilings. Many bars are reserved for men only (by law of the establishment, or by the law of tradition), and even where women are 'allowed', cultural convention often dictates you don't go in without a male companion. That's the situation, however distasteful it may be to liberated westerners – and trying to buck the system will quite possibly lead to trouble. So, as an outsider, it's much better to go with the flow and only visit the places where women can go without attracting unwanted attention. Always try to get some local female advice first.

Because of these prevailing attitudes, it can be hard to specifically meet and talk with local women in the countries you're travelling through. It may require being invited into a home, although because many women (mostly non-white) have received little or no education, sometimes language barriers can be a problem. However, this is changing to some extent because more recently a surprising number of girls have had the opportunity to stay at school while the boys are sent away to work. This means that in some countries, many of the staff in tourist offices, government departments and so on are educated, young to middle-aged black women, and this can be as good a place as any to try striking up a conversation. In rural areas, a good starting point might be women teachers at a local school, or staff at a health centre.

When you're actually travelling, the best advice on what can and can't be undertaken safely will come from local women. Unfortunately, many white women are likely to be appalled at the idea of lone travel and will do their best to discourage you with horrendous stories, often of dubious accuracy. Having said that, although the countries in this region are considerably safer than some other parts of the world, hitching alone is not recommended. However, if you decide to thumb it, you should refuse a lift if the driver is drunk (sadly a common condition) or the car is chock-a-block with men (for example, military vehicles). Use common sense and things should go well.

GAY & LESBIAN TRAVELLERS

All the countries covered in this book are conservative in their attitudes towards gays and lesbians, and gay sexual relationships are culturally taboo – although some homosexual activity, especially among younger men, does occur in some areas. Male and female homosexuality is illegal in Malawi. Only male homosexuality is illegal in Mozambique and Zambia, although the legal status of lesbians is almost certainly an oversight rather than actual acceptance. In most places, open displays of affection are generally frowned upon, whatever your orientation, and shows insensitivity to local feelings.

DISABLED TRAVELLERS

People who don't walk will not have an easy time in Malawi. Even though there are more disabled people per head of population here than in the west, there are very few facilities. A few official buildings are constructed with ramps and lifts – but not many, and probably not the ones you want to visit. Some major hotels also have ramps.

SENIOR TRAVELLERS

Malawi is generally good for senior travellers (on the assumption that they want to rough it less than the younger folk) as facilities such as hotels and restaurants of a good or high standard are generally available. Many senior white South Africans tour Malawi independently – look out for the caravan convoys – or visit with organised package tours.

MALAWI

MALAWI

TRAVEL WITH CHILDREN

From a practical point of view, Malawi is a fairly good place to holiday with kids. There is a small domestic tourism industry, particularly on the lake shore, and many places are used to catering for families, although it's unlikely you'll come all the way here for the kind of beach holiday you could have at home. Horses, boats and bikes can also be hired in many places. If you are also going to Zambia on your trip, the attractions usually provide entertainment enough: large wild animals in the national parks are a major draw, and even bored teenagers have been known to get a bit excited at Victoria Falls.

In most countries in the region, family rooms and chalets are available for only slightly more than the price of a double. Arranging an extra bed or two so that children can share a standard adult double is generally not a problem.

Malawi is a relatively small country, so distances between 'sights' are not too long, although parents need to have a good supply of distractions to hand. ('Let's count how many black goats we can see...') Another advantage: compared to some other parts of the world, there's less in the way of nasty diseases here, and good (if expensive) medical services can generally be reached fairly quickly if you don't stray too far from the main centres.

Lonely Planet's *Travel with Children* by Maureen Wheeler provides more sound advice, and several ideas for games on the bus.

DANGERS & ANNOYANCES

For travellers, Malawi used to be one of the safest countries in Africa – the national characteristic seemed to be friendliness, politeness and trustworthiness (possibly because Banda's iron grip on the country had created a cowed and subdued population). House breaking and theft from cars was a problem in cities, but muggings and violence were very rare. However, the changing political scene and the ever-increasing levels of unemployment seem to have created a slightly different atmosphere. Reports now indicate that the levels of violent robberies against tourists are beginning to increase, particularly in the popular lake shore areas such as Monkey Bay, Cape Maclear and Nkhata Bay.

While robbery can never be condoned, this problem shouldn't be blamed entirely on Malawians. It is also partly due to the increased number of tourists in the area, some of whom are incredibly insensitive when it comes to displays of wealth and possessions, or downright irresponsible when it comes to walking in unlit areas late at night.

Whatever the reason, the situation should be put into perspective: Malawi is not dangerous; generally it's still much safer than many other parts of the Southern Africa region. As one traveller put it 'everywhere in Africa there's always a bit of danger, but it can always be avoided. Malawi has just caught up, that's all'.

We've also heard reports of a scam operated at a couple of lakeside lodges used by backpackers, particularly in Senga Bay. Guests are encouraged to keep their money in a safe for security, but while it's there some items go missing – usually just one or two notes or travellers' cheques from a bundle in the hope it won't be noticed. The owner and local police are reported to show a distinct lack of interest in these cases of robbery.

Other potential dangers at Lake Malawi include hippos, especially in remote areas, and mosquitoes, which can transmit malaria in any low-lying area – see Health, earlier in this chapter.

On the economic front, as the black market is now non-existent, former money-changers in Malawi have got a new scam: they ask you to break the US$100 bill they have into tens and twenties. Naturally, the US$100 is a fake.

LEGAL MATTERS

Cannabis (more often called grass, hemp, 'Malawi gold', 'Malawi black' or *chamba)* can be easily bought in many parts of

Malawi, especially in some lake shore resorts. A 'cob' (sausage-shaped bundle about the size of two fists) sells for anything between US$2 and US$20, depending on quality, scarcity of supply and gullibility of the buyer. However, just because there's loads of grass around and plenty of stoned travellers, don't be fooled into thinking it is legal in Malawi. Buying, selling, possession and use are all serious offences. The maximum penalty is life imprisonment or a fine of US$35,000. Tourists caught may be fined a lesser amount and then deported. Some dealers are police informers, and the police have been known to raid camp sites, arrest offenders, and then allow them to go free on payment of a large unofficial 'fine'. Either way it can be expensive and unpleasant. If you're a smoker, bear this in mind.

BUSINESS HOURS
Offices and shops in the main towns usually open Monday to Friday, from 7.30 am or 8 am to 5 pm, with an hour for lunch between noon and 1 pm. Many shops open Saturday morning also. In smaller towns, shops and stalls are open most days, but keep informal hours.

Bank hours are usually from 8 am to 1 pm or 2 pm, Monday through Friday. If you arrive or leave by air at Lilongwe or Blantyre, the airport banks usually open to coincide with international flights, but not always. Banks in small towns may open only two or three mornings per week. In rural areas, there's a system of 'roving' banks (basically an armoured van), which operate for about an hour on one or two days of the week only (for more details see the Money section earlier in this chapter).

Post and telephone offices usually open 7.30 or 8 am to 4.30 or 5 pm Monday through Friday. In Blantyre and Lilongwe, they also open for shorter hours at weekends (see those chapters for details).

PUBLIC HOLIDAYS
Aside from Christmas Day, Boxing Day, New Year's Day, and Easter Friday and Monday, public holidays include:

16 January
John Chilembwe Day
3 March
Martyrs' Day
1 May
Labour Day
14 June
Freedom Day
6 July
Republic Day
2nd Monday in October
Mother's Day
2nd Monday in December
National Tree Planting Day

When one of the above dates falls on a weekend, normally the following Monday is a public holiday. In northern Malawi and along the lake, many people are Muslim and observe Islamic festivals.

ACTIVITIES
For those who like to be active, there's plenty to keep you occupied in Malawi. For those who like lounging on the beach doing little, there's plenty to keep *you* happy too.

Water Sports
As you might expect in a country dominated by a lake, there are plenty of water sports available in Malawi.

The lake's population of colourful fish (see the Flora & Fauna section in the Facts about Malawi chapter) attracts visitors for **scuba diving**. The fresh water is warm (although thin wetsuits are still recommended) and generally clear (depending on season), and weather conditions usually favourable. Remember if you are a diver that Lake Malawi is 475m above sea level, so your decompression calculations should be adjusted accordingly. Places with scuba gear for hire include Aqua Africa in Nkhata Bay, Rift Lake Charters at Club Makokola, plus several more places at Cape Maclear and other hotels on the southern lake shore. (For more information, see those sections.) Some of these outfits also organise boat cruises on

MALAWI

the lake, over several days, visiting various dive sites. Instruction courses leading to internationally recognised certificates are also available. Even if you're not qualified to dive, you can still enjoy Lake Malawi's underwater world. Most hotels and camps along the lake shore rent out equipment for **snorkelling**.

Many of the more up-market places along the lake also have facilities for **water-skiing** or **windsurfing**. You can also go **sailing**, or join luxurious 'sail safaris' where everything is done for you. There's even some enterprising outfits running **kayaking/canoeing**. These are detailed under the individual places listed in the Lake Shore chapter.

Fishing

The fish species of Malawi that are of no interest to anglers are covered in the Flora & Fauna section of the Facts about Malawi chapter, and in the Lake Shore chapter. These include the colourful cichlid species which attract snorkellers, and the various small fish which are netted by local people to eat or sell in markets. For rod and line anglers, the Malawi Tourism Department and Angling Society of Malawi (PO Box 744, Blantyre) produce the following information.

Lake Malawi Larger fish in Lake Malawi include *mpasa* (also called lake salmon), *ncheni* (or lake tiger) – well-known as a spectacular fighter, *sungwa* (a type of perch), plus *kampango* and *vundu* (both catfish). Light tackle is best; a two kg sungwa gives good sport on a one kg line. Most fish will take anything that moves and spinners of the Abu Flax or Droppen type are taken as readily as small Effzet spoons. In deeper water Abu's Pirk or Toby can be used.

Lake tiger are normally taken one to two metres below the surface in deep open water, and offer exciting angling. In the Senga Bay area, river mouths with heavy reed beds are good spots for kampango or vundu. (There's little difficulty with snagging, but a boat less than five metres is recommended.) For lake salmon the northern parts of the lake are better.

Popular fishing spots for visiting anglers include Nkopola Lodge and Club Makokola on the southern lake shore; accommodation and safe parking for vehicles is available, and boats can be hired (although this should be arranged in advance if possible). Places to head for include Boadzulu Island and White Rock. Anglers with local knowledge and contacts launch boats from Mangochi or Palm Beach, further south, or from Senga Bay.

There is no season, and fishing is allowed at any time, although it's best between September and April.

> **Warning**
> If you take a boat out on Lake Malawi, note that the weather can be severe, and changes occur very quickly. This is an inland sea, with waves over five metres high recorded in storms. Visitors should always get local opinion about conditions before setting off, and leave details of plans (where you are going, for how long) with someone responsible. ∎

Upper Shire River This river flows out of Lake Malawi, through Lake Malombe and then through various cataracts and waterfalls as it skirts to the west of the Shire Highlands. The sungwa is found here, although it's not as large as the ones in the lake.

Lower Shire River Below the last cataract – Kapichira Falls – the Lower Shire begins. The tiger fish here are relatively small (four to seven kg) but have a reputation as fierce fighters. Tackle should be upgraded accordingly. A popular combination is 5.5 to seven kg line, wire trace and big silver lures or wooden plugs. Also in this area are vundu weighing up to 15 kg and barbel (up to 28 kg). These fish have swum upstream from the Zambezi River, and heavy tackle is needed to land them. Fishing is usually from a boat. For visitors, this can be arranged at Majete Safari Lodge.

The fishing season here is May to November in the dry season, but no licences are required.

Zomba, Mulanje & Nyika For discerning anglers, the highland areas of the Zomba Plateau, Mt Mulanje and the Nyika Plateau offer good trout fishing. On Mulanje, rivers can be fished at the foot of the mountain or on the upper slopes around Chambe and Lichenya. The record for trout caught on the mountain is 1.5 kg. The Zomba Plateau has many streams, plus the well-stocked Mlunguzi Dam. On the Nyika Plateau (a national park), three dams and several fast streams have been stocked with trout. Fly-fishing only is allowed, and flies must be tied on single hooks.

The fishing season for Nyika is September to May. Day licences can be bought from the park office. On Mulanje and Zomba the season is September to May. You should bring your own rod and tackle, but if you happen to run out of flies they can be bought in Zomba town, where there is a fishing-fly factory.

Game Viewing & Bird-Watching

Malawi has several national parks and game reserves, where wild animals can be seen, either from the comfort of a vehicle, from horseback, or on a walking trail. For more details see the National Parks & Game Reserves section in the Facts about Malawi chapter.

For bird-watchers, Malawi is a real draw because there is a good range of habitats in a relatively small area, and species occur here from the Central, Southern and East African regions. Over 600 of Africa's 900-plus species have been recorded here, and a serious birder might well tick off a list of 250 or more in a two to three week trip around the country. For advice on field guides see Books, earlier in this chapter. For an idea of species that occur in Malawi, see the Flora & Fauna section in the Facts about Malawi chapter.

Hiking

The main areas for hiking are the Nyika Plateau (in the north of Malawi) and Mt Mulanje (in the south). Other areas include the Zomba Plateau, near the town of the same name, and

various smaller peaks around Blantyre. The areas between them offer a range of routes and conditions, suitable for walkers of all standards. You can go hiking for a few hours, or trekking for several days. Full details are provided in the relevant sections.

The Mountain Club of Malawi is a disparate organisation mainly for Malawians and foreign residents. Occasional club nights and walking 'meets' (outings) are arranged, but they don't normally cater for tourists. However, visitors are welcome to join club activities, especially members of other walking and climbing organisations, although it is not always possible to help with transport, equipment and so on. A newsletter is produced every two months and is available from the Tourist Office in Blantyre, or direct from the club, PO Box 240, Blantyre.

Rock Climbing

Mulanje is Malawi's main climbing area, with some spectacular routes (including the longest in Africa), although local climbers also visit smaller crags and outcrops around the country. The *Guide to Mulanje Massif* describes many climbing routes.

Horse-Riding

Most of Malawi is too low for horses to remain healthy due to the presence of tsetse flies. The main area for riding is the Nyika Plateau, where you can go on morning and afternoon rides, or longer horseback safaris. On the Zomba Plateau is the only dressage school in Africa north of the Limpopo: the Zomba Gymkhana Club. (For more details see the relevant sections.)

ACCOMMODATION

Malawi's choice and range of places to stay has expanded rapidly in the last few years. At the middle and top-end of the market, several smart new hotels and lodges have been built at various places along the lake and in the national parks. Additionally, former government-owned places have been privatised or leased to private management, and many have changed beyond recognition,

MALAWI

with greatly improved facilities and services (although rates have gone up). This situation is still on-going, and although we have tried to keep up with latest developments in this book, you should expect more changes by the time you arrive.

Prices in a top-end hotel or lodge generally range from US$100 to US$200 for a double ensuite room, with all facilities like TV, air-con and telephone, including taxes and breakfast. At the very top of the scale in Malawi you may pay US$200 per person per night, although in such places (for example, Mvuu Lodge in Liwonde) this includes all meals and activities such as game drives. Most places in this bracket have two or three charge bands: visitors from overseas pay 'international' rates (that is, the full price); visitors from other Southern African countries pay about 25% less; Malawi residents get a 50% discount. Some places also give discounts in the low season. Where possible we have quoted international high season rates throughout this chapter.

Middle-bracket hotel rates range from about US$30 to US$100 per double, including taxes, usually with ensuite bathroom and breakfast, but without any of the fancy trimmings found at the top-end places. Quality of service at a smaller place, however, can be just as good or even better than at the pricey establishments.

In the national parks and along the lake shore, there are many places offering camping and self-catering chalets or cabins. Some camp sites are pretty basic, while others have good facilities such as hot showers and security fences. 'Self-catering' in Malawi either means you get the use of a fully equipped kitchen, or the kitchen is staffed by cooks and helpers; you just bring your food – they prepare it to your instructions (and wash up). The accommodation fee you pay (US$10 to US$25) covers this, although tips are always appreciated.

At the bottom end of the price range, in almost every town there is either a council resthouse, government resthouse, or both. Prices vary but can be as little as US$1 for a room in a council resthouse and US$5 a double in a government resthouse, but conditions are generally spartan to say the least and downright disgusting at worst. Some places also have cheaper dormitory accommodation as well. Camping is generally permitted at either type of resthouse.

The last few years have also seen a dramatic rise in the number of privately owned hostels for independent budget travellers and backpackers. Most of these are along the lake shore, but there are a few in the cities too. Prices range from US$1 for a dorm bed up to about US$5 per person for a double or triple. Camping is usually about US$1 to US$2.

In most middle and top-end hotels (and even a few low-budget ones), the overnight cost includes breakfast. Breakfasts may be the full works, including eggs, sausage, cold meats etc, or a 'continental breakfast', which normally means tea and toast. Only in the top-end places should you expect croissants, pastries, marmalade and so on.

Definitions of single and double rooms are not always consistent. It may be determined by the number of beds rather than the size of the beds or the number of people. Therefore it is not unusual for two people to share a single room, paying either the single rate or something just a bit higher. If you want to save money, it always worth asking about this.

Three points worth making if you intend staying at mostly top-end hotels during your time in Malawi. First, if you've got the time and inclination, contact a couple of travel agents in Malawi or in your own country to see if they can get you hotel prices cheaper than the standard 'rack rates'. Second, consider buying a 'Prokard' which gets you discounts of 20% and various other benefits in all hotels in Malawi belonging to the Protea group (Capital, Lilongwe and Lingadzi Hotels in Lilongwe, Mt Soche in Blantyre, Mzuzu Hotel, Nkopola Lodge on the lake shore and Ku Chawe Inn, Zomba), and all other hotels belonging to the group throughout Africa, for a one-off payment of US$35. Thirdly, if you are considering staying at a Protea hotel, use their Central

Reservations Office in Blantyre (☎ 620071) to see if there are any mid-week discounts or other special offers.

For accommodation in National Parks and Game Reserves see that section in the Facts about Malawi chapter.

Accommodation & Food Taxes

All middle and top-end hotels and restaurants charge 10% service charge and a whopping 20% tax. (Despite the new government's claimed intent to promote Malawi as a tourist destination, in early 1996 this tax was increased from 10%, almost overnight, sending the country's hotel and tourist industry into confusion and leading to price hikes across the board.) You should therefore add 30% to the cost shown on menus and tariff sheets. If in doubt, ask if the price is inclusive or not, as it can make quite a difference. Wherever possible in this book we have shown prices inclusive of these taxes.

The 10% service charge officially means that tipping is not necessary, but this is not all it seems as hotels and restaurants who have the 10% service charge have to pass on 60% of this to the Ministry of Tourism, for use in a general marketing fund, so that the staff actually receive only 4% of the total you pay for your room and meal. ■

FOOD

Your choice of food in Malawi is as broad as your choice of accommodation. If you eat in local Malawian restaurants or are invited to eat in somebody's home, you will almost certainly be offered the regional staple called *nsima*, a thick dough-like substance made from maize flour (same as *ugali* in East Africa, or *nshima* and *mealie meal pap* further south). When fresh and cooked well, this is tasty and filling. It's usually eaten with a *relish*, a sauce of some kind, such as beef or vegetable stew, beans or fish. This is usually determined by the time of year, the availability of ingredients, or the type of place you are eating at. Instead of nsima you might get *kondowole*, made from cassava flour, which is more rubbery and (to western taste buds) less tasty than nsima. At bottom-end eating-houses, such Malawian fare will probably be your only choice, with prices between US$1 and US$1.50.

All over Malawi you'll find fresh fruit and vegetables for sale at shops, markets and road-side stalls. Depending on the season, these include bananas, pineapples, tomatoes, pawpaw (papaya), mangoes, avocados, carrots and potatoes. Ideal if you're self-catering, or just want a picnic. Fresh bread can be bought in most towns. PTC supermarkets (part of former president Banda's omnipresent Press Group) are found all over Malawi, stocking locally produced and imported goods. Malawian specials to look out for are guava jam and peanut butter.

In cities and large towns, or areas more used to tourists, you can find cheap restaurants serving traditional Malawian food and other options like fish or chicken with rice or chips (fries), usually for around US$2. You'll also find slightly fancier places doing European or American-style food such as burgers, fried chicken and so on, or straightforward curries. Prices are normally around US$3 to US$5, again depending on the surroundings as much as the food itself, and if you eat in or takeaway. Most also serve cheaper snacks, such as sandwiches or sausage rolls for US$1 to US$2.

Most mid-range hotels and restaurants serve European-style food: steaks, chicken, fish, served with vegetables and chips or rice. The ingredients are more or less the same wherever you go; the price you pay is determined by the quality of the cooking, presentation and service; usually between US$5 and US$10.

At top-end hotels and restaurants in cities and along the lake shore, you can find the straightforward international standards mentioned above, plus more elaborate French, British or Italian cuisine. Blantyre and Lilongwe also have places doing Indian, Korean and Portuguese food. At most top-end establishments, main-course prices range from around US$8 to US$15.

DRINKS

You can buy tea and coffee in many places, from up-market hotels and restaurants to the lowliest local eating house. International fizzy drinks, such as Coke and Pepsi, are widely available. As always, price reflects the standard of the establishment rather than the taste in your cup.

Traditional beer is made from maize, brewed in the villages and drunk from communal pots with great ceremony at special occasions, and with less ado in everyday situations. This product is also commercially brewed as Chibuku, and sold all over the country in large red and blue cartons. For most Europeans, the thick texture (not unlike weak porridge) and bittersweet taste is not appealing.

Most visitors, and many Malawians, prefer the beer produced by Danish company Carlsberg at its Blantyre brewery (the only one in Africa). There are three main types of beer: 'greens' (lager), 'browns' (more like a British ale) and 'golds' (a stronger brew).

ENTERTAINMENT
Nightclubs, bars and discos in Blantyre and Lilongwe are covered in those chapters.

THINGS TO BUY
For intrepid shoppers, Malawi offers a wide range of curios and souvenirs. Some of these items can be described as craft-work, while others are works of art, although the distinction between 'art' and 'craft' is blurred in Malawi, as elsewhere. (This is discussed further under Arts in the Facts about Malawi chapter.)

The most commonly seen items for sale are made of wood, mostly traditional in design although you do see some unusual contemporary stuff. Most carvings are of animals and people, ornaments such as bowls and chess sets, and the very popular chief's chair; a two-piece three-legged stool with a high back decorated with pictures.

You can also find plenty of objects made from grass and palm fronds, such as baskets and boxes, or intricate models of cars and lorries, and even overland trucks! Contemporary soapstone carvings, paintings, clay

One of the most distinctive creations of Malawian crafts is the Chief's Chair. These ornately carved pieces make a popular souvenir.

pots and figures, and malachite jewellery is also available.

You can buy all these items at road-side stalls or curio shops (details of places to shop are provided throughout this book). Prices are usually not fixed, so you have to bargain. Some western visitors have difficulty with this concept, and are scared of being 'overcharged', but the principle is in fact very straightforward: the salesman (they are all men) tries to get as much as he can, while you pay only as much as you want. More details on bargaining are given under Money earlier in this chapter. However, if you prefer not to haggle, there are some shops in Blantyre and Lilongwe which use price tags.

In markets all over Malawi you can buy *chitenjas*, sheets of brightly coloured cloth that local women use as wraps, cloaks, scarves and baby carriers. They make nice souvenirs and have practical value for women travelling, especially if heading for the beach or rural areas where shorts are frowned upon.

Getting There & Away

AIR

Malawi's main airport for international flights (from neighbouring countries in Africa, and from further afield) is in Lilongwe. There is also an airport in Blantyre but this has only a few direct international flights per week. If you want to fly to/from Blantyre, it is more common to take a domestic flight between there and Lilongwe. In this case, all customs and immigration is done in Lilongwe.

Buying Tickets

Your first step, if you're flying into Malawi, is buying a plane ticket. This can be an intimidating and time-consuming business, so it's always worth taking time to research the market, especially for a relatively little-visited country like Malawi. Start as soon as you can: some cheap tickets must be bought months in advance, and some popular flights sell out early.

To buy a ticket, you must contact a travel agent (travel agency). It's normally not worth contacting airlines as they rarely supply the cheapest tickets. As well as providing a range of fares, travel agents provide you with a choice of airlines too.

To get an idea of your options, look at advertisements in newspapers and magazines (some are listed below), then phone several travel agents. Tell them where you want to go, and when, and they will offer you three main choices: airline, fare and route. Once you've got a few quotes, you can start deciding which is the best option for you. Other points to consider are the duration of the journey, the departure and arrival times, and any restrictions on the ticket. (See Restrictions in the boxed Air Travel Glossary.)

You may discover that the cheapest flights are on bad quality airlines which leave you at the world's least favourite airport in mid-journey for 14 hours, or land you at Lilongwe in the middle of the night. Or that the cheap flights in the advertisement are fully booked, 'but we have another one that costs a bit more...'. Or that the agent may claim to have the last two seats available for the whole month, which they will hold for two hours only. These are all old tricks. Don't panic – keep ringing around.

You may also find that the cheapest flights are advertised by obscure 'bucket shops' (see the boxed Air Travel Glossary). Many such firms are honest, but there are a few rogues who will take your money and disappear. If you feel suspicious, don't pay all the money at once – leave a small deposit and pay the balance when you get the ticket. If they insist on cash in advance, go somewhere else. And once you have the ticket, ring the airline to confirm that you are actually booked onto the flight.

You may decide to opt for a more reliable deal by paying more than the rock-bottom fare. You can go to a better-known travel agent (such as STA, who have offices worldwide, Campus Travel in the UK, Council Travel in the USA or Travel CUTS in Canada) or to a small independent agent, where your money is also safe if they are 'bonded' – a member of a trade organisation that guarantees to protect your money in case of problems, such as the Association of British Travel Agents (ABTA), or the Australian Federation of Travel Agents (AFTA).

Once you have your ticket, keep a note of the number, flight numbers, dates and times and other details, and keep the information somewhere separate. The easiest thing to do is take a few photocopies – carry one with you and leave another at home. If the ticket is lost or stolen, this will help you get a replacement.

It's sensible to buy travel insurance as early as possible. If you get it the week before you fly, you may find, for example, that you're not covered for delays to your flight caused by industrial action.

Travellers with Special Needs

If you have special needs of any sort – you've

Air Travel Glossary

Apex Apex, or 'advance purchase excursion' is a discounted ticket which must be paid for in advance. There are penalties if you wish to change it.

Baggage Allowance This will be written on your ticket: usually one 20 kg item to go in the hold, plus one item of hand luggage.

Bucket Shop An unbonded travel agency specialising in discounted airline tickets.

Bumped Just because you have a confirmed seat doesn't mean you're going to get on the plane – see Overbooking.

Cancellation Penalties If you have to cancel or change an Apex ticket there are often heavy penalties involved. Insurance can sometimes be taken out against these penalties. Some airlines impose penalties on regular tickets as well, particularly against 'no show' passengers.

Check In Airlines ask you to check in a certain time ahead of the flight departure (usually 1½ hours on international flights). If you fail to check in on time and the flight is overbooked the airline can cancel your booking and give your seat to somebody else.

Confirmation Having a ticket written out with the flight and date you want doesn't mean you have a seat until the agent has checked with the airline that your status is 'OK' or confirmed. Meanwhile you could just be 'on request'.

Discounted Tickets There are two types of discounted fares – officially discounted (see Promotional Fares) and unofficially discounted. The lowest prices often impose drawbacks like flying with unpopular airlines, inconvenient schedules, or unpleasant routes and connections. A discounted ticket can save you other things than money – you may be able to pay Apex prices without the associated Apex advance booking and other requirements. Discounted tickets only exist where there is fierce competition.

Full Fares Airlines traditionally offer first class (coded F), business class (coded J) and economy class (coded Y) tickets. These days there are so many promotional and discounted fares available from the regular economy class that few passengers pay full economy fare.

Lost Tickets If you lose your airline ticket an airline will usually treat it like a travellers' cheque and, after inquiries, issue you with another one. Legally, however, an airline is entitled to treat it like cash and if you lose it then it's gone forever. Take good care of your tickets.

Non-Discounted Tickets These are tickets you buy straight from the airline (not through a travel agent). Normally this is not the cheapest way of doing things, but some bargains can occasionally be uncovered with persistence.

No Shows No shows are passengers who fail to show up for their flight, sometimes due to unexpected delays or disasters, sometimes due to simply forgetting, sometimes because they made more than one booking and didn't bother to cancel the one they didn't want. Full fare passengers who fail to turn up are sometimes entitled to travel on a later flight. The rest of us are penalised (see Cancellation Penalties).

On Request An unconfirmed booking for a flight, see Confirmation.

Open Jaws A return ticket where you fly out to one place but return from another. If available this can save you backtracking to your arrival point.

Overbooking Airlines hate to fly empty seats and since every flight has some passengers who fail to

---

broken a leg, you're vegetarian, travelling in a wheelchair, taking the baby, terrified of flying – you should let the airline know as soon as possible so that they can make arrangements accordingly. You should remind them when you reconfirm your booking (at least 72 hours before departure) and again when you check in at the airport. It may also be worth ringing round the airlines before you make your booking to find out how they can handle your particular needs.

Airports and airlines can be surprisingly helpful, but they do need advance warning.

Most international airports will provide escorts where needed, and there should be ramps, lifts and accessible toilets and reachable phones. Aircraft toilets, however, are likely to present a problem; travellers should discuss this with the airline at an early stage and, if necessary, with their doctor.

Guide dogs for the blind will often have to travel in a specially pressurised baggage compartment with other animals, away from their owner; though smaller guide dogs may be admitted to the cabin. All guide dogs will be subject to the same quarantine laws (six months in isolation etc) as any other animal show up (see No Shows) airlines often book more passengers than they have seats. Usually the excess passengers balance those who fail to show up but occasionally somebody gets bumped. If this happens guess who it is most likely to be? The passengers who check in late.

Promotional Fares Officially discounted fares like Apex fares which are available from travel agents or direct from the airline.

Reconfirmation At least 72 hours prior to departure time of an onward or return flight you must contact the airline and 'reconfirm' that you intend to be on the flight. If you don't do this the airline can delete your name from the passenger list and you could lose your seat. You don't have to reconfirm the first flight on your itinerary or if your stopover is less than 72 hours. It doesn't hurt to reconfirm more than once.

Restrictions Discounted tickets often have various restrictions on them – advance purchase is the most usual one (see Apex). Others are restrictions on the minimum and maximum period you must be away, such as a minimum of 14 days or a maximum of one year. See Cancellation Penalties.

RTW Tickets RTW stands for Round The World – an increasingly popular option for many travellers. The official airline RTW tickets are usually put together by a combination of two airlines, and permit you to fly anywhere you want on their route systems so long as you don't backtrack. Other restrictions are that you (usually) must book the first sector in advance and cancellation penalties then apply. There may be restrictions on how many stops you are permitted and usually the tickets are valid for 90 days up to a year. An alternative type of RTW ticket is one put together by a travel agent using a combination of discounted tickets.

Standby A discounted ticket where you only fly if there is a seat free at the last moment. Standby fares are usually only available on domestic routes.

Tickets Out An entry requirement for many countries is that you have an onward or return ticket, in other words, a ticket out of the country. If you're not sure what you intend to do next, the easiest solution is to buy the cheapest onward ticket to a neighbouring country or a ticket from a reliable airline which can later be refunded if you do not use it.

Transferred Tickets Airline tickets cannot be transferred from one person to another. Travellers sometimes try to sell the return half of their ticket, but officials can ask you to prove that you are the person named on the ticket. This is unlikely to happen on domestic flights; on an international flight tickets may be compared with passports.

Travel Agencies Travel agencies vary widely and you should ensure you use one that suits your needs. Some simply handle tours while full-service agencies handle everything from tours and tickets to car rental and hotel bookings. A good one will do all these things and can save you a lot of money but if all you want is a ticket at the lowest possible price, then you really need an agency specialising in discounted tickets. A discounted ticket agency, however, may not be useful for other things, like hotel bookings.

Travel Periods Some officially discounted fares, Apex fares in particular, vary with the time of year. There is often a low (off-peak) season and a high (peak) season. Sometimes there's an intermediate or shoulder season as well. At peak times, when everyone wants to fly, not only will the officially discounted fares be higher but so will unofficially discounted fares or there may simply be no discounted tickets available. Usually the fare depends on your outward flight – if you depart in the high season and return in the low season, you pay the high-season fare. ■

when entering or returning to countries currently free of rabies such as Britain or Australia.

Deaf travellers can ask for airport and in-flight announcements to be written down for them.

Children under two travel for 10% of the standard fare (or free on some airlines), as long as they don't occupy a seat. They don't get a baggage allowance either. 'Skycots' should be provided by the airline if requested in advance; these will take a child weighing up to about 10 kg. Children between two and 12 can usually occupy a seat for half to

two-thirds of the full fare, and do get a baggage allowance. Push chairs can often be taken as hand luggage.

UK & Ireland

From the UK, airlines flying to Malawi include British Airways, Ethiopian Airlines, KLM, Kenya Airways, South African Airways and Air Zimbabwe. Some of these carriers also serve Ireland, or you may have to reach London on a separate flight. High season return fares from London to Lilongwe start at around UK£580 for airlines with long mid-flight connecting times, going

> ### Warning
> Use the air fares quoted in this book as a guide only. They are approximate and based on the rates advertised by travel agents at the time of going to press. Airlines mentioned in this book are not necessarily recommended.
>
> Note also that the travel information of this nature is particularly vulnerable to change: prices for international flights are volatile, routes are introduced and cancelled, schedules change, special deals come and go, and rules and visa requirements are amended. Airlines and governments seem to take a perverse pleasure in making price structures and regulations as complicated as possible. You should check directly with the airline or a travel agent to make sure you understand how a fare (and the ticket you may buy) works.
>
> You should get opinions, quotes and advice from as many airlines (although they rarely supply the cheapest tickets) and travel agents as possible before you part with your hard-earned cash. The details given in this chapter should be regarded as pointers and are not a substitute for your own careful, up-to-date research. ■

up to UK£720 for something more direct. Low season fares are around UK£100 cheaper.

Discount Travel Agencies London is normally the best place to buy a ticket, although these days specialist travel agents outside the capital are often just as cheap and can be friendlier and easier to deal with. Flight agents advertise in weekend newspapers, travel magazines and listings magazines such as *Time Out* in London. Also in London check the freebie papers such as *TNT* aimed at Aussies, Kiwis and other long-term visitors. *SA Times*, for homesick South Africans, is particularly useful. In London, the following agents are main players and good places to start your price comparisons:

Africa Travel Centre, 21 Leigh St, London WC1H
  9QX (☎ (0171) 387 1211)
Bridge the World, 52 Chalk Farm Rd, Camden Town
  London NW1 8AN (☎ (0171) 911 0900)
Campus Travel, 52 Grosvenor Gardens, London
  SW1W OAG (☎ (0171) 730 8111)
    Also with offices in large YHA Adventure Shops
    and university/colleges around the country (tele-
    phone bookings ☎ (0171) 730 2101, (0161) 273
    1721 or (0131) 668 3303).
STA Travel, 74-88 Old Brompton Rd, London SW7
  (☎ (0171) 361 6262)
    117 Euston Rd, London NW1 2SX
    (☎ (0171) 465 0486)
    Also with branches in Manchester, Bristol, and
    most large university towns.

Trailfinders, 42-48 Earls Court Rd, London W8
  (☎ (0171) 938 3366)
    Also with offices in Manchester, Bristol, and
    several others.

Outside London, others to try include the following (again, this is just a list to get you started on price comparisons):

Footloose Adventure Travel, 105 Leeds Rd, Ilkley,
  West Yorkshire LS29 8EG (☎ (01943) 604030)
Quest Worldwide, 29 Castle St, Kingston, Surrey KT1
  1ST (☎ (0181) 547 3322)
Travel Bug, 597 Cheetham Hill Rd, Manchester M8
  5EJ (☎ (0161) 721 4000)
Trips Worldwide, 9 Byron Place, Bristol BS8 1JT
  (☎ (0117) 987 2626)
USIT Travel, 19 Aston Quay, Dublin, Ireland
  (☎ (01) 679 8833)

The Rest of Europe

You can fly to Malawi from many European capitals. Travel agents advertise in the same kinds of papers and magazines as they do in the UK. Places to start comparisons include:

France
    Council Travel, Rue St Augustine, 2Sme, Paris
    (☎ (01) 42 66 20 87)
    Council Travel, 22 Rue des Pyramides, 1Sre,
    Paris (☎ (01) 44 55 55 44)
Germany
    Alternativ Tours, Wilmersdorferstrasse 94,
    Berlin (☎ (030) 881 2089)
    SRID Reisen, Bergerstrasse 1178, Frankfurt
    (☎ (069) 43 01 91)

SRS Studenten Reise Service, Marienstrasse 23,
Berlin (☎ (030) 281 5033)
Italy
CTS, Via Genova 16, off Via Nazionale, Roma
(☎ (06) 46 791)
Netherlands
NBBS, Rokin 38, Amsterdam
(☎ (020) 624 0989)
Malibu Travel, Damrak 30, Amsterdam
(☎ (020) 623 6814)
Spain
TIVE, Calle Jos, Ortega y Gasset, Madrid
(☎ (91) 401 1300)
Switzerland
SSR, Leonhardstrasse 5-10, Zürich
(☎ (01) 261 2956)

USA & Canada

From North America, a flight to Malawi will
go via Europe or South Africa. It may be
cheaper to fly on an economy hop from the
US to London and then buy a discount travel-
agency ticket from there to Malawi. Canadi-
ans also will probably find the best deals
travelling via London.

The best way to find a flight is by checking
the Sunday travel sections in the major newspapers such as the *Los Angeles Times*, the
San Francisco Examiner or *Chronicle*, or the
New York Times. The student travel bureaux
– STA or Council Travel – are also worth a
go, but in the USA you must have proof of
student status or be under 26 years of age to
qualify for their discounted fares. Also recommended for North Americans is the
newsletter *Travel Unlimited* (PO Box 1058,
Allston, MA 02134) which publishes details
of the cheapest airfares and courier possibil-
ities for destinations all over the world.
Travel CUTS has offices in all major Canadian cities. The *Toronto Globe & Mail* and
the *Vancouver Sun* carry travel agents'
advertisements. The magazine *Great Expeditions* (PO Box 8000-411, Abbotsford, BC
V2S 6H1) is also very useful.

Discount Travel Agencies Although North
Americans won't get the great deals that are
available in London, there are a few discount
agencies which keep a lookout for the best
airfare bargains. (Some more places are

listed in the Overland Tours section below.)
To comply with regulations, these are sometimes associated with specific travel clubs.

CHA, 333 River Rd, Vanier, Ottawa, Ontario KIL
8H9
Canadian International Student Services, 80 Rich-
mond St W (1202), Toronto, Ontario M5H 2A4
(☎ (416) 364-2738)
Council on International Educational Exchange, 205
East 42nd St, New York, NY 10017
STA Travel, 166 Geary St, Suite 702, San Francisco,
CA 94108 (☎ (415) 391 8407)
48 East 11th St, New York, NY 10017
(☎ (212) 486 0503)
Suite 507, 2500 Wilshire Blvd, Los Angeles, CA
90057 (☎ (213) 380-2184)
Travel International, 114 Forrest Ave, Suite 205,
Narbeth, PA 19072 (☎ (215) 668 2182)
Uni Travel, PO Box 12485, St Louis, MO 63132
(☎ (314) 569 2501)
Whole World Travel, Suite 400, 17 East 45th St, New
York, NY 10017 (☎ (212) 986 9470)

Australia & New Zealand

To reach Malawi from Australasia, you'll
probably have to go via South Africa or
Zimbabwe. Airlines flying between Australia and Southern Africa include Qantas,
Air Zimbabwe and South African Airways.
Between New Zealand and Southern Africa
you must go via Australia.

In Australia, the best place to start
looking for flights are the advertisements
in newspapers such as the Saturday editions of the *Sydney Morning Herald* and
the *Age*. Agents to start with include STA
Travel and Flight Centres International.
(Some more places are listed in the Overland Tours section later.)

Standard return flights between Australia
and Southern Africa start at around A$1800,
and you can find round the world (RTW)
tickets which include a stop in Southern
Africa for around A$2300. This is also
cheaper than a standard one-way ticket, and
means you can come home via Europe or the
USA. Another option for Australasians not
pressed for time is a RTW ticket or a return
ticket to Europe with a stopover in Nairobi,
from where Malawi can be reached by
regional flight or overland.

Whichever way you get to Southern Africa, discuss your options with several travel agents before buying. Few have had much experience with inexpensive routings to Africa.

Discount Travel Agencies In Australia and New Zealand, inexpensive travel is available mainly from STA Travel, with branches in all capital cities and on most university campuses.

ACT
>   Ground floor, 13-15 Garema Place, Canberra 2601 (☎ (06) 247 8633)

New South Wales
>   855 George St, Sydney, NSW 2007 (☎ (02) 9212 1255)

Queensland
>   Shops 25 & 26, 111-117 Adelaide St, Brisbane Qld 4000 (☎ (07) 221 9388)

South Australia
>   235 Rundle St, Adelaide, SA 5000 (☎ (08) 223 2426)

Victoria
>   222 Faraday St, Carlton, Victoria 3053 (☎ (03) 9349 2411)

Western Australia
>   53 Market St, Fremantle, WA 6160 (☎ (09) 430 5553)

New Zealand
>   10 High St, Auckland (☎ (09) 309 0458)

Other Destinations in Africa

If you're travelling to Malawi from other destinations in Southern or East Africa (or going in the other direction), Air Malawi has a pretty good regional network. Destinations include: Harare, four times per week (around US$150 one-way); Nairobi, with flights twice per week (US$315); Lusaka, with flights twice per week (US$135); Johannesburg, with flights five times per week (US$250); Maputo (US$300) and Beira, with flights to both cities twice per week (US$200).

The following regional airlines also serve Malawi, usually flying on the days Air Malawi doesn't, with fares mostly on a par.

Air Zimbabwe, with flights five times per week to/from Harare (with connections to Victoria Falls, Dar es Salaam and several other parts of Southern Africa).

Kenya Airways, with flights once per week to/from Nairobi.

South African Airways, with flights four times per week to/from Jo'burg (with connections to Durban, Cape Town etc).

Zambian Express, flying once per week to/from Lusaka.

You can also fly between Lilongwe and Dar es Salaam, Kilimanjaro International Airport (KIA) or Zanzibar in Tanzania. Lilongwe to Dar es Salaam costs around US$200 one-way or US$300 return, on either Air Malawi or Air Tanzania. KIA is much nearer Tanzania's main safari areas so, if you're going to fly from Lilongwe, you might as well go all the way to KIA, which means changing in Dar es Salaam then taking one of the daily flights to KIA for US$75, or to Zanzibar for US$33. (However, as this airline can be unpredictable, it may be easier to go from Dar es Salaam to Moshi or Arusha by bus or train, and to Zanzibar by boat).

Leaving Malawi

If you're leaving Malawi by air, return flights to Europe on Ethiopian Airlines (twice weekly) cost US$700. Kenya Airways flies once weekly to London for around US$750. Air Zimbabwe flies to London for US$840 in the low season and US$940 in the high season. South African Airways fly to London twice per week from Lilongwe and twice from Blantyre, costing US$950 in the low season and US$1045 in the high season. On British Airways (thrice-weekly) or KLM (twice-weekly) it's around US$1000 in the low season and US$1100 in the high season. Even if you're not coming back, it's usually cheaper to buy an economy excursion ticket than a standard one-way ticket. A good travel agent (see the Lilongwe and Blantyre chapters) will be able to advise you on this.

Lilongwe airport has a pharmacy, post office, bookshop, banks and car hire desks, plus a restaurant and bar overlooking the runway, where you can use up the last of your kwacha before flying out (although beware of waiters overcharging hugely here). Blantyre also has a small bar-cafeteria, bookshop and Avis car hire desk.

Airport Taxes
For non-resident visitors flying out of Lilongwe or Blantyre, the airport departure tax for international flights is US$20.

LAND
You may enter Malawi by one of its land borders, either because you've flown into a nearby country (such as South Africa or Kenya) or because you've come all the way from home overland. More independent travellers arrive in Malawi overland than by air.

Malawi shares borders with Mozambique, Tanzania and Zambia. All border posts open from 6 am to 6 pm (possibly open later and shut earlier, but never the other way around). Malawi does not directly border Zimbabwe, but there is a lot of traffic between these two countries passing across a neck of Mozambique territory called the Tete Corridor.

If you're bringing a car into Malawi without a carnet (for example, if you're a nonresident of South Africa with a South African registered car), a temporary import permit is US$3 (payable in kwacha at the current rate, or SA rands or US dollars at a disadvantageous rate), and compulsory third party insurance is US$9 for one month. When you leave Malawi another US$3 Temporary Import Permit handling fee is payable. Receipts are issued.

Mozambique
If you are heading from Malawi into Mozambique, note that every foreigner entering Mozambique by land is subject to an official immigration tax of US$5 or R 10. Although you don't always get a receipt this seems to be legitimate – there's a notice about it up on every embassy wall.

Cars must also pay, but rates seem to vary between borders and according to who's on duty. For example, travellers crossing at Mulanje/Milange have paid just R 10 or US$5 for a temporary import permit, while others crossing at Mwanza/Zóbuè have been charged R 20. For large vehicles (over three tonnes) it's double or treble this. If you're driving, check the current rates when you get your visa. On top of this drivers pay R 100 or US$35 for one month's third party insurance.

Bus If you're heading for the part of Mozambique south of the Zambezi, you should go via Mwanza and Zóbuè (by far the busiest and most popular border crossing) to Tete. The most direct way of doing this is by taking one of the buses between Blantyre and Harare (see Zimbabwe, later in this chapter), which can drop you at Tete (from where buses go to Beira and Maputo) or at Changara (where the roads to Harare and Beira branch off). You can also do the trip in stages by taking a local bus from Blantyre to the Malawi border post at Mwanza (three km west of Mwanza town), then walking or hitching the six km to Zóbuè (pronounced Zobway), the Mozambique border post. If you get stuck at the border, the *Mwanza Motel* has decent rooms for US$10/16. There are plenty of moneychangers at both border posts, dealing in kwacha, Zimbabwe dollars, US dollars and meticais, but rates are low.

If you're heading for central Mozambique from Malawi, you can cross the border on the road between Nsanje and the bridge over the Zambezi at Vila de Sena. There are two or three buses per day from Blantyre to Nsanje, from where minibuses go to the border. (Some buses go all the way to the border too.) From the Mozambique side, minibuses go to Vila Nova and on to Nhamilabue and Vila de Sena. From here you can reach Caia, where an unreliable vehicle ferry crosses the Zambezi. The Vila de Sena bridge, the Caia ferry and the roads in the area are all due for renovation in 1997 and 1998, and this will make transport on these routes, and to Beira and Quelimane, more frequent and comfortable.

If you're heading for northern Mozambique, the main road crossing point is on the route between Mangochi and Cuamba.

MALAWI

Minibuses run a few times per day between Mangochi and the last Malawi town of Namwera, where there are resthouses if you need one (the *Masongola* is recommended), or all the way to the Malawi border post at Chiponde (10 km from Namwera) for US$2. If there's no bus on this last bit, you can walk, or take a local bicycle-taxi between Namwera and Chiponde for US$3. It's six km to the Mozambique border post at Mandimba. You might be able to hitch, or use a bicycle-taxi (US$2). Mandimba has a couple of *pensãos* (cheap resthouses), and there's usually a daily *chapa* (bush bus) between here and Cuamba (US$4). The road between Cuamba and Nampula is bad so most people take the train (see the Mozambique chapter). It's also possible to travel by train from Malawi to Cuamba (see the following Train section).

Your other road option between Malawi and northern Mozambique is the route between Blantyre and Mocuba. There are regular buses between Blantyre and Mulanje town which go on to the Malawi border post at Muloza (the fare is US$3). From here you walk about one km to the Mozambique border post at Milange, from where it's another few km into Milange *vila* (town) itself. There are bicycle-taxis for US$1. There's a pensão and bank here if you need one. From Milange there's usually a chapa or truck about every other day in the dry season to Mocuba (US$4), where you can find transport on to Quelimane or Nampula. But if you're heading straight for Nampula anyway, you're probably better off going by train.

Train If you're heading to northern Mozambique (that is, to Nacala, Pemba or Mozambique Island), the best way to travel is via the train between Cuamba and Nampula. You can reach Cuamba by road from Mandimba (see above) or by train from Malawi. On the Malawi side there's a twice-weekly (currently Monday and Thursday mornings, but this may change) passenger train from Balaka, via Liwonde, to the border at Nayuchi (rail crossing only) which costs

US$2. Here, you walk about one km to the Mozambique border post (which seems to be called something like 'Interlagho') and the point where you catch a Mozambique freight train (also usually twice-weekly – but not necessarily the same two days each week) to Cuamba. The fare is US$1.50, payable in meticais. There are moneychangers at Nayuchi. From Cuamba there are three passenger trains per week to Nampula (US$3) and freight trains with a wagon for passengers most other days. Three separate train rides, none of which connect, plus a bad line between the border and Cuamba (especially in the rainy season) means this trip can take a day or a week, depending on your luck.

Boat & Truck The Malawian ferry *Ilala* is covered in the main Getting Around chapter. It stops at Likoma Island, Malawian territory within Mozambique's waters, twice per week. From here a local boat goes every other day across to Cobuè (pronounced Kobway) on the Mozambique mainland. The fare is US$0.60. From here infrequent trucks go to Lichinga (two days), which is joined by a good road and a terrible railway line to Cuamba, from where you can take the train (see Train, earlier). Alternatively, you can go by boat from Likoma to Metangula (about 100 km south of Cobuè), but this is less regular and takes a couple of days. There are also Mozambican boats going between Cobuè and Metangula, especially in the wet season when the road is bad. There are immigration offices at Likoma, Cobuè and Metangula – all very straightforward.

Tanzania

The only land crossing between Malawi and Tanzania is at the Songwe River bridge north of Kaporo, in the far north-western tip of Malawi. The road is tar all the way between Karonga (the first/last town in Malawi) and Mbeya (Tanzania), although it's pristine in some places and terrible in others. (A new bridge is planned further upstream, but it's likely that the current border crossing will remain the most heavily used, with the best transport options.)

Note that if you're going from Malawi to Tanzania, the border posts both close at 6 pm. However, Tanzania's time is an hour ahead of Malawi's, so the Malawian officials will cheerfully stamp you through at 5.30 pm (their time) but once you cross the bridge it's 6.30 pm, and the Tanzanian border is shut. You can either sleep on the spot (not advisable, as some fairly unsavoury characters frequent the area) or pay the guards 'overtime' to let you through. Better still, if it's getting late, stay in Karonga or somewhere else on the Malawi side and continue your journey next day. We have heard that the Tanzania border may stay open to 8 pm on some nights, but as travel at night is not recommended, it's still best to go though with plenty of daylight to spare.

When entering Malawi, also beware of a new scam that the Malawi border guards are playing here, involving imaginary 'errors' on your visa or passport which can only be sorted out for a US$20 fee. The poor blokes probably haven't been paid for months, so it's hard to blame them, but this kind of game just isn't on. Politely ask to see their commanding officer, or written regulations about the 'fee', and you may find it swiftly waived.

Bus If you want to go the whole way between Lilongwe and Dar es Salaam in one go, there's a weekly (sometimes twice-weekly) bus operated by Metro Coach Company. In Lilongwe, their office is at the Council Resthouse, opposite the market. There is also supposed to be a direct bus service between Mzuzu and Dar (via Karonga and Mbeya), but days and times are vague, so inquire at the bus station in Mzuzu.

Most people go from Malawi to Tanzania by bus in stages. On the Malawi side, there are three buses per day between Mzuzu and Karonga. Between Karonga and the Songwe Bridge border (via Kaporo) is a twice-daily bus (US$0.50), and occasional minibuses (US$1). It's a few hundred metres across the bridge to the Tanzania border post on the other side. The Tanzanian officials here used to have a reputation for being among the toughest in Africa, but as Tanzania's entry

and exit regulations have been relaxed, so the guys at Songwe Bridge have mellowed a bit too.

From the Tanzania border post there's no public transport, so you'll have to walk or hitch about seven km to the junction with the road between Kyela and Mbeya. Alternatively, enterprising (and over-enthusiastic) local youths on bicycles will pedal you there for US$1. You can also change money with them. If you're heading north, there's no need to go into Kyela along this route as the town is five km south-east of the junction and in the wrong direction for Mbeya. From the junction you can find a bus (there's two or three each day) or a lift to Mbeya, where you can pick up a bus or train to Dar es Salaam.

There are plans to tar the road between Karonga and Mpulungu (Zambia) via Chitipa and Nakonde (see the Grand Plans boxed text below). From Nakonde, the Tanzanian town of Tunduma is just across the border. In the next few years, if the road is completed, this will probably be an easier way to go between Malawi and Tanzania.

Boat & Truck The *Ilala* serves various ports on Lake Malawi (see the Getting Around chapter). At certain times of year it runs up to the far northern end of the lake into Tanzanian waters, to the small town of Itungi, near Kyela (which has regular transport links with Mbeya). If you were coming from Tanzania, you could get on the boat at Itungi and ride down the lake as far as, say, Nkhata Bay. But as the boat runs only once per week, and does not always go to Itungi, this may involve a lot of unnecessary waiting around. However, if you wanted to go north on the boat, from Malawi to Tanzania, this would be easier. If it didn't go all the way to Itungi, you simply get off at Nkhata Bay or Kaporo, and continue by land.

The *Ilala* also goes across the lake between Nkhata Bay and Mbamba Bay – a small town on the eastern (Tanzanian) side of the lake. From here you could go by truck or pick-up to the town of Songea, about 200 km inland. From here though you're only real option is to go north, through Njombe,

MALAWI

to join the TAZARA railway, or the main road between Mbeya and Dar es Salaam, at Makambako. The road east from Songea towards the Tanzanian coast is in very bad condition, with occasional trucks the only form of transport.

At the northern end of the lake a Tanzanian ship called the *Songea* operates between Itungi and Mbamba Bay, and there are apparently plans for it to start calling at Nkhata Bay, giving another option for lake transport between Malawi and Tanzania. Note however that the *Ilala* is notoriously prone to delays, and the Tanzanian boats are no better, sometimes leaving and arriving *days* after they're supposed to.

Zambia

The main border crossing point between Malawi and Zambia is about 30 km east of Chipata, on the main road between Lusaka and Lilongwe.

The other possible route, between Karonga and Tunduma, via Chitipa (in the far north-west of Malawi) and Nyala (the Zambia border post) is much more difficult since the road is very bad. It is rarely used by drivers, and there are no buses. However, in the next few years this may change (see the Grand Plans boxed text below).

Bus If you want to go direct between Lilongwe and Lusaka there's a twice-weekly service between Lilongwe and Harare via Lusaka, run by a company called March Coach. In Lilongwe you can book in advance at the Stagecoach depot (not the bus station) near the PTC Hypermarket on Kamuzu Procession Rd. In Lusaka, buses leave from the Intercity Bus Station in Dedan Kimathi Rd. Either way, tickets cost about US$15. (From Lilongwe to Harare is US$37.)

You can also do this journey in stages using local buses, but this involves a lot of messing around and also means taking a taxi or hitching between the border posts, so it works out to be only a little cheaper. But if the express buses are booked up there are fairly regular buses and minibuses from Lilongwe to the Malawi border post, two km

west of the town of Mchinji, from where it's about 12 km to the Zambia border post. Local shared taxis and minibuses cost about US$1.50, and it's fairly easy to hitch a ride.

From the Zambian side of the border there is a daily bus to Lusaka, otherwise you can find local buses to Chipata (about 30 km west of the border), and get a bus to Lusaka from there. In Chipata there's nothing to see, but there are some places to stay if you get stuck. You might also get off the bus here if you're heading for South Luangwa National Park. (For more details, see the Zambia chapter.)

Grand Plans for the Karonga to Chitipa Road

If you're travelling by road in northern Malawi, or crossing into Tanzania or Zambia, you might like to note that there are plans to completely upgrade the road from Karonga (on the northern bank of Lake Malawi) to Chitipa (on the Malawi-Zambia border) through Nakonde and Mbala to Mpulungu on the southern tip of Lake Tanganyika.

If the plans come to reality, this will no doubt improve communications between Tanzania, Zambia and Malawi. Buses will start to run here, and moving between northern Malawi and northern Zambia will become much easier. If you need to go this way ask around for the latest situation.

Ironically, this new road follows a route originally planned by the African Lakes Corporation over a hundred years ago, to link the north of Lake Malawi with the south of Lake Tanganyika, forming a continuous 'highway' for many hundreds of miles through Central Africa. It was named the Stevenson Road, after one of the Glasgow businessmen who helped found the African Lakes Corporation in 1878 and later became its chairman, but the project was abandoned after the death of the senior engineer, one James Stewart. This was the cousin of another James Stewart who had earlier inspired and helped to found the Livingstonia missions (see History in the Facts about Malawi chapter.) His journals were later published as a book *From Nyassa to Tanganyika*. If the new road is built his plans will have finally been realised. ■

Zimbabwe

Although Zimbabwe does not border Malawi, there are two international express services between Blantyre and Harare, via Tete (Mozambique). Stagecoach runs a comfortable coach three times per week in each direction. The 10-hour journey is virtually non-stop so you need to bring enough food and drink. The one-way fare is just under US$50, payable in Malawi kwacha, or Zimbabwe dollars in Harare. More information is available from the Stagecoach depots in Blantyre and Lilongwe. There's also a smaller operator called Munorurama which runs daily buses between Blantyre and Harare. They leave Blantyre's Chileka Road bus station at 6 am and arrive in Harare some time between late afternoon and midnight. Coming the other way the times are the same. Fares are US$15, payable in Malawi kwacha, Zimbabwe dollars or SA rand. This bus also runs between Blantyre and Monkey Bay, and between Harare and Beitbridge on the South African border. For inquiries visit the Munorurama office, near Wayfarers backpackers lodge (see the Blantyre chapter for details). When crossing the borders between Malawi, Mozambique and Zimbabwe, expect large queues and long delays.

ORGANISED TOURS

There are two ways of reaching Malawi on an organised tour. You can take an all-inclusive tour which includes the flight from your home country, or you can come overland all the way. The former is preferred by people with less free time, the latter is often an option for those with more time to spare. Another alternative, somewhere between the two, is to fly to a nearby country, such as Kenya, Zimbabwe or South Africa, and join an overland tour from there, either to or through Malawi.

All-Inclusive Tours

All-inclusive tours usually include your international flight, transport around the country, accommodation, food, guides, excursions and so on. Around the world there are many companies featuring Malawi in their brochures. (Several also feature Zambia, but few include Mozambique.) You

can either join other people on a scheduled departure, or have arrangements tailored to suit your own needs exactly. The second option is normally more expensive. For travellers who want a 'half-way house' between an all-inclusive tour and completely independent travel, some companies provide self-guided itineraries, including pre-booked flights, vehicle hire and accommodation where required, but let you decide on exactly where and when you want to go.

It always pays to shop around for deals. As with flights, the best place to begin looking for advertisements is in the weekend newspapers and travel magazines.

While it would be difficult to provide a comprehensive rundown of everyone selling tours in Malawi, the following list will provide some idea of the range available. Give them a call, ask for a brochure, see what appeals, and take it from there.

Tour Companies Based in Britain

Abercrombie & Kent, Sloane Square House, Holbein Place, London SW1 (☎ (0171) 730 9600). Up-market luxury safaris all over Africa, including Malawi, Zambia and Mozambique.

Adrenaline Pump, (Safari Drive Ltd), Wessex House, 127 High Street, Hungerford, RG17 0DL (☎ (01488) 681611; fax (01488) 685055). Fast heartbeat specialists, based in and around Victoria Falls, offering white-water rafting, canoeing, microlight flights, bungy jumping and hiking in wildlife areas.

Adrift, Hyde Park House, Manfred Rd, London SW15 2RS (☎ (0181) 874 4969; fax (0181) 875 9236). Rafting trips on the Zambezi River.

Africa Exclusive, Hamilton House, 66 Palmerston Rd, Northampton NN1 5EX (☎ (01604) 28979; fax (01604) 39879). Custom itineraries all over East and Southern Africa.

Art of Travel, 268 Lavender Hill, London SW11 1LJ, (☎ (0171) 738 2038; fax (0171) 738 1893). Scheduled and tailor-made tours and safaris all over East and Southern Africa.

Cycle Active, 4 Bermondsey Mews, Otley, West Yorkshire LS21 1SN, (☎ (01943) 46 2105). Mountain bike tours in Africa, including Malawi.

Discover Adventure, 5 Netherhampton Cottage, Netherhampton Rd, Netherhampton, Salisbury, Wilts (☎ (01722) 74 1123). Mountain bike tours in various parts of the world, including Malawi.

Dragoman, Camp Green, Kenton Rd, Debenham, Stowmarket, Suffolk IP14 6LA (☎ (01728) 861133; fax (01728) 861127). Smart end of the overland tour market, with short and long trips throughout Africa, including Zambia and Malawi. One of the first outfits to go into Mozambique.

Explore Worldwide Ltd, 1 Frederick St, Aldershot, Hampshire GU11 1LQ (☎ (01252) 344161; fax (01252) 315935). Good value small group tours, focusing on adventure and hands-on activities. Includes Malawi and Zambia.

Exodus, 9 Weir Rd, London SW12 0LT (☎ (0181) 673 0859; fax (0181) 673 0779). Tours and safaris, for a wide range of budgets and interests. Includes a Kenya to Zimbabwe trip taking in Malawi and Victoria Falls.

Frontiers, 18 Albermarle St, London W1X 3HA, (☎ (0171) 493 0798; fax (0171) 629 5569). Customised safaris for families on a budget throughout Southern Africa.

Guerba, 101 Eden Vale Rd, Westbury, Wiltshire BA13 3QX (☎ (01373) 858956; fax (01373) 838351). Short and long trips and safaris by truck throughout Africa.

In the Saddle, Laurel Cottage, Baughurst Rd, Ramsdell, Tadley Hampshire RG26 5SH (☎ (01256) 851665; fax (01256) 851667). Horse-riding tours around the world, including Malawi.

Okavango Tours & Safaris, Gadd House, Arcadia Ave, London N3 2TJ (☎ (0181) 343 3283; fax (0181) 343 3287). Small specialist outfit with top-class, good-value tours all over Southern Africa.

Peregrine Holidays, 40/41 South Parade, Summertown, Oxford OX2 7JP (☎ (01865) 511642; fax (01865) 512583). Up-market wildlife and botanical safaris.

Safari Consultants, Orchard House, Upper Rd, Little Cornard, Suffolk CO10 0NZ (☎ (01787) 228494; fax (01787) 228096). Specialists in tailor-made wildlife safaris in East and Southern Africa.

Safari Drive, Wessex House, 127 High St, Hungerford RG17 0DL (☎ (01488) 681611; fax (01488) 685055). Experienced and specialised, providing fully kitted-out self-drive 4WD vehicles and equipment, and a range of escorted or self-guided itineraries throughout Southern Africa, including Zambia. Non-self-drive tailor-made itineraries and wildlife safaris all over Southern Africa are also arranged.

Scott Dunn World, Fovant Mews, 12 Noyna Rd, London SW17 7PH (☎ (0181) 767 0202; fax (0181) 767 2026). Scheduled tours and exclusive tailor-made safari options all over Africa, including Malawi and Zambia.

Sunvil Discovery, Sunvil House, Upper Square, Old Isleworth TW7 7BJ (☎ (0181) 568 4499; fax (0181) 568 8330). Imaginative, flexible and good value fly-drive packages and tours in Southern Africa, plus exclusive tailor-made safaris in Zambia. Sunvil are also the only UK-based company offering mid-price tours in Zambia.

Wild Africa Safaris, Orange Square, 202 Ebury St, London, SW1W 8UN (☎ (0171) 259 9909; fax (0171) 259 9949). Upmarket tours including Zimbabwe and Botswana, plus speciality safaris, including tiger fishing, canoeing, walking, rail safaris and even (very expensive) trips by Catalina flying boat.

Wildlife Worldwide, Naturetrek, Chautara, Bighton Airesford, Hampshire SO24 9RB (☎ (01962) 733051; fax (01962) 733368). Specialising in wildlife safaris all over Africa, including Malawi and Zambia.

Worldwide Journeys & Expeditions, 8 Comeragh Rd, London W14 9HP (☎ (0171) 381 8638; fax (0171) 381 0836). Good range of active tours, treks and safaris, including Malawi, Mozambique and Zambia.

Tour Companies Based in South Africa

African Routes, 164 Northway, Durban North 4051 (☎ (031) 833348; fax (031) 837234). Friendly and very reasonably priced company with overland tours and hiking trips throughout Southern Africa.

Afro Ventures, PO Box 2339, Randburg 2125 (☎ (011) 886 1524; fax (011) 886 2349). Wide range of tours all over Southern Africa, with various transport and accommodation options to keep costs low if required.

Alternative Photographic Expeditions, 18 Waltham Rd, Ronderbosh East, Cape Town (☎ (021) 696 2342). Budget or tailor-made trips all over Southern Africa.

Drifters, PO Box 48434, Roosevelt Park, Johannesburg (☎ (011) 888 1160). No-frills, fun-packed, hands-on group travel by vehicle (also bike, horse and canoe) all over Southern Africa.

Shumba Adventures, PO Box 330, Johannesburg 2000 ☎ (011) 321 0579; fax (011) 838 7322; e-mail freeworld @ milkyway.co.za). A good-time crowd offering no-frills truck trips around Southern Africa, including full-moon beach parties in northern Mozambique.

Wayfarer Adventures, 4 Norwich Ave, Observatory, Cape Town 7925 (☎ (021) 470792; fax (021) 474675). Tours throughout Southern Africa.

Wilderness Safaris, PO Box 651171, Benmore 2010 (☎ (011) 884 1458; fax (011) 883 6255). A long-standing mid-range company with a wide range of tours all over Southern Africa, including Malawi, using lodges and permanent campsites, plus 'mobile safaris' which cover more ground, offering standard game viewing or more specialist bushwalking, bird-watching, canoeing and photography.

MALAWI

Wild Frontiers, PO Box 844, Halfway House 1685 (☎ (011) 315 4838; fax (011) 315 4850). Middle price range canoeing and walking trips.

Tour Companies Based in the USA

The following companies include East and Southern Africa:

Abercrombie & Kent, 1420 Kensington Rd, Oak Brook, IL 60521 (☎ (708) 954 2944)

Africa Adventure Company, 1620 S Federal Hwy, Pompano Beach, FL 33062 (☎ (305) 781 3933)

Born Free Safaris, 12504 Riverside Drive, North Hollywood CA 91607 (☎ (800) 206 4600; fax (805) 285 8316)

Bushtracks, PO Box 4163, Menlo Park, CA 94026 (☎ (415) 326 8689; fax (415) 321 4456)

Desert & Delta Safaris, 16179 E Whittier Blvd, Whittier, CA 90603 (☎ (213) 947 5100)

Journeys, 1536 NW 23rd Ave, Portland, OR 97210 (☎ (503) 226 7200)

Ker & Downey Inc, 13201 Northwest Freeway Suite 850, Houston, TX 77040 (☎ (713) 744 5260; fax (713) 895 8753)

Mountain Travel-Sobek, 6420 Fairmount Ave, El Cerrito, CA 94530 (☎ (800) 227 2384; fax (510) 525 7710)

Spector Travel, 31 St James Ave, Boston, MA 02116 (☎ (617) 338 0111). Budget tours all over Africa, plus discounted airfares.

Voyagers, PO Box 915, Ithaca, NY (☎ (800) 633 0299)

Wilderness Travel, 801 Alston Way, Berkeley, CA 94710 (☎ (800) 368 2794, ext 114)

Most of the agencies selling all-inclusive tours in Malawi and other parts of Southern Africa also sell overland tours and are listed under Overland Tours, following.

Overland Tours

Many people who arrive in Southern Africa by land come on an organised trip in an 'overland truck', travelling with about 15 to 28 other people, a couple of drivers/leaders, plus tents and other equipment. Food is bought along the way and the group cooks and eats together.

For people with time to spare, especially if lone travel does not appeal, these trips are ideal. Most of the hassles (such as border crossings) are taken care of by the leader. Disadvantages include a fairly fixed itinerary and the possibility of spending a long

time with other people. Having said that, overland truck tours are extremely popular.

Many overland truck companies are based in Britain, so most trans-Africa tours start in London and travel to Nairobi, then all the way down to Harare or Johannesburg, usually via Malawi or Zambia. Some go in the opposite direction. Tours can be 'slow' or 'fast', depending or the number of places visited along the way. Prices vary according to itinerary and duration.

Many people don't have the time for long-distance trips between Europe and Southern Africa, so most of the overland outfits also arrange shorter trips, for example Nairobi to Harare, via Malawi and Zambia, or Cape Town to Harare via Mozambique. Most overland companies can arrange your flight as well, and many specialist travel agencies sell flights and tours.

Overland Companies Based in the UK

Acacia, 27d Stable Way, Latimer Rd, London W10 6QX (☎ (0181) 960 5747; fax (0181) 960 1414)

Africa Explored, Rose Cottage, Summerleaze, Magor Newport NP6 3DE (☎ (01633) 880224; fax (01633) 882128)

African Trails, 126b Chiswick High Rd, London W4 1PU (☎ (0181) 742 7724; fax (0181) 742 8621)

Dragoman, Camp Green, Kenton Rd, Debenham, Stowmarket, Suffolk IP14 6LA (☎ (01728) 861133; fax (01728) 861127)

Economic Expeditions, 29 Cunnington St, London W4 5ER (☎ (0181) 995 7707; fax (0181) 742 7707)

Encounter Overland, 267 Old Brompton Rd, London SW5 9JA (☎ (0171) 370 6845; fax (0171) 244 9737)

Exodus Overland, 9 Weir Rd, London SW12 0LT (☎ (0181) 673 0859; fax (0181) 673 0779)

Guerba, 101 Eden Vale Rd, Westbury, Wiltshire BA13 3QX (☎ (01373) 858956; fax (01373) 838351)

Kumuka, 40 Earls Court Rd, London W8 6EJ (☎ (0171) 937 8855; fax (0171) 937 6664)

Phoenix, College Farm, Far St, Wymeswold, Leicestershire LE12 6TZ (☎ (01509) 881818; fax (01509) 881822)

Tracks, 12 Abingdon Rd, London W8 6AF (☎ (0171) 937 3028; fax (0171) 937 3176)

TransAfrique, 9 Rockspray Grove, Walnut Tree, Milton Keynes MK7 7AE (☎ (01908) 378028; fax (01908) 366382)

Truck Africa, 37 Ranelagh Gardens Mansions, London SW6 3UQ (☎ (0171) 731 6142; fax (0171) 371 7445)

MALAWI

You can book direct or through some of the tour and flight agencies listed in the Air section, earlier in this chapter. In North America, Australasia and other parts of the world, overland companies are represented by specialist adventure travel agencies. Some are listed below, and in the Air section. Also check advertisements in magazines and newspapers listed in the Air section.

Adventure Travel Agencies – Australia

Adventure World, 73 Walker St, North Sydney, NSW 2060 (☎ (02) 9956 7766)

Africa Travel Centre, Level 12, 456 Kent St, Sydney, NSW 2000 (☎ (02) 9267 3048)

African Wildlife Safaris, 259 Coventry St, South Melbourne, Vic 3205 (☎ (03) 9696 2899)

Peregrine Travel, 258 Lonsdale St, Melbourne, Vic 3000 (☎ (03) 9663 8611)

Adventure Travel Agencies – New Zealand

Adventure World, 101 Great South Rd, Remuera, PO Box 74008, Auckland (☎ (09) 524 5118)

Africa Travel Shop, Auckland (☎ 09 520 2000)

Destinations, 4 Durham St East, PO Box 6232, Auckland (☎ (09) 309 0464)

Adventure Travel Agencies – USA & Canada

Adventure Center, 1311 63rd St, Emeryville, CA 91608 (☎ (510) 654 1879 or (800) 2278747)

Africa Travel Centre, 23830 Route 99, Edmonds, WA 98026 (☎ (206) 672 3697; fax (206) 672 9678)

Himalayan Travel (☎ (203) 359 3711)

Market Square Tours, 54 Donald St, Winnipeg, MB, R3C 1L6 (☎ (800) 661 3830)

Safari Center (☎ (310) 546 441, (800) 223 6046)

Trek Holidays, 8412, 109 St, Edmonton, Alberta T6G 1E2 (☎ (800) 661 7265)

Getting Around

You can travel around Malawi by air, road, rail or boat. Distances between major centres are quite short, and Malawi has generally good roads and public transport systems, making independent travel here a joy.

AIR

Air Malawi has at least two flights a day between Lilongwe and Blantyre, for US$55 one-way, and three flights a week between Lilongwe and Mzuzu for US$55 one-way. You can also fly from Lilongwe or Blantyre to Club Makokola on Lake Malawi's southern shore (you don't have to be a guest at the club), from where you can reach other points on the lake. Internal flights are usually reliable, and can be paid for in kwacha.

There is only one air charter company operating in Malawi, although others may start up as the demand from the growing tourist trade increases. Sefofane Malawi (☎ 781393; fax 781397) links the major towns and tourist centres around the country. Fares vary according to the number of people in your group, so you should always contact the company for a quotation. As a guide, however, a charter flight from Lilongwe to Salima (on the lake) is US$95, and to Liwonde National Park US$145.

BUS

Most buses around Malawi are operated by a private company called Stagecoach, and come in several different types. Top of the range is Coachline, a daily luxury service that runs non-stop between Blantyre and Lilongwe (US$17) and between Lilongwe and Mzuzu (US$19) with air-con, toilet, free newspapers and food, steward service and top-quality drivers. Anyone who's been scared by the more cavalier attitude of bus drivers elsewhere in Africa cannot help but be impressed – they slow down on corners, hoot before overtaking trucks, *and* use their rear-view mirrors.

Next comes Express, fast comfortable buses between the main towns with limited stops and no standing passengers allowed, and InterCity, similar to Express buses but with more stops. As a rule of thumb, Express buses charge between US$2 and US$2.50 per 100 km, and InterCity buses slightly less. Some sample routes, prices and times (note that these are approximate and depend very much on the road quality, which changes from year to year):

Route	Fare	Duration
Blantyre to Lilongwe	US$7	5 hours
Blantyre to Mulanje	US$2	2 hours
Lilongwe to MonkeyBay	US$4	5 hours
Lilongwe to Mzuzu	US$4	7 hours
Karonga to Mzuz	US$3	4 hours
Mzuzu to Nkhata Bay	US$1	1 hour
Mzuzu to Chitimba (Livingstonia turn-off)	US$3	3 hours
Zomba to Monkey Bay	US$4	3 hours

Stagecoach also run local services which cover the quieter rural routes and tend to be slow and crowded, but are often the only public transport available.

As well as the above, there are a few smaller outfits which compete with Stagecoach; these include Yanu Yanu and Nyika Express. There are also local minibus services around towns and to outlying villages, or along the roads which the big buses can't manage. Prices are about the same as Stagecoach, or slightly more, depending on the severity of the route.

Reservations

For Coachline and Express buses you can buy tickets in advance and have a reserved seat. The day before is usually sufficient for Express buses, but on the Coachline bus a week's notice is sometimes required, particularly for Friday and Sunday services.

Bus Stations

All towns have a main bus station where long-distance and local buses arrive and leave. In Blantyre the luxury Coachline service goes to/from the Mt Soche Hotel; in Lilongwe, it goes to/from the Capital Hotel and the Stagecoach depot near PTC Hypermarket on Kamuzu Procession Rd.

TRAIN

The main railway line is centred on Blantyre, from where passenger trains go daily Monday through Friday to/from Balaka (north-west of Zomba). The fare is US$2. There's also a twice-weekly service between Limbe and Nsanje (in the far south of Malawi) for which the fare is US$3. Trains are very slow and crowded, and only slightly cheaper than the bus, so they are rarely used by visitors. The line to Lilongwe, via Salima (just west of the lake) no longer carries passenger trains.

There is also a service between Balaka and Nayuchi (on the border with Mozambique), via Liwonde (at the south end of the lake). This connects vaguely with services in Mozambique. For details see the Getting There & Away chapter.

CAR & MOTORCYCLE

The main route through Malawi runs from the north of the country down to Mzuzu, then through the centre of the country to Lilongwe, and onto Blantyre in the south. Like other main routes, it's mostly good-quality tar, but in recent years several stretches of road have not received maintenance and are now very badly potholed. In some areas these have made driving slow, difficult and dangerous. For example, in 1996 the main road north of Karonga was so bad that no Express buses would run along it. Even Tanzanian truck drivers refused to use it – it was *that* bad.

Main roads are numbered. Major routes include: the M1 from Karonga in the north, via Mzuzu, Lilongwe and Blantyre, to Mulanje in the south; and the M5 lake shore road.

Secondary roads are usually graded dirt and, like the main tar roads, vary in condition. Some are well-maintained and easy to drive on in a normal car, others are very bad, especially after the rains, and slow even with 4WD. Rural routes are not so good, and after heavy rain they are often impassable, sometimes for weeks.

Car Hire

Most car hire companies are based in Blantyre and Lilongwe, although there are a few elsewhere. Those with offices in more than one city can arrange pick-up-drop-off deals. International agencies include Avis, while there are several independent outfits with cheaper rates. Whoever you hire from, be prepared for a car not up to European, American or South African standards. Check the tyres and as much else as you can; if anything is worn or broken, demand repairs or a discount.

Self-drive rates for a small car start at US$25 to US$35 per day, plus around US$0.30 per km. Unlimited mileage (minimum seven days) costs US$50 to US$55 per day. Larger cars are around US$45 to US$65 per day, plus around US$0.50 per km. To this add 20% government tax, plus another US$5 to US$7 per day for insurance.

Car rental companies in Malawi include the following. Contact them direct or go through an agent (see the Travel Agencies & Tours sections in the Lilongwe and Blantyre chapters).

Avis, PO Box 51059, Limbe (central reservations ☎ 672429); Lilongwe (☎ 723113, 723812); Blantyre (☎ 623792). Avis also has offices at Lilongwe and Blantyre airports, plus desks at some large hotels.
SS Rent-a-Car, PO Box 997, Kamuzu Procession Rd, Lilongwe (☎ 721179); PO Box 2282, Glyn Jones Rd, Blantyre (☎ 636836)
U-Drive Car Rentals (central reservations ☎ 645966; fax 645869)

Fuel

The cost of fuel is fixed throughout the country: US$0.65 for petrol, slightly less for diesel. Most towns have a petrol station. Supplies are usually reliable and distances between petrol stations are not long in Malawi, you rarely need to worry about running dry. However, the quality of fuel is not excellent: you may notice your fuel consumption increase, and a tendency for the engine to stall more easily than normal.

In Your Own Vehicle

Explaining how to bring your own vehicle through Africa to Malawi is beyond the scope of this book. Some manuals for trans-African overlanders are listed under Books in the Facts for the Visitor chapter.

To visit Malawi, Mozambique, Zimbabwe and Zambia you can easily get temporary import permits at the border, as long as you have the proper paperwork – international vehicle registration documents detailing the vehicle's particulars, an international driving permit, plus proof of liability insurance and current registration. Further south, the good news for drivers is that thanks to the Southern African Customs Union, you don't need a carnet de passage to travel through Botswana, Lesotho, Namibia, South Africa and Swaziland.

Of course, to travel across Africa by car or motorbike you should be mechanically competent and carry a good collection of spares. Once again, this kind of thing is covered in the overland manuals.

BICYCLE

Cycling is a cheap, convenient, healthy, environmentally sound and above all a fun way to travel. We heard from a traveller who had started out from Cairo the 'normal' way, but got so fed up with trucks and buses by the time he got to Nairobi that he bought a bike and carried on through Tanzania and Malawi on that. This was a slower way of travelling, and his planned eight-month trip turned into a year, but he was having such a good time on the bike that he wrote off his return ticket and carried on pedalling around Africa for several more months.

Getting to Malawi overland by bike is beyond the scope of this book, but flying from home *with* your bike is perfectly possible. You can dismantle the bike, and put the pieces in a large bag or box, but it's much easier simply to wheel your bike to the check-in desk, where it should be treated as a piece of baggage (some airlines don't even include it in the weight). Also this way the baggage handlers see a bike and are unlikely to pile suitcases on top of it. Some travellers say that if your bike doesn't stand up to airline baggage handlers it won't last long in

---

Driving in Malawi

Whether you drive a hire car or your own vehicle in Malawi (or beyond), you should be prepared for local attitudes towards motor vehicles, which may differ from what you're used to at home.

Generally speaking, driving standards are bad and drivers are unpredictable. Be ready for cars overtaking on blind corners and hills. In all the countries covered by this book, traffic officially drives on the left – although you wouldn't always know it.

Road standards vary considerably, from smooth highways to dirt tracks. The hardest roads to drive on are tar roads which have not been repaired for many years and are full of bone-crunching potholes. In many countries roads tend to break up after a few years, but get completely repaired once every 10 to 20 years – usually paid for by foreign aid money. Unfortunately, there never seems to be any money provided for maintenance. Decades of aid to Africa and still the donors haven't learnt.

Other things to be prepared for include children playing on busy highways and cyclists on the wrong side of the road. You should also be vigilant about livestock. Goats run fast, but often go the wrong way *into* your path; cows have a better sense of direction, but are slower, and make a hell of a dent in your paintwork. If you see kids with flags or sticks, it may mean they're leading a herd. Slow down, even if you can't see any cows. (Especially if you can't see any cows.) If you see tree branches in the road, these are the local version of warning triangles; there's probably a broken-down vehicle on the road ahead.

All of these things become much harder to deal with in the dark, and it's simply not advisable to drive at night. You can't see children, cyclists and livestock, and the chances of an accident are high. There's also other vehicles to worry about; many have faulty lights – or none at all.

There are a few other quirks. For example, if you're stuck behind a slow-moving truck or car, some local drivers use their right-side indicator to say it's OK for you to overtake. Other drivers use it to say the exact opposite – something is coming the other way. The moral of the tale is never overtake unless you can see the road ahead is completely clear. ■

Africa anyway, but that's a matter of opinion. If you do go for the non-dismantle approach, you'll probably still have to remove the pedals and turn the handlebars sideways so that it takes up less space in the aircraft's hold. Check all this with the airline well in advance, preferably before you pay for your ticket.

Once in Malawi, the country is very good for cycling. Distances between towns and places of interest are relatively short, and roads are mostly in good condition (even when they're badly potholed it's less of a problem for bikes than cars, as two wheels can weave between the bumps more easily). On main roads, cyclists have to contend with cars, trucks and buses that seem to take delight in getting as close as possible when overtaking. Keep your wits about you when the traffic is heavy, and be prepared to take evasive action onto the verge as local cyclists frequently have to do. A rear-view mirror is useful in these situations, and cruising with a Walkman on is asking for trouble. Malawi's network of rural roads is ideal for cycling, although mountain bikes will cope more easily with the dirt surfaces. Places where mountain bike touring is particularly good include: the area between Blantyre and Mt Mulanje (where you can do a marvellous circuit of the mountain, including a pass called the Fort Lister Gap); the road along the base of the Thyolo Escarpment southeast of Chikwawa; the 'old' road between Mulanje and Zomba; the road from Lilongwe to Lake Malawi, via Ntchisi and Nkhotakota Game Reserve; the old road along the lake shore between Nkhata Bay and Chitimba; the route from Mzimba to Rumphi, via Kazuni in Vwaza Marsh Game Reserve; and Nyika National Park.

As with cars and motorbikes, you won't necessarily be able to buy that crucial gizmo for your bike when it breaks down somewhere in the back of beyond, so carry sufficient spares, and have a good idea of how to fit them.

HITCHING

On the main routes in Malawi, especially between Mzuzu, Lilongwe, Zomba, Blantyre and the southern lake shore, hitching free lifts, in the western fashion, is fairly easy. At weekends well-off residents and expatriates living in Blantyre and Lilongwe make a beeline for Salima, Cape Maclear and the southern lake shore, so it's easy to get a lift there on Friday (and on Sunday in the opposite direction). Note however, that just because we say hitching is possible it doesn't necessarily mean we recommend it.

Once you get off the main routes, hitching in the western sense becomes very hard, simply because there are very few vehicles to give free lifts. The only vehicles you're likely to see are trucks or pick-ups, carrying goods and acting as an unofficial transport service (called *matola)* for local people in rural areas. Normally if you get a lift here, payment is expected (which is fair enough, as the locals have to pay). The fare is about the same as a bus (that is, around US$2 per 100 km). The distinction between hitching and public transport is blurred here, and while it cannot be proclaimed safe, problems are extremely unlikely. Anyway, in most cases it's your only choice.

All over the country you will see Malawi government cars (with MG number plates). These are of course always on important official business, although sometimes the drivers do stop to assist stranded travellers. Check whether a payment is expected in this case.

BOAT

A 'steamer' (passenger boat) called the MV *Ilala II* plies up and down Lake Malawi, once per week in each direction, between Monkey Bay in the south and Chilumba in the north, stopping at about a dozen lakeside towns and villages on the way. (It also sometimes continues north to Kambwe near Karonga, and Itungi in Tanzania.) Local people use the boat as a cheap method of public transport, but many visitors take a cruise just for the experience. The whole trip, from one end of the line to the other, takes about three days. A round trip takes a week.

Note however, that this boat is notoriously

prone to delays. It can sometimes be a day late, especially towards the end of the schedule. The official, and infinitely flexible, schedule is as follows (only main ports shown):

Northbound

Port	Arrival	Departure
Monkey Bay	–	10 am or 2 pm (Fri)
Chipoka	5 pm or 8 pm	10 pm
Nkhotakota	5 am (Sat)	6 am
Likoma Island	11 am	2 pm
Nkhata Bay	7 pm	5 am (Sun)
Chilumba	5.30 pm	–

Southbound

Chilumba	–	3 am (Mon)
Nkhata Bay	4.30 pm	2.30 am (Tues)
Likoma Island	8.30 am	11.30 am
Nkhotakota	4.30 pm	5.30 pm
Chipoka	1 am (Wed)	3 am
Monkey Bay	3 pm (Wed)	–

The *Ilala* has three classes: Cabin, First Class Deck and Economy. The cabins, which were once luxurious, are still in reasonable condition. The First Class Deck is generally quite spacious, with seats, a small area of sunshade and a bar. Economy is the lower deck – dark and crowded, with engine fumes permeating from below.

Ilala Sample Routes & Fares (US$)

Route	Cabin	First Class Deck	Economy
Monkey Bay to Chilumba	93.00	73.00	14.00
Monkey Bay to Nkhata Bay	66.00	50.00	10.00
Nkhata Bay to Nkhotakota	30.00	23.00	4.50
Nkhata Bay to Likoma	18.00	11.00	2.00
Nkhata Bay to Mbamba Bay	16.00	10.00	2.00

Reservations are usually required for the cabins. You can reserve at any of the major ports, or at the ship's official agent Soche Tours & Travel which has offices in Blantyre and Lilongwe (see those chapters for details). They would also be able to help you with the latest timetable information. For First and Deck class, tickets for the boat are only sold when it's sighted, so queueing tends to start about a day before the boat is due to arrive. On the other hand, there's no question of anyone being refused – it just keeps filling up!

If you travel economy, you'll probably be allowed on to the First Class Deck to buy a beer, which you can then make last several hours. Food is available on *Ilala*, served from the galley on the economy deck: meals of beans, rice and vegetables are less than US$1.

When the boat stops at lakeside towns or villages, the water is too shallow for it to come close. The *Ilala's* lifeboat, and small village boats, are used to ferry passengers ashore, while local people come out in canoes and sell fruit, dried fish and other food.

There are occasionally nasty storms out on the lake, so be ready for some pitching and rolling.

Another boat called the MV *Mtendere* was out of service in 1996. There are rumours of a refit, so it may be relaunched, probably running to a similar schedule that fits in between the *Ilala* (that is, so there's a boat twice per week in each direction). An older boat called the *Chauncy Maples* sometimes runs on the lake, although it also was out of service in 1996. A voyage would be historically fascinating but possibly slow and uncomfortable.

For more details on boats to/from Mozambique see the Getting There & Away chapter.

MALAWI

Steamer Names

Many visitors to Malawi wonder how the lake steamers got their names. Here's how: the *Ilala II* is named after a boat used by Scottish missionaries who founded a mission at Cape Maclear in the late 19th century. In turn this was named after the local tribe of Chitambo, the place where the explorer David Livingstone died in 1873.

The *Chauncy Maples* is named after one of the first bishops of Central Africa, who helped found the mission on Likoma Island, and was drowned in Lake Malawi in 1895. *Mtendere* means 'freedom' in Chichewa, and was given this name after Malawi's independence in 1964. ■

LOCAL TRANSPORT
Bus & Minibus

The cities and large towns, such as Lilongwe, Mzuzu, Zomba, Blantyre and Limbe, have local transport systems. Homesick Brits will love the veteran double-decker London Generals which cruise the main highway between Blantyre and Limbe. Other towns have more conventional minibuses for local trips. Full details of local routes are given in each city/town section.

Taxi

Taxis operate in the main towns only. You can find them outside bus stations, airports or large hotels. There are no meters, so rates are negotiable, particularly on airport runs. Check the price at the start of the journey. More details given in individual city/town sections.

ORGANISED TOURS

Tour companies based outside Malawi are listed in the Getting There & Away chapter. Inside Malawi, there are several companies organising tours around the country, ranging from a few days in just one or two national parks, to two or three weeks around the whole country, with optional extensions into Zambia as well. Tours may be 'mobile' (that is, moving from lodge to lodge, or camp to camp, every few days), while others are based in just one place, with excursions each day. Most are vehicle-based although some outfits also organise walking trips, or specialise in horseback safaris, or boating on the lake. Tour companies that have been recommended include:

Central African Wilderness Safaris, PO Box 489, Lilongwe (☎ 781393/781153; fax 781397, e-mail wildsaf@eo.wn.apc.org)

Heart of Africa Safaris (& Nyika Horse Safaris), PO Box 8, Lilongwe (☎/fax 740848)

Land and Lake Safaris, PO Box 2140, Lilongwe (☎/fax 744408)

Malawi's safari scene is much smaller than, say, South Africa's or Kenya's, and most tours are aimed at the middle and top end of the market. Central African Wilderness Safaris operate regular departures (one or two per month, starting at US$100 per day); the others operate on demand. All do 'tailor-made' trips, and prefer to take bookings in advance (most of their clients come from agents and operators overseas). However, if you're in Malawi and fancy joining a trip, it's always worth giving them a ring to see what they've got going. Alternatively, there are a couple of tour agencies in Lilongwe and Blantyre (see those chapters for details) who can assist you with this.

Lilongwe

History

The capital of Malawi is a pleasantly landscaped but sprawling city of limited interest to visitors. The city was initially established around the turn of the century as a British colonial administrative centre, after a local chief requested protection from warlike neighbours. It grew quickly into a small settler town. Its central position, on the junction of the country's main north-south route and the road to Northern Rhodesia (later Zambia), meant that by the 1960s it was the second-largest urban area in Malawi. In 1968 plans were announced to move the country's administrative centre from Blantyre to Lilongwe, which was more central. The construction of ministerial buildings was largely funded by South Africa (for more details see History in the Facts about Malawi chapter), and Lilongwe was officially declared the new capital in 1975.

Orientation

Lilongwe has two centres: the New City – usually called City Centre – which has ministries, embassies, some smart hotels, a shopping centre, airline offices and some travel agents; and the Old Town, with a good range of places to stay (including cheapies and camping), the bus station, the market, several restaurants and cafés. More importantly, Old Town has soul, whereas City Centre is a surprisingly quiet and rather sterile place. The two centres are at least three km apart, and minibuses run between them.

The heart of Old Town is the market on Malangalanga Rd. On one side of the market is the main bus station. On the other side is a narrow road lined with bars and cheap hotels. This road seems to have no official name but is called 'Devil St' by most locals. Malangalanga Rd meets Glyn Jones Rd, which is the main road to/from Blantyre, running down to the bridge over the Lilongwe River. This street is lined with cheaper shops selling cloths, material, hardware and so on. This part of Old Town used to be called the Asian Quarter; now the streets south of Glyn Jones Rd are called Area 1, and those to the north are Area 2. At the bottom of hill is a roundabout. Beyond here is Area 3. Go straight on to reach the Golf Club on the left. If you go right at the roundabout, you're on Kamuzu Procession Rd. This is the smart part of Old Town, with more expensive shops, restaurants and supermarkets, a shopping mall called the Nico Centre, the Lilongwe Hotel, banks, travel agents, and so on.

The heart of City Centre (if this place can be said to have a heart) is Capital City Shopping Centre, a collection of office buildings and mini-malls around a circular car park reached from Independence Drive. Here you will find several shops and travel agents, gift shops, some cafés and restaurants, a bank and post office and the US Information Service. Nearby is another large PTC Hypermarket, the British Council and most of the embassies. Further out are several ministries, more offices, a couple of smart hotels and the posh suburbs.

Information

Tourist Offices The tourist office is on Kamuzu Procession Rd, a couple of buildings south of the Lilongwe Hotel. The people are friendly, but information they're able to provide is limited. For information on tours, flights and hotels you're better off at a travel agency; several are listed under Travel & Tour Agencies, following.

For long-distance public transport information, the Stagecoach depot (☎ 740111, 731854) is next to the Nico Centre, only 50 m or so from the PTC Hypermarket on the corner of Kamuzu Procession and Kenyatta roads, and has details on Coachline and other services.

For information on national parks and reserves, try the National Parks & Wildlife

MALAWI

PLACES TO STAY
2 Annie's Lodge
12 Capital Hotel
21 Capital City Motel
23 Lingadzi Inn
30 Lilongwe Hotel
40 The Gap
42 Golden Peacock Hotel &
   Korea Garden Restaurant
43 St Peter's Guesthouse
44 Lilongwe Golf Club
   (Camping)
46 Council Resthouse

PLACES TO EAT
15 Golden Dragon
   Restaurant

27 Modi's
31 Huts
38 Annie's Coffee House
39 Gazebo Restaurant

OTHER
1 Hollywood Nightclub
3 Petrol Station
4 Adventist Health Centre
5 UK High Commission
6 Zambia High Commission
7 France Embassy
8 German Embassy
9 US Embassy
10 City Centre Post Office
11 Capital City
   Shopping Centre

13 Minibuses to Old Town
14 Zimbabwe High Commission
16 British Council Library
17 PTC Hypermarket
18 ADL House
   (Travel Agents, Clinic)
19 Commercial Bank &
   Mozambique High Commission
20 Reserve Bank Building
22 Entrance to Lilongwe
   Nature Sanctuary
24 Department of Forestry
25 Lilongwe Central
   Hospital
26 Immigration Office &
   National Parks &
   Wildlife Office

28 Commercial Bank
   of Malawi
29 Minibuses to
   City Centre
32 National Bank
   of Malawi
33 Nico Shopping Centre
34 Stagecoach Bus Depot
35 Old Town Post Office
36 Police
37 Town Hall (Cinema)
41 Petrol Station
45 Map Sales Office
47 Market
48 Local Bus Park
49 Long-Distance
   Bus Station

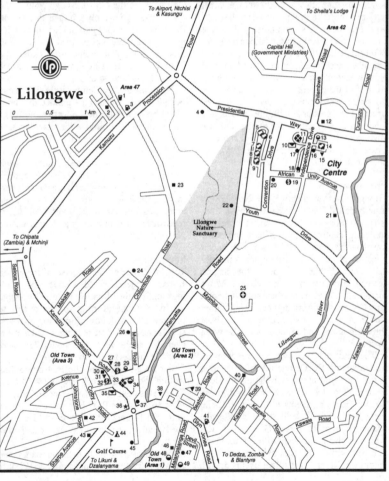

office (☎ 723566, 723676; PO Box 30131), although they mostly just handle reservations for government camps and lodges. Although this can be done by post or phone, it's better to call in person if possible; the office is on Murray Rd, in Old Town. (See also National Parks in the Facts about Malawi chapter, outlining likely future changes.)

For information on forest reserves and resthouses, the Department of Forestry office (☎ 781000) is off Chilambula Rd, between Old Town and City Centre.

Foreign Embassies For details on embassies, consulates and high commissions, see Embassies in the Facts for the Visitor chapter.

Immigration Office For visa extensions, the Immigration office (☎ 722995) is on Murray Rd, in Old Town, next to the National Parks & Wildlife office.

Money For changing money in Lilongwe there are branches of the National and Commercial banks on Kamuzu Procession Rd. In the same area are a couple of exchange bureaux where the rates are about 5% better, and there's no commission or charges for cash. If you've got time, it takes about 10 minutes to shop around the banks and bureaux, and might be worth doing as rates and commissions can vary considerably. Beware of moneychangers at the gate of the Golf Club and some other places – see Dangers & Annoyances in the Facts for the Visitor chapter.

Post & Communications Lilongwe has two main post offices. The GPO in Old Town is on Kamuzu Procession Rd, open weekdays from 8 am to 5 pm. The other is at Capital City Shopping Centre, which is open the same hours. For details of postal rates etc, see Post & Communications in the Facts for the Visitor chapter. Receiving poste restante mail addressed to GPO Lilongwe is a bit of a lottery: most poste restante mail goes to Old Town, but some mail mysteriously lands

at City Centre, so the only way to avoid this is to have your letters addressed specifically Old Town or City Centre. If you're using Amex clients' mail, the office is at Manica Travel, ADL House, City Centre.

For telephone calls and faxes, the public office is in Capital City Shopping Centre, in the depths of Centre House Arcade, opposite the entrance to Kandodo supermarket. You can also make international calls from any of the large hotels. For rates, see the Facts for the Visitor chapter.

Travel & Tour Agencies In Old Town, along Kamuzu Procession Rd, there are a few travel agencies dealing mainly in outbound flights. These include: Midland Travel (☎ 741876, 744444) and Rainbow Travel (☎ 740963, 740306). In Capital City Shopping Centre, there are several more, including Air Tour and Travel (☎ 781053, 781362) and Soche Tours & Travel (☎ 782377, 781409). Nearby, in ADL House, is Manica Travel, the Amex representative (☎ 760024). Good agents have information on the routes and fares of several airlines, and mean you don't have to visit all the individual airline offices to compare deals.

Also in ADL House is the Central African Wilderness Safaris Travel Shop (☎ 723527; fax 781397; e-mail wildsaf@eo.wn. apc.org), PO Box 489. This is an advisory service and booking agency, and can help you with hotels, internal flight reservations, air charter, accommodation bookings for the national parks in Malawi and Zambia, short or long safaris, car hire, and so on.

Bookshops In Old Town there's a TBS bookshop in the Nico Centre and a smaller one at the Lilongwe Hotel. Both have international and local newspapers and magazines, as well as a reasonable range of books, including paperback novels, plus a surprisingly good stock of African literature, local guidebooks and other books on Malawian subjects. In the Capital City Shopping Centre, the Central Bookshop has a similar selection.

MALAWI

Map Office The Department of Surveys public map office is about 500m south of the roundabout where Glyn Jones Rd meets Kamuzu Procession Rd. For more details on what's available see Maps in the Facts for the Visitor chapter.

Libraries & Cultural Centres The main National Library is just off Independence Drive in City Centre, open Monday to Friday, from 8 am to 5 pm (Saturday to 3 pm). Nearby is the British Council library. The US Information Service library (which has air-con) is in the Old Mutual Building in the Capital City Shopping Centre. Both places open Monday to Friday, 9 am to 5 pm and Saturday morning to noon. They allow nonmembers to read books and magazines in the library but not to take away. The USIS shows the previous day's CBS evening news at lunchtimes. Both places also show films on some afternoons and evenings. Check their notice boards for details.

Medical Services. For private medical consultations or blood tests, City Centre Clinic (☎ 782154) in the Capital City Shopping Centre has been recommended. Ask for doctors Mwale, Ndovi or Kazembe. A consultation is US$7; all medication and treatment, if required, is extra.

There are a few dental surgeries in town: Family Dental Clinic (☎ 780853) in ADL House, or Acropolis Dental Studio (☎ 783634), both in City Centre. The Adventist Health Centre (☎ 731819), also in City Centre, has also been recommended for eye care and dental problems. (If you have an embassy in Lilongwe, and the time to contact it first, staff there will be able to advise on recommended doctors and dentists.)

If things are serious, you should use that travel insurance you never thought you'd need, and go home. But if this is not possible, the main government hospital in Lilongwe is the Lilongwe (formerly Kamuzu) Central Hospital (☎ 721555) on Nationalist Rd. Conditions and facilities here, however, are not good. If you do have to stay overnight, you can ask for an 'Expat Bed' (essentially a private ward) which costs about US$40 per night. If you have malaria, Lilongwe Central Hospital *is* a good place, as the people here really know about this illness, and charge a nominal fee for testing. If your test proves positive, it probably won't have the drugs to treat it, but you can get some treatments at one of the pharmacies in town.

Other hospitals/clinics in Lilongwe include Likuni Hospital (☎ 721400, 721282, 721073), a private charitable institution with public wards, private rooms, and some expatriate European doctors on the staff. There are still some shortages, but locals say if you have to be in hospital here, this is the best place to be. Likuni Hospital, in the suburb of Likuni, is seven km south-west of Lilongwe Old Town. You can get there by taxi (US$15) or by one of the regular minibuses that run up and down Glyn Jones Rd.

For medicines and other things like shampoo, tampons and condoms, there are MPL pharmacies at the Nico Centre in Old Town and at Capital City Shopping Centre.

Emergency The emergency phone number for the police and ambulance service is ☎ 199 (in Lilongwe and Blantyre only), but there are never enough vehicles or petrol; if you do need assistance in the case of, say, a robbery, you'll probably have to go to the police station by car or taxi and bring an officer back to the scene of the crime. Once you've contacted the police, put aside several hours while a statement is laboriously taken. If you have a serious injury (for example, from a car crash) don't waste time phoning an ambulance – get a taxi straight to hospital.

Shopping Centres & Supermarkets In City Centre, the main place is Capital City Shopping Centre off Presidential Way, reached from Independence Drive. Here you will find several shops and travel agents, gift shops, some cafés and restaurants, a bank and post office. Nearby is a large PTC Hypermarket, which has an in-store bakery and sells food and other goods, much of it imported from South Africa or Europe and sold at similar prices. You can buy CDs (US$28 to US$45) and video tapes for VCRs (US$8) here.

In Old Town, along Kamuzu Procession Rd in Area 3, there's another PTC Hypermarket (with the same type of stock and a bakery) at the Nico Centre, which also has a bookshop, pharmacy and several other shops. On the other side of the road is a Kandodo supermarket where the stock is similar but more limited.

Film & Video Central African Studio in Capital City Shopping Centre has a good stock of print film, and can do passport photos on the spot. Developing and printing is also available. In Old Town, Lee Photographic in the Nico Centre is similar. See Photography & Video in the Facts for the Visitor chapter for an idea of prices.

Gas Travellers with vehicles and large camping gas cylinders, can get refills at the IGL (Industrial Gases Ltd) depot in the northern industrial area, about five km north of the city centre, east of the main road towards Kasungu and the airport, near Central Hatcheries (signposted).

Things to See & Do

For curios and crafts the main place is the car park outside the post office in Old Town, on Kamuzu Procession Rd. But to see what the people of Malawi buy, go to the city's main **market** on Malangalanga Rd, near the bus station in Old Town, worth a visit even if you don't want to buy anything. In the last few years this place has become considerably more crowded, mainly because at the last election the UDF promised vendors and stallholders freedom to trade (after they'd been hassled for years by members of the MCP's Young Pioneers for not carrying party cards or not making political donations) and now any attempt to limit or control the number of traders is seen as a break of promise. However, there's still room to walk between the stalls (just) and it's always lively and colourful (although cameras are not appreciated here, especially in the metal-

working section which has a bit of a rough edge). But apart from dustbins and saucepans made from oil drums, you can tour the other parts of the market, where everything is sold from car and bike parts, empty plastic containers, wood and charcoal to sugar, fruit, vegetables, toothpaste, batteries, dried fish and live chickens.

A visit to the **Nature Sanctuary** is more soothing and highly recommended. It's off Kenyatta Rd, between Old Town and City Centre, open every day from 7.30 am to 5 pm, and covers over 150 hectares of indigenous woodland that escaped development when the capital city was moved here in 1972. There's a wildlife information centre and a series of walking trails through the trees that you can follow. The Lingadzi River flows through the reserve, and contains crocodiles. Birds are surprisingly varied for such a small area, and many bird-watchers rate this sanctuary highly. Mammals include duiker, vervet monkey, porcupine and bushpig. You'll also see hyena, leopard and even tiger – unfortunately in cages. After your stroll, you can relax at *Annie's au Naturelle*, a nice open-air café near the entrance.

Train buffs may want to chug out to the **train station** (built in 1979, closed in 1992, wrecked by 1993), where two Glasgow-made steam locomotives stand forgotten in a patch of rapidly growing grass and trees. To get here by car or taxi, take the main road north, the continuation of Kamuzu Procession Rd towards the airport and Kasungu until it crosses the railway line (about five km from the Presidential Way roundabout). Turn at the next street on the left, towards Area 25, and continue for three km. Then turn left again and travel for 500m to reach the station. Minibuses run from the market to Area 25, passing within one km of the station.

The public gallery overlooking the **tobacco auction floors** at the vast Auction Holdings Ltd warehouse may interest you (see the boxed text below). This is about seven km north of the city centre, in the Kenango industrial area east of the main road

MALAWI

Tobacco

Tobacco is Malawi's most important cash crop, accounting for more than 60% of the country's export earnings, and Lilongwe is the selling, buying and processing centre of this vital industry. Most activity takes place in the Kenango industrial area on the north side of Lilongwe, which seems to be made up largely of tobacco processing factories, and is also the site of the huge and impressive tobacco auction rooms (called auction 'floors').

Tobacco was first grown in Malawi by a settler called John Buchanan, who planted the crop on his farm near Blantyre in the 1880s. Large-scale tobacco farming started in the Central Province, in the area around Lilongwe, in the 1920s and has grown steadily in importance ever since. Two types of tobacco are produced in Malawi: 'flue' which is a standard quality leaf; and 'burley' which is a higher quality leaf and much in demand from cigarette manufacturers around the world. Malawi is the world's largest producer of burley.

Tobacco is grown on large plantations, or by individual farmers on small farms. The leaves are harvested and dried, either naturally in the sun or in a heated drying room, and then brought to Lilongwe for sale. (In southern Malawi the crops go to auction in Limbe.) On the auction floors, auctioneers sell tobacco on behalf of the growers. It is bought by agents and dealers who resell on to the tobacco processors. The tobacco comes into the auction rooms in large bales weighing between 80 kg and 100 kg. The leaves have been dried but the remaining moisture content they retain determines their value - if it's too dry, the flavour is impaired; if it's too wet, mould will set in and the bale is worthless.

The bales are displayed in long lines across the auction floor, which is the size of several large aircraft hangars. Buyers will have inspected the tobacco leaves in advance, employing a skilled eye, nose and 'feel', then move down the line in a small group with an auctioneer, pausing briefly at each bale to put in their bids, which are recorded by the auctioneer in a rapid-fire language which is completely unintelligible to outsiders. It takes an average of just six seconds to sell a bale, and often the auctioneer and buyers hardly miss a step as they move swiftly down the line.

As soon as the buyers reach the end of the line, they move straight onto the next (there may be as many as 100 lines, each containing 100 bales) and the sale continues. Barrow boys whisk the sold tobacco off the floor, and within an hour a new line of bales is in place ready for the next group of auctioneers and buyers. The sold tobacco is taken to one of the nearby processing plants; some goes by truck, but a few processors are so close to the auction floors it simply goes on a conveyor belt.

A small proportion of tobacco gets made into cigarettes for the local market, but more than 90% gets processed in Malawi (the leaves are stripped of their 'core' and shredded into small pieces) before being exported to be made into cigarettes abroad. Most processed tobacco goes by road to Johannesburg in South Africa, and then onto Durban to be shipped to various countries around the world, but an increasingly large amount goes by rail to the port of Nacala in Mozambique, and is shipped out from there.

The price for tobacco in 1996 was between US$1.50 and US$2 per kg. Every day during the six-month harvesting and selling season, the auctions shift somewhere between 13,000 and 15,000 bales of tobacco. This raises a daily turnover of around US$2 million, and explains the rather sardonic sign on the wall of the main auction hall. It says 'Thank you for smoking'. ∎

towards Kasungu. It cannot easily be visited independently unless you have a car. Alternatively, Land & Lake (see under Tours, below) arranges visits, or you can go by taxi.

If you're the sporting type, Lilongwe Golf Club offers daily membership for US$7. This allows you to enter the club, and use the bar or restaurant (see Places to Eat). To use the **sports facilities** there's a small extra charge: swimming pool, squash or tennis – about US$1; 18 holes of golf US$3.50; hire of golf clubs US$3.50.

Tours

Land & Lake (☎ /fax 744408) offers short

trips around the city, and excursions to surrounding mountains and forest reserves such as Dedza or Dzalanyama. They also do longer tours and safaris around the country.

Places to Stay – bottom end

If you're on public transport and short of cash, there are several cheap options around the bus station. Nearest is the *Council Resthouse*, where basic rooms in the old wing are US$4, and better ones in the new wing are US$6 (US$8 ensuite). Three or four people can share a double for no extra charge. There's also a bar and restaurant. Slightly nearer town on Devil St, next to the market, is the dark *Bwaila Lodge*. Basic singles here cost US$4 and ensuite doubles cost US$7. At the top of Devil St is the newer and cleaner *Msungama Resthouse*, charging US$7 for a double with shared bathrooms. Nearby is the *Mulanje Resthouse* with doubles for US$6, or US$7 with breakfast. At the bottom of the street is the *Ambassador Resthouse* with clean ensuite doubles for US$17 – a bit pricey for the area, which, although not as diabolical as its name would suggest, is far from desirable, and not at all for the faint-hearted.

If you've got this kind of money, you're much better off at the *Golden Peacock Hotel* (☎ 742638), still known affectionately as the Golden Cockroach, although these days it is very clean and safe, with ensuite doubles for US$17, and standard doubles/triples for US$10/12. It's on the corner of Johnstone Rd and Lister Ave, in Area 3. Next door is the Korea Garden Restaurant which is well signposted.

In the same part of town is *St Peter's Guesthouse*: quiet, clean and safe at US$4 a bed in doubles or triples and US$7 for a private double, with breakfast for an additional US$1. Unfortunately this place is nearly always full. If you do get in here, remember it's a church place and behave accordingly. Another good cheap place is *Annie's Coffee House* (see Places to Eat) which has a small dorm upstairs for US$3 per person. If you want to skip Devil St, this is the nearest place to the bus station, and a safe place to sit down with a drink to get your bearings.

The Gap, a South African-run backpackers lodge, in the suburbs of Old Town is popular with budget travellers. Beds in the dorm are US$3, camping US$1.50, breakfast US$1, snacks US$1 to US$2 and meals are around US$3. There's fairly safe parking for vehicles. To get here from the bus station go to Glyn Jones Rd and turn right, up the hill, then first left, and through the back streets, past the Muslim Sports Club.

For campers, *Lilongwe Golf Club* in Area 3 has been popular for a long time, although its prices have shot up in the last few years.

However, for US$7 per person you get a clean site with guards, hot showers and picnic tables. Unfortunately there have been a few incidents of theft; tents near the perimeter have been slashed at night. It's probably safer to put your tent near the hut used by the guards. Included in the fee is day membership of the club, so you can use the bar, restaurant, swimming pool and some of the sporting facilities. Lilongwe's other campground is 25 km out of town at *Safari Camp Ethnic Lodge* (for details see Outside Lilongwe, below).

Places to Stay – middle

All rooms in this category have ensuite bathrooms and include breakfast in the room price, unless otherwise stated.

Central & Suburbs The cheapest place in this bracket is *Annie's Lodge* (☎ 721590), a suburban house with local flavour in Area 47, just off Kamuzu Procession Rd, north of Old Town. Self-contained singles/doubles are US$30/35. Nearer City Centre, north of Youth Drive, is the *Capital City Motel* (☎ 784531; fax 784245) where smart but characterless ensuite singles/doubles are US$38/45. In a similar position, on Chilambula Rd, is the *Lingadzi Inn* (☎ 720644), which is clean and friendly but a little frayed around the edges, with a nice large garden, an incredibly small restaurant, and rooms for US$50/65.

In the suburb of Biwi, just off the road towards Blantyre, is the *Kalikuti Hotel* (☎ 721248), where singles/doubles are US$40/50. Rooms are nothing special but OK for this price. Couples can share a single.

Worth hunting out if you've got a car or don't mind taking taxis, is *Sheila's Lodge* (☎ 734258; fax 723806) off Blantyre St in Area 42, north of the Capital Hotel. This is a large converted suburban house, quiet, with a nice garden and self-contained rooms for US$39/52. In the restaurant, sandwiches and snacks are US$1.50 to US$3, Malawian meals around US$3, and other meals around US$5. It's signposted off Blantyre St, and off

MALAWI

the main road into town from the airport, Kasungu and the north.

Outside Lilongwe Another option, if you've got your own transport and don't need to be in the city, is the German-managed and strangely-titled *Safari Camp Ethnic Lodge* (☎ /fax 721458). This collection of tasteful chalets around a restaurant/bar overlooking Kamuzu Dam is about 25 km west of Lilongwe, on the road towards Dzalanyama. Singles/doubles are US$30/45 including taxes and breakfast. Camping is US$3. Overland drivers are welcome (but trucks only by arrangement). Use of the camp's car-service bay is US$1. Kayaks and windsurfers can be hired free of charge. The owners are actively involved in local conservation education projects, and can also assist with safaris, flights, car hire and trips around the country. Food in the restaurant has a Teutonic flavour: schnitzel or zwiebelrostbraten costs around US$10. Toasted sandwiches are US$5.

Places to Stay – top end

All rooms in this category have ensuite bathrooms and include breakfast in the room price, unless otherwise stated.

In the heart of Old Town on Kamuzu Procession Rd is the *Lilongwe Hotel* (☎ 740488; fax 740505, central reservations Blantyre ☎ 620071). Unlike many top-end places in other cities around the world, this is not a bland high-rise block, but a pleasant collection of accommodation 'wings' set around small areas of garden. Single/double ensuite rooms cost US$120/145. Facilities include a travel desk and swimming pool. Staff are efficient and friendly, and the hotel has a comfortable atmosphere. The bar is popular, and gets lively in the evening. The Patio Restaurant, with an open-air terrace, serves drinks, snacks and light meals, starting at US$3. For business travellers and the more well-heeled tourists this is a popular lunch spot and meeting place. For evening meals, the Malingundi Restaurant is more stylish, with main courses between US$6 and US$8.

The smartest place to stay in Lilongwe is the *Capital Hotel* (☎ 783388; fax 781273). This gets 'Premier' status within the South African-based Malawi Protea group (central reservations, Blantyre ☎ 620071), and is used mainly by top-end tourists, business travellers and diplomats, with all facilities and rooms at US$150/195 (or US$180/230 for superior rooms). As a full international-class hotel, however, it is rather lacking in character. The coffee shop and outside terrace restaurant offer snacks and light meals for around US$6, while the *Dzalanyama Greenery Restaurant* (inside) has starters for around US$6, and main courses from US$8 for steaks up to US$20 for prawns. The hotel also has a gift shop, bookshop, pharmacy, business centre (which also handles Coachline bookings), swimming pool, several airline offices, plus car hire and travel desks. Both the Lilongwe and the Capital hotels are due for refurbishment in 1997, so there may be some changes by the time you arrive.

Places to Eat – cheap

If you're on a tight budget, finding cheap eats in Lilongwe is no hardship. The market stalls sell fruit, vegetables and some tinned foods, and the shops in Old Town have a good range of local and imported stuff which is not too pricey. For fresh bread visit the *Capital Bakery*, just off the main street in Old Town, second left coming up from the bridge. Also around the market, and in the back streets off Kamuzu Procession Rd in Area 3, are several stalls selling deep fried cassava or potato chips and roasted meat, at very cheap prices. The PTC Hypermarkets in Old Town and in City Centre are both well stocked (mostly with goods from South Africa), though prices of most things are on a par with Europe. They also have their own bakery selling delicious hot brown bread.

For sit-down food, one of the best places in this bracket is *Annie's Coffee House*, just off Glyn Jones Rd between Areas 1 and 2, in Old Town. Coffee is US$0.50 and chocolate cake just over US$1. Good value snacks, meals (around US$2) and cold drinks are also available. (Annie also has another café at the nature sanctuary – see Things to See & Do, earlier in this chapter.) Also in this area is the clean, no frills *Gazebo Restaurant*, which serves good curries for around US$3 to US$4, snacks for US$1 to US$2 and ice cream (but no alcohol).

In Area 3 on Kamuzu Procession Rd, there are a couple of cheap places to try. *Sunset Restaurant*, behind the insurance building opposite the Commercial Bank, serves standard fry-ups like fish and chips for just US$2, and local dishes like nsima and meat for just over US$1. The nearby *Byee! Takeaway*, which also has shady outdoor seating (admittedly in a car park), offers similar food at similar prices. Also nearby is *The Summer Park*, a very pleasant garden area, where ice creams are US$0.60, sundaes US$1.50, burgers US$2 and full meals US$3. On the other side of the road is the recently arrived *Southern Fried Chicken*, all the way from good ole South Africa, where takeaway burgers and the like cost US$2 to US$4.

In City Centre there's good, cheap street food available at lunchtimes around the PTC Hypermarket, which is where local office workers eat. A plate of meat, vegetables and rice costs US$1. At *Desiderata Restaurant* in Capital City Shopping Centre, the waiters go placidly but the food is OK, with local dishes for just over US$1, and other meals like fish or chicken and chips for US$2. In the same block, facing the car park is *Tasty Takeaway*. Their menu board when we visited proudly announced the sale of 'fish gizzards, chicken offal, beans, beef and chips'. They also sell burgers and soft drinks.

Places to Eat – more expensive

Most of the middle and top-end hotels listed earlier in this chapter have restaurants open to nonresidents where standards and prices are on a par with the hotel.

In City Centre, the *Restaurant Koreana* (☎ 781004) on the ground floor of Gemini House, an office block in Capital City Shopping Centre, specialises in Korean and East Asian food, where starters are around US$1,

soups US$1.50, main dishes US$4 to US$7, and side dishes US$1 to US$2 (closed Sundays). Nearby is the long-standing *Causerie* (☎ 783828) where good-value steaks, fish and curries start at US$5 and prawns are US$13.

In the same area is the *Golden Dragon Restaurant* (☎ 780414) off Independence Drive, near the British Council Library, with Chinese food (closed Mondays); large dishes are US$3 to US$5, smaller ones US$1 to US$2, plus tax. They also serve takeaways (same prices but no tax).

In Old Town, there are several more options. *Huts* (☎ 744756), just down from the Lilongwe Hotel, serves good Indian food. Main courses are around US$7, and a three-course meal comes to between US$10 and US$15 including taxes. Almost opposite is *Modi's* (☎ 743965) (pronounced Moodies, possibly because their slogan runs 'Modi's – where the foodie is goodie'), which also serves curries, steaks, chicken and fish dishes, always acceptable, sometimes marvellous, with prices about the same as Huts. At the Golden Peacock Hotel (see Places to Stay) is the *Korea Garden Restaurant*, with prices a bit lower than the Koreana and a slightly rustic outdoor setting.

Le Bistro Cordon Rouge at Lilongwe Golf Club has a good reputation, with light meals from US$2 to US$5, and full blow-outs for around US$8. This is good value, but non-members must pay an additional US$7 to get in.

Entertainment

Lilongwe's home-grown nightlife scene is not immediately obvious for outsiders: but if you dig beneath the surface a little, there are some fine places to pass an hour or three in the evening. In Old Town, along the notorious Devil St, are several bars which play music loud and late. Some are little more than bottle stores with upturned crates for seats. Although this area cannot be said to be completely safe, it's not too dangerous either, and we've heard from several travellers who have had good times here. They report most Malawians are friendly and happy to talk to strangers, especially (like anywhere else) after a few drinks. However, if you go here, take enough money for an evening's supply of beer and nothing else you can't afford to lose.

Less rough, and just as 'authentic' is the Zebra Disco at the Lingadzi Inn (see Places to Stay), which plays mostly African music to a mostly Malawian clientele; it's open Friday and Saturday nights, with a cover charge of US$1.50. Smarter again is the non-residents bar at the Lilongwe Hotel which often has a disco or live music (US$2 cover charge), although good entertainment can be had on the wall outside, watching old taxis stall on the steep ramp into the nearby car park.

Also recommended (although you'll need a car or taxi to get there) are the local bars near the petrol station in Area 47, where most of the entertainment consists of talking, and sometimes listening, to other drinkers. Nearby is the smarter Hollywood Nightclub, attracting a smart mix of European, Asian and well-to-do Malawian regulars, playing mostly western music, with a cover charge at weekends of US$3.

At the Town Hall, on the corner of Glyn Jones and Kamuzu Procession roads, is J&J Cinema, showing mostly kung fu, Van Damme, thud and blunder films for less than US$1. The British Council and USIS also occasionally show films (see Libraries & Cultural Centres, earlier in this chapter).

Getting There & Away

Air Lilongwe International Airport is on the north side of the city. Getting to/from the airport is covered in the Getting Around Lilongwe section below. For details on domestic flights from Lilongwe to other cities in Malawi, and on international flights between Lilongwe and the rest of the world, see the Getting Around and Getting There & Away chapters. If you need to fly out of Lilongwe, the following airlines have offices in the city:

Air Malawi (☎ 720966/782132), with offices at the Lilongwe and Capital Hotels

Air Tanzania (☎ 783636/784471), Capital City Shopping Centre
Kenya Airways (☎ 784227/784330), Capital City Shopping Centre
KLM (☎ 781413), Capital Hotel
South African Airways (☎ 760470), Capital Hotel

These offices are useful if you have reservations to confirm, but if you're buying a ticket you're usually better off going to an agent (see Information, earlier in this chapter) as prices should be the same or less (unless the airline has a special offer) and it will save you a lot of shopping around.

Bus There are Coachline services three times per day between Lilongwe and Blantyre (US$17), and once per day between Lilongwe and Mzuzu (US$19) via Kasungu (US$8). You can make reservations at the Coachline office at the Stagecoach bus depot (☎ 740111, 731854) next to the Nico Centre, only 50m or so from the entrance to the PTC Hypermarket in Old Town, or at the Lilongwe Hotel or Capital Hotel. A small outfit called Nyika Shuttle (☎ 622950) is undercutting Coachline, with fares of US$10 on the Lilongwe to Blantyre run.

There are also four Express buses each day between Lilongwe and Blantyre, either direct (four to five hours) for US$7 or via Zomba (five to six hours) for US$8, and several InterCity buses (slightly cheaper but slower). Other Express fares to/from Lilongwe are: to/from Kasungu, US$3; to/from Mzuzu, US$9; to/from Mangochi (for Monkey Bay), US$5; to/from Zomba, US$7; to/from Mchinji, US$2. You can buy advance tickets for Express buses (but not for InterCity buses) at the Stagecoach long-distance bus station near the market.

Getting Around

Getting around Lilongwe can be tiresome, especially if you don't have your own transport, as the city is very spread out. It's also confusing for newcomers as a lot of the main avenues look the same. Most visitors, however, will probably stay in the compact Old Town and getting around will not be such a problem, only having to head for City Centre to buy a visa or search for long lost letters at the poste restante.

The Airport The main airport is 24 km north of Lilongwe. A taxi will cost about US$17 if you're trying to get from the airport to town, but less than this the other way. If you're short of cash, a local bus goes from the Stagecoach bus station near the market in Old Town to the commercial part of the airport (about 200m from the passenger terminal) for just US$1. It's best to go to the local bus park the day before to check departure times (if any) as this service is irregular, and hard to pin down. If you're trying to find it at the airport you may have a long wait. Your alternative is to hitch (walk 500m to the last turn-off after the commercial area) or hoof it from the terminal to the main road (three km), where regular minibuses run into Lilongwe.

Bus There are minibus routes all over Lilongwe, linking the centre with the outer suburbs. The most useful service for visitors is from Old Town to City Centre. Minibuses leave from the local bus park opposite the main Stagecoach bus station near the market in Old Town. They pass along Glyn Jones and Kamuzu Procession roads, turning right into Kenyatta Rd near the PTC Hypermarket (there's a bus stop here), then up Kenyatta Rd, right into Youth Drive and then up Convention Drive or Independence Drive to terminate. Coming back the route is reversed. From City Centre back to Old Town, the bus stop is at the north end of Independence Drive. Either way the fare is US$0.30.

Taxi The best place to find taxis is at the main hotels. There's also a rank near the PTC Hypermarket in City Centre. Between Old Town and City Centre is US$4 or US$5. For fares to/from the airport see The Airport section, earlier.

AROUND LILONGWE

Places within a short journey from Lilongwe include the forest resthouses of Dzalanyama, Ntchisi and Dedza. The latter two are a bit

further away, and covered in the Central Malawi chapter.

Dzalanyama

Dzalanyama is a forest reserve in a range of hills about 50 km by road to the south-west of Lilongwe. The hills run in a roughly northwest to south-east line, and their watershed forms the border between Malawi and Mozambique. The highest point is a peak called Silamwezi (1713m). The hills are covered in miombo forest, and the region is protected because the rainfall here flows into Kamuzu Dam and is the water supply for Lilongwe.

It's a great place to go for a couple of nights, but unfortunately there is no public transport to the resthouse, so to visit you need a car (or a bike – local men do it on their heavy steel bicycles with huge piles of firewood on the back).

The name Dzalanyama means 'place of meat' from the number of game animals that used to live here. Much of this has been hunted over the years, although there are still small buck, and even leopard and hyena, but these are rarely seen. There are, however, several good walks in the surrounding forest which is particularly rich in birdlife. It might be interesting to walk up to the watershed; the views over Malawi and Mozambique are reported to be splendid, but you should ask locally about the presence of mines in the border area (the resthouse caretaker or staff at the nearby forest office may be able to help). Other walks in this areas are covered in *Day Outings from Lilongwe* mentioned under Books in the Facts for the Visitor chapter.

Places to Stay Within the reserve is a pleasant little *resthouse* run by the Department of Forestry which is open to visitors. There are four bedrooms with two beds each (with sheets and blankets), plus a bathroom, lounge, dining room and kitchen. The caretaker doubles as cook, but you must supply all the food you need, as nothing is available. To stay here costs about US$3 per person. You pay the caretaker who issues a receipt, or you can book and pay in advance at the Department of Forestry offices in Lilongwe (see Information earlier in this chapter for details). The fee is good value, even though the resthouse is getting a bit tumbledown these days. It's a shame that the money effectively goes to the government, to be swallowed up by administration costs, rather than even a bit of it being reinvested in the resthouse.

Getting There & Away To get here from the centre of Lilongwe's Old Town take Glyn Jones Rd west to Livingstone Rd round-about. From here continue south-west through the outer suburb of Likuni, past *Safari Camp Ethnic Lodge* (25 km from Lilongwe, see Places to Stay) and then on for another seven km to reach the forest gate, where you have to sign the book (but no fee is payable). From here it's about another 20 km to 25 km through the forest. There's a couple of junctions but the resthouse is signposted. The roads are bad in places, so the drive takes about 1½ hours.

Central Malawi

This chapter covers most parts of Malawi's Central Province (which has Lilongwe at its centre), and the Viphya Plateau. (The lake shore region of the Central Province is covered in the Lake Shore chapter.) Places are described roughly from south to north.

DEDZA

Dedza is a small town 85 km south of Lilongwe, just off the main road to/from Blantyre, and easily reached by bus or car. Overlooking the town is Dedza Mountain Forest Reserve, which has some pleasant walks and offers spectacular views from the highest points.

You can walk to the summit of Dedza Mountain (2198m) in two to three hours. The path starts near the golf club and heads towards a large communications aerial – check directions at the nearby government

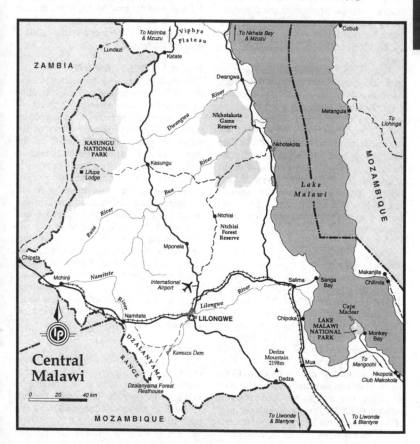

resthouse. Beyond here there's a maze of paths, but a reasonable sense of direction will take you to the top. The vegetation is mostly pine plantation but there are patches of indigenous forest on the higher slopes. Other walks in this areas are covered in *Day Outings from Lilongwe* mentioned in the Books section of the Facts for the Visitor chapter.

On the north-western outskirts of the town, just where the road through the town turns off the main road between Lilongwe and Blantyre, is Dedza Pottery, with fine hand-crafted and manufactured ceramic products (aimed squarely at the expat and visitor market) and an excellent *coffee shop* where the pastries are as fine as the pottery: try the blueberry cheesecake at US$0.50 a slice.

If you're staying at the College of Forestry resthouse (see Places to Stay, following), you can walk in the surrounding Chingoni Forest Reserve. Again this is a mix of plantation and indigenous woodland, with a couple of rocky outcrops offering views and reasonably good bird-watching. It's an easy three to four hour walk between Dedza and the college, on paths along the edge of the forest reserve and through a couple of local villages. You'd have to ask directions (a landmark is Dedza Secondary School) and the services of a local guide might be a good investment.

Places to Stay

Cheap places to stay include the *Mini Hotel* on the Blantyre side of town, charging US$1.50 per person. The nearby *Rainbow Resthouse* is slightly better. The *Government Resthouse* on the edge of town near the golf course, on the lower slopes of the mountain, is also reported to be OK. It charges US$4 per person. There's also a *Forestry Resthouse* in the College of Forestry about 10 km north of Dedza; more easily reached by those with a car. You can get more details from the college (☎ 220275) or from the Department of Forestry office in Lilongwe (see Information in the Lilongwe chapter for details).

Getting There & Away

All buses between Lilongwe and Blantyre or Zomba go through Dedza town, which lies a few km off the main road. The Express bus fare to Dedza from Lilongwe is US$2, from Blantyre it's US$5.

MCHINJI

Mchinji is about 115 km west of Lilongwe, near the border with Zambia. If you get stuck here overnight this small town has several shops, a supermarket, some local bars and restaurants, and some cheap places to stay. The *Tiyeseko Motel*, a few blocks off the right side of the road as you come in from Lilongwe, is quiet and charges US$7 per room. *Andrews Motel*, nearer the road, is cheaper but noisier.

NTCHISI FOREST RESERVE

This small and rarely visited reserve is about 80 km north of Lilongwe, near the large village of Ntchisi (pronounced 'Ncheesee'). At the centre of the reserve is Ntchisi Mountain, which offers splendid views of the surrounding area. The vegetation on the higher slopes is mainly evergreen forest – reckoned to be one of the best examples in the country – with large buttressed trees. The lower slopes consist of miombo forest. Birdlife is varied, and mammals include blue monkey, bushpig and duiker. Elephant used to occur here, but it's not known if any survived the recent increase in poaching. From the resthouse (see information following) you can walk to the summit of Ntchisi Mountain by following a track and various paths through the forest. From the resthouse the peak is about four km, so allow about three hours for a there-and-back walk, more if you enjoy bird-watching.

Places to Stay

The Department of Forestry has a resthouse at Ntchisi Forest Reserve which is open to the public. It is similar to the one at Dzalanyama (see the Lilongwe chapter), although it's seldom used and a bit run-down these days. This is made up for by excellent views to the east, across Lake Malawi (sometimes as far as Likoma Island and Cape Maclear). The resthouse was originally built as a 'hill station' for the colonial district commissioner who came here to escape the heat of his normal base in Nkhotakota.

The resthouse has five rooms, and prices and arrangements (including the services of the caretaker/cook) are the same as at Dzalanyama. You can also camp here. More information is available from the Department of Forestry offices in Lilongwe (see Information in the Lilongwe chapter for details).

Getting There & Away

The nearest settlement of any size is Ntchisi village, on the dirt road between Lilongwe and Nkhotakota (which also passes through Nkhotakota Game Reserve – see the Around Nkhotakota section in the Lake Shore chapter for details). About 12 km south of here, the forest reserve is signposted to the east. It's another 16 km along here, through a village called Chindembwe, to the reserve entrance and resthouse. There is public transport between Lilongwe and Nkhotakota (via Ntchisi village and the forest reserve junction), but none to the resthouse itself, so a trip here is only really possible for keen hikers or those with wheels.

KASUNGU

Kasungu is a fairly large town, about 130 km north of Lilongwe, where the roads to Nkhotakota and Kasungu National Park branch off the main north-south road between Lilongwe and Mzuzu. There are no major attractions, although the busy market off the main street is worth a look around. You might find yourself changing transport or overnighting here on the way to the national park.

The town is about two km east of the main north-south road. There's a petrol station on the junction, and a few minibuses stop here, but most public transport goes to/from the bus station in town, just north of the main street.

Places to Stay & Eat

The cheapest option is the none-too-clean *Council Resthouse*, on the main street oppo-

site the National Bank of Malawi. Mats on the floor cost US$0.20, while a room with two beds is US$2.50. More comfortable is the *Kasungu Inn*, at the eastern end of town, 2.5 km from the main junction, where clean ensuite rooms cost US$12/17, including breakfast. They also serve lunches and dinners. In between these two places (in price and position) is a *Government Resthouse* – closed when we passed through but likely to reopen.

There are several cheap local restaurants on the main street and around the market. The *Golden Dish* has good food and reasonably clean surroundings.

Getting There & Away

Kasungu can be reached on the daily Coachline luxury bus service between Lilongwe and Mzuzu. The fare is US$8 (for details on reservations, see Getting There & Away in the Lilongwe chapter). There are also Express and InterCity buses several times a day; the fare between Lilongwe and Kasungu is US$3.

KASUNGU NATIONAL PARK

Kasungu National Park lies to the west of Kasungu town, along the border with Zambia. It covers more than 2000 sq km, making it the second-largest park in the country, after Nyika National Park. The landscape is mainly flat or gently rolling hills, with a few rocky outcrops rising above the plain. The soil is mostly sandy and the vegetation is classed as miombo woodland. The woodland is interspersed by wide, marshy river courses, called *dambos*, where reeds and grasses grow. The park also has a small lake, called Lifupa Dam.

Although trees in miombo woodland are normally well spaced, allowing bush and grass to grow in between, giving the woods a 'parkland' appearance, the vegetation in Kasungu is relatively dense. This is because the park's population of elephant (who would naturally act as 'gardeners' by keeping the growth controlled) has been seriously reduced since the 1970s by poaching.

It is estimated that about 300 elephant still

MALAWI

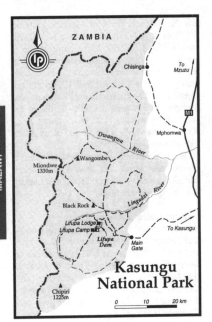

Kasungu
National Park

although most of these are closed during the rainy season and may not reopen until June each year. (If you don't have wheels, you can still go into the park – see Getting There & Away). Since 1995 Kasungu National Park has been receiving aid money from the European Union, to assist with anti-poaching efforts and management. It is likely that all tracks in the park will be upgraded in the next few years. Animal populations may also recover.

Game drives (day or night) are organised by the lodge (see Places to Stay). Walking is also permitted in the park. A guide is obligatory for game viewing or bird-watching beyond the confines of the lodge, but this is no problem as the guides always see more than you do on your own, and can explain about the animals, birds, and vegetation, helping you get more from your visit.

For morning or evening walks of about two hours through the woodland around the dam, the national park guides cost US$2 and the lodge guides charge US$10 (but they are better trained). You can go for longer (all day if you like); the lodge will arrange for an armed scout to come as well, although close encounters with large dangerous animals are unlikely. A good place to aim for is Black Rock, which is a good viewpoint (although the aerial on top spoils the feel of the wilderness). Other hills good for a walk are Miondwe, straddling the park boundary and the border with Zambia, and Wangombe ('hill of the cow'), about 23 km north of Lifupa Dam.

Places to Stay

Lifupa Lodge (☎ 253439) is in a wonderful position overlooking the dam. Animals often come to the opposite bank to drink, and sometimes even walk through the lodge grounds on their way to the water. Formerly run by the Department of National Parks & Wildlife, this was leased to private management in 1996 and is being completely rebuilt and renovated. Very comfortable twin-bedded ensuite rondavels will probably cost in the region of US$100 to US$150, which will include all accommodation and meals,

remain in the park, and the chances of seeing some are fairly good in the dry season. Other large mammals occurring here include buffalo, zebra, and several antelope species, and the dam contains a group of hippo. Predators include lion and leopard, but these are very rarely seen. Lack of management over the last 20 years or so means the park cannot be termed a major game-viewing destination.

But if you've come to Malawi for more than members of the 'big five', Kasungu is well worth a visit. The vegetation is lush and the birdlife is also excellent, with woodland and grassland species, as well as waders around the dam. The park also contains a number of historical sites. These include old iron kilns used by local people in this area before it was made a national park, and some very faint rock paintings that are assumed to be pre-Bantu.

Things to Do

If you have your own vehicle, you can tour the park on its good network of tracks, park fees, game drives, walks, boat trips and so on. The lodge also has a bar, game-viewing platform, restaurant, information room and small gift shop. For more information, you can contact the lodges reservation office in Lilongwe (☎ 780576) or any good tour agent.

Nearby, also overlooking the dam, *Lifupa Camp* (run by the same people, but not physically connected to the lodge) has simple chalets with shared showers and toilets from US$30 per person. There's a kitchen where you can prepare your own food, and for a small extra fee the cook and staff will do everything for you. This price includes one game drive or walk. Camping is US$2. The camp has a small bar and, if you don't feel like cooking, a range of snacks and meals are available.

Getting There & Away

The park entrance is 35 km west of Kasungu town. If you're in your own car coming from the south, turn left (west) off the main road, just before the turn-off to Kasungu town. The road leads past a grand palace (built by former president Banda) and winds through farmland and villages. There are a few forks and junctions, but the park is signposted and local people will always point the way if you get lost. At the park gate, you pay your entrance fees (for details see the National Parks section in the Facts about Malawi chapter). Once in the park, it's 17 km by the shortest route to the lodge and camp.

If you don't have a car, get to Kasungu town by bus (see Kasungu, earlier), and then phone the lodge (the easiest place to call from, and to wait, is Kasungu Inn). Their supply vehicle comes to town two or three times per week, and if there's space they'll give you a lift into the park. If you don't hit the right day, and don't want to wait, they will make a special journey to collect you. The charge for this is US$20. For a lift out, you can talk to other guests at the camp, or wait until the next supply run.

VIPHYA PLATEAU

The Viphya Plateau is a broad highland area,

running like a backbone through north-central Malawi, from Katate in the south, almost to Mzuzu. Despite its name, this area is not flat but consists mostly of rolling hills, cut by river valleys. In some areas, pointed rocky peaks rise sharply above the surrounding hills. Not surprisingly, the area is also called the Viphya Mountains.

Much of the area is pine plantation, and much of the rest is dense bush, so the area does not lend itself readily to long-distance hiking (although at least one set of hardy individuals have walked from here down to Lake Malawi). However, the road journey between Kasungu and Mzuzu is beautiful, especially if the sun is shining (but don't be surprised if there's dense mist and rain), and there are two wonderful forest resthouses to stop at, where you can base yourself for a day or two's strolling, and enjoy the surrounding scenery.

Luwawa Forest Resthouse

This resthouse lies 10 km east of the main road between Kasungu and Mzuzu, in a forest clearing overlooking a small dam. There are four rooms with four beds in each, separate bathrooms, a central kitchen plus lounge and dining area. The beds have sheets and blankets, the lounge has a roaring wood fire, the showers are hot, the toilets are clean, and the resident caretaker keeps the whole place spick-and-span. To stay here costs US$2.50 per person. An absolute bargain. You must supply your own food, but the caretaker will also cook (he's very good) and wash up, for which an extra tip is appropriate. Camping is allowed here for US$1.50 per person, and the caretaker will probably allow you to use a bathroom inside.

You can reserve a room here in advance by writing to the Plantations Manager (Resthouse Reservations), Viphya Plantations, PO Chikangawa, or by going to the Department of Forestry offices in Lilongwe and booking in person. If this is not possible, you can just turn up, and if the place isn't fully booked, you can stay. (Even if the place is booked, often people simply don't arrive, so you may be lucky anyway.) Reservations are not required for camping.

Getting There & Away
Because the resthouse is off the road, it's most suitable for visitors with a car. To get here, from Kasungu take the main road towards Mzuzu. About 110 km from Kasungu you'll see a sign to Luwawa. Ignore this. Continue for another nine km, until you see a sign that says 'Luwawa 10 km'. Take this dirt road to reach the resthouse. Coming from Mzuzu, continue past the junction where the road from Mzimba joins from the right. After eight km you'll see a sign saying 'Luwawa D73'. Ignore this, and continue for another eight km to the 'Luwawa 10 km' sign mentioned above.

Kasito Lodge
Kasito Lodge is another forest resthouse, very similar to the one at Luwawa (described above). If anything it's better, as it was rebuilt in 1980 following a fire, and is in very good condition (hence the 'lodge' title). It's the sort of place you might plan to stop off for a night, and end up staying two or three days. Sometimes called Chikangawa Resthouse, this place is much easier to reach for those without wheels as it's less than a km west of the main road between Kasungu and Mzuzu. There are five rooms, with two, three or four beds. The caretaker here is also a good cook (the lodge is used by some tour

companies and he can prepare four-course meals for groups of eight without batting an eyelid), but as at Luwawa Resthouse you must bring your own food. A bed costs US$3, and a tip for the cook is usually appropriate. The booking procedure is the same as at the Luwawa Resthouse. Camping costs US$1.50.

If the lodge is full when you arrive, nearby are two other places to stay: *Resthouse No 2*, where things are slightly less comfortable, and *The Annex* which is more basic again, with six beds in a room for US$2.50 per person.

An interesting short walk is to the nearby charcoal kilns, where several large mud-brick igloos steam and smoke.

Getting There & Away
To get here by car, from the south continue past the turn-off to Luwawa and the main junction where the road goes to Mzimba. Keep on the main road for 27 km beyond the Mzimba junction, and you'll see a Kasito Lodge sign on the left (west) side of the road. Go down this dirt road for 500m to reach the lodge. Coming from the north, you pass a large wood factory at Chikangawa village, and the turn-off to the lodge is a few km beyond here on the right. If you're travelling by bus, ask the driver to drop you at the resthouse, about three km before or after Chikangawa (depending which way you're coming from).

Blantyre & Limbe

Blantyre is the main commercial and industrial centre of Malawi. It stretches for about 20 km, merging into its 'sister city' Limbe. In colonial times, Limbe was established as a smart European quarter, while Blantyre was considered less desirable, but today there's little of any interest for visitors in Limbe, and nearly all visitors stay in Blantyre. Many find that Blantyre has a bit more of a buzz than Lilongwe (if any of

Malawi's sleepy cities can be said to buzz at all) but most travellers stop only for a few days, mainly to send or receive mail, buy maps and books, or to pick up a Mozambique visa. Whatever, Blantyre is a pleasant place, with some interesting sights, several enjoyable restaurants, cafés and bars to while away the time and a fair selection of places to stay. Despite the sprawling suburbs and townships surrounding Blantyre, the city

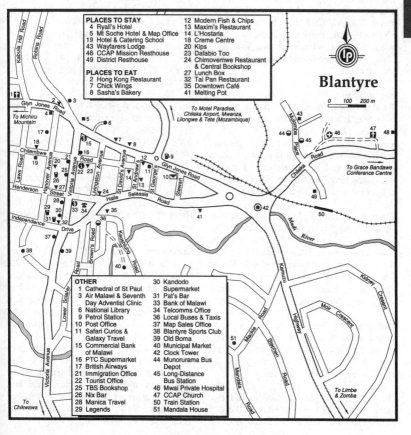

PLACES TO STAY
4 Ryall's Hotel
5 Mt Soche Hotel & Map Office
19 Hotel & Catering School
43 Wayfarers Lodge
48 CCAP Mission Resthouse
49 District Resthouse

PLACES TO EAT
2 Hong Kong Restaurant
7 Chick Wings
8 Sasha's Bakery
12 Modern Fish & Chips
13 Maxim's Restaurant
14 L'Hostaria
18 Creme Centre
20 Kips
23 Dalabio Too
24 Chimovemwe Restaurant & Central Bookshop
27 Lunch Box
32 Tai Pan Restaurant
35 Downtown Café
41 Melting Pot

To Motel Paradise, Chileka Airport, Mwanza, Lilongwe & Tete (Mozambique)

Blantyre

0   100   200 m

To Michiru Mountain

To Grace Bandawe Conference Centre

To Limbe & Zomba

To Chikwawa

OTHER
1 Cathedral of St Paul
3 Air Malawi & Seventh Day Adventist Clinic
6 National Library
9 Petrol Station
10 Post Office
11 Safari Curios & Galaxy Travel
15 Commercial Bank of Malawi
16 PTC Supermarket
17 British Airways
21 Immigration Office
22 Tourist Office
25 TBS Bookshop
26 Nix Bar
28 Manica Travel
29 Legends
30 Kandodo Supermarket
31 Pat's Bar
33 Bank of Malawi
34 Telcomms Office
36 Local Buses & Taxis
37 Map Sales Office
38 Blantyre Sports Club
39 Old Boma
40 Municipal Market
42 Clock Tower
44 Munorurama Bus Depot
45 Long-Distance Bus Station
46 Mwai Private Hospital
47 CCAP Church
50 Train Station
51 Mandala House

centre is very compact with most of the places of importance to travellers well within easy walking distance. (Unless stated otherwise, every address in this section is in Blantyre, rather than Limbe.)

Orientation

Central Blantyre's main street is Victoria Ave. Along here are several shops, the tourist office, map office, banks, change bureaux and travel agencies. To the east of Victoria Ave is Haile Selassie Rd, which contains many more shops. At the northern end of Victoria Ave is the Mt Soche Hotel and a junction with Glyn Jones Rd. East of here is a major roundabout (traffic circle), from where Kamuzu Hwy leads towards Limbe. The road going north-east from the roundabout is the bus and train stations, Wayfarers Lodge, and the main road towards the airport and Mwanza.

Information

Tourist Office The tourist office is on Victoria Ave. It's open 7.30 am to noon, and 1 to 5 pm. There's not much in the way of leaflets and give-aways, but the people here make quite an effort to provide information and assistance. Even if they can't help you with something specific, they'll probably be able to put you onto someone who can.

Foreign Embassies Most embassies, consulates and high commissions are in Lilongwe. However, there's a Mozambique consulate between Blantyre and Limbe on Kamuzu Hwy, near the junction with Hynde Rd. See Embassies in the Malawi Facts for the Visitor chapter for information about visas, costs, and so on.

Immigration Office For visa extensions, the Immigration office is in Building Society House, on Victoria Ave. It's open 7.30 am to noon, 1.30 am to 4 pm, Monday to Friday and 7.30 am to noon on Saturday.

Money For changing money in Blantyre there are branches of the National Bank of Malawi and the Commercial Bank on Victoria Ave. Both are open from 8 am to 2 pm. Nearby are the Manica Travel and Finance Bank change bureaux, both open from 8 am to 5 pm and on Saturday mornings. If you've got time, it's worth shopping around the banks and bureaux, as rates and commissions can vary considerably.

Post & Communications Blantyre's main post office (GPO) is on Glyn Jones Rd, open Monday to Friday from 7.30 am to 4.30 pm; Saturday from 8 to 10 am; and Sunday from 9 to 10 am. The poste restante is here. If you're using the Amex mail service, the office is at Manica Travel, Victoria Ave.

For telephone calls and faxes the Telcomms office is on Henderson St, just off Victoria Ave. It is open weekdays from 7 am to 5.30 pm, and weekends from 8 am to 2 pm. For rates, see the Facts for the Visitor chapter. Photocopying and other secretarial services are also offered here.

Travel & Tour Agencies Most travel agencies are based on or just off Victoria Ave. These include Airtour & Travel (☎ 622918), AMI Travel (☎ 624733) and Manica Travel (☎ 624533). The switched-on Galaxy Travel (☎ 633637) is on Glyn Jones Rd. Most of the above deal mainly in outbound international flights. Soche Tours & Travel (☎ 620777), on the corner of Chilembwe Ave and Hanover Rd, books flights and also arranges sightseeing tours.

Bookshops There's a TBS bookshop on Victoria Ave and a smaller one at the Mt Soche Hotel. Both have international and local newspapers and magazines, as well as a range of books including paperback novels, African literature, local guidebooks and other books on Malawian subjects.

For an even wider selection, visit the Central Bookshop on the corner of Livingstone Ave and Haile Selassie Rd. It also stocks stationary, books and guides about other parts of Southern Africa, local language dictionaries and a selection of antiquarian books on Malawi and Africa. There's also a pleasant coffee shop.

DAVID ELSE

DAVID ELSE

DAVID WALL

BRUNO FRANÇAIS

Malawi
Top Left: Sunday best, southern Malawi
Top Right: Rural women, southern Malawi
Bottom Left: Village boy from Karonga, northern Malawi
Bottom Right: Fisherman's daughter, Nkopola, southern Malawi

BRUNO FRANÇAIS

DAVID ELSE

DAVID ELSE

DAVID ELSE

BRUNO FRANÇAIS

DAVID ELSE

A	B
C	D
E	F

Malawi

A: Selling produce near Blantyre
B: Public laundry, Mangochi
C: Chia Lagoon, near Nkhotakota

D: Charcoal burners in the Viphya Mountains
E: Tea and corn crops, Limbe area
F: Tea plantations below Mt Mulanje

The Wildlife Society bookshop at the Heritage Centre in Limbe, next to the Shire Highlands Hotel, also has a good selection, specialising in natural history and national parks, but with more general subjects too.

Map Office The Department of Surveys public map office is on the corner of Victoria Ave and Independence Drive. For more details on what's available see Maps in the Facts for the Visitor chapter.

Libraries & Cultural Centres The National Library is just off Glyn Jones Rd, reached by a dirt road round the back of the Mt Soche Hotel. It's open Monday to Friday from 8 am to 5 pm, and Saturday to 3 pm. The British Council library is in the building on Victoria Ave, and is open Tuesday to Friday from 8 am to 5 pm, Monday afternoons 2 to 5 pm and Saturday mornings 8 am to noon. Nonmembers can read books and magazines in the library, but not take them away. It shows films on some afternoons and evenings. Check the noticeboards for details. The French Cultural Centre is on Kamuzu Hwy, towards Limbe.

Medical Centres & Pharmacies If you have an embassy in Malawi (see the list in the Facts for the Visitor chapter), and are able to contact them first, they will normally be able to advise on recommended doctors and dentists in Blantyre. In case they are not able to help, some suggested places are listed here.

If you think you've got malaria and need a blood test, go to the Malaria Test Centre at Queen Elizabeth Central Hospital (☎ 630333), the main government hospital in Blantyre, on Kamuzu Hwy. This service is free, but a donation is welcomed.

For private medical consultations and/or blood tests, Mwai Private Hospital, in the Mission grounds between the bus station and St Michael's CCAP Church, has been recommended by travellers. A consultation is US$10; all drugs and treatment are extra.

For medical or dental problems, the Seventh Day Adventist Clinic (☎ 620488, 620006), near the Hong Kong Restaurant,

has also been recommended. A doctor's consultation costs US$6, and a malaria test is US$10. Hours are 7.30 to 11.30 am, 1.30 to 3.30 pm Monday to Thursday, 7.30 to noon on Friday, closed Saturday, 9 to 11.30 am on Sunday.

If things are more serious, you should use that travel insurance you never thought you'd need, and go home. But if this is not possible the Seventh Day Adventist Hospital near the clinic (see above) accepts emergencies any time.

For medicines and other things like shampoo, tampons and condoms there's a large MPL pharmacy on Victoria Ave, and several smaller ones around the city centre.

Emergency As in Lilongwe, the emergency phone number for the police and ambulance service is ☎ 199. Refer to Emergency in the Lilongwe chapter for advice on how to minimise delays.

Supermarkets The main PTC supermarket on the corner of Victoria Ave and Chilembwe Rd sells food and other goods, much of it imported from South Africa or Europe, and sold at similar prices. A bit further down Victoria Ave is a Kandodo supermarket where the stock is similar, slightly cheaper but more limited. Traders sell fruit and vegetables outside both places.

Film & Video Colour Film Processors at the top of Victoria Ave has a good stock of print film, and can do passport photos on the spot. Developing and printing is also available. See the Photography & Video section in the Facts for the Visitor chapter for an idea of prices.

Gas Overland drivers can refill their camping cylinders at IGL (Industrial Gases Ltd) on Johnstone Rd in the industrial area, off Kamuzu Hwy, near Queen Elizabeth Hospital.

Things to See & Do
There are **craft stalls** outside the PTC supermarket on Victoria Ave, and smarter (fixed

MALAWI

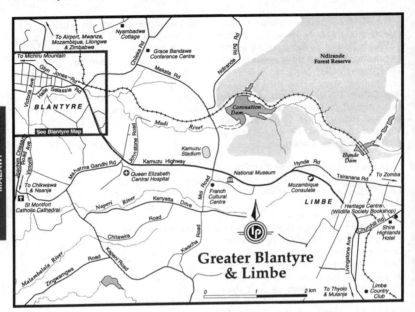

Greater Blantyre & Limbe

price) arts and crafts at Safari Curios on Glyn Jones Rd and Gangecraft on Victoria Ave, near the tourist office. But to see what Malawians buy you could visit the **Municipal Market** on Kaoshiung Rd (also called Mandala Rd), behind the local bus station. The relatively new buildings give it a more formal feel than the hectic market in Lilongwe, but it's still worth a visit even if you don't want to buy anything.

Up the hill from here is **Mandala House**, a large two-storey colonial-style building which was the headquarters of the African Lakes Corporation from the end of the 19th century (for more details see the boxed text below). It is the oldest remaining European building in Malawi. The outside is quite interesting, but the interior been completely renovated, so there's little to see inside.

Probably the most impressive thing to see in Blantyre is the **CCAP Church**, officially called the Church of St Michael and All Angels, in the mission grounds, just off Chileka Rd, beyond the bus station. This was

built by missionaries of the Established Church of Scotland, who came to Malawi a few years after their brethren of the Free Church had founded the first Livingstonia mission station at Cape Maclear (for more details see History in the Facts about Malawi chapter). Their leader was the Rev Clement Scott. With no training in architectural design or construction skills, and only local handmade bricks and wood available, Scott planned and then oversaw the building of this magnificent church, complete with dome, towers, arches and bay windows. Although extensively renovated in the 1970s, what you see today is pretty much how it looked the day it was completed in 1891. After more than a century of service, St Michael's is about to be replaced by a new modern church. In 1996 this was under construction nearby.

Blantyre also has the **Cathedral of St Paul**, on Glyn Jones Rd, about 500m west of the Mt Soche Hotel, and the Catholic **Cathedral of St Montfort**, on Joachim Chissano

Rd (the road towards Chikwawa and Nsanje), south of the city centre.

Other historical buildings of interest in Blantyre include the **Old Boma** (colonial administration office), at the junction of Victoria Ave and Haile Selassie Rd. This was originally the centre of government for the whole Nyasaland Protectorate, under the first commissioner Sir Harry Johnston, until the capital was moved to Zomba in 1891.

Malawi's **National Museum** is midway

Mandala & the African Lakes Corporation

In 1878 a group of Scottish businessmen, who had been involved in setting up and supporting the Livingstonia mission expedition of 1875, founded the Livingstonia Central African Mission Company to develop the route along the Zambezi and Shire rivers, and introduce trade to the area. The company appointed two brothers called John and Frederick Moir as joint managers, and they came to the Shire Highlands in 1878 and established a base near the Church of Scotland mission at Blantyre. The company's headquarters and trade name became known as Mandala, the local name given to John Moir because of the spectacles he wore (the word means something like 'pools of water').

Mandala trading posts were established along the Shire River, in the highlands and along the lake shore. Even when the company changed its name to become the African Lakes Corporation in the early 20th century, the Mandala name was kept, and you can still see Mandala Group shops and garages all over the country today. ■

---

between Blantyre and Limbe, just off the Kamuzu Hwy. There's a good display of traditional weapons and artefacts, some donated by an American family whose ancestor had collected them during colonial times. There are also exhibits relating to European exploration and slavery. In the museum garden are some examples of indigenous architecture and some old colonial agricultural machinery, plus an old bus and fire engine, originally shipped out from Britain.

If you're the sporting type, **Blantyre Sports Club** offers daily membership for US$5. This allows you to enter the club, and use the bar or restaurant. To use the pool or gym, or to play squash or tennis, is another US$0.60. Nine holes of golf costs US$2. Equipment can be hired.

If you enjoy less structured exercise, a walk on **Michiru Mountain** is a good way to pass a day. See Around Blantyre, at the end of this section.

If you're of a less active inclination, a visit to the **Carlsberg Brewery** is quite interesting. The Blantyre brewery is the only Carlsberg establishment in Africa, and they arrange tours most afternoons for groups of four or more people. You must phone the public relations department in advance (☎ 670022, 670133) to make an appointment, but there's no charge for the tour. If you're alone, it's usually worth phoning to see if there's a group you can join. The tour ends with a free tasting session.

Places to Stay – bottom end

If you've come by public transport and are short of cash, there are several options in the area around the bus and train stations. By far the most popular is *Wayfarers Lodge* (formerly Doogles), a dedicated backpackers' place where camping is US$2 per person and a bed in the dorm costs US$4. There's a high fence, four security guards, a bar, and a good atmosphere. The staff are friendly and know a lot about travel in Malawi. The walls are covered in maps and information. A couple of local budget tour outfits run excursions from here too. Tea, coffee, snacks and meals

Mandala House, the oldest European building in Malawi and former headquarters of the African Lakes Corporation.

are available, and there are several cheap places to eat just outside the gate. It also provides a visa service if you're heading for Mozambique. This place has links with Wayfarers in Harare and can arrange door to door transport, using the long-distance bus.

Cheaper than Wayfarers, but nowhere near as good, is the *District Resthouse* near the train station, where old, very basic single/doubles are US$1/2 and new rooms cost US$2/3. The toilets are filthy, and security questionable. So-called VIP rooms are US$4. If you *really* want to save money, and are travelling to/from Harare on the Munorurama bus, there's a free *'guesthouse'* (a bare room with mats on the floor) for passengers at their depot next to the main bus station.

More expensive, but still good value, is the *Grace Bandawe Conference Centre* (☎ 634267). This is a small, friendly church hostel on Chileka Rd, about two km from the city centre, with clean ensuite singles/doubles for US$10/14. Breakfast is US$2, and other meals cost around US$3.50. At the nearby *CCAP Mission Resthouse* (behind Phoenix School) a bed in the dormitory costs US$5. This place is spartan, clean and quiet, with big lockers to keep your gear safe – although you need your own padlock.

Camping There is a camp site and caravan park at Motel Paradise, which is about four km from the centre of town on the road to the airport. It costs US$3 per person.

Nyambadwe Cottage (☎ 633561) off Chileka Rd, Nyambadwe, also has camping facilities for US$3 per person.

Places to Stay – middle & top-end

Most places in this range include breakfast unless otherwise stated.

Cheapest in this range is *Nyambadwe Cottage* (☎ 633561), in the quiet suburb of Nyambadwe, off Chileka Rd, with straightforward singles/doubles at US$17/22 (US$4 extra for ensuite). If they are full ask about the associated *Chichiri Cottage*, between Blantyre and Limbe, which is the same price.

Also quiet and good-value in this range is *Motel Paradise* (☎ 623338), about four km

from central Blantyre on the road to the airport, where clean ensuite rooms cost US$30/40. There's safe parking, and also a camp site and caravan park which costs US$3 per person. The nearby casino and nightclub may make things less tranquil at weekends.

In town, you could consider the *Hotel & Catering School* (☎ 621866) on Chilembwe Rd, where clean ensuite rooms are US$35/55 (although the doubles are small, and there are no twins). It's quiet, with safe parking, and the pleasant restaurant serves four-course meals for US$7, but you may need to book in advance.

Blantyre's best is the *Mt Soche Hotel* (☎ 620588), part of the South African-run Protea chain (Malawi central reservations Blantyre ☎ 620071), where international standard ensuite single/double rooms with air-con and TV cost US$150/195. Superior rooms are US$175/230. Facilities at the hotel include a pool, extensive gardens, health club and bar. There are also two restaurants: the very smart *Michiru*, where steaks, fish and chicken dishes are around US$12 and specials such as prawns are around US$17; or the less formal *Gypsy's* where main courses are around US$8. This place is favoured by business travellers, UN workers and visiting diplomats.

Some visitors have recommended the smaller *Ryall's Hotel* as being better value, with standard rooms priced at US$85/100 and superior rooms costing US$100/115. The plush *21 Restaurant* has steaks for US$10, other main meals for around US$7, curries for US$6 and specialities such as seafood for US$17. There's also a small coffee shop.

Places to Stay – Limbe

For most visitors, there's no real need to stay in Limbe, but if you do find yourself here, there are basic rooms with filthy facilities for US$2 at the *Council Resthouse* near the bus station.

If you're looking for better quality, the *Shire Highlands Hotel* (☎ 640055; fax 640063) is an old colonial-style place which had half a face-lift in the 1980s and now needs another. Rooms are fine though, with ensuite singles/doubles for US$78/91, including breakfast. There's a swimming pool, and a restaurant with snacks for around US$3, light meals for US$4 and main meals from US$6.

On the outskirts of town, heading towards Mulanje, is *Limbe Country Club*, where camping costs US$5 per person. This includes day membership of the club, so you can use the showers, bar and restaurant, or the pool, squash courts and golf course for a small additional fee.

Places to Eat – cheap

For very cheap eats, there are stalls around the bus station selling fried potatoes and fish for around US$0.50. If you're self-catering, the supermarkets are well stocked with all you need, including fresh bread. Sasha's Bakery on Glyn Jones Rd is also good. Fruit and vegetables are sold by traders outside the supermarkets.

For cheap local food, try the *Downtown Café*, near the local bus station, or the *Kuyesa Restaurant* next door (open to 7.30 pm).

A good cheap place for takeaway food is *Lunch Box* in Henderson St (open 7.30 am to 2 pm only) which offers curry and rice or chicken and chips for US$1.50, and burgers for US$1. Other takeaway outlets include *Chick Wings* (open evenings) on Glyn Jones Rd, where chicken and chips cost US$3, curries cost US$2 and burgers (including vegetarian) are around US$2.50. *Kips*, on Hanover Ave, has food at prices a bit lower and also serves ice cream.

For straightforward African dishes and fry-ups try the *Chimovemwe Restaurant*, under the Central Bookshop. Prices for most meals are around US$1 to US$2, and beers are also served. In the evening it's more like a bar with food than a restaurant with beer. The *Modern Fish & Chips* on Glyn Jones Rd has similar food, but a quieter atmosphere.

Popular for a splurge is *Nico's Gelateria*, where genuine Italian ice creams and cappuccinos are US$2, and pizzas are around US$3. Another place for takeaway pizza (US$1 per slice) and ice cream (US$1 a cone) is *Dafabio Too* opposite the PTC. Or try the *Creme Centre*, which also serves waffles, kebabs and burgers, opposite the Hotel & Catering School.

Places to Eat – more expensive

Two perennial favourites are the Greek-owned *Melting Pot* (☎ 623697) on Haile Selassie Rd and *Maxim's* (☎ 620856) on St Andrew's Rd, both open lunchtimes and evenings from 6 to 10 pm. Steaks start at US$8, chicken dishes at US$7, fish or moussaka at US$6 and curry specials at around US$3.50. The decor is decidedly 60s, and at both places the atmosphere is great when they're full, but deadly when they're not.

Up from here in style and taste is the Italian-flavoured *L'Hostaria* (☎ 625052, 636025), near Maxim's, where you can enjoy a rustic terrace setting and large pizzas and pastas from US$4 to US$6, with small dishes and starters for around US$2 to US$3.

The best restaurants in Blantyre are the *21 Restaurant* at Ryall's (the hotel was originally opened in 1921) and the *Michiru* at the Mt Soche Hotel. For more details, see Places to Stay, earlier. Also good quality and popular is *Greens Restaurant* (☎ 636375) in the suburb of Sunnyside, off the road towards Chikwawa, serving à la carte European food, with main courses from US$9.

The *Hong Kong Restaurant* (☎ 620859), near the Mt Soche Hotel, has all the usual Chinese dishes: you can eat a small selection for between US$5 and US$7, or splash out and go up to US$10 or US$15. The *Tai Pan Restaurant* (☎ 622260), on the corner of Victoria Ave and Independence Drive, has similar rates. Both places are open for lunch and dinner to 10 pm. Both also serve takeaways, for the same prices less 30%, as no tax is payable.

The *Copper Bowl* at Blantyre Sports Club (☎ 621173), at the bottom of Hanover Ave, has a very good menu, and is very popular. Meals start at around US$10, plus US$5 temporary membership fee. There's also a dress code: no jeans or shorts, and gents must wear a tie on Sunday.

In Limbe, the *Royal Taj* (Indian) at the

MALAWI

southern end of Churchill Rd, and the *Nali* (Portuguese/Mozambican) near the Shire Highlands Hotel have both been recommended, with most meals in the region of US$8 to US$10.

Entertainment

Bars in central Blantyre include Pat's (in a yard set back from the junction of Victoria Ave and Independence Drive), which is a serious drinking den during the day and gets wild late at night, especially when there's a disco, and Nix Bar on Hanover Ave (which also serves snacks). The Chimovemwe Restaurant, under the Central Bookshop, is more like a bar at night, with music and gaming machines.

For smarter surroundings the Sportsman's Bar at the Mt Soche Hotel is favoured by Malawian businessmen. The downstairs bar at Ryall's Hotel is also popular. For more tranquil surroundings, try the terrace bar in the garden of the Mt Soche, where snacks are also available for around US$3.

The bar at the Blantyre Sports Club is usually lively, the centre of expatriate life, and also frequented by well-to-do Malawians. You need to pay a temporary membership fee of US$5 before you can drink here, unless you're already a member of a club with reciprocal rights. Nearby is Legends, a smart but friendly place, a cross between an English pub and a 60s American bar, with draft beer, snacks, and live music some evenings.

For music, Blantyre has livened up considerably in the last few years. Places with bands or discos (usually weekends, but sometimes midweek) include the Taj Mahal Night Club, above Nix Bar, off Hanover Ave, and La Casa (formerly the Flamingo Club), off Chileka Rd, which has jazz on Sundays. Bands also play at the Mt Soche and Shire Highlands hotels. Entrance is about US$3. All these places attract a mix of clients, and the favourite place to be seems to rotate between them on about six-monthly intervals. To find out what's going on is easy: most events are publicised on flyers stuck to walls and lampposts all over town.

Blantyre's main sports venue is Kamuzu Stadium between the city centre and Limbe. This is also Malawi's national stadium: international football and other events are held here.

Getting There & Away

Bus For getting to/from Blantyre, there are Coachline services three times per day between Lilongwe and Blantyre (US$17), and once per day between Lilongwe and Mzuzu (US$19) via Kasungu (US$8). The Mzuzu service ties in with one of the Blantyre buses, so it's possible to go all the way between Blantyre and Mzuzu in a day if you need to. The Coachline luxury service goes to/from the Mt Soche Hotel (the booking office is also here). A small outfit called Nyika Shuttle (☎ 622950) is undercutting Coachline, with fares of US$10 on the Blantyre to Lilongwe run.

Blantyre has two bus stations – the main one for long-distance Express and InterCity buses is on Chileka Rd, just outside the centre near the train station and Wayfarers Lodge; most local transport goes from a smaller station in the centre of town, near the junction of Browns and Kaoshiung Rds. Things are not so clear-cut on the ground though, as some buses seem to use both, so if in doubt ask if your bus goes to/from 'town' or Chileka Rd.

Long-distance express bus fares to/from Blantyre are as follows: Lilongwe US$7 (US$8 via Zomba) Zomba US$1.50; Mulanje US$2 (for the Mozambique border an extra US$0.60); Mwanza US$2.50; Nkhata Bay US$15; and Karonga US$22.

There are also two services to/from Harare (Stagecoach and Munorurama); for details see the Getting There & Away chapter.

Train There's a daily train on weekdays between Blantyre and Balaka (where you can change for the service to Nayuchi, on the Mozambique border – see the Getting There & Away chapter). It departs Blantyre at 5 am, and gets to Balaka officially at 9.30 am, but usually arrives some time between 10 am and noon. Going the other way it departs late morning or early afternoon and arrives in Blantyre about four to seven hours later. The fare is US$2, or US$4 if you go all the way between Blantyre and Nayuchi. Your other train option is from Limbe to Nsanje in the far south; there are two trains per week and the fare is US$3.

Getting Around

The Airport There used to be an Air Malawi bus between the Mt Soche Hotel and Blantyre's Chileka airport, but it was not running when we passed through due to 'too many passengers'. Ask around, in case something starts up again. Between the city and the airport by taxi is US$10 (although rates are negotiable, especially when going *from* the city). If your budget doesn't run to taxis, frequent local buses between Blantyre centre and Chileka township pass the airport gate. The fare is US$0.35.

Bus Blantyre is a compact city, so it's unlikely you'll need to use public transport to get around. If you need to reach Limbe, regular Cityline buses run from the town bus station, along Glyn Jones Rd and Kamuzu Hwy to Limbe bus station. The one-way fare is US$0.30.

Taxi You can find taxis at the Mt Soche Hotel or at the bus stations. A taxi across town is US$1 to US$2. From Blantyre to Limbe is between US$5 and US$10.

AROUND BLANTYRE

Blantyre is surrounded by three large hills (officially labelled mountains) called Mt Soche, Mt Ndirande and Michiru Mountain. Once a year the Mountain Club of Malawi links all the summits in a 'Three Peaks of Blantyre' walk circuit, but you can to the top at any other time of the year (weather permitting). The slopes of all three mountains have been declared forest reserves. Further to the north-east, off the road to Zomba is Chiradzulu Mountain; the slopes of this peak are also a forest reserve.

Mt Ndirande & Mt Soche

Mt Ndirande lies north-east of Blantyre, in Ndirande Forest Reserve. For casual visitors, the road to the mountain goes through a township where outsiders may not be welcome, and some walkers have been attacked on the mountain, so you should only go here with a switched-on local (preferably several). Ndirande means 'sleeping man',

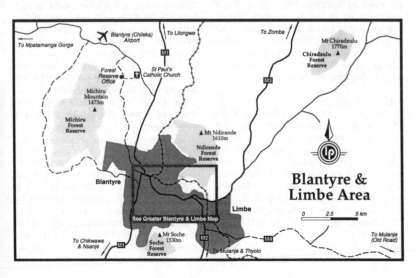

MALAWI

Tea Growing in Malawi

In southern Malawi, on the rolling hills of the Shire Highlands, between Blantyre, Limbe, Thyolo and Mulanje, the climatic conditions are ideal for growing tea, and the area is covered with plantations and estates. The first tea bushes were imported from India during the early days of the Nyasaland colony, and tea production quickly became a major industry. Growing tea is a very labour-intensive form of agriculture and only viable in countries where wages for manual workers are low. Along with tobacco and sugar, tea is a major export crop, earning money for Malawi and providing many thousands of people with jobs.

When travelling on the main road between Limbe and Mulanje, through Thyolo, you'll see the seemingly endless fields of tea, with vivid green bushes in neat lines covering the hillsides. The tea-pickers (men and women) work their way slowly down the lines, picking just a few leaves and a bud from the top of each bush and throwing them into a large basket they carry on their backs. At the end of each shift, the baskets of fresh tea leaves are taken to a collection area, where they are weighed and each worker's wages calculated. The leaves are then transported to a tea factory, where they are trimmed and dried before being packed in bags and boxes ready for export. A small proportion of low quality tea stays within the country to be sold locally.

If you have a genuine interest in tea production it may be possible to arrange a tour of an estate and factory. There is no established set-up; you simply phone an estate and ask a senior manager if it's possible to visit. You'll probably also need your own vehicle, or have to take a taxi, as most estate offices are off the main road and difficult to reach by public transport. The best place to start with is Satemwa Estate (☎ 472233), near the small town of Thyolo (pronounced 'Cho-low') on the main road between Limbe and Mulanje. The estate has *Chawani Bungalow*, which can be hired for US$50 per night. It sleeps up to eight in four double bedrooms and the price includes the services of a caretaker/cook. From the bungalow you can walk through the tea estates or go through the evergreen forest remnants on nearby Thyolo Mountain, which is a popular bird-watching spot.

Other tea estates which might allow visits include British African Estates (☎ 472266) and Namingomba Estates (☎ 472300). The tourist office in Blantyre may be able to help with more suggestions. ■

due to the shape of the mountain when seen from Blantyre.

Mt Soche is in Soche Forest Reserve, to the south of Blantyre. The path up to the summit starts at Soche Secondary School, where you can find local schoolboys to act as guides for the one-hour walk to the top. (When I asked one lad where the name 'Soche' came from, he said it was named after the big hotel in town.)

Michiru Mountain

By far the best of Blantyre's three peaks for hiking is Michiru, north-west of the city. The peak lies at the centre of Michiru Forest Reserve, a well-managed conservation area administered by the departments of Forestry and National Parks & Wildlife, with assistance from the Wildlife Society of Malawi. There are several marked walking trails starting from the Forest Reserve Office and Education Centre on the east side of the mountain. You can buy a map of the area here, which also contains a lot of useful information on the trees and wildlife. Trails

range from a short loop on the lower slopes, to an all-day hike to the summit of Michiru Peak (1470m). Both trails give excellent views of Blantyre and the surrounding area. Some of the trails have not been cut yet, although they are shown on the map, so check with the office staff about what actually exists on the ground. A scout can be hired if you'd prefer a guide. The reserve contains monkey, bushbuck, klipspringer and even leopard, but you're unlikely to see much. The variety of birds is much more rewarding – over 400 species have been recorded here.

Getting There & Away The forest reserve office is eight km out of Blantyre. There's no public transport from Blantyre to the Forest Reserve Office, so you'll have to walk or take a taxi, unless you have your own car. From near Ryall's Hotel, take Kabula Hill Rd northward, going first left onto Michiru Rd. This is tarred, passing through a select suburb and then through a township area. At the end of the tar (about three km from Blantyre) a dirt road leads through the lightly forested area at the foot of the mountain. There are several turnings to the left, but ignore all these until you reach one signposted 'car park and nature trails'. This takes you to the Forest Reserve Office and the start of the trails.

If you don't want to get a taxi the whole way, you could take it to the end of the end of the tar road or down the dirt road as far as the driver is prepared to go. From the end of the tar, the walk through the forest to the office is interesting in itself. You may be able to get a lift back from other visitors.

Another option is to approach Michiru from the main road between Blantyre and Chileka Airport. Take any bus or minibus (US$0.30) heading towards the airport and get out at St Paul's Catholic Church, about two km after the roundabout. From here a small track leads south-west towards the mountain. The office can be seen among the trees, but it takes about 1½ hours to walk here. The track becomes a path, and there are many other paths in the area, so the route can be confusing. There are always people around who will point in the right direction.

MALAWI

Southern Malawi

The Southern Province of Malawi, with Blantyre roughly at its centre, lies between the southern end of Lake Malawi and the far southern tip of the country. This chapter covers all places in this area, except the lake shore (covered in the Lake Shore chapter). Main features of this area include Zomba town and Zomba Plateau, plus Malawi's flagship, Liwonde National Park. It also includes the rarely visited Lower Shire area, which includes Lengwe National Park and Majete Game Reserve. Southern Malawi is also home to the highland wilderness of Mt Mulanje. Places are described in a roughly north to south direction.

BALAKA

This small town on the main road between Lilongwe and Zomba is unremarkable (although the splendid modern basilica church is worth a look), but you may find yourself here if you get the train to/from Blantyre, or travel to/from Mozambique by rail (via Nayuchi and Liwonde). For full details see the Getting Around and Getting There & Away chapters. For a place to stay, try the *Kudya Motel* near the bus and train stations.

LIWONDE

You may come to Liwonde town on the main road between Lilongwe and Zomba if you're heading for Liwonde National Park or for Mozambique by rail, as the train to the border passes through here. The town is divided by the Shire River, flowing south from Lake Malombe, crossed by the main road on a barrage. The train station is on the east side of the river, but most places to stay are on the west side. Most buses also stop on the west side, and there are frequent connections to Blantyre (via Zomba), Mangochi and Lilongwe.

Places to Stay

Cheap options include the optimistically named *Liwonde Holiday Resort*, just off the main road, where small basic rooms cost US$2 per person and meals cost about US$1. The nicer *Liwonde Motel*, on the main road itself, has clean ensuite rooms with hot showers for US$6/7 and meals from US$2 to US$3.

Better than these, but at a price, is *Kudya Discovery Lodge* (☎ 532333), 1.5 km off the main road, where good rooms with verandas overlooking gardens and the hippo-filled river cost from US$30/40, plus US$3 for air-con. Breakfast and light meals are around US$5, and other meals around US$8. Camping costs US$2.50. There's a bar overlooking the river, a swimming pool and boat rides available. Hippos graze on the lawn at night so be careful on your way back from the bar.

If you've got wheels, another option is the pleasant *Mpaweni Motel*, three km from town on the road to Mangochi. Clean, self-contained rondavels cost US$10, for one to three people, which includes breakfast for one person. Extra breakfasts are US$1.20. Smaller rondavels are US$7, and single/double rooms cost US$3/5. There's safe parking, a nice garden, restaurant and bar.

LIWONDE NATIONAL PARK

Liwonde National Park is the best in Malawi; well-managed with a relatively good stock of game and beautiful scenery. It lies to the south of Lake Malawi, and includes part of Lake Malombe, the Shire River and the eastern Upper Shire Plain.

Literally thousands of hippo and crocodile live in the river, and there are several hundred elephant in the park, plus plenty of antelope (including impala, bushbuck and kudu). There are also two reintroduced rhino, called Justerini and Brooks – because they're sponsored by J&B Whisky. Most game is seen in the northern half of the park; the second half of the dry season is optimum for viewing because the animals congregate along the river. The combination of riverine, mopane and grassland habitats also means birdlife is very varied.

MALAWI

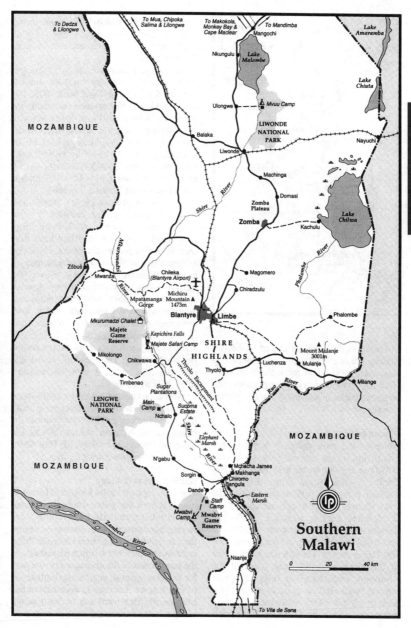

Southern
Malawi

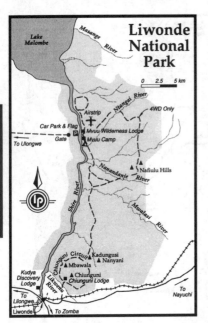

Tracks in the park are closed in the wet season, although the main lodge and camp stay open as you can reach them by boat. National park entrance fees are payable – see National Parks in the Facts for the Visitor chapter for details.

Places to Stay

Close to the park entrance is *Chiunguni Lodge,* run by the national park; the cost is US$8 per bed. By far the best place is Mvuu Camp, a privately run camp, deep in the northern part of the park on the banks of the river. There's a range of options: chalets and comfortable walk-in tents for US$34 per person; small dome tents for US$20 per person; or you can camp in your own tent for US$10 per person. The ablution block is one of the cleanest we've seen north of the Limpopo, and there's a fully equipped kitchen (with staff on hand to help) if you want to self-cater. Or you can eat at the camp restaurant where breakfast is US$6, full

breakfast US$9, lunch US$12 and dinner US$14. This is an open-plan thatched affair which overlooks the river, and also has a bar (beers US$1).

To keep you occupied, the camp arranges game-viewing trips by boat or vehicle (US$18 for 2½ hours) and walks (US$10). The walks are highly recommended; the guides know their birds, and there's a chance of spotting mammals at close quarters too. A complete full-board package in a chalet (including all meals, game drives, walks and boat rides) costs US$85. The same deal if you stay in a dome tent is US$70. Children between two and 12 get half price.

For more discerning clients, there's also *Mvuu Wilderness Lodge,* completely separate from the camp, with four large fully-ensuite double tents. They have their own balconies overlooking a water hole that attracts game and birds. With a maximum of only eight guests, this place is relaxed and intimate, with knowledgeable and attentive staff, and excellent food. New additions include a swimming pool and a luxury honeymoon suite, complete with exclusive open-air bathroom! This is luxury and exclusivity at a price though: US$200 per person per night, which includes full board and activities (day or night game drives, boat rides, bird walks etc).

Most travel agents in Malawi, and several in South Africa and overseas, organise bookings for Mvuu Lodge. Otherwise, contact the operators direct: Central African Wilderness Safaris in Lilongwe (see Travel & Tour Agencies in the Lilongwe chapter for details).

Getting There & Away

The main park gate is six km east of Liwonde town. There's no public transport beyond here into the park itself, but hitching is not impossible, especially at weekends. From the gate to Mvuu Wilderness Lodge & Camp is 28 km by park track (often impassable in the rainy season). Another way into the park for vehicles (open all year) is via the dirt road from Ulongwe (between Liwonde town and Mangochi). This leads for 14 km through villages to the gate on the western boundary, two km from the river. There's a car park near the river bank (with a watchman) to leave your car; you hoist a flag, and a boat from Mvuu comes to pick you up. This service is free if you're staying at the camp or lodge. The disadvantage, of course, is that you won't have your car, but if you use this route because it's the rainy season you wouldn't be able to drive far anyway.

An alternative for those without wheels is the boat transfer service up the Shire River offered by Waterline (☎ /fax 532552), based near Kudya Discovery Lodge (see Liwonde Places to Stay, earlier). If you've got the time and money this is by far the best way to approach, spotting elephant, hippo, crocodile and a host of water birds on the way. They will drop you at Mvuu Lodge, and wait, returning within 24 hours, for around US$42 per person for groups over two. If you want to stay a few days, a drop-off and later pick-up service costs around US$66 per person. You can either pre-arrange a lift out, or radio them when you're ready to leave. Even if you don't want to stay at Mvuu, you can just go for a three hour wildlife-spotting boat trip, which costs US$50 for one person, and around US$25 each for groups of two or more.

ZOMBA

Zomba is a large town sitting at the foot of the Zomba Plateau, a sheer-sided mountain which dominates the surrounding area. Zomba was the capital of Malawi from the late 19th century until the mid-1970s (although parliament stayed here when the ministries moved to Lilongwe) and there are many old colonial buildings which, although faded, are still quite interesting. These include the first colonial governor's residence, now a hotel (see Places to Stay). Nearby are the former residency gardens, now a botanic garden open to the public. On the eastern outskirts of town, the University of Malawi has its main campus.

Other things to see include the very lively market (one of the largest in Malawi), the King's African Rifles war memorial (on the road towards Blantyre) and the CCAP Mission School and Clock Tower (built in 1926). There's also the Zomba Gymkhana Club, another colonial relic, where you can get meals and drinks in pleasant surroundings (see below). Unfortunately, you can't play polo any more – the pitch has been converted for football – but there is a golf course. Golf clubs and caddies can be hired for less than US$1 each.

If you have a particular interest in fly fishing you may like to visit the fly factory on the main road on the east side of town. Combined with these attractions, the leafy 'upper' suburbs on the foothills of the mountain make Zomba well worth a day's strolling around.

For some more serious walking, the Zomba Plateau is another major attraction. The mountain is also popular for bird-watching or fishing, or simply picnicking at one of the many splendid viewpoints. For details, see the Zomba Plateau section, below.

Places to Stay & Eat

The *Council Resthouse* opposite the bus station is the cheapest place in town; the rooms are clean but the toilet block is disgusting. Singles/doubles cost US$2/3 (or US$5 for ensuite) and there may be some dorm beds for US$0.50. There's a noisy bar and a good restaurant, with several other cheap eating-houses nearby. The manager will store gear if you want to travel light up to the plateau.

For something better try the nearby *Ndindeye Motel*, down a dirt road past the brightly painted Zomba Tavern. Large clean rooms cost US$3/6 or US$7/13 for rooms with ensuite, including breakfast. The restaurant serves meals from US$2.

Up the hill and price scale from here is the *Government Hostel*, in actuality a fairly smart hotel used by ministers when parliament is in session and open to the public the rest of the time. It's in the house of the first colonial governor, Sir Harry Johnston, complete with large semi-circular veranda, twin towers and balconies. Unfortunately the furniture is all modern, and does not fit in with the style and atmosphere of the building itself. Ensuite rooms cost US$50/60,

MALAWI

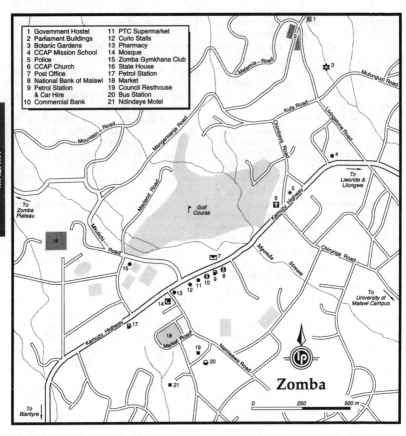

1 Government Hostel	11 PTC Supermarket
2 Parliament Buildings	12 Curio Stalls
3 Botanic Gardens	13 Pharmacy
4 CCAP Mission School	14 Mosque
5 Police	15 Zomba Gymkhana Club
6 CCAP Church	16 State House
7 Post Office	17 Petrol Station
8 National Bank of Malawi	18 Market
9 Petrol Station	19 Council Resthouse
& Car Hire	20 Bus Station
10 Commercial Bank	21 Ndindeye Motel

Zomba

including breakfast and satellite TV. Main dishes in the restaurant are around US$3 to US$5, and the set menu is US$10.

At the old colonial *Zomba Gymkhana Club*, on the road towards the plateau, temporary membership is US$3 which allows you to have a meal or a drink inside. Camping is also allowed here for US$3, which includes membership, but as there's no fence, security might be questionable.

Getting There & Away

Zomba is on one of the main routes between Lilongwe and Blantyre, and there are frequent buses and minibuses throughout the day. To/from Blantyre is US$1.50; to/from Lilongwe is US$7; to/from Monkey Bay is US$4; and to/from Liwonde US$1. There's no transport up to the plateau, so you'll have to take a taxi the eight km for US$10.

ZOMBA PLATEAU

The Zomba Plateau looms over the town of Zomba with sheer escarpments rising over a thousand metres above the plain. This plateau is not wilderness, like Malawi's other highland areas Mt Mulanje and the Nyika Plateau; there's a road to the top, and some

Southern Zomba Plateau

areas have been planted with pines. There's also a hotel, a camp site, some other places to stay and several picnic places to cater for visitors (mainly local residents who come up at the weekend), plus a permanent population of forestry workers. Several large houses, set in private grounds, have also been built along the southern edge of the plateau.

The top of the Zomba Plateau is covered by a network of drivable tracks and walking paths that wind through pine forest or patches of indigenous woodland. There are several narrow ridges along the edge of the

escarpment, with viewpoints offering dramatic panoramas over the plains below. The plateau also has streams, waterfalls and a couple of small lakes, where fishing is allowed. Some people prefer to drive around, but Zomba is also a good place for hiking or strolling (depending on your inclination), and the cool air makes a welcome change from the heat of the lowland areas.

Things to See & Do

A few km from the Ku Chawe Inn and the Forest Camp Site is **Mandala Falls**, a pleasant waterfall, and **Mlunguzi Dam**, where fishing is allowed. (There are plans to enlarge the dam, which will push the body of water back upstream almost to the foot of Mandala Falls.) Also near the camp site is a Trout Farm, and north of here is **Williams Falls**, another fairly impressive cascade.

A popular place to visit is **Chingwe's Hole**, on the western side of the plateau, which is supposedly bottomless and the basis of various local legends, although now largely overgrown and not especially impressive. Nearby, however, is a splendid viewpoint, looking westward over the Shire Valley.

For even more impressive views, head for the eastern side of the plateau, where **Queen's View** (named after Queen Elizabeth, wife of King George VI, who visited Zomba in 1957) and **Emperor's View** (after Emperor Haile Selassie of Ethiopia, here in 1964) overlook Zomba town and out towards Mulanje.

All these places can be reached by car or by foot. For more details on hiking options see Hiking on the Zomba Plateau, later in this chapter.

Places to Stay & Eat

Options in Zomba town are covered earlier in this chapter. On the plateau, the *Ku Chawe Inn* (☎ 522342, fax 522509) is a top-quality hotel built right on the edge of the escarpment with excellent views over the surrounding plains. The old hotel unfortunately burnt down a few years ago, and the new place opened in 1996. Very smart singles/doubles cost US$104/171. There's a good restaurant and bar, where they keep a fire going on cold nights, and the terraced gardens are particularly pleasant. This hotel is part of the Protea group, so you can book a room through their central reservations if required (Blantyre ☎ 620071).

Nearby is the fully equipped *CCAP Cottage*, also with excellent views. The whole cottage sleeps eight people in three bedrooms, and can be hired by Christian churchgoers for US$30 per night for the whole cottage. (For reservations and information the CCAP office (☎ 522942) is in Zomba town, behind the CCAP school.) About two km from here, at *Plateau Stables* (☎ 522143), the home of Lieutenant Colonel Brian Burgess, you can rent a comfortable, fully equipped and serviced cottage with two double bedrooms, for US$120 per night.

If you're camping, near the Ku Chawe is the aptly named *Forest Camp Site*, among large pine trees. It costs US$1 per person; there are toilets and wood-fired hot showers. It's one of those places which is beautiful in sunlight and a bit miserable in mist. You've got a 50:50 chance. There's also the remote *Chitinji Camp Site* on the western side of the plateau near Malumbe Peak, which is very basic (one long-drop loo, no showers, and water from the stream) and to all intents and purposes abandoned.

The final option is the *Kachere Forest Resthouse*, originally the home of a colonial officer serving on board the HMS *Guendolin* (see Mangochi in the Lake Shore chapter for more information). It's four km off the Up Road (the junction is about half-way up the Up Road), and simple but adequate accommodation costs US$3 per person per night. A cook is on hand in the kitchen but you must bring all your food. You can reserve at the Department of Forestry office in Lilongwe (☎ 781000), or by phoning the Zomba Upper Slopes forest officer (☎ 522638). The office is also just off the Up Road, a few hundred metres past Wico Sawmills.

You can get drinks, snacks and meals at the smart *Ku Chawe Inn*, even if you're not a guest. The buffet breakfast is particularly recommended. If you're self-catering at one of the other places listed here, you should bring most of what you need from Zomba town, as there's no shop or market on the plateau. Local children sell fruit, vegetables, peanuts and (sometimes) local bread on the roadside between the hotel and the camp site.

Getting There & Away

If you're driving, from Zomba town a tarred road leads through the outskirts, past State House and then steeply up the escarpment to the top of the plateau (about eight km). After the last junction, the road is one-way only, and called the Up Road. The Down Road descends further to the east. There's no public transport up to the plateau, so you'll have to take a taxi (the fare from Zomba town is about US$10) or you can try hitching (every morning a van brings hotel workers up). Another option is to get a taxi part of the way, say to the start of the Up Road, then simply walk. There are excellent views, often missed by drivers who have to concentrate on the narrow turns! Another option is to hire a car for the day; the petrol station on the main road near the banks has a small fleet, and there's also an Avis representative on the street down to the market, opposite the mosque.

The Potato Path If you decide to walk all the way, you can take a route called the Potato Path, which goes straight up and over the plateau linking Zomba town and the Domasi Valley. The valley has fertile soil and a reliable water supply ideal for growing vegetables (including potatoes). The local people carry the vegetables to the big market in Zomba town along this path, making it well worn and easy to follow.

The start of the path is signposted at a sharp left-hand bend on the Up Road about two km from Zomba town. The path climbs steeply, through woodland, crossing a forestry track and the Down Road, to reach the top of the plateau near the hotel. Allow two to three hours for the ascent.

Hiking on the Zomba Plateau

Zomba is a forest reserve, and composed of two main areas, divided by the Domasi Valley. The northern section has been set aside as a wilderness area. There are no tracks or paths, and visitors are not encouraged to walk here. On the southern section of the plateau, there's a maze of paths and tracks, and you can go where you like. For help with orientation, there's even a model of the plateau in a hut by the Ku Chawe Inn. Some visitors use the tracks to drive around the plateau, but hikers are unlikely to see more than a few cars, especially on weekdays.

Guidebooks & Maps If you want more detail than that provided here, a small pamphlet called *Zomba Mountain, A Walkers' Guide* may be available for sale in the reception of the Ku Chawe Inn (see Places to Stay above). This was written in 1975, and much has changed since then, but it contains many route descriptions, as well as some useful background information. For complete information, the Zomba Plateau is covered in Lonely Planet's *Trekking in East Africa*.

For detailed mapping, the Zomba Plateau is covered by the government survey 1:50,000 sheet 1535/A4 which shows most paths and tracks on the plateau, although some new tracks have been constructed since the map was published. Much more useful is *A Guide to Zomba Plateau*, a single sheet map with information on the back, including several suggested hiking routes, produced by the Wildlife Society in 1990. It's available in Blantyre and at the Ku Chawe Inn, for around US$1.50.

Hiking Routes With a map and some initiative there are many options for hiking on the Zomba Plateau. An interesting destination, if you're staying at the Ku Chawe Inn or the Forest Camp Site is the small but picturesque Williams Falls (about an hour's walk away). From here you could follow forest tracks and the Potato Path to Ngondola Village (about three hours from the camp site) on the edge of the Domasi Valley, where you get a good view of the northern half of the Zomba Plateau. The rolling open grassland of the north contrasts sharply with the pine forests of the south, showing how the whole plateau would have appeared before the plantations were established. From here you could return to the hotel or camp site on the track which crosses the Mlunguzi River, passing north and west of Chagwa Peak (a path goes up to the summit if you want to make a diversion).

If you're feeling energetic, you could consider a complete circuit of the plateau, which includes many of Zomba's highlights including the summit of Malumbe Peak (2085m), Chingwe's Hole, Queen's and Emperor's View and the Mlunguzi Dam. The whole

MALAWI

circuit takes five to six hours of walking. From near the hotel, go west and follow the tarred road up to Skyline View (a viewpoint and site of the cableway which used to link the plantations on the plateau with the sawmill outside Zomba town), then follow the ridge up towards Nawimbe Peak, where a firetower near the summit can be clearly seen. From the summit of Nawimbe Peak follow the firebreak along the ridge crest, which can be rocky and overgrown in places, to reach the radio masts on the summit of Malumbe Peak – the highest point on the plateau. From here tracks and paths lead to Chingwe's Hole (about three to four hours from the start), and the viewpoint described in

Things to See & Do, earlier. Then you head 'inland' following the Outer Circular Drive across the plateau to eventually reach Emperor's View (also described above). A track runs along the top of the escarpment (keeping the edge to the left) to reach Queen's View. From here you can follow more tracks and paths between Mlunguzi Peak and Chagwa Dam, down through woodland to reach Mlunguzi Dam, from where you can return to the hotel or camp site.

Around Zomba
Lake Chilwa The second largest of Malawi's lakes lies about 30 km east of Zomba. Forget

---

The Mail Runners
From the late 19th century, the colonial authorities administering Malawi (then called the British Central African Protectorate) developed a well-organised and far-reaching postal service. At the time, the main 'gateway' to the country (and to much of the surrounding region) was Chiromo on the Lower Shire River. Steamers from the Indian Ocean coast would come up the Zambezi River through Portuguese territory (later Mozambique) then up the Shire River and unload at Chiromo. The country's first post office was built here in 1891. From here mail would be distributed to Chikwawa, Blantyre, Zomba and other settlements throughout the protectorate, including various points on Lake Nyasa (where steamers were also used), and further beyond Karonga into southern Tanganyika (later Tanzania), Rhodesia (later Zambia and Zimbabwe) and the Belgian Congo (later Zaïre).

There were very few roads at this time, so the post was carried by mail runners – local Africans who would literally run between post offices with a bag of mail on their heads. These journeys obviously took many days to complete, so post offices doubled as resthouses for the runners. Other resthouses were built at roughly 30 km intervals along the main routes, and a system of relays was developed to reduce lost time. The route between Blantyre and Zomba (the two main settlements) was busy, and surprisingly fast. The runners would meet at Namaka resthouse – the halfway point, now the museum – exchange bags, then return the same way. Using this method, post took just a day. By 1896, the runners were going at night, so that letters posted in Blantyre in the evening were delivered next morning in Zomba.

In colonial times the mail runners, who carried bags of mail on their heads, were issued with rifles for protection from wild animals.

The first mail runners wore uniforms of white tunics and shorts, and ran in bare feet. It was soon realised that white does not stay white long when the wearer runs through the African bush for days at a time, so it was later changed to blue. At first the runners were allowed to carry spears as protection against wild animals. They were later issued with rifles. As early as 1894, the postmaster general, one Ernest Harrhy, wrote the following report: 'In February, two carriers carrying mail bags between Mpimbi and Zomba were confronted by several lions. Deeming discretion to be the better part of valour, they sought safety in the high branches of a friendly tree, and waited until their leonine majesties condescended to move on to pastures new.' A later report noted that 'cases have occurred where mail men have been driven to take refuge in a tree, and leave the bags at the foot to be smelled and pawed and discarded as inedible by disappointed beasts of prey...'

Despite these dangers, the mail runners continued pounding the tracks of Nyasaland until the mid-1930s, when bicycles were issued. Roads were also being improved by this time and the first postal van was introduced in 1942. ■

about beaches though, as this shallow lake is surrounded by reed beds, swamp and marsh – excellent bird-watching territory, and an interesting place to visit if you just want to get off the main track for a day or two.

By far the easiest way to get here is along the road from Zomba to the peaceful lakeside fishing village of Kachulu. There's a couple of basic local resthouses, but not much in the way of food, so you're probably better off bringing your own from Zomba. You can stroll along the shore, or local fishermen will be happy to take you out in a boat. Rates seem vague, as very few visitors come here and boat rental is a new concept; about US$5 for a morning or afternoon trip would be fair.

Namaka Postal Museum At a small settlement called Namaka, about 20 km south of Zomba on the main road towards Blantyre, is a slightly incongruous, but well-kept and fascinating Postal Museum. It is also called the Mtengatenga Museum, after the *tengatenga* (porters) who were the first mail runners in the country at the end of the 19th century – see the boxed text.

The museum is a converted resthouse, originally built for the runners on the route between Blantyre and Zomba. It contains various exhibits including samples of stamps and postmarks from the earliest days of the protectorate to the present time; pictures of early postmen and post offices; and a fine collection of post boxes. Entrance is free.

MULANJE

This small town is the centre of Malawi's tea-growing industry. You may stay overnight here if you're heading for Mozambique, but most travellers pass through on the way to Mt Mulanje, the vast massif which dominates the town and much of the surrounding area (see Mt Mulanje, following).

For a place to stay, two of the cheapest are the *Council Resthouse* and the *Zimbabwe Guesthouse*, both with doubles from US$2, or US$4 with cold shower. The Zimbabwe has a very lively bar. Just downhill from the bus station is the quieter *Mulanje Motel*, also with rooms for US$2. Next door is the

smarter *Mulanje View Motel*, with a better choice of rooms, from US$3.50 for single to US$8 for ensuite doubles, including breakfast. There is a bar and good-value food in the restaurant.

Camping is possible at *Mulanje Golf Club*, on the eastern outskirts of town. The cost is US$2.50, which includes day membership, so you can use the showers, bar and swimming pool, and enjoy the fabulous views of Mt Mulanje from the terrace.

About three km north of the market and bus station, back towards Blantyre, is the 'suburb' of Chitikali. This is where the road to Likabula (the base for trekking on Mt Mulanje) turns off, so you might leave the bus or overnight here. There's a couple of cheap local resthouses, none very appealing, but the *Chikuli*, opposite the petrol station, seems the best. The nearby *Fukafuka Nightclub & Restaurant* also has rooms but is very noisy.

Getting There & Away
Buses go to/from Blantyre's Chileka Rd bus station about six times per day; the fare is US$2. If you're heading for the Mozambique border, a minibus there from Mulanje town is US$0.60. For more details see the Getting There & Away chapter.

Mt Mulanje

Mt Mulanje (also called the Mulanje Massif or the Mulanje Plateau) rises steeply and suddenly from the undulating plain to the highlands, surrounded by near-vertical cliffs of bare rock, many over a thousand metres high. The cliffs are dissected by vegetated valleys, where rivers drop in spectacular waterfalls. It is often misty in this region and Mulanje's high peaks sometimes jut out above the cloud. Appropriately, one of its local names is 'The Island in the Sky'.

The stunning scenery, easy access, clear paths and a series of well-maintained huts make Mt Mulanje a fine hiking and trekking area. Although a few people come to the base

MALAWI

Mt Mulanje

0   5   10 km

To Mpasa | To Njumwa | Nazombe

Phalombe

Mchese Mountain
▲ Mchese Peak 765m

Phalombe River

Fort Lister Gap

Nambiya Estate

Nkhulambe

Tinyade Estate

Thuchila River

Likulezi Mission

Litakala Peak 2368m

Sombani Plateau

Chigaru Peak 2654m ▲

Chambe Peak 2557m

Chambe Forest Station

Thuchila Hut

Chinzama Hut

Namasile Peak 2687m ▲

Sombani Hut

▲ Matambale Peak 2643m

Chambe Basin

Nandalanda Peak 2590m ▲

Ruo Basin

Chambe Hut

Chisepo Junction

▲ Khuto Peak

Chinzama Peak 2663m

Chambe Plateau Path

Chapaluka Path

North Peak ▲ 2891m

Chisepo Shelter

Dzole Peak 2715m

Minunu Hut

Muloza River

Likabula Forest Station

Skyline

Lichenya Path

West Peak ▲ 2686m

Nakodzwe Peak 2964m ▲

Ruo River

Madzeka Basin

Nayawani North Peak 2284m ▲

Nayawani Shelf

CCAP Mission & Guesthouse

Chilemba Peak 2355m ▲

Sapitwa Peak 3001m ▲

Madzeka Hut

▲ Nayawani South Peak 2345m

Chilemba Col

Lichenya Basin

Likabula River

Hydroelectric Power Station

Waterfall

▲ Manene Peak 2640m

CCAP Cottage

Lichenya Hut (ruin)

South Peak ▲ 2637m

Lujeri River

Nadonetsa

Ndiza River (Little Ruo)

Airstrip (disused)

Chitikali (Likabula Junction)

Boma Path

Lichenya Plateau

Office No. 3 Lujeri Tea Estate

To Blantyre & Limbe

Mulanje

Lichenya River

Lujeri Tea Factory

Likabula River

M2

Mini Mini Estate

Muloza

To Mozambique

of the mountain for a day visit, most come to spend at least a few days on the upper plateau, walking between huts or heading for lofty peaks.

Mt Mulanje measures about 30 km west to east and 25 km north to south, with an area of at least 600 sq km. On its north-east corner is the outlier, Mchese Mountain (also spelt Michese), separated from the main massif by the Fort Lister Gap. Although sometimes called a plateau, implying that it's flat on top, Mulanje is composed of several separate broad river basins, all separated by a series of rocky peaks and ridges. The highest peak

on Mulanje is Sapitwa, at just over 3000m (9840 ft) above sea level, the highest point in Malawi and in all of Southern Africa north of Lesotho and the Drakensberg. There are several other peaks on the massif above 2500m, and you can reach most of the summits without technical climbing (although sections of steep scrambling are sometimes involved). If you prefer a less demanding trek, Mulanje's basins and valleys provide fine walking through undisturbed country, while the peaks themselves create a dramatic backdrop.

Mt Mulanje has been gazetted as a forest

reserve, and non-indigenous pine has been planted on some of the upper slopes. However, the artificial plantations cover only a small part of the massif and you can enjoy most of your trekking through untampered natural surroundings.

The Department of Forestry, the Ministry of Natural Resources, and the government of Malawi should be congratulated for maintaining the paths and huts on Mt Mulanje. By preserving this place of beauty and ecological importance in its natural state, its benefits can be enjoyed both by visitors and by the people of Malawi. An independent body called the Mulanje Mountain Conservation Trust may be established to assist in this task.

INFORMATION & REGULATIONS

Hiking and trekking on Mt Mulanje is controlled by the forest station (☎ 465218) at Likabula (also spelt Likhabula and Likhubula), about 15 km from Mulanje town, 10 km north of the main road. Likabula is at the foot of two of the main paths up the massif. Even if you're taking another route, you must go to the forest station to register and make reservations for the mountain huts.

No charge is made to enter the forest reserve, but you pay your hut or camping fees here. This is also the best place to arrange guides and porters, if you want them. The office is open 7 am to noon, 1 pm to 5 pm every day, including

weekends and most holidays. The tourist attendant at Likabula is a very friendly lady called Dorothy. She will make sure the porters you take are registered, and will answer any questions about huts and facilities on the mountain.

Camping is permitted only near huts, and nowhere else on the massif. Open fires, even by the huts, are not allowed. This is especially important during the latter part of the dry season, from August to October, when there is a serious fire risk. Also forbidden is the picking or collecting of plants and animals.

Guidebooks & Maps

The *Guide to Mulanje Massif*, by Frank Eastwood, has information on ascent routes and main peaks, but nothing on the routes between the huts. It also includes a large section on Mulanje's rock-climbing routes, and information on geology and wildlife. A chapter on long walks in Malawi is included in Lonely Planet's *Trekking in East Africa*, which covers several routes on Mt Mulanje as well as the Nyika and Zomba plateaux, and other areas. The Department of Forestry produces a information leaflet for visitors which contains a map of the Mulanje area.

If you need detailed maps, Mt Mulanje is covered by the government survey 1:50,000 sheet number 1535 D3 which shows most

Warnings
Mt Mulanje is a big mountain with notoriously unpredictable weather, and you should be prepared for bad conditions at any time of the year. Even during dry periods, it's not uncommon to get rain, cold winds and thick mists which can occur very suddenly. It is easy to get lost.

The worst period is between May and August when periods of low cloud and drizzle (called *chiperones*) can last for several days. Even on the main paths you can miss a junction, or mistake a firebreak for a path. At this time temperatures can drop below freezing, especially at night. Snow has been recorded here on more than one occasion. None of this is much of a problem as long as you've got some warm, waterproof gear. If you haven't, you risk suffering from severe exposure. It's not unknown for hikers to get lost and die up here. In conditions of poor visibility you should keep to the main paths, and take extra care.

If you're on Mulanje in the wet season, or after periods of heavy rain, beware of streams becoming suddenly swollen and impassable. Do not try to cross them. Wait until the flood subsides, sometimes after a few hours, or adjust your route to cross in safety further upstream.

The massif is criss-crossed with firebreaks, some of which are followed by paths, but as these can become overgrown you should be prepared for 'extra' or 'missing' firebreaks in the route descriptions. Some footpath junctions are signposted, but you shouldn't rely on this as signs may be destroyed by fire or simply go missing. ■

paths, and all the huts, except Minunu Hut (at approximate grid reference 826377). The 1:30,000 *Tourist Map of Mulanje* covers a similar area, overprinted with extra information for walkers.

Guides & Porters

It is not obligatory to use guides and porters, but porters make the trekking easier, especially for the first day's steep walk from Likabula Forest Station. Guides are not really necessary to show you the routes between huts (especially as most porters will act as guides anyway), but they may be necessary if you plan to go up some peaks.

As you arrive in Likabula you'll be besieged by hopeful locals looking for work. Some are forestry workers, others are 'schoolboys' (although because of the way the Malawian education system works, they can be up to 25 years old) working in holiday periods to raise money for school fees. You may also be approached by porters looking for work in Mulanje town or at Chitikali (Likabula Junction), but you should arrange porters only at Likabula.

The Likabula Forest Station keeps a list of registered porters, who are known to be reliable. Always check your porter is on the list. Some schoolboys are not on the list but are known by the Forestry staff. Most speak good English, and are generally honest and hard-working. They will stay with you while you're trekking, or go ahead with the bags and wait at the hut – whatever you prefer.

The Department of Forestry, with the agreement of the porters, has set a standard rate of US$4 per day per porter (not per hiker), payable in kwacha. The maximum weight carried is 18 kg. The daily rate is payable however long or short the day, or however hard or easy the walking. If your porter is also to act as a guide up the peaks, an extra fee may be payable. Before agreeing to anything though, check with the forestry office that your guide is familiar with the routes you want to do. To avoid misunderstandings, the total fee for the whole trip should be agreed before departure, and written down, then paid at the end of the trip.

From this money the porter will provide his own food while on trek, so some of it (say 25%) may be required in advance. Make sure your porter brings everything he needs, and tell him that no other food can be provided. Even if you do this you'll still feel guilty when you stop for lunch while the porters sit and watch you, so take a few extra packets of biscuits for them.

You may want to tip your porter/s if the service has been good. A rule of thumb is to pay something around an extra day's wage for every three to five days.

Supplies

There are no shops on the massif, and only a very small local store at Likabula. Mulanje town has a supermarket (near the Likabula junction), with enough to provide for a trek, and a market selling fruit and vegetables.

PLACES TO STAY
Below the Mountain

Details of places in Mulanje town are given in that section. At Likabula Forest Station, there's the very good *Forestry Resthouse*, spotlessly clean, with a kitchen, comfortable lounge and several twin bedrooms. The charge is US$3 per person per night, which includes the services of a cook. You can camp in the grounds of the forest station for US$0.35 per tent, or outside the resthouse for US$1.25, including use of the kitchen facilities.

The *Likabula CCAP Mission Guest House*, next to the forest station, has self-contained chalets for US$2.25 per person (or US$5 for the whole chalet – sleeps four), or you can sleep in the dormitory for US$1.50. Camping is US$0.75 per tent. Meals are available. There are usually school or church groups staying at the mission.

We've heard rumours that a new luxury tented camp may be built in the Likabula area, so if this is your style ask around for details when you arrive.

On the Mountain

On Mt Mulanje are six *forestry huts*. (There used to be seven, but Lichenya Hut burnt down in 1995, and there are no immediate plans to rebuild.) Each hut is equipped with benches, tables, open fires and plenty of wood. Some huts have sleeping platforms (no mattresses); in others you just sleep on the floor. You provide your own food, cooking gear, candles, sleeping bag and stove (although you can cook on the fire). Each hut has a caretaker who chops wood, lights fires and brings water, for which a small tip should be paid. The huts are (from west to east): Chambe (sleeps 14 people); Thuchila (pronounced 'Chuchila') (sleeps 16); Minunu (also spelt Mununu or Mnunu; sleeps four); Chinzama (sleeps 12); Madzeka (sleeps 12); and Sombani (sleeps eight).

Reservations and payments for huts can be made at Likabula Forest Station on arrival. (It's also possible to reserve in advance by writing to the Forest Officer, PO Box 50, Mulanje.) The huts cost US$1 per person per night – an absolute bargain, although this may rise in the future. Some huts may be full at weekends and during holidays, but you can usually adjust your route and go to another. As the reservation system doesn't require a deposit, some local residents book huts and then don't turn up. It's worth checking to see if this has happened.

The only other place to stay on the massif is the *CCAP Cottage*, on the Lichenya Plateau, run by Likabula CCAP Mission. This hut is quite near the site of the Lichenya forestry hut which burnt down, which means there is still a place to stay in this part of the massif. The hut is similar to the forestry huts, but there are utensils in the kitchen, and mattresses and blankets in the bedrooms. For this extra luxury you pay US$1.25 per night. You can reserve and pay for the cottage at the mission.

There is a small mud and thatch shelter at Chisepo, at the start of the route up Sapitwa Peak, but this is normally only used in emergencies, or for hardy walkers aiming to bag the summit by sunrise.

Camping is permitted outside the huts (US$0.60 per person), but not allowed anywhere else on the massif. You can use the hut for cooking and eating in.

GETTING THERE & AWAY

Buses between Blantyre and Mulanje town are detailed under Mulanje Getting There & Away, earlier in this chapter. The dirt road to Likabula turns off the main tarred Blantyre-Mulanje road about two km before (west of) the centre of the town, signposted to Likabula Pool and Phalombe. There is one bus a day from Blantyre to Phalombe, leaving in the early morning, and going through Likabula. If you're coming from Blantyre on the bus which goes to Mulanje town or hitching, ask to be dropped at Chitikali (Likabula Junction). From there, you can wait for the irregular minibus which runs between Mulanje town and Phalombe (via Likabula), which costs US$0.20. Alternatively, you can hitch; a ride in a pick-up is US$0.30. Or you can walk (10 km, two to three hours). It's a pleasant hike along the dirt road through tea estates, with good views of the south-west face of Mt Mulanje beyond the tea plantations on your right.

HIKING & TREKKING ROUTES

There are about six main routes from the plains up onto the higher parts of Mt Mulanje. Of these, three start at Likabula Forest Station, where all visitors have to register and pay. Once you're on top of the massif, there's a whole network of paths linking the various huts and peaks. We outline some choices in this section, but many different permutations are possible. You can stay up here trekking for a week or more or, if time is limited, some short hikes are possible, taking two or three days. It normally takes about three to six hours to walk between one hut and the next, which means you can walk in the morning, dump your kit, then go out to explore a nearby peak or valley in the afternoon. You can spend two or more nights at one hut if you want, and go out in a different direction each day, or just sit in the sun and take it easy.

The Mulanje Traverse

This route is one of many traverses that can be made across the Mulanje Massif. It begins at Likabula and ends at Fort Lister on the

MALAWI

north-east side of the massif. The route described here can be done in four days, but there are several variations which can extend this period, and plenty of opportunities for sidetracking, to scale a few peaks and ridges or explore small valleys. You could also add an extra stop about halfway through for a rest day.

Stage 1: Likabula Forest Station to Chambe Hut (seven km; two to five hours)

This stage takes you up onto the plateau. There are two options: the Chambe Plateau path, also called the Skyline Path, which is short and steep (2 to 4 hours); and the Chapaluka Path which takes longer (3½ to five hours) but is less steep, and more scenic. (The 'Skyline' is the aerial cableway which is used to bring wood down from the plantations on the plateau. On the way up the Skyline Path you'll see forestry workers coming down the steps with huge planks of wood balanced on their heads. What's even more amazing is they apologise and stand aside while you stroll up.)

From the top of the plateau, you pass through forest and the Chambe forest station, to reach Chambe Hut. There are good views of the south-east face of Chambe Peak from the hut's veranda.

Sidetrack: Chambe Peak

If you fancy conquering this spectacular peak on the same day as your ascent of the plateau, be sure to leave Likabula early; it will take you five to seven hours to get to the top and back to Chambe Hut. The path is not always clear, so you may need a guide.

About two to 2½ hours from the hut, you reach a large cairn on a broad level part of the ridge at the foot of the main face. You might be happy with reaching this point, which offers excellent views over the Chambe Basin to the escarpment edge and the plains far below. The next stage of the route requires some steep scrambling on bare rock – which can be intimidating – and should definitely be avoided after rain. The summit of Chambe Peak (2557m) is marked

by a large concrete-and-metal beacon which is not visible until you're almost on it.

The views from the summit of Chambe Peak in clear weather are superb; you can see most of Mulanje's main peaks, and much of the western side of the massif. Long stretches of the escarpment that surrounds the massif can also be seen, and below this the plains stretch out towards the Zomba Plateau in the north and the mountains of Mozambique in the south. It is often possible to see the waters of Lake Chilwa, to the north-east. On very clear days Lake Malombe, at the southern tip of Lake Malawi, can also be spotted.

To get back to Chambe Hut, retrace the route. Go slowly on the way down; it's easy to go off route, and just as easy to slip and fall on some of the steeper sections.

Stage 2: Chambe Hut to Thuchila Hut (12 km; four to five hours)

The start of this stage can be complicated to find as there are other paths all over the place, so if you haven't got a porter ask the hut caretaker to show you the first half km or so. You cross a large col, where the Chambe Basin is joined to the main massif, and reach a junction (about one to 1½ hours from Chambe Hut) where you go straight on, up a steep path. (The path to the right leads to the old Lichenya Hut.) To the left are fine views down into the Thuchila Valley. About two hours from the hut, you reach Chisepo Junction, where a path on the right leads up to the summit of Sapitwa Peak. The main path takes you across the edge of the Thuchila basin – a very scenic section – to reach Thuchila Hut.

Sidetrack: Sapitwa Peak

The summit of Sapitwa is the highest point on Mulanje, at 3001m. You can walk to the top, but it's a toughie, and the upper section involves some scrambling and tricky walking among large boulders and dense vegetation. From Chisepo Junction you should allow three to five hours for the ascent, plus four to four for descent. From either Chambe or Thuchila, add another four to five hours onto the times for doing the peak itself, or plan to spend a night at the very basic Chisepo shelter.

Perhaps not surprisingly, 'Sapitwa' in the local language means 'don't go there'.

From the junction, the route is clearly shown, for most of the way, by red marks painted on the rocks. This spoils the feel of untouched wilderness, but it stops a lot of people from getting lost. There are also a few marks missing, just to keep you on your toes! As you get near the summit you can see the top, but the route winds tortuously through an area of huge boulders and dense vegetation.

The views from the top, when you do finally make it, are worth the slog. On a clear day, you get a panoramic vista of the whole plateau, the other nearby peaks, the edge of the escarpment and the plains far below.

Stage 3: Thuchila Hut to Sombani Hut (12 km; four to five hours) This stage takes you over a small col and down into the Ruo Basin (the top of the large Ruo River valley. At a clear junction, about two hours from Thuchila Hut, turn right to drop and cross two streams and climb steeply up to reach Chinzama Hut (where you can stop if you want an easy day).

From Chinzama Hut aim eastward as the path climbs up the valley side, through grass and bush and across patches of rocks, to reach a small col. Cross into the next valley and drop through rolling grassland, to reach a junction. Take the left path (the right path leads to Madzeka Hut) and go through grassland to cross a wooden bridge and some small streams to reach Sombani Hut, about two hours from Chinzama Hut.

Sidetrack: Namasile Peak The large mountain that dominates the view, directly opposite Sombani Hut, is Namasile. To get to the top of this peak takes 2½ to three hours of ascent, plus 1½ to 2½ hours descent. The path to the summit, steep and strenuous in places but not technically difficult, spirals round the north side of the mountain and approaches the summit from the west (the 'back' of the mountain when viewed from Sombani Hut).

From the hut aim north down a clear path to cross the stream in the valley bottom on a wooden bridge. On the opposite bank is a fork. Keep straight on (right leads towards the Fort Lister Gap), up a firebreak to its end. From here the path is marked by occasional cairns, but you should have a map or a guide for this route, as getting lost is a real possibility. The route takes you below the main cliffs of the peak (about 1½ to two hours from the hut) and then up a broad vegetated gully. When you see the summit beacon you'll think you're nearly there, but now comes the hard bit! The path crosses bare rock and enters an area of large boulders and dense vegetation, then zigzags up over boulders and grassy slopes approaching the summit from the north-east. Scramble over large rocks to reach the summit (2687m), about three hours from the hut.

Views from the summit of Namasile Peak, over the north-eastern side of Mt Mulanje are excellent: across the Ruo and Madzeka basins and the upper part of the Sombani River valley. To the north-east the escarpment drops to the Fort Lister Gap, with the separate peak of Mchese beyond.

Return to Sombani Hut by the same route. Take care on the way down; it's easy to miss cairns and go off route.

Stage 4: Sombani Hut to Fort Lister Gap (five km; two to three hours) This stage takes you off the plateau, heading in a northerly direction. The path leads through some patches of indigenous forest, with great views over the surrounding plains, and keeps descending, although it is not as steep as the Chambe path coming up. There's a lot of forks, so a porter is useful to show you the way. If you're hiking alone though, the rule of thumb at every fork is 'keep going down'. For the last section you follow a dirt track. Camping is possible at Fort Lister forest station (US$0.35).

Fort Lister to Phalombe From the Gap to Phalombe village is another eight km along the dirt road. It's in bad condition (there was a major landslide in the area in 1991) and there's little or no traffic, so you'll have to walk (about two hours). But it's a pleasant

walk, through a couple of small villages. Most porters include this section in the fee you pay for the final day.

From Phalombe you can get a bus or pick-up back to Likabula or Mulanje. One bus a day goes direct to Blantyre (US$3), on the 'old road' (to the north of the main road through Thyolo). There's also transport to Zomba.

Alternative Descents From Sombani Hut you can extend your trek by another day and come down the south side of the massif to Lujeri Tea Estate. You can go to Madzeka Hut, sleep there, and then descend steeply beside the Little Ruo River (also called the Ndiza River). This is so steep it includes ladders for some sections. Some of these get damaged during rainy seasons and may not be replaced, which makes the route impass-able. If the route is open it takes three to five hours from Madzeka to descend, then go through Nadonetsa (a scattered village) to reach Office No. Three, at Lujeri Tea Estate.

Alternatively, stay your last night at Minunu Hut, and descend to Lujeri beside the ('Big') Ruo River. From Minunu Hut to the hydroelectric power station takes about three to four hours. From there to Office No. 3 is 10 km on a good dirt road (allow another three hours).

From Office No. 3 it's still 13 km to the main road that goes back to Mulanje town and Blantyre. You may be lucky and find somebody in the office with a car or a tractor who can help you with a lift. If you're out of luck, you'll have to start walking. From the office, follow the dirt road through the tea plantation. After three km, keep the tea factory on your left, go over a large river bridge, turn left, and follow this road for about nine km to reach the main tarred road. Wait here for a bus (several each day) or try hitching.

The Chambe-Lichenya Loop

This short route is good if you want to get a taste of Mt Mulanje but haven't got time for a traverse of the whole massif, as described above. It starts and finishes at Likabula forest station, so access is no problem. A trek on this route takes three days and two nights, but could be shortened to two days.

Stage 1: Likabula to Chambe Hut This section of the route is the same as Stage 1 of the Mulanje Traverse. The optional sidetrack up Chambe Peak is also described in the Mulanje Traverse section.

Stage 2: Chambe Hut to CCAP Cottage Follow the directions in Stage 2 of the Mulanje Traverse described earlier in this chapter. At the junction, about one to 1½ hours from Chambe hut, turn right (straight on leads to Thuchila), and descend through natural forest. The path levels out and crosses several small streams, the headwaters of the Likabula River. Down to the right is the Likabula Valley, while up to the left are North Peak and West Peak, outliers of Sapitwa.

Continue into the Lichenya Basin, past the site of Lichenya Hut and loop round by the

---

Mulanje's Pine Plantations

The pine plantations on Mulanje were first established by the colonial government in the early 1950s, mainly around Chambe and, to a lesser extent, Sombani. The sides of the massif are too steep for a road, so all the timber is sawn by hand and then carried down on a cable-way (called the 'skyline') or balanced on the heads of forest labourers.

The plantations provide employment for local people and wood for the whole of southern Malawi. A bad side effect, apart from plantations being ugly, is the tendency of pine trees to spread slowly across the natural grassland as seeds are blown by the wind. These artificial trees disturb the established ecological balance. The Wildlife Society of Malawi recommends pulling up any young pine trees that you see growing outside the plantation areas. ■

old airstrip. Just beyond here is the frighteningly steep Boma Path that goes down to Mulanje town. Don't take the path, but stop at the top to enjoy the good views over the escarpment.

Head north to reach the CCAP Cottage, about one hour from Lichenya Hut. The total time for this stage is four to five hours.

Stage 3: CCAP Cottage to Likabula

From the col, drop to a junction. Go left, then downhill through forest, to eventually reach the Likabula River. Wade through, or jump from rock to rock, and go up the far bank to reach the dirt track between the Mulanje-Phalombe road and the forest station. This stage takes four to five hours, plus 1½ to 2½ hours if you do the sidetrack up Chilemba Peak.

The Lower Shire

The southern limit of the Shire Highlands area (with Blantyre at its heart) is marked by the Thyolo Escarpment (also called the Shire Escarpment). Beyond here, the land falls to form the Lower Shire Valley, sometimes simply called the 'far south' – a thin spine of territory jutting deep into Mozambique, and one of the least-visited areas of Malawi.

The main road south from Blantyre plunges down the escarpment in a series of hairpin bends, with excellent views over the Shire River and out towards the Zambezi River on the hazy horizon. Even when it's cool in Blantyre and on the highlands, it can be blisteringly hot down here – the sharp change of temperature and landscape, in less than 30 km, is striking.

The plentiful water and warm climate is ideal for sugar-cane growing, and a large part of the Lower Shire has been turned over to plantation. In the 1970s there were plans to develop the agricultural potential of the area even further and turn it into a 'regional breadbasket'. For various reasons the plan was shelved; most people here practice subsistence farming – a lifestyle which is becoming increasingly precarious.

Beyond the foot of the escarpment, about 50 km south-west of Blantyre, the main road crosses the Shire River near the small town of Chikwawa. Other main settlements include Nchalo, Bangula and Nsanje. This area also contains the lowland Lengwe National Park and the reserves of Majete and Mwavbi. East of Lengwe is the Elephant Marsh, a vast area of seasonally flooded swampland. There's also a number of interesting historic sites.

MAJETE GAME RESERVE

Majete Game Reserve lies about 30 km directly to the west of Blantyre, in the area between the Shire River and the border with Mozambique. The landscape is mainly hills, covered in fairly open miombo woodland, with denser patches of forest alongside the river. Animals recorded here include elephant, sable, kudu, hartebeest, waterbuck, bushbuck and duiker, but few remain due to a lack of control and heavy poaching in the last 20 years or so. You may see a few small bushbuck, but anything large and smart enough to survive poachers will be very hard to find, so it's best to forget about mammals completely and appreciate the reserve simply as a beautiful wilderness area. Standard game reserve fees must be paid (see National Parks in the Facts about Malawi chapter).

Things to See & Do

Walking is allowed in the reserve, although officially you need to be accompanied by a game scout. You can go from the gate to the Mkurumadzi chalet (see Places to Stay below) in a day, stay the night and walk back. It's a splendid route alongside the river, and past the impressive series of falls and cataracts. The people at Majete Safari Camp (see Places to Stay, following) will give you advice on the route and current conditions. Hardy hikers could consider the possibility of continuing north from the chalet, alongside the Shire River to Mpatamanga Gorge, where the old road between Mwanza and

Blantyre crosses the river on a bridge. From here occasional transport goes to Blantyre via Chileka.

Bird-watching is good, in the area round the camp and alongside the river, and fishing here is said to be excellent, with small but fierce tigerfish. Majete Safari Camp organises excursions by foot, boat and ox-cart into the reserve and to the Kapichira Falls, or to Lengwe National Park (described later in this chapter) by vehicle and along the Lower and Upper Shire River (in a converted lifeboat which once belonged to the *Guendolin* – see the Mangochi section). Trips can also be arranged to the site of Livingstone's camp, to the graves of various explorers and missionaries, and to the later disembarking point for early settlers travelling from the lower Shire Valley to the highlands.

A dam and hydroelectric power station is being built at Kapichira. Through 1997 and 1998 you should expect to see construction vehicles in the area. When the work is completed a small lake will have been formed on the Shire River above the dam.

Places to Stay

The best place to stay is *Majete Safari Camp* (☎ 423204) PO Box 2648, Blantyre, outside the reserve, only a few km from the entrance gate. This is a useful base for exploring the whole area. Owned and run by the father and son team of John and Shane Marshall, the relaxed and friendly camp has terraced grounds on the banks of the Shire River. It overlooks the Matitu Falls, southernmost of the Shire Cataracts (of which Kapichira Falls is the largest and best known) which separate the Upper and Lower Shire. (This was the barrier to Livingstone's exploration by boat in 1858/9. See History in the Facts about Malawi chapter for more details.) The camp caters for all budgets with comfortable ensuite chalets at around US$80 per person full board, simpler chalets and permanent tents from US$20, and camping for US$3. There's a bar, a staffed kitchen for self-catering, or you can buy meals.

Inside the reserve, accommodation is limited to a small, slightly tumbledown *chalet* in the north-eastern sector, near the junction of the Mkurumadzi and Shire Rivers, which costs US$5 per person.

The Majete Chapel
An interesting feature of Majete Safari Camp is the small chapel, built in an 'Afro-Saxon' style. The owners have dedicated the chapel to 'the wilderness', rather than to a saint, and there's a large open window looking out across the river where the wilderness forms a fine backdrop. Another window is planned to have stained glass windows, and the church will deliberately have no door, so people can come and go as they like.

The church is also to have a bell. When Livingstone camped just below Matitu Falls in 1858 he wrote that his wish was to 'live to hear a church bell ring out across the Shire River'. He was probably speaking metaphorically – he wanted to bring Christianity to the whole area – but the chapel at Majete will finally fulfil his words. ■

Getting There & Away

Majete Safari Camp is 15 km north of Chikwawa, on the tar road to Majete Game Reserve gate. If travelling by car, leave the main road between Blantyre and Nsanje just south of the Shire River and drive through Chikwawa town. The camp is signposted on your right, down a dirt road.

If travelling by bus, the nearest you can get is Chikwawa; there are several buses per day to/from Blantyre. From here you can try hitching (good at weekends, as the camp is popular with Blantyre residents) or phone the camp for a lift (there is a small charge). If you get stuck as night falls, Chikwawa has a couple of local resthouses, bars and eating houses.

The road between Mwanza (near the Mozambique border on the Tete Corridor road) and Chikwawa, via Mikolongo is due to be upgraded in 1997. If you're coming from Mozambique, this would be an ideal way to enter Malawi, allowing a visit to Majete and other parts of the Lower Shire area before continuing to Blantyre.

LENGWE NATIONAL PARK

Some 75 km from Blantyre, Lengwe is Malawi's southernmost national park. The soil and climate are ideal for sugar cane, so much of the surrounding area has been turned into plantation. Within the park boundary, the vegetation consists mostly of deciduous woodland and thicket, some patches of open acacia woodland and grassy *dambo* (marshy river course). Mammals occurring here include, most notably, nyala – at the northern limit of its distribution in Africa. The park also contains bushbuck, impala, duiker, kudu and baboon. However, sightings are harder than in some other parks because of the dense vegetation, and because numbers have been reduced by poaching. Buffalo occur here, but are rarely seen. You may also notice hyena and leopard droppings, but you'll be very lucky indeed to see the actual animal. Admiring the large and varied bird population is likely to be more rewarding.

Standard national park entrance fees (see National Parks in the Facts about Malawi chapter) must be paid at the gate. Once in the park, only the eastern area is open to visitors, and even here many of the tracks for vehicles are often impassable. Rather than trying to drive around, it's more rewarding to walk in the park or spend some time at the pleasant hides overlooking water holes, one of which is within walking distance of the main camp.

Places to Stay

You can pitch your tent at the park's *main camp* for US$3 per person, or use one of their furnished chalets for US$12 per person, which includes the use of a kitchen and services of a cook, but is still on the pricey side, although these chalets are more comfortable than in some other parks and reserves. You must bring all your own food, but there is a small shop selling a few basics as well as beers and soft drinks.

Another option if you got your own vehicle is the *Sucoma Club*, a sports club or 'mess' for managerial staff at the Sucoma sugar plantation, reached from the small town of Nchalo, about 25 km south of Chikwawa, and about 18 km from the national park gate. The entrance to the plantation is on the edge of the town centre, where the buses stop. The club, however, is about seven km from here, through endless canefields on the banks of the Shire River, and can only be reached by a car. There's also a bar and restaurant here, and comfortable bungalow accommodation (US$10 per person) which has to be reserved in advance (☎ 428200; ask for the finance and administration officer). The club has a couple of boats which can be hired to cruise on the river (see the Elephant Marsh section, later in this chapter). Part of the estate has been turned into a secure reserve for nyala and other wildlife that may be threatened in the national parks.

If the club sounds a bit neocolonial for your tastes, in Nchalo itself is a *Government Resthouse*, a couple of other basic lodging houses, a bank and a supermarket.

Getting There & Away

If travelling by car, follow the directions under Getting There & Away of the Majete Game Reserve section earlier in this chapter to the bridge over the Shire River, then continue on the main road towards Nchalo. Nine km from the bridge is a signpost indicating Lengwe park to the right. Ignore this and continue for another 11 km until you reach another signpost. Turn right (west) here, and follow a straight dirt road through sugar cane plantation for nine km to reach another national park signpost, where you turn left and continue for one km to reach the park entrance.

If travelling by public transport, take the bus from Blantyre towards Nchalo, and get out at the second junction mentioned above. The park entrance is another 10 km to the west through sugar plantations. If you're without wheels you may be able to hitch to within a few km of the entrance gate on a tractor, although officially you're not allowed to enter the park on foot. The park is rarely visited, so waiting for a lift to the main camp might take a day or longer.

BANGULA

This small town (or large village) is on a junction where the road from Blantyre splits: one branch continues south to Nsanje and the Mozambique border (see the Malawi Getting There & Away chapter), the other branch goes north-east to Chiromo and Makhanga. There's no bus station, but all transport stops at the junction. If you need to overnight here, there's a cheap *Government Resthouse* and a few local eating houses.

MWABVI GAME RESERVE

In the southernmost tip of Malawi, Mwabvi is the country's smallest (under 350 sq km) and least-visited game reserve, with a genuine wilderness atmosphere. The landscape consists of hilly, sandstone ridges covered by mixed and mopane woodland vegetation, with numerous small rocky gorges formed by fast flowing streams and rivers running eastward into the Shire River. The scenery is quite unlike any other part of Malawi, and there are spectacular views over the Shire and Zambezi rivers. The reserve's western boundary is the border with Mozambique. Inside the reserve is a *camp*, with a couple of very basic huts. You can camp here also.

Like many other reserves, Mwabvi was virtually abandoned in the 1980s and early 1990s, and it suffered from the ravages of poaching. The reserve edges have been inhabited by people, and effectively 'written off' so its area is smaller than shown on most maps. Rhino and lion were once recorded here, but apart from a few buffalo and nyala it's unlikely that any large game remains today.

Getting There & Away

At the time of writing access was possible only with a car or great determination; the gate and reserve office is reached from the main road between Chikwawa and Nsanje by following a dirt road southward, from just east of the village of Sorgin, about 10 km west of Bangula. You pass near another small village called Dande.

The Wildlife Society of Malawi is cur-

rently involved in various rehabilitation projects, aiming to protect the reserve by encouraging local people to benefit from its resources. This may also improve access for visitors, so if you want to visit it would be worth enquiring about the latest situation at the Wildlife Society bookshop in Limbe (see Bookshops in the Blantyre & Limbe chapter) or at Majete Safari Camp (see the Majete Game Reserve Places to Stay section, earlier in this chapter).

ELEPHANT MARSH

The Elephant Marsh is a large area of seasonally flooded plain on the Shire River about 30 km downstream from Chikwawa, just south of the vast Sucoma sugar cane estates. Despite the name there are no elephants here any more, although vast herds inhabited the area less then a hundred years ago. Some hippo and crocodile occur in quiet areas, but the wildlife consists of a spectacular selection of birds – predominantly water species, but with many others too. This is one of the best bird-watching areas in Malawi, so most visitors are keen bird-watchers, but it's well worth considering a visit here if you simply want to sample this peaceful and very unusual landscape. The marsh is well off the beaten track, but its eastern side is not too difficult to reach. For more details on vegetation and wildlife, a copy of the *Day Outings from Blantyre* booklet produced by the Wildlife Society of Malawi is very useful.

Traditionally, local people from the surrounding area come to the marsh in drought periods when water was scarce on the higher ground. Rice, maize and other crops grow in these conditions (which is why the sugar plantation was established on the northern edge of the marsh). It is also an important fishing area. In recent years, pressures on the land elsewhere has caused the temporary population of the marsh to become more permanent and start to grow. The Wildlife Society is involved in various schemes to help local people continue to harvest the marsh without destroying it through overuse, or by the introduction of grazing animals such as goats.

Places to Stay
As mornings and evenings are the best time to see birds (it's also not so hot), travellers without wheels may find it convenient to overnight in Makhanga. This also gives you a chance to arrange a boat the day before. There's a couple of local *resthouses*; the one on the right of the road towards Muona, about a hundred metres after you cross the railway tracks, is very basic but otherwise OK. They sell cold drinks, but food must be ordered long in advance.

If you've got a car, you could stay in Bangula, Sucoma Club or Majete Safari Camp, depending on the level of comfort you require.

Getting There & Away
The only way to see the marsh properly is by boat. The Sucoma Club (mentioned earlier in this chapter under Lengwe Places to Stay) has two boats (*Poop Deck* and *Poop Deck II*) which can be hired by the public, but both were recently reported out of order. It might be worth ringing to see if they've been fixed. Another option is to stay at Majete Safari Camp (see the Majete Places to Stay section, earlier); boat trips from there to the Elephant Marsh are planned.

A third option (the only one for budget travellers) is to go out in a local boat. A place where such boats can be hired is the Fisheries Depot at a place called Mchacha Landing or Mchacha James (locals seem to call it simply 'James') on the east side of the marsh, north of Bangula, about five km from the smaller village of Makhanga.

Mchacha James can easily be reached by car, via tar roads as far as Bangula and Makhanga. If you're on public transport, get off the bus at Bangula, from where local pick-ups run a few times per day to Makhanga. (Another option to consider might be the train from Limbe to Nsanje, which goes through Makhanga.)

From Makhanga, aim northward on the road towards the village of Muona. After about two km a dirt track leads west through villages and small fields to Mchacha James. The route is not signposted, so you'll have to get directions (ask for 'James'); it might be worth arranging a local guide in Makhanga.

Local boat owners may offer to take you in dug-out canoes, but there's also a couple of more stable rowing boats for hire. The rate is very negotiable; around US$10 per boat for a morning or afternoon trip seems to be fair. The rowing-boat owners also speak English and can tell you a lot about the birds, fish and human inhabitants of the marsh.

Eastern Marsh
We heard from a keen travelling bird-watcher who reported that an area called the Eastern Marsh, downstream of the main Elephant Marsh, was easy to reach and worth a visit. About three km east of Bangula, south of Chiromo, on the west side of the Shire River (the east side is in Mozambique) an old railway embankment leaves the road and runs through the edge of this small marsh for about six km to rejoin the main line and the road to Nsanje about five km south of Bangula. You can apparently walk along this embankment; it provides good views over the marsh.

CHIROMO
For dedicated historians, Chiromo might be worth a visit. This small village, about five km north-east of Bangula, was an important staging post in the days of the early British settlers in Malawi, and the site of the protectorate's very first post office.

The explorer David Livingstone travelled in this area in the 1850s and 1860s, while following the Shire River upstream from the Zambezi River (see the main History section in the Facts about Malawi chapter for details). Through the rest of the 19th century and into the early 20th century foreign travellers heading for Lake Malawi or the Highlands around Blantyre would also come this way. From the Indian Ocean port of Quelimane (then in Portuguese East Africa) and the smaller port of Chinde (a British 'concession'), they would go by boat up the

Zambezi River and then into the Shire River. For about 80 km the Shire formed the border between British and Portuguese territory, but at Chiromo the border followed another large river called the Ruo (which rises in Mt Mulanje) and the Shire flowed through wholly British territory. Thus Chiromo became an important gateway to the whole British Central African region.

In the early 20th century a railway was constructed between Blantyre and the Portuguese port of Beira. The line crossed the Shire at Chiromo, and ran roughly parallel to the river as it flowed southward. The line crossed the Zambezi at Vila de Sena (for more details on this bridge see the Mozambique chapter). Passengers on larger steamers would alight at Chiromo and continue their journey by road or rail.

The original railway bridge has been replaced, but the one that remains is probably

50 years old – and quite impressive – designed to carry cars and trains over the river. There's also some ancient traffic lights which warn vehicles of approaching trains (they still run between Blantyre and Nsanje, but not into Mozambique), but the bulbs were last replaced some time before independence. Today a man with a flag does the job.

The old train station and original post office at Chiromo have fallen down, but you can walk among some of the other ruined buildings which date from colonial times. The jetty where the steamers used to land has gone too, but you can reach the confluence of the Shire and Ruo rivers for a good view of the bridge and a peek across the border into Mozambique.

For details of transport into Mozambique from this part of Malawi, see the main Getting There & Away chapter.

Early Missionary Graves

The Shire River was the gateway for early explorers, missionaries, settlers and those in colonial service to the area now called Malawi, and the far south of the country is dotted with the graves of these early arrivals.

Near Majete Safari Camp, at the site where Livingstone and subsequent travellers were forced to end their journey by boat (see History in the Facts about Malawi chapter), is the grave of one Richard Thornton, a British explorer and geologist who travelled with Livingstone on the Zambezi River in the late 1850s before going freelance for a while and working for a German expedition on Kilimanjaro in today's Tanzania. He rejoined Livingstone in 1862 on the Zambezi and Shire expeditions, but died of dysentery in 1863.

Downstream a few km, near the bridge over the Shire River east of Chikwawa, is the grave of the Rev Carter Scudamore, an early Universities Mission in Central Africa (UMCA) missionary who also died here in 1863. He was buried alongside the mission physician Dr J Dickinson, and the site is marked by a gravestone. Also on the banks of the Shire is a grave to Herbert Rhodes, brother of the more famous Cecil, who died here in the 1890s. The gravestone by the bridge is easy to find, but the others take local knowledge – if you're staying at Majete Safari Camp, they can help.

Near Chiromo, on the south-west side of the Shire is another graveyard. This takes some searching out as it is now completely overgrown. Coming from Chiromo, heading towards Bangula, it's on the left, 1.5 km from the bridge just after a small group of huts which seem to be called Chikanzi. The inscriptions make sober reading, and remind today's visitors of the less-glorious aspects of colonial ambition in Africa:

Charles Carvin, Gunner, HMS *Mosquito*, died 1891;
Samuel Hodges, Stoker, HMS *Herald*, died 1890, age 28;
CW Joubert Pauw, died 1906, age 25;
Dennis O'Connel, Her Majesties Customs, died 1907, age 27;
'Wee Archie' beloved son of Agnes Todd and WK Keiller, born May 1896, died November 1896. ■

BRUNO FRANÇAIS

DAVID ELSE

DAVID ELSE

DAVID ELSE

Malawi

Top Left: Mt Mulanje has the loftiest peaks between Tanzania and Lesotho.
Top Right: Livingstonia Mission, northern Malawi, founded in 1894.
Bottom Left: Below Mt Mulanje, workmen cut planks using a local style saw-pit.
Bottom Right: Sombani hut on Mt Mulanje. The mountain is a popular walking area.

Malawi

Top: View of Nkhata Bay, a popular Lake Malawi resort town
Bottom: Near Likoma Island, Malawian territory close to the Mozambican lake shore

Northern Malawi

The Northern Province of Malawi, with the provincial capital Mzuzu roughly at its centre, runs from the Viphya Plateau to the far northern tip of the country. This chapter covers most parts of the Northern Province, except the Viphya Plateau itself (covered in the Central Malawi chapter) and the lake shore (see the Lake Shore chapter). Places covered in this chapter includes the towns of Mzuzu and Rumphi, Nyika National Park and the Vwaza Marsh Game Reserve. Places are described in a roughly south to north direction.

MZUZU

Mzuzu – 'the Capital of the North' – has grown considerably in the last decade or so, changing from a sleepy frontier town to a fairly large administrative centre. Officially classed as a city (if only by Malawian standards), this place may be your first taste of 'civilisation' for quite a while if you've come from the north.

Here, there are banks where you can exchange money (see the Money section in the Facts for the Visitor chapter for details), shops, a post office, a supermarket, a pharmacy, petrol stations and other facilities.

Most visitors stay for at least one night, as it's a useful stopover on the main north to south route or a jumping-off point for the roads to Nyika and Vwaza, or to Nkhata Bay and Nkhotakota. Mzuzu has a surprisingly good selection of places to stay and eat.

The museum on M'Mbelwa Rd, just off the main street, has good quality, well-labelled displays on the customs and traditions of local tribes, the history of African and European peoples in northern Malawi, and a section on indigenous plants and wildlife. It's open Monday through Friday, 8 am to noon and 1 to 5 pm. Entrance is free, but a donation to the museum or the young curator (who is always around to talk or answer questions) may be appropriate.

Places to Stay

Most budget travellers head for the *CCAP Resthouse*, just off Boardman Rd, about 500m north-east of the bus station. It costs US$3 per person, in safe, clean rooms with two, three or four beds. There's also a self-contained double. The separate bathrooms are clean too. Good value food (Malawian or chicken and chips) is served in the restaurant. The resthouse is part of the CCAP (Church of Central Africa Presbyterian) 'estate' in Mzuzu, originally founded by Scottish missionaries, and now containing a church, schools, workshops and so on. (British visitors will recognise the line of houses just like highland crofts.)

Also near the bus station is the *Flame Tree Guesthouse*, where a friendly Malawian called Mrs Phipps runs a bed & breakfast in the English tradition for US$6 per person, or US$4 if you don't want breakfast. This place is a real little gem (there are only three bedrooms, with two beds each, and you share the rest of the house with the family) but unfortunately it's often full, although always worth trying. Flame Tree Lodge on Lake Malawi at Chintheche is run by her husband Tony and there's sometimes transport between the two places.

If you're really short of cash, try the *Jambo Resthouse*, run by the city council, on M'Mbelwa Rd. Basic rooms here cost US$1 per person. Smarter double rooms out the back are US$2.50. The bathrooms are bearable, but what you'd expect in this price range. Nearby are another couple of private resthouses and several cheap bars and eating houses.

Slightly more up-market is the *Chenda Hotel*, just to the east of the bus station and connected to the Chenda Entertainment Centre. The Centre is basically a huge bar, with music or discos some evenings. In the hotel, clean ensuite single/double rooms are US$10/15 including breakfast. The restaurant has Malawian food for around US$2,

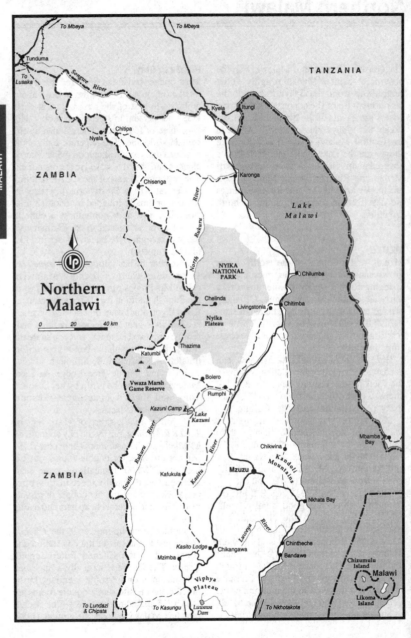

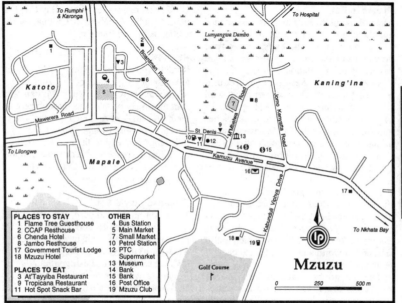

MALAWI

PLACES TO STAY
1 Flame Tree Guesthouse
2 CCAP Resthouse
6 Chenda Hotel
8 Jambo Resthouse
17 Government Tourist Lodge
18 Mzuzu Hotel

PLACES TO EAT
3 At'Tayyiba Restaurant
9 Tropicana Restaurant
11 Hot Spot Snack Bar

OTHER
4 Bus Station
5 Main Market
7 Small Market
10 Petrol Station
12 PTC Supermarket
13 Museum
14 Bank
15 Bank
16 Post Office
19 Mzuzu Club

Mzuzu

0   250   500 m

and western-style main dishes for between US$2.50 and US$5. The hotel also seems to be the local HQ for the AFORD political party, and the large banner in the restaurant which says 'Thank you Malawi Army' refers to the period in 1992 when the MCP Young Pioneers were routed by the military. (See the entry in History in the Facts about Malawi chapter.)

In a quieter setting is the *Government Tourist Lodge*, on the eastern side of town. It's about one km from the roundabout, on the right side of the Nkhata Bay road. Formerly the plain old Government Resthouse, it has been revamped by the Hotel Training School and offers (as its signboard proudly states) 'accommodation, meals and an assortment of drinks and camping services'. Clean and tidy single/double rooms cost US$12/20 with breakfast. Two rooms each share a separate toilet and bathroom. Camping on a fenced grassy site is US$2, or US$3 if you want to use the hot showers in

the bathrooms. Evening meals are around US$3, or US$7 for a three-course special. There is a garden bar and a nice terrace with views over the surrounding farmland.

A cheaper place, if you want to be outside town, is the *Kaka Hotel*, five km along the road towards Rumphi. Reasonable singles/doubles are US$2.50/6, with breakfast.

Top of the range in Mzuzu is the *Mzuzu Hotel* (☎ 332622, central reservations Blantyre ☎ 620071) on the east side of town, overlooking the golf course. This hotel is run by the South African Protea group, so conditions and facilities are of a relatively high standard. Ensuite rooms with air-con, phone and full buffet breakfast cost US$104/135. There's also a restaurant and coffee shop, where appetisers are around US$3, light meals around US$5, and main courses from US$5 to US$10. There is a quiet bar for residents, while next to the hotel the *Choma Bar* provides evening entertainment with a loud local flavour.

Places to Eat

Most of the places to stay have restaurants, and these are listed in the above section.

For low-budget eats, there's street food around the market, several shops and a good bakery by the bus station.

The *Tropicana Restaurant* is recommended for an excellent cheap meal, with large portions, and a nice veranda giving it a vaguely Mediterranean feel. Sandwiches and snacks start at US$1, Malawian meals around US$2 and western staples like fish or chicken and rice or chips are around US$2.50. Specials, like a half chicken, start at US$3.

Nearby, the *Hot Spot Snack Bar* (next to the Kool Spot Bottle Store) has similar fare and prices, but lacks the Tropicana's pleasant ambience. Near the Chenda Hotel is *Bamboo's Boozer & Takeaway* which is also similar, but worth a mention for the name if nothing else.

There's no beer at the Muslim-run *At'Tayyiba Restaurant* near the bus station (the name means something like 'goodly sustenance'), but the food is good: fish and chips, or beef and rice or nsima cost around US$1.50 to US$2.

For more stylish surroundings, visit the restaurant at *Mzuzu Club*, next to the Mzuzu Hotel, where temporary membership is US$1. The restaurant serves good Malawian and western-style food, including steaks, from US$3 to US$8. There's also a bar and a fenced-in snooker table.

Getting There & Away

There are daily Coachline services between Mzuzu and Lilongwe (US$19) via Kasungu (US$8). They leave the Mzuzu Hotel (not the bus station) at 5 am and get to Lilongwe before noon, in time to connect with the afternoon Coachline service to Blantyre (US$17). Coming the other way, you can leave Blantyre on the first coach, change at Lilongwe around noon and still be in Mzuzu by evening. There are also Express and Inter-City services from the bus station near the market. Some sample one-way fares are: Lilongwe US$9; Kasungu US$6; Rumphi

US$2; Karonga US$6; Nkhata Bay US$1. If you're heading for Nyika or Chitipa, see the section below on Rumphi.

RUMPHI

Rumphi (pronounced 'Rumpy') is a small town about 70 km north of Mzuzu, and east of the main road between Mzuzu and Karonga. Most people pass through here on their way to Vwaza Marsh or the Nyika Plateau, but from Rumphi you can also get to Livingstonia and to the northern outpost of Chitipa (from where you can enter Zambia and Tanzania – see the Getting There & Away chapter for details).

Places to Stay & Eat

The government resthouse, near the police station, was closed for renovation when we passed through, but might be worth checking when (or if) it reopens. In the centre, behind the Admarc depot, is the *Yagontha Hideout Resthouse* with simple but OK rooms for US$2 per person. There's sometimes hot water, food is usually available and it's close to the bus stop. On the edge of town, as you come in from Mzuzu, is the friendly and good-value *Simphakawa Inn*, where clean ensuite rooms with hot showers cost US$3.50 (for one or two people).

Getting There & Away

Buses between Mzuzu and Karonga call at Rumphi. To/from Mzuzu is US$2. There are also minibuses for the same price. In the dry season a daily bus goes up the old road to Livingstonia. There are also buses to Chitipa (via Zambia Resthouse Junction or Chelinda, in Nyika National Park) but these only run in the dry season when the road is good. If you're aiming for Nyika, it's best to get the bus from Mzuzu (if it's running), as it's often full by the time it reaches Rumphi.

VWAZA MARSH GAME RESERVE

This pleasant and all-too-frequently overlooked reserve is well worth visiting if you are in Rumphi or on your way up to Nyika. It lies south of the Nyika Plateau on the border with Zambia, covering 970 sq km.

Mr Ngoma's House

About 20 km north of the junction where the Rumphi road turns west off the main north-south road, you pass (on your left, if heading north) a remarkable two storey building constructed of scrap metal, old car parts, brightly painted wood, ancient beds and disused road signs. This is the house of Mr SS Ngoma, one of Africa's great eccentrics, who spends most of his time sitting on his front porch watching the world go by.

Mr Ngoma, in the nicest possible way, is obsessed with his forthcoming death, and has already built his coffin, grave and tombstone. He welcomes visitors, and will happily show you around his bizarre house. (It was once a shop, and the sign still says Grocery, but the shelves have been empty for years). It has several bedrooms (even though he lives alone) which he seems to use in rotation, a 'mortuary', a 'hospital', a chapel (complete with ancient record player with a speaker wired to the veranda so that hymns can be played to the local inhabitants), an intriguing upstairs toilet, a couple of bells, hundreds of letters, cards and photos from admirers all over the world and even a telephone which he says is linked directly to God and other friends who have already gone to heaven.

Mr Ngoma is weird but likeable, and a visit to his house will never be forgotten. On leaving you should sign the visitors book (he's on his sixth) and make a small donation. ■

Mr SS Ngoma, one of Africa's great eccentrics, welcomes visitors to his unique home.

Access by car is easy, and pretty straightforward by public transport. Once in the reserve, walking is permitted and a lot of game can be seen from the main camp, making Vwaza an ideal destination for travellers without their own transport.

There's a range of vegetation and habitats in the reserve. In the north is Vwaza Marsh itself and a large area of swamp surrounded by miombo woodland. There are also smaller areas of mopane and acacia woodland. Draining out of the marshland is the Luwewe River, which runs north to south through the middle of the reserve and eventually joins the South Rukuru River, which flows east to form the reserve's southern border. Lake Kazuni, in the far south-east of the reserve, is filled and drained by this river.

Lake Kazuni supports a good population of hippo, and despite extensive poaching several hundred elephant inhabit the reserve, and can often be seen around the lake. Other mammals in the park include buffalo (rumoured to be particularly aggressive here), waterbuck, eland, roan, sable, hartebeest, zebra, impala and puku, all surprisingly easy to see from the area around the lake. The birdlife is also excellent; this is one of the best places in Malawi for waders.

There are a number of driveable tracks in the reserve, but these are generally only suitable for 4WD vehicles. Walking is permitted around Lake Kazuni (you must be accompanied by a game scout), and is particularly rewarding.

Note that game management, accommodation and access at Vwaza are likely to improve in the future, as the reserve will be included in the redevelopment scheme planned for Nyika (see that section later in this chapter for more details).

For details of entry fees, see National Parks in the Facts about Malawi chapter.

Places to Stay

Currently, the only place to stay is the camp at Lake Kazuni, where dilapidated walk-in tents with two beds cost US$5 per person. Washing and toilet facilities are also a bit basic, but chances are you'll have the camp (plus the scenery and the animals) completely to yourself. If you have your own tent, camping is permitted.

Getting There & Away

If you are on public transport, there are fairly

frequent pick-ups and minibuses running from Rumphi to Bolero. About 10 km from Rumphi there's a junction on the left (west) where an unsignposted dirt road leads to Vwaza. (Ask to be dropped at Vwaza junction, also called Kazuni junction.) From there it is 19 km to the entrance gate and the nearby camp site. Most days there's a pick-up or two between Rumphi and Kazuni village (ask around in Rumphi), about 15 minutes' walk from the entrance gate, from which the camp at Lake Kazuni is easily reached. The ride costs US$2. For a small extra fee the driver will drop you at the gate. In the dry season, there's a daily bus from Rumphi which goes on the 'old road' to Mzimba on the Viphya Plateau (described in the Central Malawi chapter), passing through Kazuni village.

If you are driving, note that all of these roads deteriorate badly in the rainy season. If you are heading from Vwaza to Nyika, beware the 'short cut' which avoids doubling back and brings you out on the Nyika road just before Thazima village. This road is in very bad condition, and likely to take longer than going back the way you came.

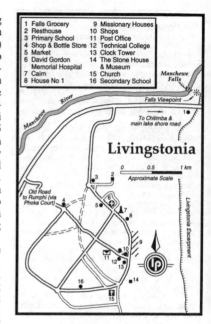

1 Falls Grocery	9 Missionary Houses
2 Resthouse	10 Shops
3 Primary School	11 Post Office
4 Shop & Bottle Store	12 Technical College
5 Market	13 Clock Tower
6 David Gordon Memorial Hospital	14 The Stone House & Museum
7 Cairn	15 Church
8 House No 1	16 Secondary School

LIVINGSTONIA

Livingstone's death in 1873 rekindled British missionary zeal and support for missions in Central Africa (for more details see the History section of the Facts about Malawi chapter). In 1875, a group of missionaries from the Free Church of Scotland arrived at Lake Malawi and built a new mission on the lake shore at Cape Maclear, which they named Livingstonia after the great man himself. Their early mission site was malarial and unsuccessful, so it was moved north along the shore to a place called Bandawe. Again, conditions were not ideal so in 1894 the Livingstonia Mission, led by the indefatigable Dr Laws, was moved to an area of high ground between the eastern escarpment of the Nyika Plateau and Lake Malawi. This site was successful and the mission station flourished and developed into a small town, which is still thriving today.

Livingstonia is a fascinating place; like a small piece of Scotland teleported into the heart of Africa. Although not easy to reach, it's well worth making an effort to get here. The town is quiet and restful, and an ideal place to base yourself for a day or two as a break from hard travel in Zambia or Tanzania or to recover from the rigours of beachlife on Lake Malawi.

Facilities include a post office (where you can make phone calls) and a mobile bank that comes on the first and third Mondays of every month. There's also the Khondowe Craft Shop selling carvings and clothing made by local people. (Khondowe was the original name of this area, before it was changed to Livingstonia.)

Things to See & Do

The fascinating **museum** in the Stone House (see Places to Stay) is open Monday through Saturday, plus Sunday afternoons, 8 am to noon and 2 to 5 pm. Entrance is US$0.30. The exhibits tell the story of early European exploration and missionary work in Malawi. Many original items that once belonged to Livingstone and his followers are still here, including an amazing collection of magic lantern slides.

Near the Stone House is the **church**, dating from 1894 and built in Scottish style. It has a beautiful stained-glass window of David Livingstone and his two companions, Juma and Guze (sometimes spelt Chuma and Suzi), his sextant and medicine chest, and Lake Malawi in the background. The church is often locked, but the keys are held at the museum or by the Head of Station, who lives nearby (ask for directions at the museum).

A short distance from the church is the **secondary school**, complete with Victorian facade. Other places of interest include the **old post office** and **clock tower** (now a small bookshop), the nearby **industrial block**, built in the early 1900s as a training centre, now a technical college, and a huge **bell** on a pedestal that is now a memorial to the Laws family.

Up the road from here is the **David Gordon Memorial Hospital**, once the biggest hospital in Central Africa. Nearby, a **stone cairn** marks the place where Dr Laws and his African companion Uriah Chirwa camped in 1894 when they reached this area and decided to build the mission. Also nearby is **House Number 1**, the original home of Dr Laws before he moved into the Stone House.

Outside the Stone House you might notice some huge letters almost hidden by the grass, designed to be read by anyone who happened to be flying over Livingstonia in a small plane. They read *Ephesians 2-14* (see the boxed text opposite).

There are several good walks in the area. You can visit the **Manchewe Falls**, about three km from the town. This is a spectacular waterfall, about 50m high, with a cave behind it where local people used to hide from slave traders some 100 years ago. There are several paths leading to the falls, and several young boys hanging around the resthouse who will show you the way for a small fee. Allow an hour going down and 1½ hours

back up. Alternatively, if you're walking to Chitimba, you can go via the falls on the way down.

A longer walk goes to **Mountain Viewpoint** overlooking Livingstonia, following the route of an old track built by early missionaries up to Nyika Plateau. A local guide is recommended. Allow five to six hours for the return trip.

Ephesians 2:14

In February 1959, as colonial rule was coming to an end in Malawi (then called Nyasaland), various pro-independence movements were active in the north and violence had escalated in the Karonga and Rumphi districts surrounding Livingstonia

The missionaries were thought to be in danger, so the government sent a small plane over the town to drop a message saying that the European missionaries could be evacuated if necessary. The missionaries were instructed to display a large symbol on the grass outside the church: 'V' if in danger and 'I' if they were safe, which a plane returning next day would be able to see.

The missionaries decided against evacuation, but also wanted to tell the outside world that despite extreme racial tension in Malawi they were living in peace and harmony with their African neighbours. Using bricks they spelt out *Ephesians 2:14* in large letters that could be clearly seen from the air.

Back at base, the government officials presumably turned to the appropriate page in the Bible and read:

'For He is our peace who hath made both one, and hath broken down the middle wall of partition between us.'

The bricks were later relaid outside the Stone House and whitewashed, where they remain to this day. They haven't been painted for a while and are getting overgrown, so anyone in a plane flying over the site these days may have to look quite hard to spot the message. ■

Places to Stay & Eat

The *Stone House* (☎ 368223), close to the clock tower, used to be one of the best resthouses in Malawi. Built by the missionaries early this century, it still contains the original furniture and has superb views. Unfortunately it has seen little maintenance in the last 10 years or so, and although the rooms are very clean, the house itself is getting a bit tatty round the edges (Dr Laws and his colleagues must be turning in their graves). However, it's still quite atmospheric, and good value at US$2.50 per night. There is a friendly caretaker, clean bathrooms with flush toilets and occasional hot water. You can camp on the lawn for US$1.50 and still use the bathrooms. Meals (soup, followed by beans, vegetables or meat with rice, plus tea) can be had for around US$2 if you order in advance. Breakfast of tea and pancakes (US$0.50) is also available. You can provide your own food for the cook to prepare, or simply use the kitchen to cook for yourself, for which a small tip should be paid to the kitchen staff.

There's another *resthouse*, where the views are even better, and if you have just staggered up the escarpment road it's about 15 minutes closer than the Stone House. At US$2 it's also a bit cheaper than the Stone House at US$2, although facilities are a little more basic (for example, there's never any hot water in the bathrooms) but otherwise it's fine. Camping, meals and use of the kitchen are also available here for the same price as the Stone House. From the garden you can see Lake Malawi and the beautiful curved spit of land on the north side of the bay that appears in the picture in the church window.

Some enterprising locals have plans to open private resthouses near the mission area. Nothing was finished (or even started) when we passed through, but it might be worth asking around when you're there to see if anything has materialised. There are also a couple of camp sites on the road up the escarpment, where local people have tried to earn a few bucks from the passing tourist trade. Facilities are basic (almost non-existent) but they're a cheap place to sleep. One of the nicest is at *Falls Grocery*, on the road right opposite the path to Manchewe Falls, where the friendly shopkeeper, Mr Edwin, lets you pitch a tent for US$0.60. There is a tumbledown toilet, and water comes from the stream nearby, but the shop is very well stocked with food and drink (including beer).

If you're self catering, there are some shops in Livingstonia town itself, selling a fairly good range of basic groceries. There's also a market on the road between the resthouse and the hospital. The shop near Admarc roundabout sells beer.

Getting There & Away

Getting to Livingstonia can be tricky. From the main north-south road between Karonga and Mzuzu, the road to Livingstonia turns west at Chitimba. From here it forces its way up the escarpment in a series of acute hairpin bends (20 to be precise – they're numbered) with a bad road surface, steep gradients, and pretty frightening drops to add to the fun. There is no public transport up or down this road but you can hitch: there's normally two or three hardy vehicles each day. At the bottom, just wait at the turn off. At the top, ask at the shops (the owners often go to Mzuzu for supplies) for a lift, or ask one of the young boys who hang around the resthouses to look around for you – they normally know what's going on. A lift in a pick-up costs about US$1. If there's nothing going when you want it, a private hire to the foot of the escarpment will cost about US$10. If you're driving, this road is usually OK for 4WD cars, and passable with 2WD in the dry season.

The alternative is to walk: this is 25 km, but it's steep, so it takes five hours to reach Livingstonia from Chitimba if you follow the road. There are short cuts which can cut it to three or four hours, but these are even steeper. Local children will offer to carry your pack for a negotiable price (usually about US$2). Going down the escarpment road is obviously easier on foot; it takes three to four hours. Take care though: we heard from a traveller who unfortunately was mugged on this road. This may have been an isolated incident – probably hundreds of travellers walk up here every year – but it may be worth checking the latest situation before you set off, or taking a local guide.

The other way to reach Livingstonia, especially useful if you're coming from the south, is to go to Rumphi (see earlier in this chapter), and catch the daily bus from there which goes up the old road (to the west of the main north-south road, and roughly parallel to it) to Livingstonia. Sometimes it only goes as far as Phoka Court, from where you'll have to walk the last seven km to Livingstonia. As well as the bus, private minibuses and pick-ups also cover this route. They all charge between US$1 and US$3 for a ride, depending on the state of the road. Note however, that there's only transport along this road in the dry season: in the wet it's often impassable.

A final option is to walk to Livingstonia from Nyika National Park. See the Nyika National Park section below for details.

CHITIPA

You'll pass through this frontier town if you're going between the extreme north of Malawi and Zambia. If you need a place to stay, there's a *government resthouse*. We've heard from other travellers who recommended the *Javet Resthouse* run by Mr Suali. Due to the lack of transport few people travel this way, but a new road may be built in the future – see the Getting There & Away chapter.

Nyika National Park

The Nyika Plateau is in the north of Malawi, overlapping the border with Zambia. It is completely different to Mount Mulanje, Malawi's other major mountain area, in both size and character. It was declared a national park in 1965, making it Malawi's oldest, and has also been extended since then, so that it is now the largest in the country. The plateau is roughly oval in shape, about 80 km long and almost 50 km across at its widest points, covering some 3000 sq km as well as an area in Zambian territory. Most of the area is at about 2000m above sea level. Although called a plateau, the Nyika is by no means flat: it consists mainly of rolling grassy hills split by forested valleys and surrounded by steep escarpments. There are several peaks

on the western, northern and eastern sides which rise above 2000m, with great views over the surrounding valleys and plains. The highest point on Nyika is Nganda Peak (2607m), which overlooks the northern section of the plateau and from where you can see the plains of Zambia in one direction and the distant mountains of Tanzania in the other, as well as the waters of Lake Malawi shining in the distance.

The wild, open nature of the Nyika Plateau attracts visitors who come to drive or ride around the park's vast network of game-viewing tracks, to admire the birds and animals, take a horseback safari, study the flowers, try a spot of fishing, or simply sit in the sun and absorb the magnificent scenery. Some of the park's main attractions are the series of short walks and longer hikes or treks that are possible.

Park entrance fees must be paid. For details see National Parks in the Facts about Malawi chapter.

Note At the time of research plans were announced that are likely to change the nature of the Nyika Plateau considerably. Following several years of neglect, during which poaching has become a major problem, the national park authorities will be provided with funds (from the German government) so that the area can be completely rehabilitated. The main changes to affect visitors will be: moving the park headquarters from Chelinda Camp to Thazima Gate; a new all-weather access road from Rumphi to Chelinda Camp via Thazima; new tracks and roads around the park; renovation of the existing park accommodation; construction of a new lodge and possibly more. It is not clear how long it will take for these various plans to see fruition. Of course, the landscape itself will remain the same, and the quality of the game viewing will probably improve, thanks to increased anti-poaching measures, staff training and better all-round management. In any event, some of the descriptions in this book are likely to be out of date by the time you arrive, so be prepared for changes.

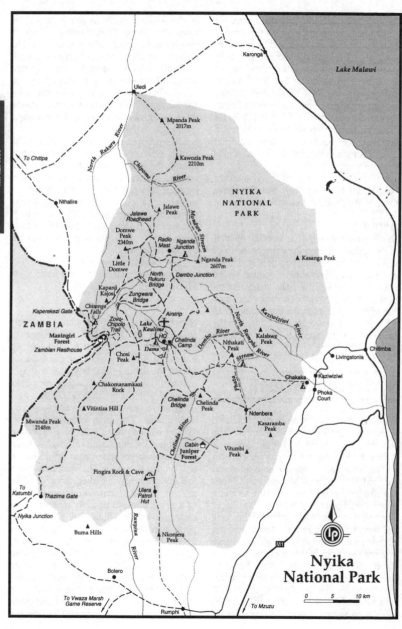

Nyika
National Park

FLORA & FAUNA

The vegetation on Nyika is unique in Malawi (and unusual in Africa) and worthy of special attention. About 1800m above sea level, most of Nyika is covered in rolling hills of montane grassland. The land below this altitude, in valleys and on the escarpment edges, is covered in light open miombo woodland, and in between the two vegetation zones you can often see areas of large protea bushes. Other areas are covered in dense evergreen forests, which are thought to be remnants of the extensive forests that once grew all over Malawi, as well as southern Tanzania, northern Zambia, and Mozambique. The plateau also contains small areas of damp grassy bog.

This range of flora attracts a varied selection of wildlife, and a major feature of a visit to Nyika is the number of birds and animals you are likely to see. Because of the general lack of trees and bushes, spotting is easy too. (In fact, many animals seem to deliberately pose on the skyline for that classic wildlife shot.) Most common are the large roan antelope and the smaller reedbuck, which move about through the grassland in herds. From a car or on foot, you'll also see zebra, warthog and eland (although, because they are a favourite target for poachers, these are very shy). Walking quietly, and crossing hilltops slowly, you might also see klipspringer, jackal, duiker and hartebeest. You might even catch a glimpse of hyena and leopard, but you'll be more likely to see their footprints and droppings. In the woodland areas, you may see blue monkey. More than 250 species of bird have been recorded in the park.

Nyika is also famous for its wildflowers. The best time to see them is during the rains, but conditions are also good in August and September, when the grassland is covered in colour and small outcrops turn into veritable rock-gardens. Over 120 species of orchid alone grow on the plateau.

Lake Kaulime is the only natural lake on the plateau and is the subject of many local stories and beliefs. In the days before Nyika was a park, local people came here to pray for rain, or throw in white beads as a sign of respect for their ancestors. If you listen hard you're supposed to be able to hear the sound of doves calling, or women pounding maize. The lake was thought to be bottomless, and on a misty day it does have a certain air of mystery about it, but it's actually not that deep: you can often see roan antelope wading through it, eating reed shoots.

Warnings

It can get surprisingly cold on Nyika, especially at night from June to August, when frosts are not uncommon. Log fires are provided in the chalets, but bring a warm sleeping bag if you're camping.

During dry periods, sectors of the park are burnt to prevent larger fires later in the season. Before setting off to drive or walk in the park, enquire at the park office about whether burning is taking place; if it is, avoid the area. ■

INFORMATION, MAPS & GUIDEBOOKS

The national park produces a small booklet with good background information on Nyika's wildlife and vegetation. There are also leaflets and displays in the information centre at Chelinda Camp. *A Visitor's Guide to Nyika National Park* by Sigrid Johnson is available in Blantyre and Lilongwe bookshops (but not, it seems, at Nyika itself) and is a good investment if you plan more than a cursory visit here.

The map we provide in this book will be enough to guide you round the park's network of game viewing tracks if you're touring on two or four wheels, and will also be sufficient for orientation while walking, though a park scout (ranger) is obliged to accompany you.

If you want to know more about the surroundings, you may want more detailed maps. The entire Nyika Plateau is covered by the government survey 1:250,000 map sheet 2, but many of the park tracks are not shown. The plateau is also covered by twelve 1:50,000 maps: 1033 B1 to B4, 1033 D1 to D4, 1034 A1 and A3, 1034 C1 and C3. (Chelinda Camp area is covered by 1033 D2.) These have excellent topographical

History of Nyika

The word 'nyika' means wilderness, and this particular expanse of high open wilderness has probably existed in its current form for many centuries. A small population of hunter-gatherers is believed to have inhabited the area more than 3000 years ago, and ancient rock paintings have been found at Fingira Cave, at the southern end of the plateau. When the Bantu people arrived in northern Malawi, most stayed on the plains below Nyika. The plateau was a place to hunt and smelt iron, but it was never settled in a big way.

The first Europeans to see Nyika were Scottish missionaries, who reached this area in 1894 (as described in the History section of the Facts about Malawi chapter. The mission station they built, between Nyika's eastern edge and Lake Malawi, was named Livingstonia, and is still a thriving centre today.

Scientists and naturalists who visited Nyika in the early 20th century recognised the biological importance of the area, and in 1933 measures were taken to protect the stands of juniper trees on the southern part of the plateau from bushfires. In 1948 this section was made into a forest reserve, and at the same time pine plantations were established around Chelinda, near the centre of the plateau.

There were later plans to extend the plantations and develop the area as a source of wood for a proposed pulp mill on Lake Malawi, but access for logging vehicles proved difficult and the scheme was abandoned. Plantations were, however, established on the Viphya Plateau (discussed in the Central Malawi chapter of this book), and plans for a Lake Malawi mill were never shelved completely (see the Lake Shore chapter for more details).

In 1965 the whole of the upper Nyika plateau was made a national park, and in 1976 this area was extended further to include the lower slopes of the plateau, which are an important water catchment area. This most recent boundary extension included several small settlements, and the people living here were relocated to areas outside the park. When they moved they took the names of their villages with them and now, in the area bordering the park, there are several settlements which share names with valleys and other features inside the park itself. ∎

detail but, once again, do not show all the park tracks.

A chapter on long walks in Malawi is included in Lonely Planet's *Trekking in East Africa*, which covers several routes on Nyika, plus Mulanje, Zomba and some other areas.

THINGS TO SEE & DO

As well as (or while) looking at birds, animals and flowers, several other activities are possible on Nyika.

Walking

Although you are not allowed to *enter* the park on foot, once inside the park walking is allowed. For short distances you can go alone, but for anything more than a few km, officially you must be accompanied by a scout (park ranger). This is usually easy to arrange with a day's notice at the park office.

Around Chelinda Camp, various paths and tracks wind through the plantation woodland, and these can be followed for several hours without the need of a guide. You can't really get lost as a large dirt road

circles the woodland area, so if you keep going you'll eventually come across it, and can then follow it back to the camp. Alternatively, you can go south of the camp on the park track towards Chelinda Bridge which passes two small artificial lakes called Dams 2 and 3. These are pleasant spots for bird-watching, and if you're patient you'll probably see roan and other animals coming to drink. From Dam 3 a footpath (indistinct in places) follows the small Chelinda River upstream back towards Chelinda Camp. If the path is unclear, keep left to avoid boggy sections. Alternatively, if you feel energetic, from Dam 3 you can head south then west on the park track which eventually loops round to meet the main access road between Chelinda and Thazima near Lake Kaulime. To get back to Chelinda from here makes a 20 km circuit.

If you've come by car, you can drive around the park, leaving it at various points to visit places of interest. Several short walks are available from the Zambian Resthouse (see Places to Stay). Also in this area is the Zovo-Chipolo Trail, a short circular route established to introduce visitors to the three main habitats on Nyika (montane grassland, evergreen forest and bog).

The word 'zovo' means 'elephant' in the local Tumbuka language. One was killed in the forest by a man called Chipolo. Elephant were once common in these patches of woodland, but are now believed to occupy only the far northern part of the park.

The trail starts about 16 km from Chelinda, just north-west of the junction of the main Thazima-Chelinda access road and the road to Nthalire. There's a signpost and car park. (It takes about half an hour to walk round the trail.)

Short walks are also possible around the Juniper Forest, in the southern part of the park. There's a small cabin here (see Places to Stay). The close combination of forest and grassland makes this a popular area for bird-watchers.

North of the Juniper Forest is Chelinda Peak, one of the few peaks in the area with exposed rock at its summit. Despite its impressive title, Chelinda Peak is only slightly higher than many of the surrounding hills, but it is crossed by a footpath which cuts off a large loop in the park track. You can leave your car at Chelinda Bridge.

In contrast to the rolling hills around Chelinda Peak and the Juniper Forest, the short walk to Jalawe Peak, in the north of the park, goes along the steep escarpment of the Chipome Valley, which separates the main part of the plateau from its northerly outliers Kawozia and Mpande. You can park at the Jalawe Roadhead, about 35 km from Chelinda Camp, and then follow the path down across a flat area of grass before it rises again up the side of Jalawe itself. Beyond the summit the path continues to a rocky outcrop overlooking the floor of the Chipome Valley, some 1000m below. With the help of binoculars, you used to be able to see elephant down here, but in several visits over the last seven years we've never seen any. (If poaching is controlled as part of the new rehabilitation scheme, the tuskers may make a comeback.) Beyond the valley, the land rises steeply again to the peak of Kawozia

(also called Kamozya) and beyond to the twin peaks of Mpanda, the northernmost summit in the park.

Hikes & Treks

If you want something more challenging than a short walk; several longer hikes, treks and trails are possible on Nyika, lasting anything from two days to a week or longer. These are described in more detail at the end of this section.

Horse-Riding

If walking seems like too much hard work, it's possible to ride a horse across the fine open grassland of the Nyika. On a horse you can get quite close to some of the game (such as zebra, eland and roan) as they seem less perturbed by the sound of hooves than cars or human footsteps. A company called Nyika Horse Safaris (part of Heart of Africa Safaris) have stables near Chelinda Camp and you can go riding for a couple of hours (US$10 per hour) or all day (US$50). Normally, you must give the stables notice the day before, or in the morning for an afternoon ride. They have horses suitable for beginners and experts.

If you want to explore Nyika further, this company runs longer luxury horse safaris, from two to 10 days, according to your time, budget or hardiness. Day rides from Chelinda Camp cost US$150 per person per day, all inclusive. More exciting are the mobile safaris, which move from camp to camp around the plateau, using pack horses or back up vehicles to carry large tents, showers and food. These cost US$180 per person per day. For more information contact Heart of Africa Safaris (☎ /fax 740848), PO Box 8, Lilongwe , or any good travel agent in Malawi.

Fishing

Nyika is reckoned by anglers to offer some of the best rainbow trout fishing in Malawi, if not *the* best. The fishing tradition here goes back to the early 20th century when the streams were stocked with trout, originally from Britain. Fishing is allowed in the three dams near Chelinda Camp and in the streams which flow into and out of them. A daily fishing licence costs US$4, and allows you a bag of six fish. Rods can be hired for US$2, but are not in good condition. Only fly fishing is permitted here. The use of spinners or lures is prohibited. Fly fishing requires more skill, and is a way of ensuring Nyika's stocks are not over-fished. An information sheet with more details about conditions and recommended tackle, compiled by Denis Tweedle, Fisheries Advisor, is available at the park HQ.

Night Drives

If you have your own vehicle, you are allowed to drive at night in the park – which can some-times be a good time to see leopard. You need to go with a scout (US$2), and can hire a powerful searchlight for another US$2.

PLACES TO STAY

As outlined in the introduction, big changes are planned for Nyika. More than anything else, the accommodation situation is likely to alter drastically in the next few years, as the chalets and camp site are improved and a new lodge is built. The exact timescale for these changes is not known, and the following information will probably be out of date by the time you arrive.

Nyika National Park's main accommodation centre is *Chelinda Camp*. The camp has self-contained chalets with two bedrooms (each with two beds), bathroom, kitchen and dining area, costing US$20 for the whole chalet or US$10 per room. There are also blocks of double bedrooms, with a shared bathroom and common room, for US$10. All have fireplaces, firewood, electricity and hot water. A fully equipped central kitchen (with staff to assist with cooking) and lounge area is open to all visitors.

The camp site, about two km north of the park office, costs US$3 per night if you use your own tent. Large tents with beds inside are available for US$8. The youth hostel is mainly for school groups but can be used if the chalets and bedrooms are full (US$5 per person).

Near the Juniper Forest (in the southern part of the park, about 30 km from Chelinda by winding park track) is a small cabin with one room containing four beds and basic furniture (US$4 per person), but this may be removed as part of the rehabilitation plan. A caretaker lives nearby.

Accommodation is also available at the *Zambian Resthouse*, in Zambian territory, to the left of the track from Thazima Gate to Chelinda, about 45 km from the gate. There are no border formalities. The resthouse is well maintained, with bedrooms (sleeping about 10 people in total), a lounge, and a well-equipped kitchen. A caretaker and cook are on duty all the time, and a notice board has good information on short walking routes in the area. To hire the whole rest-house costs US$100 per night, or US$15 per person. Camping may also be allowed. You may have to pay Zambian national park fees, which are US$5 per person. You can turn up on spec, and if nobody else has reserved the resthouse, you can stay. If you would like to reserve, in Zambia contact Robin Pope Safaris (☎ Mfuwe (062) 45090; fax 45051), PO Box 320154, Lusaka, or in Malawi contact Central African Wilderness Safaris (☎ 723527; fax 723548), PO Box 489, Lilongwe.

GETTING THERE & AWAY
Car

The main entrance to Nyika National Park is at Thazima Gate (pronounced 'Tazima', and often spelt this way). If you're driving, the road from Rumphi is straightforward; ignore all turns to left and right until you reach a major fork called Nyika Junction, 44 km from Rumphi, where you go right to the gate (54 km from Rumphi). Chelinda Camp is another 55 km from the gate through the park. In 1996 this was a fair dirt road, with bad patches, but it may well have been tarred by the time you visit, as part of the great Nyika improvement project mentioned above. The other park entrance is Kaperekezi Gate, on the west side of the park, passed if you're travelling to or from Chitipa and Nthalire, but rarely used by visitors. You cannot reach Chelinda by car from Livingstonia or any other town on the east side of the plateau, despite a road being indicated on some old maps.

Bus

There's a daily bus in each direction between Mzuzu and Chitipa, via Rumphi, going through the park via Thazima and Kaperekezi gates with a loop up to Chelinda. (If the bus doesn't go to Chelinda, ask the driver to drop you at the Zambian Resthouse junction, from where you can walk or hitch the 12 km to Chelinda. This is against park regulations, as no entry to the park is allowed unless you are in or on a vehicle, although local staff do it all the time and nobody seems to mind). This bus only runs in the dry season when the road is in good condition, and even then it can still be a problem getting on at Rumphi as it's often full by the time it reaches here. It's best to get on in Mzuzu. When the road is tarred to Chelinda (as planned) the bus will run all year.

If you miss the bus, or it's full, most days there's a bus from Rumphi to Katumbi, passing Nyika Junction, from where it's a 10 km walk or hitch to Thazima Gate. You can wait at the gate for a lift to Chelinda (this is the method used by park staff and their families). If you get stuck, the rangers at the gate will let you camp there. Some vehicles come through the park, going towards Nthalire and Chitipa, which means they turn left at the Zambian Resthouse junction. You might be able to get a lift to here and walk or hitch the rest of the way to Chelinda.

It is also possible to reach Chelinda by bus from the north, from Chitipa via Nthalire and Kaperekezi Gate and Zambian Resthouse junction, from where you follow the directions given earlier.

Bicycle

Nyika is an ideal place for two-wheeled travellers. For details on access follow the directions given under the Car section earlier. Although pedestrians are not allowed to enter the park, people on bikes can. Once in the park the network of dirt roads is ideal for mountain biking. You can base yourself at Chelinda and go for day rides in various directions, or do a 'wilderness ride' and stay out overnight.

It is also possible to ride from Chelinda to Livingstonia (although some of the descents are so steep you have to get off and carry your bike), following a similar route to the three-day hike described in the Hiking & Trekking section which follows. If you're heading north this is a particularly good diversion away from the main road between Mzuzu and Karonga. The chief game scout at Nyika, Manfred Kmwenda, has accompanied groups of mountain bikers from Chelinda to Livingstonia on several occasions, and is essential if you're to find the correct route. Even though his bike is a single gear black bedstead he has no problem keeping up, and is very knowledgeable about the wildlife and so on.

HIKING & TREKKING ROUTES

As well as the shorter walks that are possible around Chelinda Camp and other parts of the park (described above), various long-distance hiking or trekking routes are possible on Nyika. For walking routes of more than one day, you must provide all the equipment and food you need. Guides are obligatory and porters available if required. Camp sites are not fixed, although in practice the better sites are used more frequently. No facilities of any kind exist at the sites. For maps and guidebooks on the plateau, see the Information, Maps & Guidebooks section earlier.

Guides & Porters

All hikers and trekkers on Nyika must be accompanied by a park ranger, called a scout, who will act as guide. Other scouts are available for hire as porters if you need them. Scouts cost US$10 per day, porters US$15. If you're booking accommodation (see Places to Stay) in advance, scouts can also be arranged then. Alternatively, they can be hired at the park office with a day's notice. Guides and porters have their own sleeping bags, tent, cooking pots, and food.

The chief scout, Manfred Kmwenda, has

been working here for many years and is very knowledgeable about trails and other walking options around the park. He may be available to guide you himself, but if he's not free he will arrange another scout suitable for the type of route you want to do.

All the scouts speak English, and are generally very pleasant, quite knowledgeable about the birds and wildlife, and good company on a long trek. They receive no extra money from the park for this work, so a tip (of around US$1 or US$2 per day) at the end of your trek is appropriate if the service has been good.

If your trek finishes outside the park, you must pay for your scout's public transport back to Chelinda, and an 'allowance' if he stays out another night. For Livingstonia, a single fee of US$10 seems to cover transport, accommodation and other incidentals.

Even though you've got a guide it's still important to be familiar with the route, conditions, likely times and so on, as the scouts are very fit, and their ideas about daily distances may be different to yours! Let your scout know how long you want to walk for each day, and whether you are 'strong' or 'not so strong'.

Wilderness Trails

A series of walking routes called Wilderness Trails (based on the South African concept) has been set by the national park authorities, varying in length from one day to more than a week. These trails are not marked, and often do not even follow a path or track. On some sections you simply find your own way through forest, or across open grassland, using the local knowledge of your guide. There are many variations to each trail (particularly the longer ones) and the actual route you take may depend on the time of year, where you're likely to see wildlife, the skill of the guide, or just how you're feeling on the day. Although you will see plenty of game while walking, a wilderness trail of this nature is not intended to allow you to stalk zebra or antelope to get better photos, but rather to see such animals as part of the wider environment. To get full enjoyment from a

wilderness trail, you must also appreciate the birds, the vegetation, the landscape and the splendid feelings of space and isolation that walking on Nyika provides.

Some of the wilderness trails are out-and-back routes, others start and finish at different points. The best areas for trekking are the escarpments on the plateau edge, so most of the trails are in these areas, and you need to allow at least another day at either end of the trail to walk from, and back to, Chelinda Camp. If you have a car, these first stages can usually be covered by vehicle.

You don't have to keep to these wilderness trails. They are provided only as suggestions by the park authorities. Basically, you can go anywhere you like for as long as you like. All you need is a guide to go with you, and enough equipment and food to keep going.

The Nyika Highlights Route

This is not an official wilderness trail, like the ones set by the park, as it follows paths and tracks for much of the way, rather than going through open country. The title is not official either; it's got this name because it takes in many of Nyika's main attractions including Lake Kaulime, the Zovo-Chipolo Forest, Chisanga Falls, Domwe Peak, the western escarpment and Nganda Peak, the highest point on the plateau. This trek starts and finishes at Chelinda Camp and takes four days, although you could do it in three at a push. It can be done in either direction. The daily distances are quite long, although there are no major gradients to contend with. Alternatively you could stretch it over five days.

Stage 1: Chelinda Camp to Chisanga Falls (29 km, 7 to 8 hours) From the start at Chelinda, the route passes Lake Kaulime then cuts through the grassland to Zambian Resthouse junction and passes Zovo-Chipolo Forest, where there's a nature trail (see Walking above). It then follows the border track between Malawi and Zambia until you reach a path going down through woodland to reach Chisanga Falls. There is a good place to camp above the falls.

Stage 2: Chisanga Falls to Domwe Peak

(17 km, 6 to 7 hours) From Chisanga Falls, the route gains the edge of the western escarpment with splendid views over the North Rukuru Valley and into Zambia. Domwe Peak (2340m) is the highest point on the western escarpment and a particularly good viewpoint.

Stage 3: Domwe Peak to Lower Mondwe Stream

(17 km, 5 to 6 hours) From Domwe Peak, the route strikes out across the heart of the plateau, through classic montane grassland scenery to reach to Lower Mondwe Stream, below Nganda Peak, where there's a choice of camp sites, all of them slightly damp. Allow another two to three hours to go up and down Nganda Peak (2607m) the highest point on the Nyika Plateau. From the summit, the whole rolling expanse of the plateau spreads away towards the south, and to the north-east you can often see the glistening waters of Lake Malawi.

Stage 4: Lower Mondwe Stream to Chelinda Camp

(20 km, 6 to 7 hours) You can do the Nganda Peak walk the next day (Stage 4), before heading home. The route cuts across the top of the North Rumphi Valley then aims south all the way back to Chelinda Camp.

The Livingstonia Route

This route follows tracks and paths for its entire length, and drops dramatically down the wooded escarpment on the eastern edge of the plateau, leaving the park and going via the villages of Chakaka and Phoka Court to reach the old mission station of Livingstonia. Daily distances are not long, and most of the route is downhill. The route takes three days, with the possibility of a fourth if you can't find a lift out of Livingstonia. If you're short of time, and feeling fit, the first two stages can be done in one day, but it's long and hard. This route cannot be done in reverse.

Stage 1: Chelinda Camp to Phata Stream

(18 km, 6 to 7 hours) From the start at Chelinda Camp the route goes south then east from Chelinda, across fine rolling grassland, passing south of Nthakati Peak, and crossing several small streams to reach the larger Phata Stream, which makes a good camp site.

Stage 2: Phata Stream to Chakaka Village

(12 km, 5 to 6 hours) From Phata Stream, the route continues eastward over the crest of a large broad ridge marking the eastern edge of the escarpment. The route then follows a secondary ridge through forest, bush and long grass to leave the park and descend very steeply to eventually reach the huts and small fields of Chakaka village.

Stage 3: Chakaka to Livingstonia

(16 km, 5 to 6 hours) From Chakaka village, a small dirt road winds down the valley beside the large North Rumphi River to reach the main dirt road between Livingstonia and Rumphi at a small village called Phoka Court. Some final switchbacks over steep ridges lead you to Livingstonia. (For full details on places to stay here, see the Livingstonia section earlier.)

The Lake Shore

Lake Malawi is probably the country's number one attraction, and many visitors travel along the lake shore, from village to village, or beach to beach, without ever going to the highlands of the interior. Whilst not recommending that anyone should do this (thereby missing more than half of the country), this chapter covers every place on the shore (and a few places just inland), in a roughly north to south direction.

Lake Shore Divisions
The shore of Lake Malawi is divided into three ill-defined and rather uneven parts. The Northern Lake Shore runs from the Songwe River border, through Karonga and Chilumba, down to where the Kandoli Mountains (east of Mzuzu) plunge directly into the lake, forming an effective barrier to land transport. The Central Lake Shore runs from Nkhata Bay, through Chintheche, Nkhotakota, down to Senga Bay, near Salima. The Southern Lake Shore runs from Monkey Bay to Mangochi, where the Shire River flows out of the lake and into Lake Malombe. Beyond here is Liwonde National Park – covered in the Southern Malawi chapter of this book. ■

The Northern Lake Shore

KARONGA

Karonga is the regional centre of the far north of the country, and could be your first or last town if you're travelling between Malawi and Tanzania. The town is strung out for about two km along the main street between a roundabout on the north-south road and the lake shore. Facilities include a post office and the only permanent bank north of Mzuzu.

Although fairly sleepy today, Karonga has seen its share of action in the past. At the end of the 19th century, the African Lakes Corporation waged a 'private war' against the army of Sultan Mlozi, a powerful Swahili-Arab slave trader who was based here. Later, during WWI, colonial British soldiers, with African conscripts, repelled a German invasion from the neighbouring colony of Deutsch Ost-Afrika (later to become Tanzania). This is reported to be the only WWI land battle to be fought on Malawian territory. (Another battle took place on the lake – see Mangochi, later in this chapter.)

Places to Stay & Eat
A popular and good-value place is the *Tukumbugwe Hotel*, by the roundabout on the main road. Small rooms cost US$4, larger ensuite rooms US$7. North of the roundabout, on the road to Kaporo, is the *Chombe Hotel & Restaurant*, charging US$3 per person, with good food. Also near the roundabout is the new market and bus park, several cheap eating houses (including the recommended *Cross Roads and Karonga Restaurant*) and a couple of bottle shops and bars.

Heading from the roundabout towards the lake, you reach *Safari Lodge* where clean, self-contained rooms with mosquito nets cost US$7, including a hearty breakfast. Nearby *Bazuka Lodge* charges US$5 for rooms with attached bathroom. Budget travellers can go for *Kankhununu Guesthouse*, behind the old market, off the main street, where small rooms cost US$1.50. It's certainly nothing special but clean enough and quite adequate for a night.

At the end of the road, go left to reach the gloomy *Council Resthouse* with rooms for just US$1. Or turn right to reach friendly *Mufwa Lakeside Centre*; it's worth the long, hot walk from the roundabout, with clean singles/doubles for US$4/6, and camping for US$1 per person. There is plenty of shade, good food for US$2, and cold beer. Not far away is *Club Marina*, also with cold beer and smart ensuite rooms for US$10/15 with hot showers and breakfast. You can camp here,

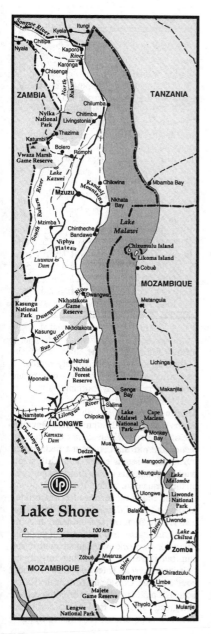

Lake Shore

0   50   100 km

and use the shower for a small fee. Staff can advise on places in town to change money (including Tanzanian shillings) if the bank is closed.

Getting There & Away

Buses run at least three times a day to/from Mzuzu for US$6. Going from Karonga to Mzuzu, it might be worth getting the bus from the Stagecoach depot, as it's sometimes full by the time it gets to the main bus park in town. Between Karonga and the Tanzania border at Songwe Bridge a bus costs US$0.50, and a minibus US$1 (for more details see the Getting There & Away chapter). There's no bus to Chitipa (on the Zambia border) but there are plans to tar the road between Karonga and Nakonde (the Zambia-Tanzania border town), via Chitipa, so in the next few years buses will no doubt start running this way too.

CHILUMBA

This is a steamer port, just east of the main north-south road about 80 km south of Karonga and 20 km north of Chitimba. You might get off the boat here if you're heading for Livingstonia. Places to stay seem limited to the very basic *Jetty Resthouse* which charges US$1 for a bed and almost the same for a paltry breakfast.

CHITIMBA

This is the junction where the Livingstonia road turns off the main north-south lake shore road. If you get stuck here for the night there's the very basic but friendly *Florence Bay Resthouse*, on the junction, where you can sleep for US$0.50 per night. Mr Obie and Mike run the place. Cheap food and beer are on sale, and you can safely leave your bag here if you only want to go to Livingstonia for the day. Next door is the similar *Nyabweka Restaurant & Resthouse*, which some travellers have also rated highly.

For a longer stay, *Des's Chitimba Beach Campsite* is popular with overland trucks and independent travellers; there are chalets for US$3, camping for US$1.50, and a lively bar right on the beach. The beer is usually cold, and a meal costs around US$3. Des (the locals pronounce his name 'Daze', perhaps not uncoincidentally) is a some-time overland driver, and arranges water-skiing, snorkelling and boat trips. The camp site is a few hundred metres east of the main road, about one km north of the Livingstonia turn-off.

A bus between Chitimba and Mzuzu is US$3. Chitimba to/from Karonga is US$2.

Around Chitimba

About five km south of Chitimba, very close to the lake shore, is *M'Buta Tourist Lodge & Camping*, where pleasant, self-contained double chalets, with a kitchen and mosquito-netted veranda, cost US$14, or US$24 if you want the kitchen fully-equipped. Ensuite rooms (basically a chalet without the kitchen) cost US$6/8, and camping is US$0.50. Breakfast is US$1.50 and main meals cost about US$3.

A further five km south is the *Chombe Motel*, with rooms for around US$10. The more basic but pleasant *Nyamkamba Lodge* has rooms (for one or two people) for US$3; camping costs US$1 per person.

The historic mission town of **Livingstonia** is 25 km inland from Chitimba. It is covered in detail in the Northern Malawi chapter.

The Central Lake Shore

NKHATA BAY

The town of Nkhata Bay spreads round a large lake inlet, about 50 km east of Mzuzu. This is probably the most scenic of Malawi's lake shore towns, and a few travellers have even described it as 'Caribbean'. That may be a touch too fanciful, although at sunrise and sunset it does become quite picturesque.

It's a busy place: the Lake Malawi steamer docks here, and buses go regularly to/from Mzuzu or along the lake shore to Salima and Monkey Bay. In the last few years, Nkhata Bay has started to rival Cape Maclear as a budget travellers' destination, and there are several good places to stay. Despite the

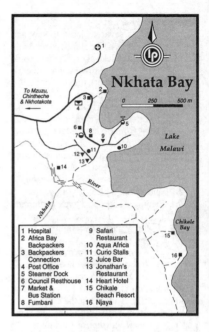

Nkhata Bay

To Mzuzu, Chintheche & Nkhotakota

Lake Malawi

Nkhata River

Chikale Bay

1 Hospital	9 Safari
2 Africa Bay	Restaurant
Backpackers	10 Aqua Africa
3 Backpackers	11 Curio Stalls
Connection	12 Juice Bar
4 Post Office	13 Jonathan's
5 Steamer Dock	Restaurant
6 Council Resthouse	14 Heart Hotel
7 Market &	15 Chikale
Bus Station	Beach Resort
8 Fumbani	16 Njaya

influx of foreigners, the town retains its Malawian feel. There's a lively market, a post office, and a bank where you can change money every weekday morning.

Things to Do

Aqua Africa (☎ 352284) in Nkhata Bay runs **diving** courses which have been recommended. Prices start at about US$35 for an introductory scuba experience (for people with qualifications but no diving experience in the past year). A five day scuba diving course, leading to an internationally recognised certificate, costs US$100. These courses are popular, and the team at Aqua Africa run at least two per week. You should try to book a week or two in advance if you can, but if by any chance they're full you only have to wait a few days for the next course to start. Outside the town is the Kalwe Forest, which closely resembles the coastal evergreen forests of East Africa and offers excellent opportunities for bird-watching.

Places to Stay & Eat

Nkhata Bay has several places to stay and eat, all strung out in a line along the road into town and along the lake shore. As you come down the hill into the town centre (there's only one road in and out), on your right, just past the post office, is *Backpackers Connection* (☎ 352302), formerly the Kadanga Lake Facing Hotel, vaguely connected to other Backpackers Connection lodges in other parts of Southern Africa, run by the ebullient Ian Colclough. It's on a steep bank above the road, with good views over the bay. Secure single/double rooms are US$3.50/5, camping is US$1 and there's a place to park vehicles if you're driving. There's a bar, restaurant, clean bathrooms and a storage room for baggage if you want to travel light to Likoma Island or elsewhere.

Next on your left, down by the lake, is *Africa Bay Backpackers*, with simple beach chalets (where fishermen come and go early in the morning) for US$1.50 per person. Food is usually available in the evening.

At the bottom of the hill is the bus stand and the *Council Resthouse* (a dump, with rooms from US$1.50 per person). The road then passes the market and a couple of local eating houses, including the *Fumbani* which has a vast menu and some small cheap rooms. Beyond here is the *Safari Restaurant*, a popular travellers' haunt with another great view across the bay, where you can get omelettes and sandwiches for US$1, pizza and moussaka for US$2, and other meals like chicken for US$2.50. Just past here is the ferry jetty, Aqua Africa and the road's end.

If you turn right onto a dirt road just before the Safari Restaurant, you pass an area of woodcarvers' stalls and a small street leading back towards the bus stop. On this street is the *Juice Bar* run by Sandra and Paul, where you can get fresh fruit drinks and milk shakes for US$0.30, salads for US$2, and some of the largest and most healthy-looking sandwiches in Malawi for just over US$1.

If you continue along the dirt road, you pass *Jonathan's Restaurant*, a mellow shack with a vast menu of good meals for around US$2. Several travellers have written to recommend this place. On from here, past the police station, is another small turning which leads to the *Heart Hotel*, a friendly, no-frills place to stay with a definite African village feel, and one of the few tourist places in town that is Malawian-run. Many shoestring travellers have recommended this place too. The owner, Philip, says whatever the other resthouses in town charge, he'll always be the cheapest. Camping costs US$0.35, you can sleep on the floor for US$0.60, or take the luxury option of a bed in the new building with electricity for US$1 (with breakfast). Meals cost US$2. (Another new resthouse is being built by the junction, and might be worth checking when it's finished.)

Back on the dirt road, you cross a bridge and head uphill and down dale for 20 minutes (it always seems longer with a backpack) to reach Chikale Bay, the next bay round from the main town. Here are two places which are fast becoming legendary on the traveller's grapevine. One is *Njaya*, the first backpackers' place in the area, run by English couple Claire and Paul, where reed chalets (on the beach or up the hill) with beds and mosquito nets cost US$5 (for one or two people). Camping or a mat in the dorm on the beach is US$1.50, or you can take the luxury ensuite double chalet (complete with bath tub overlooking the lake) for US$20. The breezy bar overlooks the lake, and food includes burgers and homemade sausages for US$1.50, vegie pizza for US$2, and meaty pizza or risotto for US$3. You can get your laundry done, and there's even a visa service if you're heading for Mozambique. And don't forget to say 'Hi' to resident artist Van the Man. Some of the money from this place goes to support a local centre for the blind.

The other place (next door to Nyaja) is the smarter *Chikale Beach Resort* where brick ensuite double chalets cost US$8, and triples cost US$11. Camping is US$2. In the bar and restaurant right on the fabulous beach, you can get a full breakfast for US$3, a continental breakfast for US$1 and other meals for about US$2 to US$3.

Unfortunately, security became a bit of a problem in Nkhata Bay during 1996. Some travellers were attacked and robbed when walking outside the town centre (especially to/from Chikale), and a few people had bags snatched near the bus station while looking for a place to stay (thieves love new arrivals). To combat this, the various hotels, lodges, restaurants and Aqua Africa have got together and will 'lend' their watchmen to anyone walking to Chikale or elsewhere. Use this service and you'll have no worries.

Getting There & Away

All buses go to and from the bus stop at the bottom of the hill, next to the market. A bus between Nkhata Bay and Mzuzu is US$1; to/from Chintheche is US$1; and to/from Nkhotakota is US$3. Many travellers also come or go on the lake steamers which call at Nkhata Bay on their way to/from Karonga, Likoma Island, Nkhotakota, or the ports in Tanzania. For more details see the Getting Around and Getting There & Away chapters.

THE CHINTHECHE STRIP

Chintheche (pronounced 'Chin-tech-ee') is a largish village about 40 km south of Nkhata Bay. Although this place is unremarkable in itself (there are a few shops, a market, a mosque and a bank open twice a week), nearby is a long stretch of lake shore where several camp sites, hotels and lodges have been built, all with various 'feels' and catering for different types of visitor. They all lie about two to five km east of the main M5 road that runs between Nkhata Bay and Nkhotakota. Getting there usually involves a drive or walk along a dirt track through sandy forest, villages or local farmland. Most of the places are signposted off the main road, but at minor junctions on the track there may be no signs (the local people seem to like them as decorations or firewood) so you may have to ask directions.

As with the rest of this chapter, places are described north to south. If you're travelling by bus, the Express services may not stop at every turn-off, so you may have alight at the nearest place, and walk or hitch the last few km. InterCity buses stop at more places. There are also minibuses along this road which stop almost anywhere on request.

Places to Stay & Eat

In Chintheche village itself there are a few local resthouses, but a better option if you're short of cash is the typically under-used *Forest Resthouse*, where beds in functional and clean cabins cost US$2.50. Each room has two to four beds and its own bathroom. There's a lounge and dining area, with an outside kitchen where you can self-cater or ask the cook to prepare meals – but you must bring all your own food. There are also some basic rooms for US$1.50, and camping is US$1.25. The resthouse is signposted down a track, half a km off the main road next to the large signpost for the Katoto Beach Motel. The only drawback is that it's not on the beach – you have to walk about a km through the forest, but it's a pleasant enough stroll. A new chalet is under construction although, rather strangely for a forest department, it's being built with brick.

At the *Katoto Beach Motel*, about 800m off the main road, simple ensuite chalets cost US$6/7, and VIP chalets (overlooking the beach) US$11/13. Management has spared no expense on fittings – you get veneered cabinets, TVs, fans and full-length mirrors in the VIP chalets – but the concrete is overpowering and the whole place could do with a lick of paint. Camping is US$2, breakfast US$1 to US$4, and meals around US$3. It's popular with Malawian organisations who use it for conferences and workshops.

Half a km south of here, another dirt track leads to *London Cottage*, where 10 closely sited ensuite chalets cost US$3 per person, or US$7 for the whole chalet (up to six people). Camping is US$3 per tent. The front row of chalets overlooks the beach, and there's also a bar and restaurant. About two km down the road, and another two km along a dirt track, is *Flame Tree Lodge* (☎ 357276), run by a friendly English-Malawian couple. It's on a beautiful spit of sand and rock jutting into the lake. Smart self-contained chalets are US$10/$14, with no extra charge for children sharing. Camping is US$2, and the showers are hot. This is a pleasant, quiet place suitable for families or small groups. There's a small bar and bookshop/library, and the restaurant serves meals like steak, chicken and stew for US$3. Breakfast (with homemade jam) is US$1.50. This place is connected to Flame Tree Bed & Breakfast in Mzuzu (see that section) and transport runs between the two at least once a week.

Next along, about two km further south and 2.5 km off the main road, is the turn-off to *Sombani Lodge*, where prices and facilities are about the same as at Flame Tree. In between these two lodges, an old Malawian man by the name of Hamilton is building a resthouse which should be open 'sometime soon'.

Another 1.5 km along the main road, a tar road leads for two km to *Chintheche Inn*, originally built by the government as staff quarters for a proposed paper mill (see the boxed text below on the Chintheche Paper Mill Threat), and later taken over by the Department of Tourism. The setting is idyllic, with clean and comfortable rooms for US$15/20, including breakfast. Camping is US$2. Unfortunately, this place never became popular as the management was sloppy and food supplies were irregular. Now it's rarely used, as other places with better staff and reliable menus have opened in the vicinity. It's likely, however, that the hotel will be leased out to private management, in which case things are likely to improve.

Chintheche Paper Mill Threat
The Chintheche Inn was built in the 1970s as staff quarters for a proposed paper mill planned for this area. For various reasons the plan was shelved, but never abandoned completely. In 1996 it was reported that the paper mill plans may be brought out of mothballs, as an overseas industrial investor had promised millions of dollars to the government if allowed to build here.

This would certainly earn much-needed foreign exchange for the country, and provide jobs, but conservationists (and some powerful donor nations) argue that it will pollute the lake and endanger fish stocks, thereby affecting tourism and fishing – two of Malawi's other vital industries. At the time of writing, a decision was in the balance. ■

Nearby, *Vyatowa Lodge & Camping* is under construction.

Further down the main road, one km south of the Chintheche Inn turn-off, is a signpost to the CCAP School (also called New Bandawe). Go down here, turn right in the school grounds, and continue for 2.5 km along a dirt track to reach *Nkhwazi Lake Camp*, a good-quality camp site run by an English-South African couple, where camping on the grass is US$1.50, and in thatched reed shelters US$2. There are clean ablution blocks and wash-up facilities, and a good bar and restaurant with meals for around US$3 to US$5. The camp overlooks a small sandy cove, and nearby is a longer beach. There are plans for chalets. The camp also has scuba gear and a motorboat for divers or anglers to hire. Snorkelling in the area is also good.

Continuing south down the main road you cross a river bridge and reach the turn-off to Bandawe (one of the early Livingstonia Mission sites, and also called Old Bandawe) and *Makuzi Lodge*, another 3.5 km down the track. Makuzi Lodge is run by Jane Jackson, an old Malawi hand and skilled diver, who knows the lake and surrounding mountains very well. Her lodge used to be famous for its grassy campsite, simple cabins and laidback atmosphere, but when we oassed through Jane had plans for a small and exclusive lodge with ensuite chalets for between US$100 and US$150 per person, including excellent food and various activities. These plans may take a while to realise though, so check the current situation before arriving. Although on-spec guests are welcomed, reservations through Central African Wilderness Safaris in Lilongwe (see under Travel & Tour Agencies in the Lilongwe chapter) are preferred. Jane has good connections with the nearby village, and is assisting with school-building and the care of local children.

The main road runs alongside the lake for a while, then seven km from the Makuzi turn-off (about 55 km from Nkhata Bay) is a

MALAWI

sign to *Kande Beach Camp*. This place is a very basic camp site with long-drop toilets and a long, open bar, but it is extremely popular with overland trucks. Good times and partying is the name of the game here. Individual campers are charged US$1.50.

Another seven km further south is the vastly different *Mwaya Beach Camp*, owned by Kristin and run by the amiable Mr Robinson, where the atmosphere is quiet and restful, and the entrance track allegedly designed to wind through trees and cross weak bridges to keep the overland trucks out! Simple chalets cost US$3 per person, and camping is US$1.25. There's a bar, where the music volume is never too loud, and food includes pancakes, banana bread, scones, pasta, beanburgers, or meals of chicken and fish for US$2 to US$4. Clean drinking water is free.

Old Bandawe & Makuzi Hill

Near Makuzi Lodge is the site of Bandawe mission station, established by UMCA missionaries in the 1890s after they moved from their original position at Cape Maclear, before moving to the more successful site at today's Livingstonia. This site is often called Old Bandawe, to distinguish it from New Bandawe, built nearer the main road in the 1920s and still a thriving mission and secondary school today. All that remains today is a few huts and the church the missionaries built, which has a new roof and is still used on Sundays. It is a simple, square building with a series of low steps in a semi-circle facing the altar, instead of pews, contrasting sharply with the more European style church later built at Livingstonia.

Also nearby is a graveyard where various missionaries are buried, in a line facing the lake, surrounded by a series of low white walls which seem to pen them in. A single grave lies outside the wall – our guide said it contained the body of a shipwrecked sailor who was not known to be a Christian.

Overlooking the lodge is Makuzi Hill, which has spiritual significance for the local people. For some unknown reason (geological, meteorological or magical) small bolts of lightning have been seen shooting a few metres *up* from rocks on the hill. There are also several caves, where the Tonga people would hide from Ngoni warriors or Swahili-Arab slavers in the 19th century. ■

DWANGWA

This town has grown up around a large sugar-cane plantation established on the lake shore plain. There is a market, petrol station and local resthouse. About 20 km north of here is *Heidi's Hide-out*, still being completed when we passed though, with simple clean and airy rooms for US$3 and camping for US$1. There's a bar and small restaurant, and a beach nearby.

NKHOTAKOTA

This is reputedly one of the oldest market towns in Africa and was once the main centre of the slave trade in this region. The town itself is strung out along the main north-south road, and along another road which runs down to the lake. The bus station and a small group of resthouses are about two km off the main road, from where it's another two km to the lake itself.

Things to see in the area include the mission (if you come on a Sunday the singing from the church is wonderful). Nearby is a tree under which Livingstone the explorer reportedly camped on one of his expeditions. It is said that he met here with a local chief called Jumbe and tried to persuade him to abandon the slave trade (described in full under History in the Facts about Malawi chapter). A second tree marks the spot where Livingstone camped on a subsequent visit. Another attraction is the hippo pool at Jalo, a few km north of town. Local guides will show you the way (Nelson and Den, who are also artists, have been recommended). They may also try to show you the hot springs, just south of town on the main road, but this is not worth the bother.

Places to Stay & Eat

On the main road, there's a *Council Resthouse*, a couple of bars and nightclubs, a supermarket, bank and petrol station. As you go into town from the main road, after about 1.5 km you reach the mission hospital. In the grounds is the *Livingstone Resthouse & Restaurant* where basic but acceptable rooms cost US$2/3. Doubles have their own bathroom. Good food costs from US$1 to US$2, and the range includes curries, western style dishes and Malawian meals.

Carry on down the road towards the lake for 500m to reach the *Pick & Pay Resthouse*, run by friendly Philip Banda. It's clean, and has electricity and showers (cold water only). Rates are similar to the Livingstone. There's also camping and safe parking for vehicles for US$1. All the rooms have mosquito nets, and the restaurant is reported to be the best in town, although *Alekeni Anene Restaurant* next door is keeping the competition fierce.

Another two km down the road, near the jetty where the boats go out to meet the lake steamers (it's too shallow to dock) is the *District Council Lake Shore Resthouse*. Tatty rooms cost US$2, and should be avoided, but the resthouse itself is well worth a visit. It seems to have been built largely from old boats and motor parts. The windows on the staircase are still attached to the car doors they came out of, and the terrace balustrade is a fine collection of crankshafts and axles. It's a good place for a sundowner beer overlooking the lake, especially if you're waiting for the *Ilala*. The bar is a popular nightspot.

Getting There & Away
Buses between Nkhotakota and Nkhata Bay cost US$3.50; to/from Salima is US$2; and to/from Lilongwe is US$5. You can also come/go by lake steamer – see the Getting Around chapter for details.

Around Nkhotakota
About 11 km south of the Nkhotakota turn-off is *Sani Beach Resort*, a few km off the main lake shore road, on the lake, with simple chalets for US$3 and camping for US$1. Two km beyond here is the turn-off to the smarter *Njobvu Safari Camp* (☎ 292227), on the lake shore about four km off the main road, which has comfortable chalets for US$10 per person. Numbers are limited to 16 guests at any one time, keeping the place quiet and friendly. Camping is US$3. There's a bar and restaurant.

Nkhotakota Game Reserve lies west of the main north-south lake shore road, covering a broad area of the Rift Valley escarpment. It's the largest reserve in Malawi but it was virtually abandoned by the Department of National Parks & Wildlife during the 1980s and early 1990s, and poaching was rampant. The main dirt road between Nkhotakota and Lilongwe (via Ntchisi) passes through the southern portion of the reserve, but there are hardly any other roads or vehicle tracks, so the best way to explore it is by foot (you must be accompanied by a game scout).

Big game is limited, and difficult to see in the dense vegetation, but walking here is reported to be an excellent way to sample true Malawian wilderness. There's a mix of miombo woodland and patches of evergreen forest, and the reserve is crossed by several large rivers, so the birdlife is varied and rewarding. Accommodation is limited to some dilapidated rondavels at Chipata Camp, a ranger post and reserve headquarters, about five km north of the dirt road towards Lilongwe, about 35 km from Nkhotakota town. The charge is US$5 per night, and camping is allowed. (There are also two other camp sites in the reserve.) You can hire a ranger/guide here. Reserve entrance fees must also be paid (see under National Parks in the Facts about Malawi chapter).

An internationally funded rehabilitation scheme is planned for the reserve in the late 1990s, so expect some changes to access, accommodation and management by the time you arrive. If you don't have your own car, and prefer not to chance the vagaries of public transport, trips to the reserve are arranged from Njobvu Safari Camp, from US$17 per person, including transport, lunch and entrance fees. If you have a good guide, who knows about trees and birds, you can have a very pleasant day out.

About 24 km south of Nkhotakota is the entrance to **Chia Lagoon**, a large bay linked to the main lake by a narrow channel, crossed by a bridge near the main road. Local people fish here using large triangular nets on poles, and seem to be resigned to having their photos taken by tourists on the bridge.

MALAWI

SALIMA

The town of Salima is about 20 km from the lake, where the main road to/from Lilongwe meets the main lake shore road. Salima itself is nothing special but it's the jumping off point for Senga Bay, a popular destination for visitors (see below for details).

Places to Stay

If you get stuck in Salima for the night there are a few options – none very inspiring. Right next to the bus station is the *Everest Resthouse*, charging US$2 per person; the showers don't work but the staff will bring hot water in a bucket. The restaurant is good. Opposite is the basic and grotty *Council Resthouse*, which has dorm beds for US$0.30 and doubles for US$2.50. Just over the railway tracks is the slightly better *Mwayma Lodge*. Better then all these, but more expensive, is the *Mai Tsalani Motel* near the PTC supermarket, about 10 minutes walk from the bus station. It is clean and friendly, with a surprisingly good restaurant. Basic double ensuite rooms are US$3; singles are cheaper. The bus to Blantyre goes from outside the door.

If you're heading for Monkey Bay, you wait for lifts or the bus at the junction about two km west of the town. If you get stuck, the *Malambi Inn* has bearable rooms for US$2/3. There are several bars and cheap eats places nearby.

Getting There & Away

To reach Salima from Lilongwe, there are four express buses per day, costing US$2. One of these buses continues all the way to Senga Bay, arriving late afternoon. It leaves to come back to Lilongwe at 6 am. If you miss this, there are local minibuses and pickups between Salima and Senga Bay town for US$1. There are also buses to/from Mzuzu (via Nkhotakota and Nkhata Bay) and to/from Blantyre (via Mangochi).

SENGA BAY

Senga Bay is a large inlet at the eastern end of the broad peninsula that juts into the lake from Salima. The lake seems to be remarkably clear here, and the beaches are also good. The town of Senga Bay (marked simply as Senga on some maps) lies at the end of the road that runs east from Salima. Here, and stretched along the bay itself – over a distance of about 10 km – are several places to stay, ranging from cheap camp sites to one of the classiest hotels in the whole of Malawi.

Things to Do

At Senga Bay, most of the lake shore establishments arrange **water sports**, such as windsurfing, water-skiing, snorkelling and boat rides. A popular destination is the nearby island, known locally as Lizard Island, home to fish eagles, cormorants and, surprisingly, huge lizards. The whole island is spattered white with cormorant droppings and it stinks, but don't let that put you off.

Alternatively, from Senga Bay town, you can go **hiking** in the nearby Senga Hills. There are a few trails but nothing well-established, so they can be hard to follow if the grass is long. It's worth persevering though, as the walks through the woodland up to viewpoints overlooking the lake are well worth the effort. It's best to hire a local guide from your hotel to show you the way (and also because there have been isolated incidents of robbery and harassment here). Go early morning or late afternoon: it's cooler, and the light is better for photographs. **Bird-watching** in the area is also excellent, with a good range of habitats in close proximity.

Another good place for a walk are the **hippo pools** about half an hour's walk up the lake shore beyond Steps camp site. Again, a local guide is recommended, and we've heard that the hippos have a reputation for being timid, but aggressive when pushed, so you'll either see nothing at all or have a chance of being attacked.

If you prefer **shopping** to walking and wildlife, you'll also love Senga Bay: along the main road through the town are loads of handicraft stalls which have about the best range you'll find anywhere.

Places to Stay & Eat

As you head towards Senga Bay, about 17 km from Salima a road branches off to the right. This leads (after another five km) to *The Wheelhouse*, where camping costs US$1.50 and boat rides are available. This place used to be famous for its circular bar on stilts out in the lake. Now the lake level has dropped, the bar stands stranded high above the sand, and loses some of its attraction, but it's still a popular place with overland trucks and anyone else with a vehicle (there's no public transport). The bar also serves pub food and snacks.

A few km along the coast nearby is *Crystal Waters Hotel*, where a standard double chalet is US$14, plus another US$14 if you want air-con, and another US$7 if you want to try the waterbed. Camping on terra firma is US$1, but the setting is nothing special and, again, this place can only easily be reached by those with wheels.

Back on the main Salima to Senga Bay road, after a few more km, another road branches off to the right, leading to the *Kambiri Lake Shore Hotel*. Somebody has made an effort here, with pleasant buildings and manicured grounds, but rooms do not overlook the lake and are rather functional, and a touch on the pricey side with singles/twins at US$40/75, although spotlessly clean. Meals cost US$4 to US$7.

If you follow the main road from Salima all the way to Senga Bay town, you come to the main street, lined with curio sellers. Buses stop here. At the western end of this street a dirt road leads off to the right (south) to three places, all next to each other, about 2.5 km from town. The first-built and still the best of the bunch is *Carolina's Lakeside Chalets* where straightforward ensuite rooms are US$14 for one or two people. There are nets and hot water. Camping costs US$1.50, and meals range from US$3 to US$5. Shady gardens overlook the lake, even though Carolina (who planted them) has moved on to pastures new. The new owner is a Muslim guy, so doesn't sell beer. However, he has no problem about you going to the bar next door and bringing home

a carry-out. The place has a restful feel, although this may change when the new blocks of luxury rooms are completed.

Next door is *Baobab Chalets* where rooms are US$10, camping is US$1 and meals about US$3. The 'camp site' is a patch of ground near the bar and the toilets could do with a good clean. Also next door is *S Chiphango Chalets*, a low-key place where basic chalets cost US$7 for one or two people. There is no food or bar, but there is a kitchen for self-catering.

Back in the town, just off the main street behind the curio stalls, is *Hippo Hide Resthouse*, a real backpackers' lodge, where no-frills rooms, with bedding and nets, cost US$1.50 per person and camping is US$1. Meals are US$2 to US$3, and they have cold beer and hot showers. The beach is just a few hundred metres away, and the friendly staff arrange boat trips to nearby islands, and hikes in the hills or to the nearby hippo pools. They also have snorkel gear for hire.

The main road continues through the town, for another two km, all the way to the imposing gates of the *Livingstonia Beach Hotel* (☎ 744022; fax 744483). This is a very smart place, where the architecture is a successful mix of old colonial, African and even something vaguely Mediterranean, set in lush gardens, with picture-postcard views over the lake. Style and luxury don't come cheap though – ensuite rooms cost US$130/170 a single/double, and chalets are US$170/185, including breakfast and taxes. The owners are from Holland, so this is probably one of the few places in Southern Africa where you can get an English breakfast *or* a Dutch breakfast, complete with specially imported Gouda. Various water sports and boat trips are available: you can hire dinghies for US$10 per hour, sailboards for US$6 per hour and canoes or snorkel gear for US$3; boat trips to nearby islands or hippo pools start at US$10 per person. Water-skiing costs US$15 per lap. The hotel has a tennis court, and organises guided walks or bird-watching trips to viewpoints in the hills, and car excursions

MALAWI

to various places of interest in the area (such as Mua Mission and the nearby fish farm).

Next door to the Livingstonia Beach Hotel is *Steps Camp Site*, run by the same management, and reckoned by some travellers to be the best campground in Malawi. It's clean and safe, with flat pitches, electric hook-ups and spotless showers and toilets. There's also a place to wash clothes and pots and pans, as well as a bar and a takeaway kitchen serving fast food, snacks and fresh bread. Once again, quality at a price: US$4 per person for camping. Costly by Malawian standards, but good value compared with some other parts of Southern Africa. Beers at the bar are at top-end hotel prices, and burger and chips (admittedly fine quality) will set you back US$7. Water sports and activities are available at the Livingstonia Beach Hotel (see paragraph above for prices).

Two other options in this area are the low-budget *Feel at Home Resthouse*, on the main road between the hotel and the town, and *Chigumukile Forestry Resthouse*, frequently overlooked but very good value (US$3 per person), on the lake shore beyond Steps camp site.

Getting There & Away

First get to Salima (for bus details, see the Salima Getting There & Away section). From here, local pick-ups run to/from Senga Bay for about US$1. Pick-ups will drop you in the main street of Senga Bay town. If you want a lift all the way to Livingstonia Beach and Steps Camp Site, or to Carolina's, negotiate an extra fee with the driver.

CHIPOKA

This is the nearest port to Lilongwe, and quite busy, although few tourists come here. *Lake View Lodge* is quiet and clean, but has no water, for US$3 a double. There's also a couple of cheap local restaurants.

MUA

Mua is a small town between Salima and Balaka, near the turn-off to Monkey Bay. There has been a mission here since the beginning of the century, and today there is a large church, school and hospital. Of interest to tourists is the **Kungoni Crafts** shop, full of paintings and wood sculptures by local people who have been encouraged in their work by one of the priests at the mission. Some of the work is of very high quality, covering religious and traditional secular subjects, and prices are reasonable. Nearby is a workshop where you can see the carvers in action. The area is set in gardens, and there's a small zoo, where the animals seem reasonably well cared for. Due to open in 1997 is the **Chamare Museum**, an exhibition of traditional indigenous arts, crafts, weapons, clothing, implements and ornaments (both modern and old). Visitors who have been allowed a sneak preview say there's nothing like it anywhere else in Malawi, and few others in Southern Africa, so it will be well worth a visit.

Monkey Bay & Cape Maclear

Monkey Bay is Malawi's main port, on the eastern side of the Nankumba Peninsula, towards the southern end of the lake. There's no beach or attractions here, so most travellers arriving by bus or boat head for the nearby delights of Cape Maclear as soon as possible.

MONKEY BAY

If you do get stuck for a night, there are a few places to stay: the *District Council Resthouse* near the bus station has grotty rooms for US$1 per person. Nicer is *Zawadi Lodge* where rooms are US$3. Camping is allowed in the yard, but no fence means security is very questionable. For eats, try *Gary's Café* opposite. Monkey Bay also has a market, a supermarket and an excellent bakery, plus a roving bank on Monday and Thursday mornings, where you can change travellers' cheques. (This bank may not be reliable

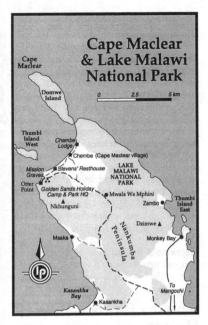

Cape Maclear & Lake Malawi National Park

though, so you're better off changing elsewhere before you arrive.)

Getting There & Away

Many travellers arrive or leave on one of the lake steamers. For details of the timetable and prices see the Getting There & Away and Getting Around chapters. The port is within easy walking distance of the bus station. Buses go regularly to/from Blantyre for US$6 (via Mangochi, US$1.25), but there's very little going north because the road to/from Mua (on the main road between Salima and Balaka) is in bad condition. If it's fixed, transport to Salima (and on to Lilongwe or up the lake shore road) will start again, so ask around if you're heading that way.

If you're a pan-continental traveller in a hurry, get the weekly bus which goes from Monkey Bay all the way to Beitbridge on the South African border, via Blantyre, Tete and Harare. And pack a very long novel.

CAPE MACLEAR

Technically, Cape Maclear is a spit of land on the tip of an island at the end of the Nankumba Peninsula, jutting into Lake Malawi. It's about 20 km by road from Monkey Bay. On the mainland shore nearby is a large bay and beach which everybody – but everybody – knows as Cape Maclear. The village spreads along the beach is technically called Chembe, but this usually gets called Cape Maclear as well.

Technicalities aside, Cape Maclear has become a travellers' by-word for sun, sand, rest and recreation – the closest thing you'll find to an Indian Ocean beach in inland Africa (though the 'ocean' here is a freshwater lake) – and most people passing through Malawi stay here at one time or another. Some never quite get round to leaving. Most travellers like it because it's cheap, friendly and beautiful. For others, the plentiful supply of 'Malawi Gold' (see Legal Matters in the Facts for the Visitor chapter) is another attraction. You'll meet people here you last saw in Cape Town, Harare, Nairobi, Zanzibar or wherever. It's the sort of place where you sit on the beach, have a few beers, and the next thing you know your visa's run out.

Despite an increased influx of visitors over the last few years, this place hasn't lost its village feel. Most people are friendly because the outsiders bring money and jobs to the area. Others are less happy when they see their sons and daughters adopting western ways (loud t-shirts, dope and arguments), and when food prices for locals are double what they are in non-touristy places.

Much of the lake shore and peninsula around Cape Maclear, the lake itself and several offshore islands are part of Lake Malawi National Park, one of the few freshwater marine parks in Africa. The park headquarters is at Golden Sands Holiday Resort (see Places to Stay, following).

Things to See

Near the entrance gate to the Golden Sands Holiday Resort and park headquarters, a small path leads towards the hills overlooking the bay. A few hundred metres up here is

MALAWI

a small group of **missionary graves**, marking the last resting place of Dr William Black and other missionaries (three European and one African) who attempted to establish the first Livingstonia Mission here in 1875 (see History in the Facts about Malawi chapter for more details). Also near the gate is a large **baobab tree**. An early photograph taken in 1888 shows the same tree, looking the same – almost branch for branch – which indicates how slowly these trees grow, and how long they can live.

Also worth a visit, just inside the Golden Sands area, is the **Lake Malawi National Park Museum & Aquarium**. This is part of the **Visitor Centre**, a project organised by the Department of National Parks & Wildlife and the US Peace Corps. Aimed mainly at local schools, this is open to the public.

Things to Do

Naturally, most activities revolve around the lake, and water sports are a big thing here. Depending on your budget, several of the lodges and resthouses arrange windsurfing, water-skiing and various types of boat trips, which usually include snorkelling.

Boat Trips Local youths organise day trips to nearby islands for about US$10 to US$40 for a boat, or around US$4 per person, including snorkelling and lunch (fish cooked on an open fire, with rice and a few other bits and pieces). Before arranging anything though, check with other travellers for recommendations; some of the lads are very good, but others can be sharks.

Snorkelling If you prefer to do things on your own, hire some snorkel gear (prices start at about US$2 – but check the quality of your mask) and head for Otter Point, less than a km beyond the park headquarters at Golden Sands. This small rocky peninsula and nearby islet are very popular with fish and snorkellers. There is an underwater snorkelling trail here, which you can follow with the help of a waterproof map, which is included in *Guide to the Fishes of Lake Malawi* (see Books in the Facts for the Visitor chapter).

Diving There are also two fully geared-up dive schools: Cape Maclear Scuba Shack at Stevens' Resthouse, and Lake Divers at Golden Sands. They both have highly qualified instructors and offer learn-to-dive courses and a range of options for people already experienced. Their prices are similar, but it is worth checking if there are any special deals. More important than this, talk to anybody you can who has done a dive and get personal recommendations. A five day course, leading to NAUI or PADI qualifications costs US$130 to US$150. For those already qualified, shore dives are US$15, boat dives US$20 and night dives US$30.

Kayaking & Sailing Another aquatic option is **kayaking** offered by Kayak Africa, with a base on the beach near Stevens'. They have top-of-the-range sea-kayaks which can be used by experts or beginners, and arrange three day guided island hopping trips for US$150 per person all inclusive (meals, tents, hammocks, solar showers). Longer trips work out at about US$45 per day. People who have done this trip rave about it. You can either turn up and arrange to go after a day or two, or make arrangements in advance through a travel agent in Lilongwe.

Yet another option is **sailing** with a German-run outfit called Hello Afrika, with a base at Chembe Lodge (see Places to Stay, following). A sunset cruise on their eight metre catamaran is US$8 per person, a full-day cruise US$20, and a stylish three day cruise (including all meals) US$150. All trips can be combined with snorkelling or diving. Book through Hello Afrika direct (☎ /fax 584334, or in South Africa (☎ (011) 706 1210; fax (011) 463 3001) or go through Central African Wilderness Safaris (☎ 781393; fax 781397) in Lilongwe.

Hiking If you tire of the lake, or just want a day on dry land, there's a very good range of hikes and walks in the hills that form a horseshoe around the plain behind the

The Baobab

One of the great symbols of Africa, the baobab tree, with its bizarre appearance, is surrounded by myth and folklore, and has a multitude of uses for local people and for wildlife. In Malawi, baobabs are found principally on the lake shore, on Likoma Island and in the areas along the Shire River.

Stories have been passed down through the generations about how God, angry with the baobab, pulled it out and flung it back into the ground headfirst. With branches that look just like a root system when the tree is leafless, it is easy to see how this and many other similar stories came about. (Further south, in Namibia and Botswana, San people (Bushmen) tell a story about God giving all the animals a seed to plant. The hyena, angry at being left until last, planted his allocated seed, the baobab, upside down.)

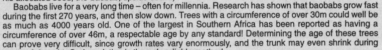

Baobabs live for a very long time – often for millennia. Research has shown that baobabs grow fast during the first 270 years, and then slow down. Trees with a circumference of over 30m could well be as much as 4000 years old. One of the largest in Southern Africa has been reported as having a circumference of over 46m, a respectable age by any standard! Determining the age of these trees can prove very difficult, since growth rates vary enormously, and the trunk may even shrink during years of drought. Carbon dating is the only reliable method.

The wood of this tree is very light and almost spongy in appearance. When the tree dies, within a few months it will have rotted down to a mass of fibre. Baobabs produce big white flowers in October, each bloom only lasting 24 hours. They are pollinated by the fruit bat and it's interesting to note that the distributions of fruit bats and baobabs throughout Africa are very similar. They may also be pollinated by ants. Large oval fruits containing seeds are produced in April and May.

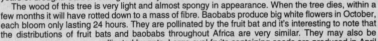

The uses of this tree seem to be endless. Although not suitable for hut construction, the very light fibrous wood can be used in the manufacture of paper and also as floats for fishing nets. The interior of the trunk frequently dies off, leaving a hollow shell – excellent for use as a water trap; a nesting site for birds and reptiles; a place of refuge for both humans and animals; and as a storage room. The fibrous bark makes a very strong thread, used for making nets, sacks, instrumental strings and even cloth.

All parts of the tree seem to have some nutritional value. The fruits are very rich in protein and vitamins, and are a favourite food of elephants and baboons. The seeds can be ground and roasted. The leaves can be eaten as a type of spinach. Animals eat the fruit, leaves, and flowers as well as young roots. Elephants strip and eat the bark. In times of drought they will also dig out and eat the inner wood, which has a water content of up to 40%. The baobab has medicinal uses too: the leaves are used to treat diarrhoea and fevers. The bark can also be used in the treatment of fevers, and used to be sold commercially for this purpose.

More modern uses for the baobab include the WWI gun emplacement and ammunition store that was built in the branches of a tree at Karonga in northern Malawi. Finally, we should not forget Major Trollip, who, whilst stationed at Katima Mulilo in Namibia, installed a flush toilet in his local hollow baobab. It remains there to this day. ■

village and beach. You can go alone or arrange a guide, either from the village or at the park headquarters: the park rate is US$10 for a full-day trip. The main path starts by the missionary graves described in Things to See, earlier. From here the path leads up through woodland and through a small valley to a col formed between a small spur and the main peak of Nkhunguni, the highest

and westernmost peak on the Nankumba Peninsula. The col offers great views over the Cape Maclear plain, the lake and surrounding islands. If you go for the summit it's three hours walking up and about the same coming down.

Another interesting place to visit on foot is Mwala Wa Mphini ('the rock of the tribal face scars'), which is just off the main dirt road into Cape Maclear, about five km from the park headquarters. This huge boulder is a national monument covered in lines and patters which seem to have been gouged out by long-forgotten artists, but are in fact a natural geological formation. If you want a longer walk, a small lakeside path leads south-west from Otter Point, through woodland above the shore, for about four km to a small fishing village called Msaka (which has a small bar/shop serving cold drinks). From here a track leads inland (west) to meet the main dirt road between Cape Maclear and Monkey Bay. Turn left and head back towards Cape Maclear, passing Mwala Wa Mphini on the way. The whole circuit is about 16 km and takes four to five hours.

Places to Stay & Eat

In the last few years the number of places to stay at Cape Maclear has grown considerably. Through most of the 1980s the choice was Stevens' Resthouse and Golden Sands Holiday Resort, and that was it. Now there are at least eight places – but not always the same eight. They come and go like grains of sand, so expect some new arrivals and some closures by the time you arrive. All the places are on the beach, spread over about five km, described here west to east.

The main dirt road that turns off the Monkey Bay road leads all the way to the gates of the Lake Malawi National Park headquarters, at the far western end of Cape Maclear. This is also *Golden Sands Holiday Resort*, run by the parks department, with basic chalets and camping for US$3 per person and ensuite rondavels for US$5 per person. As it's inside the national park you have to pay park fees too (for details see National Parks in the Facts for the Visitor chapter). The beach here is cleaner and the atmosphere is generally quieter (one traveller said 'more sensible') than some other places in Cape Maclear; suitable for families and people who don't want to drink and smoke all night.

There are adequate central showers (cold water only) and toilets, and there is electricity until 9 pm each evening. In the main building there's a bar and kitchen where staff will prepare your food, or you can cook yourself. If you camp, watch out for the monkeys – they'll run off with anything edible. If you're in a group it's worth renting one rondavel to store your gear – you also get your own bathroom, which is in better condition than the communal ones inside. (For those interested in history, the park headquarters building was once a hotel, used briefly as a stopping-off point for 'flying-boat' aircraft going between London and Johannesburg in 1949 and 1950.)

Nearby is the national park Visitor Centre (see Things to See, earlier) where you can also arrange lodgings with a local family in Cape Maclear village. This scheme is called the *Visitor Stay Experience*, run by the national park in co-operation with the US Peace Corps. You stay for about 24 hours and do everything the family does – collect water from the lake, help with cooking traditional food, and so on. It costs US$6.

Next along the beach, about 1.5 km from Golden Sands, is *Emanuel's Campsite*, where it costs US$1 per person to pitch a tent, or US$1.25 for a very basic room with a mattress on the floor. It's clean and quiet, with a bar but no food is available. Next along is *Mr Banda's Store*, where you can buy cold drinks, bread, tinned foods and groceries if you're self-catering or picnicking on the beach. Near here is *Chip's Bar* which serves, naturally, deep fried potato pieces plus a few other takeaway snacks at budget prices.

A bit further along, and back from the beach, is the *Top Quiet Resthouse*, with simple clean rooms around a sandy courtyard for US$1 per person, or US$3 if you want an attached shower. Meals cost US$2 to US$3.

Close by is the legendary *Stevens' Resthouse*, run by the Stevens family (two brothers and a son) for as long as anyone can remember. This used to be one of *the* places to stay on the backpackers' Cape to Cairo route, but there's stiff competition these days and it's lost some of its once-legendary friendliness and laid-back atmosphere.

Clean singles are US$1, doubles US$2 (or US$3 for ensuite). Breakfast is US$0.50, and other meals US$1.50 to US$2. The bar on the beach is still a popular place to go for a drink and meet other travellers, especially at sunset, even though the building itself is not very attractive. In fact, it's amazing that anyone able to build a bar in such a fabulous position can come up with something so ugly.

A bit further along the beach are two more places. *The Ritz* has camping for US$0.60, but it's only just worth that, with basic facilities and no bar or restaurant. Next door is *The Gap*, where camping is the same price, and simple rooms are US$1. Snacks start at US$1, or you can buy burgers and chips or similar for US$2 to US$3. The South African-Malawian management claim to sell the coldest beer in Cape Maclear and have a generator to keep the fridge going. They have links with the place of the same name in Lilongwe, and it's worth asking about transport between the two – there's usually something once a week.

Along from here are two local places: the *Bodzalakani Resthouse* (it means 'don't tell lies') with very basic rooms for US$1 and camping for US$0.60. Almost opposite is *Mayi Tsalani Resthouse* ('left behind') where facilities are better and prices slightly higher.

From here it's another 1.5 km to *Ba'Blue* where camping is US$0.60. This is a very relaxed hang-out – the sort of place you turn up for a day and stay a week. When we passed through, the kitchen and bar-restaurant were still under construction, and chalets may go up also, so ask around when you arrive. Full moon parties here attract scores of travellers from everywhere between Nairobi and Victoria Falls. (As we went to press, the word was that Ba'Blue had already closed. Something similar is bound to evolve here soon.)

Last in the line, right at the far end of Cape Maclear beach, is *Chembe Lodge*, up a few grades in quality and style from anything else in the area. It's got permanent walk-in tents under thatch shelters, set in beautiful gardens, overlooking a very nice bit of beach, at the foot of some small wooded hills. Singles/doubles cost US$22/25 (US$25/32 July through September, Easter, Christmas and New Year) including breakfast. Other meals cost US$3.50 to US$5, and there's a very nice bar. Sailboard hire is free for guests; water-skiing and sailing (see Things to Do, earlier) can also be arranged. For advance bookings see the Hello Afrika numbers above.

If you decide not to eat at any of the places listed above, your other option is a beach barbecue. From the moment you arrive you'll be approached by young kids who want to make one for you. This is not a bad way to spend an evening, but you'll need to bargain over the price, which is about US$2 for fish, rice, tomato and onion. Once again, talk to other travellers and get personal recommendations before committing to anything.

Another place to consider, if Cape Maclear sounds too frenetic, is *Pumulani Lodge*, near Kasankha village, on a small hill overlooking the lake (high enough to catch the breeze, near enough to reach the beach) about 12 km off the dirt road from Monkey Bay to Cape Maclear. Camping here costs US$3, and full board accommodation in smart chalets is US$30 per person. If you don't have your own vehicle, get to Gary's Café (☎ 587296) in Monkey Bay: there's transport to the lodge every day (except Sunday) at 5 pm.

Getting There & Away

When the dirt road beyond Monkey Bay is in good condition there's a Stagecoach Inter-City (that is, slow) bus all the way to Cape Maclear from Blantyre (via Mangochi). The fare is US$5. It leaves Blantyre at 9 am and arrives around 5 pm, 'sleeping' at Golden Sands and returning to Blantyre early next day. The Monkey Bay to Cape Maclear section is US$0.50. Alternatively, the Stevens' truck does the run between Cape Maclear and Monkey Bay a couple of times a day for US$1 per person. The guys at Gary's Café will tell you when it's due.

MALAWI

The Southern Lake Shore

THE MONKEY BAY – MANGOCHI ROAD

From Monkey Bay the main lake shore road runs south to Mangochi, which marks the southern tip of the lake. Along this stretch of lake are several places to stay, catering for all tastes and budgets. A selection is described here, arranged north to south.

Leaving Monkey Bay, you pass the junction for Cape Maclear and then the road west to Mua. Continue for another 18 km to reach the turn-off to *Nanchengwa Lodge*, reached by a dirt track through baobabs, 1.5 km west of the main road. This is a friendly lodge for backpackers and overlanders, in a fishing village on a small bay, with camping above the beach for US$1.50, a bed in the dorm for US$3 or rooms for US$9. There's a bar and

food is available, plus a whole range of activities like snorkelling, hiking, diving and horse-riding.

A few km further south is *Sun & Sand Holiday Resort* on a huge site, with a 1960s British Butlins feel, where single/double chalets are US$10/18, and self-catering cottages sleeping seven people are US$70. Beyond here is the preferable *Boadzulu Lodge*, set in nice gardens on a beach, where ensuite double chalets with a small kitchen cost US$19/32 with breakfast, plus US$5 for extra children. For self-catering you can hire kitchen equipment for another US$8, or eat in the restaurant where main meals are US$3 to US$4.

Next along is *Club Makokola* (☎ 584244; fax 584417, or Blantyre ☎ 670500), a full-on Mediterranean-style holiday resort with 70 chalets, two swimming pools, restaurants, bars, water sports, golf course, floodlit football fields, squash, tennis and volleyball

---

Cichlid Fish

There are over 600 species of fish in Lake Malawi. Most of these are of the family *Cichlidae* – cichlids – and 99% of these are endemic to the lake. This is the largest family of fish in Africa, totalling about 850 species, most of which are concentrated in the Rift Valley lakes.

Chambo, familiar to anyone who has eaten in a restaurant in Malawi, are one type of cichlid. Other types include the small utaka, the chisawasawa and the kambuzi, as well as the larger ndunduma and ncheni. The largest species is the sungwa, which is widely distributed in sub-Saharan Africa.

But Lake Malawi is most famous for the small, brightly coloured cichlids known as mbuna. These remain in very localised territories and do not interbreed with other species. Therefore as well as being attractive to snorkellers and divers, they have provided a fascinating insight into the process of evolution. Different species only evolve through many years of gradual changes in shape and colour. It is thought that many species of mbuna remain unidentified, particularly in the region of the north-eastern coast of the lake.

Cichlids have evolved over the millennia from one common species into many hundreds, yet they have continued to co-exist. This has been achieved by different species developing different mechanisms for feeding on different types or layers of plankton and algae. Chambo eat phytoplankton which they filter out of the water through their mouths. Some mbuna have specialised teeth to scrape algae off the rocks; others specialise in scraping the algae off aquatic plants. There are also 'snail eaters', with strong flat teeth for crushing shells, 'sand diggers' which filter insects and small animals out of the sand, and 'zooplankton eaters', which have tube-like mouths for picking up minute creatures. Other species include those which are plant-eaters and fish-eaters. All of these different feeding mechanisms depend principally on the shape and size of the cichlid head and mouth, and on the nature of the pharyngeal bone at the back of the throat. The evolution of these special adaptations have ensured that each species is able to deal with a particular type of food.

Equally fascinating is the cichlid breeding process. The male establishes a nest, and then, benefiting from his bright colours, lures a female in. She starts to lay eggs, which she immediately takes into her mouth for protection. Part of the male's guise is a pattern near his tail resembling the eggs. The female tries to pick these up as well, at which point the males releases sperm into the water which the female inevitably inhales. This process is repeated until all or most of the eggs are fertilised. Once the eggs hatch the mother continues to hold the tiny fish in her mouth, letting them out increasingly often to feed. Any sign of danger and they go straight back into her mouth. ■

courts and a long strip of private beachfront. Club Mak (as it informally calls itself) also has a luxury cruise boat; you can go out for the day, or longer if required, to visit islands or other hotels along the lake. At the time of writing, the club was undergoing a US$1 million revamp, so vast improvements are expected. Comfortable ensuite rooms in bungalows cost US$90/144 for singles/doubles. Club Makokola has its own airport, served by daily scheduled Air Malawi flights to/from Blantyre and Lilongwe. For water sports, Rift Lake Charters (☎ 584473) are based at the club, and arrange boat trips to the islands, sailing, windsurfing, diving, luxury cruises and 'sail safaris'. For scuba diving lessons and equipment hire Scuba Blue (☎ 584576) are also based at Club Makokola.

Just one km down the road from here is another top-end establishment: *Nkopola Lodge*, part of the Protea Hotels group (central reservations Blantyre ☎ 620071), where pleasant chalets and rooms set in attractive – almost manicured – gardens overlooking a beach on the lake, cost US$90/150, including tax and breakfast. The restaurant serves à la carte, with main meals around US$5 to US$8; there are special weekend buffets for US$12. Overlooking the lake, with splendid views, is a raised 'deck bar'. A local band plays on weekends, and traditional dancers perform some evenings. Various water sports are available; sailboards, canoes and dinghies are free for guests, motor boats about US$40 per hour and water-skiing US$5 per lap. The lodge also has a short nature trail, winding through the huge boulders and dense bush that cover the lake shore just north of the hotel.

Next door to Nkopola Lodge is *Nkopola Beach Club* where no-frills double ensuite chalets cost a good-value US$30. There are also double walk-in tents for US$12. Alternatively, you can pitch your own tent here for US$6 or park a caravan for US$18. The communal ablution blocks are clean, and there's a small bar and restaurant overlooking the lake. The atmosphere is calm and peaceful, and seems popular with families.

Next down the road is *Mulangani Holiday Resort*, a vast place of limited appeal with chalets for US$50/60 with breakfast, and walk-in tents for US$10 per person. Camping in your own tent is US$5. There's a conference hall here which is very popular with government departments: when we passed through, the whole place was fully booked with Health Department officials on a weekend seminar. (The same day we happened to visit a local clinic which was running out of medicines.)

Last in the line is *Palm Beach Leisure Resort*, a fairly smart place set on lawns and a beautiful beach surrounded by (not surprisingly) a grove of palm trees. Ensuite chalets cost US$22 per person, and camping is US$5. The restaurant serves small breakfasts and snacks for US$2, big breakfasts and meals for around US$4. Boat owners from Lilongwe and Blantyre favour this place, as there's a good launch area.

MANGOCHI

Mangochi lies at the southern end of Lake Malawi, a few km from the shore, straddling the Shire River which flows into Lake Malombe. This place was once an important slave market, and then an administrative centre in colonial days, when it was known as Fort Johnston. Relics of these times include many Muslim people and the Queen Victoria clock tower. Nearby is a memorial to the people who died when a steamer on the lake called MV *Viphya* sank in a violent storm in 1946. The Shire Bridge is also scenic, and the museum may be worth a visit when it finally reopens. Other sights include the gun from HMS *Guendolin* (see boxed text below), the Cathedral, and the Malindi Pottery showroom on the road towards Liwonde. Facilities include several shops and supermarkets, a post office and bank.

Places to Stay & Eat

Near the bus station, the *Chinyangala Resthouse* has dingy rooms for US$1 per person, and the better (but only slightly) *Impala Resthouse* charges US$1.50/$2, plus US$1 for a fan. A better choice is the clean and airy *Domasi Resthouse*, near the PTC supermarket, with rooms for US$2. Another good option is the *Forestry Resthouse* on the riverside just north of the bridge, with clean rooms and self-catering kitchen, plus cook, for US$3 per person. Nearby, the *Holiday Motel* has a pleasant atmosphere and reasonable rooms for US$2/$4, or US$7/8 for ensuite. Couples can share a single. There's also a large bar and restaurant. The *Ice Cream Bar* on the main road near the petrol station also serves food and is worth a visit.

Getting There & Away

There are several buses each day between Blantyre and Monkey Bay, via Mangochi. The bus station is on the edge of the town centre, but transport on the main road also stops at the filling station near the junction where the road into town branches off the main road. Buses between Mangochi and Liwonde cost US$1.50. To/from Blantyre is US$4. Minibuses between Mangochi and the Mozambique border at Chiponde (via Namwera) cost US$2 (for more details on the route to Mozambique see the Getting There & Away chapter).

Around Mangochi

The road south of Mangochi runs alongside **Lake Malombe** and is very scenic, although thick reed beds mean no beaches. However, there is a healthy weaving industry here, and you can buy baskets, mats, hats, chairs and curios made from grass, straw, reed and palm leaf at very good prices.

One other interesting area is **Mangochi Mountain**, at the southern end of Lake Malawi. This is a hilly, tree-covered area, which is protected as a forest reserve. There are the ruins of an old colonial fort here, and elephants from the nearby Liwonde National Park sometimes migrate up into the forested hills during the rainy season.

If you *really* want to get away from it all, you could aim for **Ngapandi Estate**, north of Mangochi in the strip of territory wedged between the lake's eastern shore and Mozambique. The fully furnished *Ngapandi*

The HMS *Guendolin*

The HMS *Guendolin* was a military boat, made in Britain and assembled in Mangochi in 1899. For many years it was the largest boat on the lake (340 tons), with a top speed of 12 knots, and equipped with two powerful guns. The colonial authorities regarded such a show of strength necessary firstly to deter slave traders, who crossed the lake in dhows with their human cargo, and secondly because both rival colonial powers Germany and Portugal had territory facing Lake Malawi (then Lake Nyasa) and were believed to have designs on increasing their influence in the region.

The Germans also had a gunboat, called *Herman von Wissemann*, but despite the territorial disputes of their governments the captains of the two ships were reported to be great friends and drinking partners, often meeting at various points around the lake for a chat and a few beers.

When WWI was declared in 1914, the *Guendolin* was ordered to destroy the German boat. The British captain knew where the *von Wissemann* would be, as they had previously arranged one of their regular get-togethers. But the German captain was unaware that war had broken out, and his ship was completely unprepared. Abandoning the usual British principle of fair play, the *Guendolin* steamed in close, then bombed the *von Wissemann* and rendered it unusable. The German captain and crew were then informed of the commencement of hostilities and taken prisoner. This rather unsporting event happened to be the first British naval victory of WWI, and Lake Malawi's only recorded 'battle at sea'.

In 1940 the *Guendolin* was converted to a passenger ship, and one of the guns set up as a memorial in Mangochi, near the clock tower. Some years later the ship was scrapped. All that remains today is the gun. ■

---

holiday cottage, sleeping eight people, can be hired for US$5 per person per night. This is only really an option for drivers: to reach it take the road from Mangochi, up the steep escarpment road through Kwilembe, then forking left (north) through Mchokola. Nearby is Namizimu Forest Reserve and Msondole Mountain. You must book in advance: contact Mapanga headquarters (☎ 651799; fax 651646).

LIKOMA & CHIZUMULU ISLANDS

The islands of Likoma and Chizumulu are in the northern part of Lake Malawi, within the

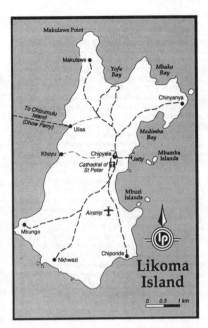

Makulawe Point
Makulawe
Yofu Bay
Mbako Bay
Chinyanya
To Chizumulu Island (Dhow Ferry)
Ulisa
Madimba Bay
Khuyu
Chipyela
Jetty
Mbamba Islands
Cathedral of St Peter
Mbuzi Islands
Airstrip
Mbungo
Chiponde
Nkhwazi

Likoma Island

0   0.5   1 km

MALAWI

territorial waters of Mozambique but part of Malawi and linked to the rest of the country by the steamer service.

Likoma is the largest island, and something of an enigma: it's not a paradise isle in the usual sense, although it does have some excellent beaches (mostly on the southern coast) and snorkelling, but has more of a sparse beauty which some, but not all, visitors will appreciate. The island is fairly flat, mostly dry and sandy since it lies in the rainshadow of the Mozambique shore. Baobabs are a common feature of the landscape, but big trees are generally scarce, resulting in little shade. There are some marshy areas of coastline, particularly in the east, while the north and west are more rocky.

The island is highly populated, with about 6000 people living within the 17 sq km area. There are therefore extensive plantations, mainly of cassava. Cashews, rice and mangoes are also grown.

Visitors seem to fall into two categories: those who love it and stay for days or weeks, and those who are disappointed and leave as soon as possible. Either way, you'll meet few other tourists. Chizumulu Island in particular can be a perfect hideaway.

Things to See & Do
Unless you are rich enough to charter a plane, steamer schedules mean being here at least three days, so you'll have to relax whether you like it or not! Likoma Island has some lovely, long stretches of sandy beach, mostly along the southern coast but also notably at Jofu in the north. Crocodiles have killed a couple of people in recent years, so take care where you swim. Ask around locally before diving in.

Likoma is small enough to explore on foot, although bear in mind the lack of shade and the high midday temperatures. Akuzike Resthouse has produced a map of the island, showing the best beaches, areas of interest and suggesting a number of **walks**. Also remember when wandering that the people here live a very traditional way of life. This isn't the Costa del Sol – so keep your clothing and behaviour suitably modest.

The impressive Anglican **Cathedral of St Peter** (see the boxed text below) should not be missed, but it is kept locked unless there is a service in progress. For another slant on local religion talk to Eddie at the Akuzike (see Places to Stay & Eat, following) – he can introduce you to a local witch doctor.

The **market place** is something of a curiosity; it is very neat with stone-lined walkways. It was built in 1985 by a German-funded development project, but only recently have the locals been tempted from their traditional trading area down by the port, where there's plenty of water to wash fish. There is also a bizarre tree in the square – an old baobab which has been overtaken by a strangler fig, and has rotted away from underneath so that it is now used by the locals as storeroom.

A dhow ferry runs from the west coast of Likoma to Chizumulu once or twice a day (fare US$0.30), but it's a very choppy ride

Likoma Missionaries & the Cathedral of St Peter

European involvement on Likoma Island began in 1882 when members of UMCA (Universities Mission to Central Africa) established a base here, some 18 years after their initial attempt to establish missions on the Shire Highlands and along the lower reaches of the Shire River (see History in the Facts about Malawi chapter). Leaders of the party were Will Johnson and Chauncy Maples. They chose the island because it would be safe from attacks from the warlike Ngoni and Yao people, who were still actively involved in slaving in the area.

Chauncy Maples became the first bishop of Likoma. He died only a few months after being appointed, drowning in the lake off Monkey Bay. (For many years he was remembered in the name of a steam boat which carried passengers up and down the lake.)

Despite the setback, missionary work and development on the island continued. Between 1903 and 1905 a huge cathedral was built, probably inspired by the church which had been built by the missionaries at Blantyre (see that chapter), and under the guidance of a missionary-architect called Frank George who went to become the archdeacon. The cathedral on Likoma Island was dedicated to St Peter and is still standing today, and is one of Malawi's most remarkable buildings. It is generally known simply as the Anglican Cathedral.

Measuring over 100m long by 25m wide (for British travellers, that's the size of Winchester Cathedral), the cathedral has stained glass windows and elaborate choir stalls carved from soapstone. The crucifix above the altar was carved from wood from the tree where Livingstone's heart was buried, near Lake Bangweulu in Zambia. It was sited on a part of the island called Chipyela, meaning 'place of burning', as the early UMCA arrivals had witnessed some suspected witches being burnt alive here. The island's main settlement grew up around the cathedral, and is still called Chipyela today.

The UMCA missionaries remained on Likoma until the 1940s. During that time they'd been hard at work – claiming 100% literacy among the local population at one point. The cathedral fell into bad repair, but was restored in the 1970s and 1980s, and local people are evidently very proud of it.

There is still a mission on the island, and there are now two bishops, one American and one Italian. Recently, however, a resurgence in the belief and use of witchcraft has been reported among the local people. As in the rest of Malawi, this has been partly caused by the rise in the number of people dying of AIDS. Western conventional medicine is perceived as ineffectual, creating fear in the villages and a return to traditional beliefs. ∎

when the wind is blowing. The snorkelling off Chizumulu is reported to be better than Likoma, and Kubira Lodge can arrange dives; they are fully equipped with scuba gear.

Places to Stay & Eat

In Chipyela, Likoma Island's main settlement, the *Akuzike Resthouse* is justifiably popular, not far from the jetty, with rooms which open out onto a very pleasant central courtyard. It is clean and good value at US$3 per person, with running water and mosquito nets. There is also a coffee shop next door.

Similar in price is the *Quiet & Cool Resthouse*, which also has a restaurant. Between the Akuzike and the port is the small *Sun 'n Sand Resthouse* charging US$4 for ensuite rooms, although we heard recently this might have closed. There's also reported to be a *Government Resthouse* about half a km south of the cathedral, but this seems to have been leased to private management and is due to undergo improvements. You can camp

free of charge on the beach on the west side of the island but it would be worth asking about security before you do this.

A luxury lodge called *Kaya Mawa* is under construction on the south-west corner of the island, due for completion in 1997. We've also been told about another new place called *Chiponde Beach Lodge*, at the south-east end of the island, charging US$10 per person.

Apart from the places mentioned above, there are a few other restaurants/bars, but you should order meals in advance if possible. Try *the women's restaurant* near the jetty. Wherever you go, don't expect a huge menu – the staples here are fish, nsima and rice. If you want to be sure of vegetables, fruit and eggs it's best to bring your own.

On Chizumulu Island you can stay at *Kubira Lodge*, with very friendly staff, on a good beach about 20 minutes walk north of where the dhow ferry crosses from Likoma. Double rooms are US$2.50, camping is US$0.60 and there is a pleasant bar which has been built in a baobab tree. You can also try the new *Tionge Resthouse & Restaurant*, where prices are the same.

Getting There & Away

Most people travel to Likoma Island by lake steamer – see the Getting Around chapter for details. The boat usually stops for about an hour, so even if you were heading elsewhere, you might be able to nip ashore to have a quick look at the cathedral. (Check you've got time with the captain first though.)

The island is only about 10 km off the coast of Mozambique, and dhows sail to the town of Cobuè (Kobway), which has an immigration office, from where you can continue through Mozambique. For more details see the main Getting There & Away chapter.

MALAWI

Map Index

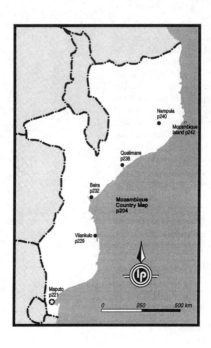

Mozambique

For 17 years Mozambique was all but paralysed in the grip of a brutal civil war that ended in 1992. Although the fighting is over, Mozambique is still a desperately poor country, but one whose people are generous and open. The beaches are the best on the whole east coast of Africa and a few southern resorts are once again filling with fun-and-sun seekers. Further north – in the area neighbouring Malawi – the roads are bad and other facilities haphazard, so travel here is for the more adventurous. Wherever you go in Mozambique it's fascinating and well worth the time and effort.

Mozambique
Area: 801,590 sq km
Population: 18.5 million
Population Growth Rate: 4.3%
Capital: Maputo
Head of State: President Joaquim Chissano
Official Language: Portuguese
Currency: meticais
Exchange Rate: US$1 = Mt 11,125
Per Capita GNP: US$80 (Purchasing power parity: US$610)
Literacy: 33%
Infant Mortality Rate: around 20%

Facts about the Country

HISTORY

The early history of Mozambique *(Moçambique* in Portuguese) is covered along with the history of Malawi and other parts of the region in the Facts about Malawi chapter.

The Early Colonial Period

Vasco da Gama, the Portuguese navigator, first arrived on the Mozambique coast in 1498. He found several powerful Swahili-Arab outposts such as Quelimane and Ilha de Moçambique. The Portuguese needed supply points on their sea route from Europe to India and so established their own bases, which brought them into conflict with the Swahili-Arabs. Further incentive to stay came from the lucrative trade in gold brought from the interior, and they set up a number of trading enclaves and forts. By the end of the 1600s ivory took over as the main trading commodity, and by the mid-1700s slaves were added to the list. It is thought that up to one million Mozambicans were sold as slaves over the next hundred years.

Initially, the Portuguese remained on the coast and it wasn't until the late 17th century that colonisation began in earnest with the setting up of privately owned agricultural estates on land granted by the Portuguese crown or obtained by conquest from African chiefs.

The 1880s heralded the 'Scramble for Africa'. The major European colonial powers (Britain, France and Germany) allowed Portugal to keep their territory (known then as Portuguese East Africa) in exchange for huge land concessions being granted to foreign companies in the northern two-thirds of the country. The southern third remained in Portuguese hands.

The Early 20th Century

By the early 20th century a pattern was established in Mozambique. Rather than putting any effort into developing the country, the Portuguese simply rented out the available resources. This included human labour hired to neighbouring countries, particularly South Africa and Rhodesia, thus removing a large proportion of the male labour force. Transit routes were built from the coastal ports to further service neighbours' needs – for example, the rail link between Beira and Mutare.

In the late 1920s the fascist leader Salazar came to power in Portugal. He sealed off the colonies from non-Portuguese investment, allowing Portugal to profit directly. The

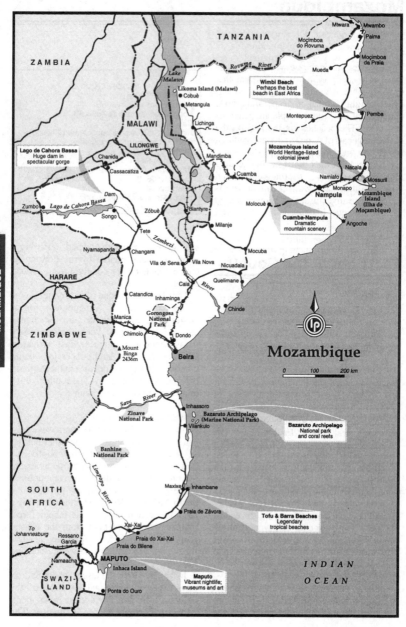

Mozambique

0   100   200 km

Wimbi Beach
Perhaps the best
beach in East Africa

Lago de Cahora Bassa
Huge dam in
spectacular gorge

Mozambique Island
World Heritage-listed
colonial jewel

Cuamba-Nampula
Dramatic
mountain scenery

Bazaruto Archipelago
National park
and coral reefs

Tofu & Barra Beaches
Legendary
tropical beaches

Maputo
Vibrant nightlife;
museums and art

TANZANIA
ZAMBIA
MALAWI
LILONGWE
HARARE
ZIMBABWE
SOUTH
AFRICA
SWAZI-
LAND

INDIAN
OCEAN

Mtwara
Mwambo
Paima
Moçimboa
do Rovuma
Moçimboa
da Praia
Mueda
Rovuma River
Lake
Malawi
Likoma Island (Malawi)
Cobuè
Metangula
Lichinga
Metoro
Montepuez
Pemba
Mandimba
Namialo
Nacala
Cuamba
Mossuril
Mozambique
Island
(Ilha de
Moçambique)
Monapo
Nampula
Molocuè
Angoche
Chanida
Cassacatiza
Zóbuè
Blantyre
Milanje
Mocuba
Songo
Zumbo
Lago de Cahora Bassa
Dam
Tete
Zambezi
Nyamapanda
Changara
Vila de Sena
Vila Nova
Nicuadala
Quelimane
Catandica
Caia
River
Chinde
Inhaminga
Manica
Gorongosa
National
Park
Chimoio
Dondo
Mount
Binga
2436m
Belira
Save
River
Inhassoro
Zinave
National Park
Bazaruto Archipelago
(Marine National Park)
Vilankulo
Banhine
National Park
Limpopo River
Maxixe
Inhambane
Praia de Závora
To
Johannesburg
Xai-Xai
Ressano
Garcia
Praia do Xai-Xai
Praia do Bilene
Namaacha
MAPUTO
Inhaca Island
Ponta do Ouro

cultivation of cash crops (mainly cotton and rice) was introduced. All men over 15 years old had to work on the plantations for six months of every year for a minimal wage. Labourers were often chained. These harsh conditions led to a further exodus of Mozambican men.

Forced cultivation of the cash crops led to a dramatic decrease in production of food crops. Famines became frequent during the 1940s and 1950s, and many Mozambicans died of starvation. There wasn't even a pretence of social investment in the African population; of the few schools and hospitals that did exist, most were in the cities and reserved for Portuguese, other whites and privileged African *asimilados*.

The War of Independence

In June 1960, at Mueda in northern Mozambique, an official meeting was held by villagers protesting peacefully about taxes. Portuguese troops opened fire on the crowd and killed up to 600 people. This kindled the rise of the independence struggle, and resistance to colonial rule coalesced in 1962 with the formation of Frelimo – the Mozambique Liberation Front.

Led by the charismatic Eduardo Mondlane, Frelimo's aim was the complete liberation of Mozambique. By 1966 it had liberated two northern provinces, but progress was slow, and the war dragged on into the 1970s. The Portuguese attempted to eliminate rural support for Frelimo with a scorched earth campaign and by resettling people in fenced-off villages.

The final blow for the Portuguese was the overthrow of the fascist regime in 1974. On 25 June 1975, the independent People's Republic of Mozambique was proclaimed. Mondlane had been killed during the war, so Samora Machel was sworn in as the country's first president.

Independence

The Portuguese pulled out virtually overnight and left the country in a state of chaos: there were few skilled professionals and virtually no infrastructure; capital reserves were withdrawn and the economy took a nose-dive. The make things even harder for the new government, acts of sabotage by the Portuguese, such as filling the drainage system of a half-finished hotel in Maputo with concrete, were common.

Suddenly faced with the task of running the country, Frelimo was committed to a policy of radical social change. Advisors from the then USSR and East Germany arrived, although their 'advice' seemed to centre around over-exploitation of natural reserves such as fish and timber stocks. Mozambique's Marxist links and policies inevitably caused concern in the west and in South Africa – which saw itself as the last line of defence against Communism in the region.

South Africa expelled tens of thousands of Mozambican miners, raising unemployment still further and causing a large fall in foreign revenue. At the same time Mozambique bravely complied with UN-sponsored sanctions against Rhodesia (following Ian Smith's Unilateral Declaration of Independence), thus putting even greater pressure on its own economy.

Despite these setbacks, Frelimo forged ahead with its socialist programme. Private ownership of land was abolished, paving the way for the creation of state farms and peasant co-operatives. Rented property was nationalised, as were schools, banks and insurance companies, while private practice in medicine and law was abolished in an attempt to disperse skilled labour. Education assumed a high priority; literacy programmes were launched with the aim of teaching 100,000 people to read and write each year. Much assistance was received from foreign volunteers, notably from Sweden. Maoist-style 'barefoot doctors' provided basic health services, such as vaccinations, and taught about hygiene and sanitation.

However, by 1983 the country was almost bankrupt. Money was valueless and shops were empty. While collectivisation of agriculture had worked in some areas, in many others it was a complete disaster and one which Frelimo failed to recognise for

MOZAMBIQUE

many years. The crisis was compounded by a disastrous three year drought and by South African and Rhodesian moves to destabilise Mozambique because the ANC and ZAPU (both fighting for majority rule) had bases there.

Onto this scene came the Mozambique National Resistance – Renamo. They had been established in the mid-1970s by Rhodesia as part of the destabilisation policy. After Zimbabwe's independence their training had been taken over by South Africa – and then they started to cause serious trouble.

The Civil War

Renamo had been created solely by external forces, rather than by internal political motives. There were no aims beyond the wholesale destruction of social and communications infrastructure within Mozambique and thus the destabilisation of the government and the country. Commentators have also pointed out that this was not really a 'civil' war, but one between Mozambique's Frelimo government and the external forces which created Renamo.

Recruitment was sometimes voluntary, but frequently by force. Roads, bridges, railways, schools and clinics were destroyed. Villagers were rounded up and anyone with skills – teachers, medical workers, etc – was shot. Atrocities were committed on a massive and horrific scale. Samora Machel later claimed that Renamo had caused the destruction of 900 rural shops, 495 primary schools, 86 health posts and 140 villages.

Ironically, some of the problem stemmed from the Frelimo re-education camps, established after independence, where inmates included any political opponents as well as common criminals, and appalling abuses of human rights took place. Rather than establishing respect for the state authority, the result was to provide a fertile recruitment ground for Renamo.

The drought and famine of 1983 brought the country to its knees. Some western countries provided food aid, but Renamo (still backed by South Africa) attacked relief trucks and burned grain stores. Frelimo was forced to

change: Mozambique was to be opened up to the west, and in return the west agreed to help with food aid, although most came too late for the thousands who were dying.

On 16 March 1984, South Africa and Mozambique signed the Nkomati Accord. South Africa undertook to withdraw its support of Renamo; Mozambique agreed to expel the ANC and open the country to South African investment. For Mozambique, this was a strange mixture of courage and naivety, yet they abided by the agreement. South Africa, however, exploited the situation to the full and Renamo activity did not diminish. The truth finally surfaced in late 1985: after a joint Zimbabwean-Mozambican military offensive against Renamo in which 1500 guerrillas were killed or captured, proof was found that not only had Pretoria continued to supply the rebels, but senior advisers had regularly flown in to train recruits and check on progress.

Samora Machel died in a plane crash in 1986, and his place was taken by Joaquim Chissano. The war between the Frelimo government and the Renamo rebels continued. By the late 1980s, however, political change was sweeping through the region. The new president of South Africa, FW de Klerk, made it much harder for right-wing factions to supply Renamo.

More changes came in 1990. Frelimo ditched its Marxist ideology and announced that Mozambique would switch to a market

---

Land Mine Statistics

* It may cost as little as US$3 to produce a land mine.
* It costs US$300 to US$1000 to remove one.
* In Mozambique, every time a land mine goes off an average of 1.45 people are killed and 1.27 are wounded. Households with a land mine victim are 40% more likely to experience difficulty in providing food for the family.

Sources: First two figures from *Hidden Killers*, US State Department, 1993. Third figures from International Committee of the Red Cross, 1994. Quoted in British Medical Journal, Vol 311, September 1995. ∎

economy, state enterprises would be privatised, and multiparty elections were to be scheduled. Not everyone, particularly the rural peasants, was happy with these changes, but it pulled the carpet from under Renamo.

For a while, Renamo prevaricated over direct talks with the government, but it was clear there was no more mileage in banditry. Following two rounds of talks in Rome during 1990, a cease-fire of sorts was arranged. This was followed by a fully fledged peace agreement in October 1992.

Modern Times
Renamo was allowed to operate as a political party, so a 'manifesto' was hastily written. Elections were planned and several thousand United Nations observers and peacekeepers (in an operation called ONUMOZ) were drafted in to assist during the transitional period. Contrary to many expectations, the elections held in October 1994 went remarkably smoothly.

The outcome was a win for Frelimo and Joaquim Chissano remained as President. Renamo agreed to abide by the results. The UN scaled down operations, causing a sharp rise in local unemployment.

There is a very long way to go before Mozambique's problems are over. The economy is still in a shambles and although peace seems to be solid it could still fall apart at any time. But for the first time in many years the outlook is hopeful.

GEOGRAPHY
Mozambique is a large country, some 2000 km north to south, with a 2500 km coastline and an area of just over 800,000 sq km. Topographically, the country consists of a coastal plain, 100 to 200 km wide in the south, narrower in the north, rising to mountains and plateaux on the borders with Zimbabwe, Zambia and Malawi. The highest peak is Mount Binga (2436m) in the Chimanimani Mountains on the border of Mozambique and Zimbabwe. Two of Southern Africa's largest rivers – the Zambezi and the Limpopo – flow through the country. Other major rivers are the Save (also written Savé) and the Rovuma (which forms the northern border with Tanzania).

CLIMATE
In such a large country, there are many regional variations, but generally the dry season runs from April to September, during which time daytime maximums on the coast are around 24°C to 27°C, and cooler inland. In the wet season temperatures range from 27°C to 31°C, with high humidity, but once again it's cooler inland.

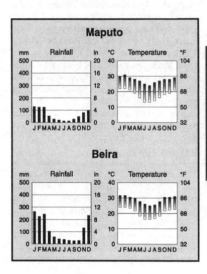

NATIONAL PARKS
Mozambique's population of large mammals was severely depleted during the war, but many visitors are attracted by the country's excellent marine life in the Bazaruto Archipelago Marine National Park, a group of reefs and islands off the coast between Inhambane and Beira. There are also three national parks on the mainland: Gorongosa, Zinave and Banhine, but none of these can be visited at present because of a lack of facilities, lack of animals and the presence of

MOZAMBIQUE

land mines. Gorongosa was actually a base for the Renamo fighters during the civil war, but has been rehabilitated and may reopen in 1997. The Maputo Elephant Reserve, south of Maputo city, is also being rehabilitated and also may reopen in 1997. For the latest news contact ENT (National Tourist Organisation) or any travel agent in Maputo, or (for Gorongosa) Albatours in Beira.

GOVERNMENT & POLITICS

Representatives of political parties are elected to the National Assembly by universal adult suffrage, using a system of proportional representation. The president is elected separately. Following the October 1994 elections, politics continues to be dominated by the Frelimo and Renamo parties. There are between 10 and 15 minor parties, some with a few seats in the National Assembly, others with none at all, because of a 5% cut-off rule. Political allegiance tends to be on a regional (or ethnic) basis: Renamo enjoys considerable support in the central provinces of Zambezia, Sofala and Nampula, while Frelimo is stronger in the north and south.

The next general and presidential elections are due in 1999. Local analysts report that Frelimo is losing some of its popularity as voters become disillusioned with the country's slow progress. Renamo appeals to nationalist sentiments, and even accuses Frelimo of too much collaboration with Western backers. Generally speaking, President Chissano is regarded by most observers as an honourable leader, although reports of corruption and mismanagement among some senior government figures has cost Frelimo further support.

POPULATION & PEOPLE

The population of Mozambique is around 18 million. There are 16 main ethnic groups (tribes). The main (or most significant) are: Makua, the country's largest group, inhabiting the northern provinces of Cabo Delgado, Niassa and Nampula; Makonde, also a northern group, famous for their carvings; Sena, in the central provinces of Sofala, Manica and Tete; and Shangaan, who dominate the southern provinces of Gaza and Maputo.

Minor groups are: Lomwe, Chuabo, Marende, and Mwani (in the north); Yao and Nyanja (Niassa province); Nyungwe (centre); Shona, (Manica province and other areas bordering Zimbabwe); Tswa (Inhambane province); Ronga, Chope and Tsonga (south). There is also a small population (1%) of native Portuguese, plus small numbers of other European and Asian residents.

ARTS

Mozambique has a rich artistic tradition which, incredible as it may seem, continues to thrive after decades of colonial occupation and civil war. Today Mozambique produces some of the finest art in Africa, and was the only African country to exhibit in the Contemporary Art Pavilion at Expo 92 in Spain.

Literature

As elsewhere in Africa, traditions and stories were preserved and transmitted orally from generation to generation. It was not until this century that the written word assumed more importance, although local literature was not encouraged, and often deliberately repressed, by the colonial regime. In 1918, the newspaper *O Brado Africano* was founded by a group of black and mixed race journalists in Lourenço Marques (now Maputo). For many years this paper provided a platform for writers declaring first an African and then a Mozambican identity. Two of the most famous nationalist poets of

---

Mozambique's Provinces

Mozambique is divided administratively into 10 provinces, each with a capital city, a governor, and some autonomy. These give rise to acute inter-provincial rivalries – although these may also be based on ethnic differences. The provinces (and their capitals) are: Cabo Delgado (Pemba); Niassa (Lichinga); Nampula (Nampula); Zambezia (Quelimane); Tete (Tete); Manica (Chimoio); Sofala (Beira); Gaza (Xai-Xai); Inhambane (Inhambane); and Maputo (Maputo). The city of Maputo is also regarded as an 11th province. ■

this period were Rui de Noronha and Noemia de Sousa.

In the late 1940s Jose Craveirinha started to write poetry about the social reality of the Mozambican people. His subjects were the slums, the miners and the prostitutes, but his poems called for resistance and rebellion and this eventually led to his arrest by the colonial authorities. He is now recognised as one of Mozambique's most outstanding writers, and his work, including *Poem of the Future Citizen*, is recognised worldwide.

A contemporary of Craveirinha's was another nationalist called Luis Bernado Honwana. He is famous for short stories such as *We Killed Mangey Dog* and *Dina*.

As the armed struggle for independence gained strength, Frelimo freedom fighters began to write poems reflecting their life in the forest, their marches and the ambushes. One of the finest of these guerrilla poets was Marcelino dos Santos. Others included Sergio Vieira and Jorge Rebelo.

With Mozambique's independence in 1975, writers and poets felt able to produce literature free of interference. The newfound freedom was soon shattered by Frelimo's war against the Renamo rebels, but new writers emerged, including Mia Couto, whose works include *Voices Made Night* and *The Tale of the Two Who Returned from the Dead*. Other writers from this period include Ungulani Ba Ka Khossa, Lina Magaia, Heliodoro Baptista and Eduardo White. A significant development in 1982 was the establishment of the Mozambique Writers' Association, which has been active in both publishing new material and in advancing the spread of indigenous literature throughout the country.

A recently published book to look out for is *A Shattering of Silence*, by Farida Karodia, which describes a young girl's journey through Mozambique following the death of her family. One reviewer called it 'a spirited response to the brutalising effects of war'.

Visual Arts

The sculpture of the Makonde people from northern Mozambique is recognised as one of Africa's most sophisticated art forms (and is found in many other neighbouring countries). Some work is traditional, but many Makonde artists have developed contemporary styles. One of the leading members of the new generation of Makonde sculptors is Nkatunga, whose work portrays different aspects of rural life. Others include Miguel Valingue and Makamo, who specialises in huge intricate carvings of tortuous figures. Although not working in the Makonde style, Chissano is another sculptor whose work has won international recognition.

A number of very talented painters have emerged in Mozambique since the 1950s. Probably the most famous is Malangatana, whose vibrant art is now exhibited around the world. Since pre-independence days he has had strong connections with Frelimo, and at one time was imprisoned by the Portuguese colonial authorities. Other internationally famous artists from this period include Bertina Lopes, whose work reflects her research into African images, colours, designs and themes, and Robert Chichorro, known for his paintings which deal with childhood memories. More recently, a new generation of artists has emerged, including Naguib, Victor Sousa and Idasse.

All of the painters and sculptors mentioned above have work on exhibition in the National Art Museum in Maputo, and a visit there is highly recommended.

Among the most obvious forms of Mozambican art are the murals painted on walls at special sites in towns and cities, most notably in Maputo. The largest and most famous is opposite the Heroes' Circle, near the airport, which is 95m long and reflects many stories and images of the Revolution. Malangatana was one of the best known mural painters, and his work includes a mural in the gardens of the Natural History Museum on the theme of 'the people's struggle in the context of nature'.

Music

Traditional music is widely played in Mozambique. The Makonde in the north are

MOZAMBIQUE

noted for their wind instruments, known as *lupembe*. These are usually made from animal horn, less often with wood or gourds. In the south the Chope musicians play the *marimba*, a form of xylophone found throughout Southern Africa, and are famous for their marimba orchestras. Traditional drums, chimes and rattles are found everywhere.

Modern music flourishes in the cities, and the live music scene in Maputo is excellent. Marrabenta is perhaps the most typical Mozambican music – with a light style inspired by traditional rural *majika* rhythms. Marrabenta has also inspired its own styles of dance and fashion. The Orquestra Marrabenta was a state-funded band who emerged after independence, following Samora Machel's efforts to promote and encourage local African culture of all forms. They split in 1989, but several former members then formed Ghorwane, an Afro-Jazz band who have achieved some international fame. They often play live at the Centro Social do Desportivo in Maputo. Other Mozambican musicians producing pop music with a traditional flavour include Yana and Mingas. Yana is also well known as a teacher and promoter of other groups.

Another state-funded band called Grupo RM was popular in the late 1980s and the early 1990s and played an important role in promoting modern Mozambican music abroad. Other musicians to achieve recognition since the end of the war include Stuart, Roberto Chidsondso, Jose Barata and Elvira Viegas.

Places to buy music in Maputo are listed in that section.

RELIGION

Like the other countries of Southern Africa, animist religions have existed in Mozambique for thousands of years, and many people retain their traditional beliefs, sometimes alongside an established religion.

Islam was introduced to the coastal regions by Arab traders after the 7th century, and Christianity was first introduced by Portuguese Catholic missionary-explorers who arrived in the 16th century. Today, about 25% of the population are Muslim, mostly inhabiting the northern provinces and coastal areas, and about 20% are Catholic. There are some twenty Protestant groups, including Methodists, Baptists, Lutheran and Salvation Army, plus many local African-Zionist churches, especially in areas bordering Malawi and Zimbabwe.

LANGUAGE

Each of the major ethnic groups listed in Population & People have their own vernacular language. The common tongue and official language of Mozambique is Portuguese. As teenagers and young adults had their education interrupted by the war, Portuguese tends to be spoken by older people and the very young. English is not widely spoken outside the tourist areas of the south, so some basic Portuguese is essential for visitors.

Portuguese Pronunciation

The following should give you a rough idea, but listening to how local people speak will be your best guide.

ã	(as in *amanhã*) pronounced 'y' as in year, quite nasal
ão	(as in *pensão*) pronounced 'ow' as in how
ç	(as in *Moçambique*) pronounced 'z' like in zebra, although slightly softer – more like 'zsh'
c	(as in *como esta?*) pronounced 'k' as in kitten
ch	(as in *chá*) pronounced 'sh' as in shake
é	(as in *café*) pronounced as in French
h	(as in *banho*) pronounced 'y' as in you
m	(as in *sim*) is often dropped or pronounced 'n'
s	(as in *como esta?*) pronounced 'sh' as in finish (not as soft as 'sh' in shake)
qu	(as in *quanto*) pronounced 'qu' as in queen
qu	(as in *quiosque*) pronounced 'k' as in kiosk
x	(as in *Maxixe*) pronounced 'sh' as in shake
z	(as in *faz favor*) pronounced 'jz'

Greetings & Civilities

Excuse me/Please.
Faz favor.
Thank you.
Obrigado. (if spoken by a man)
Obrigada. (if spoken by a woman)
friend
amigo
Good morning.
Bom dia.
Good afternoon.
Boa tarde.
Good evening.
Bom noite.
How are you?
Como está ?
I am fine, thank you.
Muito bem obrigado. (if spoken by a man)
Obrigada. (if spoken by a woman)
What's your name?
Como se chama?
No problem/Never mind.
Não faz mal.

Essentials

I don't understand.
Não compreendo.
I don't speak Portuguese.
Não falo Português.
I am lost.
Estou perdido.
Have you got ...? Is there ...?
Tem ...?

Ladies' (toilet)	*Senhoras*
Men's (toilet)	*Senhors*

Yes.	*Sim.*
No.	*Não.*
No/Never/Nothing.	*Nada.*

Places to Stay

hotel	*hotel/pousada*
cheap hotel	*pensão*
hotel room	*quarto*
single/double	*simple/duplo*
bed	*cama*
toilet/bathroom	*casa da banho*

Do you have a room?
Tem um quarto?
room for married couples
casal

Places to Eat

breakfast	*pequeno almoço*
dinner	*jantar*
lunch	*almoço*
market	*mercado*
menu	*card pio*
menu (a set meal)	*menu*
restaurant	*restaurante*
snack-bar/food stall	*quiosque*
the bill	*quanto*
the receipt	*recibo*

Food & Drink

bread	*pão*
chicken	*frango/galinha*
chips/fries	*batata frita*
crayfish	*lagostim*
eggs	*ovos*
fish	*peixe*
fruit	*fruta*
lobster	*lagosta*
meat	*carne*
potatoes	*batata*
prawns	*camarão*
rice	*arroz*
salt	*sal*
scrambled eggs	*ovos mexidos*
squid (calamari)	*lulas*
steak	*bifel*
steak sandwich	*prego*
sugar	*açucar*
vegetables	*legumes*

beer	*cerveja*
mineral water	*agua mineral*
tea	*chá*
water	*agua*

Getting Around

Road/Street	*Rua*
main road	*estrada nacional*
Avenue	*Avenida*
Square	*Praça*
corner	*esquina*

MOZAMBIQUE

beach	*praia*
beach road/esplanade	*marginal*
town	*vila*
house	*casa*

Transport

bus	*ônibus/bus/*
	machimbombo
ticket	*bilhete*
train	*comboio*
wagon (train)	*vagão*

local truck converted to carry people
    chapa-cem or *chapa*
How many kilometres to ...?
    Quantos kilometros até ...?

Other Useful Words & Phrases

all	*todos*
here	*aqui*
cheap	*barato*
expensive	*caro*
too expensive	*muito caro*
left	*a esquerda*
right	*a direita*
perhaps	*talvez*
tomorrow	*amanhã*
When?	*Quando?*
Where?	*Onde?*

How much (does this cost)?
    Quanto custa?
Write it down, please.
    Escrever, por favor.
May I? (Use before entering a house,
    taking a photo etc)
    Dá licença?
Customs
    Alfandega

Facts for the Visitor

TOURIST OFFICES

Mozambique has a single ENT (National Tourist Organisation) office in Maputo (see that section for details). In South Africa, ENT is represented by Mozambique National Tourist Co (☎ (011) 339 7275; fax 339 7295), PO Box 31991, Braamfontein, Johannesburg, 2017. They can arrange anything (visas, car hire, flights, etc) and advise on bus travel, camp sites, diving and so on. They also represent several hotels and diving/fishing outfits in Mozambique. In other countries, such as the UK and USA, Mozambique's embassies can send tourist information on request.

VISAS

Visas are required by all visitors. Mozambique has embassies in most neighbouring African countries and a handful around the world. Visas generally cost US$10 to US$15 (or equivalent) for one-month single-entry tourist visas ($5 for transit, US$30 for three-month, multiple-entry). In some places, such as Malawi, the visa fee is payable in local currency and therefore can work out cheaper; elsewhere you must pay in US dollars or SA rands cash.

For visa extensions, each provincial capital has an immigration office. The cost varies and the service takes two to three days.

EMBASSIES
Mozambican Embassies Abroad

Around the world, places with Mozambique embassies include Belgium, France, Italy, Portugal, Sweden, the UK and the USA. Citizens of other countries should check in the phone directory of their own capital city. Mozambique also has embassies in the following neighbouring countries: Malawi (Lilongwe and Limbe), South Africa (Johannesburg, Pretoria, Cape Town, Durban and Richards Bay), Swaziland, Tanzania, Zambia and Zimbabwe. Elsewhere in Africa there are Mozambique embassies in Ethiopia and Kenya.

France
    Mozambique Embassy, 82 Rue Laugier, Paris 75017 (☎ (01) 47 64 91 32)
Malawi
    Mozambique High Commission, Commercial Bank Building, African Unity Ave, Capital City, Lilongwe (☎ 784100); and Kamuzu Highway, Limbe (☎ 643189)

South Africa
Mozambique High Commission, Glencairn Building, 73 Market St, Johannesburg (☎ (011) 23 4907)
Tanzania
Mozambique High Commission, 25 Garden Ave, Dar es Salaam (☎ 33062)
UK
Mozambique High Commission, 21 Fitzroy Sq, London W1P 5HJ (☎ (0171) 383 3800)
USA
Mozambique Embassy (☎ (202) 293 7146)
Zambia
Mozambique High Commission, 46 Mulungushi Village, Kundalile Rd, Lusaka (☎ 290451)
Zimbabwe
Mozambique High Commission, 152 Herbert Chitepo Ave, Harare (☎ 790837)

Foreign Embassies in Mozambique

All foreign embassies listed here are in Maputo. Countries with representation include:

France
1419 Avenida Julius Nyerere (☎ 491461)
Italy
130 Rua Pereira Marinho (☎ 491520)
Portugal
720 Avenida Julius Nyerere (☎ 490316)
Sweden & Finland
On Ave J Nyerere, near the Hotel Polana (to be joined by Denmark and Norway)
UK
310 Avenida Vladimir Lenine (☎ 492151)
USA
193 Avenida Kenneth Kaunda

The following neighbouring countries, for which you may need a visa, also have high commissions:

Malawi
75 Avenida Kenneth Kaunda (☎ 491468; open for applications from 8 am to noon; visas cost US$23, and are issued in three days)
South Africa
745 Avenida Julius Nyerere (☎ 490059)
Swaziland
608 Avenida do Zimbabwe (☎ 492451; open from 8 am to noon, 2 pm to 4 pm; visas cost R30 or US$5)
Tanzania
852 Avenida Martires da Machava (☎ 490110; open from 8 am to noon; visas cost from US$20, up to US$50 for British and some other Commonwealth citizens)

Zambia
1266 Avenida Kenneth Kaunda (☎ 492452; open 6 to noon, 2 pm to 5 pm; visas cost US$20 and take two days to issue)
Zimbabwe
Ave Martires da Machava (☎ 490404)

MONEY

Currency

Mozambique's currency is the meticais (pronounced *meticash* and abbreviated Mt). Most commonly used notes include 500, 1000, 5000 and 10,000. Because of the exchange rate, you'll always be carrying large bundles around. Notes for 50,000 and 100,000 are available but difficult to use for cheap items as nobody ever has change.

Currency Exchange

Inflation is high and the exchange rates shown here are likely to be wrong by the time you arrive. Prices throughout this chapter are quoted in US dollars, which are likely to remain more constant. We have converted prices at the official bank rate; if you use change bureaux, things will work out a bit cheaper. Official bank rates at the time of going to print were as follows:

US$1	=	Mt 11,125
UK £1	=	Mt 17,288
DM1	=	Mt 7338
SA R1	=	Mt 2466

Changing Money

The most readily accepted currencies are US dollars and South African rands. In the south of the country you can pay for a lot of things (such as accommodation) with rands direct. Other international currencies (eg UK pounds, German marks) will also be accepted in Maputo, but with less ease elsewhere around the country.

The main banks for changing money are Banco Standard Totta, Banco Commercial de Moçambique (BCM) and Banco Popular de Desenvolvimento (BPD). The latter two have branches all over the country.

Bank charges and commissions are high (especially for travellers' cheques, for which

MOZAMBIQUE

they also need to see your receipt – yes, the slip you're supposed to keep separate), so in reality the rate works out about 10% less than shown. Banks are also very slow. There are some private change bureaux in Maputo and other large towns where you can get about 5% higher than the bank rate – without commission for cash and with quicker service. Many supermarkets and shops selling imported goods will also change cash dollars or rands into meticais. The rate is about 5% to 10% higher than the bank and very quick. Rip-offs are unlikely. However, changing on the street itself is not safe anywhere.

POST & COMMUNICATIONS

Mail between Maputo and the outside world is not too bad (it costs US$1 for any international letter outside Africa – most letters take about two weeks), but the country's domestic postal system is a disaster. One letter took 52 days to reach Johannesburg from Vilankulo, and another took over three months from Tete to Australia!

Mozambique's telephone service has been completely overhauled, and efficient public phone offices can be found in most towns. They are open all day, plus evenings and weekends. Calls inside Mozambique are US$0.50 per minute during daytime, half this at night. International calls connect quickly, and the cost is US$5 to South Africa and US$13 for three minutes to anywhere in Europe, the USA or Australia. In Beira and Maputo faxes can be sent from the post office or the telephone office for the same rate as a call.

Codes for main centres include: Maputo 01; Beira 03; Nampula 06; Quelimane 04. Omit the zero if phoning from outside the country. Mozambique's international code is 258.

BOOKS

There is not a huge number of books in English about Mozambique, and some titles may take some searching out, but there are enough to provide all the information you might need before or during your trip. Some general titles on the region are listed in the Malawi Books section. Literature by

Mozambican writers is covered under Arts in the Facts about the Country section.

Most books are published in different editions by different publishers in different countries. As a result, a book might be a hardcover rarity in one country while it's readily available in paperback in another. Fortunately, bookshops and libraries search by title or author, so your local bookshop or library is best placed to advise you on the availability of the following recommendations.

History, Politics & Background

If you can only read one book about Mozambique it should be *Kalashnikovs and Zombie Cucumbers*, by Nick Middleton. The writer has done his share of 'real' travelling (hitching on trucks, staying in filthy hotels, etc) and a lot of background study, which is presented in an entertaining and very informative way. He covers colonial times, the war, South African and super-power involvement, aid and development, plus various aspects of the country today as it emerges from almost 20 years of fighting.

Apartheid's Contras, by William Minter, is an inquiry into the roots of the civil wars in Angola and Mozambique and the role of South Africa in continuing the conflicts. *The Harrowing of Mozambique*, by William Finnigan (subtitled *A Complicated War*), covers the same subject. Both books are well researched and provide further information on the issues raised in *Kalashnikovs*.

And Still They Dance, by Stephanie Urdang, is a study of womens' roles in the wars and struggles for change in Mozambique. *Assignments in Africa*, by Per Wästberg, includes a large section on Mozambique, where this Swedish journalist spent some time in the early years of independence, talking to poets and artists who had been given mundane jobs by the new government.

Liberating the Law, by Sachs & Welsh (Zed Books, London), describes how the colonial Portuguese laws of Mozambique were rewritten by the Frelimo government into an international-African legal system.

Arts & Culture

A whole range of beautiful colour large-format books were produced when Mozambique exhibited at the cultural arena of Expo 92 in Spain. Available from BIP in Maputo, these include: *Artistas de Moçambique*, an overview and celebration of the country's principal artists; *Mascaras*, a study of traditional masks; *Ilha de Moçambique*, about the former island capital, and two general books called *Olhar Moçambique*.

MAPS

The Maputo listings magazine *Time Out* produces a good map of Mozambique, with street plans of Maputo and Beira, available from BIP (see the Maputo Information section) for US$10, and some BP petrol stations for US$7.50.

NEWSPAPERS

Mozambique's main national newspapers are *Notícias* (Maputo and the south) and *Diário* (Beira and the centre/north); both are in Portuguese. English-language publications include *Time Out*, a listings magazine, and *MozambiqueFile*, produced monthly by the official news agency, with good coverage of politics and current affairs.

RADIO & TV

Mozambique has a surprising number of radio channels, mostly broadcasting in Portuguese or local languages. Radio Maputo is an English language service, broadcasting at 1 pm and 8 pm on 88 FM. The country has two TV channels: the state-run TVM and the commercial RTK, both with programmes in the evenings only. Portuguese TV is also available, beamed straight to the former colony by satellite.

PHOTOGRAPHY & VIDEO

General photographic hints are given in the Malawi Facts for the Visitor chapter. Film for cameras is available in Maputo and some other cities (Kodak 100 ASA 36-print film sells for US$7, Fuji slide film for US$12 to US$15) but spares and repairs are difficult to come by.

Even though the war is over, the authorities are still sensitive: you shouldn't photograph public buildings (eg Maputo station or city hall) or anything connected with the military.

HEALTH

The health precautions you need to take in Mozambique are no different from those elsewhere in the region, and discussed fully in the main Health section. If you swim in Lake Niassa (what Mozambique calls Lake Malawi), remember that it is infected with bilharzia. Details on hospitals in Maputo and Beira are given in those sections.

DANGERS

It has been estimated that more than one million land mines – laid by both sides during the war – remain unexploded in Mozambique. Some minefields have warning signs, but most are unmarked and often only discovered when someone gets blown to bits. For this reason it is simply not safe to go wandering off into the bush *anywhere* without first seeking local advice, and even then your safety is not guaranteed – the number of local people you see who have had one or both legs amputated is proof enough of that.

Stay on roads and well worn tracks where other people have obviously gone before. Take special care on road verges in rural areas – for example, if you want to head into the bushes for a pee. We have even heard of men setting off mines while standing *on* the road and pissing into the verge.

There are also a lot of guns in Mozambique, and a lot of desperately poor people. Armed robberies – aimed mostly at people driving cars around Maputo – used to be completely unknown, but since 1996 several incidents have been reported.

LEGAL MATTERS

The use or possession of recreational drugs is not legal in Mozambique. However, grass is available in several places along the coast where an influx of travellers has inevitably created a demand. If you're a smoker and get

MOZAMBIQUE

busted, the police will throw the book at you. Expect a very long jail term, or demands for a very large bribe.

BUSINESS HOURS

Banks are open from 8 to 11 am or noon, and shops and offices from 7.30 or 8 am until noon, then from 2 pm to between 4 pm and 6 pm, from Monday through Friday. Shops open Saturday morning, and possibly from 3 to 6 pm as well.

PUBLIC HOLIDAYS

The following public holidays are observed: 1 January (New Year), 3 February (Heroes' Day), 7 April (Women's Day), 1 May (Workers' Day), 25 June (Independence Day), 7 September (Victory Day), 25 September (Revolution Day) and 25 December (Christmas).

ACTIVITIES

Although Mozambique has great potential for anybody keen on wild animals or hiking (or both), the presence of land mines in most national parks and mountain areas means these activities are not yet available. Water sports (diving, snorkelling, sailing, fishing) are popular on the coast and are covered in more detail in the coastal sections.

ACCOMMODATION

As you might expect after many years of war, Mozambique's tourist infrastructure has seriously deteriorated. This situation is gradually changing, but in the meantime don't expect too much. If you're on a budget, Mozambique is a very good place to carry a tent: there are campgrounds at many places along the coast. Otherwise, the cheapest hotels (*pensãos*) start at around US$5/8 for singles/doubles, and you don't get much for your money. For US$15/20 there are some better options (sometimes called *pousadas*). A bed in a mid-range hotel costs from US$30, but even here basics such as electricity and running water are often in short supply. Two people travelling together will find some hotels charge different rates according to the size or number of beds you

use; many have a cheaper (casal) rate for married couples.

In the cities and coastal resorts there are better hotels with reliable facilities, but from around US$50 per person and upwards these are pricey for what you get compared to neighbouring countries.

FOOD

Staple foods include maize, rice and millet, eaten by local people with a sauce of beans, vegetables or fish. This kind of food is sold for around US$0.50 to US$1 at stalls and basic eating houses – these are usually found in markets and around bus stations. In the morning they also sell tea and very cheap egg or fish sandwiches.

Up in style and cost from here, most towns have a straightforward *salão da cha* or *restaurante* where you can get coffee or a pastry for around US$0.50, snacks and light meals such as omelettes, *pregos* (thin steak sandwiches) or burgers for US$1 to US$2. Most of these places also offer meals; the straightforward ones charge from US$2 to US$4 for meat stew or fried chicken, served with rice or chips. Bread is often served but you may be charged around US$0.50 extra for this. Slightly fancier restaurants charge US$3 to US$6, although this will often also include soup and bread. In cities like Maputo and Beira most mid-range restaurants charge between US$4 and US$7 for a main course and up to US$12 or US$15 for 'specials'.

Mozambique differs from many other countries in the region because fresh seafood is so plentiful. Even in small places you can get fresh fish, prawns, calamari and crayfish. A good meal of fried fish and rice starts at US$2, while prices for a big plate of king prawns start at about US$10 – not cheap if you're on a tight budget, but very good value compared to prices you might pay in Europe.

DRINKS

Local beers include 3M and Laurenço, but you can also buy South African imported beer in many places. For a 330 ml can, you'll pay US$1 at a street stall, and US$1.50 to US$2 in a smarter bar.

Getting There & Away

AIR

Mozambique's national carrier is Linhas Aéreas de Moçambique (LAM). There are five flights per week between Maputo and Johannesburg (US$180 single), and weekly flights between Maputo and Harare via Beira. Harare to Beira costs US$60.

Regional airlines serving Mozambique include: Air Malawi, with flights between Maputo and Lilongwe for about US$300; South African Airways, which flies daily between Jo'burg and Maputo for around US$300 return; and Metavia Airlines, with daily flights between Jo'burg and Maputo (via Nelspruit) for US$170 one way, US$250 excursion.

For long-haul flights, Air Portugal (TAP) and Air France each go to Europe three times per week starting at US$1300 one way and US$1700 return (it's much cheaper to fly to Jo'burg and get a ticket to Europe there).

The airport departure tax for international flights is US$10, payable in US dollars or SA rand, cash.

LAND

Mozambique has land borders with Malawi, South Africa, Swaziland, Tanzania, Zambia and Zimbabwe. Every foreigner entering Mozambique must pay an immigration tax of US$5 or R10 at the border. This seems to be legit – there's a notice about it on embassy walls – but make sure you get a receipt or stamp in your passport to show you've paid, otherwise you'll get trouble at the first road-block (a few km up the road).

Cars must also pay, but rates seem to vary between borders. For example, drivers crossing at Milange have paid just US$5 or R10 for a Temporary Import Permit (TIP), while those at Zóbuè have paid US$20 or R20 (exchange rates seem irrelevant). At Machipanda charges of US$35 or R70 have been known. If you're driving, check the current rates when you get your visa. Drivers also pay R100 or US$35 at the border for one

month's compulsory third party insurance. Wherever you cross, insist on TIP and insurance forms if the officials claim to have run out, otherwise you'll be fined at the first roadblock.

Malawi

The main land border with Malawi is at Zóbuè, on the 'Tete Corridor' road linking Blantyre and Harare (Zimbabwe). From Tete there are buses to the Mozambique border. You'll then have to hitch or walk the few km to the Malawi border, from where it's easy to hitch or get a minibus to Mwanza and on to Blantyre. Other land border crossing points include Milange, Mandimba and Nsanje. For more details see the Malawi Getting There & Away chapter.

South Africa

Bus From Maputo minibuses go from outside the train station, or the stands near the junction of Avenidas Guerra Popular and Zedequias Manganhela, to the Ressano Garcia border (US$3) or all the way to Komatipoort (US$5). From the South African side there's transport to Nelspruit and Jo'burg.

The Panthera Azul is a daily direct luxury bus between Maputo and Jo'burg (via Manzini, Swaziland) with on-board food, music, video and toilet. It departs from the company's office (☎ 494238; open every day) on Ave Mao Tse Tung at 8 am Monday to Friday, later at weekends. The journey takes eight hours and costs US$45. There's also a thrice-weekly service to/from Durban (12 hours, US$55). You can buy tickets in advance.

Train A thrice-weekly South African train connects Maputo with Jo'burg (via Komatipoort, Nelspruit and Pretoria). It leaves Maputo on Monday, Wednesday and Friday at noon, arriving the next day at 3.30 pm. Jo'burg to Maputo departs Sunday, Tuesday and Thursday at 5.45 pm, arriving 10 am next day. The cost is US$23/16/9 (payable in meticais or rand) for 1st/2nd/3rd class, including bedding in 1st and 2nd. You

MOZAMBIQUE

have to leave the train at the border crossings; watch your gear or take it with you. An alternative is to catch the daily train between Jo'burg and Komatipoort (US$12), and a minibus between Komatipoort and Maputo (US$5).

Swaziland

Minibuses operate from outside Maputo train station, or the stands near the junction of Avenidas Guerra Popular and Zedequais Manganhela, to the border at Namaacha (US$3), from where buses go to Mbabane and Manzini.

Tanzania

Intrepid travellers heading overland for Tanzania must travel from Pemba to Palma, but there's little traffic north of Moçimboa da Praia. From there, transport north to Namiranga (the Mozambique border post), and on to the Rovuma River (the border), a further 10 km, is even more scarce. You may have to walk, but local boys work as porters for a small fee. There's no bridge or ferry – only canoes. In the wet season roads are impassable and the river too fast for canoes, so the border is effectively closed. On the Tanzania side there's a long wait for transport (or another long walk) to Mwambo (the Tanzania border post), from where transport goes most days to Mtwara. Roads are very bad – ask around for the *Canadian Spirit* ferry, which goes to/from Dar es Salaam.

We heard from a traveller who had crossed at the even more remote border of Moçimboa do Rovuma, travelling by tractor from Mueda and by foot to Newala, from where occasional trucks run to Mtwara.

There are rumoured plans for improved roads in this area and a bridge across the river. If they're true, expect big changes on this route some time in the future.

Zambia

You can cross the border between Cassacatiza and Chanida, north-west of Tete, but few travellers go this way; most go through Malawi. Land mines and bandits may be a danger on this route.

Tanzania to Mozambique by Dhow (The Joys of Travel)

We heard from a traveller who had sailed from Msimbati in a Tanzanian dhow. The wind was coming from the south, but the captain promised to take him to Pemba in a day and a night for 10,000 Tanzanian shillings (about US$20). After four days of tacking and being blown backwards they hadn't even reached Moçimboa (less than half way) and were running out of food. The desperate traveller jumped ship with another local, and somehow managed to get ashore without being eaten by sharks. There followed a three hour slog though thigh-deep mud and mangrove swamps to reach dry land. The main road which he'd been told was 'near' the shore turned out to be several hours away, and he stayed for a night in a remote fishing village.

The next day's walk across hot sand and rocks gave him blisters, but he finally reached a road with occasional transport, found a truck to Moçimboa and then another to Pemba, by which time his blisters had gone septic and he could hardly walk.

The moral of the tale is this: the monsoon winds along the East African coast blow north to south from November to February, and south to north from April to September. Never try to go against the wind. ∎

Zimbabwe

There are two main crossing points between Mozambique and Zimbabwe: Nyamapanda on the Tete Corridor; and Machipanda on the Beira to Harare road. Both routes are very busy, with hundreds of trucks and holiday-makers, so hitching is not too difficult. If you're coming from Zimbabwe, you can get free detailed road information, and the latest on import and tourist immigration fees, from The Beira Corridor Group (☎ 739302/3; fax 721956), 207 Josiah Tongogara Ave, Harare.

SEA & LAKE
Malawi

It is possible to cross between Mozambique and Malawi by boats on Lake Malawi via

Likoma Island and Cobuè, although this is a slow and rarely travelled route. For more details see the Malawi Getting There & Away chapter.

South Africa
We've heard about a Unicorn Lines cargo ship sailing weekly between Durban and Nacala, with reasonably priced passenger accommodation. For details in South Africa phone (☎ (031) 301 1476), or ask at a backpacker's lodge in Durban. For details in Mozambique, see the Nacala section.

Tanzania
Some travellers go between Mozambique and Tanzania by local dhow. Pemba to Mtwara is about US$20. Other ports include Msimbati (south of Mtwara) and Moçimboa da Praia, which all have customs and immigration posts.

Getting Around

AIR
For getting around by air inside Mozambique, LAM serves internal routes between Maputo, Beira, Nampula, Quelimane and Tete, plus some other centres. Flights can be paid for in local currency. Sample fares: Maputo to Beira US$120 (daily); Beira to Nampula US$110 (five times weekly); Beira to Quelimane or Tete US$90; and Beira to Pemba US$120 (twice weekly). All large towns have a LAM office. Flights are frequently delayed or cancelled, and baggage frequently lost or tampered with. Metavia Airlines has twice-weekly flights between Maputo and the Bazaruto Archipelago.

A private charter airline called Sabin Air flies three times per week between Beira and Maputo, for US$140 one way, and to any other destination in Mozambique or Southern Africa on request. Even if you don't plan to hire a plane, it's worth ringing to see if spare seats are available on one of their charter flights. Expect to pay slightly more than the equivalent LAM fare.

ROAD
Owing to lack of maintenance and sabotage during the war, Mozambique's roads are generally in pretty poor shape. With the help of foreign aid, repairs are under way, and the situation will gradually improve, but for now travelling by road takes time. For example, the 500 km from Beira to Vilankulo (a combination of good and bad roads) takes from eight to 10 hours by car and up to 16 by bus. Beira to Maputo takes two days by bus. We've heard horror stories of Beira to Quelimane (350 km) taking five days by bus.

Bus
Where the roads are well maintained good buses connect major towns, usually at least once per day. There are three main private operators – Transportes Olivieras in southern Mozambique, Transportes Virginia in the centre and TransNorte in the north. All have express and stopping services; there's a minimal difference in price, but expresses are quicker (or less slow). Some sample fares: Maputo to Maxixe US$4.50; Maputo to Vilankulo US$7; Maputo to Beira US$18; Beira to Tete US$10; Beira to Vilankulo US$12; Quelimane to Nampula US$11; Nampula to Nacala US$2.50.

Where roads are bad, or in rural areas, you'll probably have to use converted passenger trucks (called *chapa-cems*, short for tin-one-hundreds and usually just called *chapas*) or normal trucks *(camions)* to get around.

Cities and large towns have bus stations, but in smaller places transport usually leaves from the start of the road towards the destination. You may have to ask around for directions. Long distance buses or chapas all tend to leave early (between 4 and 6 am), although sometimes chapas simply leave when full – you get there early just in case then hang around until noon.

Car
If you're driving your own vehicle in Mozambique, the police have a reputation for finding imaginary problems with vehicles for which large 'fines' are imposed.

We've heard from people who have been fined for doing U-turns, not wearing seat belts, even for wearing sunglasses. We've also heard from drivers who have been north to south through the whole country without a single police problem, giving away no more than a few soft drinks and packets of cigarettes in the interests of international understanding. Sure, there are lots of road blocks and the cops can seem intimidating when they speak loudly in Portuguese from behind dark glasses. But if you smile, say 'bom dia', look like you've got all day to stop and chat, and of course have your vehicle and papers in 100% order, you should have no problem. If a policeman does try it on, stand your ground or ask to see a superior officer. If you obey all road rules (including the 30 kph speed limit in towns and over bridges, seat belts at all times, carry warning triangles, stick reflective strips on your car) there's less chance of being pulled over in the first place.

Rental Cars can be hired in Maputo and Beira, where Avis, Hertz and a few small independent operators have depots. The large companies charge about US$35 per day for a small car, plus about US$0.35 per km. Collision and theft damage waiver is another US$15 per day. Smaller outfits can undercut this; contact them direct or through a travel agency (see the Maputo and Beira sections for more details).

TRAIN

Trains run through various parts of Mozambique, connecting neighbouring countries to the Indian Ocean. The line between Maputo and Johannesburg (South Africa) is described in the Getting There & Away section. Another useful line runs between Nacala and Liwonde (Malawi), via Nampula and Cuamba; more details are provided in the Nampula section, and in the Malawi Getting There & Away chapter.

BOAT

Mozambique has a long coastline, but very little in the way of organised ferry services

between the towns and cities on the coast. There is a regular service between Quelimane and Beira, but otherwise you'll have to ask around at ports and harbours. Chances improve the further north you go: for example, small freighters and dhows go between Quelimane, Nacala and Pemba for negotiable fees of around US$10.

ORGANISED TOURS

Companies specialising in tours around Mozambique include the following (all based in South Africa): Mozambique Adventure Tours (☎ (011) 787 0774) and African Adventures (☎ (012) 320 5663) for overland tours; Go Africa Tours (☎ (011) 487 1254) for flight and accommodation packages; Off Beat Safaris (☎ (01528) 35777) for overland activities; and Marine Safaris (☎ (012) 9989989) for fishing and diving. Tours are also arranged by the Mozambique National Tourist Co (☎ (011) 339 7275; fax (011) 339 7295) – see under Tourist Offices in the Facts for the Visitor section of this chapter for more details.

Maputo

Maputo, formerly called Lourenço Marques (or 'LM'), was once renowned as a beautiful city and rated by world travellers alongside Cape Town and Rio. But after almost twenty years of war and deprivation it is very run-down today, with crumbling buildings and dirty streets. Nevertheless, it is still an interesting place, with a very lively atmosphere. As the situation in the country improves, so do the facilities in the city – new shops and restaurants open, hotels are refurbished, nightclubs reawaken and streets are cleared and repaired. Old-timers say Maputo is already regaining some of its old charm.

Orientation

The first thing to strike you about Maputo is its size. The city is spread over a vast area and the streets (set in a grid pattern) are incredibly long and straight. For example,

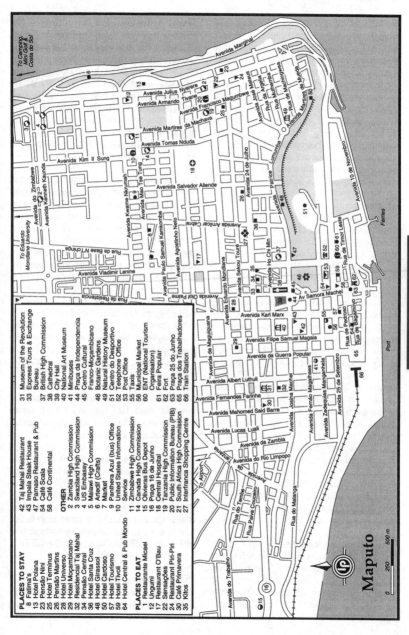

MOZAMBIQUE

Maputo

PLACES TO STAY
8   Fatima's
13   Hotel Polana
23   Pensão Nini
25   Hotel Terminus
26   Pensão Martins
28   Hotel Universo
29   Hotel Moçambicano
32   Residencial Taj Mahal
34   Pensão Central
36   Hotel Santa Cruz
48   Hotel Girasol
50   Hotel Cardoso
57   Hotel Tourismo
59   Hotel Tivoli
64   Hotel Central & Pub Mondo

PLACES TO EAT
1   Restaurante Micael
12   Ungumi
17   O'Bau
22   Sensações
24   Restaurant Piri-Piri
30   Café Primavera
35   Kitos

42   Taj Mahal Restaurant
43   Impala Steak House
47   Parnaso Restaurant & Pub
54   Café Scala
58   Café Continental

OTHER
2   Zambia High Commission
3   Swaziland High Commission
4   US Embassy
5   Malawi High Commission
6   Artedif (Crafts)
7   Market
9   Panthera Azul (bus) Office
10   United States Information
     Service
11   Zimbabwe High Commission
14   Canada High Commission
15   Olivieras Bus Depot
16   Praça 16 de Junho
18   Central Hospital
19   Tanzania High Commission
20   Public Information Bureau (PIB)
21   South Africa High Commission
27   Interfranca Shopping Centre

31   Museum of the Revolution
33   Express Tours & Exchange
     Bureau
37   British High Commission
38   Cathedral
39   City Hall
40   National Art Museum
41   Minibuses
44   Praça da Independencia
45   Centro Cultural
     Franco-Moçambicano
46   Botanic Gardens
49   Natural History Museum
51   Centro do Desportivo
52   Telephone Office
53   Post Office
55   Taxis
56   Municipal Market
60   ENT (National Tourism
     Organisation)
61   Feira Popular
62   Fort
63   Praça 25 do Junho
65   Praça dos Trabalhadores
66   Train Station

Avenida 24 de Julho, the main east-west drag, is about five km from end to end. Another main street, Avenida Eduardo Mondlane, runs two blocks to the north. Avenida 25 de Setembro runs parallel to the south; on or just off this street are the railway and minibus stations, bars, cafés, restaurants, banks, travel agencies, post and telephone offices, parks and museums. East of the centre, in an area formed by Avenidas Kaunda, Nyerere, Nkrumah and Lenine, are many embassies. East of here, the Marginal (beach road) runs alongside the not especially attractive Costa do Sol.

Information

Tourist Office ENT (the National Tourism Organisation) is at 1179 Avenida 25 de Setembro, above Lusoglobo Travel. The people are friendly, but don't know much about matters of interest to tourists, although they can often direct you to someone who does. For background information an excellent source is the BIP (Public Information Bureau) (☎ 490200) on the corner of Avenidas Eduardo Mondlane and Francisco Magumbwe, where you can buy maps, leaflets and books, or browse in the reference library. Much of the material is in English.

Money In Maputo, branches of the main banks are around the junction of Avenidas 25 de Setembro and Samora Machel. The bank at the Hotel Polana is open afternoons. Maputo's change bureaux include: AfriCambio, next to Hotel Tivoli, Avenida 25 de Setembro; Expresso Cambio, Avenida 24 de Julho; and at the Hotel Polana (also open afternoons and Sundays). Cash from Visa cards is available at BCM and Standard Totta banks, but this process is reported to take a very long time.

Post & Communications The CTT (main post office) is on Avenida 25 de Setembro. There is a poste restante here. The telephone office is on the same street (corner of Avenida Lenine) on the ground floor of a high-rise building, and open from 7.30 am to 9 pm every day.

Travel Agencies Most travel agencies in Maputo deal only with outbound flights, although a few also handle car hire and local tours. These include: Kwezi Travel (☎ 400628) – English-speaking, South-African managed; SET Travel (☎ 422363) at the Hotel Tourismo; Mextur Travel (☎ 428427) in the high-rise building on the corner of Avenidas Lenine and 25 de Setembro; Cotur (☎ 424341) at 1242 Avenida Karl Marx; and Mozambique Travel & Tours (☎ 424002).

Bookshops & Music Stores The BIP has books about Mozambique. Sensações, on the junction of Avenidas Mondlane and Nyerere, has a big selection of paperbacks, newspapers and magazines from South Africa, the USA and Europe, plus imported CDs featuring international and local musicians. CDs and tapes are also sold at the Clube Sportivo, the base of local-band-made-good Ghorwan.

Libraries & Cultural Centres The National Library is on Avenida 25 de Setembro, next to the main post office. Most items here are in Portuguese. More useful for non-Portuguese speakers are: the British Council, Rua John Issa, near the British High Commission; Centro Cultural Franco-Moçambicano, Praça da Independencia; and the United States Information Service, corner of Avenidas Mao Tse Tung and Kim Il Sung. All these places have libraries, regular exhibitions and film shows.

Medical Services Maputo's main Central Hospital, off Avenida Mondlane, charges US$1 for a malaria test and US$2.50 for general consultations in the *Clinica Especial* (☎ 424663). If you need overnight care, private rooms for US$100 are available. For private doctors and hospitals your embassy will advise; Clinic Cruz Azul (☎ 422787) has been recommended.

Things to See & Do

The oldest historic site is the **fort** on Praça 25 do Junho, where you can patrol the ramparts, look at the old cannons, or just sit and rest in the grassy courtyard. A must-see is the **train station**, designed and built in the early 1900s by a certain Mr Eiffel, who was also responsible for something or other in Paris. Recently renovated, it looks more like a palace, with polished wood and marble decorations, topped by a gigantic copper dome. The **cathedral** on Praça da Independencia is a more modern affair, although often closed to visitors. Nearby are the **Botanic Gardens** and the large **Camara Municipal** (City Hall), complete with pillars and portico, built in 1945. Also nearby is the more modest **Casa de Ferro** (iron house), designed in Europe in the late 19th century as a governor's residence, but built from metal plates which strangely enough proved unsuitable for tropical conditions.

The **Museum of the Revolution**, Avenida 24 de Julho (open daily from 9 am to noon, 2 pm to 6 pm, except Saturday morning; US$0.05) is worth a visit, but you need a guide-translator (which can be arranged in advance) to get a lot out of it, unless you read Portuguese. Also interesting are the **Money Museum** (Museu da Moeda) on Praça 25 do Junho, with exhibits of local currency from early barter-tokens to modern day bills, and the **Natural History Museum**, south-east of the city centre (open weekdays from 8 am to noon, 2 pm to 4 pm; free), where exhibits include a shark collection and a fascinating display of elephant foetuses at different stages of development.

The **National Art Museum** on Avenida Ho Chi Min has a truly wonderful permanent collection of Mozambique's finest contemporary artists. Entrance is free and a visit is very highly recommended.

A lively and colourful place to visit is the **Municipal Market** (Mercado Municipal) on Avenida 25 de Setembro, where fruit, vegetables, spices and basketwork are sold. (For craft markets see Things to Buy further on in this section.)

Places to Stay – bottom end

The *Parque Municipal de Campismo*, on the Marginal about 1.5 km north-east of the Hotel Polana, is a bit of a ghetto, but there are a few small patches of grass to stick tents on for US$2 per person. Running water is sporadic, and security is questionable unless you're in a vehicle or group.

For budget travellers, the best option is *Fatima's* (no phone, but you can book ahead on fax 400425), at 1317 Ave Mao Tse Tung. It's a house in the suburbs with rooms for US$7.50 per person, dorm beds US$5 and camping for US$3. Breakfast, meals and drinks are sold, and there are shops nearby. Fatima is a veteran backpacker, speaks English (plus about 10 other languages) and knows everything there is to know about Maputo and Mozambique. The only problem with this place is it's popularity – it's often full.

Other than this, good cheap accommodation is very hard to find. If you're really desperate *Hotel Girassol*, a large round building on Avenida Lumumba, has bare filthy rooms for US$5 per person. Better is *Pensão Central* 1957 Avenida 24 de Julho, where OK rooms cost US$7/14, although the bathrooms are antiquated. In the same league is the friendly *Pensão Nini*, Avenida Julius Nyerere, charging US$15 for a basic double.

Hotel Santa Cruz (☎ 420147) on Avenida 24 de Julho has straightforward rooms from US$16/18. The *Hotel Universo*, corner of Avenidas Eduardo Mondlane and Karl Marx, has run-down and gloomy rooms for US$20/22, but is worth considering as Transportes Virginia buses go to/from here (see Getting There & Away, following). Much better value is *Residencial Taj Mahal* (☎ 732122), Avenida Ho Chi Min, where clean rooms are US$15/20, breakfast US$2 and meals US$3 to US$6. The surrounding streets are not especially safe at night. Better again is the outwardly-tatty *Hotel Central*, near the train station, where surprisingly smart rooms are US$15 per person.

Places to Stay – middle & top end

Most hotels in this range include breakfast, unless otherwise stated. In the city centre, the former state-run *Hotel Tourismo* and *Hotel Tivoli* are due for major renovation, so make inquiries when you arrive. On the edge of the centre, and best value in this range, is the

MOZAMBIQUE

very pleasant *Pensão Martins* (☎ 424930; fax 429645), Avenida 24 de Julho, where rooms cost US$45/60 (US$65/80 ensuite). Also good is the *Hotel Moçambicano* (☎ 429252; fax 423124), off Avenida Eduardo Mondlane, with pool, restaurant and safe parking, charging US$60/80. Similar is *Hotel Terminus* (☎ 491333; fax 491284), on Ave Magumbwe, where small but smart 'economy' rooms (single or double) cost US$65, and larger 'standard' rooms are US$85. Breakfast is US$5, and other meals in the recommended restaurant start at US$8 for a simple main course, and US$12 for specials.

If you want to be outside the city consider the *Hotel-Restaurant Costa do Sol*, at the end of the Marginal about seven km from Avenida Julius Nyerere. Simple airy ensuite double rooms are US$50. The restaurant has meals in the US$3 to US$5 range, up to US$7 for specials, and is very popular at weekends when live bands play.

Towards the upper end of the range is *Hotel Cardoso* (☎ 4910715; fax 491804), Avenida Martires de Mueda, with singles from US$100 to US$170, doubles from US$140 to US$200. Top of the lot is the fabulous *Hotel Polana* (☎ 491001; fax 491480) on Avenida Julius Nyerere. It's of an international standard with all the facilities you'd want and prices to match: doubles cost from US$180, although some cheaper rooms on the upper floors are available. The food (eaten in luxurious surroundings) is good value if you've got spare cash. Snacks and light meals are US$5 to US$8, and all-you-can-eat buffet lunches and dinners are US$18.

Places to Eat – cheap
Shoestringers should head for the *market* on the junction of Avenidas Lenine and Mao Tse Tung, where you can get bread, tinned foods, fruit and vegetables. In the mornings stalls sell tea and egg or fish sandwiches for around US$0.50. Near the junction of Avenidas Samora Machel and 25 de Setembro is a bakery, with people on the street outside selling butter, jam, fish and other fillings.

For a decent coffee and cakes, the *Café*

Continental on Avenida 25 de Setembro is popular. Opposite, the friendly *Café Scala* is similar and also has snacks like toasted cheese sandwiches. Other good places are *Kitos* and *Café Primavera*, both on Avenida 24 de Julho, where you can get cakes and sandwiches for less than US$1, and snacks (such as burgers) from US$1.50 to US$2. Another cheap pleasant place is *Lanchonete* at the train station.

One of the best places to go for good-value eats is the *Feira Popular*, a fun-fair on Avenida 25 de Setembro, which has dodgems, swings and about 20 small bars and restaurants. Most do Mozambican standards like steaks and seafood, ranging from US$3 to US$5, up to about US$8 for prawns, and you can also eat Greek, Chinese or Ethiopian fare. The Feira is popular from Thursday to Sunday nights (when some of the bars become discos) and quiet at other times. Stroll around, have a beer, check a few menus, then take your pick.

Places to Eat – more expensive
Several of the hotels listed in the section above also have restaurants. Other places to try include *Parnaso Restaurant & Pub*, near the British Embassy, which does pregos and burgers for US$1.50, fish dishes for US$3.50, meat, chicken and pasta dishes for US$4 to US$6, and prawns for US$10, which is pretty much standard price for this type of place.

Good value in this range is the ever-popular *Restaurant Piri-Piri*, at the far eastern end of Avenida 24 de Julho, offering spicy chicken and seafood dishes for about US$5.

Carnivores can head for the *Impala Steak House*, on the corner of Avenidas Karl Marx and Josina Machel. The food is good, the service rapid and prices reasonable – around US$6 for a main course. They also have fish dishes for around US$4.50.

For something a bit better, go to *Restaurant O'Bau* on Avenida Lenine, a small place with a large TV, and good meals such as fish from US$4 and meat dishes from US$5 to US$7.

Mozambique

Top Left: Pemba, northern Mozambique. Most visitors come for the beaches and reefs.
Top Right: Across Mozambique, poor roads mean travel by truck is the norm.
Bottom Left: Church, Mozambique Island.
Bottom Right: Governor's Palace on Mozambique Island, the 19th century capital.

Mozambique

Top Left: Fishermen mend nets by the Church of Santo Antonio, Mozambique Island.
Top Right: Mozambique Island's waterfront; the island escaped civil war damage.
Bottom: Nampula, northern Mozambique. The cathedral is impressive but bad roads and
    wrecked cars show the country still needs a great deal of rebuilding.

On the slightly sleazy Rua de Bagamoyo, near the train station, *Pub Mundo* is very popular with expats (particularly South Africans) and does good meals for around US$5. Next door, *Maxim's* has a more local feel. The nearby *Snack Bar Rossio*, opposite the Hotel Central, has also been recommended. Smarter, but still affordable, is *Sensações* (see Bookshops & Music Stores earlier) where burgers are around US$6 and pizzas and pasta US$7.50.

There are several mid-range restaurants in Maputo, offering flavours from around the world and mostly charging US$5 to US$8 per main course. These include *Tai Pan* (Chinese) on Rua de Pedroso, near the train station; the *Taj Mahal Restaurant* (Indian) on Avenida Filipe Samuel Magaia; *El Greco* (Italian) on Avenida Julius Nyerere; *Restaurante Micael* (Brazilian) on Rua da Resistencia; *Zé Verde* (Portuguese) on Avenida Angola.

By far the smartest place in town is *Ungumi*, a restored colonial house near the Hotel Polana, which has the best cuisine in the country. The decor is quietly luxurious (the pictures on the wall are worth thousands of dollars) and main courses start at about US$30. If you go for a full à la carte meal reckon on US$70 to US$100 per person, with wine. At lunchtime, the very reasonable daily menu (four courses plus coffee) costs US$29.

Entertainment

Ciné Africa on Avenida 24 de Julho shows films of various nationality and dubious standard dubbed into Portuguese or with subtitles. Entrance is US$0.30. For better quality, try Ciné Scala on Avenida 25 de Setembro. Most of the cultural centres mentioned previously also show films about once or twice per week. Theatres include Teatro Avenida on Avenida 25 de Setembro, where most performances are in Portuguese, and the Centro Cultural Franco-Moçambicano, which has a more international flavour.

Maputo has a thriving nightlife with many pubs, clubs, bars and discos. Friday and Saturday nights are very lively, but there's rarely any action until about 11 pm. And then it goes until dawn. A good place is the Feira Popular, described in Places to Eat, which has a choice of bars and discos. Taxis wait by the main gate to take you home afterwards. For something a bit smarter, the previously mentioned Pub Mundo and Maxim's on Rua de Bagamoyo are also popular. On the same street, a pick-up joint, with strip-shows, is Club Luso (apparently no pun intended). Other places which have been recommended include Eagles Bar at the Centro Social do Desportivo (also the place to see football and basketball), and the smarter Complexo Mini-Golf on the Marginal, with restaurant, swimming pool and disco.

For live bands and discos try: Clube Kwuana, in the insalubrious suburb of Xipamanine, specialising in Rumba (Zaïrean) and African music; Buzio, near the Marginal, with a mix or European and African sounds; and Sunsplash, near the Catembe ferry jetty, with rap music and a young clientele. Cover charges are usually from US$2 to US$3. Other places for live music include Tchova Xita Duma on Rua Muthemba, Pensão Martin and Restaurant Costa do Sol, all with jazz and traditional bands.

Things to Buy

On Saturday mornings there's a craft market on Praça 25 do Junho. Other places to buy crafts are the stalls outside Café Continental, Restaurant Piri-Piri or the Hotel Polana. All have wooden carvings, masks, ornaments made from wood, soapstone or malachite, and models made from wire. Items range from tacky souvenirs to works of near-genius and all prices are negotiable. Pottery and basketware are sold on the Marginal roundabout, downhill from the Hotel Polana. Nearby is Artedif, where craft items (especially leatherwork) made by disabled people are sold. Some of the stuff is good and prices are reasonable. Moçambique Arte is a more expensive gallery with some excellent pieces and a calm atmosphere. It's on Avenida Karl Marx just down from the Impala Steak House.

MOZAMBIQUE

Getting There & Away

Air Details of flights between Maputo and places in Mozambique or other countries are given in the Getting There & Away and Getting Around sections of this chapter. Airport tax is US$20 for international flights, US$10 for regional flights.

Airlines with offices in Maputo include:

Air France
  15 Avenida Karl Marx (☎ 420337)
LAM
  Corner of Avenidas 25 de Setembro and Karl Marx, next to Hotel Turismo (☎ 426001)
Metavia
  Maputo Airport (☎ 465487)
SAA
  Avenida Samora Machel, near Café Continental (☎ 420740/2)
Sabin Air
  Maputo Airport (☎ 465108)
TAP
  Avenida 25 de Setembro, next to Hotel Tivoli

Bus For long-distance transport between Maputo and destinations in southern Mozambique, the Olivieras Transportes depot is on Avenida 24 de Julho, just beyond Praça 16 de Junho, about three km from the city centre. Buses run up Avenida 24 de Julho to the praça. A taxi from the city centre to the depot is US$4. Some sample fares from Maputo to: Xai-Xai US$2.30; Maxixe US$4.50; Vilankulo US$7; Beira US$18.

Transportes Virginia buses go to/from the Hotel Universo, and there's a booking office inside the hotel where you can buy your tickets a day in advance (Vilankulo US$7.50, Beira US$20).

Getting Around

The Airport Buses from Maputo city centre run along Avenidas Angola and Acordos de Lusaka, to within about one km of the airport. Alternatively, a taxi to/from downtown will cost between US$7 and US$10.

Bus Maputo's city bus service is hard to fathom as there are no route numbers, only a nameboard of the final destination. Chapas (converted trucks and yellow minibuses) also operate on some routes but don't even have nameboards. There are bus stands outside the Natural History Museum, at the train station and near the municipal market. Routes of use to visitors include the Costa do Sol service, which goes from the city centre along the Marginal (beach road). Bus fares are US$0.15, any distance.

Car If you need to hire a car to get around the city, or to go further afield, Hertz's main Maputo office is on Avenida 24 de Julho (fax 426077); they also have a branch at the Hotel Polana (☎ 491001) and the airport (☎ 465534). Avis is based at Maputo airport (☎ 465140; fax 465493). Some sample prices are given in the Mozambique Getting Around section. Smaller outfits in Maputo include Auto-Car (☎ 423733), 1022 Avenida Karl Marx, and Interfranca (☎ 427253).

Taxi Taxis are generally black and green, although there are many informal operators using unmarked cars, but neither cruise for business. There are ranks near the train station and central market (daytime) and outside the Feira Popular (evenings). You can also find them outside top-end hotels and at the Olivieras bus depot. Across the city centre will cost about US$4. Between the centre and suburbs US$5 to US$7.

AROUND MAPUTO

Across the bay from Maputo is the small town of **Catembe**, and a fairly pleasant area to stroll around. The ferry runs roughly two-hourly and costs US$0.10 per person (double at weekends). A major attraction is *Restaurante Diogo*, near the ferry jetty, specialising in prawns and other seafood.

Inhaca Island lies about 40 km offshore. Attractions here include classic tropical beaches and reefs, and the recommended *Lucas Restaurant* (seafood meals for US$8 to US$10). Accommodation options are limited to the mid-range *Inhaca Hotel* (☎ 34098), charging US$40 per person, although they may have some cheaper rooms for around US$12, or a small *campground* about two km from the hotel, where guides can be hired. Or you can ask around the village near the hotel – some locals rent out rooms. To get there, unreliable local dhows charge US$8 per person. Alternatively you can take a day tour. SET Travel Agency at the Hotel Tourismo represents several boat and plane outfits who run trips starting at about US$50 per person. Other organised excursions from Maputo visit **Macaneta Beach** and **Incomati River Camp** (US$60 including lunch). You can stay overnight at the camp (☎ 494466), which is tastefully built from local materials, for US$50 per person, all inclusive.

A cheaper destination is **Xefina Grande Island**, just off the Costa do Sol. Local boats from the fishing village four km from the end of the tar road will take you over. Ask at Restaurant Costa do Sol for the current price.

Southern Mozambique

This section covers the southern part of Mozambique, ie the area south of the Save River (also spelt Savé, Sabe or Sabi). This includes the provinces of Maputo, Gaza and Inhambane. Places are described from south to north.

BILENE

Bilene is a resort (full name: Praia do Bilene), about 100 km north of Maputo, with a good beach and long lagoon separated from the ocean by sandy spits and islands. It's 40 km off the main road; the junction is at Macina, from where pick-ups run throughout the day to/from Bilene (US$1).

At the north end of the beach is *Campismo Palmieras* – a clean, shady campground and very popular with South African families; US$8 per site plus US$5 per person. They also have no-frills three/four-person chalets for US$35 ($40 with linen), which share loos and hot showers with the campsite. There's a restaurant and bar. Half a km further along the beach is *Parque Flors*, run by ENT, where camping is US$5 and chalets US$15; water is scarce and security questionable, although

it might be worth checking in case things change.

Your other options are the ENT-run *Complexo Lagoa Azul*, at the south end of the beach, where clean, fully furnished and equipped self-contained two bedroom (four bed) chalets cost US$50 ($40 mid-week). There's a small charge for extra people, so if you're in a group this is a good deal. There is also safe parking. Nearby is a group of blue and pink holiday cottages for CFM (national railway) employees, but tourists can also stay; a functional double is US$25, or US$35 for four.

There are several places to eat along the beach road, including *Pavilão Tamar* – a small bar-restaurant with snacks around US$1 to US$2.50 and meals from US$4 to US$5; and *Tchin Tchin*, where prices are about the same. There's also a market and a couple of shops selling bread and groceries.

XAI-XAI

Pronounced 'Shy-Shy', this is a large straggling town on the main road just north of the Limpopo River. Most visitors head for the beach at Praia do Xai-Xai, about eight km off the main road. The large *Hotel Xai-Xai* is due a major revamp, and *Complexo Halley* has nothing-special ensuite rooms for US$35. Nearby is *Xai-Xai Camping* where it costs US$4 to pitch a tent plus US$2.50 per person, or US$8 if you want to hire a rondavel. There's a bar and meals are available (chicken and chips US$2.50, prawns and chips US$6.50). In a corner of the campgrounds is *Xai-Xai Diving & Fishing Charters* (☎ 22942), with camping for US$5 and basic bungalows for US$8 per person. Full fishing boat charter is US$45 per person per day. A dive is US$17. About 10 km north along the sandy beach road is another *camp site* (with cabins). It has been recommended as safe and pleasant.

To reach Praia do Xai-Xai, there's a direct bus which leaves Maputo at 6 am every morning, arriving four hours later. It returns to Maputo at 1 pm. The one-way fare is US$2.80. Alternatively you can do the trip in stages: minibuses between Maputo and

Xai-Xai town cost US$2; a pick-up between town and Praia is US$0.20.

PRAIA DE ZÁVORA

About 150 km north of Xai-Xai, and 17 km off the main road down a sandy track, is Praia de Závora and the friendly *Závora Lodge*, which offers accommodation, camping (around US$4), and good food in the US$4 to US$6 range. The beach and reef are wonderful and snorkelling gear can be hired.

MAXIXE & INHAMBANE

About 450 km north-east of Maputo, Maxixe ('Masheesh') is a little town from where you cross a bay to the sleepy provincial capital of Inhambane. Everybody goes by boat, as the road journey round is over 60 km. Dhows charge US$0.15 and take 20 minutes to two hours, depending on the wind. Motorboats charge US$0.30.

Places to Stay & Eat

In Maxixe, the *Oceana Hotel* between the bus park and the market has very basic rooms for US$6 (ensuite US$10) and reasonably priced food. The *Pousada de Maxixe* on the main road is similar in quality and price. Best deal is *Campismo de Maxixe* near the jetty, a clean campground with excellent security and hot showers. Backpackers' sites cost US$4.50 (one to four people), and caravan pitches with electric hook-ups are US$11. Self-contained fully furnished bungalows (one or two people) are US$25, and simpler beach houses US$18. Food is available, and the English-speaking manager is a good source of information regarding fishing, boat permits, etc. You can park a car here if you want to visit Inhambane, or go to Linga Linga, a resort which can only be reached by sea, about 12 km up the coast. Best for food is *Restaurant Dom Carlos*, near the bus park, with main meals from US$3 to US$5. *Quiosque o Veleiro* right by the jetty is a great place for a cold beer or snack while watching the dhows come and go.

In Inhambane, your choice is more limited. The overpriced *Inhambane Hotel* charges US$15 per room (US$18 ensuite).

Meals are available. Other places to eat or drink include *Bar Tuno* and *Restaurant Tic Tic* near the market. On the same street is Palms Bazar shop and information centre, mainly to assist South African investors (there are a lot around). They also assist with changing money.

About 15 km outside Inhambane, where the roads to Tofu and Barra split, is *Bar Babalaza*, which is also a shop and restaurant. Campers are welcome and simple cabins are planned.

Getting There & Away

A bus between Maputo and Maxixe or Inhambane is US$4.50. If you're heading north from Inhambane, take the ferry to Maxixe and get transport there. A bus between Maxixe and Vilankulo is US$2.

TOFU & BARRA BEACHES

The long, beautiful beaches of Tofu and Barra were legendary years ago and are fast regaining their former fame. Tofu is more accessible and more developed, with a hotel and holiday cottages. Barra is harder to reach but quieter, with a better setting: clean sand dunes with surf on one side and mangroves and palm groves on the other, where parrots and monkeys do their tropical stuff. If South African fishermen stop driving along the beach in ugly 4WDs it will be perfect. Like so many other places in Mozambique there are several projects under construction here, so expect changes and additions when you arrive.

Places to Stay

At Tofu Beach, *Complexo Turistico* has rooms for US$35 but is due for a major revamp. Nearby, the South African-run *Albatroz Fishing Camp* charges US$25 per person.

Low-budget travellers should head for the excellent *Barra Beach Backpackers*, run by John Henderson, who founded The Last Resort in Vilankulo; camping costs US$3.50 and simple single/doubles go for US$4.50/5.50. There's a kitchen, hot and cold water and various water sports. High-budget travellers should go next door to *Great Barra Reef Resort* (☎ (09258) 232220), where an English couple called Eric and Mel are constructing luxury bungalows which will cost US$80 per person when finished. There will also be a pool, bar and restaurant, plus boating, diving and fishing gear for hire.

Getting There & Away

From Inhambane there's a tar road for 20 km all the way to Tofu. After 15 km a sand road splits off left to Barra (reached after another eight km). For driving, a 4WD is recommended, or you can leave your car safely at Bar Babalaza and arrange a transfer. There are regular chapas from Inhambane to Tofu ($0.50), or you can hitch. There are also chapas to Barra village school, from where it's a four km walk through the palm trees to Barra Beach Backpackers. Local boys will show you the way and carry your pack for a small fee.

VILANKULO (formerly Vilanculos)

This small, spread-out town is about 20 km east of the main north-south road, and is becoming increasingly popular with travellers. It has wonderful beaches and is the main gateway to the Bazaruto Archipelago. Buses from Maputo and the south terminate at the northern end of town, near the Dona Ana Hotel. There is also a bank here.

Places to Stay & Eat

Most travellers head for *The Last Resort*, on the beach, where camping is US$3 and simple cabins US$3.50. There's a shady lounge-bar where you can while away the high-noon heat. Cheap food is available, although the service is a little disorganised. There's also a book-swap and information board. The manager can advise on hikes in the area, snorkelling and diving, the current rates for speedboats and dhows to the islands, and places to stay once you get there. Naturally, it's often quite busy. Nearby is *Simbira Lodge*, with huts for US$2.50 and camping US$2. It's used by overland trucks as they can't reach

The Last Resort and it's not on the beach, although the food is said to be better. Both places are about two km from the bus terminus.

Other options are the vast *Campismo de Vilankulo* (or Campismo Dodo) where camping in your tent or one of their empty marquees costs US$3.50, or the friendly and peaceful *Casa Josef*, with cool rooms in thatched cottages for US$3.50 per person, up to US$12 for an ensuite double. The bathrooms are clean, with running water, and camping is sometimes possible. Overlooking the harbour, the once-grand

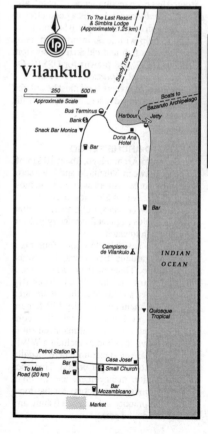

Dona Ana Hotel has spartan ensuite rooms, with excellent views, for US$9/16. Breakfast is US$2; other meals cost from US$4 to US$7. Nearby is *Margie's House* (ask for 'Casa de Margarita'), where a comfortable room or hut is US$8.50 per person. Breakfast is US$2.50 and other meals US$3.50. Snorkel gear can be hired.

For food, if you're self catering, the *mercado* in town has fish and fresh vegetables. Nearby are several *shops*. Vilankulo seems remarkably well supplied with bars; there are several along the road between the town centre and the Dona Ana; some do food in the US$2 to US$4 range. *Snack Bar Monica* has been recommended. There's also *Bar Mozambicano*, which is a good place to stop for a drink; the people who run it are happy to help with local information. Food here includes fish and chicken dishes from US$5 to US$7, and prawns for US$10. On the beach road, *Quiosque Tropical* is a mellow local bar where food must be ordered several hours in advance, but is worth the wait.

BAZARUTO ARCHIPELAGO

The Bazaruto Archipelago, about 10 km off the coast between Vilankulo and Inhassoro, is rated by some visitors as among the most beautiful places in Africa. It's all here: azure waters, sandy beaches, palm trees, pristine coral reefs, plus tropical fish to goggle at and big game fish to catch.

There are several islets plus four main islands: Magaruque, Benguerra, St Carolina and Bazaruto. Three of these were made a national park in the 1970s. Recently Bazaruto was added, and the whole area between the mainland and the 150 fathom mark is now protected as a world-class conservation area. Funding and management is provided by various bodies including WWF, who have a base on Bazaruto. There's a daily entrance fee of US$4 per person. This goes to conservation management and to small projects (clinics and schools) for the local people who practice subsistence fishing and farming inside the park.

Places to Stay & Eat

Development is carefully controlled, but there are several places to stay – most at the top end of the price-range, with accommodation between US$100 and US$250 per person per night, all inclusive, although most give special lower rates out of season. All usually require advance booking to their head office or through a specialist travel agency, but if you turn up at Vilankulo or Inhassoro and talk to one of the boat owners with a radio link to the islands you might be able to arrange something on the spot.

Ilha de Magaruque, on the island of the same name, has always been a flagship lodge: it was originally founded by tycoon-entrepreneur Joaquim Alves in colonial days and later became the favourite haunt of various rich and famous personalities. It's reported to be the best place for diving and various types of sea fishing; top quality boats and all equipment can be hired. They also have water-skis and sailboards. The lodge is run by Zimbabwe-based Landela Safaris (☎ Harare 734043; fax 706366), who plan a multi-million dollar refit in 1997, so expect big changes and even more exclusivity by 1998.

On Benguerra Island, there's *Benguella Lodge* (☎ South Africa (011) 483 2734) and *Marlin Lodge*, while Bazaruto Island has *Bazaruto Lodge* (☎ South Africa (011) 447 4454) and *Sabal Lodge*. for reservations or information you can also contact one of the tour agents listed in the Maputo section. St Carolina Island also has a lodge which is currently run-down but due for major renovation in the future.

Most of the lodges can be visited for the day (although a small fee may be payable if you don't take a meal). For example, Ilha de Magaruque is a popular destination from Vilankulo; you can hire scuba or water-sport gear, and feast on a splendid buffet lunch. The people at The Last Resort have all the details.

The archipelago's only concession to backpackers is *Gabriel's Lodge*, on Benguerra Island, where camping costs US$5 and simple chalets US$6. Bazaruto Island has *Zengelemo Campsite*, run by the national park. Guided walks can be arranged. You're supposed to get a permit to stay here from the District Agricultural Officer *(Direcão Distrital de Agricultura)* in Vilankulo or Inhassoro. Again, The Last Resort has details.

Getting There & Away
If you stay at one of the smart lodges, transfer by speedboat will be arranged for you, from either Vilankulo or Inhassoro, for around US$100 per return trip. If you want to go for the day, a speedboat costs about US$120 from Vilankulo to Magaruque, and US$200 from Vilankulo to Bazaruto Island. From Inhassoro to Bazaruto with Hutnic Adventures (see under Inhassoro, following) is about US$60 for two people.

Alternatively you can go by dhow from Vilankulo to Magaruque or Benguerra. There are public boats, which run to no fixed schedule, but most travellers get a group together and hire a dhow for the day. This can be arranged at the harbour or through The Last Resort, and costs about US$15 per boat per day. The one-way voyage can take anything from two to six hours, depending on the wind and tide. If you want to spend a few days on, say, Benguerra just tell the guys when you want to be picked up, but don't pay anything until you're safely back on the mainland!

INHASSORO
This small town is a jumping-off point for Bazaruto and St Carolina islands, and a popular spot for South African anglers. There are a couple of well-stocked shops and a bakery, and buses a few times per day to/from Vilankulo and the Save River bridge.

Inhassoro Hotel has rooms for US$3 per person but no water, although this may change. *Hotel Seta* has simple, breezy cabins for US$6 per person and camping for US$5.

An outfit called Hutnic Adventures runs fishing holidays for US$70 per person per day and include a fully kitted boat, comfortable tent accommodation and two meals per day. On top of this you pay US$1 per litre of fuel used. They also offer all-day fishing, water-skiing or parasailing trips, trips to St Carolina and Bazaruto islands, and have diving and snorkelling gear for hire.

Central Mozambique

This section covers the central areas of Mozambique, between the Save River and the Zambezi River (spelt Zambeze in Portuguese). This includes the provinces of Manica, Tete and Sofala, the city of Beira and the towns of Tete and Chimoio, on the 'corridor routes' to/from Malawi and Zimbabwe. Places are described roughly south to north.

BEIRA
This is the second-largest city in Mozambique, a major port and the terminal of the oil pipeline and railway to Zimbabwe. The central area is more compact than Maputo's and the old Mediterranean-style buildings give this place some faded glamour, making it definitely worth visiting for a day or two.

Orientation & Information
The heart of the city is the *Praça* (main square). On or around this square are shops, banks, post and telephone offices, supermarkets (some may change cash dollars), a pharmacy and the LAM office. There's also the friendly English-speaking Albatour Travel Agency (☎ 328980), upstairs next to Café Capri, for flight and tour bookings and help with general tourist inquiries. Several main streets radiate out from the Praça, meeting other streets, squares and intersections making the layout quite confusing at first – especially as there are few street signs. The main street into the city is Avenida Eduardo Mondlane. Most public transport terminates on a small street between the southern end of Eduardo Mondlane and the Praça. South-east of the Praça, various streets lead to the *marginal* (coast road) called Avenida das FPLM. This runs alongside the ocean, past the newly renovated hospital (malaria testing available), to

MOZAMBIQUE

MOZAMBIQUE

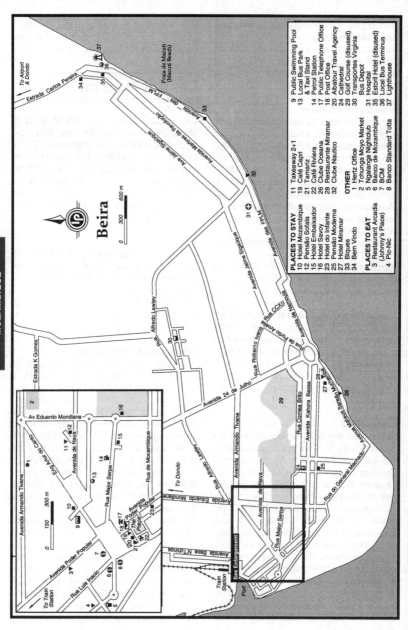

Beira

0   300   600 m

PLACES TO STAY
10 Hotel Mozambique
12 Pensão Sofala
15 Hotel Embaixador
16 Hotel Savoy
23 Hotel do Infante
25 Pensão Moderna
27 Hotel Miramar
33 Biques
34 Bem Vindo

PLACES TO EAT
3 Restaurant Arcadia
   (Johnny's Place)
4 Pic-Nic
11 Takeaway 2+1
19 Café Capri
21 Tamariz
22 Café Riviera
26 Clube Oceana
28 Restaurante Miramar
32 Clube Nautico

OTHER
1 Hertz Office
2 Tchunga Moyo Market
5 Ngalanga Nightclub
6 Banco de Mozambique
7 BCM
8 Banco Standard Totta
9 Public Swimming Pool
13 Local Bus Park
   & Taxi Stand
14 Petrol Station
17 Public Telephone Office
18 Post Office
20 Abatour Travel Agency
24 Cathedral
29 Golf Course (disused)
30 Transportes Virginia
31 Hospital
   Bus Depot
35 Estoril Hotel (disused)
36 Local Bus Terminus
37 Lighthouse

Macuti Beach and the landmark Estoril Hotel and lighthouse.

Warning The lack of street signs means that nobody knows their name – so bear this in mind if asking for directions. Also, the few maps of Beira that do exist disagree on some names anyway. For example Avenida Eduardo Mondlane is also called Avenida Samora Machel, while Avenida Kahora Bassa may also be called Eduardo Mondlane!

Things to See & Do
The **cathedral** is on Avenida Kahora Bassa, south-east of the centre. At one time it was glistening white but it's looking a bit grimy now. The lively market at **Tchunga Moyo** ('brave heart') is full of imported goods, contraband and some unsavoury characters, so travel light and walk carefully here. The old part of the **port** is also worth a look, if only to see all the wrecked vessels. Most people head for the seashore, to the east of the centre, where **Praia de Macuti** is a fine beach, with fairly clean water and a couple of places to stay and eat nearby. Near the red and white **lighthouse** at the far end of the beach another **shipwreck** is spectacularly washed up on the beach.

Places to Stay – bottom end
For shoestringers, the cheapest place in town is the scruffy *Bem Vindo*, right behind the Hotel Estoril (currently disused) in Macuti Beach, nine km from the centre and just a minute's walk from the beach. It's actually a scrap-metal yard, but the big man who runs it is friendly enough. Camping is US$1, and basic rooms cost from US$2 to US$3 per person. The toilets and showers leave a hell of a lot to be desired. To get there catch a 'Macuti' or 'Estoril' bus or minibus and ride to the end (the fare is US$0.15). A taxi costs US$2.50. A far better choice is nearby *Biques*, right on the beach, where camping is US$2 and the showers are spotless. The on-site English-speaking bar also has food, and is a popular evening spot for well-to-do locals and expats. Chalets are planned.

In town, the cheapest we found was *Pensão Sofala* on Avenida de Naya, a brothel with filthy toilets and rooms for US$4/6. Far better is the *Hotel Savoy* a few blocks away, where clean airy rooms are US$5/9, or US$11 for doubles with reasonable bathrooms. Also good value is the quiet *Pensão Moderna*, two small blocks south of the cathedral, where comfortable rooms are US$8/15. The restaurant offers breakfast for US$1.50 and main meals for around US$4. There's also the *Monaco Hotel*, behind the Hotel Mozambique, charging US$8.50/16, and the *Messa da Policia*, near the bus park, which has cheap rooms and food (chicken and chips for $1.50).

Up the price band a bit, but still good value, is the *Hotel Miramar* (☎ 3222830), just off the Marginal, where very clean ensuite rooms with hot water and air-con cost US$12/17. There's also safe parking.

Places to Stay – middle & top end
Most places in this range include breakfast. Central and good value is the *Hotel do Infante* (☎ 323042), just south of the main Praça, where clean ensuite rooms (some with balcony) cost US$20/22 (plus US$4 for air-con). The roof-top restaurant is also good. Up a grade is the *Hotel Embaixador* east of the Praça, where smart rooms with TV start at US$30/35; or US$45/55 with air-con (travellers' cheques accepted). Best in town is the *Hotel Mozambique* (☎ 325011), a blue and white high-rise that dominates the city centre, where rooms are US$50/65.

Places to Eat
Several of the hotels and pensãos listed above also have restaurants where non-guests can eat. Otherwise, if you're self-catering you can buy tins and vegetables in the shops around the main Praça or at the nearby central market. You can buy fresh fish and prawns (around US$5 per kg) from the sellers on Macuti Beach.

A cheap place is *Tamariz*, on the Praça, where meals start at less than US$1, rising to US$2 for chicken and chips. Nearby are several pavement cafés where you can rest from the sun and absorb the atmosphere: the

Riviera, *Capri* and *La Scala* all have coffees, soft drinks, meals and snacks at reasonable prices. Near Pensão Sofala *Takeaway 2 + 1* has outside seats, snacks from US$1 and meals for around US$2, and smarter dining upstairs.

For something more substantial, *Pic-Nic* is a lavishly decorated friendly place north of the Praça, open daily for lunch and dinner with main meals from US$4 and seafood around US$9. The restaurant at the *train station* may not be the first place you'd think of, but the food is fine and good value with main meals at US$5. Nearby, with similar prices and better ambience (including an outside terrace) is *Restaurante Arcadia* also known as *Johnny's Place*.

On Macuti Beach is *Clube Nautico*, a popular place with main meals from US$5 to US$7 and seafood from US$9. The manager speaks English and no membership is required. There's also a swimming pool, showers and games room. Nearby is the well-positioned *Clube Oceana*, which is quieter than the Nautico with slightly lower prices, and *Restaurante Miramar*, with not such a good view but with good food and prices about the same as the Oceana.

Entertainment

The two most popular bars in town seem to be the above-mentioned Clube Nautico and Biques (good for meeting other travellers). Clube Oceana is more of a local place with live music or discos at weekends. In town, the smart Ngalanga Nightclub is open every night, with a US$2 cover charge.

Getting There & Away

Air LAM has daily flights to/from Maputo, and a few times per week to/from Quelimane and Nampula. You can also fly to/from Harare in Zimbabwe (see the main Getting There & Away section in this chapter).

Bus For long-distance buses the Transportes Virginia depot is off Rua Alfredo Lawley. Most buses leave around 5 am, and can fill up even earlier, so it's best to get your ticket the day before. The office is open from 8 am to noon then 2 to 4 pm. You can sleep at the depot too – most locals seem to. The buses stop at Tchunga Moyo market to pick up passengers, but may be full by the time they get there. Some sample prices from Beira: Tete US$6.50; Vilankulo US$5.50; Maputo US$20 (two days). Transport along the road to/from Zimbabwe also goes from here: to Chimoio ($2) at 6 am, 10 am and 3 pm; Machipanda ($3) 4 am and noon.

In 1996 there was no bus from Beira to Quelimane because the road was too bad. Trucks and cars were getting through, so you could hitch – but don't expect a picnic. We received the following advice from a traveller who went this way:

From Beira, to reach Quelimane, you should hitch or bus to the Caia road junction just past Dondo, on the road to Chimoio. Walk up the dirt road, which is the main national highway north, where you will find a huge crowd of people waiting for transport. Sit down and join them. Eventually a truck will come, for which there will inevitably be a scramble. You will then have a 230 km journey which will take at least 10 hours. This will get you to Caia, on the bank of the Zambezi. You will arrive at night, and since there is nowhere to stay, your best option is to bed down at the truck yard with all the others. There is a vehicle ferry across the Zambezi, but it won't necessarily be working. If this is the case there will be huge numbers of trucks waiting for it to be fixed. Foot passengers can find canoes across the river. On the other side, there are infrequent trucks or chapas to Quelimane. The whole Beira to Quelimane trip takes between one and two days and cost about US$15 to US$20 in total.

Andrew Chilton

Car If you're driving to Quelimane, much of the advice above will be useful. An alternative route is via the railway bridge at Vila de Sena, which has been converted to take cars too. The roads on either side of the bridge are in bad condition, although there are plans to renovate them in 1997 and 1998.

If you're driving between Beira and Mutare (Zimbabwe) the road is generally fine and being upgraded in several places. For more details see the main Getting There & Away section in this chapter.

Train There is a thrice-weekly train between Beira and Machipanda (the Zimbabwe border), which stops *everywhere* on the way, and is very slow. Sample fares to Chimoio: 1st class US$3.50; 2nd US$3; 3rd US$1.50.

Boat Once a week a rusty ferry chugs between Beira and Quelimane, allegedly in 24 hours. The fare is US$20 for a seat under shade on the deck. Inquire at the port.

Getting Around
The Airport A taxi between Beira airport and the city centre or Macuti is between US$5 and US$10, depending on your bargaining skills. There's also a public bus between town and the airport.

Bus & Minibus For getting around town, the local transport hub is the bus park, just east of the main Praça. From here to Macuti costs US$0.15; to near the Virginia bus depot is US$0.20 (you have to walk the last 500m).

Car If you need a car to get around the city, or to travel further, Avis is based at Beira airport (☎ 301263; fax 301265), while Hertz is on Avenida Armando Tivane (☎ 322315).

Taxi You can find taxis (black with a green roof) near the bus park. From the centre of town to Macuti or the Virginia bus depot is US$3.

CHIMOIO
Chimoio is an unremarkable town where you may find yourself overnighting on the route between Zimbabwe and Beira. Places to stay include *Pensão Flor de Vougua*, one block west of the main street near the post office, with reasonable rooms from US$5 per person. There are several cheap restaurants and snack bars on and around the main street. The *Motel Moino*, a mock windmill on the main road towards Beira, has doubles for US$13 and reportedly a good restaurant, with main meals from US$3.50. Best in town is *Executive Manica Hotel* (☎ 23135), signposted off the eastern bypass road, where excellent rooms are US$30/40 with breakfast. They also have safe parking and a petrol station.

Around Chimoio
Buses to/from Tete run along the road east of Zimbabwe's Eastern Highlands. This goes through **Catandica** (which has a resthouse, shop and petrol station) and **Changara** (the junction with the road to/from Harare). From Chimoio you could also reach Gorongosa National Park, if it didn't have land mines.

TETE
Tete is a large town on the 'corridor route' through Mozambique between Blantyre (Malawi) and Harare (Zimbabwe). The road crosses the Zambezi River on a very impressive suspension bridge, but apart from that Tete has few sights. You may find yourself here if you're hitching, or breaking away from the beaten track going to/from Zambia, taking the Beira road via Catandica or visiting the Cahora Bassa Dam.

Places to Stay & Eat
Cheapest is the basic *Pensão Alves*, in the upper part of the town centre, five blocks from the river, which charges US$2. On the same street is the *Hotel Kassuende* where ensuite singles/doubles are US$8/10. Between these two places is *Pastelaria Confianca* and *Snack Bar 2002*, both with good cheap eats. At the centre of town is *Hotel Zambeze*, where clean and cool ensuite rooms are US$7/9 (US$9/11 with a fan and US$15/18 with air-con). Meals are around US$4, and nearby is the *mercado* (market) with several very cheap eating houses. Down on the river bank, almost under the bridge, is the *Piscina*, which has rooms for US$18 and camping for US$2. There's also food in the evenings, loud music some nights and an empty pool. Next door is *Restaurant Freita*, a popular expat hang-out with shady outside seating, cold beers, snacks around US$1 and good meals for US$5 (prawns US$8). About 20 km out of Tete, on the road to/from the Malawi border at Zóbuè, is the small town of Moatize. On the main street, *Café Agua* has been recommended for safe camping and good cheap food.

MOZAMBIQUE

The Cahora Bassa Dam

About 150 km north-west of Tete, the Zambezi River is dammed by the Barragem de Cahora Bassa. It was built in the 1970s – one of the largest civil engineering projects in Africa. Today, it is still a grand sight. Set in stunning scenery at the head of a magnificent gorge, the dam has created Lago de Cahora Bassa, a vast lake 270 km long, stretching back to the confluence of the Zambezi and the Luangwa rivers on the border with Zambia. Although not as big in area as Lake Kariba, it has a far greater power potential – capable of generating more than 4000 megawatts of energy.

The project was initiated by the Portuguese colonial government (who called it Cabora Bassa) in the late 1960s. The dam was intended to control floods, and to store water for irrigating plantations on the Lower Zambezi. Later the plan was enlarged to include a hydroelectric power station, with South Africa agreeing to buy most of the energy. The construction contracts were signed in 1969 and, despite repeated attacks by Frelimo forces, then fighting for independence, construction continued through the early 1970s.

The massive Cahora Bassa dam, a classic example of a major African development project which turned into a white elephant.

It was a scheme of enormous proportions. The underground hall containing the turbines is twice the size of St Paul's Cathedral in London. To move all the equipment needed for the work, existing roads and railways had to be modified, one of the results of which is the impressive suspension bridge across the Zambezi at Tete. Resettlement of people in the area was not as great a problem as around Kariba, but 24,000 new homes had to be built. The dam was completed and the lake began filling by 1974.

Despite these superlatives, the Cahora Bassa Dam has to be one of the greatest white elephants of Africa, if not the world. One of the main problems is that in the 20 years or more since completion it has supplied a tiny proportion of its capable power output. This is because the power lines to South Africa and to other parts of Mozambique were destroyed by Renamo rebels in the civil war after independence. (The disruption to South Africa is particularly ironic as this country supplied most of Renamo's support. It may have been an act of revenge against the signing of the Nkomati Accord when South Africa apparently agreed to discontinue backing Renamo.)

In 1996 the power station was being repaired and rehabilitated. The lines are due to be fixed through 1997 and 1998 – estimates of the repair bill are in the region of US$150 million. In 1996 the power station supplied just Tete and Songo.

Another problem with the dam has been the invasion of water hyacinth – an aquatic weed, which has also invaded Lake Kariba, Lake Victoria and several other lakes in Africa. Introduced from South America, this plant grows at a phenomenal rate, doubling its mass every week if conditions are very favourable. It covers vast areas of the lake's surface, encourages water evaporation and consumes large quantities of oxygen in the water, so affecting the balance of aquatic life. It is virtually impossible to eradicate, since it produces seeds which cannot be removed from the lake bottom.

And if that wasn't enough, silt has also been reported as a major problem. Although a lot silt is taken out by the Kariba and Kafue dams (upstream of Cahora Bassa), a great deal is added via the Luangwa River. This has increased over the last few decades as overgrazing and inefficient farming leads to a rapid increase in soil erosion and run-off. It remains unclear how long the lifespan of Cahora Bassa will be. Estimates have varied between 35 and 1000 years. That is, nobody really knows!

Until recently the dam was a sensitive site, but it can now be visited by tourists. This is easy for those with their own wheels, but there is a daily bus from Songo, the dam's service town (it leaves from the Hotel Kassuende in Tete – US$2.50), or you can hitch. Before arriving, though, you have to get *declaração* (statement of permission to visit) at the Tete offices of HCB (Hydroelectrica de Cahora Bassa, pronounced *ach-ceh-beh*) in Tete. From the Hotel Zambeze in Tete, go uphill and left at the crossroads. Along this street about 100 metres, the office is on your right in an apartment block above a hardware shop called Somac. On the 1st floor is a clerk who speaks English. He will take you to the *chef* on the 2nd floor, and he will issue permission (free of charge), either on the spot or next day. This you present to the police at the checkpoint about five km before Songo, which is about eight km by road from the dam itself. Tours of the dam (which take you into the underground turbine rooms) are run a few times per week. If you need to overnight in Songo, the *Pousada Sete Montes* has rooms for around US$10. ■

Getting There & Away

Southbound buses (Beira US$6.50, Maputo US$25) go from the bus station about 500m along the street from Pensão Alves. Northbound transport goes from near the market.

Northern Mozambique

This section covers the area of Mozambique closest to Malawi – north of the Zambezi River, including the provinces of Zambezia, Nampula, Niassa and Cabo Delgado. Places are described roughly south to north.

QUELIMANE

Quelimane (pronounced 'Kelimarne' or 'Kelimarny') is a large town on an estuary about 10 km upstream from the ocean. There are some beaches nearby and the town has a pleasant coastal feel. You can change money at the BPD on Avenida 1 de Julho. The LAM office is nearby. The town has few sights, although the old Portuguese church near the port and the newer cathedral on Avenida 7 de Setembro are both worth a look. The waterfront is a pleasant place to stroll, especially in the evening.

Places to Stay

There are a few cheap dives near the bus park: *Pensão Moderno* is reported to be OK but there's little else worth recommending. Cheapest in the centre is *Pensão Ideal* on Avenida Samuel Magaia, charging US$7 for simple rooms (one or two people), US$11 with air-con, US$13 for ensuite. It's clean and friendly, but problems with water and power make only simple rooms worth taking. They also do meals like fish for US$3, beef for US$4 and chicken for US$6. Next up in price is *Hotel Zambeze* on Ave Acordos de Lusaka, charging US$12/18 for simple singles/doubles, and US$15/22 for smarter ensuites, plus US$2 for breakfast. Meals are US$3.50 to US$6. Not quite so nice is *Pensão Quelimane*, a two-storey building (no sign) on Avenida Eduardo Mondlane, with rooms for US$15 (one or two people). A room for two or three with ensuite

is US$30. Breakfast is US$1, and other meals US$4 to US$7. A bit smarter is *Hotel 1 de Julho* (☎ 213067) with reasonable rooms for US$15/30.

Top of the range, but very costly for what you get, is *Hotel Chuabo* (☎ 213181; fax 213812), where visitors pay (hard currency only) US$85/140 for single/twin rooms with fridge, TV and air-con. The restaurant charges US$4 for fish or beef dishes, US$10 for prawns and US$30 for crayfish.

Places to Eat

Café Nicola on Avenida 1 de Julho, has snacks for around US$1.50 and meals around US$3. At the nearby *Salao Palladium* prices are similar. The *Salao Aguila* next to Cinema Aguila is also good, especially for coffee, cakes and ice cream. Nearby is the small and friendly *Barette Verde*, where meals start at just over US$1.

Entertainment

The most popular bars in town are *Bar Refeba* on the waterfront, and *Bar Aquerio* in the gardens near the City Hall. Both are open-air, serving cold beers, and food from US$4 to US$5. Refeba is a disco at weekends. Aquerio has ice cream and a pond complete with ducks and fountains. If you want something more lively, *Club Palmera* behind the petrol station on Avenida Josina Machel has discos most nights. *Bar Far West*, near the Pensão Quelimane, has also been recommended.

Getting There & Away

Quelimane is 25 km south of the main road; the junction is at Nicuadala, from where a chapa to town is US$0.70. The bus park is near the market on the edge of town. You might be able to find a direct chapa to/from Nampula (US$15), otherwise change at Mocuba. Local ferries go to Chinde, near the mouth of the Zambezi, twice per week for US$5 per person.

MOCUBA

Mocuba is on the main route between Quelimane and Nampula, and the junction of

MOZAMBIQUE

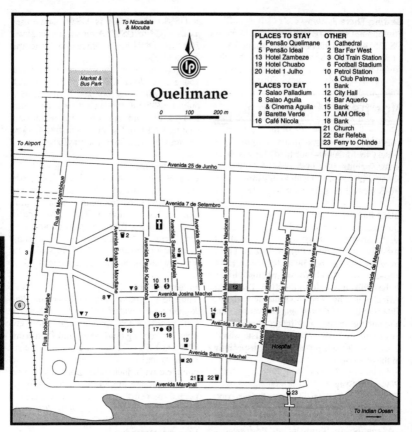

Quelimane

PLACES TO STAY	OTHER
4 Pensão Quelimane	1 Cathedral
5 Pensão Ideal	2 Bar Far West
13 Hotel Zambeze	3 Old Train Station
19 Hotel Chuabo	6 Football Stadium
20 Hotel 1 Julho	10 Petrol Station
	& Club Palmera
PLACES TO EAT	11 Bank
7 Salao Palladium	12 City Hall
8 Salao Aguila	14 Bar Aquerio
& Cinema Aguila	15 Bank
9 Barette Verde	17 LAM Office
16 Café Nicola	18 Bank
	21 Church
	22 Bar Refeba
	23 Ferry to Chinde

the road to/from south-east Malawi. *Pensão Cruzeiro*, on the main street, has reasonable rooms for US$15 (one or two people) and meals for around US$3 to US$4. Coffees and cakes are US$0.50. Just down the hill, *Pensão São Christorao* is cheaper at US$4 per person, but very dirty.

Quelimane buses (US$3.50) and chapas (US$4.50) go to/from the market east of the main street. Chapas to Nampula (US$10) go from the north end of the main street. There's a truck to/from Milange about every other day in the dry season; ask around or walk a few km out of town to the Milange road

junction and wait for a ride there. Expect to pay about US$5.

MILANGE

This small town is the border between Mozambique and south-east Malawi. About 20 km west of here is the Malawian town of Mulanje, and overlooking them both is the mountain of the same name. *Pensão-Restaurante Esplanade* has reasonable singles/doubles for US$5/8, and meals for around US$3. The bank changes US dollars or SA rands, and money changers will swap meticais for Malawian kwacha, and give a better rate for your bucks. For transport to Malawi see the main Getting There & Away section in this chapter.

MOLOCUÈ

Pronounced 'Molok-way', this pleasant town, high enough to be cool, is a refuelling point between Mocuba and Nampula. If a chapa stops here for the night, most passengers sleep on the veranda of the *Pensão São Antonio* on the main square; alternatively, clean ensuite doubles cost US$15. The food is good: chicken or beef and rice with soup goes for US$3.50. There's another *pensão* nearby with rooms for US$9, and a third just off the square charging US$6 for adequate singles/doubles.

NAMPULA

Nampula is a bustling city, and you'll inevitably spend time here changing transport or money. The main drag is Avenida Paulo Kankomba; it runs from the train station to a large traffic circle. Most hotels, restaurants, bars, banks and an exchange bureau are on or near this street. The lively **market** and large **cathedral** are worth a look, and there are several other fine **old colonial buildings** dotted around the town. You can while away a few hours at the CFVM Piscina (swimming pool), which has clean water, lush lawns, shady seating, a bar and restaurant, plus music in the evenings (US$2 entrance fee). There's also an excellent **museum** (with explanations in English and Portuguese), and a **cinema**.

Places to Stay & Eat

Cheapest in town include *Restaurante-Pensão Central* on Avenida Kankomba near the station, *Pensão Marques*, on the same street, and *Pensão Nampula* just off it; all are dingy and dirty with beds for US$2.50 and single/double rooms at US$3/5. Much better is *Pensão Parques*, where a bed in a small dorm is US$4, doubles are US$8 and triples US$12. Rooms are clean, the staff friendly and the food downstairs good value (meals US$3, snacks US$1.50). With negotiation you may be allowed to pitch a tent on the flat roof. Other choices include *Pousada Francisca* near the traffic circle, and *Pensão Avenida* near the telephone office, both at around US$4/8.

Better value is *Hotel Brazilia*, where clean ensuite doubles with running water cost US$8, or US$10 with air-con. The restaurant serves coffee and snacks, plus meals from around US$2. Similar but more pricey is the *Residential Monte Carlo*, near the market. Clean ensuite doubles cost US$13, but the main draw of this place is the rooftop restaurant, which has discos at weekends.

More up-market options include the soulless *Hotel Lurio*, where ensuite singles/doubles are US$16/25 (casals US$20). The nearby *Hotel Tropicale* (☎ 3220) charges US$30/40 for rooms with air-con. It's better than the Lurio (and ought to be at twice the price), although still poor value.

Apart from those mentioned above, food is available in several other places. Shoestringers should head for the old *vagão* at the train station, where cheap beers and eats are served during the day. There's also a *wagon-turned-takeaway* down the street from the cinema, near the secondary school, which is a good place to meet local students.

There are several restaurants on Avenida Kankomba. Smartest of these is *Clube Tenis*, with outside seating under shady trees and good meals (omelettes for US$1.50, fish US$3.50, meat dishes US$6.50 and crayfish US$15). There's music and dancing some nights. It's not really a club – anyone can enter – and there doesn't seem to be any tennis either.

Other up-market alternatives are *Restaurant Lord*, with main courses around US$5, and the Italian-style *Restaurant Carlos* (popular with expats and well-to-do locals), which serves pizzas and pastas for around US$5 to US$8, plus seafood from US$10.

Getting There & Away

Bus From Nampula, east-bound buses and chapas go from outside the rail station or from about 500m eastwards down the road. West-bound transport goes from near the Gani petrol station on the main road about

MOZAMBIQUE

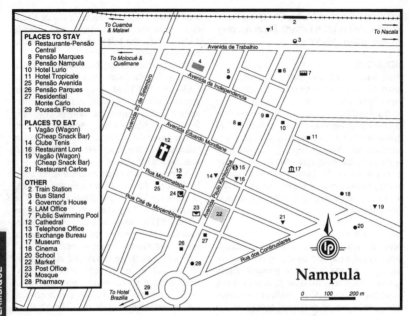

PLACES TO STAY
6 Restaurante-Pensão
   Central
8 Pensão Marques
9 Pensão Nampula
10 Hotel Lurio
11 Hotel Tropicale
25 Pensão Avenida
26 Pensão Parques
27 Residential
   Monte Carlo
29 Pousada Francisca

PLACES TO EAT
1 Vagão (Wagon)
   (Cheap Snack Bar)
14 Clube Tenis
16 Restaurant Lord
19 Vagão (Wagon)
   (Cheap Snack Bar)
21 Restaurant Carlos

OTHER
2 Train Station
3 Bus Stand
4 Governor's House
5 LAM Office
7 Public Swimming Pool
12 Cathedral
13 Telephone Office
15 Exchange Bureau
17 Museum
18 Cinema
20 School
22 Market
23 Post Office
24 Mosque
28 Pharmacy

Nampula

0   100   200 m

2.5 km west of the train station. Fares: Nacala US$2.50, Pemba US$10, Mozambique Island US$3.50, Quelimane US$11 and Mocuba US$5.

Train Thrice-weekly passenger trains go between Nampula and Cuamba. The fare is US$3 (3rd class only). It's very crowded (you need to keep a good eye on your bags), but since the track was renovated the journey takes less than a day (it used to take up to two weeks!). There are also freight trains, with an extra wagon for passengers – the fare is also US$3. Drivers can avoid the terrible road by loading vehicles onto this train for around US$80 per tonne, plus about US$10 in tips to the guys who help with ramps and tying down. The process is straightforward and you can ride with your car to make sure it's not tampered with.

There are also trains between Nampula and Nacala (US$2) but most people go by road.

ANGOCHE

This small coastal town has a wonderful beach and peaceful atmosphere, especially from Monday to Friday. At the weekends it swells with good-time Nampulans and livens up a bit. There are two small pensãos and a couple of bars and restaurants. Chapas run daily to/from Nampula for US$3.

CUAMBA

You'll pass through this town if you travel by road or rail between Nampula and Malawi. Pensãos include *São Miguel* (US$7 a double, with a good bar) and *Namaacha* (US$5), plus some restaurants, shops and a market. For details on the train see the Nampula section above or the Malawi Getting There & Away chapter.

Around Cuamba

The scenery between Cuamba and Nampula is incredibly beautiful. The plains are dotted with rocky hills, some of them small inselbergs and others great massifs with sheer sides and forested tops sticking through the clouds. It would be tempting to walk and hike here, but until the area is declared free from mines it will have to remain a dream. Watch this space though.

LICHINGA

Lichinga is the capital of Niassa Province, the most remote and least-visited part of Mozambique. Part of this area includes Lago Niassa (the Mozambican name for Lake Malawi). The town has most facilities, including a large market, hospital, bank, airport and immigration office. The cheapest places to stay are *Pensão Lichinga* and *Hotel Rival*, which both offer food. Up a grade is *Pousada Lichinga*.

You can reach Lichinga from Cuamba; there is a railway, but the line is very bad and trains unreliable. The dirt road is in good condition to Mandimba (near the Malawi border) and reasonable from there to Lichinga, with chapas and trucks a few times per week. Another option is the weekly LAM flight to/from Maputo, via Nampula and Beira.

For intrepid travellers, it's also possible to reach Lichinga from Malawi, via Likoma Island and Cobuè. For details see the Malawi Getting There & Away chapter.

MOZAMBIQUE ISLAND

Mozambique Island (Ilha de Moçambique) is a fascinating town, 2.5 km long and about three km off the mainland (linked by a bridge). The island was one of the first places Portuguese explorers landed in this region, at the end of the 15th century, although before they arrived the island had been visited by Arabs, plus people from Madagascar, Persia and other parts of East Africa and the Indian Ocean. The island-town remained the capital of Portugal's East African colony until the late 19th century.

Today, the island is home to people of many different hues and several different faiths. There are mosques, churches, and a Hindu temple, plus various colonial buildings including a fort, a palace and a vast

hospital. They date from between the 16th and 19th centuries, and are mostly decayed and decrepit, although a few have been restored in the last few years. A *marginal* (coast road) runs along the east side of the island, with splendid views out across the ocean. Forget about swimming – the beach is the island's toilet – but if you like old relics and a time-warp atmosphere don't miss 'Ilha'.

Things to See

Most things to see are in the northern half of the island (this section has been declared a World Heritage Site by the United Nations Education, Scientific and Cultural Organisation). In the southern half of the island most people live in cramped dwellings in poor *bairros* (suburbs) – perhaps overlooked by UNESCO.

The number one attraction is the **Palace and Chapel of São Paulo** – the former governor's residence – dating from the 1700s. This large building overlooks a large square inlaid with patterned stones, and the straits on the west side of the island. Most of it is now a **museum**, containing original furniture and ornaments – from Portugal, Arabia, Goa, India and even China. It's a fascinating place, but what's even more amazing is that it is still here and in good condition, following almost 20 years of civil strife on the mainland. In the chapel, note the altar and the pulpit, and the upper windows linked to the palace so the governor could receive mass without having to mix with commoners. Behind the palace is the **Church of the Misercordia** – overshadowed by its large neighbour but well worth a look. Attached to this is the **Museum of Sacred Art**, containing religious ornaments, paintings and carvings. The museum is housed in the former hospital of the Holy House of Mercy, a religious guild which operated in several Portuguese colonies from the early 1500s onwards, providing charitable assistance to the poor and sick. Both museums are open all day from Wednesday to Saturday, closed lunchtimes, and also on Sunday morning. They are free, but a small tip (US$0.50 to $1) for the guide is appreciated.

At the north end of the island is the **Fort of**

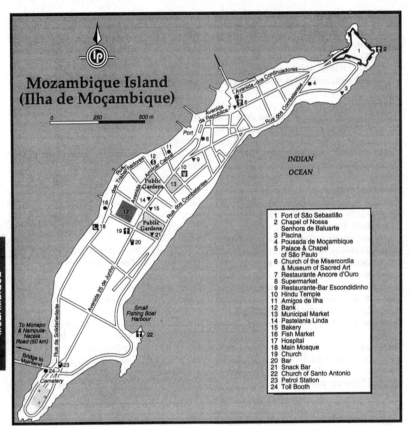

Mozambique Island
(Ilha de Moçambique)

0   250   500 m

INDIAN
OCEAN

1 Fort of São Sebastião
2 Chapel of Nossa
   Senhora de Baluarte
3 Piscina
4 Pousada de Moçambique
5 Palace & Chapel
   of São Paulo
6 Church of the Misercordia
   & Museum of Sacred Art
7 Restaurante Ancore d'Ouro
8 Supermarket
9 Restaurante-Bar Escondidinho
10 Hindu Temple
11 Amigos de Ilha
12 Bank
13 Municipal Market
14 Pastelania Linda
15 Bakery
16 Fish Market
17 Hospital
18 Main Mosque
19 Church
20 Bar
21 Snack Bar
22 Church of Santo Antonio
23 Petrol Station
24 Toll Booth

São Sebastião, built by the Portuguese around a spring which was the only reliable source of drinking water on the island. The fort is still in remarkably good condition; it is open all the time and entry is free. Immediately beyond the fort, right on the tip of the island, is the **Chapel of Nossa Senhora de Baluarte** – reported to be the oldest standing building in the southern hemisphere. Towards the southern end of the island, on a headland, is the small **Church of Santo Antonio**. Fishing boats moor nearby.

In the main town are several more recent buildings. Look out for the beautifully restored **bank** on Avenida Amilcar Cabral, and the three huge ornate colonial **administration offices** overlooking the gardens east of the hospital. They seem to be disused now, but are still in reasonable condition. Near the municipal market is a **Hindu temple**. There is also a **cemetery** at the southern end of the island with Christian, Muslim and Hindu graves.

Amigos de Ilha (Friends of Ilha) is a cultural and conservation organisation. They have an office near the bank and might be able to help with more specific details or information on other places to see around the island.

Places to Stay & Eat

At the time of writing the only place to stay was *Pousada de Moçambique*, an old hotel which is not quite as tumbledown as the rest of the town, where simple single rooms are US$7, and ensuite doubles US$12. There's no water and cheaper rooms are often 'full'. For food and drinks, most popular is the *Piscina*, overlooking the ocean near the Pousada; there's no water in the swimming pool but the meals (mainly seafood, from US$3) are good.

There's a cheap *eating house* in the municipal market, where you can also buy fruit and vegetables, although there's also a good selection at the *fish market* near the mosque. There's a *supermarket* near the port office. Other places for cheap eats include the *snack bar* in a converted shipping container in the gardens between the hospital and the sea. The island's *bakery* is near nearby. Ilha also has some other good local restaurant-bars, although not all of them serve food all of the time, so for evening meals you should inquire during the day (and possibly order then); try *Pastelania Linda*, near the bakery, *Escondidinho*, a block north-east of the municipal market, and *Restaurante Ancore d'Ouro* near the palace.

Getting There & Away

Ilha can be reached by direct bus from Nampula ($3.50). Alternatively, take anything between Nampula and Nacala, drop at Monapo, and take a local chapa from there. Ilha is 50 km from the main road. Leaving Ilha, the bus goes from the Pousada and chapas go from the municipal market or from the near the bridge toll booth. In your own car, it costs US$2 to cross the bridge – the toll booth is on the island side. Another option is by boat to Chocas – ask around at the quay by the palace or the harbour near the fish market.

CHOCAS

This small village, near Mossuril on the mainland across from Mozambique Island, has a good beach and a nice little *complexio* where ensuite cabins cost US$28. There's also a restaurant with good meals starting at around US$4. You can hire a motor boat across to Ilha for US$30, or go by dhow for US$10. To reach Chocas by road, take any transport between Monapo and Ilha and drop at the junction signposted Mossuril, 24 km from Monapo. From there you'll have to walk or hitch. Chances of a lift are good at the weekend, as Chocas is popular with local day-trippers from Nampula or Nacala.

NACALA

Nacala itself has nothing to attract tourists, but ships to/from South Africa stop here so it's become something of a gateway (or exit) town. The main street runs from the train station near the port up to Nacala Alta (the higher town); most things of interest or use to travellers are on or just off this street.

Places to Stay & Eat

Cheapest is the *pensão* above the video shop, just off the main street, where basic twin rooms are US$9, or you can get a bed in a small dorm for US$4.50. Up from here is *Hotel Nacala* (☎ 526036), which might have been smart and modern once, charging US$22/32 for a room (US$25/42 for air-con), including breakfast.

Another option is the *Finnida Compound* – for aid workers but open to the public at US$25 for double self-contained units (with a kitchen). It's in Nacala Alta, 100m behind the BP petrol station. Phone in advance (☎ 526363 mornings, ☎ 520268 afternoons), and arrive during office hours.

For cheap eats, the *market* has fresh vegetables, and the surrounding *shops* are well stocked. Opposite the market is *Café Carioca*, selling fresh bread, coffee, cakes and soft drinks. Round the corner is *Restaurant Sandokan*, the smartest place in town, with good meals for US$4.50 (lobster for US$9). There's also a bar with TV and an outside terrace. Next door is the less pricey *Restaurant O Casarao* which also has an outside disco at weekends, and opposite is a cheap *snack bar*.

MOZAMBIQUE

Getting There & Away

Trains go to Nampula (US$2) but most people go by road (bus US$2, chapa US$2.50, from near the market). Monapo (for Mozambique Island) and Namialo (for Pemba) are also reached on any transport between Nacala and Nampula. The office for Unicorn Line ships to Durban is opposite the train station.

PEMBA

Pemba is a coastal town, at the mouth of a huge bay, with some interesting buildings (particularly in Baixa – the low/old town) and a pleasant lively atmosphere. The viewpoint over the bay near the governor's house is good at sunset.

Most visitors come for the beaches and coral reefs – reckoned to be some of the best in Southern Africa – at Wimbi (also spelt Wimbe), about five km east of the town itself. The reef is so close you don't need to hire a boat. The fledgling tourist industry (bars, restaurants, diving, snorkelling, boating, fishing etc) is due for a boost in the next few years, as many new developments are planned. (In fact, by the time you arrive Pemba may be unrecognisable from this description.)

The Makonde workshop on the road between town and the beach has distinctive wooden carvings for sale at very good prices. They also work ivory but no documentation is available, so it's probably illegal to even touch the stuff. For items of a more practical nature, the town itself has banks, supermarkets and shops. The Tourist Office (☎ 2538) is in Wimbi Conches (a shell shop) near the Complexio Nautilus, run by a lady called Fatima (she speaks English).

Places to Stay & Eat

Top of the range is the landmark *Hotel Cabo Delgado*, charging US$27/32 for air-con ensuite singles/doubles. The rooms are nothing special for this price but the restaurant is reported to be reasonable. Other places include *Hotel VIP Pemba*, with air-con ensuite rooms at US$20. *Pensão Baia* is one of the cheapest options: it is clean, safe and friendly with rooms (single or double) for US$10. Both places also have bars and offer food with prices on a par with their room rates.

Good value snacks and meals can be had at the *Pemba Takeaway*, near the Hotel Cabo Delgado, where the menu is in English and Portuguese; burgers are from US$1, omelettes from US$1.50 and pizzas from US$2. There's also a small seating area and beers for sale. More pricey is the restaurant at *Complexio Shiva*, which also has a disco at weekends. For cheaper eats and drinks try any of the bars in the *feira* near the Hotel Cabo Delgado. For late night revelry the Chick Disco is also here.

Wimbi Beach *Complexio Nautilus* has ensuite bungalows at US$55 for one, two or three people. Breakfast is US$1.50, snacks and light meals cost from US$4 to US$6, and dinners start at US$8, up to US$15 for seafood. Jet skis, fishing boats, diving gear and sailboards can be hired. Alternative places to eat include the nearby *Sol e Mar Restaurant* (fish and chips US$5, other seafood US$6 to US$8) and *Celmar Takeaway* (cheap snacks). At the far end of the beach is *Restaurante Wimbe* (aka Aeroclube), where prices are about the same as Sol e Mar but the setting is nicer and the bar more popular.

Be prepared for changes: several more hotels and restaurants are planned in this area, plus a top-end resort complex. There is also talk of a campsite, to be set up by a South African guy who runs a diving and boating outfit called Clube Sportivo Indico. For details, talk to Fatima at the Tourist Office.

Getting There & Away

Pemba can be reached by bus or chapa from Nampula (US$10). Coming from Nacala, change at Namialo, although the bus from Nampula is often full by the time it gets here. Pemba's bus station is on the Nampula road about three km from the centre. If you arrive late there are some basic restaurants where some people sleep on the floor until morning. If you're heading north, transport to

Moçimboa da Praia is limited to trucks and chapas, although there are plans to improve the road and buses may start running. Your other option is to leave/reach Pemba by dhow: ask around at the port, or chat to Fatima at the Tourist Office.

MOÇIMBOA DA PRAIA

This is the first/last town of any size on the coast of northern Mozambique. It is a fairly important harbour for dhows, and we've heard from travellers who have got rides here to Tanzania or Pemba (see the Getting There & Away and Getting Around sections in this chapter for more details). If you leave/enter Mozambique here, it's essential to get your passport stamped at the Immigration Office.

There are a couple of cheap pensãos and places to eat. Tanzanian shillings are accepted between here and the border. Trucks go between Moçimboa and Palma a few times per week; the fare is US$9 and the place to wait is about 500m north of where the transport from Pemba drops you.

PALMA

This small town is stretched out for more than a kilometre down a narrow road to the sea. There is an immigration post here. The only place to stay seems to be *Hotel Palma* – cheap, but small and dark. Travelling between here and Tanzania is described in the Getting There & Away section of this chapter.

MOZAMBIQUE

Map Index

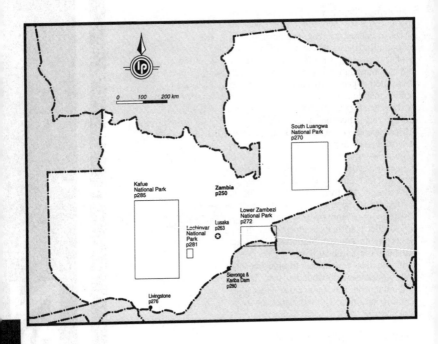

South Luangwa
National Park
p270

Kafue
National Park
p285

Zambia
p250

Lower Zambezi
National Park
p272

Lochinvar
National
Park
p281

Lusaka
p263

Siavonga &
Kariba Dam
p280

Livingstone
p276

0   100   200 km

ZAMBIA

Zambia

Zambia is a challenge for independent travellers: distances between major towns or places of interest are long; getting around by car or public transport takes persistence (particularly once you get off the main routes); and accommodation choices for any budget are limited, especially outside the few tourist centres that do exist.

However, for many people these challenges are the very attraction of Zambia. The 'real Africa' handle is often overworked, but here it still seems to apply. Zambia has several genuinely wild national parks and wildlife areas, and some of the finest scenery in Africa. The premier park – South Luangwa – is only 280 km from Lilongwe, and many visitors combine a visit to Malawi with a short trip into Zambia. Some go further: two of Southern Africa's major tourist highlights are in southern Zambia – Victoria Falls and the Zambezi River.

If you like your travel trouble-free and your wilderness neatly bundled then Zambia will not appeal. But if you enjoy a raw edge, Zambia could be just the place you're looking for.

Note This chapter concentrates on the eastern, western and southern parts of Zambia. For travellers heading beyond these areas, some outline information on northern Zambia is also provided.

Facts about the Country

HISTORY
The early history of Zambia is included with the history of Malawi and other parts of the region in the Facts about Malawi chapter.

The Late 18th Century
The first Europeans to enter the area now called Zambia were Portuguese explorers. (For more details on this period see the

Zambia
Area: 752,615 sq km
Population: 9.5 million
Population Growth Rate: 3.5%
Capital: Lusaka
Head of State: President Frederick Chiluba
Official Language: English
Currency: Zambian kwacha
Exchange Rate: ZK 1290 = US$1
Per Capita GNP: US$280 (Purchasing power parity: US$860)
Literacy: 73%
Infant Mortality Rate: around 10%

Mozambique chapter.) In the 1790s, several groups travelled from Angola in the west as far as the headwaters of the Zambezi River. Around the same time another group travelled inland from Mozambique in the east, as far as the area between Lakes Mweru and Bangweulu.

However, the Portuguese were not the first non-Africans to reach this area. For several centuries before their arrival, Swahili-Arab slave-traders had gradually penetrated the region from their city-states on the east coast of Africa. Often in collaboration with the chiefs of powerful local tribes, the slave-traders captured many people from today's Zambia. They were taken across Lake Malawi and through Mozambique or Tanzania to be sold in the slave markets of Zanzibar. (For more details on the slave trade, see the Malawi History section.) These slavers established the routes from the coast to the interior which were later followed by the Portuguese and other European explorers.

The 19th Century
In the 1820s the effects of the *Difaqane* ('the scattering of the tribes' following the rise of the powerful Zulu nation in today's South Africa) rippled through to Zambia. Matabele migrants moved into western Zimbabwe and threatened the Makololo (also spelt

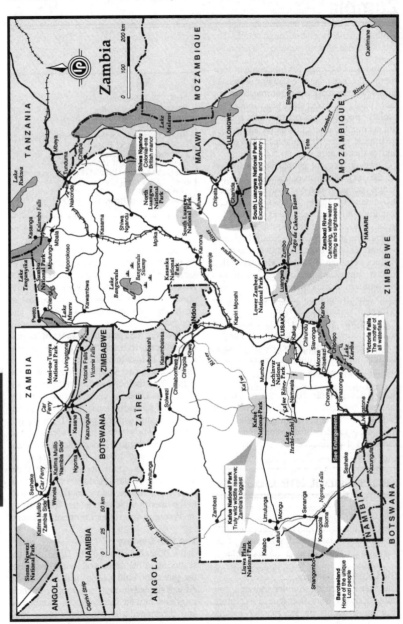

Zambia

0   100   200 km

TANZANIA

MOZAMBIQUE

MALAWI

Lake Malawi

LILONGWE

Lake Tanganyika

Lake Rukwa

Kalambo Falls

Kasanga

Mbala

Mpulungu

Mpulungu

Mporokoso

Kawambwa

Kasama

Chilubi

Nakonde

Tunduma

Mbeya

Chitipa

Shiwa Ngandu
Colonial-era
British manor

North
Luangwa
National Park

Mfuwe

Chipata

Chama

South Luangwa National Park
Exceptional wildlife and scenery

Mpika

Shiwa
Ngandu

Lake
Bangweulu

Bangweulu
Swamp

Kasanka
National Park

Serenje

Kanona

Luangwa

Blantyre

MOZAMBIQUE

Tete

Zumbo

Lago de Cahora Bassa

Zambezi River
Canoeing, white-water
rafting and sightseeing

HARARE

Pweto

Chiengi

Lake
Mweru

Sumbu
National Park

Kapiri Mposhi

Lower Zambezi
National Park

Luangwa

Zumbo

Ndola

Lusaka

Kafue

ZAMBIA

Mosi-oa-Tunya
National Park

Livingstone

Victoria Falls

Victoria Falls

ZIMBABWE

Car
Ferry

Kasane

Kazungula

BOTSWANA

ZAÏRE

Lubumbashi

Kasumbalesa

Solwezi

Chililabombwe

Chingola

Kitwe

Mumbwa

Kafue River

Kafue
National Park

Lochinvar
National
Park

Namwala

Chirundu

Siavonga

Lake
Kariba

Kariba

Chisekesi

Monze

Choma

Chongo

Sinazongwe

Siavonga

Victoria Falls
The mother of
all waterfalls

ZIMBABWE

See Enlargement

Livingstone

Kazungula

NAMIBIA

BOTSWANA

Seshe ke

Kafue National Park
Truly wild wildlife reserve;
Zambia's biggest

Mwinilunga

Zambezi

Zambezi River

ANGOLA

Kabompo

Lukulu

Mongu

Lealui

Senanga

Ngonye Falls

Liuwa Plain
National Park

Kalabo

Lake
Itezhi-Tezhi

Kalongola
Sioma

Shangombo

Barotseland
Home of the unique
Lozi people

0   25   50 km

Sioma Ngwezi
National Park

Caprivi Strip

ANGOLA

NAMIBIA

ZAMBIA

ZIMBABWE

BOTSWANA

Katima Mulilo
'Zambia Side'

Katima Mulilo
'Namibia Side'

Car Ferry

Wenela

Ngoma

Kasane

Kazungula

Sesheke

ZAMBIA

Makalolo), who in turn moved into southern Zambia and displaced the Tonga people. The Makololo also took advantage of a period of unrest among the Lozi people on the Upper Zambezi and occupied their territory.

Celebrated British explorer David Livingstone travelled up the Zambezi River in the early 1850s, searching for a route into the interior of Southern Africa and with the aim of introducing Christianity and the principles of European civilisation to combat the horrors of the slave trade. In 1855, Livingstone reached the giant waterfall which he called Victoria Falls. Subsequent explorations through the 1860s took him north from the Zambezi, up the Shire River into Malawi (more details in the Malawi Facts about the Country chapter).

Livingstone's work and writings inspired missionaries to come to the area north of the Zambezi, and close on their heels came explorers, hunters and prospectors searching for whatever the country had to offer. The 'new' territory did not escape the notice of one Cecil John Rhodes, who was already establishing mines and a vast business empire in South Africa. Rhodes' British South Africa Company (BSAC) laid claim to the area in the early 1890s and this move was backed by the British government in 1895: partly to help combat slavery, but also to prevent further Portuguese expansion in the region.

The 20th Century

For the next few decades, like many other parts of Southern Africa, Zambia's history was largely influenced by BSAC activities. Initially, two territories were created: Northwestern Rhodesia and North-eastern Rhodesia, but these were combined in 1911 to become Northern Rhodesia. In 1907, the town of Livingstone (not to be confused with Livingstonia in Malawi) became the capital.

At around the same time, vast deposits of copper ore were discovered in the northern-central part of the territory (the area now called the Copperbelt). The indigenous people are thought to have mined here for centuries, but now large European-style mines were established and local Africans were employed as labourers. They may have had little choice: they needed money to pay the hut tax which had been introduced, and their only other source of income had gone when much of their farmland was appropriated by the European settlers.

To export the copper, the BSAC constructed a railway between the mines and Livingstone, from where it could be transported onwards to South Africa. This line was part of Rhodes' grand plan to build a railway from Cape Town to Cairo, passing through British territory all the way. (His dream was never realised, but travellers today can at least go from Cape Town to Zambia by train and pass over the Victoria Falls bridge – one of the line's most dramatic sights.)

In 1924, the colony was put under direct British control and in 1935 the capital was moved to the more central town of Lusaka. In the following years settlers pushed for federation with Southern Rhodesia and Nyasaland (present-day Zimbabwe and Malawi), to make them less dependent on the rule of the colonial authorities in London. For various reasons (including WWII) the Federation of Rhodesia and Nyasaland did not come about until 1953.

Meanwhile, African nationalism was becoming a more dominant force in the region. The United National Independence Party (UNIP) was founded by one Kenneth Kaunda; he spoke out against the federation with Southern Rhodesia and Nyasaland on the grounds that it promoted the rights of white settlers to the detriment of the local African population.

Through the late 1950s and early 1960s, many African countries gained independence. The Federation was dissolved in 1963 and Northern Rhodesia became independent in 1964. It took the name Zambia from the Zambezi river which flows through the west of the country and forms the southern border with Rhodesia (later to become Zimbabwe). By this time the British government had generated huge sums in taxes from Northern Rhodesia, yet had spent only a small part of this money on the colony. Today, Zambia still suffers from the effects of this staggering loss of capital and lack of investment.

Independence

On independence, Zambia inherited a British style multiparty political system. Kenneth Kaunda, as leader of the majority UNIP, became the new republic's first president. The other main party was the African National Congress, led by Harry Nkumbula.

Kaunda remained in power for the next 27 years, largely because during 1972 he disbanded the Zambian ANC, created the 'second republic', and declared UNIP the sole legal party with himself as sole presidential candidate.

Through the rest of the 1970s, Kaunda's rule in Zambia was based upon 'humanism' – his own mix of Marxist ideals and traditional African values. The civil service was increased and nearly all private business nationalised (including the copper mines), but corruption and mismanagement, exacerbated by a fall in the world copper price, meant that by the end of the 1970s Zambia had become one of the poorest countries in the world.

Despite the domestic situation Kaunda supported several liberation movements in neighbouring countries: the Zimbabwe Patriotic Front (ZAPU and ZANU), the ANC (of South Africa), Frelimo (Mozambique), and Swapo (Namibia). Naturally, neighbouring governments saw the liberation movements as rebels and terrorists, so they regarded Zambia as an enemy too. Through the 1970s, landlocked Zambia's imports and exports were severely restricted as rail routes to the coast (through Mozambique, Rhodesia and South Africa) were closed.

The 1980s

By the early 1980s Rhodesia had become Zimbabwe and the TAZARA railway line to Dar es Salaam (Tanzania) was complete, giving Zambia access to the sea. Kaunda was able to take his country off a war footing but things were hardly rosy: the economy was on the brink of collapse; foreign exchange

reserves were almost exhausted; there were serious shortages of food, fuel and other basic commodities; and both the crime and unemployment rates had risen sharply. The constant threat of saboteurs and spies had left its mark too: foreign travellers passing through Zambia in the 1980s were regularly hassled at borders and roadblocks by underpaid and ill-disciplined officials.

In 1986, an attempt was made to diversify the economy and to do something about the country's balance of payments. Zambia received economic aid from the International Monetary Fund (IMF), but their conditions were severe: basic food subsidies were withdrawn and the currency (the kwacha) was floated. The resultant rise in food prices led to serious country-wide riots in which many people lost their lives, forcing Kaunda to restore subsidies.

The 1990s

The winds of change blowing through Africa and the world in the late 1980s, coupled with Zambia's disastrous domestic situation, meant something had to give. In mid-1990, another round of violent street protests against increased food prices quickly transformed into a general demand for the return of multiparty politics, and Kaunda was forced to accede to public opinion.

He attempted to fob off the population with a snap referendum in late 1990 but, as protests grew more vocal, he was forced to amend the constitution, legalise opposition parties and set full elections for October 1991. Kaunda and UNIP were resoundingly defeated by Frederick Chiluba, the former chairman of the Zambian Congress of Trade Unions, and the Movement for Multiparty Democracy. To his credit, Kaunda bowed out gracefully and Chiluba became president.

Chiluba moved quickly to encourage the return of the IMF and World Bank. Exchange controls were liberalised to attract investors, particularly from South Africa, but tough austerity measures were also introduced – and these were less than appealing to the average Zambian. Food prices soared, the value of the kwacha continued to fall, the civil service was rationalised and nationalised state industries privatised or simply closed, leading to many thousands of people losing their jobs. For many Zambians things were even worse than they were in the 1980s.

By the mid-1990s the lack of visible change in Zambia allowed Kaunda to confidently re-enter the political arena. He attracted strong support from large areas of the country, but leading up to elections in November 1996 Chiluba and the MMD were accused of unfair practices, causing Kaunda and UNIP to withdraw in protest. Chiluba took advantage of the situation, won a landslide victory and remained in firm control.

Shortly after the election, Chiluba ordered the arrest of two independent monitors who claimed the elections were rigged. Two days later, a group of journalists were suspended from their jobs, apparently because their reports of the MMD's role in the election did not contain the required degree of enthusiasm.

However, it was reported by independent sources that a majority of Zambians accepted the result, even if they knew it was rigged, many in the hope that at least Zambia would remain peaceful. The international donors also seemed satisfied: aid money continues to flow in. Despite these positive aspects, the sad fact is that with a continued debt crisis, high unemployment, high inflation and a rapidly growing population, Zambia's troubles are far from over.

GEOGRAPHY

Landlocked Zambia is one of Africa's most eccentric legacies of colonialism. Shaped like a contorted figure-of-eight 750,000 sq km in area, its borders do not correspond to any tribal or linguistic area.

Zambia sits on an undulating plateau which slopes to the south. Areas of high ground include the Copperbelt Highlands and the Nyika Plateau, on the border with Malawi, which contains Mwanda Peak (2148m), the country's highest point.

Zambia's main rivers are: the Zambezi, which rises in the west of the country and forms the border between Zambia and

Namibia, Botswana and Zimbabwe; the Kafue, which rises in the highlands between Zambia and Zaïre, and flows into the Zambezi south of Lusaka; and the Luangwa, which rises in the north and also flows into the Zambezi, to the east of Lusaka.

CLIMATE

Along with much of Southern Africa, Zambia's altitude creates a temperate climate. There are three distinct seasons: cool and dry from May to August; hot and dry from September to October; and rainy between November and April (summer). Rainfall is higher in the north of the country than in the south.

NATIONAL PARKS

Zambia has 19 national parks and 31 game management areas (GMAs) created as 'buffer-zones' surrounding the parks. This figure seems impressive, but many parks are difficult to reach and others are just lines on the map which, after decades of poaching, clearing and general bad management, no longer protect (or even contain) much in the way of wildlife.

Zambia's parks have been called Southern Africa's best kept secret, but in the last few years the cover has been blown and wildlife aficionados now come from all over the world to see the impressive populations of birds and mammals, or to take part in walking safaris for which Zambia's parks are particularly well known. In many cases, the downturn of the 1970s and 1980s has been reversed and several 'high-profile' parks are relatively well managed again, often with the co-operation of international conservation bodies and donor governments.

Throughout the mid-1990s many improvements were made, including the construction of new roads and tracks and the privatisation of (formerly state-run) lodges and camps in the parks. These changes are likely to continue for the next few years, and full details are given in the relevant national park sections. We have tried to keep up with developments, but in several parks you should expect to find alterations by the time you arrive.

ZAMBIA

The Parks

Zambia's 'high profile' parks are: South Luangwa, Lower Zambezi, Kafue and Mosi-oa-Tunya (Victoria Falls). There are also plans to upgrade and promote smaller parks such as Lochinvar. Less well-known parks include Liuwa Plain, Sioma Ngwezi, Sumbu and North Luangwa, all featured in the itineraries of exclusive safari companies (see Organised Tours in the Getting Around section). Kasanka National Park, on the road towards northern Zambia, has been leased to a private operator. This scheme may be extended to other parks (although it's likely that those considered beyond redemption will be abandoned).

Costs

Entry to South and North Luangwa and Lower Zambezi costs US$15 per person per day; to Kafue, Lochinvar and Sumbu it is US$10. Other parks cost US$5, US$3 or nothing, depending on location or facilities. A vehicle is US$5. Zambian residents pay around 30% of these rates.

Places to Stay

Parks usually have four types of accommodation: camping, where you provide all you need, costs about US$5 per person; self-catering places, where facilities include basic huts and a staffed kitchen (you just provide your own food) cost between US$10 and US$25; mid-range 'fully-catered' lodges charge between US$50 and US$100 per person, including all meals; and top-end lodges, exclusive and luxurious, cost around US$200 to US$250, which normally includes park fees, activities (such as walks and game drives), transfers, drinks and laundry.

These prices are 'international rates' (ie what most overseas visitors pay). The regional rate (for residents of other Southern African countries) is about 25% less; Zambian residents pay around 50%. We have also quoted high (dry) season rates. In the rains, most lodges close. Those that stay open offer considerable 'green season' discounts.

Some places are in the park, others are just outside it; there's little practical difference, although of course you don't pay park entrance fees until you actually go in. Except for the camp sites and chalets, it's usually necessary to book accommodation in advance, either through the lodge, or through an agent in Lusaka or abroad.

Access

Most guests at the up-market places fly in to the nearest airstrip on a chartered plane. Other visitors come by road in their own vehicle or as part of a tour. For independent travellers without wheels or big bucks, getting to the parks can be hard, but there are some options which make things practicable – most notably at South Luangwa, but also at some of the other parks. Details are given in the relevant sections.

POPULATION

In 1996 Zambia's population was estimated at about 9.5 million. However, population density is about 11 people per sq km – one of the lightest in the world. Most unusual for a developing country, more than 50% of Zambia's population lives in urban areas (mostly Lusaka and the cities of the Copperbelt).

LANGUAGE

There are about 35 different ethnic groups (or 'tribes') in Zambia, all with their own language. (The actual number varies according to definition.) Main groups and languages include: Bemba in the north and centre; Tonga in the south; Nyanja in the east (the same as Chewa in Malawi); and Lozi in the west. English has become an essential national and official language; it is widely spoken across the country – even in quite remote areas.

Facts for the Visitor

TOURIST OFFICES

In Zambia, there are tourist offices in Lusaka and Livingstone. Outside of Africa, the

Zambia National Tourist Board's offices include:

Australia
c/o Orbitair, 36 Clarence St, Sydney, NSW 2000 (☎ (02) 9299 5300; fax 9299 4580)
South Africa
Finance House, Oppenheimer Rd, Johannesburg (☎ (011) 622 9206; fax 622 7424)
UK
2 Palace Gate, Kensington, London W8 5NG (☎ (0171) 589 6343; fax 225 3221)
USA
237 East 52nd St, New York, NY 10022, (☎ (212) 308 2155; fax 758 1319)

VISAS & DOCUMENTS

All visitors need a visa except citizens of any Commonwealth country or Ireland – although you may be told otherwise. The price can vary according to your nationality, but most people pay US$25 for a single entry visa (maximum stay three months). The only exception to these regulations is that British citizens must now have a visa (unless they are going to Zambia as part of a fully organised tour). This is apparently in response to Britain making visas obligatory for Zambian nationals. Whatever the reason, visas cost UK£33 single entry, UK£45 multiple entry. However, visa requirements are constantly under review. In Sydney, Australian travellers are told they need a visa for Zambia, while in London Aussies are told they don't need one. The moral is to always phone your nearest high commission or embassy.

Visa extensions are available at the Immigration Office on the 2nd floor of Memaco House, Cairo Rd in Lusaka: the process is quick, easy and free. Going beyond the three month maximum is tricky, and costs US$400. It might be easier to leave the country then re-enter on a new visa.

If you're coming from Zimbabwe and you haven't obtained a visa in advance, you can get one at the Kariba and Victoria Falls border posts. It's normally no hassle, but sometimes only seven-day transit visas (US$10) are issued. These must be extended in Lusaka if you plan to stay longer.

EMBASSIES

Zambian Embassies Abroad

Around the world, places with a Zambian embassy or high commission include Canada, France, the UK and the USA. Citizens of other countries should check in the phone directory of their own capital city. Zambia also has embassies or high commissions in the following neighbouring countries: Angola, Botswana, Malawi, Mozambique, Tanzania, Zaïre (Kinshasa and Lubumbashi) and Zimbabwe. Elsewhere in Africa there are Zambian embassies in Kenya and South Africa.

Botswana
Zambia High Commission, Zambia House, The Mall, PO Box 362, Gaborone (☎ 351951)
Canada
Zambia High Commission, 130 Albert St, 1610 Ottawa, Ontario K1P 5G4
France
Zambia Embassy, 76 Ave O'Jena, 75116, Paris
Malawi
Zambia High Commission, Convention Drive, Capital City, Lilongwe (☎ 782100/635)
Mozambique
Zambia High Commission, 1266 Avenida Kenneth Kaunda, Maputo (☎ 492452)
Namibia
Zambia High Commission, 22 Sam Nujoma Drive, corner of Republic Rd, PO Box 22882, Windhoek (☎ 237610; fax 228162)
UK
Zambia High Commission, 2 Palace Gate, London W8 5NG (☎ 0171 589 6655)
USA
Zambia Embassy, 2419 Massachusetts NW, Washington DC 20008 (☎ (202) 265 9717)
Zimbabwe
Zambia High Commission, 6th floor, Zambia House, Union Ave, PO Box 4698, Harare (☎ 790851)

Foreign Embassies in Zambia

Foreign embassies, consulates and high commissions listed here are in Lusaka unless otherwise stated. 'Home' countries with representation include:

Canada
United Nations Ave, opposite Tanzania High Commission (☎ 254176)
UK
Independence Ave (☎ 251133; fax 235798)

ZAMBIA

USA
    Independence Ave (☎ 250955; fax 254861)

The following neighbouring countries also have embassies or high commissions:

Botswana
    Haile Selassie Ave, near the Tanzania High Commission (☎ 250555)
Malawi
    Woodgate House, Cairo Rd (☎ 228296)
Mozambique
    46 Mulungushi Village, Kundalile Rd (☎ 290451)
Namibia
    6968 Kabanga Rd, Rhodes Park (☎ 252250)
Tanzania
    Ujaama House, United Nations Ave (☎ 253320). Open from 9 am to noon. Visas are US$20 for Aussies, while Americans, Brits and most Europeans are charged US$50. The process takes one or two days.
Zaïre
    1124 Parirenyetwa Rd (☎ 229044). Open from 9 am to noon. One month single entry visas cost US$20, with a 'letter of introduction' from your own embassy (standard procedure). If you apply early, you can pick it up the same afternoon. There's also a Zaïre consulate at Mpelembe House, Broadway Rd, Ndola (☎ 614247).
Zimbabwe
    4th floor, Memaco House, Cairo Rd (☎ 229382). Open from 8 am to 1 pm for visas. Single entry costs US$30. The process takes seven days.

MONEY
Currency
Zambia's unit of currency is the kwacha (abbreviated to ZK, or Kw). The largest bank note is ZK 500; other denominations are 100, 50 and 20. In 1996, the production of bank notes had not kept up with the inflation rate, so to save carrying large wads of cash, many mid-range and top-end hotels, lodges, shops and restaurants accept international credit cards.

Currency Exchange
For the past few years inflation has been running very high, so quoting prices in kwacha is not helpful because they will have undoubtedly changed by the time you arrive. Therefore, we have used US dollars (US$) in this chapter. Although the actual exchange rate will have changed by the time you reach

Zambia, the cost of things in US$ (or any other hard currency) will not have altered much. At the time of writing, the exchange rates were:

US$1	=	ZK 1290
UK£1	=	ZK 2120
DM1	=	ZK 770
SA R1	=	ZK 290

Changing Money
You can change money at Standard Chartered Bank or Barclays which both have many branches around the country. You can get cash advances (US dollars or kwacha) with a Visa card at Barclays Bank on Cairo Rd in Lusaka, but it can be an all-day process. Don't rely on cash-for-plastic in other towns.

Because the currency has been deregulated, there are foreign exchange ('forex') bureaux in most large towns whose rates are generally around 5% better (with faster service) than the banks. There's no real black market. You might get a few kwacha more on the street, but the chances of con-men or robberies make this not worth the risk. If you get stuck when banks and bureaux are closed, try changing money at a hotel, or at a shop which sells imported items.

POST & COMMUNICATIONS
The costs of sending a letter are: inside Zambia US$0.30; to Europe US$1; USA & Australia US$1.50. International letters from Lusaka are surprisingly quick (three or four days to Europe), but from elsewhere in the country the post is less reliable and much slower.

There are public phones in Lusaka and in most large towns. From telephone offices, trunk calls (eg Lusaka to Livingstone) are about US$0.50 per minute; international calls to Europe or Australia cost about US$25 for three minutes (minimum charge). Zambia's international dialling code is 260.

If your communication wants to stretch beyond telephones, you can send/receive faxes at several places in Lusaka, and get

Zambia

Top: Lower Zambezi National Park, east of Lusaka. As well as gazelle, you can see zebra, lion and cheetah, and some of the 400 species of birds discovered here.

Bottom: South Luangwa National Park, eastern Zambia, on the Luangwa River. Wildlife is varied and the park is relatively easy to reach.

DAVID ELSE

DAVID WALL

DAVID ELSE

DAVID ELSE

Zambia

Top: Mongu, western Zambia. The town is linked to the Zambezi by an 8 km canal.
Middle: Kids near Chipata, eastern Zambia.
Bottom: The rarely visited Ngonye Falls on the upper Zambezi.
Right: Victoria Falls, Zambia's biggest tourist attraction.

access to the Internet – see the Lusaka section for details.

BOOKS

Books and magazines covering general aspects of Southern Africa (politics, history, wildlife etc) are listed in the Malawi Facts for the Visitor chapter; many include sections on Zambia.

If you need more specific information on Zambia, especially if you're driving your own vehicle or spending some time in the national parks, a good recent book is *Zambia* by Chris McIntyre. The author and his contributors are experts on the region, and the wildlife sections are well written.

A less practical but highly recommended publication is *Zambia*, a large-format book by Richard Vaughan with photographs by Ian Murphy. It covers the natural beauty of Zambia's landscape and wildlife, and the less 'touristy' aspects, such as city life and mining, to create a complete and fascinating picture. Another large format book worth looking out for is *Spirit of the Zambezi* by Jeff & Fiona Sutchbury; it is a personal and knowledgeable account of three decades spent living and working in, on and around the great river between Zambia and Zimbabwe, illustrated with beautiful photos. Both books are too big to carry while travelling but make excellent trip souvenirs.

Other recommended books include *Kakuli* by Norman Carr, who has spent a lifetime working with animals and people in the South Luangwa National Park (see that section for more details). Although this book is a personalised selection of wildlife and human observations made over a decade, deeper issues are also raised, and some practical solutions to today's conservation problems suggested. Covering related subjects but in a strikingly different way is *Survivors Song* by Delia & Mark Owens. The authors rose to fame with their Botswana-based book *Cry of the Kalahari*; this more recent title picks up their story in Zambia's North Luangwa National Park, where they launch themselves single-mindedly (some say arrogantly) into the

difficult fight against elephant poachers, putting their lives and their relationship on the line. Dramatic and immensely readable, but with a powerful message that cannot be ignored, this book has all the ingredients for a Hollywood movie. It can only be a matter of time before one is made.

NEWSPAPERS & ON-LINE INFORMATION

Zambia has several national newspapers; the best seems to be *The Post* ('the paper that digs deeper'), containing good coverage of home news and political events, plus limited overseas news. The Post also has a web site on http://www.zamnet.zm. Zamnet announces itself as 'Zambia's only Internet site'.

PHOTOGRAPHY

In Lusaka slide and print film can be bought at Phoenix Photos on Cairo Rd, and next door at Royal Photographics. Prices for a 36-exposure print film (Fuji, Kodak or Agfa) range from US$3 to US$5. Slide film is US$9. Both places also do passport photos ($3 for four), developing and printing.

Possibly more than any other country in the region, officials in Zambia do not like you photographing public buildings, bridges, airports or anything else which could be considered strategic. If in doubt, ask – or better still, save your camera for the national parks.

HEALTH

General advice is given in the Health section of the Malawi Facts for the Visitor chapter. Generally speaking, medical facilities are poor, and many hospitals suffer from shortages. There are private hospitals for those who can pay (and this includes you – see Travel Insurance in Malawi Facts for the Visitor). If you need medical assistance while in Lusaka, some facilities are listed in that section. If you need more directions contact your embassy, or make inquiries at the reception of a large hotel.

ZAMBIA

DANGERS

The main danger for visitors is the chance of being robbed or mugged, especially in Lusaka. (For more details see the Lusaka section.) Wherever you go, don't make yourself a target for thieves by behaving imprudently (eg walking the streets late at night) or by showing off your wealth (eg wearing jewellery, carrying cameras).

BUSINESS HOURS

Offices open Monday through Friday from 8 or 9 am to 4 or 5 pm, with an hour for lunch sometime between noon and 2 pm. Shops keep the same hours from Monday to Saturday. In Lusaka, some supermarkets open Sunday mornings from 9 am to 1 pm. Banks open from around 8 am to 2 or 3 pm Monday to Saturday, except Thursday (when they close at noon), and Saturday (11 am or noon). Post offices open from 8 or 9 am to 4 or 4.30 pm, Monday to Friday (Saturday to noon in Lusaka).

PUBLIC HOLIDAYS

The following days are public holidays: 1 January, second Monday in March (Youth Day), Good Friday and Easter Monday, 1 May (Workers Day), 25 May (Africa Day), first Monday and Tuesday in July (Heroes Day and Unity Day), 1 August (Farmers Day), 24 October (Independence Day), 25 & 26 December.

ACCOMMODATION

For travellers on a tight budget, good inexpensive accommodation is rare. Some towns have government resthouses, which are cheap but in a bad state of repair. Recently, many have been renovated by the Hostels Board and are now clean, with good food and facilities. Naturally, prices have also gone up, but they are now far better value.

Many hotels (particularly bottom-end) charge by the room. Thus two, three or even four people travelling together can get some real, if crowded, bargains. Solos may find some prices steep, although negotiation is always a possibility.

Most middle and top-end hotels quote prices in foreign currency, usually US$. You can pay in kwacha, but the hotel's exchange rate may be less favourable than a bank's. These hotels often have three charge-bands: visitors pay 'international' rates (ie the full whack); locals get up to 50% discount; regional residents about 25%. We have used international rates throughout this chapter. All but the cheapest hotels include breakfast in their overnight rate.

Another feature of all but the cheapest joints is the extra charges: 10% for service (which technically means tipping is not required) and a whopping 20% government tax. Wherever possible in this book we've quoted the all-inclusive rates, but it's always worth checking when asking the price of a room. The same taxes are applied to meals in smarter restaurants.

For national park accommodation, see the National Parks section in the earlier Facts about the Country section.

Getting There & Away

AIR

Zambia's international airport is Lusaka, although some regional flights go to/from Livingstone (near Victoria Falls), or Mfuwe (South Luangwa National Park). If you're coming from Europe, airlines serving Zambia include Air Zimbabwe, British Airways, Ethiopian Airlines, KLM, Kenya Airways, Air France and South African Airways. High season return fares from London to Lusaka start at around £580, going up to £700. Low season fares are about £100 cheaper. Returns from Lusaka to Europe range from US$750 on Ethiopian Airlines to US$1100 on British Airways.

If you're coming from elsewhere in Southern or East Africa several regional airlines include Lusaka and Livingstone on their networks. These include Air Malawi, Air Tanzania, Aero Zambia, Inter Air and South African Airways.

If you're flying out of Lusaka, departure tax for international flights is US$20.

LAND

Zambia shares borders with eight other countries so there's a huge number of crossing points. Most border posts are open from 6 am to 6 pm (8 pm at Victoria Falls). If you're bringing a car into Zambia without a carnet, a temporary import permit is free, and compulsory third party insurance is US$6 per month.

Botswana

The only crossing point between Zambia and Botswana is the ferry across the Zambezi River at Kazungula, about 60 km west of Victoria Falls. This is rarely used by travellers as most cross the Zambezi at Victoria Falls, between Zambia and Zimbabwe.

Malawi

The main border crossing point between Zambia and Malawi is east of Chipata, on the main road between Lusaka and Lilongwe. For details see the Malawi Getting There & Away chapter.

Mozambique

The main border crossing between Zambia and Mozambique is between Chanida and Cassacatiza (also written Cassa Catiza) in south-eastern Zambia, but very few travellers take this route, as most go through Malawi (see the Getting There & Away chapter for details). We did hear of an intrepid traveller who went to the Zambian town of Luangwa, crossed by canoe to the Mozambique town of Zumbo, and then worked his way slowly to Tete by truck and

chapa. However, this crossing may not be officially open to tourists, even though locals go back and forth all the time, so don't expect guaranteed entry. You should also take local advice on the safety of this route; both bandits and land mines are reported to be dangers here.

Namibia

The only border crossing point between Zambia and Namibia is at the Zambian village of Katima Mulilo, on the west bank of the Zambezi River, near Sesheke. The Namibian border post is called Wenela, near the large Namibian town of Katima Mulilo. (The geography here is complicated, with four countries meeting at the Zambezi River. Locals refer to 'Katima Mulilo Zambia side' and 'Katima Mulilo Namibia side'.)

Buses between Livingstone and Sesheke, via Kazungula, go twice a day in each direction. The fare is US$6 to US$8, and the trip takes seven hours (because of bad potholes between Kazungula and Sesheke). The bus may terminate in Sesheke or continue another five km to the 'pontoon' (ferry) on the east bank of the Zambezi.

The ferry charges US$15 (40 rand or 30 pula) for foreign cars. Foot passengers ride free. If the ferry isn't running, canoes make the trip free of charge (the paddler is paid by the local council). If the council paddler cannot be found (not unusual), there are also 'private' canoes for US$0.20 per person.

Once on the west bank, it's 500m to the Zambia border post, and then less than one km to the Namibia border post (Wenela). From here to Katima Mulilo ('Namibia side') is five km. There's no bus, but a lift in a pick-up costs N$2 (US$0.50).

Note If you're heading into Zambia from Namibia, there's no bank at Katima Mulilo Zambia side, although there is one at Sesheke. If you plan to cross the Zambezi and head for Livingstone this is no problem, but if you're heading north towards Mongu, you'll have to find the local money changers who lurk around the ferry. Rand and Namibian dollars are always in demand, and

ZAMBIA

changing is low-key and hassle free. Rates vary but at the time of writing N$10 bought around 2800 kwacha. If you don't get hold of enough kwacha, Namibian dollars (but not SA rand) are accepted in larger hotels, shops and petrol stations in Senanga (where you can also buy more kwacha). Therefore, if you're heading for Mongu, take enough N$ to change into kwacha to get you there.

Grand Plans

In the next few years, a bridge may be built between Sesheke (Zambia) and Katima Mulilo (Namibia), and the roads from Sesheke to Livingstone and Mongu upgraded. This forms part of a grand long-term transport scheme to link Southern Africa's outer reaches to Walvis Bay (Namibia), which is currently being developed as a major port for the whole region. As part of the same scheme the roads from Katima Mulilo through the Caprivi Strip and between Livingstone and Lusaka are also due for upgrading. Be prepared for changes, but don't hold your breath. ■

South Africa

If you need direct land travel between Zambia and South Africa, consider the Trans-Zambezi Express, a luxury coach between Lusaka and Johannesburg. The one-way fare is US$115. Book at Bushwackers (☎ 250310) in the Lusaka Holiday Inn, or in Jo'burg (☎ (011) 7732160). Global Travel in Lusaka also runs a similar service, via Harare – see under the following Zimbabwe section.

Tanzania

The main Zambia-Tanzania border crossing point is between Nakonde and Tunduma, used by the Great North Road and the TAZARA railway line. Most travellers use the train, as bus rides are very long and slow, and often involve changing at the border anyway.

Train There are usually two international express trains per week in both directions between Kapiri Mposhi and Dar es Salaam, although trains can sometimes be cancelled

and the timetable is subject to change. Express departures from Kapiri Mposhi are Tuesday and Friday at 2 pm, and the trip takes 36 hours. The fare is US$60/40/24 in 1st/2nd/3rd class (1st and 2nd are sleeping compartments). The fare between Lusaka and Mbeya is US$33/22/13. A student discount is easy to obtain, even without a student card.

You'll be visited by border officials on the train (visas are essential for Tanzania). You'll also be disturbed by money changers. If you're sure of the rates it's worth changing, but take care – these guys are sharks. The train buffet uses the correct currency in each country.

Coming from Lusaka, book your ticket in advance (see the Lusaka section), but if they are full here, don't despair: we've heard from travellers who bought tickets on the spot at Kapiri Mposhi without trouble.

There are also slower ordinary trains between Kapiri Mposhi and the border, and between the border and Dar es Salaam.

Zaïre

The main crossing point is between Chililabombwe and Kasumbalesa, on the main road between Ndola and Lubumbashi. There is a daily bus service from Lusaka to Chililabombwe, then shared taxis to the border, but from there you must walk to Kasumbalesa. Between Kasumbalesa and Lubumbashi there are pick-ups and taxis.

Zimbabwe

The main crossing points between Zambia and Zimbabwe are: Chirundu, on the main road between Lusaka and Harare; Kariba, about 50 km from Chirundu; and Victoria Falls – the most popular crossing for travellers.

If you need to go direct, there are several buses each day between Lusaka and Harare, via Chirundu; the trip takes nine hours and costs US$7. An alternative is the thrice weekly luxury bus run by Big 5 Travel in Lusaka (☎ 229237/9), an eight hour journey via Kariba. A single fare is US$22. (For details in Zimbabwe, call (Harare) 700332.) Most travellers cross at Victoria Falls. For getting between Livingstone and the Zambia border post, see the Livingstone section. It's a one-km walk between the Zambia and Zimbabwe border posts, but you're rewarded with great views of the Falls from the Zambezi Bridge. The Zimbabwe border post is one km from Victoria Falls town.

LAKE

Tanzania & Burundi

There's a ferry called the *Liemba* on Lake Tanganyika. Recent reports suggest there is no service to Burundi (although this may start again) and the timetable is very flexible. It's supposed to depart Mpulungu (Zambia) on Friday, arriving at Kigoma (Tanzania) on Sunday, via other Tanzanian ports. Another ferry called the *Mwengoza* covers the same route, officially leaving Mpulungu every Tuesday.

The international fare between Mpulungu and Kigoma is US$50 for a 1st class (cabin), US$40 for second class and US$25 for economy class, payable in US dollars. To minimise the cost, you can buy a ticket to Kipili (Tanzania) in dollars, and then buy another ticket for the rest of the journey in Tanzanian shillings on the boat. Port tax is US$2.

Both ferries carry cars; loading is by crane, and Mpulungu to Kigoma costs US$130, plus US$30 'handling'.

Getting Around

AIR

Zambia Airways no longer exists. Internal flights are operated by Aero Zambia (☎ 226111) and Zambia Express (☎ 227965). One-way fares are around US$80 for Lusaka to/from Kitwe, and US$130 for Lusaka to/from Livingstone. Proflight Air Services (☎ 263686; fax 261214) flies regularly between the main tourist destinations around the country; many services tie in with long-haul international flight arrivals. Sample fares from Lusaka: Mfuwe (South Luangwa National Park) US$135/240 one way/return; Living-stone US$125/220; Kafue National Park US$180 return. Mfuwe to Livingstone is US$260 one way.

For private charter, operators include Pro-flight and Zambia Express (see above) plus Roan Air (☎ 223839; fax 222904). Safari specialists are Lunga Air Shuttle, linking the Lower Zambezi, South Luangwa and Kafue parks.

All air companies listed here are based in Lusaka. Most travel agencies in Lusaka and Livingstone can also arrange air charters, and it might be easier doing it this way than going to the air company direct.

BUS

Travelling around Zambia by bus can be hard and tiring. Many roads are badly potholed. The national bus company, UBZ, has disappeared and all buses are now privately-owned. Fares are standardised, so it's not normally worth shopping around. Many routes are served by minibuses (usually quicker) and big buses (slower and slightly cheaper).

Some sample fares: Lusaka to Living-stone, US$7; Lusaka to Kapiri Mposhi, US$2; Lusaka to Mpulungu, about US$8. Long-distance buses on main routes tend to leave punctually, although arrival times can be unpredictable. On local services buses leave when full and journey times are even more uncertain. In rural areas the 'bus' is often a truck or pick-up carrying goods as well as people.

TRAIN

Other than the TAZARA railway (see the earlier Getting There & Away section), the country's main line runs from Lusaka south to Livingstone and north to Kitwe.

Lusaka to Livingstone express trains depart Monday, Wednesday and Friday at 7 pm, arriving the next morning (between 6 am and noon). From Livingstone to Lusaka they run Tuesday, Thursday and Saturday, departing at 8 pm and arriving the next morning. Fares are US$7/5/4 in 1st/2nd/3rd class. An ordinary train runs every day in both directions; the fare is slightly less but it's very slow.

On the Lusaka-Kitwe line there are ordinary trains only both ways daily at 8 pm, arriving next morning. Fares are US$6/$5.50/$3. This train goes via Kapiri Mposhi where you can change to the TAZARA line, but there's no connecting service, so you might be better going by bus.

Tickets for 1st and 2nd class can be bought in advance. Conditions on the trains vary, but 1st class is usually a sleeper compartment taking two or four people. Second class is a sleeper for three or six people. Third class is seats only. Most compartments have no lights and locks – take a torch and something to secure the door at night. Beware of bogus ticket collectors, and 'double bookings' which can be sorted out for a small fee.

If you want to avoid Lusaka, the ordinary train services are connected. For example you can go from Livingstone all the way to Kapiri Mposhi; when the train goes through Lusaka, you just stay on.

ORGANISED TOURS

Some companies run tours around Zambia as part of wider trips of Southern Africa. Many of the tour companies listed in the Malawi Getting There & Away section also offer Zambia in their brochures. Several local tour companies based in Malawi also operate in Zambia.

Tours and safaris around Zambia inevitably focus on the national parks. As these are hard to visit without a vehicle, joining a tour might be your only option. Many companies have their own lodges.

Zambia's safari scene is small and select. Most tours are aimed squarely at the top-end of the market, with 'tailor-made' tours for small groups. Companies prefer to take bookings in advance (most clients come from overseas agents). However, if you've got some cash to spare, a tour to one of Zambia's parks would be a great investment.

There are several tour companies based in Zambia. You can contact them direct, or through a good travel agent (listed in the following Lusaka section). Some tour com-

panies are listed below, others are listed in the national park sections throughout this chapter, and under Organised Tours in the Livingstone section.

Shiwa Safaris, PO Box 36655, Lusaka (☎ 223113; fax 223048). Specialising in northern Zambia, including North Luangwa, Bangweulu, and the incongruous 'country manor' at Shiwa Ngandu.

Robin Pope Safaris, PO Box 320154, Lusaka (☎ Mfuwe (062) 45090; fax 45051). Robin Pope is considered one of Zambia's leading guides, and his tours include exclusive walking safaris in South Luangwa, plus the 'unusual' parks of Kasanka, Liuwa and Nyika.

Royal Zambezi Canoeing, Findeco House, PO Box 31455, Lusaka (☎ 223952; fax 223747). A range of canoe safaris on the Lower Zambezi, from two nights to a week, for a range of budgets, either camping, staying in African villages, simple camps or luxurious lodges.

Lusaka

Central Lusaka is part traditional African and part modern; with dusty markets sitting alongside high-rise blocks. From Cairo Rd, the city centre's main street, wide boulevards lead east to the Government Area (ministries), the 'Diplomatic Triangle' (some embassies) and the smarter residential suburbs. To the west are the 'high density housing zones', for which read 'townships'.

For visitors, the main feature of Lusaka is the lack of other tourists and (therefore) tourist facilities. Unfortunately, Lusaka's other main feature is its high crime rate, especially in the centre. Consequently, many people avoid this area and go instead to the out-of-town shopping centres which have become increasingly popular. In the last few years, many airline offices and embassies have also relocated to the suburbs.

Although Zambia is a fascinating country, there's very little of interest in Lusaka itself. However, if you do have to be here for a while (eg to get a visa or change transport), it's not quite as bad as it's often painted, and there are several places where you can pass time pleasantly enough.

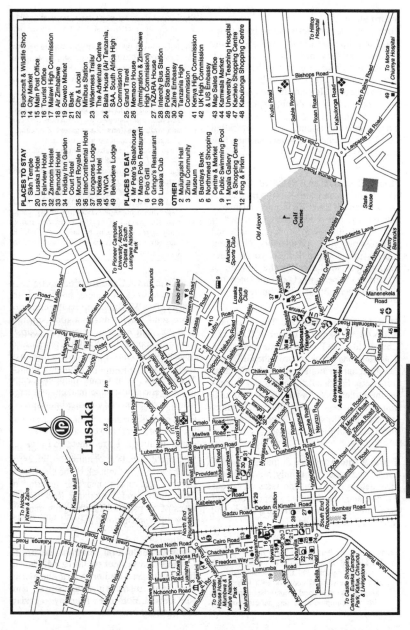

PLACES TO STAY
1 Sikh Temple
20 Lusaka Hotel
31 Fairview Hotel
32 Zamcom Hostel
33 Pamodzi Hotel
34 Holiday Inn Garden Court Hotel
35 Mount Royale Inn
36 InterContinental Hotel
37 Longacres Lodge
38 Ndeke Hotel
45 YWCA
49 Belvedere Lodge

PLACES TO EAT
4 Mr Pete's Steakhouse
7 Marco Polo Restaurant
8 Polo Grill
10 Gringo's Restaurant
39 Lusaka Club

OTHER
2 Mulungushi Hall
3 Zintu Community Centre & Market
5 Barclays Bank
6 Northmead Shopping Centre & Market
9 Public Swimming Pool
11 Mpala Gallery & Shopping Centre
12 Frog & Firkin
13 Bushcraft & Wildlife Shop
14 City Market
15 Main Post Office
16 Tourist Office
17 Malawi High Commission
18 Air Zimbabwe
19 Soweto Market
21 Bank
22 City & Local Minibus Station
23 Wilderness Trails/The Adventure Centre
24 Bata House (Air Tanzania, SAA, South Africa High Commission)
25 Grand Travel
26 Memaco House (Immigration & Zimbabwe High Commission)
27 TAZARA House
28 Intercity Bus Station
29 Police Station
30 Zaire Embassy
40 Tanzania High Commission
41 Kenya High Commission
42 UK High Commission & US Embassy
43 Map Sales Office
44 Kamwala Market
46 University Teaching Hospital
47 Kachelo Shopping Centre
48 Kabulonga Shopping Centre

Lusaka

ZAMBIA

Information

Tourist office The tourist office is on Cairo Rd. The people are friendly enough, but the information they have is fairly limited. *Lusaka Lowdown* is a freebie listings and news magazine, available from hotels, shops and travel agents. It's aimed mainly at expats and more well-to-do Zambians, but there's plenty of interest for tourists about local events and attractions. A booklet called *Lusaka at a Glance* lists hotels, airlines, tour companies etc.

Money Barclays and Standard Chartered have branches on Cairo Rd (the Barclays at the north end of Cairo Rd is quiet and quick). There are also several exchange bureaux. If you've got time, shop around as rates and commissions vary considerably. However, thieves prowl Cairo Rd, so you're safer changing elsewhere, eg the bureau at Kabulonga Supermarket or at the InterContinental Hotel (not the reception desk).

Post & Communications The main post office (GPO) is on the corner of Cairo and Church Rds. The Poste Restante is also here. The telephone office is above the GPO; you can make international calls and send faxes from here. For details of hours and charges see the earlier Facts for the Visitor section. If you need access to the Internet, Zamnet (☎ /fax 290358) at the University charges US$8 per hour for on-line use.

Travel & Tour Agencies Some travel agents handle outbound flights only, but good ones have details on routes and fares of various airlines, and can save you a lot of footslogging. Others also deal with tours, safaris and activities; these include:

Grand Travel, southern end of Cairo Rd (☎ 226073; fax 223048). This knowledgeable outfit arranges domestic, regional and international flights. It also has very good contacts with lodges and camps in the parks and around the country, and with tour companies running safaris, canoeing etc.

Big 5 Travel, Cairo Rd, near Grand Travel (☎ 288971; fax 289362). Flights, car hire (Avis agents) and coach to Zimbabwe.

Busanga Travel & Tours, Cairo Rd (☎ 220897/221694; fax 274253). Flights, plus bookings for safaris, lodges and camps in the national parks, including their own camps in Kafue National Park.

Wilderness Trails/The Adventure Centre, Ben Bella Rd (☎ 220112). Plenty of information on lodges and active/adventurous tours, such as canoeing and walking safaris (Zambia and Zimbabwe), plus info on several car hire companies.

Kachelo Travel, Kachelo Shopping Centre (☎ 263973; fax 260817). A friendly team, they can arrange flights or help you put together tours to the national parks.

Africa Tour Designers, at Castle Shopping Centre, Kafue Rd (☎ 274883/4; fax 273865). A switched-on booking service for hotels, camps and lodges all over the country, and in Zimbabwe, Botswana, Malawi and Namibia, plus adventure activities at Livingstone and the Upper Zambezi.

Bookshops On Cairo Rd, Bookworld has a reasonable stock of general books and stationary. The Wildlife Shop on the corner of Cairo and Church Rds has a good selection of books and maps of interest to tourists (proceeds support the Wildlife Conservation Society of Zambia). There's also a branch of Bookworld at Kabulonga Shopping Centre. Tower Books at the Castle Shopping Centre is also good. Most supermarkets and large hotels stock local and imported newspapers and magazines.

Maps The Map Sales Office (part of the Ministry of Lands & Natural Resources) is in a basement, at the back of the Geological Survey Department, near the junction of Government and Nationalist Rds. Survey maps of all parts of Zambia, plus maps of some cities and national parks all cost US$3.

Libraries & Cultural Centres The British Council library is just off Cairo Rd. The US Information Service library is in the Meridian Bank building near South End Roundabout. Both open Monday to Friday, and Saturday morning.

Medical Centres & Pharmacies At the University Teaching Hospital (UTH) the Emergency department charges US$15. If you need to stay longer ask for a 'High Cost Bed'. For more straightforward matters, such as malaria testing, private clinics in Lusaka include Hilltop Hospital, at the far eastern end of Kabulonga Rd, and the Monica Chiumya Hospital (☎ 260492) on Bulwe Rd, south of Leopards Hill Rd (there's also a dentist here). You must pay a US$100 deposit before they'll even look at you, but service is good, and both have pharmacies. Other places for medicines are City Pharmacy, opposite the GPO, and the stores at the large hotels.

Dangers Cairo Rd and the streets on its west side are dangerous. People get mugged regularly here and pickpockets prowl the markets and bus stations. Naturally, rich-looking tourists are a tempting target. While walking on Cairo Rd, don't be distracted by con-men pretending to sell souvenirs or change money, especially those who work in gangs. If you think you've been targeted, go into a shop or bank (many places have their own security guards) and wait until the danger has passed. Even if you're on a tight budget, Lusaka is a place to consider taking taxis.

Shopping Centres & Supermarkets Lusaka has several suburban shopping centres. These include: Kabulonga, which has a large supermarket, bottle store and change bureau; Northmead, which has all the above, plus several restaurants; Kachelo, near Kabulonga, with a restaurant, farm shop, and travel agency; and one on Joseph Mwilwa Rd which has a farm shop, outdoor equipment store and Mpapa art gallery.

Things to See
Lusaka is surprisingly well-endowed with galleries where the work of local artists is of a high quality. Try the **Henry Tayali Visual Arts Gallery** at the Showgrounds, the smaller **Mpala Gallery** on Mwilwa Rd, and the **sculpture park** at the Garden House Hotel on Mumbwa Rd, run by Mr Rossi, a well-known collector and supporter of Zambian art. **Zintu Community Museum**, Panganini Rd, shows traditional arts and crafts, on display and in production. Entrance costs US$0.50.

Places to Stay – bottom end
City Centre & Suburbs The *YWCA* takes men and women and charges US$10 per person in double rooms. It's basic but very clean and friendly. Water is limited, but buckets are provided. Another cheap option is *Emmasdale Lodge* (☎ 243692), on Great North Rd, two km past North End Roundabout, where single rooms cost US$15. Self-catering flats, sleeping one to four people, with equipped kitchen, cost US$33 – a bargain if you're in a group. Local buses pass the end of the road, or a taxi from town costs US$3.

The Salvation Army hostel has closed, partly because travellers abused the hospitality. At the *Sikh Temple*, Mumana Rd, off Katima Mulilo Rd, off Great East Rd, a bed in the yard is free, but you should leave a donation, and obey house rules (no cigarettes, booze, meat or improper behaviour), otherwise this place will close to travellers too.

Outer Lusaka *Pioneer Campsite* is signposted five km south of the Great East Rd – 18 km east of the city centre and three km east of the airport turn-off. Chalets cost US$10, camping US$5. There's a bar and meals (cooked by Mr Banda), or you can self-cater. The friendly owners run a free lift service to/from town on weekday mornings. From the city to the camp, they pick up at Kachelo Travel Agency (☎ 263973) between noon and 1 pm. Phone in advance to make arrangements.

If you're coming from the south, *Eureka Camping Park*, on a farm about 10 km south of the city, is an ideal stop-off. Chalets are US$10, camping US$5. There's meat and firewood for sale, a bar to enjoy a relaxing drink or two, and some fine showers.

ZAMBIA

Minibuses between Lusaka and Chilanga or Kafue pass the end of their drive.

Places to Stay – middle

City Centre & Suburbs Most central is the *Lusaka Hotel*, just off Cairo Rd, charging US$38/47 for singles/doubles B&B with TV and coffee facilities. It's clean and quite secure once you're through the door.

The safe and friendly *Zamcom Hostel* on Church Rd charges US$20 to US$25 per person including breakfast, with good evening meals for US$5. Nearby is the similar *Hubert Young Hostel*, closed for renovation when we passed through, but worth trying when it reopens. *Mount Royale Inn*, a few blocks away on Suez Rd, has modern airy single/double rooms for US$25/36. Breakfast is US$2, and other meals cost from US$2 to US$7. There's a pool and safe parking.

Also worth trying are the revamped government hostels: *Longacres Lodge*, off Haile Selassie Ave, where reasonable doubles cost US$33 with breakfast; and *Belvedere Lodge* (☎ 263680) Leopards Hill Rd, where ensuite rooms cost US$36, including three full meals. Extra people (one or two) pay only for food (breakfast US$3, dinner US$6).

Up in price is the *Ndeke Hotel* (☎ 252779; fax 252779), just south of the junction of Haile Selassie Ave and Los Angeles Blvd. Ensuite doubles cost US$32/56 (after 6 pm they're half price) with breakfast. There's a bar, restaurant, pool and 'travellers stand-by' rates available (see under Outer Lusaka, following). Less spartan is *The Fairview* (☎ 212954; fax 218432), on Church Rd, with small but clean and comfortable ensuite doubles for US$60. Evening meals cost US$6, and there's a terrace bar (although it seems to be a bit of a pick-up zone, so single women may feel uncomfortable here).

Outer Lusaka Out of town, your options include some places on the Kafue road. Five km south of the centre, opposite the Castle Shopping Centre is the small *Kafue Road Garden Hotel* (☎ 252422) with ensuite rooms for US$32/56. A few km further down

this road is *Andrews Motel* (☎ 272106) with straightforward ensuite rooms (some with air-conditioning) for US$35 for one or two people plus breakfast. A family suite, with two rooms sleeping four people, costs a very reasonable US$50. Both the above places can be reached by taxi (about US$4).

On the Mongu road, six km west of the centre, the large but spacious *Garden House Hotel* (☎ 289328) has rooms for US$34/40 B&B. Along with the Ndeke and Kafue Road Garden hotels (part of the same group) this place offers 'travellers stand-by' rates: if you arrive after 6 pm, rooms are half price.

Places to Stay – top end

All places in this bracket include breakfast.

City Centre *The Holiday Inn Garden Court* (formerly the Ridgeway) (☎ 251666/252796; fax 254115) on Church Rd, has singles/doubles for US$105/130. On the ground floor is Steers Restaurant (steaks from US$6) and McGinty's Pub – both of which are part of South African chains. There's also a poolside bar and garden grill, where snacks cost from US$4 to US$8, and full meals are around US$12. The nearby *Pamodzi Hotel* (☎ 254455; fax 254005), charges US$120/130. The Jacaranda Restaurant serves evening buffet specials for US$12 and the Rendezvous has more up-market fare.

Top of the tree is the *InterContinental Hotel* (☎ 250600, fax 251880), Haile Selassie Ave, where rooms are US$130/150. The Pool Terrace has snacks from US$5, the Brasserie does light meals from US$8 and a buffet for US$14, and the Makumbi Restaurant offers full-blown a la carte meals starting at US$10 and ending somewhere near the horizon.

All three top-end hotels have business centres (secretarial services, photocopies, faxes etc), swimming pools, hair salons, boutiques, travel desks and bookshops. The Pamodzi has a gym and massage room. The InterContinental has tennis courts, a pharmacy and a Barclays Bank change bureau.

Outer Lusaka If you don't need to be in town, one of Lusaka's finest options is *Lilayi Lodge* (☎ 228682/3; fax 222906; e-mail lilayi@zamnet.zm), set in a private game reserve, about eight km off Kafue Rd, 11 km south of the centre (signposted). Very comfortable ensuite bungalows cost US$80 for one person and US$90 for two. This also includes game viewing on the reserve. A four course evening meal is US$15. Buffet lunches are served at weekends. If you don't have wheels, a transfer from town costs US$20, or US$40 from the airport. Full board, including transfers, is US$150/230. The ambience here is peaceful and the staff are friendly and quietly efficient.

Places to Eat – cheap

If you're on a tight budget the Shoprite supermarket on Cairo Rd is the cheapest option; it has fresh bread and a good selection of foods. For cheap meals, there are *basic eating houses* near the local and intercity bus stations, but the setting is far from pleasant. You're better off at a *petrol station snack bar*; try the Caltex (open to 5 pm) just beyond North End Roundabout, or the Mobil (open until midnight) on the corner of Church and Kabelenga Rds, where burgers, pies and chips start at about US$1. The BP at Castle Shopping Centre has similar offerings, plus specials like souvlaki for US$3.

Along Cairo Rd, there's a number *snackbars* and *takeaways* offering chicken and chips and other fried food, with snacks around US$1 and meals starting at US$2. These include the long-standing *Rooster King*, at the south end of Cairo Rd, and the nearby *BiteRite*.

Places to Eat – more expensive

Most of the hotels listed above have restaurants and coffee shops, where prices and standards reflect the quality of the establishment.

Of the restaurants in town, a favourite is *Mr Pete's Steakhouse*, Panganini Rd, where meals are around US$8. A close rival in popularity is the *Frog & Firkin* (see under Entertainment below), with 'pub grub' from US$4.

Most other restaurants are in the suburbs.

El Toro at Kachelo Shopping Centre, has snacks from US$1.50 and light meals from US$2 to US$4 in a pleasant open-air setting. *Jaylin* (☎ 252206) at the Lusaka Club in Longacres is open to non-members. It's not much to look at, but the food is excellent and good value: main meals are around US$8 to US$10. Near the showgrounds is the *Marco Polo Restaurant*, a smart place with Italian specialities and a terrazzo overlooking the polo field. Opposite, the less fancy and cheaper *Polo Grill* has outdoor seating under shade.

The buffet lunches at *Lilayi Lodge* (see Places to Stay – top end, Outer Lusaka) are a weekend institution where you can revel in a huge choice of fine foods for US$20. Many people come for the day, to swim in the pool or walk in the game reserve.

Entertainment

Mr Pete's (see Places to Eat – more expensive) has music at weekends; US$4 cover, free if you eat. Also highly recommended is the *Frog & Firkin*, Kabelenga Rd, a British-style brewery-pub, that is very popular with Zambians. It has a good, lively mixed crowd; music on Tuesday, Wednesday and Thursday; there's no cover charge; and 500 ml of perfect draught for US$2.

If you've got wheels, and a taste for the bizarre, try *Mike's Car Wash* on Kafue Rd, south of the centre; it has a 24-hour drive-in bar, with snacks and live music, plus vehicle spares and repairs.

The public swimming pool, east of Addis Ababa Drive, is clean with a pleasant shaded area, and small snack bar. It's a good place to pass the day (entrance costs US$1; closed Monday). Several hotels have pools and if you buy food or drinks you can normally swim for free.

Things to Buy

For curios go to Bushcraft or the Wildlife Shop on the corner of Church and Cairo Rds, Zintu at the Holiday Inn or on Panganini Rd, and the shop at the YWCA (see Places to Stay). For CDs of African and Western music (around US$25) try Sounds at Kabulonga Shopping Centre, or Dunga Disc on

ZAMBIA

Kabelenga Rd. The Shoprite supermarket on Cairo Rd has a surprisingly good selection of cassettes (Western stuff, plus Zambian traditional and modern music) for US$3 to US$4. Street hawkers sell bootleg cassettes for US$2 or less.

For general goods, cheap eats, curios and carvings go to the stalls at Northmead Shopping Centre, on the Great East Rd. It's safer here than the markets in town, but pickpockets are not uncommon.

Getting There & Away

Air If you need to fly out of Lusaka, the following airlines have offices in the city.

Aero Zambia, ZNIB House, near TAZARA House, Independence Ave (☎ 226111)
Air France, 8 Chindo Rd, Woodlands (☎ 264930; fax 271212)
Air Malawi, ZNIB House, near TAZARA House, Independence Ave (☎ 254455)
Air Tanzania, Bata House, Cairo Rd (☎ 228295)
Air Zimbabwe, Kariba House, Chachacha Rd (☎ 221750/225431)
British Airways, Holiday Inn (☎ 250073/255320)
Kenya Airways, Findeco House, Cairo Rd (☎ 228484)
KLM, Pamodzi Hotel (☎ 254455)
South African Airways, Bata House, Cairo Rd (☎ 221508)
Royal Swazi, Farmers House, Cairo Rd (☎ 224222)
Zambia Express (☎ 227965/222060)

These offices are useful if you have reservations to confirm, but for buying a ticket you're better off going to an agent (see Travel & Tour Agencies in the Information section) as prices are usually the same and it will save you a lot of shopping around.

Bus Lusaka has two depots: City Bus Station, near Kulima Tower, at the southern end of Freedom Way, for local services (including surrounding towns such as Kafue), and the Intercity Bus Station on Dedan Kimathi Rd, for long distance (including cross-border) routes. The UBZ station on Chachacha Rd is mostly disused, but some services may go from here in the future as the other depots become more crowded.

Here are some sample fares from Lusaka:

Kafue US$1; Kapiri Mposhi US$4.50; Livingstone US$8; Chipata US$8.50 (express), US$5.50 (slow); Kitwe US$6.50; Mongu US$8.50; Siavonga US$3.50; Nakonde US$13.50; Mpulungu US$13. On most routes there are several buses daily in each direction.

Hitching Although we don't recommend hitching, the place to wait if you're heading from Lusaka along the Great East Rd is the bus stop just beyond the turn-off to the airport. (You can retreat to Pioneer camp if it gets late.) If you're heading south it's best to get to the junction 10 km beyond Kafue town, where the roads to Kariba and Livingstone divide; there's a basic local resthouse if you get stuck.

Train The main Lusaka train station is on Dedan Kimathi Rd. Reservations and tickets for Zambia Railways trains can be made here. For TAZARA reservations go to TAZARA House, on the corner of Dedan Kimathi Rd and Independence Ave. For more details on trains see the main Getting Around section.

Getting Around

The Airport Lusaka International Airport is about 20 km east from the centre. Taxis *from* the airport cost US$25, but from town *to* the airport it's US$10 to US$20, depending on the time of day. There's no airport bus, but the big hotels all have courtesy buses to meet international flights. The best deal is the post office bus, which runs two or three times per day between the GPO in town and the airport post office, and charges US$1.50 each way.

Bus For getting around Lusaka, local buses run along the city's main roads, but there are no route numbers and the buses don't have name boards, so the system is difficult to work out. From the suburbs to the centre you just wait at a bus stop until a bus comes a long, with the ticket boy shouting 'town'. Going from the centre outwards, you can go to the local bus station, or get onto the main road heading roughly towards where you want to go and wait at the first bus stop. Sample fares: centre to Longacres is US$0.20; centre to Kabulonga US$0.50.

Rental Car If you need a car for getting around Lusaka (or further afield), there are several rental companies. Avis has offices at Big 5 Tours on Cairo Rd (☎ 229238; fax 221978), at the airport (☎ 271058) and at the Pamodzi and InterContinental Hotels. Hertz has offices at Mulungushi Hall Conference Centre (☎ 291542/7; fax 291533) and at the airport (☎ 271331). Both charge around US$50 per day for a small saloon car, plus US$0.50 per km, with reductions and free kms after five days. Local companies include: Bushwackers (☎ 253869), US$25 per day, plus US$0.20 per km; Juls, US$55 per day, plus US$0.30 per km; and Chigwaza, US$30 per day, US$0.25 per km. All are represented by most travel agents. Add 20% to 25% tax to all rates. In Zambia most rental cars come with a driver; you pay a daily allowance, but not insurance or collision damage waivers.

Taxi Taxis are recognised by the numbers painted on the door. There are taxi ranks at the main hotels, and you can also hail a cab in the street. Fares are negotiable, but as a guide: centre to Holiday Inn or Pamodzi US$2 to US$3; centre to Kabulonga US$4. Always check the fare before getting in the taxi.

Tours A company called Day-trippers (☎ 262281) offers a series of excursions in and around Lusaka. Some hotels and travel agents have their brochure.

Eastern Zambia

This section covers the area between the border town of Chipata and Lusaka (the part of Zambia most easily reached from Malawi) and includes the South Luangwa and Lower Zambezi national parks. Places are described from east to west.

CHIPATA

Chipata is the 'gateway' to South Luangwa National Park, and you may find yourself overnighting here if stuck between transport. The bus station and market are one km north of the main street in the old part of town. For changing money there are two banks.

Places to Stay & Eat

Kapata Resthouse near the bus station costs US$5 a double; it's fairly safe but dirty. Most of the other places are in the new part of town, about 1.5 km away. At the *Zambian Wildlife Conservation Society campground*, just north of the main street, you can pitch a tent for US$2. The nearby *Kamocho Guest House* has singles for US$12, and basic doubles for US$16 ($18 for ensuite). About three km west of town, where the road to Luangwa branches north, there's the friendly *Chipata Motel* with clean ensuite double rooms for US$14 with breakfast.

SOUTH LUANGWA NATIONAL PARK

For scenery and variety of animals, South Luangwa is probably the best park in Zambia, and one of the best in the whole of Africa. Vegetation ranges from dense woodland to open grassy plains, and oxbow lagoons act as natural water holes. Mammals include lion, buffalo, zebra and Thornicroft's giraffe (a subspecies); Cookson's wildebeest is also endemic. The park also contains elephant (one of the largest concentrations in Africa) and is particularly noted for its leopard. Antelope species include bushbuck, waterbuck, impala and puku. In the Luangwa River you'll see hippo and crocodile. The birdlife is tremendous.

Lodges and camps run tours (in open-top vehicles), night drives and walking safaris, either for the day or longer (staying overnight in the bush). Horse-riding is also available in the area. One way or another, in South Luangwa you can get pretty close to the 'real Africa', and although it's hard to visit on the cheap, there are more options for the budget-conscious than in some other Zambian parks.

For details on entrance fees see under

ZAMBIA

South Luangwa National Park

National Parks in the Facts about the Country section.

Places to Stay & Eat

As with all the parks in Zambia, South Luangwa will change dramatically in the next few years, as new lodges and camps are opened and state-run hotels are privatised. Except for the camp sites and chalets, it's usually necessary to book accommodation in advance, either direct to the lodge or through an agent in Lusaka or overseas. Many places are just outside the park boundary, so you don't pay park fees when staying there. Note that most are seasonal – open from April to October/December. Notable exceptions are Flatdogs, Wildlife Camp and Kapani, which are accessible all year.

Most campers and overlanders head for *Flatdogs*, just outside the park near the Mfuwe Gate entrance, overlooking the river. Camping costs US$5, and self-catering chalets are US$15. There is a small bar and

you can buy snacks and fresh vegetables. The camp is run by a guy called Jake who is a good source of local information. He also runs Rancho los Pajeros horse riding, and organises game drives (day and night) in the park for US$25.

A few km to the west is the well-maintained *Wildlife Camp* (☎ (062) 45026), where camping costs US$5, self-catering family chalets (sleeping up to four) are US$15 per person, and pleasant ensuite chalets are US$20. There's a bar which serves snacks and meals. Game drives are US$20 ($25 at night). This place is popular, so bookings for chalets may be necessary at busy times.

South of Mfuwe Gate, just outside the park on the east bank of the river, are three top-end lodges. Most famous, and probably most popular, is *Kapani Lodge* (☎ (062) 45015; fax 45025), built by Norman Carr (see the boxed text later on the history of South Luangwa) about 10 years ago. Norman recently relinquished the helm at Kapani and the lodge is run by his young and knowledgeable team of safari guides, but a major feature of the lodge are his afternoon talks on the history and wildlife of the park. Open all year, accommodation is in thatched cottages overlooking a lagoon. Kapani runs bush camps and walking safaris. It costs from US$200 to stay; the price includes all meals and accommodation, all game drives and walks, park fees and transfer to/from the airport.

In the same area and price band is *Chinzombo Safari Lodge* (☎ (062) 45053 or Lusaka 225976), very close to the river bank and with excellent views and comfortable ensuite bungalows. Also nearby is the tastefully designed *Nkwali Lodge* (Robin Pope Safaris, see the Organised Tours section) with walk-in tents and delightful open-air bathrooms. Both these places organise walking safaris: Robin Pope leads many personally, while Chinzombo include fully portered colonial-style expeditions. About 15 km south of here is the mid-range *Tundwe Lodge* (Busanga Travel and Tours – see the Lusaka section), which also has wheelchair access.

North of Mfuwe Gate are several more

History of South Luangwa

The history of South Luangwa National Park is inextricably linked with the story of Norman Carr, a leading wildlife figure who has been based in the area since 1939. He is sometimes known as the 'George Adamson of Zambia' because he raised two lions and returned them to the wild, but his influence and contribution to conservation in Africa goes much deeper.

In 1938, the North and South Luangwa game reserves were created to protect and control wildlife populations – notably elephant. A year later Norman Carr became a ranger here. With the full backing of the area's traditional leader, Carr created Chief Nsefu's Private Game Reserve in 1950 and opened it to the public (until this time reserves had been for the animals only). All visitor fees were paid directly to the chief, thus benefiting both wildlife and local people. Thirty years later 'community involvement' became a buzzword when conservationists finally realised that the survival of habitats and animals depends on the co-operation of local people.

Norman Carr was years ahead of his time in other fields too. He built Nsefu Camp, the first public camp in the country, and developed walking safaris (a totally new concept then, though commonplace today), to introduce visitors to African bush conditions away from the confines of a vehicle.

In the following decades other game reserves were created, more tourists came to Luangwa and more camps were built along the river, including Chinzombo – owned by Norman Carr's increasingly busy safari company. In 1972, Nsefu and several game reserves were combined to form the South Luangwa National Park. Despite the new title, from the mid-1970s poaching of elephant and rhino became an increasing problem. In 1980 Carr and several other people founded the Save the Rhino Trust; funds raised helped the government parks department combat the poachers.

In 1984, Norman Carr opened yet another camp – Kapani Lodge – and continued to operate safaris from this base. He retired from 'active service' in the early 1990s, but still lives in the Luangwa Valley and meets guests at the lodge on most days. ■

top-end places including *Chibembe Safari Lodge* and *Nsefu Camp* (Wilderness Trails – see the Lusaka section) and *Tena Tena* (Robin Pope – see the Organised Tours section). *Tafika Camp* is a touch less fancy and a bit cheaper than most, with boat and canoe trips on the river, and microlight flights. Inside the park on the west bank is the small and exclusive *Kaingo Camp* (Shenton Safaris, ☎ 062 45064; fax 45036). As this book went to press, we heard that the formerly state-run *Mfuwe Lodge* had been bought by Malawi-based Club Makokola. They plan a complete rebuild and will offer a range of walking and vehicle safaris. If you're coming from Malawi, you can get more details from Club Makokola (listed in the Lake Shore chapter).

Places to Eat

If you come in or out by air, or with your own vehicle, take time to visit the unlikely but splendid *Moondogs Café,* at Mfuwe Airport, where luxuries like cold beers, tacos, waffles and salads grace the menu. Next door is Magenge Crafts, full of locally made curios and art: some tasteful, some weird (check out the ceramic hats!).

Getting There & Away

Most people reach South Luangwa by air: about 20 km from the main gate is Mfuwe Airport. (There are services from within Zambia and on Air Malawi, twice weekly.) Lodge transfer vehicles meet all clients with reservations.

If you have your own vehicle, Mfuwe Gate and the surrounding lodges and camps are easily reached from Chipata. In the dry season it's usually in poor to reasonable condition, and takes two to three hours. In the wet season it can take all day (or be simply impassable).

If you're on a tight budget, local pick-ups run from Chipata to Mfuwe village, near the main gate, at least once daily (the fare is US$5), from where you can walk to Flatdogs or hitch to the Wildlife Camp. Some travellers hitch all the way: the junction by the Chipata Motel is the best place to wait for a lift. To tour the park, all the camp sites and lodges arrange game drives.

CHIRUNDU

This border town is on the main road between Lusaka and Harare. On the Zambia side, the *Nyambadwe Motel* has rooms for

US$15, and allows camping for US$5. There are also some shops, a few truckers' bars, a bank and a clutch of money changers.

The best place to stay is *Gwabi Lodge*, 11 km from Chirundu towards Lower Zambezi National Park. Rondavels cost US$65 per person including a three-course dinner and full breakfast. The 'travellers rate' (smaller dinner, light breakfast) is US$50. Camping costs US$3.50. The lodge has marvellous lush grounds, although the campground is a bit dusty, and the view from the swimming pool and bar is one of the best in Africa. Boat rides are available. The owners of the lodge are tireless conservationists, involved in several wildlife education schemes in the surrounding area. The same team also plans to open a new lodge and camp site on the edge of the park.

Getting There & Away
Minibuses between Lusaka and Chirundu cost US$3. To/from Siavonga or the Kariba border crossing it's US$0.50. To reach Gwabi Lodge from Chirundu town, head north up the dirt road on the east side of town (signposted). Unless you've got your own wheels, you'll have to hitch or walk.

LOWER ZAMBEZI NATIONAL PARK
The Lower Zambezi National Park covers an area of about 4000 sq km on the north bank, roughly opposite Zimbabwe's Mana Pools. The main gate is at Chongwe, on the western boundary. To the east the park ends at the Mpata Gorge. The eastern boundary runs roughly parallel to the Luangwa River (which also forms part of the border with Mozambique).

Most people visit as part of a tour, but self-drivers can reach the park. A track runs roughly parallel to the river, but it is in very bad condition once you get about 25 km from the gate. There are also several game-viewing loops, but these change from year to year.

For details on entrance fees see under National Parks in the Facts about the Country section.

Places to Stay
For most places in the Lower Zambezi park it's usually necessary to book accommodation in advance, either direct (contacts in brackets in this section, where applicable) or through an agent in Lusaka or overseas.

As pioneers in this area, the expertise of *Chiawa Camp* (☎ Lusaka 261588; fax 262683)

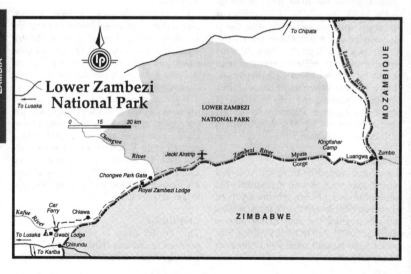

Lower Zambezi – Ecology & History

The Lower Zambezi National Park consists of two main features: the Zambezi river plain, a strip about 90 km long and between 10 and 20 km wide which contains a mixture of woodland and grassland; and the more heavily wooded Zambezi Escarpment, between the river plain and the central plateau to the north. Several perennial rivers flow through the park, and there are also some pans and swampy areas. There are several islands on the Zambezi itself; some are large, based around rock outcrops and covered in old trees, and feature in the writings of early explorers such as Livingstone and Selous. Others are nothing more than temporary sand banks with grass and low bush. Towards the eastern side of the park the flood plain narrows and the escarpments close in, forming a hilly landscape, until at the spectacular Mpata Gorge the Zambezi River is forced through a narrow gap between steep orange cliffs.

Naturally, such a varied range of habitats supports a wide range of animals. The elephant population has been ravaged by poaching, but small herds are often seen. Other mammals include bushbuck, impala, zebra and buffalo. Predators include lion and cheetah, and over 400 species of bird have been recorded here.

The rich wildlife led to the park's creation in the 1950s; it was sponsored by a group of US and world conservation agencies and was originally called the International Game Park. It was renamed Lower Zambezi in the 1970s, but during the war in Rhodesia-Zimbabwe, the park became a heavily mined front-line battle zone. The conservationists pulled out and for most of the 1980s the park was ignored, except by poachers.

In 1989, Chiawa Camp became the first tourist lodge to open in the park itself. Access tracks and an airstrip were built, and other tasks included mine-clearing, anti-poaching patrols and some restocking of game. But the commitment paid off and by 1990 Lower Zambezi Park was back on the map. It became known as a wild, untouched, and rather specialist place, where the game were still timid and had to be stalked to be viewed.

In the early 1990s several canoe safari operators established seasonal camps along the banks of the Zambezi, and a few more lodges were built in the area bordering the park, but essentially it retained its raw and exclusive atmosphere. Unfortunately, poaching also continued: many elephant and buffalo retreated across the Zambezi to the comparative safety of Zimbabwe's Mana Pools National Park.

In 1996, Zambia's Ministry of Tourism leased 11 new lodge sites in the park. This will alter the nature of the park considerably: on the plus side, it will make it easier to visit, but a minus is that the park will lose some of its pristine atmosphere.

There are other pros and cons which echo current conservation debates all over Africa. The new developments have raised concerns among environmentalists who saw the whole region's visitor-carrying capacity as pretty near full from lodges and activities on the Zimbabwe side, even before the Zambia side opened up. Supporters of the developments point out that this area was badly affected by poaching, and that the presence of tourists and guides will by default 'patrol' the area. More importantly, the new developments will provide employment and income for local people, as will associated spin-offs such as curio stalls. Both sides agree that only if local people benefit from wildlife conservation can the survival of habitat and animals be ensured.

Whatever the arguments, the Lower Zambezi Park remains a special place and any visit there is likely to be memorable. ∎

ZAMBIA

is highly regarded, and has to be paid for: US$215 per person per night, full board in luxury tents with ensuite and running water. However, this also includes park fees, boat trips, fishing, game drives and walks.

From 1997, several new camps will be built – although most are likely to be on the costly side. Companies with concessions include Safari Par Excellence, Sobek and Royal Zambezi Lodge. There are also plans for at least one camp site, providing an option for self-contained travellers. Travel and tour agents in Lusaka will have details.

Just outside the park, in the game man-agement area west of Chongwe River, are several more options. These include *Royal Zambezi Lodge* (☎ Lusaka 223952; fax 223504/223747), a small luxury tented camp, with a restaurant overlooking the river and splendid aerial bar built around the branches of a huge tree. The international charge of US$230 per person covers all accommodation, game viewing trips by boat or by vehicle. Fishing and canoeing trips are also arranged. In the same area are *Kwalata Lodge* and *Kayila Lodge*: also bookable through agents in Lusaka or overseas.

Just outside the park's east boundary 25 km

upstream from Luangwa town, is *Kingfisher Camp*, run by the indestructible Alistair Gellatly. It is a quiet and very authentic place – comfortable with no unnecessary frills – below the steep escarpment wall overlooking the river. The cost is US$150 per person all inclusive (with transfers). The game-viewing is good (by foot or boat), as is the fishing, and you can also go by boat to the spectacular Mpata Gorge. An associated lodge will be opened in the park during 1997. For more details contact a tour agent in Lusaka.

Getting There & Away

Most of the lodges and camps (on the west side of the park) arrange transfers for guests, either to the airstrip at Jecki, or by road from Lusaka to Gwabi Lodge (see under Chirundu, earlier), and then by boat down the Zambezi into the park itself. Unless you're pushed for time, the latter option is highly recommended.

Another way to see the park is from a canoe. Several operators run canoe trips: they usually start at Gwabi Lodge, and stop for two or three nights at seasonal camps on the Zambezi or simply pitch tents and mosquito nets on the midstream islands. See Organised Tours in the Getting Around section of this chapter.

The park is not suitable for travellers without a car. Even if you manage to hitch *to* the park (there's no public transport), once you're there you need a vehicle to get around as entrance without one is not allowed.

Southern Zambia

This section covers the area between Livingstone and the town of Kafue (just south of Lusaka), where the highlights include Victoria Falls and Lake Kariba. The places are described roughly west to east and south to north.

VICTORIA FALLS

The Zambian side of Victoria Falls is sometimes forgotten, but it provides an entirely separate experience to its Zimbabwean counterpart. First of all, the views are different: you can sidle right up to the falling water, walk a steep track down to the base of the falls and follow spindly walkways perched over the abyss. The panoramas may not be as picture-postcard-perfect as those in Zimbabwe, but they allow closer observation of the mesmerising water, and the less manicured surroundings create a pristine atmosphere.

Mosi-oa-Tunya National Park

Mosi-oa-Tunya, Zambia's smallest national park, is comprised of two sections: the Victoria Falls area; and the game park, further west along the riverbank. Admission to the park is US$3.

Victoria Falls Area From the park entry gate, a network of paths leads through the thick vegetation to the various viewpoints. For a good view of the Zambezi Bridge and main river gorges, take the path alongside the customs fence. For close-up shots, nothing beats the Eastern Cataract or Knife Edge Point, reached by crossing a hair-raising (but perfectly safe) footbridge. If the water is low or the wind favourable, you'll be treated to a magnificent view of the falls, as well as the yawning abyss below the bridge. Otherwise, your vision will be obliterated by drenching spray. You can also descend to the Boiling Pot for a view of the river as it passes through a dynamic whirlpool.

Near the falls is a line of **curio stalls** with an excellent selection of crafts. Nearby is a small **museum**, built on an archaeological site, with some displays from the excavation.

Game Park The insignificant little Mosi-oa-Tunya Game Park, north of the Maramba River, once had a few indigenous rhino but they were all poached. In 1994, they were replaced by six white rhino from South Africa. These may well be among the most endangered creatures on earth, but to the credit of the park guards they've survived for at least two years now. A short guided walking safari in the park costs about US$0.50.

Organised Tours

To organise tours in the Victoria Falls area, there are tour desks at the Hotel InterContinental and Rainbow Lodge (see Places to Stay & Eat, following). They arrange evening booze cruises on the Zambezi for around US$40; non-guests are welcome. Quick tours of Mosi-oa-Tunya National Park cost US$20. If you're interested in white-water rafting, bungy jumping or microlight flights, see Safari Par Excellence (☎ 323349; fax 323542) at the Hotel InterContinental, or Sobek (☎ 321830; fax 321539) in Livingstone. Helicopter flights over the Falls and gorges are organised by Del-Air (☎ /fax 321850). More tour companies are listed in the following Livingstone section.

Places to Stay & Eat

The *Hotel InterContinental* (☎ 321121; fax 321128) offers single/double rooms for US$145/180. Rates are negotiable in the low season. *Rainbow Lodge* (☎ 322473) is less organised, with double rondavels for US$60. For meals, Rainbow Lodge has a standard restaurant, but if money is no object the InterContinental offers finer dining with theme nights: Chinese, Italian, western etc. Weekend buffets are fairly good value, costing around US$16 per person.

The rather barren *campground* is between the InterContinental and Rainbow Lodge and is administered by the latter. Although it's in a good location, your belongings should be locked up in the hotel baggage room when you're away from your tent. Camping costs US$5 per night; this includes the use of hotel facilities, since there are none at the campground, but watch for hippos grazing on the hotel lawns.

Your other option in the Falls area is *Taita Falcon Lodge* (☎ /fax 321850). Downstream from the Zambezi Bridge, it is perched right on the edge of the gorge with splendid views of the river (and white-water rafters) far below. Accommodation in bungalows built with local materials costs from

US$100 per person, including full board and transfers from Livingstone.

Day Trips to Zimbabwe

If you want to pop over to the Zimbabwe side of the Falls, it's straightforward but you still have to go through customs and immigration formalities at the Zambia and Zimbabwe border posts. You should get an early start because queues can be long, particularly in the late morning and early afternoon. Most people walk across (and get great views from the Zambezi Bridge), although there is a twice-daily train service too (ask at Livingstone station).

Getting There & Away

Important information about the road between Victoria Falls and Livingstone is given under Getting There & Away in the Livingstone section below.

LIVINGSTONE

The first European settlement in the Victoria Falls area was Old Drift, a 'wild west' trading post on the Zambian bank, established shortly after David Livingstone's reports about the falls began attracting traders to the area. At the turn of the century, the settlement shifted to its present site and was named after the great explorer.

The Zambezi Gorge was first bridged when the planned Cape-to-Cairo railway came through between 1902 and 1904, bringing the first influx of tourists. The town of Livingstone became the tourism hub for the Victoria Falls area, but in the 1970s (when Zambia started down the road to economic and political chaos) it was eclipsed by the town of Victoria Falls in neighbouring Zimbabwe.

Nowadays, things are changing again and Livingstone is once more a bastion of commerce and an up-and-coming escape from the tourist jungle on the other side of the falls.

Information

Tourist Office The friendly tourist office (☎ 321404) on Mosi-oa-Tunya Rd is fine for information on happenings in Livingstone

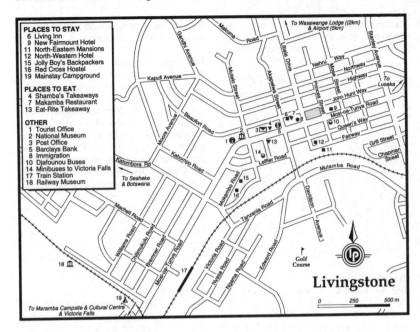

PLACES TO STAY
6 Living Inn
9 New Fairmount Hotel
11 North-Eastern Mansions
12 North-Western Hotel
15 Jolly Boy's Backpackers
16 Red Cross Hostel
19 Mainstay Campground

PLACES TO EAT
4 Shamba's Takeaways
7 Makamba Restaurant
13 Eat-Rite Takeaway

OTHER
1 Tourist Office
2 National Museum
3 Post Office
5 Barclays Bank
8 Immigration
10 Djafounou Buses
14 Minibuses to Victoria Falls
17 Train Station
18 Railway Museum

Livingstone

and can arrange hotel and rafting bookings. But their practice of charging tourists just for advertising leaflets and brochures really isn't on.

Money To exchange currency or travellers' cheques, there's a bank on Mosi-oa-Tunya Rd. Alternatively try the New Fairmount Hotel.

Things to See

The **Railway Museum** (☎ 321820) – technically known as the Zambezi Sawmills Locomotive Sheds National Monument – lies west of Mosi-oa-Tunya Rd. The yards fell into disuse in 1973, and now contain a motley collection of old engines and rolling stock. Inside are lots of rail-related antiques plus information and exhibits about railway history. The museum is open daily from 8.30 am to 4.30 pm and admission is US$5 but unless you're a railway buff, it isn't worth it. However, if you're genuinely interested and can't pay that much, it's often possible to work out some sort of discount.

The **National Museum** (☎ 321204), adjacent to the tourist office, has an interesting collection of archaeological and anthropological relics including a copy of a Neanderthal skull estimated to be over 100,000 years old. There are also examples of ritual artefacts and Tonga material crafts, an African village mock-up, a collection of David Livingstone items and a display of Africa maps dating back to 1690. Ask Mr Sitale to show you the back room where they keep an amazing – and rather horrifying – collection of witchcraft paraphernalia. Admission is a whopping (but eminently negotiable) US$5.

About five km south of Livingstone, towards Victoria Falls, is the **Maramba Cultural Centre**. On Saturday from 3 to 5 pm they stage traditional dance performances. Admission is a phenomenal US$0.03.

Organised Tours

Bwaato Adventures (☎ 324227; fax 321490), at the New Fairmount Hotel, offers breakfast or lunchtime booze cruises for US$25 per person and sundowner cruises for US$20. Game drives in the Mosi-oa-Tunya National Park cost US$28 per person (minimum four), including drinks, plus US$3 per person admission. Livingstone Safaris, run by Dave Lewis, operates three-hour game drives to Mosi-oa-Tunya National Park for US$15 per person. Dave is a qualified guide and particularly adept at locating the park's rhino. Book through the Mainstay campground or Jolly Boy's Backpackers (see Places to Stay, below for details of both). Makora Quest Tours (☎ 321679; fax 320732) runs day tours through scenic and historical attractions around Livingstone, including Old Drift, Mosi-oa-Tunya National Park, the museums, a local market and Victoria Falls. Other local tour companies are listed in the Victoria Falls section above.

For a longer adventure, the Botswana Bus (☎ 324278; fax 324229; PO Box 61170) run by Richard Sheppard, offers excellent inexpensive tours from Livingstone to Chobe National Park and the Okavango Delta in Botswana. The 10-day safari costs US$295, including transport, camping, meals and a guide.

Places to Stay

Livingstone has two campgrounds: the simple *Mainstay*, near the railway museum, has a bar and restaurant, and charges US$2 per person; and the better-appointed *Maramba*, off the Victoria Falls road, with bar and hot showers, costs US$5.

Livingstone's goal to attract tourists from the Zimbabwe side of the falls will be greatly assisted by the presence of *Jolly Boy's Backpackers* (☎ 324278; fax 324229), at 559 Mokambo Rd (sometimes called Mokambo Way), run by friendly Paul Quinn. Dorm beds cost US$6, camping US$2, and guests have access to the pool, sauna and cooking facilities. Breakfast and other meals are around US$3.50. You can also hire bikes

here – ideal for trips to the Falls (see the Getting There & Away section following) – at US$10 per day.

The welcoming *Red Cross Hostel* (☎ 322473), Mokambo Rd, has clean double rooms with washbasin and communal facilities for US$6.50.

The cleanest and most up-market hotel is the *New Fairmount* (☎ 320075; fax 321490), on Mosi-oa-Tunya Rd, which has self-contained rooms for US$30/35, but discounts are available in times of low occupancy. The New Fairmount also has a low-key casino, which operates evenings. The *North-Western Hotel* (☎ 320711), a deteriorating colonial structure on Fairway St, has double rooms for US$12.

The *Living Inn* (☎ 324203; fax 324205), one block off the main street at 95 John Hunt Way, has clean and acceptable rooms for US$13/22. The attached Dreamland Takeaway offers simple snacks.

Four km out of town along the airport road is *Wasawange Lodge* (☎ 324066; fax 324067), which offers a quiet alternative to in-town accommodation and a measure of basic luxury. Single/double lodges cost US$70/100.

Places to Eat

If you're self-catering the *Shoprite Chequers* supermarket has a good selection. Next door is *Eat-Rite Takeaways* which is okay for lunches, but the best choice is the *Makamba Restaurant*, a block back from the main street. Although attention focuses on the TV and music videos, the food and atmosphere are quite acceptable. Otherwise, you can resort to the several greasy takeaways along Mosi-oa-Tunya Rd.

For alcohol, try the *North-Western Hotel*, a local hang-out, or the *New Fairmount Hotel*, both of which have bars. The latter sometimes stages live music.

Getting There & Away

Between Livingstone and Victoria Falls is 11 km along the main road. Over the last few years, some people have been mugged walking here, so hiring a bike has become a popular option. However, we recently heard reports that even travellers on bikes have been attacked. There's a lot to be said for going in the group and cycling pretty fast. If this sounds too much like the Tour de France, you can search out one of the infrequent public buses (US$0.25), or get a few people together and go by taxi (US$3 to US$4 each way). Ask at Jolly Boy's Backpackers (see Places to Stay above) about the latest safety situation and public transport options.

For travel further afield, between Livingstone and Lusaka, a good value bus company is Djafounou, which stops at the North-Western Hotel. Details on trains between Livingstone and Lusaka are given in the Lusaka section. If you're hitching (to Lusaka, or into Namibia or Botswana), try the truck park near the train station.

Livingstone Island

Livingstone Island is the big chunk of rock that splits Victoria Falls into two. Thanks to Tongabezi Lodge, you can now enjoy a three-course champagne lunch here – at the 'world's most exclusive picnic spot'. Even if you're not staying at the lodge, you'll be welcome at the picnic (they do pick-ups from the Hotel Inter-Continental). The price of US$65 includes boat and car transfers (from either the Zambian or the Zimbabwean side), a three-course meal (including alcohol) and park fees. Book through Safari Par Excellence (☎ 323349) at the Inter-Continental.

If you don't mind a measure of adrenaline with your meal, you can organise your own Livingstone Island picnic. When water levels are very low – as in late winter – you can actually pick your way to Livingstone Island along stepping stones from the Zambia side. This newly popular hike makes quite a spectacle for viewers on the Zimbabwe side, but it's not for the dizzy or faint-hearted. ∎

THE ZAMBEZI RIVERFRONT

Upstream of Victoria Falls, the Zimbabwe bank of the Zambezi is protected by Zambezi National Park, but the Zambia shore is open to development, and promises to become one of the country's major tourist areas. Whether or not this is a good thing is open to debate,

but in a country desperate for tourism recognition and foreign exchange it's bound to have an impact.

Places to Stay & Eat

The finest place is *Tongabezi Lodge* (☎ 323235; fax 323224). The emphasis is on originality and luxury, and its central location makes it a favourite getaway spot for affluent Zambians, Zimbabweans and Namibians. Accommodation is either in imaginatively designed luxury tents or in river-view bungalows. For something really different, try the secluded open-air honeymoon suite, set atop a cliff with its own private garden, a sunken bathtub and a romantic four-poster bed. Rates start at US$160 per person for the tented camp and climb to US$200 for the bungalows.

Tongabezi also has a small associated camp, *Sindabezi*, on a tiny mid-river island just downstream, and a base on Livingstone Island, where they arrange overnight camping trips (normally at full moon to view the lunar rainbows over the falls) and exclusive picnics (see boxed text opposite on Livingstone Island).

Seven km east of Tongabezi is the family-owned *Thorntree Lodge* (☎ 320823; fax 320732), a tented camp on private land inside Mosi-oa-Tunya National Park. Each unit sits right on the riverbank and affords a front-row view of the Zambezi using this stretch of the Zambezi as a crossing-point. Rates are US$125 per person, including accommodation, three meals and drinks.

About 25 km upstream from Tongabezi is *Kubu Cabins* (☎ 324093; fax 324091; e-mail kubu@zamnet.zm), with thatched riverside cottages make a good base for bird-watching, walking, or visiting Victoria Falls. The charge is US$150 per person, including meals, bar and transfers. There's also a good shady *campsite* for US$10 per person. In the restaurant you can choose between African and European cuisine.

Kazungula

The friendly new backpackers' lodge *Jungle Junction* is on a lush island at Katombora

Rapids, 50 km upstream from Livingstone and eight km below Kazungula. Tented accommodation costs US$9, which includes the use of a kitchen, and transfers to/from Livingstone. There's a bar and small shop on the site. Owners Dave, Brett and Gremlin can organise village visits, sightseeing and fishing trips with locals in traditional canoes. Care is taken to ensure local people benefit directly from tourism. For information and bookings – ask at Jolly Boy's Backpackers in Livingstone (for more details see Places to Stay in Livingstone section).

Mwande

Mwande is a small village on the Zambezi about 145 km west of Livingstone. *Soka Fishing Camp* has self-catering rondavels for US$10 per person, camping for US$5. You have to book in advance – contact Gwembe Safaris (see under Choma, following) for details and directions.

CHOMA

Most visitors pass through the small town of Choma at high speed, desperate to get between Livingstone and Lusaka in a day. But Choma is worth a stopover, and worth considering as a centre for touring the south of Zambia.

The excellent little **Choma Museum & Crafts Centre** concentrates on the history and culture of the Tonga people (some of whom were relocated when the Kariba Dam was built). The building is a former school, dating from 1920s – one of the oldest preserved colonial buildings in Zambia. The craft shop has some good bargains. The museum is currently funded by Dutch aid money. This may dry up in a few years, and the museum will then be dependent on tourist support.

Places to Stay & Eat

Gwembe Safaris (☎ (032) 20169/20021; fax 20054), aka *Brooks Farm*, is signposted one km south of town, two km off the road. Pleasant chalets cost US$25/40, and there are self-catering facilities or meals provided with notice (breakfast US$5, dinner US$20).

Camping is US$5 per person; the site is grassy and shady with fire pits, a cooking and eating shelter, electric lights and plugs, plus clean toilets and showers. Meat, milk, eggs etc are available from the farm shop. Security is no problem: a sign on the gate says 'Beware of the Crocodiles'.

Getting There & Away

Regular buses to/from Lusaka cost US$6.50; to/from Livingstone is US$4.50; and to/from Sinazongwe is US$3. The thrice-weekly express train between Lusaka and Livingstone also stops here: fares to/from Lusaka are US$4.50/$4 in 1st/2nd class, slightly less to/from Livingstone.

Around Choma

About 40 km south of Choma, then 10 km off the main road, is *Wildlives Game Farm* which also has chalets and camping. To the west of Choma is Kkanga River Conservation Area, combining the game ranches of the Bruce-Miller, Green and Ross families, with camping and chalets at *Bruce-Miller's Farm*.

LAKE KARIBA

Most tourists who reach Lake Kariba visit the Zimbabwe side. The Zambia side of Kariba also has its attractions, although these are typically Zambian in nature: authentic, off the beaten track, and a bit rough around the edges.

Sinazongwe

This small town is the centre of Zambia's lake fishing industry. Places to stay include the *Crocodile Farm* campground (US$5) and *Lake View Chalets* (US$18/30). Both are run by the Brooks at Gwembe Safaris (for details see the earlier Choma Places to Stay & Eat section) and you need to go there first to make arrangements. Travellers without a car might be able to get a lift: trucks run between Choma and Sinazongwe a few times per week.

We've also heard reports of a new lodge to be opened here, connected with a new tented camp and game range on Chete Island. There are plans for an Arab-style dhow to transfer guests and a flying boat to link the island to Victoria Falls and Kariba. For details inquire at Grand Travel, Lusaka.

Chikanka Island

This privately owned island, about 10 km from Sinazongwe, has simple *chalets* for US$25/40 and a *campground* (US$5). Fishing boats can be hired, and there are plans to stock the island with plains game and turn it into a reserve. The show is run by the Brooks clan (for details see the earlier Choma Places to Stay & Eat section). Fishing boat transfers between Sinazongwe and Chikanka cost US$12. Travellers with wheels can safely park in Sinazongwe, and those without can usually link up with Gwembe Safaris vehicles. You might even be able to arrange a boat ride to Chipepo, and continue nautically towards Siavonga.

Chipepo

This small fishing village is linked by local ferry to Siavonga (see the following section) but there is no official place to stay. Minibuses run a few times per day to/from Monze, via Chisekesi.

SIAVONGA

Siavonga is the nearest most Zambians get to the seaside. On the opposite shore, just over the Kariba Dam, is Zimbabwe and the sprawling busy town of Kariba with a fancy yacht marina, hotels, restaurants and fishing-tackle shops. In comparison, Siavonga is quiet and low-key, and therefore preferred by some travellers, especially those who want to be in Africa rather than a place which desperately pretends to be anything but.

Places to Stay & Eat

East of town is the highly recommended *Eagle's Rest*, with self-catering chalets for US$15 per person. Each has bedding, shower, fridge and cooker. Bring your own food and cooking gear (if you're travelling light the friendly owner can loan you a sauce-pan or two). You can book in advance through Wilderness Trails or Africa Tour Designers in Lusaka. Camping costs US$6.

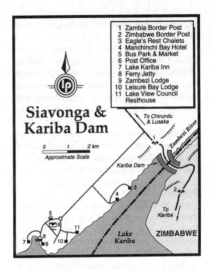

1 Zambia Border Post
2 Zimbabwe Border Post
3 Eagle's Rest Chalets
4 Manchinchi Bay Hotel
5 Bus Park & Market
6 Post Office
7 Lake Kariba Inn
8 Ferry Jetty
9 Zambezi Lodge
10 Leisure Bay Lodge
11 Lake View Council
   Resthouse

Siavonga & Kariba Dam

Nearby is the smart *Manchinchi Bay Hotel* (☎ 511599), where singles/doubles with air-con, private balconies and TV cost US$53/88 with breakfast, although this place is due to be taken over by an international hotel group so big changes, and possibly price rises, are expected.

In Siavonga town, you have several more choices. *Leisure Bay Lodge* has a pebbly beach on the lake shore and straightforward self-contained chalets for US$28/38. If you arrive after 6 pm, you get a 50% reduction. A little further down is *Lake View Council Resthouse* (☎ 511279), with basic but clean rooms at US$22 (one to four people). The Kariba North Bank bus (see under Getting There & Away, following) starts and ends its run to/from Lusaka here. There are also meals for around US$4, a bar which can get lively, and – naturally – a splendid view of the lake from the garden, where tents can be pitched for a negotiable fee. The resthouse is due for renovation, so expect improvements and possibly a price rise in future.

Two mid-range places are *Zambezi Lodge* (☎ 511148 or Lusaka 227935), with simple bungalows and splendid views for US$40/60; and *Lake Kariba Inn*, which has spacious rooms for US$57/90 full board, plus pool, sauna, gym and boats.

Another option for self-contained drivers is *Sandy Beach Camping*, about 14 km west of the road between Siavonga and Chirundu. Look for the sign about 20 km north of Siavonga, near a group of local shops called Kariba Stores.

Getting There & Away
Bus The Kariba North Bank bus leaves Lusaka between 10 am and noon daily and arrives at Siavonga four hours later. It 'sleeps' at the Council Resthouse, then leaves Siavonga at 5 am, arriving Lusaka around 9 am. The fare is US$2.50. Throughout the day, minibuses (US$3.50) also run on this route, sometimes via Chirundu (US$0.50). From Siavonga they leave from the market.

Boat A local ferry runs twice weekly between Siavonga and Chipepo (south of Monze), via Kalalezi, Kole and Kotakota. Either direction, the boat leaves at 6 am and arrives at 5 pm. A seat for the whole trip costs US$6.50. In Siavonga the jetty and Lake Kariba Waterways office are near Zambezi Lodge.

LOCHINVAR NATIONAL PARK
This small park lies to the north of Monze and includes areas of grassland and low wooded hills, part of a floodplain called the Kafue Flats, and a seasonally flooded area called Chunga Lagoon. Like many parks in Zambia, Lochinvar (and its lodge) was virtually abandoned for 20 years. There are now plans to rehabilitate the area and the accommodation, so expect changes by the time you arrive.

Mammals here include buffalo, wildebeest, hippo, zebra and kudu, although numbers have been depleted by poaching. You can also see large herds of Kafue lechwe (a subspecies of this rare aquatic antelope, related to the red lechwe found most notably in Botswana's Okavango Delta). For bird-watchers, Lochinvar is a draw – over 400 species have been recorded here (including wattled crane). Walking in the park is permitted.

Getting There & Away
If you're driving, from just north of Monze take the dirt road towards Namwala. After 25 km, turn right at a junction and continue for about another 25 km to reach the lodge. For those without wheels, minibuses go from Monze to Namwala, but you'd have to walk or chance hitching from the junction. Three km before the lodge, a left turn leads to a campsite. Chunga Lagoon (another campsite may be established here) is 15 km from the lodge. In the dry season, the lodge (and possibly Chunga Lagoon) can be reached without 4WD.

Western Zambia

This section covers most of Zambia's Western Province, which includes Barotseland, plus various other towns and points of interest along the upper Zambezi River. This

History of Barotseland

For many Zambians, Western Province *is* Barotseland – the traditional kingdom of the Lozi people. The Lozi people are thought to have arrived in the area in the 17th century, having migrated from central Zaïre. They settled the fertile floodplains of the upper Zambezi, and over the next century expanded and consolidated the kingdom, establishing a stable and well organised system of administration, ruled by their king *(Litunga)*.

The 1880s brought the European powers' 'Scramble for Africa'. The Portuguese wanted to control the upper Zambezi region to link their colonies of Angola and Mozambique, but the British South Africa Company had similar designs on the mineral rights in the area. The Litunga, Lewanika, was threatened by neighbouring Matabele, so he requested British protection. In 1900 Barotseland was officially established as a British Protectorate, and was later incorporated into the colony of Northern Rhodesia, despite Lozi hopes that they might regain some autonomy.

When Zambia became independent, this position did not change, fuelling ongoing Lozi bitterness towards the central government. Self-rule for Barotseland continues to be high on the political agenda. ■

area features increasingly on travellers' itineraries, as an alternative way to Lusaka from the south, or as a loop from Victoria Falls. Places are described from south to north and from west to east.

SESHEKE

The former capital of Barotseland, Sesheke is on the east bank of the Zambezi River, about 200 km upstream from Livingstone. Across the river is the Namibian town of Katima Mulilo (for details see the earlier Getting There & Away section).

Places to Stay & Eat

For a place to stay, the *Council Resthouse*, almost opposite the hospital, has basic rooms with two beds for US$4. Smarter ensuite rooms cost US$10. Camping is possible – rates are negotiable. The friendly staff will prepare meals for around US$2. The garden overlooks the Zambezi River, and the bar sells cold beers to accompany the wonderful views at sunset.

There's a few cheap local restaurants around the market. The bar about 50m back from where the buses stop has a pleasant atmosphere and food.

West Bank On the west bank of the river, near the ferry, the dingy *Government Rest House* is US$1.50. Next door is a new place, owned by a local businessman (who also owns the bus that runs to Senanga and

Mongu) charging between US$6 and US$10. The shacks near the bus park sell bread rolls, tins of fish and other basics. There's also a bar nearby.

Getting There & Away

For details on routes east towards Livingstone or south into Namibia see Getting There & Away earlier in this chapter. If you're staying in Zambia, you can head northward up the west bank of the Zambezi to Senanga and Mongu. There is a bus to Mongu about three times per week, charging US$15 (US$10 to Senanga).

THE NGONYE FALLS

If it wasn't for Victoria Falls about 300 km downstream, the impressive Ngonye Falls (also called Sioma Falls) would be a major attraction. On most days you'll probably have the whole place to yourself.

The falls are less than one km east of the main dirt road between Sesheke and Senanga. For drivers, access is easy. Without your own wheels, ask to be dropped (look for the Wildlife Department sign), or consider staying at *Maziba Bay Lodge*, seven km south of the falls. This place is run by two South African brothers, with help from a team of friendly (and musical) Zambians and moral support from an orphaned baby elephant. Accommodation in luxurious chalets overlooking the river costs US$150 per person (international rates), which includes all meals, trips to the falls, plus other activities such as fishing, walking, boat trips, and white-water rafting (OK, not up to Victoria Falls level, but exhilarating enough and you are the only boat on the river). Advance bookings are normally required, but if you're passing anyway you could try your luck. Camping is also available for US$10 (large groups not allowed). If you don't have wheels, transfers from Katima Mulilo cost US$30. They also run game drives to nearby **Sioma Ngwezi National Park** (some at night to see elephants round a water hole in moonlight) and have *Royal Barotse Safari Camp* in **Liuwa Plain National Park**, further to the north. (Reservations to Safarique, South Africa ☎ (012) 329 6124, fax (012) 329 6123.)

At least three other lodges (*Zambolozi, Sakazima* and *Mutemwa)* are planned or under construction in this area. If you're heading south, you may be able to get information in Lusaka. If you're heading north (from Namibia) you can get details on Maziba Bay or any other place in Western Zambia and the Caprivi Strip from Mrs Katie Sharpe at the Katima Mulilo Tourist Information Service (☎ /fax Namibia (0677) 3453).

SENANGA
If you're coming from Lusaka, Senanga has an 'end of the line' feel about it. The tar runs out here, and the dusty dirt road that continues southward towards Namibia and Zimbabwe is quiet and rarely travelled by tourists. If you've come from the south this is the first town of any size since leaving Katima Mulilo or Sesheke.

Whichever way you come, Senanga is a pleasant town, with a busy market, several shops, local bars, a petrol station, hospital, police station – even a prison. All the trapping of civilisation you could wish for.

Places to Stay & Eat
Senanga Safaris is a small hotel with comfortable double ensuite rondavels for US$16 including breakfast (camping rates negotiable). There are splendid views over the Zambezi and the plains beyond – especially

at sunset. The bar has cold beer and the restaurant serves meals for about US$4.

Nearby, *Mwanambinyi Council Resthouse* has simple rooms for US$6, breakfast US$2 and meals US$2.50. The *Government Rest House*, on the south side of town, has dingy rooms for US$1.50, but no food or camping.

Cheap places to eat include the recommended *Rita's Restaurant.*

Getting There & Away
Buses run several times per day to/from Mongu, costing around US$2.50. For details on the bus to the Namibia border see the Sesheke section above. Hitching south on trucks – paying about the same as the bus – is usually possible.

MONGU
Mongu is the largest town in Barotseland, and the capital of Western Province. It lies on an area of high ground overlooking the flat, and seemingly endless, Liuwa Plain. The town has a harbour, linked to a tributary of the Zambezi by an eight km canal. The town itself straggles over several km, but has a pleasant lively feel, so a walk along the main street is always interesting.

Places to Stay
Shoestringers' choice includes *Winters Resthouse & Pleasure Resort* where basic rooms cost US$6 for one or two people. The bar gets lively in the evenings, so get a room at the far end of the yard. Nearby is *Muzanga-Bantu Guesthouse*, with dingy rooms at US$4. Next door *Kombahari Steak House & Bar* has good local meals from US$1.

Top of the range is the *Ngulu Hotel*, about two km south of the junction of the main street and the Lusaka road. Reasonable self-contained rooms (for one or two people), with hot water, fan, TV and breakfast cost US$25, which is a bit steep for what you get, although the staff are friendly. Evening meals are around US$5, and there's a bar.

Rooms at the *Lyamba Hotel*, near the harbour, are almost as good as the Ngulu's but cost US$16 including breakfast. Evening meals cost from US$4. This hotel has a wonderful view of the plain – but unfortunately you have to sit in the carpark to get its full beauty.

Getting There & Away

Buses to Lusaka (three or four daily) cost US$8.50; Senanga (twice daily) is US$1.50.

If you're heading for Kalabo, 'long-boats' with outboard motors, carrying about 25 people, go daily from the harbour, charging US$8.50 per person for the six hour trip. When the water is high, the more comfortable Post Boat (a ferry run by the Zambian Posts & Telecommunications Corporation) also does this route.

Around Mongu

Limulunga The paramount chief of the Lozi people, the *Litunga*, has two palaces. For most of the year he lives at Lealui, on the Liuwa Plain, about 15 km north-west of Mongu. When the Zambezi waters rise, the plain floods, so the Litunga moves with his court to the higher ground of Limulunga, about 20 km north of Mongu. The ceremony surrounding the Litunga's move is called the *kuomboka* (see the boxed text for more information).

At Limulunga you can see the Litunga's palace from the outside (although no photos are allowed), but of more interest is the museum, containing exhibits about the Lozi, the Litunga and the kuomboka ceremony, including a fabulous model landscape some 20m long, with hundreds of clay figures portraying different aspects of Lozi life, which took the artist, Rainford Sililo, over a year to make.

The *Museum Rest House* has straightforward rooms for US$5 per person. No meals are available, but there is a kitchen and Limulunga village has a bar and some stores where you can buy food.

Minibuses run between Mongu and Limulunga throughout the day for US$0.50 each way.

Lealui The Litunga's low-water palace is at Lealui. It takes an effort to reach, but the journey by boat (along a canal from Mongu to a branch of the Zambezi, then upstream to Lealui) is very interesting. You go through the flat grassland of the plains, passing local people on dug-outs and other boats. The birdlife is amazing. Avoid visiting at weekends; the Litunga's *kotu* (court) is closed and you need permission from his *indunas* (advisors) to get a close look at the palace, or take

---

The Kuomboka Ceremony

Kuomboka literally means 'to get out of water onto dry ground', and celebrates the move of the *Litunga* (Lozi king) from his dry season palace to his wet season palace.

In years with good rains the Zambezi plain begins to flood in about December, and turns into an enormous lake by late March. Lealui is an area of raised ground in the floodplain which was established as the Lozi capital by Lewanika, grandfather to the current Litunga. In 1933, a winter palace was built by Yeta III on the edge of the plain, on permanently dry ground at Limulunga. Although the kuomboka was already a long-standing tradition, it was Yeta III who first made it a major ceremony.

Central to the elaborate ceremony is the royal barge called the *Nalikwanda* which carries the Litunga. This is a huge wooden canoe, painted with black and white stripes. It is considered a great honour to be one of the hundred or so paddlers on the Nalikwanda. Each paddler wears a head-dress of a scarlet beret with a piece of attached lion's mane, and a knee length skirt of animal skins.

Drums also play a leading role in the ceremony. The most important are the three royal war drums, each over a metre wide and said to be at least 170 years old. They are named Kanaona, Munanga and Mundili.

The journey takes some six hours, and follows a very tortuous course through the floodplains, the drums playing continuously. The Litunga begins the day in traditional dress, but during the journey changes into the full uniform of a British admiral, complete with all regalia and ostrich-plumed hat. This tradition started when King Lewanika was presented with the same uniform in 1902 by the British King Edward VII, in recognition of treaties signed between the Lozi and Queen Victoria.

The kuomboka does not happen every year. In 1994, 1995 and 1996 the floods were not extensive enough to require the Litunga to leave Lealui, or to allow the passage of Nalikwanda. ■

photos. Public 'long-boats' go between Mongu and Lealui once or twice per day: a place costs US$1.50 one way. There's nowhere to stay on the island. Alternatively, if you're in a small group, you can charter a boat at the harbour. A return trip by long boat with powerful outboard is US$70, and by a smaller boat with smaller engine about US$30. All prices are negotiable.

KAFUE NATIONAL PARK

Kafue National Park, about 200 km west of Lusaka, covers more than 22,000 sq km. It's the largest park in Zambia, and one of the largest in the world. Vegetation types within the park range from riverine forest along the Kafue River and its main tributaries (the Lunga and Lufupa), and around Lake Itezhi-Tezhi, through areas of open mixed woodland, to vast grassland plains on its western and northern edges – classic wildlife country. Beyond the northern plains stretch the seasonally flooded Busanga swamps.

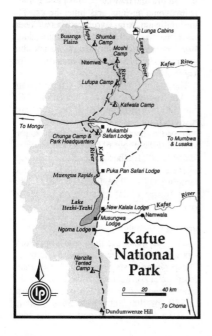

Mammals occurring here include lion, leopard, elephant and buffalo, plus hyena, crocodile and hippo. Antelope species include impala, roan, kudu, sable and red lechwe, plus sitatunga in the swamps. Birdlife is also prolific, with over 400 species recorded.

For details on entrance fees see National Parks in the Facts about the Country section.

Places to Stay

As with all the parks in Zambia, many new lodges and camps are under construction in and around Kafue National Park, and old state-owned hotels and camps will be privatised and renovated by 1997 or 1998. The park itself is also due to be developed under a new management plan, so expect some changes (even to the road layout) by the time you arrive.

Except for camp sites and chalets, it's usually necessary to book accommodation in advance, either direct to the lodge or through an agent in Lusaka or overseas. Many visitors to Kafue come as part of a tour organised by one of the lodge operators or travel agents listed in the Lusaka section.

Chunga Camp (also called Chunga Safari Village), at the park HQ, has basic rondavels overlooking the river for US$12 and camping for US$5. Kitchen staff will prepare any food you bring if required. The warden can arrange for a scout if you want to walk in the bush from the camp. On the opposite side of the river (ie just outside the park) is *Njovo Lodge* with ensuite thatched cottages, due for completion in 1997.

Also on the north-east bank is *Mukambi Safari Lodge* (☎ Lusaka 228185, fax 228184), very easy to reach from the main road, where stylish and well-designed self-contained cottages cost US$70 per person. Camping is US$10. Downstream, is the remote and exclusive *Puku Pan Safari Lodge* (☎ /fax Lusaka 260134). Near Lake Itezhi-Tezhi is the smart *New Kalala Lodge*, and *Musungwa Lodge* which also allows camping. In the far south is the luxurious *Nanzila Tented Camp* (run by Chundukwa

Trails, Livingstone). The old state-run Ngoma Lodge is closed but due for renovation.

In the north sector are three camps run by Busanga Travel and Tours (Lusaka ☎ 220897/221694; fax 274253): *Lufupa*, US$60 per person full-board including park fees, or camping for US$15; *Kafwala*, self-catering with basic huts for US$22 per person, including use of the fully serviced kitchen; and *Shumba*, more remote, overlooking the northern plains, US$60 full-board. At Lufupa game drives (day or night) cost US$15. At Shumba, the cost is US$20. Transfers to these camps from Lusaka can also be arranged. Sometimes transport for groups is already arranged and additional passengers can join for a reasonable charge. For more details visit the Busanga Trails office in Lusaka (see that section for details).

Further north and higher up the luxury scale is *Lunga Cabins* (run by African Experience, ☎ South Africa (011) 4622554; fax 4622613), or book through any good agent in Lusaka or overseas), with rates around US$250 per person per night. Also available are trips to their remote bush camp on the Busanga Plains and canoe safaris.

Getting There & Away

Kafue is huge and most park tracks are in bad condition, so the smarter lodges all have private airstrips and their guests fly in. As advance reservations are essential at these places, transfer information is provided when you book. If you're driving, the main road into Kafue National Park is from Lusaka, via Mumbwa. At the time of writing this was one of the worst roads in Zambia – vicious axle-crunching potholed tar – but it's due to be upgraded in 1997 or 1998. Coming from Lusaka, about 60 km beyond Mumbwa, another bad tar road leads south towards Kalala and Musungwa lodges. If you continue west on the main road, about 10 km before the Kafue Bridge is the turn-off to Mukambi Lodge (signposted). On the west side of the bridge, the main track into the northern sector turns off right. There is a

small guard post here where you have to pay park fees, unless you have a booking with a lodge where this is included. Opposite, the dry season track leads towards Chunga park HQ (17 km from the main road). About six km further west, is the all-weather road to Chunga (21 km from the main road).

Northern Zambia

This briefly covers a selection of places not described in the southern, eastern and western sections of this chapter. If you're heading this way, the following pointers may be useful. Places are described roughly south to north.

KAPIRI MPOSHI

Kapiri Mposhi is a busy junction town at the southern end of the TAZARA railway to/from Dar es Salaam (Tanzania), and is also on the line between Lusaka and Kitwe. Thieves and pickpockets love the crowds and confusion, so take great care here. Cheap places to stay include the bad-value *Unity Motel*. Better is the *Amity Motel*, with double rooms for US$15 including breakfast. The *Kapiri Motel* is more expensive.

The station for the TAZARA train is about 1.5 km from the centre of town and Lusaka line station. For more details on trains and buses to/from Lusaka, see that section.

If you're driving north-east from Kapiri Mposhi, after about 65km (30 km south of Mkushi) look for the signposts to *Forest Inn*, where ensuite chalets cost US$25/35 and camping US$5. The friendly owner is a good source of information on places to visit in the surrounding area.

NDOLA

Ndola – capital of the industrial Copperbelt – is a large city, rarely visited by tourists. Cheap places to stay are limited, and most hotels cater for business travellers. Try the *New Ambassador*, with doubles from US$40, or the fancy *New Savoy*, about US$80 a double. The airport is on the edge of town, and there are daily flights to/from Lusaka. For more details on transport to Lusaka see that section.

KITWE

This city is the centre of Zambia's mining business. It seems even busier than Ndola, although the centre and immediate suburbs are very compact. Shoestring travellers will find more options here than Ndola. Cheap place to stay include the *YMCA* on Independence Ave, with basic singles/doubles for US$2/3. The management is friendly. Part of the building is a brothel, but the action is fairly low-key. Up the scale from here is the *Hotel Edinburgh* with budget rooms for US$20/30 and smarter rooms for US$30/40, and the *Nkana Hotel* – around US$80 a double. For cheap eats, try the *Sweet Corner* in the centre. There are several smarter restaurants in the vicinity.

KASANKA NATIONAL PARK

Kasanka is Zambia's only privately managed national park; revenue goes to conservation and local community projects. There's an excellent range of habitats, birds and mammals, and a visit here is highly recommended. There's a comfortable lodge, charging US$140 all inclusive, plus self-catering and camp sites for US$15. The park is only accessible if you've got a vehicle or by organised tour. For details on the park, or lodge reservations, contact Grand Travel or Bushwackers Travel in Lusaka (see the Lusaka section for details).

LAKE BANGWEULU

This large shallow lake, and its associated swamps on the southern side, make up a fascinating and very rarely visited wildlife area. The luxurious *Shoebill Camp* is reported to be a spectacular place to stay, while *Nsobe Camp* offers budget self-catering for US$30 and camping for US$5. Details in Lusaka are available from the agents mentioned above. Once again, this area is restricted to fly-in visitors or drivers. Access is via the road which passes near the **David Livingstone Memorial** – marking the spot where the explorer died in 1873 (see the earlier History section for more details).

NORTH LUANGWA NATIONAL PARK

This park is large, wild, remote and spectacular, with a set-up for visitors very different to its southern namesake. There are just a few top-end camps, and access is pretty much limited to exclusive organised safaris. The famous conservationists Delia and Mark Owens (see the earlier Books section) have a base here. Tour operators covering North Luangwa are listed in the Lusaka section.

SHIWA NGANDU

Just off the main road, about 90 km north of Mpika, the incongruous mansion at Shiwa Ngandu, and the surrounding estate, was built in the 1920s by a paternalistic British aristocrat. About 20 km further west is **Kapishya Hot Springs**, where there are chalets (US$30 per person) and a camp site (US$5). Make arrangements at Shiwa Ngandu, or in advance at Grand Travel in Lusaka.

KASAMA

You might find yourself overnighting here between Lusaka and Mpulungu, especially if you're switching from the TAZARA train to local bus. Places to stay include the straightforward *Kasama Hotel*, which has doubles for US$6 and a simple restaurant. A bit further out of town (about 1.5 km from the TAZARA train station which is itself two km south of the town centre) the *Kapongolo Resthouse* has self-contained double rooms with fans and hot water for US$10.

MBALA

Mbala is 40 km from Mpulungu (the Lake Tanganyika ferry port), and you may overnight here waiting for transport connections. Cheap places to stay include the *government resthouse* and another, privately run, *resthouse* opposite the bus station. More expensive is the old colonial *Arms Hotel* and the better-value *Grasshopper Inn*.

Outside Mbala there's the *Outward Bound School* in a great spot overlooking the lake, where you can camp or possibly rent a room. Go 10 km down the road to Mpulungu, where there's a turn-off. From there it's a six km walk if you can't get a lift.

About three km from town is the **Moto Moto Museum**, a fascinating collection of artifacts relating largely to the Bemba tribe put together by a missionary who was based here for 40 years.

About 40 km to the north-west of Mbala, right on the border between Zambia and Tanzania is **Kalambo Falls**, the second highest in Africa, with a sheer drop of over 200m (double Victoria Falls). To get here is difficult without a vehicle, but we've heard from travellers who walked there and back in three or four days and reckoned it was well worth the hike. If you're thinking of doing this, consider hiring a local guide (to make necessary introductions to the chief of villages you'll pass through) and reporting briefly to the police in town, just so they don't think you're trying to leave the country illegally. (Another way of reaching the falls is by boat from Mpulungu; this involves a 20 km boat ride followed by several hours of hiking. A two-day trip makes it less of a rush. You may need a guide and police clearance this way too.)

MPULUNGU

Mpulungu is the Zambian terminal for the Lake Tanganyika ferries serving ports in Tanzania and Burundi (for more details, see the Zambia Getting There & Away section). It's a busy crossroads between East, Central and Southern Africa with a lively atmosphere. It's also very hot.

Places to stay include a couple of local *resthouses*, but highly recommended is *Nkupi Lodge*, on the east side of town, which is run by Kathy and Denish Budhia and caters especially for backpackers. You can camp (US$2) or stay in basic rondavels (not rainproof) for US$5. Further away from the town are two other lodges which are ideal places to base yourself for a few days of rest and recreation. One is for backpackers, the other a more up-market affair. Both lodges are best reached by boat – easy to hire in the

port area. Nkupi Lodge will give you the details.

If you miss the twice-weekly bus from Mpulungu to Lusaka (it's rumoured to tie in with the ferry, but don't bank on it), frequent pick-ups go between Mpulungu and Mbala, from where onward local buses run to Kasama (on the TAZARA railway) or all the way to Lusaka.

> ### Lake Tanganyika
> Sitting tightly in the western branch of the Great Rift Valley, Lake Tanganyika is the world's longest lake. It stretches almost 700 km from north to south and is the deepest in Africa (and the second deepest in the world) at more than 1.5 km. It measures over 33,000 sq km, with a total shoreline of 3000 km. Only 7% of its area and about 250 km of shoreline is Zambian territory. ■

SUMBU NATIONAL PARK

This remote park lies on the southern shore of Lake Tanganyika, west of Mpulungu. Like many other parks in Zambia, Sumbu (also spelt Nsumbu) was virtually abandoned in the 1980s and poaching virtually wiped out game stocks. In recent years, three lodges have been reopened, and conditions in the park have been improved, although the situation remains unclear. Make inquiries at agents in Lusaka or at Nkupi Lodge in Mpulungu.

NAKONDE

This small town on the southern (Zambian) side of the border between Zambia and Tanzania seems to be full of hustlers and is not an especially pleasant place, but you might find yourself changing transport here. Accommodation can be hard to find the night before and the day after the TAZARA train passes through, but your best choice is the *Kalinda Resthouse*, off the main road about 100m from the border. The *government resthouse*, about 500m from the border on the main road, is reported to be even less appealing.

Glossary

Although English is widely spoken in Malawi and Zambia, native speakers from the British Isles, Australasia and North America will notice many words which have developed different meanings locally. There are also many unusual terms which have been borrowed from Afrikaans, Portuguese and indigenous languages. This Glossary includes many of these particular 'Afro-English' words, as well as other general terms and abbreviations which may not be understood.

In African English, repetition for emphasis is common: something that burnt you would be 'hot hot'; fields after the rains are 'green green'; a crowded minibus with no more room is 'full full', and so on.

Specifically Portuguese words are listed in the Mozambique chapter.

af – derogatory reference to a black person, as bad as 'nigger' or 'abo'

AFORD – Alliance for Democracy, a Malawian political party strongest in the north of the country

ANC – African National Congress

animist – various definitions, but the most useful seems to be: 'beliefs based on the existence of the human soul, and on spirits that inhabit or are represented by natural objects and phenomena, which have the power to influence human life for good or ill'

apartheid – 'separate development of the races'; a political system in which peoples are segregated according to ethnic background

baas – boss; subservient address reserved mainly for white males

bakkie – (pronounced 'bukkie') utility or pick-up truck

BCAP – British Central Africa Protectorate, the colonial-era name for Malawi prior to the adoption of the name Nyasaland

bhundu – the bush, the wilderness

bilharzia – water-borne disease caused by minute worms which are passed on by fresh-water snails

biltong – dried and salted meat that can be made from just about anything from antelope or ostrich to mutton or beef

boerewors – spicy Afrikaner sausage of varying consistency

boma – in Zambia, Malawi and some other countries, this is a local word for 'town', or more specifically town centre, or area containing government buildings. In East Africa the same word also means fortified stockade. It is not an indigenous African word, and may be derived from the early colonial term BOMA (British Overseas Military Administration) which was applied to any government building, such as offices or forts.

braai – barbecue

BSAC – British South Africa Company; led by Cecil Rhodes this company was hugely influential in shaping Southern Africa in colonial times

buck or **bok** – any kind of antelope, also part of many species' name: reedbuck, bushbuck, springbok etc

chamba – Malawian term for grass, marijuana

chapa-cem – Mozambican term for trucks converted to carry passengers; often shortened to chapa

chibuku – local mass-produced beer, stored in tanks and served in buckets, or available in takeaway cartons (mostly in Zimbabwe and Malawi). It's good for a quick burst of euphoria and a debilitating 'babalass' (hangover).

chiperone – damp misty weather which affects southern Malawi

chitenjas – sheets of brightly coloured cloth worn by Malawian women, readily available in markets

dagga – (pronounced dakha) South African term for grass, marijuana

dambo – area of grass, reeds or swamp alongside a river course

Difaqane – (also called Mfecane) forced migration by several Southern African tribes in the face of Zulu aggression in the early 19th century; translates as 'the scattering of the tribes'. Mfecane, a Zulu word, means 'the crushing'.

donkey boiler – watertank positioned over a fire and used to heat water

drift – river ford

euphorbia – several species of cactus-like succulents which are endemic in Southern Africa

Frelimo – Frente pela Liberacão de Moçambique or Mozambique Liberation Front. After 13 years of war against the colonial Portuguese, Frelimo took power in 1975 and has held it since, ditching Marxism in 1990.

game – formerly used for any animal hunted, now means larger mammals

inselbergs – isolated rocky hills common to Southern Africa; literally means 'island mountains'

Izzit? – rhetorical question which most closely translates as 'Really?' and is used without regard to gender, person, or number of the subject. Therefore, it could mean 'Is it?', 'Are you?', 'Is he?', 'Are they?', 'Is she?', 'Are we?' etc. Also 'How izzit?', for 'How are things?', 'How's it going?' etc. Originates in South Africa but used by whites all over Southern Africa.

just now – reference to some time in the future but intended to imply a certain degree of imminence – it could be half an hour from now or two days from now, ie 'at the appropriate time'

kaffir – derogatory reference to a black person

kapenta – *Limnothrissa mioda*, an anchovy-like fish caught in Lake Kariba

kloof – ravine or small valley

kopje – pronounced, and sometimes spelt, 'koppie', an isolated hill or rocky outcrop which translates from Afrikaans as 'little head'

kraal – Afrikaans version of the Portuguese 'curral'; an enclosure for livestock or hut village, especially one surrounded by a stockade

kwacha – currency of Malawi and Zambia

larney – posh, smart, high quality (originally South African, used by impressionable whites all over Southern Africa)

lekker – (pronounced 'lakker'), very good, enjoyable or tasty

LMS – London Missionary Society

location – another word for township, more usually in rural areas

make a plan – 'sort it out'; this can refer to anything from working through a complicated procedure to circumventing bureaucracy

Malawi shandy – nonalcoholic drink made from ginger beer, Angostura bitters, orange or lemon slices, soda and ice

marimba – African xylophone, made from strips of resonant wood with various-sized gourds for sound boxes

matola – vehicle, usually a pick-up van, acting as an unofficial public transport service

mazungu – white person

mbira – thumb piano; it consists of 22 to 24 narrow iron keys mounted in rows on a wooden sound board

MCP – Malawi Congress Party; led by Dr Hastings Banda this party ruled Malawi as a one-party state from 1964 until 1994

meticais – currency of Mozambique

miombo – dry open woodland, also called brachystegia woodland

não faz mal – Portuguese expression, literally 'it doesn't make bad', ie 'no problem'

now now – not the present moment, but pretty soon after it – sometime sooner than *just now*

nsima – maize porridge; black African

staple (called *ugali* in East Africa and *mealie meal* in Southern Africa)

pan – dry flat area, often seasonal lake-bed
peg – mile post
pint – small bottle of beer or can of oil (or similar) usually around 300 to 375 ml (and not necessarily equivalent to a British or US pint)
pronking – leaping, as done by several species of antelope, apparently for sheer fun

relish – sauce of meat, vegetables, beans, etc eaten with *nsima*
Renamo – *Resistência Nacional de Moçambique* or MNR, Mozambique National Resistance. Anti-Frelimo rebels once supported by the apartheid-era regime of South Africa, now a political party.
rondavel – round, African-style hut

shebeen – an illegal township drinking establishment
sjambok – whip
slasher – hand tool with a curved blade used to cut grass or crops, hence 'to slash' means 'to cut grass'
squaredavel – see *rondavel* and work out the rest

tackies – trainers, tennis shoes, gym shoes
tambala – minor Malawian unit of currency: 100t equals 1MK (*kwacha*)
township – high-density black residential area outside a central city or town

UDF – United Democratic Front, Malawian political party that won the 1994 elections, led by Bakili Muluzi

Van der Merwe – archetypal Boer country bumpkin who is the butt of jokes throughout Southern Africa
veld – open grassland (pronounced 'felt') – variations: lowveld, highveld, bushveld, strandveld
veldskoens – comfortable shoes made of soft leather (also called 'vellies')
vlei – any low open landscape, sometimes marshy (pronounced 'flay')

Index

ABBREVIATIONS

Mal – Malawi   Moz – Mozambique   Zam – Zambia

MAPS

Beira (Moz) 232
Blantyre (Mal) 127
  Blantyre & Limbe Area 135
  Greater Blantyre & Limbe 130

Cape Maclear & Lake Malawi
  National Park (Mal) 189

Kafue National Park (Zam) 285
Kasungu National Park (Mal)
  124

Likoma Island (Mal) 197
Lilongwe (Mal) 110
Livingstone (Zam) 276
Livingstonia (Mal) 166
Liwonde National Park (Mal)
  140

Lochinvar National Park (Zam)
  281
Lower Zambezi National Park
  (Zam) 272
Lusaka (Zam) 263

Malawi 14
  Central 121
  Lake Shore 179
  map index 12
  Northern 162
  Southern 139
Maputo (Moz) 221
Mozambique 204
  map index 202
Mozambique Island 242
Mt Mulanje (Mal) 148
Mzuzu (Mal) 163

Nampula (Moz) 240
Nkhata Bay (Mal) 180
Nyika National Park (Mal) 170

Quelimane (Moz) 238

Siavonga & Kariba Dam (Zam)
  280
South Luangwa National Park
  (Zam) 270

Vilankulo (Moz) 229

Zambia 250
  map index 248
Zomba (Mal) 142
  Southern Zomba Plateau 143

BOXED TEXT

Map references are in **bold** type.

A few words of Tumbuka & Yao
  49
Accommodation & Food Taxes
  87
Air Travel Glossary 90-91
Air Travel Warning 92
Banning the Press 45
Baobabs 191
Birds of Malawi 36-8
Cahora Bassa Dam 236
Chintheche Paper Mill Threat
  183
Cichlid Fish 194
Dress Codes 47
Driving in Malawi 105
Early Missionary Graves 160
Economic Swings &
  Roundabouts 40
Effects of Colonialism 21
Ephesians 2:14 167
Everyday Health 73

Grand Plans (Sesheke to Katima
  Mulilo) 260
Grand Plans for the Karonga to
  Chitipa Road 98
Great Bilharzia Con 69
Hard Work (Missionaries) 19
Highlights (Regional) 53
History of Barotseland 282
History of Nyika 172
History of South Luangwa 271
HMS *Guendolin* 196
Horrors of Slavery 16
Islam in Malawi 48
Kuomboka Ceremony 284
Lake Tanganyika – Some
  Statistics 288
Land Mine Statistics 206
Likoma Missionaries & the
  Cathedral of St Peter 198
Livingstone Island 278
Lower Zambezi – Ecology &
  History 273
Mail Runners 146
Majete Chapel 156

Malawians in South Africa 41
Mandala & the African Lakes
  Corporation 131
Medical Kit Check List 71
Mozambique's Provinces 208
Mr Ngoma's House 165
Mulanje's Pine Plantations 154
Naming of Malawi 15
No Problem! (Health) 258
Nutrition 72
Old Bandawe & Makuzi Hill
  184
Online Services 66
Orchids of Malawi 33
Photography Hints 68
Second-hand Clothes 52
Steamer Names 107
Tanzania to Mozambique by
  Dhow (the Joys of Travel) 218
Tea Growing in Malawi 136
Tobacco 114
Warnings (Mt Mulanje) 149
Warnings (Nyika National Park)
  171

TEXT

accommodation
  Malawi 85-7
  Mozambique 216
  Zambia 258
activities, see individual
  activities
AIDS 48, 76, 198, 258
air travel
  departure tax (Mal) 95
  glossary 90-91
  to/from Malawi 89-95
  to/from Mozambique 217
  to/from Zambia 258
  within Malawi 103, 195
  within Mozambique 219
  within Zambia 261
Angoche (Moz) 240
arts & artists
  Kaunda, Berling 43
  Malangatana 209
  Malawi 42-3
  Mede, Cuthy 43
  Mozambique 208
  Mua Mission 43, 188

Balaka (Mal) 138-9
Banda, Dr Hastings 22-6, 44-5
  economic policies 40
  Islam 48
  Press Holdings 23-4
Bandawe (Mal) 184
  missionaries 19
Bangula (Mal) 158
Bantu 13-17, 41, 172
bargaining, see money
Barotseland (Zam) 283-5
Barra Beach (Moz) 228-9
Bazaruto Archipelago (Moz)
  230-1
Bazaruto Marine National Park
  (Moz) 230-1
Beira (Moz) 231-5, **232**
Bemba (14) 288
bicycle, see cycling
Bilene (Moz) 227
bilharzia 69
bird-watching 85
  birds 36-8
black market, see money
Blantyre (Mal) 127-37, **127,**
  130, 135
  entertainment 134
  getting around 135
  getting there & away 134-5
  money 128
  places to eat 133-4
  places to stay 131-3

post & communications 128
  things to see & do 129-31
  travel & tour agencies 128
boat travel
  to/from Malawi 96-8, 106
  to/from Mozambique 218-19
  to/from Zambia 261
  within Malawi 106-7
Bolero (Mal) 166
books 61-7
  conservation issues 65
  field guides 65-7
  general 64
  health 71
  history 63-4
  literature 63-4
  Lonely Planet 62
  Mozambique 214
  Mt Mulanje 149
  Nyika National Park 171
  politics 64
  road atlases 62
  Zomba Plateau 145
Boskopoid people 13
British African Estates (Mal) 136
bus travel
  to/from Malawi 95-9
  to/from Mozambique 217
  to/from Zambia 259
  within Malawi 103, 108
  within Mozambique 219
  within Zambia 261
bushwalking, see hiking
business hours
  Malawi 83
  Mozambique 216
  Zambia 258

Cahora Bassa Dam, see Lago de
  Cahora Bassa
Cape Maclear (Mal) 189-93, **189**
car hire
  Malawi 104
  Mozambique 220, 226
  Zambia 269
car travel
  Mozambique 217
  Malawi 104-5
  Zambia 259
Carr, Norman 257, 270-1
Catandica (Moz) 235
Catembe (Moz) 226
Chagwa Peak (Mal) 145
Chakaka (Mal) 177
Chambe Peak (Mal) 152
Changara (Moz) 235
Chembe (Mal) 189

Chewa 41
Chia Lagoon (Mal) 185
Chichewa 48-9
Chikale Bay (Mal) 181
Chikangawa (Mal) 126
Chikanka Island (Zam) 280
Chikanzi (Mal) 160
Chikwawa (Mal) 156, 160
children, travel with 82
Chilembwe, Reverend John 21-2
Chiluba, Frederick 252-3
Chilumba (Mal) 179
Chimoio (Moz) 235
Chinde (Moz) 21, 237
Chindembwe (Mal) 123
Chingoni Forest Reserve (Mal)
  122
Chingwe's Hole (Mal) 144
Chintheche (Mal) 183
Chintheche Strip (Mal) 182-4
Chipata (Zam) 269
Chipepo (Zam) 280
Chipoka (Mal) 41, 188
Chipyela (Mal) 198
Chiromo (Mal) 159-60
Chirundu (Zam) 271-2
Chisanga Falls (Mal) 176
Chisekesi (Zam) 280
Chissano, Joaquim 206-7
Chitikali (Mal) 147
Chitimba (Mal) 179-80
Chitipa (Mal) 169
Chizumulu Island (Mal) 196-9
Chocas (Moz) 243
Choma (Zam) 279
Christianity
  Malawi 47
  Mozambique 210
  Zambia 251
Chunga Lagoon (Zam) 281
cichlids 34
climate
  Malawi 27
  Mozambique 207
  Zambia 253
Club Makokola (Mal) 194
Cobuè (Moz) 241
colonialism, effects of 21
conservation, see environmental
  issues
Couto, Mia 209
costs, see money
Craveirinha, Jose 209
credit cards, see money
Cuamba (Moz) 240
cultural considerations 45-7
  dress codes 25, 47

cultural considerations *cont*
  photography 68
currency, *see* money
customs (Mal) 57
cycling 105-6
  Nyika National Park (Mal) 175

dance 43-4
  Gule Wamkulu 43
Dande (Mal) 158
Dedza (Mal) 121-2
Dedza Mountain Forest Reserve
  (Mal) 121
diarrhoea 74-5
Difaqane 16, 249
disabled travellers 81
diving 83
  Cape Maclear (Mal) 190
  Club Makokola (Mal) 195
  Inhassoro (Moz) 231
  Nkhata Bay (Mal) 180
  Vilankulo (Moz) 230
  Wimbi Beach (Moz) 244
  Xai-Xai (Moz) 228
documents, *see also* permits
  Malawi 55-6
  Mozambique 212
  Zambia 255
Domasi Valley (Mal) 145
Domwe Peak (Mal) 177
dress codes 25, 47
driving, *see* car travel &
  motorcycle travel
drugs, *see* legal matters
Dwangwa (Mal) 184
Dzalanyama Forest Reserve
  (Mal) 119-20

e-mail services
  Malawi 61
  Zambia 264
Eastern Marsh (Mal) 159
economy 39-41
  Mandala & the African Lakes
    Corporation 131
  policies 40
  tea 136
  tobacco 114
education 41-2
Elephant Marsh (Mal) 158-9
environmental issues 27-31
  Wildlife Society of Malawi 35

fauna 33-4
  birds 36-8
  cichlids 194
  fish 34
  mammals 33-4
fax services

Malawi 61
Mozambique 214
Zambia 264
fishing 84-5
  Bazaruto Archipelago (Moz)
    230-1
  Nyika National Park (Mal) 173
  Zomba Plateau (Mal) 141, 144
flora 31-5
  baobab tree 191
  evergreen forest 32
  flowers 33
  forest reserves 35
  miombo 32
  montane grassland 32
  mopane 31
  national parks & game reserves
    34
  orchids 33
  plantation & farmland 33
  riverine & wetlands 32
food 87
  nutrition 72
  taxes 87
forest reserves 35
Fort Johnston (Mal) 195
Fort Lister (Mal) 151, 153
Frelimo 205-7, 236
fuel 104

game reserves, *see* national parks
game-viewing 85
gay travellers 81
geography
  Malawi 26-7
  Mozambique 207
  Zambia 253
Gorongosa National Park (Mal)
  235
government & politics
  Malawi 39
  Mozambique 208
  Zambia 253-4
Great Rift Valley
  Malawi 26
  Zambia 288
Gule Wamkulu 43

health 69-80
  AIDS 76
  bilharzia 69
  diarrhoea 74-5
  hepatitis 70, 75
  HIV 76
  immunisations 70
  insurance 71
  malaria 77
  medical kit check list 71
  nutrition 72

typhoid 76
  water 72
  women's health 78-9
hepatitis 70, 75
hiking 85
  Cape Maclear (Mal) 190
  Chambe-Lichenya Loop (Mal)
    154-5
  equipment 52
  Livingstonia Route (Mal) 177
  Mt Mulanje (Mal) 151-5
  Mulanje Traverse (Mal) 151-4
  Nyika Highlights Route (Mal)
    176-7
  Nyika National Park (Mal) 175-7
  Zomba Plateau (Mal) 145-6
history 13-26, *see also*
  individual country entries
  African Lakes Corporation 178
  democracy 25
  human rights 23-4
  independence 23
  Malawi today 26
  naming of Malawi 15
  reforms 25-6
  'Scramble for Africa' 203
  Young Pioneers 24, 162-3
hitchhiking 106
HIV, *see* AIDS
holidays
  Malawi 83
  Mozambique 216
  Zambia 258
horse-riding 85, 173

immunisations 70
Inhaca Island (Moz) 226
Inhambane (Moz) 228
Inhassoro (Moz) 231
insurance
  health 71
  travel 55
Islam 47
  Malawi 48
  Mozambique 210

Jalawe Peak (Mal) 173
Jalo (Mal) 184
Johnston, Sir Harry 21

Kachulu (Mal) 147
Kafue National Park (Zam)
  285-6, **285**
Kalabo (Zam) 284
Kalalezi (Zam) 281
Kalambo Falls (Zam) 288
Kalwe Forest (Mal) 180
Kapichira Falls (Mal) 156
Kapiri Mposhi (Zam) 286

Kapishya Hot Springs (Zam) 287
Karonga (Mal) 178-9
Kasama (Zam) 287
Kasanka National Park (Zam)
  287
Kasungu (Mal) 123
Kasungu National Park (Mal)
  123-5, **124**
Katate (Mal) 125
Katima Mulilo (Zam) 259-60,
  282, 283
Kaunda, Kenneth 251-3
Kawozia Peak (Mal) 173
Kazungula (Zam) 278-9
Kazuni (Mal) 166
Kitwe (Zam) 287
Kkanga River Conservation
  Area (Zam) 279
Kole (Zam) 281
Kotakota (Zam) 281
Kwilembe (Mal) 196

Lago de Cahora Bassa (Moz)
  236
Lago Niassa (Moz) 241
Lake Bangweulu (Zam) 287
Lake Chilwa (Mal) 146
Lake Itezhi-Tezhi (Zam) 285
Lake Kariba (Zam) 279-81
Lake Kaulime (Mal) 171, 176
Lake Kazuni (Mal) 165
Lake Malawi 26-7, **179**
Lake Malawi National Park 189,
  189
Lake Malombe (Mal) 196
Lake Tanganyika (Zam) 288
Lambya 16, 41
land mines 215
languages 48-9
  Chichewa 48-9
  Portuguese 210-12
  Tumbuka 48
  Yao 48
Lealui (Zam) 284-5
legal matters
  Malawi 82-3
  Mozambique 215
Lengwe National Park (Mal) 157
lesbian travellers 81
Lichinga (Moz) 241
Likabula (Mal) 147
Likoma Island (Mal) 196-9, **197**
Lilongwe (Mal) 109-20, **110**
  entertainment 117-18
  getting around 118-19
  getting there & away 118
  history 109
  information 109-13
  orientation 109

places to eat 116-17
places to stay 114-16
things to see & do 113-4
Limbe (Mal) 127-135, *see also*
  Blantyre
Limulunga (Zam) 284
literature, *see also* books
  Malawi 44-5, 63-4
  Mozambique 208
Litunga of the Lozi 282, 284
Liuwa Plain National Park
  (Zam) 283
Livingstone (Zam) 260, 275-7,
  276
Livingstone Island (Zam) 278
Livingstone, Dr David 17-19,
  156, 159, 184, 198, 251, 287
Livingstonia (Mal) 166-69, 172,
  166
Livingstonia Beach (Mal) 188
Liwonde National Park (Mal)
  140-1, **140**
Lizard Island (Mal) 186
Lochinvar National Park (Zam)
  281, **281**
Lower Shire Valley (Mal) 155-60
Lower Zambezi National Park
  (Zam) 272-4, **272**
Lozi 250-1, 282, 284
Luangwa (Zam) 274
Lujeri Tea Estate (Mal) 154
Lusaka (Zam) 262-9, **263**
  entertainment 267
  getting around 268-9
  getting there & away 268
  information 264-5
  places to eat 267
  places to stay 265-7
  shopping 267-8
  things to see 265

Macaneta Beach (Moz) 227
Machel, Samora 205-6
Mackenzie, Charles 18
Majete Game Reserve (Mal)
  155-6
Makhanga (Mal) 158, 159
Makonde 208, 209
Makua 208
Makuzi Hill (Mal) 184
Malangatana 209
malaria 77
Malawi 13-199, **14**
  Blantyre & Limbe 127-37, **127,
    130, 135**
  Central Malawi 121-6, **121**
  Lake Shore 178-199, **179**
  Lilongwe 109-20, **110**
  Northern Malawi 161-77, **162**

Southern Malawi 138-60, **139**
Malumbe Peak (Mal) 145
Manchewe Falls (Mal) 167
Mandala Falls (Mal) 143
Mandimba (Moz) 241
Mangochi (Mal) 195-6
  Mangochi Mountain Forest
    Reserve 196
maps 51
  Mt Mulanje (Mal) 149
  Nyika National Park (Mal) 171
  Zomba Plateau (Mal) 145
Maputo (Moz) 220-7, **221**
  entertainment 225
  getting around 226
  getting there & away 226
  information 222
  places to eat 224-5
  places to stay 223-4
  shopping 225
  things to see & do 222-3
Maravi Empire 15
Matitu Falls (Mal) 156
Maxixe (Moz) 228
Mbala (Zam) 287-8
Mchacha James (Mal) 159
Mchese Mountain (Mal) 148
Mchinji (Mal) 122
Mchokola (Mal) 196
media 67-8
  censorship 45
  online services 66
Mfecane, *see* Difaqane
Mfuwe (Zam) 271
Michiru Forest Reserve (Mal)
  136-7
Michiru Mountain (Mal) 136-7
Milange (Moz) 238-9
missionaries 19-20, 160, 167,
  190
Mlunguzi Dam (Mal) 143
Moçimboa da Praia (Moz) 218,
  245
Mocuba (Moz) 237-8
Molocuè (Moz) 239
Mondlane, Eduardo 205
money 57-61
  accommodation & food taxes 87
  bargaining 60
  black market 59
  changing money 58-9
  costs 57
  credit cards 58
  currency exchange 58
  tipping 59-60
Mongu (Zam) 260, 283-5
Monkey Bay (Mal) 188-9
Monkey Bay-Mangochi Road
  (Mal) 194-5

Monze (Zam) 280, 281
Mosi-oa-Tunya Game Park (Zam) 274
Mosi-oa-Tunya National Park (Zam) 274
motorcycle travel 104-5
Mozambique 203-45, **204**
    accommodation 216
    arts 208-10
    civil war 206-7
    climate 207
    embassies 212-13
    getting around 219-20
    getting there & away 217-19
    history 203-7
    Maputo 220-7, **221**
    money 213-14
    national parks & game reserves 207-8
    post services 214
    safety 206, 215
    telephone services 214
    tourist offices 212
    visas 212
Mozambique Island (Moz) 241-3, **242**
Mpanda Peak (Mal) 173
Mpata Gorge (Zam) 273-4
Mpulungu (Zam) 288
Msaka (Mal) 192
Msondole Mountain (Mal) 196
Mt Mulanje (Mal) 147-55, **148**
    hiking 151-5
    information 149-50
    safety 149
    Sapitwa Peak 152
Mt Ndirande (Mal) 135-6
Mt Soche (Mal) 136
Mua (Mal) 188
    Mua Mission 188
Mueda (Moz) 205
Mulanje (Mal) 147
Muluzi, Bakili 25, 39
Mumbwa (Zam) 286
Muona (Mal) 159
museums
    Chamare Museum (Mal) 188
    Choma Museum (Zam) 279
    Lake Malawi National Park (Mal) 190
    Livingstonia Museum (Mal) 166
    Money Museum (Moz) 223
    Moto Moto Museum (Zam) 288
    Museum of the Revolution (Zam) 223
    Mzuzu Museum (Mal) 161
    Namaka Postal Museum (Mal) 147
    National Art Museum (Moz) 223

National Museum (Blantyre) (Mal) 131
National Museum (Livingstone) (Zam) 276
Natural History Museum (Moz) 223
Railway Museum (Livingstone) (Zam) 276
Zintu Community Museum (Zam) 265
music
    Malawi 44
    Mozambique 209-10
Mwabvi Game Reserve (Mal) 158
Mwala Wa Mphini (Mal) 191
Mwande (Zam) 279
Mwanza (Mal) 156
Mzuzu (Mal) 161-4, **163**

Nacala (Moz) 243-4
Nadonetsa (Mal) 154
Nakonde 179, 288
Namaka (Mal) 146-7
Namasile Peak (Mal) 153
Namingomba Estates (Mal) 136
Namizimu Forest Reserve (Mal) 196
Nampula (Moz) 239-40, **240**
Namwala (Zam) 281
Nankumba Peninsula (Mal) 188-9
national parks & game reserves (Mal) 34-5, (Moz) 207-8, (Zam) 253-6
    Bazaruto Marine National Park (Moz) 230-1
    Gorongosa National Park (Moz) 235
    Kafue National Park (Zam) 285-6, **285**
    Kasanka National Park (Zam) 287
    Kasungu National Park (Mal) 123-5, **124**
    Kkanga River Conservation Area (Zam) 279
    Lake Malawi National Park (Mal) 189, **189**
    Lengwe National Park (Mal) 157
    Liuwa Plain National Park (Zam) 283
    Liwonde National Park (Mal) 140-1, **140**
    Lochinvar National Park (Zam) 281, **281**
    Lower Zambezi National Park (Zam) 272-4, **272**

Majete Game Reserve (Mal) 155-6
Mosi-oa-Tunya Game Park (Zam) 274
Mosi-oa-Tunya National Park (Zam) 274
Mwabvi Game Reserve (Mal) 158
Nkhotakota Game Reserve (Mal) 185
North Luangwa National Park (Zam) 287
Nyika National Park (Zam) 169-77, **170**
Sioma Ngwezi National Park (Zam) 283
South Luangwa National Park (Zam) 269-71, **270**
Sumbu National Park (Zam) 288
Vwaza Marsh Game Reserve (Mal) 164-6
Nawimbe Peak (Mal) 146
Nchalo (Mal) 157
Ndirande Forest Reserve (Mal) 135
Ndola (Zam) 286-7
Nganda Peak (Mal) 169
Ngapandi Estate (Mal) 196
Ngoma, SS 165
Ngonde 16, 41
Ngondola (Mal) 145
Ngoni 16, 41, 198
Ngonye Falls (Zam) 282-3
Nkhata Bay (Mal) 180-2, **180**
Nkhotakota (Mal) 184
Nkhotakota Game Reserve (Mal) 185
Nkhunguni Peak (Mal) 191
North Luangwa National Park (Zam) 287
Ntchisi (Mal) 122
Ntchisi Forest Reserve (Mal) 122-3
Nthalire (Mal) 175
nutrition 72, see also health
Nyanja 208
Nyasaland 21-2
Nyika National Park (Mal) 169-77, **170**
    cycling 175
    fishing 173-4
    flora & fauna 171
    getting there & away 174-5
    hiking 175-7
    history 172
    horse-riding 173
    places to stay 174
    safety 171
    walking 172

Palma (Moz) 245
Pemba (Moz) 218, 244-5
permits, temporary import 105
Phalombe (Mal) 153
Phoka Court (Mal) 169, 177
photography 68
planning 50-4
    highlights 53
    itineraries 52-4
poaching 28
poetry
    Malawi 44-5
    Mozambique 208
population
    Malawi 41
    Mozambique 208
    Zambia 254
Portuguese 17, 203-5, 249, see
    also languages
postal services
    Malawi 61
    Mozambique 214
    Zambia 257
Praia de Závora (Moz) 228
Praia do Xai-Xai (Moz) 227
public holidays, see holidays

Quelimane (Moz) 237, **238**

refugees 41
Renamo 23, 206-7, 236
Rhodes, Cecil 20, 251
rock climbing 85
Rumphi (Mal) 164

safety
    Malawi 82
    Mozambique 215
    Mt Mulanje 149
    Nyika National Park (Mal) 171
    Zambia 258
sailing
    Cape Maclear (Mal) 190
    Club Makokola (Mal) 195
    Senga Bay (Mal) 186
Salazar, Antonio 203
Salima (Mal) 186
San 13
Sapitwa Peak (Mal) 148, 152
Satemwa Estate (Mal) 136
scuba diving, see diving
Senanga (Zam) 283
Senga Bay (Mal) 186-8
senior travellers 81
Sesheke (Zam) 260, 282
Shaka Zulu 16
Shiwa Ngandu (Zam) 287
Siavonga (Zam) 280-1, **280**
Sinazongwe (Zam) 279-80

Sioma Ngwezi National Park
    (Zam) 283
slavery
    Malawi 16-18
    Mozambique 203
    Zambia 249
snorkelling
    Cape Maclear (Mal) 190
    Inhassoro (Moz) 231
    Praia de Závora (Moz) 228
    Senga Bay (Mal) 186
    Vilankulo (Moz) 230
    Wimbi Beach (Moz) 244
Soche Forest Reserve (Mal) 136
Songo (Moz) 236
Songwe Bridge (Mal) 179
Sorgin (Mal) 158
South Luangwa National Park
    (Zam) 269-71, **270**
Stanley, Henry 19
Sucoma Sugar Plantation (Mal)
    157, 159
Sultan Mlozi 178
Sumbu National Park (Zam) 288
Swahili-Arabs 16, 203, 249

taboos, see cultural
    considerations
taxes, see money
taxi travel
    Malawi 108
telephone services
    Malawi 61
    Mozambique 214
    Zambia 256-7
Tembo, John 26
Tete (Moz) 235, 236
Thyolo (Mal) 136
Thyolo Escarpment (Mal) 155
Thyolo Mountain (Mal) 136
tipping, see money
Tofu Beach (Moz) 228-9
Tonga 41, 184, 250, 251, 279
tourist offices
    Malawi 54
    Mozambique 212
    Zambia 254-5
tours, organised
    Malawi 99-102, 108
    Mozambique 220
    Zambia 262, 264, 275, 277
train travel
    to/from Malawi 96
    to/from Mozambique 217
    to/from Zambia 260
    within Malawi 104, 134-5
    within Zambia 261-2
trekking, see hiking
Tumbuka 41, see also languages

Ulongwe (Mal) 140

Victoria Falls (Zam) 274-5
    Livingstone Island 278
video 68
Vilankulo (Moz) 229-30, **229**
Viphya Plateau (Mal) 125
visas
    Malawi 55-6
    Zambia 255
    Mozambique 212
Vwaza Marsh Game Reserve
    (Mal) 164-6

walking, see hiking
Wildlife Society of Malawi 35
Williams Falls (Mal) 144
Wimbi Beach (Moz) 244
wildlife, see fauna
windsurfing
    Cape Maclear (Mal) 190
    Club Makokola (Mal) 195
    Senga Bay (Mal) 186
witchcraft 47-8, 198
women travellers 80-1
women's health 78-9

Xai-Xai (Moz) 227-8
Xefina Grande Island (Moz) 227

Yao 16, 41, 198, 208, see also
    languages

Zambezi Escarpment (Zam) 273
Zambezi Riverfront (Zam) 278-9
Zambia 249-88, **250**
    accommodation 258
    books 257
    climate 253
    embassies 255-6
    getting around 261-2
    getting there & away 258-61
    history 249-53
    Lusaka 262-9, **263**
    money 256
    national parks & game reserves
        253-4
    post services 256-7
    safety 258
    telephone services 256
    tourist offices 254-5
    visas 255
Zomba (Mal) 141-2, **142**
Zomba Plateau (Mal) 142-6, **143**
    hiking 145-6
Zulu 16

LONELY PLANET PHRASEBOOKS

Building bridges,
Breaking barriers,
Beyond babble-on

Listen for the gems

Speak your own words

Ask your own
questions

Master of
your
own
image

- handy pocket-sized books
- easy to understand Pronunciation chapter
- clear and comprehensive Grammar chapter
- romanisation alongside script to allow ease of pronunciation
- script throughout so users can point to phrases
- extensive vocabulary sections, words and phrases for every situations
- full of cultural information and tips for the traveller

'...vital for a real DIY spirit and attitude in language learning' – Backpacker

'the phrasebooks have good cultural backgrounders and offer solid advice for challenging situations in remote locations' – San Francisco Examiner

'...they are unbeatable for their coverage of the world's more obscure languages' – The Geographical Magazine

---

Arabic (Egyptian)
Arabic (Moroccan)
Australia
 Australian English, Aboriginal and Torres Strait languages
Baltic States
 Estonian, Latvian, Lithuanian
Bengali
Burmese
Brazilian
Cantonese
Central Europe
 Czech, French, German, Hungarian, Italian and Slovak
Eastern Europe
 Bulgarian, Czech, Hungarian, Polish, Romanian and Slovak
Egyptian Arabic
Ethiopian (Amharic)
Fijian
Greek
Hindi/Urdu

Indonesian
Japanese
Korean
Lao
Latin American Spanish
Malay
Mandarin
Mediterranean Europe
 Albanian, Croatian, Greek, Italian, Macedonian, Maltese, Serbian, Slovene
Mongolian
Moroccan Arabic
Nepali
Papua New Guinea
Pilipino (Tagalog)
Quechua
Russian
Scandinavian Europe
 Danish, Finnish, Icelandic, Norwegian and Swedish

South-East Asia
 Burmese, Indonesian, Khmer, Lao, Malay, Tagalog (Pilipino), Thai and Vietnamese
Sri Lanka
Swahili
Thai
Thai Hill Tribes
Tibetan
Turkish
Ukrainian
USA
 US English, Vernacular Talk, Native American languages and Hawaiian
Vietnamese
Western Europe
 Basque, Catalan, Dutch, French, German, Irish, Italian, Portuguese, Scottish Gaelic, Spanish (Castilian) and Welsh

---

LONELY PLANET JOURNEYS

JOURNEYS is a unique collection of travel writing – published by the company that understands travel better than anyone else. It is a series for anyone who has ever experienced – or dreamed of – the magical moment when they encountered a strange culture or saw a place for the first time. They are tales to read while you're planning a trip, while you're on the road or while you're in an armchair, in front of a fire.

JOURNEYS books catch the spirit of a place, illuminate a culture, recount a crazy adventure, or introduce a fascinating way of life. They always entertain, and always enrich the experience of travel.

THE RAINBIRD
A Central African Journey
Jan Brokken
translated by Sam Garrett

The Rainbird is a classic travel story. Following in the footsteps of famous Europeans such as Albert Schweitzer and H.M. Stanley, Jan Brokken journeyed to Gabon in central Africa. A kaleidoscope of adventures and anecdotes, *The Rainbird* brilliantly chronicles the encounter between Africa and Europe as it was acted out on a side-street of history. It is also the compelling, immensely readable account of the author's own travels in one of the most remote and mysterious regions of Africa.

Jan Brokken is one of Holland's best known writers. In addition to travel narratives and literary journalism, he has published several novels and short stories. Many of his works are set in Africa, where he has travelled widely.

SONGS TO AN AFRICAN SUNSET
A Zimbabwean Story
Sekai Nzenza-Shand

Songs to an African Sunset braids vividly personal stories into an intimate picture of contemporary Zimbabwe. Returning to her family's village after many years in the West, Sekai Nzenza-Shand discovers a world where ancestor worship, polygamy and witchcraft still govern the rhythms of daily life – and where drought, deforestation and AIDS have wrought devastating changes. With insight and affection, she explores a culture torn between respect for the old ways and the irresistible pull of the new.

Sekai Nzenza-Shand was born in Zimbabwe and has lived in England and Australia. Her first novel, *Zimbabwean Woman: My Own Story*, was published in London in 1988 and her fiction has been included in the short story collections *Daughters of Africa* and *Images of the West*. Sekai currently lives in Zimbabwe.

This project has been assisted by the Commonwealth Government through the Australia Council, its arts funding and advisory body.

LONELY PLANET TRAVEL ATLASES

Lonely Planet has long been famous for the number and quality of its guidebook maps. Now we've gone one step further and in conjunction with Steinhart Katzir Publishers produced a handy companion series: Lonely Planet travel atlases – maps of a country produced in book form.

Unlike other maps, which look good but lead travellers astray, our travel atlases have been researched on the road by Lonely Planet's experienced team of writers. All details are carefully checked to ensure the atlas corresponds with the equivalent Lonely Planet guidebook.

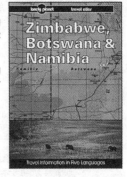

The handy atlas format means no holes, wrinkles, torn sections or constant folding and unfolding. These atlases can survive long periods on the road, unlike cumbersome fold-out maps. The comprehensive index ensures easy reference.

- full-colour throughout
- maps researched and checked by Lonely Planet authors
- place names correspond with Lonely Planet guidebooks
  – no confusing spelling differences
- legend and travelling information in English, French, German, Japanese and Spanish
- size: 230 x 160 mm

Available now:
Chile & Easter Island • Egypt • India & Bangladesh • Israel & the Palestinian Territories •Jordan, Syria & Lebanon • Kenya • Laos • Portugal • South Africa, Lesotho & Swaziland • Thailand • Vietnam • Zimbabwe, Botswana & Namibia

---

LONELY PLANET TV SERIES & VIDEOS

Lonely Planet travel guides have been brought to life on television screens around the world. Like our guides, the programmes are based on the joy of independent travel, and look honestly at some of the most exciting, picturesque and frustrating places in the world. Each show is presented by one of three travellers from Australia, England or the USA and combines an innovative mixture of video, Super-8 film, atmospheric soundscapes and original music.

Videos of each episode – containing additional footage not shown on television – are available from good book and video shops, but the availability of individual videos varies with regional screening schedules.

Video destinations include: Alaska • American Rockies • Australia – The South-East • Baja California & the Copper Canyon • Brazil • Central Asia • Chile & Easter Island • Corsica, Sicily & Sardinia – The Mediterranean Islands • East Africa (Tanzania & Zanzibar) • Ecuador & the Galapagos Islands • Greenland & Iceland • Indonesia • Israel & the Sinai Desert • Jamaica • Japan • La Ruta Maya • Morocco • New York • North India • Pacific Islands (Fiji, Solomon Islands & Vanuatu) • South India • South West China • Turkey • Vietnam • West Africa • Zimbabwe, Botswana & Namibia

The Lonely Planet TV series is produced by:
Pilot Productions
The Old Studio
18 Middle Row
London W10 5AT UK

For video availability and ordering information contact your nearest Lonely Planet office.

Music from the TV series is available on CD & cassette.

PLANET TALK

Lonely Planet's FREE quarterly newsletter

We love hearing from you and think you'd like to hear from us.

When...is the right time to see reindeer in Finland?
Where...can you hear the best palm-wine music in Ghana?
How...do you get from Asunción to Areguá by steam train?
What...is the best way to see India?

For the answer to these and many other questions read PLANET TALK.

Every issue is packed with up-to-date travel news and advice including:

- a letter from Lonely Planet co-founders Tony and Maureen Wheeler
- go behind the scenes on the road with a Lonely Planet author
- feature article on an important and topical travel issue
- a selection of recent letters from travellers
- details on forthcoming Lonely Planet promotions
- complete list of Lonely Planet products

To join our mailing list contact any Lonely Planet office.

Also available: Lonely Planet T-shirts. 100% heavyweight cotton.

LONELY PLANET ONLINE

Get the latest travel information before you leave or while you're on the road

Whether you've just begun planning your next trip, or you're chasing down specific info on currency regulations or visa requirements, check out Lonely Planet Online for up-to-the minute travel information.

As well as travel profiles of your favourite destinations (including maps and photos), you'll find current reports from our researchers and other travellers, updates on health and visas, travel advisories, and discussion of the ecological and political issues you need to be aware of as you travel.

There's also an online travellers' forum where you can share your experience of life on the road, meet travel companions and ask other travellers for their recommendations and advice. We also have plenty of links to other online sites useful to independent travellers.

And of course we have a complete and up-to-date list of all Lonely Planet travel products including guides, phrasebooks, atlases, Journeys and videos and a simple online ordering facility if you can't find the book you want elsewhere.

www.lonelyplanet.com
or
AOL keyword: lp

LONELY PLANET PRODUCTS

Lonely Planet is known worldwide for publishing practical, reliable and no-nonsense travel information in our guides and on our web site. The Lonely Planet list covers just about every accessible part of the world. Currently there are eight series: *travel guides*, *shoestring guides*, *walking guides*, *city guides*, *phrasebooks*, *audio packs*, *travel atlases* and *Journeys* – a unique collection of travel writing.

EUROPE

Amsterdam • Austria • Baltic States & Kaliningrad • Baltic States phrasebook • Britain • Central Europe on a shoestring • Central Europe phrasebook • Czech & Slovak Republics • Denmark • Dublin • Eastern Europe on a shoestring • Eastern Europe phrasebook • Finland • France • Greece • Greek phrasebook • Hungary • Iceland, Greenland & the Faroe Islands • Ireland • Italy • Mediterranean Europe on a shoestring • Mediterranean Europe phrasebook • Paris • Poland • Portugal • Portugal travel atlas • Prague • Russia, Ukraine & Belarus • Russian phrasebook • Scandinavian & Baltic Europe on a shoestring • Scandinavian Europe phrasebook • Slovenia • Spain • St Petersburg • Switzerland • Trekking in Greece • Trekking in Spain • Ukrainian phrasebook • Vienna • Walking in Britain • Walking in Switzerland • Western Europe on a shoestring • Western Europe phrasebook

NORTH AMERICA

Alaska • Backpacking in Alaska • Baja California • California & Nevada • Canada • Florida • Hawaii • Honolulu • Los Angeles • Mexico • Miami • New England • New Orleans • New York, New Jersey & Pennsylvania • Pacific Northwest USA • Rocky Mountain States • San Francisco • Southwest USA • USA phrasebook • Washington, DC & the Capital Region

CENTRAL AMERICA & THE CARIBBEAN

Bermuda • Central America on a shoestring • Costa Rica • Cuba • Eastern Caribbean • Guatemala, Belize & Yucatán: La Ruta Maya • Jamaica

SOUTH AMERICA

Argentina, Uruguay & Paraguay • Bolivia • Brazil • Brazilian phrasebook • Buenos Aires • Chile & Easter Island • Chile & Easter Island travel atlas • Colombia • Ecuador & the Galápagos Islands • Latin American Spanish phrasebook • Peru • Quechua phrasebook • Rio de Janeiro • South America on a shoestring • Trekking in the Patagonian Andes • Venezuela

Travel Literature: Full Circle: A South American Journey

ANTARCTICA

Antarctica

ISLANDS OF THE INDIAN OCEAN

Madagascar & Comoros • Maldives & Islands of the East Indian Ocean • Mauritius, Réunion & Seychelles

AFRICA

Arabic (Moroccan) phrasebook • Africa on a shoestring • Cape Town • Central Africa • East Africa • Egypt • Egypt travel atlas • Ethiopian (Amharic) phrasebook • Kenya • Kenya travel atlas • Malawi, Mozambique & Zambia • Morocco • North Africa • South Africa, Lesotho & Swaziland • South Africa, Lesotho & Swaziland travel atlas • Swahili phrasebook • Trekking in East Africa • West Africa • Zimbabwe, Botswana & Namibia • Zimbabwe, Botswana & Namibia travel atlas

Travel Literature: The Rainbird: A Central African Journey • Songs to an African Sunset: A Zimbabwean Story

MAIL ORDER

Lonely Planet products are distributed worldwide. They are also available by mail order from Lonely Planet, so if you have difficulty finding a title please write to us. North American and South American residents should write to Embarcadero West, 155 Filbert St, Suite 251, Oakland CA 94607, USA; European and African residents should write to 10 Barley Mow Passage, Chiswick, London W4 4PH; and residents of other countries to PO Box 617, Hawthorn, Victoria 3122, Australia.

NORTH-EAST ASIA

Beijing • Cantonese phrasebook • China • Hong Kong, Macau & Guangzhou • Hong Kong • Japan • Japanese phrasebook • Japanese audio pack • Korea • Korean phrasebook • Mandarin phrasebook • Mongolia • Mongolian phrasebook • North-East Asia on a shoestring • Seoul • Taiwan • Tibet • Tibet phrasebook • Tokyo

Travel Literature: Lost Japan

MIDDLE EAST & CENTRAL ASIA

Arab Gulf States • Arabic (Egyptian) phrasebook • Central Asia • Iran • Israel & the Palestinian Territories • Israel & the Palestinian Territories travel atlas • Istanbul • Jerusalem • Jordan & Syria • Jordan, Syria & Lebanon travel atlas • Middle East • Turkey • Turkish phrasebook • Yemen

Travel Literature: The Gates of Damascus • Kingdom of the Film Stars: Journey into Jordan

ALSO AVAILABLE:

Travel with Children • Traveller's Tales

INDIAN SUBCONTINENT

Bangladesh • Bengali phrasebook • Delhi • Hindi/Urdu phrasebook • India • India & Bangladesh travel atlas • Indian Himalaya • Karakoram Highway • Nepal • Nepali phrasebook • Pakistan • Rajasthan • Sri Lanka • Sri Lanka phrasebook • Trekking in the Indian Himalaya • Trekking in the Karakoram & Hindukush • Trekking in the Nepal Himalaya

Travel Literature: In Rajasthan • Shopping for Buddhas

SOUTH-EAST ASIA

Bali & Lombok • Bangkok • Burmese phrasebook • Cambodia • Ho Chi Minh City • Indonesia • Indonesian phrasebook • Indonesian audio pack • Jakarta • Java • Laos • Lao phrasebook • Laos travel atlas • Malay phrasebook • Malaysia, Singapore & Brunei • Myanmar (Burma) • Philippines • Pilipino phrasebook • Singapore • South-East Asia on a shoestring • South-East Asia phrasebook • Thailand • Thailand travel atlas • Thai phrasebook • Thai audio pack • Thai Hill Tribes phrasebook • Vietnam • Vietnamese phrasebook • Vietnam travel atlas

AUSTRALIA & THE PACIFIC

Australia • Australian phrasebook • Bushwalking in Australia • Bushwalking in Papua New Guinea • Fiji • Fijian phrasebook • Islands of Australia's Great Barrier Reef • Melbourne • Micronesia • New Caledonia • New South Wales & the ACT • New Zealand • Northern Territory • Outback Australia • Papua New Guinea • Papua New Guinea phrasebook • Queensland • Rarotonga & the Cook Islands • Samoa • Solomon Islands • South Australia • Sydney • Tahiti & French Polynesia • Tasmania • Tonga • Tramping in New Zealand • Vanuatu • Victoria • Western Australia

Travel Literature: Islands in the Clouds • Sean & David's Long Drive

THE LONELY PLANET STORY

Lonely Planet published its first book in 1973 in response to the numerous 'How did you do it?' questions Maureen and Tony Wheeler were asked after driving, bussing, hitching, sailing and railing their way from England to Australia.

Written at a kitchen table and hand collated, trimmed and stapled, *Across Asia on the Cheap* became an instant local bestseller, inspiring thoughts of another book.

Eighteen months in South-East Asia resulted in their second guide, *South-East Asia on a shoestring*, which they put together in a backstreet Chinese hotel in Singapore in 1975. The 'yellow bible', as it quickly became known to backpackers around the world, soon became *the* guide to the region. It has sold well over half a million copies and is now in its 9th edition, still retaining its familiar yellow cover.

Today there are over 240 titles, including travel guides, walking guides, language kits & phrasebooks, travel atlases and travel literature. The company is the largest independent travel publisher in the world. Although Lonely Planet initially specialised in guides to Asia, today there are few corners of the globe that have not been covered.

The emphasis continues to be on travel for independent travellers. Tony and Maureen still travel for several months of each year and play an active part in the writing, updating and quality control of Lonely Planet's guides.

They have been joined by over 70 authors and 170 staff at our offices in Melbourne (Australia), Oakland (USA), London (UK) and Paris (France). Travellers themselves also make a valuable contribution to the guides through the feedback we receive in thousands of letters each year and on our web site.

The people at Lonely Planet strongly believe that travellers can make a positive contribution to the countries they visit, both through their appreciation of the countries' culture, wildlife and natural features, and through the money they spend. In addition, the company makes a direct contribution to the countries and regions it covers. Since 1986 a percentage of the income from each book has been donated to ventures such as famine relief in Africa; aid projects in India; agricultural projects in Central America; Greenpeace's efforts to halt French nuclear testing in the Pacific; and Amnesty International.

'I hope we send the people out with the right attitude about travel. You realise when you travel that there are so many different perspectives about the world, so we hope these books will make people more interested in what they see. These are guidebooks, but you can't really guide people. All you can do is point them in the right direction.'
– Tony Wheeler

LONELY PLANET PUBLICATIONS

Australia
PO Box 617, Hawthorn 3122, Victoria
tel: (03) 9819 1877 fax: (03) 9819 6459
e-mail: talk2us@lonelyplanet.com.au

USA
Embarcadero West, 155 Filbert St, Suite 251,
Oakland, CA 94607
tel: (510) 893 8555 TOLL FREE: 800 275-8555
fax: (510) 893 8563
e-mail: info@lonelyplanet.com

UK
10 Barley Mow Passage, Chiswick,
London W4 4PH
tel: (0181) 742 3161 fax: (0181) 742 2772
e-mail: 100413.3551@compuserve.com

France:
71 bis rue du Cardinal Lemoine, 75005 Paris
tel: 1 44 32 06 20 fax: 1 46 34 72 55
e-mail: 100560.415@compuserve.com

World Wide Web: http://www.lonelyplanet.com